WITHDRAWN

STUDIES *in* READING *and Related Writing*

NEAL FRANK DOUBLEDAY

STUDIES *in* READING

and Related Writing

D. C. HEATH AND COMPANY   BOSTON

For Frances

Library of Congress Catalog Card Number: 57–5101

Copyright 1957 by D. C. HEATH AND COMPANY

Printed in the United States of America (6 A5)

Foreword

The student has a right to know why he is asked to learn particular things and to practice particular skills, and he works best when he can see distinct and immediate advantage in the knowledge and skill he gains. Explanations of purpose, therefore, are made for the student as he goes along. These explanations the instructor will wish to consider in themselves and they need not be repeated here, but perhaps a few remarks on the design of the book will be of use to him.

The selections in this book are short pieces of such writing as the college student needs to read in college work, and of such writing as is read by the intelligent adult of fairly wide interests. Short pieces of importance and of some little difficulty seem to me the best instructional material, for with them the instructor can reasonably insist on active, careful reading.

A glance through the book will show that the selections are so arranged that there is a return to certain interests, and a return to certain writers. Everywhere an effort is made to help the student see how one piece is related to another, and how reading one piece may be a preparation for reading another. But I understand that an instructor uses a textbook with his own class, and I have been careful not to make the organization so tight that chapters and parts of chapters may not be omitted at the instructor's discretion.

The selections have also been chosen to allow a close correlation between the student's reading and his writing. The suggestions for papers at the end of each chapter are designed primarily to show ways in which that correlation may be made. Of course the instructor will use them as he sees fit, and he may often prefer other assignments. Perhaps instructors doing their first teaching will find them useful, and more experienced teachers who have come to distrust the conventional "theme" as an instrument of instruction may turn to them. The range is usually from suggestions for short and simple exercises to suggestions for papers of some length.

The questions and discussion that follow something more than half of the selections are designed to help the student make the best use of his preparation time—for many students suppose that they have done all they can do when they have "read over" a passage. Sometimes the student is given necessary information; always he is directed back to the text and urged to discover exactly what it says. The instructor probably will not wish to make regular progress through the questions a fixed class procedure, but he may find, particularly in the first weeks of the term, that classroom attention to the questions is a useful check.

The student should have a good desk dictionary and a handbook; and the questions ask him to use both. Particularly he is reminded of the resources of the dictionary, and urged to make an intelligent use of them.

My debt in this book is great, and greatly dispersed. First of all it is to my students, who have, often patiently, worked through much of this material and taught me much while they were doing so. They furnish some example pieces of writing. Fellow teachers have in various ways influenced this book. Writers and publishers have been gracious in granting permission to reprint copyright material. And I owe special thanks to Mrs. Laura Smith Hawkins, to James F. Doubleday, and to Dr. Marie L. Edel of D. C. Heath and Company.

N. F. D.

Contents

First Considerations

Almost all first-year students in American colleges and universities take courses designed to improve their skills in reading and in writing. These courses recognize that most entering college students face the necessity of reading on a level to which they are unused and of writing for purposes new to them. For many students the transition is almost a leap. But this book takes the difficulties into account, and concerns itself with your immediate problems. We cannot consider them all at once. Working out from what you already know, we shall have to try to find appropriate starting points for college work. Your first question need be only this: "What ought I to expect of myself?"

You should certainly not suppose that your reading skill is fully developed—no good reader supposes that. And you should realize that in the textbooks and the magazines of mass circulation read by most high school students, great concessions are made to a lack of experience and ability on the part of readers. In this book, the selections are usually short, but the reading of them will often require your best attention. Yet if you can get the habit of active reading, you can expect that the careful reading of one selection will always make you a better reader for the next. You can expect to learn approaches to particular difficulties in reading, so that finally no kind of reading will offer problems entirely new to you. You can expect to see your reading skill developing—but not over night.

You will find a close relationship between learning to read well and learning to write well. A good reader is not necessarily a gifted writer, but he is nearly always an acceptable writer. What he has learned as a reader is the larger part of his equipment as a writer. Since language is a complex set of conventions, you cannot reasonably expect to use it well unless you know a good deal about the ways in which it has been used.

And you need to learn to use it well, both for the academic purposes of the next four years and in the callings college people follow. These needs are obvious; what may be harder to realize is that your effectiveness as a good member of society will depend in part upon how well you can make yourself understood. Whatever form your communication with your fellows takes, the best training in making your ideas clear comes in the close consideration of written material, your own and that of others. In that consideration, you can put your finger on faults and successes; you can say, "Just here the idea does not come clear," or "There communication seems complete."

i   READER AND WRITER

Our first selection is close to the college student's problems; indeed it may suggest how some of them came about. We are interested in it both as an exercise in reading and as a discussion of some important matters in reading and writing.

FROM *The Second Tree from the Corner* (1954)

E. B. WHITE

Calculating Machine

I A publisher in Chicago has sent us a pocket calculating machine by which we may test our writing to see whether it is intelligible. The calculator was developed by General Motors, who, not satisfied with giving the world a Cadillac, now dream of bringing perfect understanding to men. The machine (it is simply a celluloid card with a dial) is called the Reading-Ease Calculator and shows four grades of "reading ease"—Very Easy, Easy, Hard, and Very Hard. You count your words and syllables, set the dial, and an indicator lets you know whether anybody is going to understand what you have written. An instruction book came with it, and after mastering the simple rules we lost no time in running a test on the instruction book itself, to see how *that* writer was doing. The poor fellow! His leading essay, the one on the front cover, tested Very Hard.

II Our next step was to study the first phrase on the face of the calculator: "How to test Reading-Ease of written matter." There is, of course, no such thing as reading ease of written matter. There is the ease with which matter can be read, but that is a condition of the reader, not of the matter. Thus the inventors and distributors of this calculator get off to a poor start, with a Very Hard instruction book and a slovenly phrase. Already they have one foot caught in the brier patch of English usage.

III Not only did the author of the instruction book score badly on the front cover, but inside the book he used the word "personalize" in an essay on how to improve one's writing. A man who likes the word "personalize" is entitled to his choice, but we wonder whether he should be in the business of giving advice to writers. "Whenever possible," he wrote, "personalize your writing by directing it to the reader." As for us, we would as lief Simonize our grandmother as personalize our writing.

IV In the same envelope with the calculator, we received another training aid for writers—a booklet called "How to Write Better," by Rudolf

Flesch. This, too, we studied, and it quickly demonstrated the broncolike ability of the English language to throw whoever leaps cocksurely into the saddle. The language not only can toss a rider but knows a thousand tricks for tossing him, each more gay than the last. Dr. Flesch stayed in the saddle only a moment or two. Under the heading "Think Before You Write," he wrote, "The main thing to consider is your *purpose* in writing. Why are you sitting down to write?" And echo answered: Because, sir, it is more comfortable than standing up.

v Communication by the written word is a subtler (and more beautiful) thing than Dr. Flesch and General Motors imagine. They contend that the "average reader" is capable of reading only what tests Easy, and that the writer should write at or below this level. This is a presumptuous and degrading idea. There is no average reader, and to reach down toward this mythical character is to deny that each of us is on the way up, is ascending. ("Ascending," by the way, is a word Dr. Flesch advises writers to stay away from. Too unusual.)

vi It is our belief that no writer can improve his work until he discards the dulcet notion that the reader is feeble-minded, for writing is an act of faith, not a trick of grammar. Ascent is at the heart of the matter. A country whose writers are following a calculating machine downstairs is not ascending—if you will pardon the expression—and a writer who questions the capacity of the person at the other end of the line is not a writer at all, merely a schemer. The movies long ago decided that a wider communication could be achieved by a deliberate descent to a lower level, and they walked proudly down until they reached the cellar. Now they are groping for the light switch, hoping to find the way out.

vii We have studied Dr. Flesch's instructions diligently, but we return for guidance in these matters to an earlier American, who wrote with more patience, more confidence. "I fear chiefly," he wrote, "lest my expression may not be *extra-vagant* enough, may not wander far enough beyond the narrow limits of my daily experience, so as to be adequate to the truth of which I have been convinced. . . . Why level downward to our dullest perception always, and praise that as common sense? The commonest sense is the sense of men asleep, which they express by snoring."

viii Run that through your calculator! It may come out Hard, it may come out Easy. But it will come out whole, and it will last forever.

---

1) Does the title "Calculating Machine" refer only to the device developed by General Motors? Or does it come to have a larger reference than that?

2) Perhaps we ought to push the question a bit further. What is Mr. White objecting to? He is certainly not objecting to simple, direct writing; he would then be objecting to his own. Does vi suggest an answer?

3) When we say that a man writes simply and directly, we may be saying that he has written very carefully. A long time ago the playwright Richard Brinsley Sheridan wrote:

> You write with ease to show your breeding,
> But easy writing's curst hard reading.

Now White remarks upon the difficulty of writing well. Do you find any evidence in the piece itself that it has been written very carefully? You might first consider the transition between paragraphs.

4) Did that consideration make you aware of the organization of the piece—how the discussion proceeds from a description of a concrete thing, a "Reading-Ease Calculator," to principles about the relationship of writer to reader?

5) Is the distinction made in the second and third sentences of II a real distinction? What is the difference between White's attitude toward the "condition of the reader" and that of the contriver of the calculating device?

6) Do you object to the word "personalize"? Why should anyone? It may be a matter of association; a reader may, for instance, remember an advertisement for some mass-produced article alleged to be "personalized" by the addition of initials. But in the quoted sentence, surely, one trouble is that the word makes a confused sense. Perhaps the sentence means only "direct your writing to a reader"—a good and sensible meaning. But then what is the word "personalize" doing there anyhow?

7) Possibly we need to remark something that White takes for granted. When White says that the writer ought not to question the capacity of the reader, he does not mean that the writer assumes the reader has all the information and the ideas that *he* has. Of course the writer must assume he has something to give a reader. But he must not question his reader's capacity to understand.

8) In reading magazines or perhaps even textbooks, have you not been aware that writers have approached you as if you had no capacity—approached you as schemers, not writers? Can you not, indeed, give examples of that approach?

9) This matter is of much concern to us here at the beginning of a college course. A writer who approaches his readers as if they were feeble-minded and makes the least possible demand upon them can surely give his readers very little. It is a great part of being educated to be willing to read writers who respect their readers and who do not fear to ask some activity from them.

10) We can put the matter another way. You would not wish to resemble some writer's concept of an average reader; you would rather reach up to a writer than have him reach down to you. What textbook and instructor can help you with is just that reaching.

11) The quotation in VII is from Henry Thoreau. Thoreau italicizes and hyphenates "extravagant" in order to remind his readers of its derivation, but perhaps the sentence itself shows you what the derivation is (if it does not, your dictionary will).

12) Notice the expressions in II and IV that White uses to represent the difficulties in using the English language. We call such expressions META-PHORS; the skillful use of them accounts for some of the vividness of these passages. Of course a writer's difficulty might be described in another way. But can you think of an expression that is at once so vivid and so economi-

cal as "one foot caught in the brier patch of English usage"? What is being said of the movies in the last sentence of vi?

13) You will have noticed that the word "metaphors" is printed in SMALL CAPITALS in 12 above. The terms of literary discussion that are at all likely to be unfamiliar to the student are so printed *on their first appearance* in this text. Literary terms have the same kind of importance that the technical terms of mechanics have—they are necessary for efficient discussion. Look them up in your dictionary when you need to.

HOW GOOD WRITING COMES ABOUT   *ii*

Now we turn to another discussion of good writing, this one by a professional scholar, Samuel Eliot Morison. But you will find that it complements what E. B. White says. It offers us opportunities for the introductory discussion of matters with which we shall be much concerned, and to many of its principles we shall have later occasion to return.

Professor Morison is directing his advice to young persons doing their first writing in history, but much of what he says applies to all writing. At the same time, he suggests principles by which you may judge what you read, for good workmanlike prose will have just the qualities here urged. The essay has a wide application; and you will not often meet with so sound and sensible a discussion of the problems of college writing. Remember that the graduate students addressed are only a few years older than you are, and that their problems are not different in kind from your own.

You will find the essay easy to read, and you will probably not have to use your dictionary much. But subsequent selections will often have words unknown to you—and perhaps the questions and discussion sometimes. If you pass over any word unknown to you and not clear from its CONTEXT, your preparation is that far incomplete. It is well to get started right.

History as a Literary Art   (1946, 1953)

SAMUEL ELIOT MORISON

1 Exploring American history has been a very absorbing and exciting business now for three quarters of a century. Thousands of graduate students have produced thousands of monographs on every aspect of the history of the Americas. But the American reading public for the most part is blissfully ignorant of this vast output. When John Citizen feels the urge to read history, he goes to the novels of Kenneth Roberts or Margaret Mitchell, not to the histories of Professor this or Doctor that. Why?

11 Because American historians, in their eagerness to present facts and their laudable anxiety to tell the truth, have neglected the literary aspects

Reprinted from *By Land and By Sea* by Samuel Eliot Morison, by permission of Alfred A. Knopf, Inc. Copyright, 1953, by Priscilla B. Morison.

of their craft. They have forgotten that there is an art of writing history. . . .

III In the meantime, the American public has become so sated by dull history textbooks in school and college that it won't read history unless disguised as something else under a title such as "The Flowering of Florida," "The Epic of the East," or "The Growth of the American Republic." Or, more often, they get what history they want from historical novels.

IV Now I submit, this is a very bad situation. The tremendous plowing up of the past by well-trained scholars is all to the good, so far as it goes. Scholars know more about America's past than ever; they are opening new furrows and finding new artifacts, from aboriginal arrowheads to early twentieth-century corset stays. But they are heaping up the pay dirt for others. Journalists, novelists, and free-lance writers are the ones that extract the gold; and they deserve every ounce they get because they are the ones who know how to write histories that people care to read. What I want to see is a few more Ph.D.'s in history winning book-of-the-month adoptions and reaping the harvest of dividends. They can do it, too, if they will only use the same industry at presenting history as they do in compiling it.

V Mind you, I intend no disparagement of historians who choose to devote their entire energies to teaching. Great teachers do far more good to the cause of history than mediocre writers. Such men, for instance, as the late H. Morse Stephens, who stopped writing (which he never liked) as soon as he obtained a chair in this country, and the late Edwin F. Gay, who never began writing, inspired thousands of young men and initiated scores of valuable books. Thank God for these gifted teachers, I say; universities should seek out, encourage, and promote them far more than they do. My remarks are addressed to young people who have the urge to write history, and wish to write it effectively.

VI There are no special rules for writing history; any good manual of rhetoric or teacher of composition will supply the rules for writing English. But what terrible stuff passes for English in Ph.D. dissertations, monographs, and articles in historical reviews! Long, involved sentences that one has to read two or three times in order to grasp their meaning; poverty in vocabulary, ineptness of expression, weakness in paragraph structure, frequent misuse of words, and, of late, the introduction of pseudo-scientific and psychological jargon. There is no fundamental cure for this except better teaching of English in our schools and colleges, and by every teacher, whatever his other subjects may be. If historical writing is infinitely better in France than in America, and far better in the British Isles and Canada than in the United States, it is because every French and British teacher of history drills his pupils in their mother tongue, requiring a constant stream of essays and reports, and criticizing written work not only as history but as literature. The American university teacher who gives honor grades to students who have not yet learned to write English, for industrious compilations of facts or feats of memory, is wanting in professional pride or competency.

VII Of course, what we should all like to attain in writing history is style. "The sense for style," says Whitehead in his *Aims of Education,* "is an aesthetic sense, based on admiration for the direct attainment of a fore-seen end, simply and without waste. Style in art, style in literature, style in science, style in logic, style in practical execution, have fundamentally the same aesthetic qualities, namely attainment and restraint. Style, in its finest sense, is the last acquirement of the educated mind; it is also the most useful. It pervades the whole being. . . . Style is the ultimate morality of mind."

vIII Unfortunately, there is no royal road to style. It cannot be attained by mere industry; it can never be achieved through imitation, although it may be promoted by example. Reading the greatest literary artists among historians will help; but do not forget that what was acceptable style in 1850 might seem turgid today. We can still read Macaulay with admiration and pleasure, we can still learn paragraph structure and other things from Macaulay, but anyone who tried to imitate Macaulay today would be a pompous ass.

IX Just as Voltaire's ideal curé advises his flock not to worry about going to heaven, but to do right and probably by God's grace they will get there; so the young writer of history had better concentrate on day-by-day improvement in craftsmanship. Then perhaps he may find some day that his prose appeals to a large popular audience; that, in other words, he has achieved style through simple, honest, straightforward writing.

x A few hints as to the craft may be useful to budding historians. First and foremost, *get writing!* Young scholars generally wish to secure the last fact before writing anything, like General McClellan refusing to advance (as people said) until the last mule was shod. It is a terrible strain, isn't it, to sit down at a desk with your notes all neatly docketed, and begin to write? You pretend to your wife that you mustn't be interrupted; but, actually, you welcome a ring of the telephone, a knock at the door, or a bellow from the baby as an excuse to break off. Finally, after smoking sundry cigarettes and pacing about the house two or three times, you commit a lame paragraph or two to paper. By the time you get to the third, one bit of information you want is lacking. What a relief! Now you must go back to the library or to the archives to do some more digging. That's where you are happy! And what you turn up there leads to more questions and prolongs the delicious process of research. Half the pleas I have heard from graduate students for more time or another grant-in-aid are mere excuses to postpone the painful drudgery of writing.

XI There is the "indispensablest beauty in knowing how to get done," said Carlyle. In every research there comes a point, which you should recognize like a call of conscience, when you must get down to writing. And when you once are writing, go on writing as long as you can; there will be plenty of time later to shove in the footnotes or return to the library for extra information. Above all, *start* writing. Nothing is more pathetic than the "gonna" historian, who from graduate school on is always "gonna" write a magnum opus but never completes his research on the subject, and dies without anything to show for a lifetime's work.

xii Dictation is usually fatal to good historical writing. Write out your first draft in longhand or, if you compose easily on the typewriter, type it out yourself, revise with pencil or pen, and have it retyped clean. Don't stop to consult your notes for every clause or sentence; it is better to get what you have to say clearly in your mind and dash it off; then, after you have it down, return to your notes and compose your next few pages or paragraphs. After a little experience you may well find that you think best with your fingers on the typewriter keys or your fountain pen poised over the paper. For me, the mere writing of a few words seems to point up vague thoughts and make jumbled facts array themselves in neat order. Whichever method you choose, composing before you write or as you write, do not return to your raw material or verify facts and quotations or insert footnotes until you have written a substantial amount, an amount that will increase with practice. It is significant that two of our greatest American historians, Prescott and Parkman, were nearly blind during a good part of their active careers. They had to have the sources read to them and turn the matter over and over in their minds before they could give anything out; and when they gave, *they gave!*

xiii Now, the purpose of this quick, warm synthesis between research, thinking, and writing is to attain the three prime qualities of historical composition—clarity, vigor, and objectivity. You must think about your facts, analyze your material, and decide exactly what you mean before you can write it so that the average reader will understand. Do not fall into the fallacy of supposing that "facts speak for themselves." Most of the facts that you excavate, like other relics of past human activity, are dumb things; it is for you to make them speak by proper selection, arrangement, and emphasis. Dump your entire collection of facts on paper, and the result will be unreadable if not incomprehensible.

xiv So, too, with vigor. If your whole paragraph or chapter is but a hypothesis, say so at the beginning, but do not bore and confuse the reader with numerous "buts," "excepts," "perhapses," "howevers," and "possiblys." Use direct rather than indirect statements, the active rather than the passive voice, and make every sentence and paragraph an organic whole. Above all, if you are writing historical narrative, make it move. Do not take time out in the middle of a political or military campaign to introduce special developments or literary trends, as McMaster did to the confusion of his readers. Place those admittedly important matters in a chapter or chapters by themselves so that your reader's attention will not be lost by constant interruption.

xv That brings us to the third essential quality—objectivity. Keep the reader constantly in mind. You are not writing history for yourself or for the professors who are supposed to know more about it than you do. Assume that you are writing for intelligent people who know nothing about your particular subject but whom you wish to interest and attract. I once asked the late Senator Beveridge why his *Life of John Marshall,* despite its great length and scholarly apparatus, was so popular. He replied: "The trouble with you professors of history is that you write for each other. I write for people almost completely ignorant of American history, as I was when I began my research.". . .

XVI Above all, do not be afraid to revise and rewrite. Reading aloud is a good test—historians' wives have to stand a lot of that! A candid friend who is not a historian and so represents the audience you are trying to reach, is perhaps the best "dog" to try it on. Even if he has little critical sense, it is encouraging to have him stay awake. My good friend Lucien Price years ago listened with a pained expression to a bit of my early work. "Now, just what do you mean by that?" he asked after a long, involved, pedantic, and quote-larded paragraph. I told him in words of one syllable, or perhaps two. "Fine!" said he, "I understand that. Now write down what you said; throw the other away!"

XVII Undoubtedly the writer of history can enrich his mind and broaden his literary experience as well as better his craftsmanship by his choice of leisure reading. If he is so fortunate as to have had a classical education, no time will be better spent in making him an effective historian than in reading Latin and Greek authors. Both these ancient languages are such superb instruments of thought that a knowledge of them cures slipshod English and helps one to attain a clear, muscular style. All our greatest historical stylists—notably Prescott, Parkman, Fiske, and Frederick J. Turner—had a classical education and read the ancient historians in the original before they approached American history.

XVIII If you have little Latin and less Greek and feel unable to spare the time and effort to add them to your stock of tools, read the ancient classics in the best literary translations, such as North's Plutarch, Rawlinson's Herodotus, John J. Chapman's Æschylus, Gilbert Murray's Euripides, and, above all, Jowett's or Livingstone's Thucydides. Through them you will gain the content and spirit of the ancient classics, which will break down your provincialism, refresh your spirit, and give you a better philosophical insight into the ways of mankind than most of such works as the new science of psychology has brought forth. Moreover, you will be acquiring the same background as many of the great Americans of past generations, thus aiding your understanding of them.

XIX The reading of English classics will tend in the same direction, and will also be a painless and unconscious means of improving your literary style. Almost every English or American writer of distinction is indebted to Shakespeare and the English Bible. The Authorized Version is not only the great source book of spiritual experience of English-speaking peoples; it is a treasury of plain, pungent words and muscular phrases, beautiful in themselves and with long associations, which we are apt to replace by smooth words lacking in punch, or by hackneyed or involved phrases. Here are a few examples chosen in five minutes from my desk Bible: I Samuel i, 28: "I have lent him to the Lord." What an apt phrase for anyone bringing up their son for the Church! Why say "loaned" instead of "lent"? Isaiah xxii, 5: "For it is a day of trouble, and of treading down, and of perplexity." In brief, just what we are going through today. But most modern historians would not feel that they were giving the reader his money's worth unless they wrote: "It is an era of agitation, of a progressive decline in the standard of living, and of uncertainty as to the correct policy." Romans xi, 25: "Wise in your own conceits." This epigram has often been used, but a modern writer would be tempted to express the thought in some such cumbrous manner as "Expert within the limits of your own fallacious theories."

xx Of course much of the Biblical phraseology is obsolete, and there are other literary quarries for historians. You can find many appropriate words, phrases, similes, and epigrams in American authors such as Mark Twain, Emerson, and Thoreau. I have heard an English economist push home a point to a learned audience with a quotation from *Alice in Wonderland;* American historians might make more use of *Huckleberry Finn.*

xxi The historian can learn much from the novelist. Most writers of fiction are superior to all but the best historians in characterization and description. If you have difficulty in making people and events seem real, see if you cannot learn the technique from American novelists such as Sherwood Anderson, Joseph Hergesheimer and Margaret Mitchell. For me, the greatest master of all is Henry James. He used a relatively simple and limited vocabulary; but what miracles he wrought with it! What precise and perfect use he makes of words to convey the essence of a human situation to the reader! If you are not yet acquainted with Henry James, try the selection of his shorter novels and stories edited by Clifton Fadiman, and then read some of the longer novels, like *Roderick Hudson* and *The American.* And, incidentally, you will learn more about the top layers of American and European society in the second half of the nineteenth century than you can ever glean from the works of social historians.

xxii What is the place of imagination in history? A historian or biographer is under restrictions unknown to a novelist. He has no right to override facts by his own imagination. If he is writing on a remote or obscure subject about which few facts are available, his imagination may legitimately weave them into a pattern. But to be honest he must make clear what is fact and what is hypothesis. The quality of imagination, if properly restrained by the conditions of historical discipline, is of great assistance in enabling one to discover problems to be solved, to grasp the significance of facts, to form hypotheses, to discern causes in their first beginnings, and, above all, to relate the past creatively to the present. There are many opportunities in historical narrative for bold, imaginative expressions. "A complete statement in the imaginative form of an important truth arrests attention," wrote Emerson, "and is repeated and remembered." Imagination used in this way invests an otherwise pedestrian narrative with vivid and exciting qualities.

xxiii Finally, the historian should have frequent recourse to the book of life. The richer his personal experience, the wider his human contacts, the more likely he is to effect a living contact with his audience. In writing, similes drawn from the current experience of this mechanical age rather than those rifled from the literary baggage of past eras, are the ones that will go home to his reader. Service on a jury or a local committee may be a revelation as to the political thoughts and habits of mankind. A month's labor in a modern factory would help any young academician to clarify his ideas of labor and capital. A camping trip in the woods will tell him things about Western pioneering that he can never learn in books. The great historians, with few exceptions, are those who have not merely studied, but lived; and whose studies have ranged over a much wider field than the period or subject of which they write.

xxiv The veterans of World War II who, for the most part, have completed their studies in college or graduate school, should not regard the years of their war service as wasted. Rather should they realize that the war gave them a rich experience of life, which is the best equipment for a historian. They have "been around," they have seen mankind at his best and his worst, they have shared the joy and passion of a mighty effort, and they can read man's doings in the past with far greater understanding than if they had spent these years in sheltered academic groves.

xxv To these young men especially, and to all young men I say (as the poet Chapman said to the young Elizabethan): "Be free, all worthy spirits, and stretch yourselves!" Bring all your knowledge of life to bear on everything that you write. Never let yourself bog down in pedantry and detail. Bring History, the most humane and noble form of letters, back to the proud position she once held; knowing that your words, if they be read and remembered, will enter into the stream of life, and perhaps move men to thought and action centuries hence, as do those of Thucydides after more than two thousand years.

---

1) Here, as often in this book, the questions are intended primarily to insure a second consideration of passages especially important to us. We may start with this one: Does Morison's contention that people do not read history (in i and iii) conform to your observation? If you know a dull textbook in history, does Morison properly diagnose the causes of its dullness? Or do you know an interesting one? Is it written as Morison says history should be? (In iii Morison is making fun of himself: he and Henry Steele Commager have written a book called *The Growth of the American Republic*.)

2) Had you noticed that the introductory portion of the essay ends with v? A good reader is aware of structure. Morison's summary statement of the ills of contemporary writing in vi is a statement of ills your composition course will try to cure. Are you willing that all your instructors accept the principle in the last sentence of vi? Is it fair?

3) What do you take it Whitehead means by "Style is the ultimate morality of mind"? Notice that he says that style depends upon "attainment and restraint." The skill that is attainment we must expect to develop—we cannot have it all at once. But restraint, one would think, might be exercised fully at once. What do you take "restraint" to mean in the practice of writing—what would be CONCRETE instances of it? (You had better make sure of the word ABSTRACT, too.)

4) Style, if we mean by it only a way of writing that is pleasant and clear for a reader, is not really a mystery. Jonathan Swift has a famous EPIGRAM: "Proper words in proper places make the true definition of a style." It is a true enough definition, although it seems so impossibly inclu-

sive that one wonders at first if Swift meant it seriously. But Swift himself interprets it:

> Although . . . our English tongue is too little cultivated in this kingdom, yet the faults are nine in ten owing to affectation and not to want of understanding. When a man's thoughts are clear, the properest words will generally offer themselves first, and his own judgment will direct him in what order to place them, so as they may be best understood. Where men err against this method, it is usually on purpose, and to show their learning, their oratory, their politeness, or their knowledge of the world. In short, that simplicity without which no human performance can arrive to any great perfection is nowhere more eminently useful than in this.

Do you think Morison's advice always consistent with Swift's? Swift seems to be saying that good writing is primarily an extension of clear thinking. The beginning writer, at any rate, will do well to believe that if he can be clear, the other excellences will come after. But we had better remember the advice of Voltaire's curé (IX) and Morison's application of it; what Swift did not talk about in the quoted passage is practice.

5) It may help you in understanding VIII to have a passage by Macaulay before you. Here is a famous one:

> Thus the Puritan was made up of two different men, the one all self-abasement, penitence, gratitude, passion, the other proud, calm, inflexible, sagacious. He prostrated himself in the dust before his Maker: but he set his foot on the neck of his king. In his devotional retirement, he prayed with convulsions, and groans, and tears. He was half-maddened by glorious or terrible illusions. He heard the lyres of angels or the tempting whispers of fiends. He caught a gleam of the Beatific Vision, or woke screaming from dreams of everlasting fire. Like Vane, he thought himself intrusted with the scepter of the millennial year. Like Fleetwood, he cried in the bitterness of his soul that God had hid his face from him. But when he took his seat in the council, or girt on his sword for war, these tempestuous workings of the soul had left no perceptible trace behind them . . .

Morison says we can learn paragraph structure and other things from Macaulay. What other things? We have in Chapter X a piece by Morison himself on the Puritan. Perhaps you would like to look ahead and see how he handles this subject matter.

6) Did you notice that the first sentence of XIII is a kind of signpost—that it points ahead to the structure of XIII, XIV, and XV? Read this little three-paragraph section over again; its advice is entirely practical. What does your handbook have to say about the passive voice and about indirect constructions? Can you give an example of each?

7) Consider XV and XVI together. Do you see that XVI makes a useful suggestion about putting the principle of XV into practice? If you use your roommate, for instance, to try out a piece of writing, you will have really envisaged a reader—the thing beginning writers most often fail to do.

8) Did you notice that the five paragraphs beginning with XVII make up a section on reading? Think particularly about what Morison says are the intellectual results of wide reading.

9) Of course skill in reading is in itself the most necessary of intellectual attainments. Morison, quite properly sticking to his subject, concentrates his discussion on the influence of one's reading upon one's writing. It is well for us that he does so, because students often do not realize how intimately the skills are connected.

10) And that brings us to a comment on the design of this book. The selections are first of all for practice in reading; each has been chosen in the hope that it will be valuable to college students quite in itself. But we shall work out from these pieces of reading in two ways. We shall try to discover in our examination of the selections principles that apply to further reading. And we shall work toward pieces of writing: pieces about the selections, and pieces that offer comparable problems to those solved in the selections. Neither textbook nor classroom instruction can take the place of the wide reading Morison recommends. But they can make a beginning for it; they can help you read perceptively; and they can show you how your reading and your writing are connected, and thus hasten the influence of the one upon the other.

11) You will probably wish to consider this essay further than these questions lead you; we are never to suppose that the questions have exhausted the interest of the selection or noted all that is of importance in it. And it would be well to reread the essay before you write your first long term paper, no matter for what course it happens to be.

SUGGESTIONS FOR PAPERS

Of course your instructor will direct your papers; the suggestions for papers here and in the following chapters are intended primarily to show the sort of connection that may be made between your reading and your writing.

If a paper connected with the selections is desired for the first writing assignment, it might carry out one of these suggestions: (a) Write a discussion of the way in which a writer should think of his reader, drawing your material from both White and Morison, and making proper acknowledgment. (b) Write a restatement of the passage quoted from Macaulay in such words and sentence structure as you think appropriate to contemporary writing. (c) Write a short discussion of the vigor and simplicity of Biblical language, using paragraph xix of the Morison piece as a starting point and supplying your own examples. (d) Write two or three paragraphs on the difficulties of writing a few sentences without being tripped up by English grammar and syntax (everyone has material for this). (e) This week you will have started the reading of a number of books new to you. Consider the style of one or two of them. You will need to include short quotations. (f) Take this as a first sentence for a paragraph: "Morison's 'History as a Literary Art' may explain in part the ordinary high school graduate's ignorance of history." Develop it. (g) In this book we have another selection from Morison and another from White. Read ahead a little, and write a consideration of the relationship between theory and practice in either of the writers.

II

Paragraphs and Structure

Our first chapter was introductory; we now come to particular problems in reading, and we ought to start with something that will be useful to you at once in all your college work. We shall begin, therefore, with a consideration of sentences in the context of paragraphs, and of paragraphs in their relation to one another, for on those matters most beginning students need immediate help. So important are they that we shall discuss them in some detail, even at the risk of pointing out things you already know. Not all our discussion will be so elementary; and if the material in this section seems over-familiar, that is your good fortune.

i   PARAGRAPHS IN PATTERNS

In good writing, a paragraph is not an arbitrary division, but a planned part of the structure of the whole. An awareness of structure is one of the marks of a good reader. A good reader needs to be aware of structure because a careful writer plans his paragraphs to accomplish particular parts of his purpose in the whole composition.

When you are reading difficult material, you will find it well to ask yourself just what is accomplished in each paragraph. Often—not always—in EXPOSITION, in writing designed to set forth facts and ideas in their relationships, you can find the sentence or sentences around which the paragraph is organized. They make the statement the paragraph is designed to explain or enforce. Such sentences are key sentences or TOPIC SENTENCES, and it is convenient to mark them as you read. They often stand first in the paragraph, but by no means always; one identifies them by the kind of statement they make, not by their position. And in some paragraphs the relationship of statements is such that no one sentence is the center of organization. Then the reader must be sure that he stops on the paragraph long enough to see the relationship that binds it together.

Equally important are the sentences and expressions that function as TRANSITION. You will find between-paragraph transition usually accomplished by sentences standing at the beginnings of paragraphs, less commonly by sentences standing at the ends. And there may be transitional sentences and expressions within paragraphs, connecting one part of the development to another—these too need your attention. Sometimes a whole paragraph will have a transitional function, or will announce the subject matter of subsequent paragraphs.

An awareness of paragraph structure will help you in your general reading. You have probably been urged, and rightly, to mark your books. But every instructor has observed many students who mark their books in a fashion more likely to hinder than to help. Often such students mark emotionally, to indicate their first reactions of approval or disapproval, or to single out striking turns of phrase or impressive examples. But the reader who is aware of structure, of topic sentences, and of transition, will mark a book in such manner that when he returns to it—for instance, in review—he can follow easily from his marking the main line of discussion. When you have learned to keep in mind as you read that a paragraph has a purpose, a structure, and a relationship to the paragraphs around it, you will have accomplished a great deal.

We shall see what we can accomplish now with an eleven-paragraph unit from a good piece of academic writing, a unit that offers no great difficulty. But you will need your dictionary sometimes.

FROM *Literary Culture on the Frontier* (1948)

DIXON WECTER

I In recent years, it has become conventional to attribute . . . cultural changes to the "frontier." Nathaniel Ames, with an almanac maker's gifts of prophecy, foretold as early as 1758 that "Arts and Sciences will change the Face of Nature in their Tour from Hence over the Appalachian Mountains to the Western Ocean." While the settler was destined to transform the frontier, it was clear from the start in an equally real sense he would be transformed by it.

II These interactions happened at successive times and places—as white settlement after the Revolution flowed first into the great meadows of Kentucky and the fertile wilderness of the Ohio Valley, then early in the new century pushed on to the Illinois country and began to explore the vast Mississippi Valley, while another tongue from Virginia and the Carolinas thrust itself into the then Southwest frontier of Georgia, Alabama, and Tennessee. Eddying around points of earlier settlement like New Orleans and St. Louis, the wave of migration that had surged so promptly into the territory of the Louisiana Purchase—the "choice country with room enough" promised by President Jefferson—began before long to encroach upon Mexican dominion in Texas and later in the Far West, until both vast regions had fallen to the Federal Union by 1848. Meanwhile in 1846 the United States, by treaty with Britain, gained undisputed title to that Pacific Northwest which for a decade had been the journey's end of the famous

Oregon Trail. This, in brief, is the story of the frontier, whose march rounded out the continental expanse of the nation before the nineteenth century was half done—although areas and pockets of unsettled land remained for many decades, and the frontier was not declared officially closed until the Census of 1890. The cultural institutions and tools which shaped the mind of this frontier, through printing, reading, and writing, deserve examination.

III Within a few years after the winning of independence, hosts of settlers—carrying seeds, a few tools, and one or two indispensable books like the Bible—had begun to cross the Alleghenies toward "the meeting point between savagery and civilization," as the historian Frederick J. Turner called the frontier. It has been defined as that zone, facing the trackless public domain, where fewer than two persons lived per square mile. Socially and culturally, it was a laboratory of mixed races and folkways from the start. Success came to the young and vigorous, rather than to the heir of wealth and prestige. Even book learning mattered less than brawn, daring, and the earthy lore of soldier, woodsman, and farmer.

IV In those early days, the valves of influence opened chiefly westward. Receiving from the Eastern seaboard almost all the culture it knew, the frontier gave little or nothing in return. Once a settler made the western traverse, he rarely went home. The mind of the East, in general, felt little more than casual curiosity about the rude frontier, save as a terra incognita of romantic novelists. Soon after the dawn of the nineteenth century, travel grew easier, thanks to the building of turnpikes into the West, and the steamboats that pioneered its great rivers, and the canals that linked its waters. In the thirties and forties came the first railroads, and the conquest was assured.

V Over these roads and watercourses eagerly streamed the advance agents of civilization. One such courier was the itinerant revivalist, missionary, or circuit rider. He helped break the shell of frontier loneliness, as the grim homiletics of Cotton Mather and Jonathan Edwards gave way to the warmth of backwoods exhorters like Lorenzo Dow and Peter Cartwright. "When I hear a man preach," said Lincoln, "I like to see him act as if he were fighting bees." Emotional oratory from the pulpit, and reading matter like missionary tracts, henceforth became a powerful element in frontier culture, shaping its imagination and daily idioms. From the preacher, also, much backwoods education stemmed. As early as 1800, the Methodist General Conference made its circuit riders agents for books published under direction of the church; the greatest of its Western missionaries, Bishop Francis Asbury, shortly became an evangel of popular education. The Baptists, who shared with Methodists the primacy on the frontier, presently followed suit. From early days, Presbyterians and Congregationalists, whose Yankee tradition demanded learning in the pulpit and literacy among the flock, tended the vineyard of knowledge. Biblical scholars like Lyman Beecher and Calvin Stowe—father and husband, respectively, of Harriet Beecher Stowe—transplanted their educational interests, with powerful effect, to the Ohio country.

VI Secular education in the West owed most to that hardy perennial, the wandering schoolmaster. The first historian of Kentucky and introducer of Daniel Boone to the world, in 1784, was a Pennsylvania pedagogue, John Filson. On the frontier, this profession was no sedentary calling; the first master of a log-cabin school at Lexington, Kentucky, began one day's tasks by strangling with his bare hands a wildcat in the schoolroom. First in the South, later in the Southwest, the New England schoolmaster grew proverbial for qualities of enterprise, rather than for the cloistered pursuit of knowledge. He charged what he could get, and boarded around, while holding classes in a cabin of mud-daubed logs, where boards served for desks and shingles with bits of charcoal for slates and blackboards. Little beyond "readin', writin', and cypherin' to the rule of three" was expected of him. Nevertheless, he inducted his charges into the mystery of the printed word—chiefly by means of those aggressively American textbooks that came after Independence, like Noah Webster's blue-backed speller, Jedidiah Morse's geography, and Nicholas Pike's arithmetic ("more suitable to our meridian than those heretofore published").

VII Such books, and others on law, medicine, surveying, biography, history and fictional subjects, were carried into the West by that humble pollinator of culture, the itinerant peddler. Like the greatest of his tribe, Bronson Alcott, this type was commonly Yankee. That New England wrote, published, taught, and sold the majority of books on the frontier, in the first generation of settlement, is a fact of much significance in the shaping of the western country's neo-Puritanism.

VIII Free education was one of the pioneer's cherished ideas. The Land Ordinance of 1785 set aside section sixteen in each township for public schools; that of 1787 promised, "Schools and the means of education shall forever be encouraged." As a matter of sober fact, the dream of a great public educational system in the West did not come close to realization until the 1830's, when the taxes necessary to its support were at last levied.

IX Colleges, however, made early headway. Transylvania Seminary in Kentucky, the pioneer west of the Alleghenies, started in 1785 as little more than a grammar school; it began to confer degrees in 1802, amassed an important library, and grew to considerable prestige before sectarian quarrels sapped its usefulness. Ohio University at Athens, set up by act of the state legislature in 1804, drew sustenance from federal land grants. It bred a notable generation of schoolmasters in the New England tradition. Its president during the Van Buren era was William Holmes McGuffey, whose Eclectic Readers taught three generations of Americans good English and sound morals. Most pioneer colleges, by the yardstick of modern times, were poor in books, scholarship, and mental stimulus; but their spirit, like that of the region itself, fed upon hope. Naturally enough the fount of intellectual America remained in the East, whence came the best educators, and where backwoods sons with ambition and luck were prone to gravitate. Thanks to the religious orthodoxy of the frontier, the shadow of Yale, in the land of steady habits and Trinitarianism, and likewise that of safely Presbyterian Princeton, loomed larger across the Ohio Valley than did the influence of more liberal, heretical Harvard.

x Mechanics' institutes, local lyceums, lecture and study courses, museums featuring exhibits and talks, all promoted Western education upon the adult level. Moreover, here and there, nuclei of utopian communities—such as New Harmony, Indiana, on the lower Wabash, which drew the English socialist Robert Owen, the feminist Frances Wright, the French naturalist Charles Lesueur, and others who taught in its school—served as intellectual beacons on the prairie, even though geographically the radius of their light was small.

xi Under great handicaps—indeed with an appetite whetted by privation—the westering pioneers cherished the crumbs of book learning and culture. In an address in 1859, Henry Ward Beecher picturesquely described these emigrants: "They drive schools along with them, as shepherds drive flocks. They have herds of churches, academies, lyceums; and their religious and educational institutions go lowing along the western plains as Jacob's herds lowed along the Syrian hills."

---

1) The material here offers the writer a difficult problem of organization. If you were not aware of his problem as you read the selection, it is because he has solved it. Essentially the piece is a narrative of a complex cultural movement, involving many persons over a considerable period and throughout a wide territory. The sort of narrative structure one might use in writing an account of a relatively simple set of events would not be economical enough for the presentation of so complex material for the purposes of a compact literary history. We shall examine the structure the writer does devise.

2) The difficulty a summary historical treatment offers the reader is, of course, that of packed detail. For reasons of space the detail must be handled briefly, but it must be there to make the generalization meaningful. Our selection is easier to read than such writing often is, for it has a better-than-usual paragraph organization. But it has been left to you to see that organization. You may be used to textbooks which, by means of black-face type or other mechanical means, announce a new aspect of a subject or a new division of its treatment. Here it is assumed that the reader will be aware of structure by himself.

3) In i notice the very close connection of the three sentences, and the close connection of the last of them to the first sentence in ii. The reader who does not stop to be sure of the reference of "These interactions" gets a poor start on ii.

4) What is the relationship of ii to the rest of the piece? Notice that the last sentence of ii is an announcement of the intention of the whole.

5) We may consider ii a narrative rather than an expository paragraph. A narrative structure is determined by an order of events in a time sequence. Although a narrative paragraph may develop a topic sentence, it commonly does not. Is there a topic sentence here?

6) Paragraph ii gave us some general account of the westward movement; the purpose of iii is to define. You can distinguish two definitions.

How do they complement each other? Notice their position in the paragraph. We say that the last three sentences extend the definition. (What does "public domain" mean?)

7) Paragraphs I–III have been introductory; IV brings us to the specific subject of the piece. In IV we have an example of a simple, useful paragraph structure: the topic sentence is the initial generalization, and it is developed by restatement and by instances.

8) How many of the eleven paragraphs begin with a generalization that may be considered a topic sentence? Does x?

9) Since we are discussing the structure of a finished piece of writing, we can say that in some paragraphs the generalizations come first and that they are supported by instances. But in the writer's process of reasoning, the particulars came first, and the generalizations after as statements that covered the particulars. The generalizations are, we say, INDUCTIVE GENERALIZATIONS. Not all the particulars upon which the generalizations are based can be recorded. The writer must try to find particulars that will best represent the rest, and that will show us, clearly and economically, the basis for his generalization.

10) Now you must surely pay attention to an initial generalization; but that is not to say that you may neglect the detail. For instance, the first sentence in v is "Over these roads and watercourses eagerly streamed the advance agents of civilization." The detail of the preceding paragraph concerns the roads and watercourses; in the paragraph itself and in the next two paragraphs there are instances of the activities of the advance agents of civilization. Unless the reader ties generalization to instance, the paragraph will have no real meaning for him. Perhaps that seems too elementary to need remark, but every instructor will remember his students' attempts to use generalizations they had managed to remember but did not understand.

11) You will have realized that v, vi, and vii make up a section of the whole discussion concerned with three advance agents of civilization: the clergyman, the schoolmaster, and the peddler. The first sentence of v, then, functions as a topic sentence for the group; it is the second sentence of v that is specifically developed in the paragraph.

12) You may not have been very conscious of transition in reading this selection. That is not because you have been careless; it is because the piece is put together carefully enough so that transition need not be obtrusive. Let us see something of the way in which transition is accomplished. In v the first two sentences prepare for the between-paragraph transition in v–vi, for when we come to vi it is clear that the wandering schoolmaster is a second sort of advance agent. But there is another sort of transition: v ends with a statement about religious education; the first words of vi—"Secular education"—announce a change to a related subject. Likewise in vii: the peddler is clearly a third advance agent; but the first sentence in vii also has a close relationship to the last sentence in vi, and its first words—"Such books"—have their reference there.

13) Point out a grouping of paragraphs comparable to that of v, vi, and vii. But these paragraphs are not related in quite the same way, are hey? How will you describe the way in which they are put together?

14) Can you justify the lack of any specifically transitional expression between VII and VIII? Between X and XI?

15) What is the relationship of XI to the whole?

16) We have read Morison's "History as a Literary Art." How does Dixon Wecter's writing stand up according to the principles for good writing Morison gives us? In forming your answer, bear in mind that the essay from which our selection is excerpted first appeared in a work which by its basic scheme imposed upon all the contributing authors the necessity to be concise.

Now we shall turn to two short selections in which a fairly thorough analysis will be feasible. They present no difficulties in language or idea; we can therefore give our main attention to the ways in which the passages are put together. The first, by James Bryce, is from a chapter discussing the general characteristics of Americans in the late nineteenth century. It is complete in itself, and it is, moreover, an example of the complete development of an idea. Mark the passage as you read, but mark it lightly—you may wish upon consideration to change your markings.

FROM *The American Commonwealth* (1894)

JAMES BRYCE

[American Education] [1]

I [1] The Americans are an educated people, compared with the whole mass of the population in any European country except Switzerland, parts of Germany, Norway, Iceland, and Scotland; that is to say, the average of knowledge is higher, the habit of reading and thinking more generally diffused, than in any other country. [2] (I speak, of course, of the native Americans, excluding Negroes and recent immigrants.) [3] They know the Constitution of their own country, they follow public affairs, they join in local government and learn from it how government must be carried on, and in particular how discussion must be conducted in meetings, and its results tested at elections. [4] The Town Meeting has been the most perfect school of self-government in any modern country. [5] In villages, they still exercise their minds on theological questions, debating points of Christian doctrine with no small acuteness. [6] Women in particular, though their chief reading is fiction and theology, pick up at the public schools and from the popular magazines far more miscellaneous information than the women of any European country possess, and this naturally tells on the intelligence of the men.

II [1] That the education of the masses is nevertheless a superficial education goes without saying. [2] It is sufficient to enable them to think they know

[1] Brackets around a title indicate that it has been supplied by the editor, and in general throughout the book brackets indicate editorial addition or explanation.

something about the great problems of politics: insufficient to show them how little they know. [3] The public elementary school gives everybody the key to knowledge in making reading and writing familiar, but it has not time to teach him how to use the key, whose use is in fact, by the pressure of daily work, almost confined to the newspaper and the magazine. [4] So we may say that if the political education of the average American voter be compared with that of the average voter in Europe, it stands high; but if it be compared with the functions which the theory of the American government lays on him, which its spirit implies, which the methods of its party organization assume, its inadequacy is manifest. [5] This observation, however, is not so much a reproach to the schools, which generally do what English schools omit—instruct the child in the principles of the Constitution—as a tribute to the height of the ideal which the American conception of popular rule sets up.

III [1] For the functions of the citizen are not, as has hitherto been the case in Europe, confined to the choosing of legislators, who are then left to settle issues of policy and select executive rulers. [2] The American citizen is one of the governors of the Republic. [3] Issues are decided and rulers selected by the direct popular vote. [4] Elections are so frequent that to do his duty at them a citizen ought to be constantly watching public affairs with a full comprehension of the principles involved in them, and a judgment of the candidates derived from a criticism of their arguments as well as a recollection of their past careers. [5] The instruction received in the common schools and from the newspapers, and supposed to be developed by the practice of primaries and conventions, while it makes the voter deem himself capable of governing, does not fit him to weigh the real merits of statesmen, to discern the true grounds on which questions ought to be decided, to note the drift of events and discover the direction in which parties are being carried. [6] He is like a sailor who knows the spars and ropes of the ship and is expert in working her, but is ignorant of geography and navigation; who can perceive that some of the officers are smart and others dull, but cannot judge which of them is qualified to use the sextant or will best keep his head during a hurricane.

---

1) If we look at 1 by itself, we have an example of the simple, frequently-useful paragraph structure we saw in a number of Wecter's paragraphs. The first sentence is the topic sentence; it has two independent clauses, the second a restatement of the first. The generalization in the topic sentence is limited by the parenthetical sentence 2, and then developed by a series of particular statements, concrete examples of the intellectual attainments of average Americans. Bryce is careful, as good writers in general are careful, to get things stated fully and plainly, and to back up generalizations with instances and examples.

2) At first glance, one might say that II is just like 1 in structure. The first sentence seems to be a topic sentence; 2 and 3 develop it. You will notice that 2 and 3 make the same statement, 3 the more concretely. (The structure of either of these sentences may be called an ANTITHESIS.)

3) But if a too-hasty reader assumes that the paragraph will merely proceed with examples of superficial education and leaps over most of it to III, what trouble does he get into?

4) When we come to II:4, what happens to the structure of the paragraph?

5) We can approach the question in another way. Suppose you wished to quote the single sentence from the whole passage that would best represent its central idea. What sentence would you choose? Students asked the question are likely to pick out II:4 or III:5. Does your marking of the passage indicate either or both as particularly important? If you will compare them, you will see that II:4 is the more inclusive. What does it say that III:5 does not?

6) We can describe the structure in this way: in II:4 we have to the semicolon a summary restatement of the key idea of I; the second part of the sentence includes the idea in II:1–3 but introduces a new comparison. The new comparison is interpreted and limited by 5.

7) The last paragraph makes no new contention. It develops the comparison between the level of American education and the functions of American citizenship by examples of the duties of the American voter. Sentence 5 is a summarizing sentence; 6 is a restatement of 5 in the form of an ANALOGY, so that the discussion ends with a vivid IMAGE.

8) The structure of the whole passage, then, depends upon II:4; the passage develops to and then from that sentence. We may sometimes think of paragraphs as blocks of related information or ideas; but the comparison to blocks is inappropriate here, as it always is when ideas are related in a pattern that runs through a number of paragraphs.

9) Of course, such a pattern will not be clear without careful transition. Point out the words and expressions by which transition is accomplished.

10) Do you find that your marking of the passage is adequate? Does it indicate the structure of the passage, and therefore the relationships in ideas? Many good readers use, in addition to marking, marginal statements of key ideas, abbreviated according to their own systems or taste. (Wide outside margins have been provided in this book for just that purpose.) For example, marginal statements for the three paragraphs of our passage might be these: I. *Ams. compared most Es. highly ed.* II. *But ed. superficial; for citizen's need, inadequate.* III. *Ams. decide issues, choose exec. as well as legis.; cit. thinks self capable, actually not.* Such marginal notes are useful in review; if one finds that they are intelligible and that he can at once expand them, he has control of the passage; if they recall but little to him, he needs to reread.

11) Do you think this judgment on American education in the late nineteenth century is still valid?

FROM *The Sea Around Us* (1951)

RACHEL L. CARSON

The Birth of an Island

I Millions of years ago, a volcano built a mountain on the floor of the Atlantic. In eruption after eruption, it pushed up a great pile of volcanic rock, until it had accumulated a mass a hundred miles across at its base, reaching upward toward the surface of the sea. Finally its cone emerged as an island with an area of about 200 square miles. Thousands of years passed, and thousands of thousands. Eventually the waves of the Atlantic cut down the cone and reduced it to a shoal—all of it, that is, but a small fragment which remained above water. This fragment we know as Bermuda.

II With variations, the life story of Bermuda has been repeated by almost every one of the islands that interrupt the watery expanses of the oceans far from land. For these isolated islands in the sea are fundamentally different from the continents. The major land masses and the ocean basins are today much as they have been throughout the greater part of geologic time. But islands are ephemeral, created today, destroyed tomorrow. With few exceptions, they are the result of the violent, explosive, earth-shaking eruptions of submarine volcanoes, working perhaps for millions of years to achieve their end. It is one of the paradoxes in the ways of earth and sea that a process seemingly so destructive, so catastrophic in nature, can result in an act of creation.

III Islands have always fascinated the human mind. Perhaps it is the instinctive response of man, the land animal, welcoming a brief intrusion of earth in the vast, overwhelming expanse of sea. Here in a great ocean basin, a thousand miles from the nearest continent, with miles of water under our vessel, we come upon an island. Our imaginations can follow its slopes down through darkening waters to where it rests on the sea floor. We wonder why and how it arose here in the midst of the ocean.

IV The birth of a volcanic island is an event marked by prolonged and violent travail: the forces of the earth striving to create, and all the forces of the sea opposing. The sea floor, where an island begins, is probably nowhere more than about fifty miles thick—a thin covering over the vast bulk of the earth. In it are deep cracks and fissures, the results of unequal cooling and shrinkage in past ages. Along such lines of weakness the molten lava from the earth's interior presses up and finally bursts forth into the sea. But a submarine volcano is different from a terrestrial eruption, where the lava, molten rocks, gases, and other ejecta are hurled into the air through an open crater. Here on the bottom of the ocean the volcano has resisting it all the weight of the ocean water above it. Despite the immense pressure of, it may be, two or three miles of sea water, the new volcanic cone builds upward toward the surface, in flow after flow of lava. Once within reach of the waves, its soft ash and tuff are violently attacked, and for a long period the potential island may remain a shoal, unable to emerge. But, eventually, in new eruptions, the cone is pushed up into the air and a rampart against the attacks of the waves is built of hardened lava.

v Navigators' charts are marked with numerous, recently discovered submarine mountains. Many of these are the submerged remnants of the islands of a geologic yesterday. The same charts show islands that emerged from the sea at least fifty million years ago, and others that arose within our own memory. Among the undersea mountains marked on the charts may be the islands of tomorrow, which at this moment are forming, unseen, on the floor of the ocean and are growing upward toward its surface.

---

1) Did you look up all the words you needed to? What do "ephemeral," "paradoxes," and "catastrophic" mean? What is a "geologic yesterday"?

2) You doubtless concluded that the structure of this passage is quite different from that of the Bryce passage. The structure of each is controlled, of course, by the material and intention of the passage. But did you decide just how this passage is put together? We can say that it proceeds from a concrete and typical instance to a general statement.

3) Paragraph I is a short piece of narrative, is it not? It is carefully planned: notice that the name of the island is withheld until the narrative comes to the age in which the island was called Bermuda. Why, do you suppose, did the writer choose to begin with Bermuda, and not some other island formed in as typical a manner?

4) But obviously the central concern of the passage is not Bermuda, but the way in which volcanic islands come to be. What, then, is the relationship between I and II? Shall we say that II is an expository paragraph? Did you mark a topic sentence for it? How is transition between the two paragraphs accomplished?

5) Paragraph III is designed to establish a point of view for the reader. Miss Carson risks a brief break in structure to awaken, if she can, her reader's imagination.

6) Note how closely related I, II, and IV are. They develop by expanding restatement: I. how Bermuda was formed; II. how this typically violent process differentiates isolated islands from the continents; IV. how this process depends upon the interaction of the forces of earth and sea.

7) To the colon in the first sentence of IV we have a restatement of the central fact of I and II. It serves to connect IV to I and II after the intrusion of III. The ABSOLUTE phrases that follow the colon—"the forces of the earth striving to create, and all the forces of the sea opposing"—state the topic idea of the paragraph. And do you see that these absolute phrases also control the structure of the paragraph? How far does the development of the first of them proceed? What sentence functions as within-paragraph transition? Did your marking indicate that transition?

8) Paragraph v discusses how the process which has been described has gone on and now continues in time; and it also prepares for the rest of the chapter, which is a discussion of particular volcanic islands.

COMPRESSED DISCOURSE　*ii*

Our selection here is an admirably clear explanation of the philosophy of Communism. It offers no difficulty except the sort that necessarily accompanies the brief treatment of a highly complex subject. The author, Carl Becker, is one of the most skillful academic writers of our time. The skills you need in reading the selection are precisely those most important to your immediate purposes as college students. We here add to the consideration of structure some attention to the kind of effort the reader must make in such reading as this.

FROM *How New Will the Better World Be?* (1944)

CARL L. BECKER

[Communism]

1 The theory of Communism is at least as old as Plato (fifth century B.C.); but in its modern form it was worked out by Karl Marx during the middle of the nineteenth century. Marxian Communism, or "scientific" Socialism (both words were used at that time) was based on a few simple ideas. The fundamental idea was that the course of historical development is inevitably determined by economic forces rather than by men's ideas about what ought to happen. The organization of society at any time, and men's ideas about it, are fundamentally determined by the most important form of wealth ("factors of production"). The class which controls this form of wealth is, by virtue of its economic power, the ruling class, and will remain such as long as the form of wealth which it controls remains the most important form of wealth; and the form of government, the prevailing customs and ideas, are such as are best suited to maintain the ruling class in power. But when another form of wealth becomes the most important basis of economic power, the class which controls this new form of wealth will inevitably dispossess the old ruling class, and new institutions, customs, and ideas will be established because they are better suited to maintain the economic power of the new ruling class. Such a transfer of economic power and change of institutions and ideas constitute what Marx called a social revolution. The efficient cause of the revolution is the transfer of economic power from one class to another; the new ideas and institutions are merely the necessary consequence of such a transfer of power. In short, the efficient cause of historical development, of "progress," is a persistent and inevitable "economic class conflict."

II The liberal-democratic revolution of the eighteenth and nineteenth centuries, according to this philosophy, was the result of such an economic class conflict. It occurred because a new form of wealth ("capital") had come to be more important than the old form (land). The "capitalist class" which controlled the new form of wealth then dispossessed the old ruling class (landowning nobles), and the monarchical and feudal institutions and ideas that had maintained the landowning aristocracy in power were replaced by liberal-democratic institutions and ideas because they were better suited to maintain the power of the new ruling class of business men and bankers and lawyers. The new "freedoms"—representative government, freedom of speech and the press and religion, and freedom of competitive economic enterprise—were freedoms for the bourgeois capitalist class only. For the industrial laborers, the "proletariat," they were not freedoms at all, but merely devices for keeping them in subjection. Therefore, according to Marx, there necessarily developed within the capitalist system a new economic class conflict between the ruling class and the proletariat, and this class conflict would inevitably result in another social revolution.

III The coming revolution would be inevitable, Marx thought, because the capitalist system contained "contradictions" that would necessarily destroy it. The basic principle of the system was unrestrained competition for private profit. Such competition would enable the more intelligent and unscrupulous "capitalists" to drive the others out of business. Wealth would therefore be increasingly concentrated in the hands of a few, and the mass of the people would be reduced to the level of "wage slaves" earning a bare subsistence. But with the mass of the people impoverished, the market for goods would decline, industry would "contract," and sooner or later a series of increasingly disastrous business "crises" would end in the complete collapse of the capitalist system.

IV This would provide the necessary conditions for the social revolution, which would begin in the most highly industrialized country and spread to all the others. The revolution would be carried through, Marx seemed to think, by a spontaneous uprising of the people and the creation of a "Dictatorship of the Proletariat." Private property in land and industry would be abolished, the capitalist class would be liquidated, and the production and distribution of wealth would be directed by the government. With the revolution accomplished, the dictatorship would give way to a truly democratic government of the people. Since there would be no private property or competition for private profit, there would no longer be any "economic classes," and hence no "class conflict." The revolution would thus, according to Marx, be the end of the old world of oppression and the beginning of a new and better world of equality and justice, in which men would compete, not for private profit, but on the higher humane level of intellectual achievement and social service.

V The Marxian philosophy of history and social evolution provided the workers of Europe with a kind of religion, a fighting faith. It assured them that their present oppression was a necessary part of the nature of things, but that the nature of things was on their side and would inevitably bring for them or for their children a world purged of all injustice. Their part was to understand the law of history, and while waiting for the coming revolution to prepare for it by uniting with their brothers in all countries for promoting the class conflict against the capitalists in all countries. This the industrial workers did by organizing Socialist societies and Socialist political parties in virtually all European countries. They adopted programs of "social reform" designed to benefit the workers in particular and the poor people in general, and elected deputies to the legislatures pledged to work for these measures. Such measures, however, were at first regarded as mere temporary expedients—crumbs which could be picked up from the capitalist table pending the coming of the revolution which would end the capitalist banquet once and for all.

vi But then, towards the end of the nineteenth century, faith in the Marxian doctrine of revolution declined. For one thing, the revolution seemed a long time in coming—much longer than Marx had thought. So far from impoverishing the mass of the people, the capitalist system seemed to be enriching them. Measures of "social reform" were doing a good deal to improve the conditions of the workers, and such measures were in part carried into effect by the Socialist parties, which were able to elect more and more deputies to the legislatures. But the Socialist leaders found that the less they said about the coming revolution and the collapse of the capitalist system, the more votes they polled at the elections. Preaching the orthodox Marxian doctrine of violent revolution thus ceased to be good political tactics, and towards the end of the century the majority of the followers of Marx "revised" the orthodox Marxian doctrine. According to the "revised" doctrine, the revolution would come "gradually," by the legal democratic procedure. The great object still was the nationalization of land and industry, and the state control of the production and distribution of wealth; but this object would not necessarily be achieved by revolutionary violence and social upheaval.

vii Meantime the minority Socialistic parties in most countries retained their faith in the orthodox Marxian doctrine of revolution by violence; and after the last war they generally took the name of "Communist" to distinguish their brand of Marxism from the "Socialist" or "revisionist" brand accepted by the majority parties. In Russia the radical (Bolsheviki) party came to be directed, after the last war, by Nicolai Lenin. Lenin accepted the basic ideas of Marx, but he disagreed with Marx in respect to the methods by which the revolution could be carried out. He realized that the mass of the people in Russia knew nothing about the philosophy of Marx, and cared less. He was therefore convinced that a revolution could never be carried through to a definite end by any spontaneous uprising of the people. It would have to be carried through by a small, highly disciplined party, composed of tried and reliable persons who accepted the Communist faith with a religious conviction and zeal. The revolution, to be successful, would have to be strictly planned, begun only when circumstances were favorable, and carried through by a "dictatorship of the Communist Party" *for* the proletariat and probably in opposition to strong and persistent resistance of the mass of the people whom the revolution was designed to benefit.

VIII Acting on this plan, Lenin and the Communist Party carried through the Russian Revolution of October 1917. The event would have surprised and disconcerted Karl Marx, who confidently expected the revolution to begin in the most highly industrialized country as a result of the collapse of the capitalist system. But Russia was one of the least highly industrialized countries of Europe, one in which the capitalist system, so far from being in a state of collapse, was not even well established. The Russian Revolution was the result of two circumstances, in the nature of historical "accidents," which neither the Marxian nor any other philosophy of history could have foreseen. One of these was the sudden collapse of the czarist authority as a result of the war: had it not been for the corruption and ineptitude of the czarist government in the last war, the czarist regime would have continued in power. The other circumstance was the presence and remarkable ability of Nicolai Lenin; apart from Lenin, it is safe to say, the revolution would not have resulted in the establishment of Communism.

IX Even so, the Russian Revolution turned out very differently from what Marx, or even Lenin himself, had hoped it would. After twenty-five years only one of the great basic ideals of Communism has been realized. This is the nationalization of land and industry, and the control and direction of the production and distribution of wealth by the government. Even this was accomplished only after fifteen years, in the face of bitter resistance by the peasant farmers, and only by systematic and merciless liquidation, not only of the capitalist class, but of the nonconforming proletariat itself. The "dictatorship," which Marx and Lenin thought would be only temporary, still exists under Joseph Stalin, more absolute even than it was under Lenin. In twenty-five years much has been accomplished. The country has been rapidly industrialized, the production of wealth has been greatly increased, and on the whole more equitably distributed than it was under the czarist regime. Illiteracy has been largely abolished, the standard of life for the majority of the people has been raised, and the majority of the people accept the system of government with loyalty and devotion. But the "classless" society which Marx predicted and Lenin hoped to establish has not yet emerged; and the "freedoms" which we think essential, and which Marx thought would be secured by the revolution (political freedom, freedom of speech and the press) do not as yet exist. History, and especially history in Russia, has almost completely refuted the Marxian philosophy of history.

---

1) Since an understanding of Communism is important to us, it is well to have a dispassionate, concise, and simple account of it. But to say that our selection is concise and simple does not mean that the reader may be passive. Indeed, a concise treatment of a difficult subject requires the read-

er's effort by its very conciseness. Many students do not realize how much they can do for their reading skill just by increasing the intellectual tension under which they read. But this they must do for themselves; textbook and instructor can do no more than urge it.

2) Notice the use of quotation marks in this selection. They are not used in depreciation; they are used to mark the first appearance in the text of terms that are part of the technical vocabulary of Communism. Frequently the context defines a term at its first appearance. Beyond these terms—terms which the reader needs to recognize as technical terms—the vocabulary is unspecialized. You may find that you will need to use your dictionary less frequently than you do in some treatments of far less complex subject matter. What are the general assumptions the writer is making about his readers?

3) Our selection may be considered in two parts: The first part, I–IV, is an account of the doctrine of Marxism, primarily of the principles in *Das Kapital,* the first volume of which appeared in 1867, and which was completed after Marx's death by Friedrich Engels. Paragraphs I–IV, then, comprise a piece of exposition. The second part, V–IX, is organized as a historical narrative. Notice that it does not bring the account of the development of Communism much beyond 1940.

4) In I it is contended that Communism is based on a few simple ideas, ideas which the paragraph sets down in the order of their logical relationship. In the study of this paragraph, underlining would not help very much, for each statement in this packed exposition is important; perhaps giving each idea a number would help. But the best approach will be a list of the ideas, briefly stated in your own terms. That will insure that you read actively; and the mere setting forth of the ideas in your own way will help to fix them in your memory.

5) Notice how the ideas are connected in I—how, often, the subject, or part of the subject, of a sentence is a term picked up from the preceding sentence. What are examples? Notice, too, the number of connectives that show logical relationships: "for," "therefore," "thus."

6) Paragraph I, then, states the basic principles of Marxism. What exactly is accomplished in II, in III, and in IV—what part of the whole doctrine of Marxism is covered in each?

7) In so tight an organization, obviously, a careless reading of a part will obscure what follows it. Notice that the organization is dictated by the nature of the subject matter, for Marxism is a philosophy of history. Marxism assumes that its interpretation of the past makes it possible to predict as inevitable the developments of the future.

8) In V–IX point out the time words and the expressions that accomplish transition.

9) Paragraphs V–IX form a narrative of principles carried into practice, and in practice the principles themselves change. What great change in Communist principle, for instance, is ascribed to Lenin? Note that an understanding of this narrative of the development of Communism depends throughout upon the reader's control of I–IV.

10) Now we have some questions by which you may test your control of the piece. Try to answer them without looking back at the text.

(a) What does Marx mean by "a social revolution"? (b) According to Marx, the dominance of capitalism was itself the result of a revolution. How? (c) How did Marx interpret democracy? (d) How did Marx think the end of the capitalist system would come? Where did he think the movement would start? Why? (e) In what way would the Stalinist regime have disappointed Marx and Lenin? (f) What is the basis for contending that "History, and especially history in Russia, has almost completely refuted the Marxian philosophy of history"?

11) How did you come out? If you were unable to answer all the questions above, it may be that you read without demanding enough of yourself—that you have been accustomed to be content with the most general impression of a piece of writing. Then reading under an increased intellectual tension is a habit you will need to acquire.

12) But such questions as those in 10 may not adequately test your understanding of a complex matter, nor your ability to use and apply ideas you have gained to a further consideration of the subject. Perhaps we can in some sort test those things too. Here is a definition of "communism" from *Webster's New Collegiate Dictionary,* a remarkably adequate short definition, but a very packed one:

> A doctrine and program based upon revolutionary Marxian socialism as developed by N. Lenin and the Bolshevik party, which interprets history as a relentless class war eventually to result everywhere in the victory of the proletariat and establishment of the dictatorship of the proletariat, and which calls for regulation of all social, economic, and cultural activities through the agency of a single authoritarian party as the leader of the proletariat in all countries so as to achieve its ultimate objectives, a classless society and establishment of a world union of socialist soviet republics.[1]

Now can you, on the basis of Carl Becker's discussion, develop and interpret that definition part by part? For instance: What distinction is accomplished by modifying "Marxian socialism" by "revolutionary"? What is a particular development in doctrine and program that Lenin and the Bolshevik party are responsible for? How does Communism interpret, say, the history of the eighteenth and nineteenth centuries?—Those questions cover less than the first third of the definition.

13) Now let us consider what Carl Becker has done for the reader in our selection. The writer has done a great deal. He has given the reader the advantage of his long consideration of history, yet he has rigorously excluded every detail not essential to the understanding of Communism as a political philosophy. He has used as familiar a vocabulary as is consistent with his purpose of conciseness, and he has defined many technical terms. He has organized his material carefully: the function of each paragraph is clear; within paragraphs the sentences are woven together in a coherent fashion; and the transitions between paragraphs are clear. Although the selection is not from a textbook, it is representative of the best sort of academic writing; indeed few textbooks are as well written.

[1] By permission. From *Webster's New Collegiate Dictionary,* copyright, 1949, 1951, 1953, by G. & C. Merriam Co.

14) But the writer cannot do it all; there is much left for the reader to do. If the reader fails to recognize a word, he must be willing to look it up. Then the writing is packed; there is—compared, say, to the selection from James Bryce—relatively little restatement of idea. And the reader must be able to comprehend some abstract statements, to decide what they would mean in the concrete—what, for instance, would illustrate "the transfer of economic power from one class to another"?

15) Do you need to give the selection one more reading?

SUGGESTIONS FOR PAPERS

You might begin with some practice in writing the sort of paragraph that begins with a generalization and develops it with instance and example. One student might begin: "The farmers in Green County are active in soil conservation." Another student might write: "Traffic problems in Eastern City are nearly insolvable." Take some generalization you can develop from your own experience and observation.

But you can get quite as good practice in paragraph development in the use of our selections. Here are two suggestions: (a) Begin by quoting 11:4 of the Bryce passage, dropping the first five words and introducing the quotation by attributing it to Bryce. Use the quotation as a topic sentence, and develop it in, say, 165 words. Each of the two comparisons will need development. Watch the transition. And do not try to pick up Bryce's phrasing in your development; restate in your own words. (b) As a test of your control of the passage from *The Sea Around Us,* and of your ability to organize a paragraph, develop this topic sentence: "Volcanic islands all come into being in much the same way." (You might try it without looking back at the passage.)

For an exercise in connection with the selection by Dixon Wecter, you might pick out the name of a person you would like to know more about (for instance, Peter Cartwright, William Holmes McGuffey, or Robert Owen). Find out about him and write, for the class, a brief note that will illuminate Wecter's reference to him. (The *Dictionary of American Biography* will be a good source for the first two, the *Dictionary of National Biography* for the third.) You can easily make this an exercise in the development of a topic sentence—for instance, such a topic sentence as this: "The *Eclectic Readers* of William Holmes McGuffey had a great part in shaping the mid-nineteenth-century mind."

The Becker selection offers an opportunity for the treatment of material for particular purposes. You might assume that you are to make a brief talk on the fundamental beliefs of Marxism. Work over the first paragraph of the selection (of course acknowledging your source). You may supply concrete illustration from other paragraphs; for instance, material from 11 will illustrate the fifth and sixth sentences, and material from 111 will help to make clear the nature of the "economic class conflict" that the Marxist believes now goes on in capitalist countries. Your main problem will be the restating of the paragraph for hearers.

Or the selection might be handled in another way. It is difficult for us in the United States to realize why any country should feel hostility toward our aims and beliefs. Assume that you are an editorial writer and, drawing on Carl Becker (and acknowledging your debt), write a short editorial to explain what the Marxist interpretation of democracy is. Your assumed readers will not be the least capable of newspaper readers—editorials are directed toward the reader of better-than-average capability. Do not underestimate your reader's intelligence, but do not overestimate his information.

Words in Context

Our consideration of the structure and relationships of paragraphs has been a preliminary one to indicate ways of thinking and of talking about patterns in written material. This chapter on the ways in which words work in contexts is likewise preliminary. We are not discussing these matters in order to dismiss them; we are discussing them so that we may have principles, terms, and approaches to use in the reading and writing that follows.

MEANING IN CONTEXT *i*

The writer works in a medium that belongs to him and to his reader; if either does not possess it fully, communication may fail in some degree. The writer must try to predict what knowledge and what sort of experience his readers can bring to the reading of his piece. A particular reader may not have had just the experience, may not even possess the knowledge of words, that the writer predicted. That hazard always exists; it is just the difficulty and the fascination in reading. Language is a communal matter; but we do not possess it equally. Each of us began knowing none of it.

"Words," W. Somerset Maugham says, "are tyrannical things, they exist for their meanings, and if you will not pay attention to these, you cannot pay attention at all." Now paying attention to meanings requires alertness and discrimination. We speak for convenience of the meaning of a word; of course we know that if we were to speak precisely, we should speak of the meanings, that if "watch" means a timepiece, it also means other things, for instance, a sailor's period of duty. We understand a word according to its context, the way in which it is interwoven with other words. When we set down this fact about words it seems perfectly obvious, but in our reading and even in the classroom it is too often forgotten.

The dictionary can be your greatest help. But do use your dictionary intelligently—students often do not. Most of the words you are likely to look up have more than one definition. It is for you to decide which is closest to the writer's purpose in the sentence you are reading. For example, in a discussion by James Harvey Robinson of personal motives in the work of great writers, we have this sentence: "These facts are not recalled here as a *gratuitous* disparagement of the truly great, but to insure a full realization of the tremendous competition which all really exacting thought has to face, even in the minds of the most highly endowed mortals." A student may not know the meaning of the word here italicized. If he looks it up in *Webster's New Collegiate Dictionary,* this is what he will find [1]:

> gra·tu′i·tous (-tŭs), *adj.* [L. *gratuitus,* fr. *gratus* pleasing.] **1.** Given freely, without recompense, or regardless of merit. **2.** Not called for by the circumstances; unwarranted. **3.** *Econ.* Designating goods, or utilities, which are the free gifts of nature and not the products of effort. **4.** *Law.* Not involving a return, compensation, or consideration, as in **gratuitous contract,** one solely for the benefit of one of the parties. — **Syn.** See SUPEREROGATORY. — **gra·tu′i·tous·ly,** *adv.* — **gra·tu′i·tous·ness,** *n.*

Now if the student uses the dictionary as unintelligently as many students do, he will stop reading with the first definition and tell you that the writer is saying that certain facts are not recalled as a freely given disparagement of great men. But he needs merely to read the second definition to know that it, and not the first, fits the context in which he found "gratuitous." Or, for another example, here is a sentence by Herbert Spencer: "If he would escape the charge of political *empiricism,* he must show us some test by which he can in each case ascertain whether or not State-superintendence is desirable." Our student will have to read the sentence carefully enough to realize that here "empiricism" means something undesirable—something one would not wish to be charged with—before he can find in his dictionary the meaning that will fit this context.[2]

A word familiar to the student in only one of its senses, or a word about which he has a mistaken notion, may be more deceptive for him than a word which is wholly new to him. Take this sentence for example: "Matthew Arnold defined criticism as 'a disinterested endeavor to learn and propagate the best that is known and thought in the world.' " The sentence is full of pitfalls, for there are college freshmen who know "criticism" only in the sense of censure or faultfinding, who use "disinterested" to mean "uninterested," and who will get only a vaguely erroneous sense from "propagate." But suppose we have a student with these three misapprehensions, or any one of them. Must such a student inevitably misunderstand the sentence? Not at all. He can tell that something is the matter with his reading, that the sentence is not making a satisfactory sense. He can tell, for instance, that his meaning for "disinterested" does not seem to fit the context. His dictionary will give him a meaning that does fit.

We have, then, a principle of the greatest importance: *Words do not have their meanings alone, but in contexts.* You must be careful, therefore, to discriminate among the definitions of a word. And you must not too easily assume that if you know a word in one or two of its senses, you

[1] Reprinted by permission. From *Webster's New Collegiate Dictionary.* Copyright, 1949, 1951, 1953, by G. & C. Merriam Co.
[2] If the student wishes to know the history of a word—if, for instance, he wishes to know how "empiric" came to mean "quack"—he should consult the *Oxford New English Dictionary* (often referred to as the N. E. D. or the O. E. D.).

know it in all. Moreover, there is this to remember as you use a dictionary: its definitions are of necessity a kind of generalization, for it must give for each word a number of meanings that will approximate the senses of the word in various contexts—it cannot define for each context. A good dictionary is a wonderful thing, the result of the patient work of many minds. But it is a tool to use; and its use requires some skill and some alertness.

You need to remember, too, that in this interweaving of words we call context there arise emotions, and attitudes, and judgments. And the way in which words affect one another you have to see for yourself. If fact and judgment were always stated quite independently of one another, every reader would recognize each for itself. But when a fact and a judgment are stated together in the context of a single expression or sentence, readers do not always separate them.

So commonplace a choice as the use of one verb construction instead of another may make a judgment at the very moment a fact is stated. In a college there is credit for, let us say, square dancing. If one says, "Students earn credit for square dancing," and another says, "Students are allowed credit for square dancing," each has made his judgment as he has stated a fact. Or, if one newspaper editor writes of a proposed city sales tax as "the mayor's desperate expedient" and another writes of "the mayor's recommendation for a new source of revenue," they write of the same core of fact and make quite different judgments.

Of course an ill-intentioned writer may exploit this way of language in an attempt to befool and corrupt his readers. In our time, in any time, there is reason to be on guard against him. But you do not need to be defended from him; you have your own defence. He always depends upon some degree of carelessness in his reader—you can be alert. Although there are formulas for the exercise of that alertness, perhaps they do not help very much; it is the alertness itself that is the important thing. There is, indeed, a limit to the usefulness of any generalized discussion of the problem of meaning. It is necessary that we know the nature of the problem; but it is most fruitfully considered in particular manifestations. We turn now to a consideration of metaphor. And we shall be concerned with the problem of meaning in context after context.

METAPHOR *ii*

A dictionary, even the largest, does not and cannot define all the possible senses of every word. It will always give you the LITERAL sense, that is, the sense we now consider the simple and primary meaning. An extension of a word which has to be understood by considering together the literal sense and the context in which the word appears is called a metaphor. A dictionary defines metaphorical senses only when they are common and long established.

We have noted some metaphors in passing, and indeed you have been long familiar with metaphors, even if the term has been unfamiliar to you.

When you read in the Bryce passage that the public school gives every-body "the key to knowledge," you immediately understood "key" meta-phorically, and not literally as the instrument to turn a lock. This meta-phorical sense is so common that you were hardly aware, as you read, that the literal sense had been extended. But when you read Dixon Wecter's sentence, "In those early days, the valves of influence opened chiefly west-ward," you were probably conscious of the extension of the literal sense of the word "valves."

In order to get some initial practice in the identification of metaphor, we shall read from Sir Winston Churchill's *Their Finest Hour* the open-ing and closing passages, where we would expect a heightened style. The book is an account of the period in World War II from May, 1940, when Sir Winston became Prime Minister, to the end of the year—a period in which the very survival of Great Britain was in doubt. History itself is evi-dence of Sir Winston's effectiveness as a speaker, and his historical writing has much the same characteristics as his addresses.

Now you are to mark the metaphors as you read along through the se-lection. For instance, you will see at once that "storm" in the first sentence is not used literally to mean atmospheric disturbance, that it is used in a common metaphorical sense. Or when, later in the paragraph, you find "Germany and Italy at our throats" and "Japan glowering on the other side of the globe," you will recognize "at our throats" and "glowering" as meta-phors. Decisions about some expressions will not be quite so easy; and sometimes students may disagree about what is or is not literally used. But about these possible disagreements we need not now be very much con-cerned; we merely want to find most of the words and expressions that are clearly metaphors.

FROM *Their Finest Hour* (1949)

WINSTON S. CHURCHILL

[Britain in 1940]

[i]

1 ¹ Now at last the slowly gathered, long-pent-up fury of the storm broke upon us. ² Four or five millions of men met each other in the first shock of the most merciless of all the wars of which record has been kept. ³ Within a week the front in France, behind which we had been accus-tomed to dwell through the long years of the former war and the opening phase of this, was to be irretrievably broken. ⁴ Within three weeks the long-famed French Army was to collapse in rout and ruin, and the British Army to be hurled into the sea with all its equipment lost. ⁵ Within six weeks we were to find ourselves alone, almost disarmed, with triumphant

Germany and Italy at our throats, with the whole of Europe in Hitler's power, and Japan glowering on the other side of the globe. [6] It was amid these facts and looming prospects that I entered upon my duties as Prime Minister and Minister of Defence and addressed myself to the first task of forming a Government of all parties to conduct His Majesty's business at home and abroad by whatever means might be deemed best suited to the national interest.

II [1] Five years later almost to a day it was possible to take a more favourable view of our circumstances. [2] Italy was conquered and Mussolini slain. [3] The mighty German Army surrendered unconditionally. [4] Hitler had committed suicide. [5] In addition to the immense captures by General Eisenhower, nearly three million German soldiers were taken prisoners in twenty-four hours by Field Marshal Alexander in Italy and Field Marshal Montgomery in Germany. [6] France was liberated, rallied and revived. [7] Hand in hand with our allies, the two mightiest empires in the world, we advanced to the swift annihilation of Japanese resistance. [8] The contrast was certainly remarkable. [9] The road across these five years was long, hard, and perilous.[10] Those who perished upon it did not give their lives in vain. [11] Those who marched forward to the end will always be proud to have trodden it with honour.

[ii]

III [1] We may, I am sure, rate this tremendous year as the most splendid, as it was the most deadly, year in our long English and British story. [2] It was a great, quaintly organised England that had destroyed the Spanish Armada. [3] A strong flame of conviction and resolve carried us through the twenty-five years' conflict which William II and Marlborough waged against Louis XIV. [4] There was a famous period with Chatham. [5] There was the long struggle against Napoleon, in which our survival was secured through the domination of the seas by the British Navy under the classic leadership of Nelson and his associates. [6] A million Britons died in the First World War. [7] But nothing surpasses 1940. [8] By the end of that year this small and ancient island, with its devoted Commonwealth, Dominions and attachments under every sky, had proved itself capable of bearing the whole impact and weight of world destiny. [9] We had not flinched or wavered. [10] We had not failed. [11] The soul of the British people and race had proved invincible. [12] The citadel of the Commonwealth and Empire could not be stormed. [13] Alone, but upborne by every generous heartbeat of mankind, we had defied the tyrant in the height of his triumph.

IV [1] All our latent strength was now alive. [2] The air terror had been measured. [3] The island was intangible, inviolate. [4] Henceforward we too would have weapons with which to fight. [5] Henceforward we too would be a highly organised war machine. [6] We had shown the world that we could hold our own. [7] There were two sides to the question of Hitler's world domination. [8] Britain, whom so many had counted out, was still in the ring, far stronger than she had ever been, and gathering strength with every day. [9] Time had once again come over to our side. [10] And not only to our national side. [11] The United States was arming fast and drawing ever nearer to the conflict. [12] Soviet Russia, who with callous miscalculation had adjudged us worthless at the outbreak of the war, and had bought from Germany fleeting immunity and a share of the booty, had also become much stronger and had secured advanced positions for her own defence. [13] Japan seemed for the moment to be overawed by the evident prospect of a prolonged world war, and, anxiously watching Russia and the United States, meditated profoundly what it would be wise and profitable to do.

v [1] And now this Britain, and its far-spread association of states and dependencies, which had seemed on the verge of ruin, whose very heart was about to be pierced, had been for fifteen months concentrated upon the war problem, training its men and devoting all its infinitely varied vitalities to the struggle. [2] With a gasp of astonishment and relief the smaller neutrals and the subjugated states saw that the stars still shone in the sky. [3] Hope and within it passion burned anew in the hearts of hundreds of millions of men. [4] The good cause would triumph. [5] Right would not be trampled down. [6] The flag of Freedom, which in this fateful hour was the Union Jack, would still fly in all the winds that blew.

vi [1] But I and my faithful colleagues who brooded with accurate information at the summit of the scene had no lack of cares. [2] The shadow of the U-boat blockade already cast its chill upon us. [3] All our plans depended upon the defeat of this menace. [4] The Battle of France was lost. [5] The Battle of Britain was won. [6] The Battle of the Atlantic had now to be fought.

---

1) Did you find that marking the metaphors here required a little discrimination? For instance, did you hesitate over "dwell" in 1:3? How about "looming prospects" in 1:6? Do you remain in doubt about some words or expressions? Are you sure that you have nowhere assumed that an expression is not metaphorical just because it is familiar to you?

2) Do you find any words here that are more familiar to you in their metaphorical extensions than they are in their original and literal senses? Is not "callous" (as in "callous miscalculation" in iv:12) about as familiar metaphorically as it is literally (as in "a callus on my hand")? What does the verb "to brood" mean? Is it used literally or metaphorically in vi:1? How do you take "citadel" in iii:12?

3) What is the sense of the word "intangible" in iv:3? Is "booty" used literally in iv:12? Do you find a familiar pair of metaphors that have their origin in the sport of boxing?

4) Consider vi:4–6 as an example of an extended metaphor. Do you find other examples in the selection?

5) You found many metaphors here that, if they were separated from their context, might be considered CLICHÉS, overused expressions. Students are often warned, perhaps properly, against resorting to any much-used metaphor or other stock expression. Your handbook probably has a list of examples, and such a list might well include "verge of ruin" (v:1) or "hope burned anew" (v:3). But in some contexts there may be an advantage in the use of expressions we have responded to before, which al-

ready have emotional association for us. Are the very familiar metaphors (what are further examples?) ineffective or inappropriate here?

6) Sir Winston's metaphor "at the summit" (vi:1), which he has also used in other contexts, seemed by the time of the Geneva Conference of July, 1955, to have been established as a part of our common language. Perhaps here we can identify the source of one bit of linguistic change.

7) If you want further practice in the identification of metaphor, the selection from Dixon Wecter in Chapter II will offer an opportunity. You will find some interesting extended metaphors, and a curious, grotesque metaphorical passage quoted at the close.

We used the Churchill selection as an exercise in the identification of metaphor because the metaphors there are frequent and obvious. But we must understand that metaphor is not just a quality of emotive writing and that it is never in good writing just a decoration. Metaphor is a way in which language works, and it appears in some degree in almost all writing. The term "figure of speech" is commonly used in connection with metaphor; we will not so use it, since a "figure of speech" is usually thought of, and indeed often defined, as some form of expression other than a normal one—and metaphor is normal and inevitable. We need now to see some of the ways in which this common habit of language works.

You may have been taught that a metaphor is an implied or tacit comparison, a comparison without the "like" or the "as" that would make it a SIMILE, and often this definition is adequate. If one says "the ship plows the sea," there is a tacit comparison between, not really a ship and plow, but between their actions, and between the ship's wake and the furrow left by the plow. One may readily translate that metaphor into a simile. But such a metaphor as "they patched up their quarrel" is not readily translatable into a simile—indeed, the awkward simile one might make it into would not be at all equivalent. And many metaphors are not readily translatable into similes. We will think of a metaphor as the application of a word or expression in a way in which it is not literally used—as an extension, controlled by context, of the literal sense.

When we say *he leaps to a conclusion,* we extend the literal, physical sense of the verb *leap* to another use; when we speak of *a bitter disappointment* or *a cloudy future,* the adjectives have senses beyond their literal ones. When we hear people talk of *the light of hope* or *the morning of life,* we do not take the nouns *light* and *morning* literally. Our good slang is commonly metaphorical. Our IDIOMATIC use of prepositions may be often metaphorical—consider *look up to, look down upon, look after, overlook.* Indeed, metaphor is a part of all our discourse. Many people seem to suppose that the language of science and mechanics is quite literal, even people who themselves constantly use such metaphors as *light waves* and *radio antennae.* Modern physics, in particular, constantly resorts to metaphor. Consider this sentence: "Post-Plücker physicists have discovered that the 'cathode ray' is a stream of electrons." One of the things the sentence is saying is that *stream* is a better metaphor than *ray* for the phenomenon in question.

Sometimes we have a choice between literal and metaphorical language, but when we talk about things that cannot be perceived by the five senses, we must talk as if they could be. You will have constant occasion to observe that fact in your reading; for the moment the most forcible illustration is our way of talking about what goes on in the mind. You *grasp* an idea. You find a problem *hard.* You *struggle* with it; you *see a point* that you had been *missing.* You believe that you have *comprehended* the whole. You write a *brilliant* explanation of it. Whatever you have to say about mental activity will be expressed in metaphorical language. If you need to be convinced, try to write a few sentences in entirely literal language about what has happened to you intellectually in any one of your courses.

When a metaphor enters into standard speech, it may lose in time its original force; the concrete image that arose in the minds of the first users may, by our very familiarity with the metaphor, be blunted or lost. Some of the examples in the paragraph above are of this sort; and you can recognize it in the metaphors headline writers constantly use: *flay, probe, nip, hits, rift, bare* and the rest. Such metaphor is called DEAD or FOSSIL METAPHOR. Often we hardly recognize a dead metaphor as a metaphor at all. "Career" is, or was, literally "a running course"; we now use it almost entirely for the course of a person's life, particularly his professional life. Yet in nineteenth-century novels you can find sentences like "He ran his unhappy career quickly" in which the writer is quite conscious of the metaphor. Or, to take another example, the literal sense of "aftermath" seems strange to us, so used we are to its extension; yet Robert Louis Stevenson writes: "They were cutting aftermath on all sides, which gave the neighborhood . . . an untimely smell of hay."

A good many dead metaphors—and live ones, too—are of the sort in which a part, attribute, or characteristic stands for the whole (called a SYNECDOCHE). The slang term for policeman, *flatfoot,* is a convenient example. *Bigwig*—for an important person—is perhaps a dead metaphor for most of its users today, but a similar term *big brass* is still a live metaphor. If *red tape* is a dead metaphor for you, your dictionary will explain its origin and give it a degree of life. And see what your dictionary has to say about a historically important metaphor: *sans-culotte.*

But we are constantly finding new metaphors; we continually "carry over" a word to a new use ("metaphor" comes from a Greek verb for "to carry over"). For instance, Stevenson writes of a famous California stagecoach driver: "Along the unfenced, abominable mountain roads, he *launches* his team with small regard to human life or to the doctrine of probabilities. Flinching travellers, who behold themselves *coasting* eternity at every corner, look with natural admiration at their driver's huge, impassive, fleshy countenance." "Launches" is a nautical term in its common use, but do you see how its use here enforces the hazard of the travellers, who coast eternity? (You may need your dictionary to give you the nautical sense of "coasting.") Or, to take an instance from a different sort of writing, when James Bryce is discussing the impulse of Americans toward re-form, he writes: "Nor do their moral and religious impulses remain in the soft haze of self-complacent sentiment. The desire to expunge or cure the visible evils of the world is strong. Zeal outruns discretion, outruns the possibilities of the case, in not a few of the efforts made. . . ." This time you underline the words used metaphorically.

When a metaphor is consistently maintained throughout a sentence or a passage, we say we have an extended metaphor—you noted some extended metaphors in the Churchill selection. In two sentences from Washington Irving's "English Writers on America," we have two examples of extended metaphor, well handled though perhaps a bit too elaborate for modern taste. Irving is saying that, despite English criticism of Americans, Americans have much to gain by a study of English custom and culture:

. . . for it is in the moral feeling of the people that the deep foundations of British prosperity are laid; and however the superstructure may be time-worn, or overrun by abuses, there must be something solid in the basis, admirable in the materials, and stable in the structure of an edifice that so long has towered unshaken amidst the tempests of the world. . . . We may thus place England before us as a perpetual volume of reference, wherein are recorded sound deductions from ages of experience; and while we avoid the errors and absurdities which may have crept into the page, we may draw thence golden maxims of practical wisdom, wherein to strengthen and to embellish our national character.

But metaphor often shifts from sentence to sentence or even within sentences. Consider these sentences from Henry George's *Progress and Poverty:* "This association of poverty with progress is the great enigma of our times. It is the central fact from which spring industrial, social, and political difficulties that perplex the world, and with which statesmanship and philanthropy and education grapple in vain. From it come the clouds that overhang the future of the most progressive and self-reliant nations." In the second sentence difficulties spring from the association of poverty and progress and are grappled with; in the third sentence the metaphor is changed, and from the same association come clouds that overhang the future.

Our imaginations easily accept such a shift of metaphor as that in the sentences by Henry George. Perhaps a sentence from V. L. Parrington will be a bit more difficult. In discussing how slowly Americans in the early nineteenth century became aware of European ideas, Parrington writes: "The nineteenth century with its cargo of romanticisms had not yet crossed the Atlantic, and while Napoleon was strewing Europe with the wrecks of old empires, America was still dwelling in the twilight of a century that was loath to be gone." In the first clause we must think of the nineteenth century as a ship, and in the second of the eighteenth century as a lingering day. But such a shift as this should offer only a momentary difficulty. When a shift in metaphor causes real dismay or imaginative confusion (or sometimes amusement), we say we have a mixed metaphor. An example is the remark of a senator, not long ago, that the President was trying to cover up red ink by flights into the wild blue yonder.

A successful metaphor may supply an image for an idea. The most subtle effect of metaphor, therefore, is its way of suggesting a judgment or imposing an attitude at the very moment an idea is expressed or a person or action described. For instance, the expression "they patched up their quarrel" suggests, without explicitly stating, that the renewed relationship is temporary or questionable. And the choice of one metaphor or another may make an important change in the effect of a statement. You might compare effects in the following pairs of statements: (a) "Paul *pried into* the matter" or "Paul *looked into* the matter." (b) "The senator *battled hard* for the interests of his constituents" or "The senator was the *willing tool* of the interests in his state." (c) "The essayist *parades* his knowledge of the classics" or "The essayist *weaves* classical allusions into the *fabric* of his essays." It is quite possible, you see, that two sentences which state the same core of fact will use metaphors that suggest very different responses to it. We shall from time to time consider such metaphors. The good reader is alert for metaphors which impose attitudes and judgments, for he will wish to know how he comes by his.

iii   REFERENCE AND ALLUSION

In paragraph III of the Churchill selection you found some references to historical personages and events. Perhaps you recognized all or most of them; perhaps you merely passed over them. Perhaps you should have looked them up? Since a writer will of course make use of the information and experience he believes he shares with his readers, he will frequently refer to events or persons or writings that he expects his readers to have some knowledge of. A reader whose knowledge falls short of this expectation will find when he comes upon such references that he is losing part of the intended meaning. But ordinarily he will have no difficulty in seeing what the source of his trouble is; and if he is sufficiently interested he can look up references that he does not understand.

Now, ideally, you might be advised to look up every reference to a name or an event unfamiliar to you. You are indeed here and now advised in all your reading to exhaust the resources of your dictionary, which are greater than most students suppose them. But reference work further than the use of the dictionary is practicable for the undergraduate in most of his reading only within limits—though those limits are not nearly so narrow as our inertia makes us feel they are.

Let us suppose that an undergraduate encounters these sentences in an introductory essay in an anthology of American literature:

The Colonial leaders were familiar with the democratic ideas of John Milton and other Puritan thinkers, and they cherished the Whig liberalism of the Revolution of 1688 as expounded in John Locke's two treatises on government. When such liberal ideas went out of fashion in the England of

George III, Americans still clung to them and embodied them in their appeals to King and Parliament and in their Declaration of Independence.[1]

Now what is the position of this student? He knows something of the Declaration of Independence, something of George III, something of John Milton—at least that he wrote *Paradise Lost*. Since we are assuming an average student, we can hardly assume much more. With his information our student can gather from these sentences three ideas: that the Colonial leaders were in sympathy with the liberal political ideas of the English seventeenth century; that these ideas persisted in America as they did not in England; and that there is some connection between them and the Declaration of Independence.

Now should our student be content? His answer depends upon his purpose, his interests, and his immediate needs. He is reading from an introduction. Perhaps he would be right in judging that the general ideas he has gained will become concrete for him as he goes on in the study of American thought, and that they serve his purpose for the present. If, however, he intends to understand the political thinking of the revolutionary period, these sentences introduce him to a vital matter and he is by no means helpless in gaining at once an understanding of it.

From any textbook of English history or historical dictionary the student can learn in a few minutes that at the Revolution of 1688 Englishmen deposed King James II and invited William and Mary to the throne—perhaps the same source will inform him sufficiently about John Locke. If it does not, an encyclopedia or, more conveniently, *The Oxford Companion to English Literature* will inform him that Locke's two treatises on government (1690) were written to justify the Revolution of 1688 by means of Locke's interpretation of a political concept called "original contract." He will find that, for Locke, all government derives its authority from the original contract among all the persons in a state. By this contract, they entrust the administration of some of their affairs to a government, but retain the right to remove or alter that government when it does not serve the trust reposed in it. The student thereupon will remember, or can easily find, the passage in the Declaration which runs:

—That to secure these rights, Governments are instituted among Men, deriving their just powers from the consent of the governed.—That whenever any Form of Government becomes destructive of these ends, it is the Right of the People to alter or to abolish it, and to institute new Government. . . .

Our student, therefore, will have learned that the Declaration of Independence, in a "decent respect to the opinions of mankind," justifies the American Revolution by Locke's theory of original contract, set down eighty-six years earlier and known to the educated in all Europe. Our stu-

[1] Reprinted from *American Life in Literature* by Jay Hubbell, by permission of Harper and Brothers. Copyright, 1936, 1949, by Harper & Brothers.

dent's interests may of course take him further; he may wish to find out about Milton's political ideas; he may wish to read Locke's treatises on government themselves.

But it would be unreasonable to expect a student to consult reference books every time he encounters a passage for which his background is insufficient, although his needs and his interests should lead him to do so frequently. While you are in the process of learning to read in an adult fashion and have so much to do in order to accomplish it, this textbook may well relieve you of some of the burden by making explanatory comments or by referring you to convenient sources of information. But you are by no means relieved of all the burden. For one thing, a textbook writer cannot foresee just what information individual students will happen not to have. What is more important, you should develop an intellectual responsibility of your own. Decision about consulting sources of information is a matter of tact and judgment—not of rule.

It must be frankly acknowledged, however, that some reference will inevitably lose part of its effectiveness for the reader who does not recognize it at once. Let us look again at the references in paragraph III of the Churchill selection. At the beginning of this section it was suggested that a reader who did not recognize those references should look them up. Perhaps it occurred to you then that filling the gap was not quite so easy. Clearly, the ideal reader for that particular passage is one in whom the references will evoke a spontaneous emotional response which presupposes familiarity with the facts.

A similar reservation often holds for the sort of reference that you may know as LITERARY ALLUSION. By this term we mean some way of recalling a part of the reader's previous literary experience—ordinarily one that carries an emotional as well as an intellectual freight—and bringing it to bear upon a new consideration. Let us look at a not very difficult example. In an essay on the New England Puritans, James Russell Lowell writes: "And it was natural that men who captained or accompanied the exodus from existing forms and associations into the doubtful wilderness that led to the promised land, should find more to their purpose in the Old Testament than in the New." The allusion here to the exodus of the Children of Israel from Egypt and their journey through the wilderness to the promised land of Canaan will be recognized by readers acquainted with the Old Testament. For such persons, the allusion suggests a significant likeness between the New England Puritans and the people Moses led to found a new society.

Literary allusion is a valuable resource for the writer, since it permits him to achieve complex and subtle effects with great compression. But this very quality, as you can see, increases the difficulty of the reader in whom the allusion fails to evoke the response that the writer counted upon. You must expect to run into this difficulty, and you should try not to feel discouraged—or impatient with the writer—when you do. Your inability to recognize a particular allusion merely means that your literary experience is not yet as broad as the writer assumed. As you read more widely, you will find that your problems with allusion gradually become less frequent. In the meantime, even while you recognize that reference books have their limitations, you should get the habit of identifying allusion whenever you can. More often than you suppose, the dictionary will give you a clue.

Now let us see how the things we have been discussing throughout the chapter apply to a particular context. Our selection will furnish us with excellent examples of metaphor and allusion, and it has more meaning than may be apparent at first reading. Perhaps the questions and discussion will show you how certain difficulties in determining the full meaning of words in their context may be approached. Remember as you read the passage that it was written about a century ago, when vast territories in our country were unsettled or only partly settled.

FROM *Walking* (1862)

HENRY DAVID THOREAU

I [1] When I go out of the house for a walk, uncertain as yet whither I will bend my steps, and submit myself to my instinct to decide for me, I find, strange and whimsical as it may seem, that I finally and inevitably settle southwest, toward some particular wood or meadow or deserted pasture or hill in that direction. [2] My needle is slow to settle,—varies a few degrees, and does not always point due southwest, it is true, and it has good authority for this variation, but it always settles between west and south-southwest. [3] The future lies that way to me, and the earth seems more unexhausted and richer on that side. . . . [4] I turn round and round irresolute sometimes for a quarter of an hour, until I decide, for the thousandth time, that I will walk into the southwest or west. [5] Eastward I go only by force; but westward I go free. [6] Thither no business leads me. [7] It is hard for me to believe that I shall find fair landscapes or sufficient wildness and freedom behind the eastern horizon. [8] I am not excited by the prospect of a walk thither; but I believe that the forest which I see in the western horizon stretches uninterruptedly toward the setting sun, and there are no towns nor cities in it of enough consequence to disturb me. [9] Let me live where I will, on this side is the city, on that the wilderness, and ever I am leaving the city more and more, and withdrawing into the wilderness. [10] I should not lay so much stress on this fact, if I did not believe that something like this is the prevailing tendency of my countrymen. [11] I must walk toward Oregon, and not toward Europe. [12] And that way the nation is moving, and I may say that mankind progress from east to west. . . .

II [1] We go eastward to realise history and study the works of art and literature, retracing the steps of the race; we go westward as into the future, with a spirit of enterprise and adventure. [2] The Atlantic is a Lethean stream, in our passage over which we have had an opportunity to forget the Old World and its institutions. [3] If we do not succeed this time, there is perhaps one more chance for the race left before it arrives on the banks of the Styx; and that is in the Lethe of the Pacific, which is three times as wide.

III ¹ I know not how significant it is, or how far it is an evidence of singularity, that an individual should thus consent in his pettiest walk with the general movement of the race; but I know that something akin to the migratory instinct in birds and quadrupeds . . . affects both nations and individuals, either perennially or from time to time. . . .

IV ¹ Every sunset which I witness inspires me with the desire to go to a West as distant and as fair as that into which the sun goes down. ² He appears to migrate westward daily, and tempts us to follow him. ³ He is the Great Western Pioneer whom the nations follow. ⁴ We dream all night of those mountain-ridges in the horizon, though they may be of vapor only, which were last gilded by his rays. ⁵ The island of Atlantis, and the islands and gardens of the Hesperides, a sort of terrestrial paradise, appear to have been the Great West of the ancients, enveloped in mystery and poetry. ⁶ Who has not seen in imagination, when looking into the sunset sky, the gardens of the Hesperides, and the foundation of all those fables?

---

1) First of all, did you use your dictionary properly? There are few words here that are likely to be unfamiliar to you. But there are a number whose meaning is so controlled by context that you need to make some nice discriminations. There are, for instance, "inevitably" in the first sentence, and "realise" in II:1. And how about "irresolute" in 1:4? What does "perennially" (III:1) mean? And that common word "consent" (III:1)—does it have quite its ordinary sense in this context? Do you find a definition in your dictionary that exactly fits the sense here? Is it labeled?

2) Did you look up the proper names?

3) Perhaps no passage of comparable length in American writing represents so much of the essence of our history as do these few paragraphs from Thoreau. And for our present study they have a good deal of interest. We may think of the whole passage as a sort of extended metaphor, in which Thoreau's walk, a tiny part of the westward movement, is used to stand for the whole. The metaphor is interpreted within the passage itself, interpreted by, for instance, 1:10.

4) What is the full meaning of the first clause in II:1? It makes perfectly good sense if taken with entire literalness; Americans often do go to Europe to study the past. Is the literal meaning of "eastward" the only effective meaning? Notice that a metaphorical statement may be so made that the context interprets the metaphor, as it does here. Thoreau might have said something like this: For us, the east is the past, and the west is the future. But that statement would have required more of the reader than II:1 does.

5) This passage gives us some excellent examples of metaphors that depend upon allusion; consider II:2–3 and IV:5–6. If you did not recognize the allusions at first reading, your dictionary has given you an intellectual

control of them, and you should be able to get the sense of the sentences in which they appear. But of course the dictionary cannot give the allusions the emotional weight they carry for readers who know them in their original contexts. For example, one fortunate enough to have read the sixth book of Virgil's *Aeneid* has more to bring to II:2 than one who must understand it through the dictionary's entry for "Lethe." But by means of the dictionary one can see what Thoreau is saying. Restate II:2–3 in literal language, without any metaphor or allusion.

6) In II:3 we have an example of the sort of change and extension of meaning that sometimes happens in a piece of writing with the passing of time, in this instance a disturbing change and one that Thoreau could not possibly have foreseen. In our time many Americans have crossed the Pacific, but not on errands which allowed them to forget the Old World and its institutions.

7) What does the comparison in III between the westward movement and the migrations of birds and animals suggest?

8) Frederick Jackson Turner contended that the true point of view in our history is the Great West, and certainly he was right at least this far: through about a century of our history we not only believed in a better future, but in a future that had a direction and a location ever farther west. And we have not always been willing to "go eastward . . . retracing the steps of the race," for in our faith in the future the past has seemed useless and outworn. Notice how carefully Thoreau embodies this westward impetus. Why are his walks southwest, not due west? Do you think Thoreau believed that the westward movement could be explained entirely by such things as free land and economic opportunity? Would one have had to migrate westward to share in the westward movement?

9) Does IV suggest in any way a quality of illusion in this faith in westward future—or its possible disappointment? What is the effect of the metaphors and allusions used therein? Consider 5 particularly. Is there an allusion in "terrestrial paradise"? Notice how the image of the sunset controls the whole paragraph.

10) Does this passage help to explain the difficulties we have had as a nation in comprehending and meeting twentieth-century problems? How?

THE JARGON HABIT   *iv*

In this final section we consider a verbal stumbling block that will cause you trouble in general reading, as well as in writing. It is a repellent kind of expression that is variously called pretentious writing, gobbledygook, and JARGON. We are generally concerned in this book with what is good and effective in writing; but the jargon habit is so prevalent, so serious intellectually *and* morally, and so insidious, that we must discuss, this time, what not to do. The vice disfigures much contemporary writing; in fact, no one of us avoids it entirely. Many of the influences on students, even some of their textbooks, push them toward it.

And yet, when a particular example of jargon is pointed out, everyone recognizes it for what it is. Here is a sentence by a student: "Those who did not wish to participate in dancing sat on benches." "To participate in dancing" is jargon for "to dance." How did an admirable girl come to write a sentence like that? It is not hard to explain. "Participate" is almost a technical term in educational theory. The student's teachers had a bad habit, which they communicated to the student—who may communicate it to others, for jargon is most infectious. One finds a husky lad writing that he has "participated in football." What would you think of someone who said, when a halfback made a fifty-yard run, "Boy, how that halfback can participate in football"?

Jargon is a rhetorical matter, but it is a moral matter, too. Mark Twain calls a pretentious piece of writing "a literary cake-walk." And jargon is often a kind of strutting, to which a writer is impelled by his desire to make what he is saying impressive and more important than it really is— perhaps to himself as well as to his readers. A student, let us suppose, is writing about potato growing in his section of country, a subject that needs no apology and no inflation. He wants to say that nearly all the potatoes are shipped by truck. But he feels impelled to say, "In the overwhelming majority of cases, the shipping of the potatoes is accomplished by means of truck transport." A bit later in his paper he wants to say that some potato growers have good incomes. But he is likely to say, "It is not uncommon for some producers of potatoes to experience a high level of financial return." And before you think very harshly of him, be sure you never write such sentences.

The thing is insidious. We continually hear and read jargon, and we may easily slip into it. This writer, for instance, has to watch himself with the expression "in terms of." It does have some legitimate uses; usually it is just padding. If we want to say that a job pays well, but is night work, let us say *that,* and not "The position is desirable in terms of financial return, but in terms of the working hours would be undesirable in the case of the majority of prospective employees."

You will find jargon everywhere. The government economist talks about "accumulated savings" (as if some savings were not accumulated). The clergyman says in his sermon, "This matter is of great concern to us in terms of our spiritual life." The educationalist writes: "The majority of objective examinations which have been built by classroom teachers for informal use, and many standardized tests as well, have tended to be un-duly, if not almost exclusively, informational in character, and have tended to place a premium upon rote learning rather than upon true un-derstanding." How many of the words in that sentence do no work? The sentence can be cut down by half; perhaps it might be reduced more than this: "Most objective tests devised by classroom teachers, and many stand-ardized tests as well, do test rote learning and not understanding."

But you do not much need examples; they are all too readily available to you. And when you really pay attention to what is going on in a piece of jargon writing, you resent it. You realize that, in your own writing, jargon will spoil your relationship with your reader, and that it will becloud the sense. Perhaps reading the vigorous discussion below will help you to keep in mind the dangers of this vice in writing. (You will see that it also touches upon some of the matters we considered in the Metaphor section.) It is by the author of *1984*.

FROM *Politics and the English Language* (1946)

GEORGE ORWELL

1 . . . I am going to translate a passage of good English into modern English of the worst sort. Here is a well-known verse from *Ecclesiastes:*

"I returned, and saw under the sun, that the race is not to the swift, nor the battle to the strong, neither yet bread to the wise, nor yet riches to men of understanding, nor yet favor to men of skill; but time and chance happeneth to them all."

Here it is in modern English:

"Objective consideration of contemporary phenomena compels the conclusion that success or failure in competitive activities exhibits no tendency to be commensurate with innate capacity, but that a considerable element of the unpredictable must invariably be taken into account."

II This is a parody, but not a very gross one. . . . It will be seen that I have not made a full translation. The beginning and ending of the sentence follow the original meaning fairly closely, but in the middle the concrete illustrations—race, battle, bread—dissolve into the vague phrase "success or failure in competitive activities." This had to be so, because no modern writer of the kind I am discussing—no one capable of using phrases like "objective consideration of contemporary phenomena"—would ever tabulate his thoughts in that precise and detailed way. The whole tendency of modern prose is away from concreteness. Now analyze these two sentences a little more closely. The first contains 49 words but only 60 syllables, and all its words are those of everyday life. The second contains 38 words of 90 syllables: 18 of its words are from Latin roots, and one from Greek. The first sentence contains six vivid images, and only one phrase ("time and chance") that could be called vague. The second contains not a single fresh, arresting phrase, and in spite of its 90 syllables it gives only a shortened version of the meaning contained in the first. Yet without a doubt it is the second kind of sentence that is gaining ground in modern English. I do not want to exaggerate. This kind of writing is not yet universal, and outcrops of simplicity will occur here and there in the worst-written page. Still, if you or I were told to write a few lines on the uncertainty of human fortunes, we should probably come much nearer to my imaginary sentence than to the one from *Ecclesiastes*.

III As I have tried to show, modern writing at its worst does not consist in picking out words for the sake of their meaning and inventing images in order to make the meaning clearer. It consists in gumming together long strips of words which have already been set in order by someone else, and making the results presentable by sheer humbug. The attraction of this way of writing is that it is easy. It is easier—even quicker, once you have the habit—to say *In my opinion it is a not unjustifiable assumption that* than to say *I think.* If you use ready-made phrases, you not only don't have to hunt about for words; you also don't have to bother with the rhythms of your sentences, since these phrases are generally so arranged as to be more or less euphonious. When you are composing in a hurry—when you are dictating to a stenographer, for instance, or making a public speech—it is natural to fall into a pretentious, Latinized style. Tags like *a consideration which we should do well to bear in mind* or *a conclusion to which all of us would readily assent* will save many a sentence from coming down with a bump. By using stale metaphors, similes and idioms, you save much mental effort at the cost of leaving your meaning vague, not only for your reader but for yourself. This is the significance of mixed metaphors. The sole aim of a metaphor is to call up a visual image. When these images clash—as in *The Fascist octopus has sung its swan song, the jackboot is thrown into the melting pot*—it can be taken as certain that the writer is not seeing a mental image of the objects he is naming; in other words he is not really thinking. . . . People who write in this manner usually have a general emotional meaning—they dislike one thing and want to express solidarity with another—but they are not interested in the detail of what they are saying. A scrupulous writer, in every sentence that he writes, will ask himself at least four questions, thus: What am I trying to say? What words will express it? What image or idiom will make it clearer? Is this image fresh enough to have an effect? And he will probably ask himself two more: Could I put it more shortly? Have I said anything that is avoidably ugly? But you are not obliged to go to all this trouble. You can shirk it by simply throwing your mind open and letting the ready-made phrases come crowding in. They will construct your sentences for you—even think your thoughts for you, to a certain extent—and at need they will perform the important service of partially concealing your meaning even from yourself. . . .

IV I said earlier that the decadence of our language is probably curable. Those who deny this would argue, if they produced an argument at all, that language merely reflects existing social conditions, and that we cannot influence its development by any direct tinkering with words and constructions. So far as the general tone or spirit of a language goes, this may be true, but it is not true in detail. Silly words and expressions have often disappeared, not through any evolutionary process but owing to the conscious action of a minority. Two recent examples were *explore every avenue* and *leave no stone unturned,* which were killed by the jeers of a few journalists. There is a long list of fly-blown metaphors which could similarly be got rid of if enough people would interest themselves in the job; and it should also be possible to laugh the *not un-* formation out of existence,[1] to reduce the amount of Latin and Greek in the average sentence, to drive out foreign phrases and strayed scientific words, and, in general, to make pretentiousness unfashionable. But all these are minor points. The defense of the English language implies more than this, and perhaps it is best to start by saying what it does *not* imply.

v To begin with, it has nothing to do with archaism, with the salvaging of obsolete words and turns of speech, or with the setting-up of a "standard English" which must never be departed from. On the contrary, it is especially concerned with the scrapping of every word or idiom which has outworn its usefulness. It has nothing to do with correct grammar and syntax, which are of no importance so long as one makes one's meaning clear, or with the avoidance of Americanisms, or with having what is called a "good prose style." On the other hand it is not concerned with fake simplicity and the attempt to make written English colloquial. Nor does it even imply in every case preferring the Saxon word to the Latin one, though it does imply using the fewest and shortest words that will cover one's meaning. What is above all needed is to let the meaning choose the word, and not the other way about. In prose, the worst thing one can do with words is to surrender them. When you think of a concrete object, you think wordlessly, and then, if you want to describe the thing you have been visualizing, you probably hunt about till you find the exact words that seem to fit it. When you think of something abstract you are more inclined to use words from the start, and unless you make a conscious effort to prevent it, the existing dialect will come rushing in and do the job for you, at the expense of blurring or even changing your meaning. Probably it is better to put off using words as long as possible and get one's meaning as clear as one can through pictures or sensations. Afterwards one can choose—not simply *accept*—the phrases that will best cover the meaning, and then switch round and decide what impressions one's words are likely to make on another person. This last effort of the mind cuts out all stale or mixed images, all prefabricated phrases, needless repetitions, and humbug and vagueness generally. But one can often be in doubt about the effect of a word or a phrase, and one needs rules that one can rely on when instinct fails. I think the following rules will cover most cases:

(i) Never use a metaphor, simile or other figure of speech which you are used to seeing in print.

(ii) Never use a long word where a short one will do.

(iii) If it is possible to cut a word out, always cut it out.

(iv) Never use the passive where you can use the active.

(v) Never use a foreign phrase, a scientific word or a jargon word if you can think of an everyday English equivalent.

(vi) Break any of these rules sooner than say anything barbarous.

These rules sound elementary, and so they are, but they demand a deep change of attitude in anyone who has grown used to writing in the style

---

[1] One can cure oneself of the *not un-* formation by memorizing this sentence: *A not unblack dog was chasing a not unsmall rabbit across a not ungreen field.*

now fashionable. One could keep all of them and still write bad English, but one could not write the kind of stuff that I quoted in these five specimens at the beginning of this article.

VI I have not here been considering the literary use of language, but merely language as an instrument for expressing and not for concealing or preventing thought. Stuart Chase and others have come near to claiming that all abstract words are meaningless, and have used this as a pretext for advocating a kind of political quietism. Since you don't know what Fascism is, how can you struggle against Fascism? One need not swallow such absurdities as this, but one ought to recognize that the present political chaos is connected with the decay of language, and that one can probably bring about some improvement by starting at the verbal end. If you simplify your English, you are freed from the worst follies of orthodoxy. You cannot speak any of the necessary dialects, and when you make a stupid remark its stupidity will be obvious, even to yourself. Political language—and with variations this is true of all political parties, from Conservatives to Anarchists—is designed to make lies sound truthful and murder respectable, and to give an appearance of solidity to pure wind. One cannot change this all in a moment, but one can at least change one's own habits, and from time to time one can even, if one jeers loudly enough, send some worn-out and useless phrase—some *jackboot, Achilles' heel, hotbed, melting pot, acid test, veritable inferno* or other lump of verbal refuse—into the dustbin where it belongs.

SUGGESTIONS FOR PAPERS

A good exercise in connection with the instruction about words is to see how far it applies to assigned work for the next week in your several courses. Note down what words you have to look up and what discrimination among definitions is necessary. Record examples of metaphors and allusions with enough of their context to make them intelligible. Decide whether any use of reference books is desirable in connection with the week's work, and how far your dictionary is a sufficient reference for your needs. See if the writers of your textbooks have entirely escaped writing in jargon. A week's work may not illustrate every matter we have considered; it will illustrate a number of matters, and the rest will soon turn up. You should be able to find quite enough material for as extended a report as your instructor may wish.

For a study of metaphor you might consider the metaphors in a particular kind of writing—in a history or economics textbook, for instance—and then write a discussion of the use of metaphor there. Or you might study a group of newspaper editorials—say the editorials in one newspaper for three successive days—and discuss their use of metaphor. A somewhat more extended paper might be a discussion of metaphor for a reader to whom the term is new. Inform him about the nature and function of metaphor in general writing. Remember that even if the term is new to your reader, metaphors themselves are not. Try to use his own experience in your writing.

For an exercise on the selection from "Walking," you might assume an unpracticed reader, younger than yourself, and write *for him* a set of notes on the selection, notes which will help him see its full meaning and implication. Often expansion of a passage, using your knowledge of the allusion, would help such a reader.

A useful exercise, particularly now at the beginning of your college work, is a report on a reference work new to you, a report written to inform the class. Your handbook will have a list of reference books; and your instructor can suggest those appropriate to individual interests. Many college freshmen are quite unacquainted with the most useful and interesting reference books, the *Dictionary of American Biography*, for instance. Particularly, freshmen seem not to know the compact sort of reference work; the admirable *Encyclopedia of American History*, edited by Richard B. Morris, is one example. It would be well, too, if three or four students examined extended bibliographies in special fields of knowledge; for instance, one student might take volume III of the *Literary History of the United States* for his report. Whatever book you report on, remember that you should make clear to your readers what its resources are and how it is to be used. Look up a few matters in it and see how they are handled; do not try to depend upon the introduction.

IV

The Full Control of Meaning

W e have here four kinds of reading, each of which requires its own approach, although none offers any great difficulty. You will be able to use what you have learned in the preceding sections in reading this one. His use of what he already knows on a new problem is the special mark of a good student.

i TEXTBOOK READING IN SCIENCE

Within your first two college years you will probably use a textbook in science. You will of course learn your science in science courses, but a good many students have difficulty with the reading in science, and that is part of our concern. Pieces of scientific writing appear in several places in this book, since the reading of scientific and technical material offers no problem different in *kind* from the problems in other sorts of expository prose. But the understanding of scientific and technical material is likely to be in a greater degree cumulative than is the understanding of expository prose in other fields. That is to say that the understanding of the subject in hand grows by successive additions, the second explanation depending upon the first, the third upon the first and second, and so on throughout. Therefore, if one were reading a unit of nine paragraphs and read the first six carelessly, it is almost certain that the last three would be nearly meaningless to him, no matter how attentively he read *them*.

Our selection from a college textbook in geography will stand quite well by itself. As in many textbooks, short sections are given titles in order to make sure that the student sees at once what they are about. Do not neglect this aid. Notice too that there is a good deal of definition, and that later definitions depend upon the initial definitions. Perhaps the very first concern of a student in an elementary science course is to get its terminology straight. Our selection will be an instance. If a student does not know before he comes to the piece the difference between a *parallel* and a *meridian,* he must fix the definitions of these terms in his mind before he leaves the first paragraph. If he does not do so, surely the terms introduced later—such terms as *Tropic of Cancer* and *prime meridian*—will have no meaning for him. You may need your dictionary sometimes. It would be convenient to have a globe at hand as you read, but a map that shows parallels and meridians will illustrate what is said.

FROM *Elements of Geography* (1949)

VERNOR C. FINCH and GLENN T. TREWARTHA

[The Earth Grid. Location. Time]

I THE EARTH GRID. . . . On a true sphere that is not in motion there is neither beginning nor ending, no natural point or line of reference from which to begin to measure the relative positions of other points. If it were not for its motions and other planetary relations, the earth also would have no natural point or line from which to measure direction. Since the fact of rotation establishes the geographic poles of the earth, these serve as initial points in a scheme of imaginary lines, called the earth grid, by means of which directions and relative locations are easily indicated. Midway between the poles an imaginary circle may be drawn upon the surface. It is a "great circle," called the *equator.* Other circles may be drawn at any desired distances from the poles. They will be smaller than the equator but parallel with it. They are called *parallels.* Upon the equator and the parallels, distance may be measured east or west from any given point. The north-south members of the earth grid, or system of coordinates, are called *meridians.* They are produced by drawing any number of circles which intersect at both poles. They are all great circles, and each of them bisects the equator and every parallel. Each of these great circles is divided at the poles and forms a pair of meridians, one meridian being a semicircle extending from North Pole to South Pole. By means of all these circles, the parallels and meridians, is developed the system of lines made familiar through the grid of a geographical globe.

II LATITUDE. In the measurement of the earth it is customary to divide into quadrants the circle formed by each pair of meridians, the points of division being the poles and the two intersections with the equator. Each quadrant is divided into 90 parts, called degrees (°) of latitude, the sum of the number of degrees in the four parts being the 360 degrees of the meridian circle. The numbering of the degrees proceeds from the equator to either pole, and positions on the meridian are marked by the east-west cross lines of the parallels. By means of the parallels, latitude is reckoned from the equator (0°Lat.) northward to the North Pole (90°N.Lat.) on any meridian and, in the same way, from the equator to the South Pole (90°S.Lat.). Owing to the size of the earth, the average length of a degree of latitude is about 69 miles.

III THE LENGTH OF DEGREES OF LATITUDE. On a true sphere each degree of circumference, measured in any direction, has the same length, but this is not quite true on the earth. Because of the earth's polar flattening, degrees of latitude near the poles are slightly longer than those near the equator. The first degree of latitude from the equator has a length of 68.69 miles, while the first degree from the pole is 69.39 miles long. Each degree of latitude is divided into 60 minutes ($'$), and each minute into 60 seconds ($''$). One minute of latitude has an average length of 6,080 ft. (1 nautical mile) or about 1.15 statute miles, and one second of latitude is about 101 ft. The length of the meter, standard of measurement in the metric system, is, in theory, exactly one ten-millionth of the meridian distance from the equator to the pole.

The latitude of any place is determined by instrumental observation. It is necessary only, by means of the sextant, to measure the angle between the horizon and the zenithal position of the sun at noon. At the time of the equinoxes (about Mar. 21 and Sept. 22) the sun's rays at noon fall vertically on the equator, and the latitude of any place may be computed by subtracting from 90° the angle read on the sextant. For times other than the equinoxes the results obtained by the above method must be revised by the use of tables that show the different latitudes at which the rays of the sun fall vertically for each day in the year. Latitudes may be obtained also by instrumental observation upon the North Star (Polaris).

IV A PARALLEL OF LATITUDE, drawn through points equally distant from the equator on all meridians, may be constructed for any degree, minute, or second of latitude. On an ordinary globe grid, at small scale, only a few of the many possible parallels are shown—usually those of the multiples of 5 or 10°. Almost always, however, four fractional parallels are shown in addition to the others, because they have special significance. These are the parallels of approximately 23½°N. and S. and 66½°N. and S., respectively. Their importance is derived from their relation to the inclination of the earth's axis to the plane of the ecliptic. The parallels of 23½°N. and S. are called the Tropics of Cancer and Capricorn, respectively. They mark the limits of that portion of the earth where the solar rays ever fall vertically. The parallels of 66½°N. and S. are called, respectively, the Arctic and Antarctic Circles. They are the lines at which the midday rays of the sun are tangent to the earth's surface at the time of the shortest day of the year and at which the midnight rays are tangent at the time of the longest day.

V LONGITUDE is reckoned east or west along the parallels of latitude. Just as distances on a horizontal chalk line are measured by the vertical lines on a rule, so positions on the east-west parallels of latitude are marked by the intersections of the north-south meridians of longitude. Among the meridians there is no particular one marked by nature (as is the equator for counting latitude) from which numbering may begin. All are exactly alike, and it is possible to begin to count from any one of them as 0°Long. This was in fact done for several centuries, each important country beginning with a meridian drawn through a spot within its own borders. So much confusion resulted that, in the year 1884, the meridian passing through the Royal Astronomical Observatory at Greenwich, near London, was chosen by international agreement as the zero meridian. It is called the *prime meridian*. It intersects the equator in the Gulf of Guinea at a point which has the distinction of having 0°00′00″Long. and 0°00′00″Lat. The 360° of longitude in the equator and each parallel are numbered 180°E. and 180°W. of the prime meridian to the opposite side of the earth.

VI DEGREES OF LONGITUDE VARY IN LENGTH. All the parallels of latitude, except the equator, are less than great circles, the diameters of those near the poles being much less than that of the equator or of the other parallels near to it. Since each parallel, regardless of its circumference, is divided into 360°, it follows that the length of 1° of longitude, in miles, must decrease toward the poles. One degree of longitude on the equator, a great circle, has about the same length as an average degree of latitude (69.15 miles). At latitude 30°N. or S. the length of a degree of longitude is 59.94 miles; at 60° it is 34.60 miles; at 80° it is 12.05 miles; and at the poles it is, of course, zero.

The longitude of an unmapped place east or west of the prime meridian, or of a ship at sea, can be determined only by finding the difference in time between that place and the prime meridian. This was first accomplished by means of accurate timepieces (chronometers) carried on shipboard and set at Greenwich, or prime-meridian, time. Observation of the sun at the instant when it reached the highest point (zenith) in its daily course across the sky gave local noontime, which could then be compared directly with the chronometer, and the difference in time translated into degrees and minutes of longitude. Now, instantaneous communication by telegraph and radio makes accurate time comparison possible almost everywhere and, therefore, makes possible greatly improved determinations of longitude. This is of particular aid in geographical exploration.

VII ACCURATE LOCATION. The intersection of any two lines is a point; consequently, any point on the earth's surface may be located by determining that it lies at the intersection of a certain meridian with a certain parallel. Therefore, by exact determination of its latitude and longitude the location of any place may be expressed briefly and with great accuracy. Thus if one were to say that the dome of the National Capitol at Washington was located at 38°53′23″N.Lat. and 77°00′33″Long. west of Greenwich, one would state its exact position on the earth to within 10 paces.

VIII LONGITUDE AND TIME. The earth rotates eastward through its entire circumference of 360° of longitude in 24 hr., therefore through 15° in 1 hr. When noon (the zenith position of the sun) arrives at any meridian, it is already 1 hr. later (1:00 P.M.) on the meridian 15° east of that one, and it lacks 1 hr. of noon (11:00 A.M.) on the meridian 15° to the west of it. For the instant, it is noon on the one meridian only, but it is noon on that meridian from north pole to south pole. Four minutes later it is noon on the meridian 1° farther west. In a generation past, each town kept the time of its own meridian, which was called apparent solar time or, in common American parlance, "sun time." When rail transportation permitted rapid travel, it became awkward or impossible to change one's time a few minutes with every village passed. To avoid this necessity each railroad adopted an arbitrary time scheme which differed from that of most of the places that it passed through but was the same for considerable distances on the rail line. Unfortunately, several railroads in a region often adopted different times for their own use. Consequently, it sometimes happened that a town reached by different railroads found itself required to use, or distinguish between, several different kinds of time: its own solar time and one for each of its railways. The awkwardness and confusion of this situation led to the adoption by American railways, in 1883, of a system of *standard time*. This system, in theory, supposes that all parts of a north-south zone 15° of longitude in width adopt the solar time of the central meridian of that zone. Places within the zone that are east or west of the central meridian, instead of differing in time by a few minutes from it and from each other, all have the same time. Changes of time are then necessary only in crossing the boundary of the zone, and each change is exactly 1 hr. The timepiece is set forward (*i.e.*, later, as from 12:00 to 1:00) in traveling east, and back (*i.e.*, earlier, as from 12:00 to 11:00) in traveling west. In practice, these zones are not bounded by meridians but by irregular lines the location of which is dictated by railway convenience and political consideration. . . .

On the whole earth there should be 24 standard-time zones, each extending from pole to pole and each differing from Greenwich time by an integral number of hours. In practice the arrangement is not quite so simple, for, although most countries follow the plan, certain isolated ones have not yet adopted standard time at all, and a few small countries employ standard meridians that are not multiples of 15 and therefore do not differ from Greenwich time by exact hours. For example, Netherlands time is 19 min. faster, and Bolivian time 4 hr. 33 min. (instead of 5 hr.) slower, than Greenwich time.

IX THE INTERNATIONAL DATE LINE. The quickness with which the earth may be circumnavigated has introduced a problem of correction not only of the hour but also of the date and day of the week. The nature of this problem may clearly be seen if one imagines an airplane sufficiently fast to fly around the earth in the latitude of Chicago, let us say, in exactly 24 hr. If the flyer left Chicago, *going westward*, at noon on Monday the tenth of the month, he would keep exact pace with the apparent motion of the sun, would see it in the same position all the way, and would return to Chicago the same (to him) noon. To persons in Chicago a night would have intervened, and it would be noon of Tuesday the eleventh. The flyer would have *lost* a day. If he had flown *eastward,* he would have encountered midnight over Spain, noon of another day over Central Asia, a second night over the Pacific Ocean, and would have returned to Chicago at noon of the second day, though he had been gone only 24 hr. To him it would be noon of Wednesday the twelfth, while to those who remained it is, as before, Tuesday the eleventh. The flyer has *gained* a day. The fact that one who travels slowly by train and boat loses or gains this time by 24 time corrections of 1 hr. each does not alter the case in the least. Unless he sets his calendar ahead one day when traveling around the earth westward and sets it back when traveling eastward, it will be out of adjustment on his return. To avoid the confusion that would result from individual choice as to place of change, an *international date line* has been established at the 180th meridian. There, correction may be made uniformly, and no correction of date is necessary unless that line is crossed. Certain deviations of the date line from the 180th meridian are agreed upon to prevent confusion of day and date in certain island groups or land areas that are divided by the meridian.

---

1) The information in this selection is valuable, even necessary, to almost anyone. Locate on a globe or a map of Korea the 38th parallel, so important in recent history. Why must one change his watch in a long journey east or west? Why is it 12 noon in San Francisco when it is 3 P.M. in Boston? How can a ship be located in the trackless ocean? If you have read this piece with ordinary care, you can answer these questions, and more.

2) The mystery ship *Mary Celeste,* abandoned by her crew for some reason never known, was discovered December 5, 1872, sailing with no one at the helm at about latitude 38°20'N. and longitude 17°15'W. About where was she? On March 14, 1952, what appeared to be an island was sighted from a plane at 88°17'N., 166°13'W. The "island" was really a great mass of floating ice. Where was it in its travels when sighted?

3) We are, of course, most concerned with what reading this piece may teach us about scientific reading in general. A frequent difficulty for students is distinguishing the essential fact or principle from the illustrative detail. One need not burden his memory with the latitude and longitude of the dome of the Capitol at Washington (VII); one surely should remember that the earth rotates eastward through 15 degrees in an hour. Now if a student fails to make such distinctions, is it not likely that he is reading without really trying to understand?

4) Perhaps a careful marking of his book would help. If he marks it intelligently, he must make distinctions as he reads. He should remember that one of the purposes of marking up a book is his convenience in review. If he over-marks it, he defeats that purpose. His marks should designate salient facts and principles. But he should not mark illustrations or explanations that he will not need once principles are clear to him. Look over your own marking of this selection. Have you marked too frequently? Have you marked the relatively unimportant? How useful would your marking be in a review three months hence?

5) Some students have a difficulty they do not recognize. One can remember a verbal formula—remember what the book said—without at all understanding it. Perhaps for a time neither instructor nor student will be aware of the lack of understanding; but both will recognize it in the long run. A student with this propensity must find a method of avoiding the rote reproduction of material. (And he must do so in the rest of his work as well as in science; the tendency unchecked is fatal everywhere.)

6) Such a student would do well often to close his book and to make sure that he can put explanations in his own sentences, and in his own terms wherever technical terms are not required. If he will start his dis-

cussion in a familiar manner, that may get him away from parroting and toward understanding. He might start in some such fashion as this: "If you want to find on a map the location in latitude and longitude of your home town, you. . . ." How will you continue that sentence?

7) There is some provision for practice in this sort of restatement in the "Suggestions for Papers" at the end of this chapter. But in the ordinary course of your work, making sure that you understand as well as seem to remember is pretty much up to you.

8) Now will you try an experiment? Write down definitions of all terms of importance in the order of their first appearance. If you have trouble defining a term, perhaps the dictionary will help. When you have once defined a term, you will not, of course, define it again when it appears as part of a term, or as part of a definition. Sometimes you may have to consider what will be the important term or terms in a section. In VIII, for instance, can you find a term which, when defined, will indicate the essence of the section? Will the term "standard time-zone" do?

9) Now look over your list of definitions. How good a control of the selection has this progressive definition given you? Perhaps this selection depends upon progressive definition more than some scientific writing does, but the terms of any science are of first importance.

ii   HISTORICAL GENERALIZATION

Now we shall take two passages that have the same subject—the American character—and interpret the same general facts. Here is a suggestion about handling them: Read over both passages carefully, and more than once, before you look at any of the questions. Then see how many of the questions you can answer without going back to the passages. Finally, go back to the passages and check your answers. If you will carry out the exercise as suggested, it will indicate to you how well you comprehend the sort of generalization with which we are now working.

FROM

The Significance of the Frontier in American History
(1893)

FREDERICK JACKSON TURNER

[The American Character]

From the conditions of frontier life came intellectual traits of profound importance. The works of travelers along each frontier from colonial days onward describe certain common traits, and these traits have, while softening down, still persisted as survivals in the place of their origin, even when a higher social organization succeeded. The result is that to the frontier the American intellect owes its striking characteristics. That coarseness and strength combined with acuteness and inquisitiveness; that practical, inventive turn of mind, quick to find expedients; that masterful grasp of material things, lacking in the artistic but powerful to effect great ends; that restless, nervous energy; that dominant individualism, working for good and for evil, and withal that buoyancy and exuberance which comes with freedom—these are traits of the frontier, or traits called out elsewhere because of the existence of the frontier. Since the days when the fleet of Columbus sailed into the waters of the New World, America has been another name for opportunity, and the people of the United States have taken their tone from the incessant expansion which has not only been open but has even been forced upon them. He would be a rash prophet who should assert that the expansive character of American life has now entirely ceased. Movement has been its dominant fact, and, unless this training has no effect upon a people, the American energy will continually demand a wider field for its exercise. But never again will such gifts of free land offer themselves.

FROM *Character and Opinion in the United States* (1920)

GEORGE SANTAYANA

[The American Character]

The discovery of the new world exercised a sort of selection among the inhabitants of Europe. All the colonists, except the Negroes, were voluntary exiles. The fortunate, the deeply rooted, and the lazy remained at home; the wilder instincts or dissatisfaction of others tempted them beyond the horizon. The American is accordingly the most adventurous, or the descendant of the most adventurous, of Europeans. It is in his blood to be socially a radical, though perhaps not intellectually. What has existed in the past, especially in the remote past, seems to him not only not authoritative, but irrelevant, inferior, and outworn. He finds it rather a sorry waste of time to think about the past at all. But his enthusiasm for the future is profound; he can conceive of no more decisive way of recommending an opinion or a practice than to say that it is what everybody is coming to adopt. This expectation of what he approves, or approval of what he expects, makes up his optimism. It is the necessary faith of the pioneer.

---

1) Is each passage organized around a topic or key idea? State those key ideas in your own terms.

2) Probably the vocabulary of these passages offered you no great difficulty, but here in an early exercise a check may be appropriate. When Turner says the Americans are "quick to find expedients," what is he say-

ing that "quick to find ways of doing things" does not say? What does "to effect great ends" mean? Do you ever confuse "affect" and "effect"? What is the literal sense of "buoyancy," and the metaphorical sense as Turner uses it to describe the American intellect? Do you consider Santayana's expression "tempted them beyond the horizon" metaphorical? If, as Santayana says, "the deeply rooted" Europeans remained at home, does that metaphor imply a judgment about the Europeans who came to America?

3) Both passages seem to express a general approval of the American character. Does either, or do both, imply or suggest weaknesses that accompany the optimistic individualism of Americans? How, by what words or expressions?

4) Santayana says of the typical American, "It is in his blood to be socially a radical, though perhaps not intellectually." What does the sentence mean? Put it in your own terms. You will have to consider the context: What does "socially" mean here? See what your dictionary says about "radical," and then decide what distinction between two modes of radicalism Santayana intends.

5) Do both passages present essentially the same reason in explanation of the character of typical Americans? If they do, state that reason briefly and in your own terms. If they do not, state the reason that each of the passages offers in explanation of the character of typical Americans.

6) If you decided that the passages present different reasons in explanation of the character of typical Americans, are the reasons incompatible —can you admit that one is right without denying the other?

7) You will have noted that Santayana uses the singular "the American" as a type to represent characteristics he believes common to most Americans. Can you give examples of this habit of thought and expression from everyday discussion? Santayana in the chapter from which our passage comes speaks of such types or symbols as "that paper money of our own stamping, the legal tender of the mind." Interpret his metaphor. Does the metaphor suggest what may be a danger in this habit of thought? (To say that there may be danger in it is not to condemn it.)

The next selection is from St. John de Crèvecoeur's *Letters from an American Farmer*. The *Letters*, written for European readers, were based on Crèvecoeur's experience in Orange County in colonial New York about 1765. They are a valuable record and might be part of the reading in college courses in literature or history. Our selection from the third letter is distinguished for its early recognition that a new national character was developing in America.

Crèvecoeur's location enabled him to observe the racial mixture taking place in the New York colony, and his European background and his intelligence enabled him to realize its significance. He is, moreover, perhaps the first writer with a clear insight into what was happening in newly settled country and on the frontier. Although he discovers his representative American in the middle settlements, between the older region on the coast and the frontier, there are certain suggestions of the theory of the frontier developed much later by Turner. "He who would wish to see America in its proper light," Crèvecoeur writes, "and have a true idea of its feeble beginnings and barbarous rudiments, must visit our extended line of frontiers where the last settlers dwell."

FROM *What Is an American?* (1782)

J. HECTOR ST. JOHN DE CRÈVECOEUR

I We are a people of cultivators, scattered over an immense territory, communicating with each other by means of good roads and navigable rivers, united by the silken bands of mild government, all respecting the laws, without dreading their power, because they are equitable. We are all animated with the spirit of an industry which is unfettered and unrestrained, because each person works for himself. If he travels through our rural districts he views not the hostile castle, and the haughty mansion, contrasted with the clay-built hut and miserable cabin, where cattle and men help to keep each other warm, and dwell in meanness, smoke, and indigence. A pleasing uniformity of decent competence appears throughout our habitations. The meanest of our log-houses is a dry and comfortable habitation. Lawyer or merchant are the fairest titles our towns afford; that of a farmer is the only appellation of the rural inhabitants of our country. It must take some time ere he can reconcile himself to our dictionary, which is but short in words of dignity, and names of honour. There, on a Sunday, he sees a congregation of respectable farmers and their wives, all clad in neat homespun, well mounted, or riding in their own humble waggons. There is not among them an esquire, saving the unlettered magistrate. There he sees a parson as simple as his flock, a farmer who does not riot on the labour of others. We have no princes, for whom we toil, starve, and bleed: we are the most perfect society now existing in the world. Here man is free as he ought to be; nor is this pleasing equality so transitory as many others are. Many ages will not see the shores of our great lakes replenished with inland nations, nor the unknown bounds of North America entirely peopled. Who can tell how far it extends? Who can tell the millions of men whom it will feed and contain? for no European foot has as yet travelled half the extent of this mighty continent!

II The next wish of this traveller will be to know whence came all these people? they are a mixture of English, Scotch, Irish, French, Dutch, Germans, and Swedes. From this promiscuous breed, that race now called Americans have arisen. The eastern provinces must indeed be excepted, as being the unmixed descendants of Englishmen. I have heard many wish that they had been more intermixed also: for my part, I am no wisher, and think it much better as it has happened. They exhibit a most conspicuous figure in this great and variegated picture; they too enter for a great share in the pleasing perspective displayed in these thirteen provinces. I know it is fashionable to reflect on them, but I respect them for what they have done; for the accuracy and wisdom with which they have settled their territory; for the decency of their manners; for their early love of letters; their ancient college, the first in this hemisphere; for their industry; which to me who am but a farmer, is the criterion of everything. There never was a people, situated as they are, who with so ungrateful a soil have done more in so short a time. Do you think that the monarchical ingredients which are more prevalent in other governments, have purged them from all foul stains? Their histories assert the contrary.

III In this great American asylum, the poor of Europe have by some means met together, and in consequence of various causes; to what purpose should they ask one another what countrymen they are? Alas, two thirds of them had no country. Can a wretch who wanders about, who works and starves, whose life is a continual scene of sore affliction or pinching penury; can that man call England or any other kingdom his country? A country that had no bread for him, whose fields procured him no harvest, who met with nothing but the frowns of the rich, the severity of the laws, with jails and punishments; who owned not a single foot of the extensive surface of this planet? No! urged by a variety of motives, here they came. Every thing has tended to regenerate them; new laws, a new mode of living, a new social system; here they are become men: in Europe they were as so many useless plants, wanting vegetative mould, and refreshing showers; they withered, and were mowed down by want, hunger, and war; but now by the power of transplantation, like all other plants they have taken root and flourished! Formerly they were not numbered in any civil lists of their country, except in those of the poor; here they rank as citizens. By what invisible power has this surprising metamorphosis been performed? By that of the laws and that of their industry. The laws, the indulgent laws, protect them as they arrive, stamping on them the symbol of adoption; they receive ample rewards for their labours; these accumulated rewards procure them lands; those lands confer on them the title of freemen, and to that title every benefit is affixed which men can possibly require. This is the great operation daily performed by our laws. From whence proceed these laws? From our government. Whence the government? It is derived from the original genius and strong desire of the people ratified and confirmed by the crown. This is the great chain which links us all, this is the picture which every province exhibits, Nova Scotia excepted. There the crown has done all; either there were no people who had genius, or it was not much attended to: the consequence is, that the province is very thinly inhabited indeed; the power of the crown in conjunction with the musketos has prevented men from settling there. Yet some parts of it flourished once, and it contained a mild harmless set of people. But for the fault of a few leaders, the whole were banished. The greatest political error the crown ever committed in America, was to cut off men from a country which wanted nothing but men!

IV What attachment can a poor European emigrant have for a country where he had nothing? The knowledge of the language, the love of a few kindred as poor as himself, were the only cords that tied him: his country is now that which gives him land, bread, protection, and consequence. *Ubi panis ibi patria*,[1] is the motto of all emigrants. What then is the American, this new man? He is either an European, or the descendant of an European, hence that strange mixture of blood, which you will find in no other country. I could point out to you a family whose grandfather was an Englishman, whose wife was Dutch, whose son married a French woman, and whose present four sons have now four wives of different nations. *He* is an American, who, leaving behind him all his ancient prejudices and manners, receives new ones from the new mode of life he has embraced, the new government he obeys, and the new rank he holds. He becomes an American by being received in the broad lap of our great *Alma Mater*. Here individuals of all nations are melted into a new race of men, whose labours and posterity will one day cause great changes in the world. Americans are the western pilgrims, who are carrying along with them that great mass of arts, sciences, vigour, and industry which began long since in the east; they will finish the great circle. The Americans were once scattered all over Europe; here they are incorporated into one of the finest systems of population which has ever appeared, and which will hereafter become distinct by the power of the different climates they inhabit. The American ought therefore to love this country much better than that wherein either he or his forefathers were born. Here the rewards of his industry follow with equal steps the progress of his labour; his labour is founded on the basis of nature, *self-interest;* can it want a stronger allurement? Wives and children, who before in vain demanded of him a morsel of bread, now, fat and frolicsome, gladly help their father to clear those fields whence exuberant crops are to arise to feed and to clothe them all; without any part being claimed, either by a despotic prince, a rich abbot, or a mighty lord. Here religion demands but little of him; a small voluntary salary to the minister, and gratitude to God; can he refuse these? The American is a new man, who acts upon new principles; he must therefore entertain new ideas, and form new opinions. From involuntary idleness, servile dependence, penury, and useless labour, he has passed to toils of a very different nature, rewarded by ample subsistence.—This is an American. . . .

v Men are like plants; the goodness and flavour of the fruit proceeds from the peculiar soil and exposition in which they grow. We are nothing but what we derive from the air we breathe, the climate we inhabit, the government we obey, the system of religion we profess, and the nature of our employment.

_____

1) Perhaps at first reading you did not feel that this selection offers any special difficulties. But Crèvecoeur is a diffuse writer, whose thinking and observation are more coherent than his expression. Even a careful reader is likely to miss, the first time through, important ideas in this selection. Crèvecoeur's extension of his title in iv—"What then is the American, this new man?"—directs us. You would do well to mark all those sentences which seem of particular importance in answering the question. And that will need attention. For instance, although you will have seen at once that

[1 Where bread is, there is a fatherland.]

Crèvecoeur feels economic equality a distinguishing feature of the life he describes, did you notice that he also seems happy to find a lack of intellectual distinction? What sentence indicates that?

2) According to Crèvecoeur, did the emigrants from Europe retain much of their racial or national traditions after their settlement in New York? What does form the American character? Notice Crèvecoeur's simile "Men are like plants," and the way in which it is developed into a metaphor. What are its implications? Do you find him using it in more than one place?

3) If *Ubi panis ibi patria* is an appropriate motto for all emigrants, what does that imply? In IV Crèvecoeur says that the American's labor "is founded on the basis of nature, *self-interest*." Does he approve self-interest as the primary motive of human behavior? Crèvecoeur, V. L. Parrington says, "was something of an economic determinist." Do the paragraphs we have been considering support that judgment? (Perhaps you need to look up "determinism.")

4) Crèvecoeur's metaphors sometimes suggest judgments or impose attitudes—as we have seen that metaphors often do. For instance, he says in I that Americans are "united by the silken bands of mild government"; but in III, when he is less concerned with individual liberty and more with the unity of Americans under English law, the government is "the great chain which links us all." Have you noted other examples of such metaphors?

5) In IV Crèvecoeur attacks his subject in much the same manner that Santayana does. What are Americans like? The answer comes in the figure of a representative American generalized from observation—perhaps also from Crèvecoeur's predilections. And this figure exhibits, as no single American could, the nature of the group. At the same time, it presents a more unified concept of the nature of Americans than a collection of statements about Americans would be likely to give.

6) Is Crèvecoeur's interpretation of the American character most like that of Santayana or that of Turner? Why do you answer as you do?

7) At the Revolution, Crèvecoeur was completely out of sympathy with the revolting colonies. Can you tell on the basis of this selection why?

8) One sometimes hears a student, even a college student, maintain that he understands something he has read, but that he "can't say it." Perhaps he does understand, but he will have to say it somehow before he can make much use of his understanding. You might practice as a part of your preparation—or in class if your instructor likes—saying briefly in your own words what Crèvecoeur says diffusely in his. Ask yourself a question that will allow you to cover some considerable portion of the selection in your answer.

9) Does any one of these three discussions interpret or illuminate your own observation of the American character in any way? Do you have reason to doubt or to disagree with any one of them? Look up the popular (as distinguished from the legal) definition of "special pleading." Have you use for the term here?

10) One piece of reading is likely to illuminate, if not the next, then some other that comes up soon. How does Thoreau's "Walking" connect

with these three selections? Is it, highly informal and personal as it seems, therefore less important than, say, the passage from Turner?

READING IN THE HISTORY OF IDEAS *iii*

The next selection discusses an important question that extends over a great span of time. It is that whole set of beliefs, assumptions, and attitudes which together are often designated the Idea of Progress. Woodrow Wilson once said in an address that "all through the centuries there has been a slow, painful struggle forward, forward, up, up, a little at a time, along the entire incline, the interminable way." He was merely saying what most Americans in the nineteenth and early twentieth centuries had taken for granted.

But the Idea of Progress is centuries old. In the chapter from which our selection comes, the writer has been discussing the emergence, in the seventeenth and eighteenth centuries, of the contention that what is modern is always better than what is past. The first paragraph of our selection states a form of that contention; the rest of the selection discusses its validity. The contention, although it is not here discussed in special reference to the United States, has persisted particularly with us.

FROM *The Classical Tradition* (1949)

GILBERT HIGHET

[The Idea of Progress] [1]

I The second argument [2] is the most popular nowadays. It is this. *Human knowledge is constantly advancing. We live in a later age than the Periclean Greeks and Augustan Romans: therefore we are wiser. Therefore anything we write, or make, is better than the things written and made by the ancient Greeks and Romans.*

II The emotional pressure towards accepting this argument was strong in the Renaissance, when worlds which the ancients had never seen were being discovered every generation, every decade: worlds in the far west, in the antipodes, in the sky. But in the Renaissance the discovery of the great classical books was still too new to allow men to vaunt one achievement of thought and will above the other. All the discoveries were equally wonderful: the new world of unknown nations and strange animals found by Columbus, the new worlds revealed by science, and the new world of subtle writing and trenchant psychology and glorious myth created by antiquity. In the baroque age, on the other hand, the classics were growing

---

[1] From *The Classical Tradition* by Gilbert Highet. Copyright, 1949, by Oxford University Press, Inc.

[2 The first argument was this: "The ancients were pagans; we are Christians. Therefore our poetry is inspired by nobler emotions and deals with nobler subjects. Therefore it is better poetry."]

familiar, especially the Latin classics, less daring than the Greeks. Their thoughts had so long been current that their majesty had become customary and their daring had been equalled. Meanwhile, the science of the ancients, Vitruvius the architect, Hippocrates the doctor, and the few others, had been examined, equalled, surpassed, and discarded; while the self-perpetuating fertility of modern experimental science was asserting itself more emphatically every year. Men forgot that Lucretius and his master Epicurus and Epicurus' master Democritus had known that matter was constructed of atoms; men forgot that the Greeks had inferred, by thought alone, that the planets revolved round the sun; men forgot that Hippocrates had laid the foundations of medicine. They saw that, by experiments which had never been conceived before, modern men had found out things which had never been proved or believed possible of proof. They concluded therefore that civilized humanity as a whole had become better, and that their moral conduct, their arts, and their political intelligence had improved also. This is now the commonest attitude to the question, and looks like being the most persistent. The diagram of human history which most European and American schoolchildren have in their heads is simple. It is a line, like the line on a graph, rising continuously at a 45° angle, from the cavemen, through ancient Egypt, past Greece and Rome, through a nebulous Middle Age, past the Renaissance, upwards, ever upwards, to the ultimate splendour of to-day. Much of this belief, however, is false. Gilbert Murray summed it up by saying that we think we are better than the Greeks, because, although we could not write the superb tragic trilogy, the *Oresteia,* we can broadcast it.

III Yet part of this modern optimism is true and justified. The ancients never believed in the noblest and most ennobling ideal of modern science— that man can change and improve nature. The abolition of disease; the curtailment of labour; the suppression of physical pain; the conquest of distance, planetary and interplanetary; penetration of the heights and the depths, the deserts and the poles; interrogation of nature far beyond the limits of our own senses, and the construction of machinery to continue that questioning and then change the answers into acts—these magnificent achievements have given modern man a new freedom which raises him higher above the animals, and allows him, with justice, to boast of being wiser than his ancestors.

IV But the argument is false when applied to art, and particularly false when applied to literature. (In philosophy it is highly questionable, and in politics and social science it cannot be accepted without careful examination.) Great works of art are not produced by knowledge of the type which can be accumulated with the lapse of time, can grow richer with succeeding generations, and can then be assimilated by each new generation without difficulty. The material and the media of art are the human soul and its activities. The human soul may change, but it does not appear to grow any greater or more complex from generation to generation, nor does our knowledge of it increase very markedly from age to age. One proof of this is that the ordinary problems of living, which have been faced by every man and woman, are no less difficult to-day than they were 2,000 years ago: although, if the argument from scientific progress were universally true, we ought to have enough knowledge at our disposal to enable us to solve the great questions of education, and politics, and marriage, and moral conduct generally, without anything like the perplexities of our forefathers. . . . And is it not truer to say that to-day our scientific progress has made the problems of life not easier, but more difficult? Now that we have learnt to change the world, the world has become less stable, so that it is more difficult to understand: new problems are constantly arising, for which no clear precedents exist. And our naïve confidence in applied science has to some extent dissuaded the common man from thinking out problems of conduct as earnestly as our forefathers did, in conversation, in public debate, in meditation, and in prayer.

v To the assertion that man has progressed through the accumulation of scientific knowledge there is a counter-argument which is sometimes overlooked. This is that many arts and crafts have been forgotten during the past centuries, crafts of great value, so that our scientific advance has been partly offset by the loss of useful knowledge. Some such crafts were the property of skilled tradesmen, who never wrote their secrets down; others were part of the mass of folk-lore which has only recently perished; others again were the result of generations of skilled practice in work that is now done, more copiously but not always more satisfactorily, by machinery. For example, the pharmacopoeia could be greatly enlarged if some of the valuable herbal remedies known to country folk a few generations ago were available; but many have been lost. The art of oratory was studied by the ancients for many centuries. During that time they discovered thousands of facts about applied psychology, about propaganda, about the relation between thought, artifice, and emotion, about the use of spoken language—facts which became part of a general tradition of rhetorical training, and were lost in the Dark Ages. Men make speeches to-day, and still move their hearers; but they cannot calculate their results so surely, and the speeches themselves have a narrower influence than those of the great classical orators because the rules of the craft have been forgotten.

vi Even if we know more than the ancients, does that prove that we are better? Does it not mean that they did the great work, and that we only use it, adding a little here and there? This objection was put very forcefully by the twelfth-century philosopher Bernard of Chartres, in the famous phrase, 'We are dwarfs standing on the shoulders of giants.' However, it was taken up and turned round, wittily though falsely, by the partisans of the modern side in the Battle of the Books.[1] They pointed out that we ought not to call Plato and Vergil 'ancients' and think of ourselves as their young successors. Compared with us, Plato and Vergil and their con-

[1 The Battle of the Books is the name of a literary controversy carried on with great spirit in France and England, especially during the latter part of the seventeenth century. It was concerned with the relative merits of the "Ancients" (the classical writers of Greece and Rome) and the "Moderns." Its best known product is Jonathan Swift's *The Battle of the Books* (1704), a prose satire on the side of the Ancients.]

temporaries are young. We are the ancients. The world is growing up all the time.

VII Now, this is the commonest modern assumption, and it is one in which the deepest fallacy lies. The assumption is that the whole of human civilization can be compared to the life of a man or an animal—as a continuous process in which one single organism becomes steadily more mature. It is the great merit of Spengler to have shown, in *The Decline and Fall of the West,* that this is false, because it is over-simplified. Toynbee, in his *Study of History,* has elaborated and strengthened the view which Spengler stated. This view is that civilization all over the world, or for that matter civilization in Europe, is not one continuous process but a number of different processes. Different *societies,* groups of races, grow up at different times, forming separate civilizations (he calls them 'cultures,' but he means the set of activities we call civilizations). At any given moment there may be three or four different civilizations alive at once, all of different ages. There have been several in the past, which have died or been destroyed. One civilization can come into contact with another, can destroy it or imitate it or learn from it. But one civilization does not grow out of another and surpass it, any more than one full-size tree grows out of the top branches of another. Spengler proceeds to infer that the growth, maturity, and decay of all the different civilizations follow the same rhythmic pattern, and manifest themselves in comparable intellectual, social, and artistic phenomena. Thus he says that our present time is preparing for 'the era of warring Caesarisms'—a name he devised as early as the First World War, before the emergence of Mussolini, Hitler, and those others—and says it is *contemporary* with the Hyksos period in Egypt (c. 1680 B.C.), the Hellenistic period in Greco-Roman civilization (300–100 B.C.), and the age of the contending states in China (480–230 B.C.). (One of the smaller, but not less striking, aspects of this theory is that it helps to explain the sympathy which men of one civilization often feel for their 'contemporaries' in another, and the repulsion or lack of understanding with which they confront art or thought of a period too early or too late for them to grasp. For instance, Tacitus was a great historian; but we have not yet arrived at the period when we can fully appreciate his spiritual attitude and his strange style, because he belonged to an age later than ourselves; while the mystery religions of antiquity, the stories of the saints in primitive Christianity, and the religious beliefs of more recent 'primitives' such as the founders of Mormonism are too early for most of us to understand nowadays.)

VIII If this theory is true, the moderns in the Battle of the Books were mistaken in saying that they were later than the Greeks and Romans, and therefore wiser. They were later in absolute time, but not in relative time. Spengler holds that, on the chart of the growth of civilizations, they were at an earlier stage. Louis XIV looks like Augustus Caesar; his poets read like the Augustan poets; and the Louvre corresponded to Augustus' reconstruction of central Rome. But both the monarch and the arts of seventeenth-century France look *less mature* than those of Augustan Rome.

IX And apart from theories, the cold facts of history are enough to disprove the argument. The development of civilization has *not* been continuous since the flourishing of Greco-Roman culture. It has been interrupted. It has been set back many centuries by wars, savages, and plagues. The European of the tenth century A.D. was not ten centuries in advance of the European of the first century B.C., but, in everything but religion, many centuries behind him.

————————

1) A minor difficulty here is the number of unfamiliar words and names you may have to look up. But there is another difficulty you may not have much considered. In such generalization as this, the writer expects the reader to fill in, to supply in part the concrete instances and applications. Emerson quotes a hard saying: "He that would bring home the wealth of the Indies, must carry out the wealth of the Indies." Of course one can carry to a piece of reading only what he has, but students sometimes fail to realize what they really do have. Some of the questioning is designed to suggest what you can supply here.

2) In I your dictionary will give you the adjectives "Periclean" and "Augustan"; you may have to look up the proper nouns to get dates. You will need to fix the italicized passage in your mind, since the whole selection considers it.

3) Before we go further, let us look at the structure. It is designed to discuss in an orderly fashion the contention stated in I. Paragraph II develops and discusses the contention, and makes no judgment until the end: "Much of this belief, however, is false." Notice how this sentence leads on the discussion in III of what is true in the belief, and in IV of what is false. The piece is carefully and formally constructed. You can trace the structure through the initial statements of the topic idea in each paragraph (the first sentence or the first two sentences). And notice that with VI there is major transition, and that the structure of the whole falls into two parts.

4) How much of the italicized passage in I has Mr. Highet denied? How much truth has he allowed that it has?

5) In II "the discovery of the great classical books" refers to the rebirth —the renaissance—of interest in the work of Greek and Roman authors. What age is the "baroque age"? Consider the statement: "Men forgot that Lucretius and his master Epicurus and Epicurus' master Democritus had known that matter was constructed of atoms." The general sense—that some sort of atomic theory is very old—is clear even if one does not know the names. If you need a fuller meaning, your dictionary will take you a little way; the *Oxford Companion to Classical Literature* will take you further (try the entry for Epicurus). What does the metaphor "a nebulous Middle Age" mean? You surely will not know unless you know the literal meaning of "nebulous" first.

6) Henry David Thoreau once spoke of "improved means to unimproved ends." What sentence in II is parallel in idea? Does it seem curious to you that such a wonderfully complex device as television is should show us—to take a minor instance—pictures of puppets, one of the oldest entertainments?

7) You must have heard the contention that if the methods of science were applied consistently to human problems, they would be as efficient as they have been in the physical sciences. What, judging by what is said in IV, would be Mr. Highet's opinion?

8) What is meant by "our naïve confidence in applied science" (IV)? Do you know instances of it? Does that confidence for most of us stem from our knowledge? Physics is the most spectacular science in our time. What proportion of students in your high school took a course in physics?

9) In V there are only a few examples of lost arts and crafts—more would clog the discussion. Do you know more? If fewer persons now than in the past have the satisfaction of having a high skill, is that humanly important?

10) The quotation from Bernard of Chartres in VI may be paralleled by a quotation from T. S. Eliot: "Someone said: 'The dead writers are remote from us because we *know* so much more than they did.' Precisely, and they are that which we know." And it must have occurred to you that some of the greatest human achievements are remote beyond the reach of history. The most complex of all, the development of language—when did it come about? Who domesticated cattle?

11) You have noted that VI is transitional. What is the sign at the beginning of VII that Mr. Highet is approaching the core of his discussion?

12) In VII you are introduced to two important modern books. Eventually you will want to know more of them, but at least now when you hear or see them mentioned, you will know an important contention they make. To be sure you understand that contention, say it (or, better, write it) in your own words. You might make your approach an answer to this question: According to Spengler and Toynbee, what is wrong with the conception of history in the sentence from Woodrow Wilson quoted in the headnote (or with the parallel description in II)?

13) Do you at all recognize the feeling—described at the end of VII—of being more at home in one past age than in another?

14) Consider IX in the light of the experience of your own generation.

15) Now it is time to ask about the importance of the ideas in this selection, and to ask whether or not you agree with them. (Students are somewhat inclined to ask such questions too soon, before they have determined what the ideas *are*.) The Idea of Progress might be defended as a cheerful idea, one that makes for hope in the future. Is that defence valid? But might the Idea of Progress be accompanied by moral complacency, a tendency to feel that things will be all right whether or not one does anything about them?

16) In American experience one result of the assumption of inevitable progress is the inclination toward an uncritical acceptance of change in society and in material things. You will remember that Santayana said of the American: "This expectation of what he approves, or approval of what he expects, makes up his optimism."

17) Do you think that our frontier experience and westward expansion —a physical progress—would tend to reinforce the Idea of Progress? Does anything that we have read suggest that they would? Why?

18) The impact of Darwinism came in the United States in the 1860's. It seemed to show a progressive complexity in the development of animal life. Do you see how its influence might have so combined with the much older Idea of Progress that complexity and improvement were equated?

19) Perhaps you do not remember having seen any explicit, developed assertion of the Idea of Progress in American writing. Does that mean that you have had no acquaintance with it? Does it not mean, instead, that what is generally assumed—however important—is generally not expressed? What we take for granted is often more important than what we say. Often in our reading we need to look for the ASSUMPTION as well as to see what is explicitly said. What is IMPLICIT may be as important as what is EXPLICIT.

REPRESENTED IDEAS   *iv*

Our selection here may offer two kinds of difficulty. Its writer, Henry Adams, characteristically represents his ideas as well as states them, and a hurrying reader may underestimate the importance of a detail or a description. Moreover, you read the selection out of its context in *The Education of Henry Adams*. You have here, then, much the sort of problem that college students often face in survey courses and in their collateral reading. See if you can make a clear connection between the selection and the context the editor supplies.

The fair Adams describes, the St. Louis fair of 1904, was officially known as the Louisiana Purchase Exposition and celebrated the purchase of the Louisiana territory a century before. The "he" in the first sentence is Adams himself, since he wrote his autobiographical work in the third person. The Secretary of State in I is named in II: John Hay was Secretary of State under Presidents McKinley and Theodore Roosevelt; he was a close friend of Adams and was travelling with him.

When in IV Adams refers to himself as "a pilgrim of power," he means that he is a student of force however manifested, by the worship of the Virgin Mary in twelfth-century France, or by the new physical forces released in his own time. In his *Mont-Saint-Michel and Chartres* he had studied in detail the worship of the Virgin, for whom he believed the great cathedrals were designed. In our piece he implies that a world's fair is the nearest thing America has to the great communal effort that went into the building of the cathedrals—that a world's fair may be thought of as an attempt to represent a culture. He does not mean, of course, that such fairs involved men's minds and hearts in the same way the cathedrals did. The title of our selection means "New Force."

FROM *The Education of Henry Adams* (1907, 1918)

HENRY ADAMS

Vis Nova (1903–1904)

I . . . Ten years had passed since he last crossed the Mississippi, and he found everything new. In this great region from Pittsburgh through Ohio and Indiana, agriculture had made way for steam; tall chimneys reeked smoke on every horizon, and dirty suburbs filled with scrap-iron, scrap-paper and cinders, formed the setting of every town. Evidently, cleanliness was not to be the birthmark of the new American, but this matter of discards concerned the measure of force little, while the chimneys and cinders concerned it so much that Adams thought the Secretary of State should have rushed to the platform at every station to ask who were the people; for the American of the prime seemed to be extinct with the Shawnee and the buffalo.

II The subject grew quickly delicate. History told little about these millions of Germans and Slavs, or whatever their race-names, who had overflowed these regions as though the Rhine and the Danube had turned their floods into the Ohio. John Hay was as strange to the Mississippi River as though he had not been bred on its shores, and the city of St. Louis had turned its back on the noblest work of nature, leaving it bankrupt between its own banks. The new American showed his parentage proudly; he was the child of steam and the brother of the dynamo, and already, within less than thirty years, this mass of mixed humanities, brought together by steam, was squeezed and welded into approach to shape; a product of so much mechanical power, and bearing no distinctive marks but that of its pressure. The new American, like the new European, was the servant of the powerhouse, as the European of the twelfth century was the servant of the Church, and the features would follow the parentage.

III The St. Louis Exposition was its first creation in the twentieth century, and, for that reason, acutely interesting. One saw here a third-rate town of half-a-million people without history, education, unity, or art, and with little capital—without even an element of natural interest except the river which it studiously ignored—but doing what London, Paris, or New York would have shrunk from attempting. This new social conglomerate, with no tie but its steampower and not much of that, threw away thirty or forty million dollars on a pageant as ephemeral as a stage flat. The world had never witnessed so marvellous a phantasm; by night Arabia's crimson sands had never returned a glow half so astonishing, as one wandered among long lines of white palaces, exquisitely lighted by thousands on thousands of electric candles, soft, rich, shadowy, palpable in their sensuous depths; all in deep silence, profound solitude, listening for a voice or a foot-fall or the plash of an oar, as though the Emir Mirza were display-ing the beauties of this City of Brass, which could show nothing half so beautiful as this illumination, with its vast, white, monumental solitude, bathed in the pure light of setting suns. One enjoyed it with iniquitous rap-ture, not because of exhibits but rather because of their want. Here was a paradox like the stellar universe that fitted one's mental faults. Had there been no exhibits at all, and no visitors, one would have enjoyed it only the more.

iv Here education found new forage. That the power was wasted, the art indifferent, the economic failure complete, added just so much to the interest. The chaos of education approached a dream. One asked one's self whether this extravagance reflected the past or imaged the future; whether it was a creation of the old American or a promise of the new one. No prophet could be believed, but a pilgrim of power, without constituency to flatter, might allow himself to hope. The prospect from the Exposition was pleasant; one seemed to see almost an adequate motive for power; almost a scheme for progress. In another half-century, the people of the central val-leys should have hundreds of millions to throw away more easily than in 1900 they could throw away tens; and by that time they might know what they wanted. Possibly they might even have learned how to reach it.

v This was an optimist's hope, shared by few except pilgrims of World's Fairs, and frankly dropped by the multitude, for, east of the Mississippi, the St. Louis Exposition met a deliberate conspiracy of silence, discourag-ing, beyond measure, to an optimistic dream of future strength in Ameri-can expression. The party got back to Washington on May 24, and before sailing for Europe, Adams went over, one warm evening, to bid goodbye on the garden-porch of the White House. He found himself the first per-son who urged Mrs. Roosevelt to visit the Exposition for its beauty, and, as far as he ever knew, the last.

vi He left St. Louis May 22, 1904, and on Sunday, June 5, found him-self again in the town of Coutances, where the people of Normandy had built, towards the year 1250, an Exposition which architects still admired and tourists visited, for it was thought singularly expressive of force as well as of grace in the Virgin. On this Sunday, the Norman world was celebrat-ing a pretty church-feast—the Fête Dieu—and the streets were filled with altars to the Virgin, covered with flowers and foliage; the pavements strewn with paths of leaves and the spring handiwork of nature; the cathedral densely thronged at mass. The scene was graceful. The Virgin did not shut her costly Exposition on Sunday, or any other day, even to American Sena-tors who had shut the St. Louis Exposition to her—or for her; and a his-torical tramp would gladly have offered a candle, or even a candle-stick in her honor, if she would have taught him her relation with the deity of the Senators. The power of the Virgin had been plainly One, embracing all human activity; while the power of the Senate, or its deity, seemed—might one say—to be more or less ashamed of man and his work. The matter had no great interest as far as it concerned the somewhat obscure mental processes of Senators who could probably have given no clearer idea than priests of the deity they supposed themselves to honor—if that was indeed their purpose; but it interested a student of force, curious to measure its manifestations. Apparently the Virgin—or her Son—had no longer the force to build expositions that one cared to visit, but had the force to close them. The force was still real, serious, and, at St. Louis, had been anxiously measured in actual money-value.

----

1) Since Adams is here "a pilgrim of power," we need to know a little of his thinking about force. Adams believed that man does not really capture and control the physical forces he releases; instead they make his world and control him. A released force in its action on man accelerates, and Adams studies man as one force in himself in relation to the physical forces he has released. A world's fair is an opportunity to observe what sort of relationship is developing between man and the new forces he has been releasing.

2) But perhaps we need an illustration of Adams's idea. We may think of the matter in this way: Using a familiar metaphor, we say we have "harnessed" waterpower by building great dams. But since electricity from this waterpower creates new patterns of industry and life which we really neither plan nor foresee, the force we release may control us. Our metaphor, which represents our habitual assumption, is misleading. Not many Americans really understood this concept until the atomic bomb at Hiroshima jarred them into realization.

3) Probably, then, we understand what Adams was talking about better than many of his first readers did. Such a sentence as this comes home to us: "In the earlier stages of progress, the forces to be assimilated were simple and easy to absorb, but, as the mind of man enlarged its range, it enlarged the field of complexity, and must continue to do so, even unto chaos. . . ." This frightening idea is really behind Adams's consideration of the St. Louis fair, which represented, in Adams's view, an America trying to assimilate new forces. How well was it succeeding, according to Adams?

4) If we take at face value what Adams says in II, we must conclude that an American hope has been disappointed. Here is an instance of that hope. About 1870 Walt Whitman writes that he can conceive that the new American community has taken shape, that "perhaps even some such community already exists, in Ohio, Illinois, Missouri, or somewhere, practically fulfilling itself . . . outvying . . . all that has been hitherto shown in best ideal pictures."

5) Now Adams was not finding that ideal community in the West. What exactly is Adams saying? Has the immigrant to the United States neither adopted the American tradition nor contributed to it? Is Adams overstating his case? St. Louis, for instance, has a strong tradition of German culture. Is it without meaning? According to Adams, is anything left of Whitman's hope?

6) Consider Adams's question in IV: "One asked one's self whether this extravagance reflected the past or imaged the future." Is not the first

half of the question answered in II and III? If the exposition promises a new American, what sort of an American does it promise? A half-century has passed since Adams visited the exposition. Have Americans learned to know what they want? To reach it?

7) Why do you think Adams pays so much attention in VI to the fact that the exposition was closed on Sundays by legislative action? Consider particularly the next-to-last sentence in the paragraph. What is Adams implying about religion in America?

8) We must take it that by heredity and training Adams knew and understood the American tradition. He was the great-grandson of John Adams, the grandson of John Quincy Adams, the son of Charles Francis Adams, and secretary to his father when he was Lincoln's ambassador to Great Britain; Adams was moreover a historian of distinction. What do you think he means exactly when he says that "the American of the prime seemed to be extinct with the Shawnee and the buffalo"? (What is the sense of "prime" here?)

9) Are we to understand the sentence as a final judgment about our culture? Or is this conclusion what the St. Louis fair contributes to his education—all that he can find the fair representing or implying?

SUGGESTIONS FOR PAPERS

Some brief exercises in connection with the selection from *Elements of Geography* may be these: (a) Assume a reader younger than yourself— your brother perhaps—and give him his approximate latitude and longitude. Then explain *to him* what that location means and how you arrived at it. (b) For the same reader, explain how and why one changes his watch on a trip from Chicago to Boston. (c) Your nephew in Denver wants to hear a radio program that originates in New York at 2 P.M. Explain to him when he must tune in and why. (d) Assume that you are foreign-news editor on a newspaper, and that you have an important news story from Japan. Write a headnote for it to explain the date line and to let your readers know when the events of the news story happened *their time.*

For a writing exercise in connection with the second part of the section, you might take question 5 following the selections from Turner and Santayana and write a full answer to it. Or you might answer Crèvecoeur's question "What is an American?" according to him and in a well-organized paragraph. Find a generalization to use for a topic sentence and develop it.

An answer to question 12 following the Highet selection will make an interesting exercise. Or, if you would prefer the question in a different and perhaps more difficult form, it may be this: The quotation from Woodrow Wilson in the headnote implies that his concept of human history might be easily graphed. Is it possible to devise a graph that would represent the interpretation of human history in Spengler and Toynbee? Discuss.

Subjects for written exercises less specifically connected with the Highet selection may be these: (a) Take the quotation "We are dwarfs standing on the shoulders of giants" and explain and develop it, drawing your material both from the selection and from your general knowledge. (b) Write a short discussion called, say, "The Idea of Progress and My Generation."

A paper resembling "Vis Nova" in method may come from one of these suggestions: (a) Adams proceeds on the assumption that the effort of a community to celebrate and to represent itself should reveal something of its values. Try a piece on the same assumption. Write of a county fair you know: how does it represent its community? Or examine a college homecoming: does it represent the values of the institution or some of them? The suggestion may be extended to other activities of representative significance. (b) Examine a number of current advertisements for automobiles and decide what appeals to the reader the ad writers are making (e.g. to his judgment of material value? to his desire for prestige and power? to his interest in mechanics?). Then write a discussion of the evidence and your conclusions about it, considering what it suggests about our standards of value. The suggestion might be adapted to a consideration of advertisements for toilet soaps, perfumes, and cosmetics.

V

Formal Summary

Whenever you ask yourself, or are asked by another, what a piece of writing says, your answer must take the form of a statement of your own. Your only means of demonstrating your understanding of a passage is, you have long been aware, saying it over again in your own words. If you do that carefully and in writing, you have a summary. You cannot, of course, summarize good writing without some loss (although a summary may improve indifferent writing); but the activity of summary making enforces your attention and increases your comprehension. In effect you say when you make a summary: "This is what is important; this is the essence of the passage." And having the summary, you and your instructor have a record of your comprehension of the passage and an evidence of your degree of skill in setting forth its meaning.

You will not be concerned with the formal summary alone; for summaries may have various purposes and therefore somewhat differing forms.[1] And often your practice will better be called restatement, since in handling a piece of writing you will be considering a part or a particular aspect, or you will have a purpose that requires a statement too brief to be called a summary. But in this section we shall deal with the formal summary or PRÉCIS. Since it proceeds according to very definite principles, it is the easiest kind of restatement.

THE PRINCIPLES OF SUMMARY

Before we try the writing of summaries, we shall want to see what some of the problems of summary making are. A formal summary is a concise restatement of a passage, without comment and with nothing omitted that is essential to the development of the ideas in the passage. So far as is possible, the summary is kept in proportion to the original passage, with the same relative weight given to the ideas as was given them there. The summary should stand for the original and convey accurately *to a reader who has not read the original* the essence of it. The important thing is to make sure that your summary does stand on its own feet and is clear in itself. It is all too easy to assume that a summary is clear when it merely re-

[1] Summary in the context of course papers and the like is discussed in Chapter XIV.

minds its writer of the passage he has just read. The question the summary writer must ask about his own work is this: "Would this summary give an ordinarily intelligent reader who has not read the original passage a just and adequate understanding of what the original passage said?"

Let us take a summary of the selection from James Bryce we read in Chapter II and ask that test question about it.

The Americans are—compared to the citizens of most European countries—highly educated. They have some knowledge of the theory of their government, and they learn more by taking part in local government. In villages theological debate is still an intellectual exercise. And American women generally have more information than European women. But, although the level of education is relatively high, American education is superficial and clearly inadequate to the function the ordinary citizen should fulfill in government under the American idea of popular rule. For in the United States the citizen decides issues and selects his rulers in frequent elections, and ideally he should have a full comprehension of issues and sufficient knowledge to judge the qualifications of candidates. The average citizen's education is not at all adequate to his political responsibilities, though it may be enough to make him consider himself more competent than he is.

Consider the relationship of the structure of this summary to that of the original. And notice that the summary is a restatement, that it is not accomplished by quoting bits of the original and tacking them together.

The passage below is from a famous essay by John Stuart Mill. You will see that it states the central principle for a long essay and is, therefore, vital to the essay. Since it is clearly written, it offers the reader little difficulty; and since the ideas are very fully stated, it is easy to summarize. Read it carefully.

FROM *On Liberty* (1859)

JOHN STUART MILL

[i]

The object of this Essay is to assert one very simple principle, as entitled to govern absolutely the dealings of society with the individual in the way of compulsion and control, whether the means used be physical force in the form of legal penalties, or the moral coercion of public opinion. That principle is, that the sole end for which mankind are warranted, individually or collectively, in interfering with the liberty of action of any of their number, is self-protection. That the only purpose for which power can be rightfully exercised over any member of a civilized community, against his will, is to prevent harm to others. His own good, either physical or moral, is not a sufficient warrant. He cannot rightfully be compelled to do or forbear because it will be better for him to do so, because it will make him happier, because, in the opinions of others, to do so would be wise, or even right. These are good reasons for remonstrating with him, or reasoning with him, or persuading him, or entreating him, but not for compelling him, or visiting him with any evil in case he do otherwise. To justify that, the conduct from which it is desired to deter him, must be calculated to produce evil to some one else. The only part of the conduct of any one, for which he is amenable to society, is that which concerns others. In the part which merely concerns himself, his independence is, of right, absolute. Over himself, over his own body and mind, the individual is sovereign.

————————————

1) Are you sure you have control of all the words in their context, for instance "amenable," "coercion," and "sovereign"?

2) This passage will take a good deal of reduction; Mill develops his principle by restating it. If you could quote but one sentence to represent the whole, which sentence would you choose?

3) Twenty students asked to write summaries of this passage will produce twenty variant summaries, but the best of them will resemble each other closely. We shall look at some student summaries; here is one:

> The object of this essay is to state that every member of a community has the right to do as he pleases without being subjected to persuasion by some other person to do what is morally and physically right for him. The only time a person would be justified in compelling him or making him forbear would be when it is for the well being of another individual.

Now students at first thought are likely to say that this summary is more or less adequate, although they may find it awkward. It seems to be consistent with the passage; at least the passage does say something like this. But what is the test? Will this summary clearly state Mill's principle for a reader who has not read the Mill passage? Does not the summary fail to make clear that Mill's essential concern here is the relationship between the individual and society? The summary might be taken to describe right relations between any two persons. Indeed, would not one reading it by itself so take it?

4) Here is another summary:

> The object of this Essay is to assert the principle that the only purpose for which power can be rightfully exercised over any member of a civilized community, against his will, is to prevent harm to others. If a person is doing something wherein he is hurting himself only, he cannot be forced to stop. Only when his practices injure others can he be remonstrated with.

In what respect is this better than the first? Yet does it pass our test of a good summary? How about the last sentence? What else needs revision?

5) This seems to be an adequate summary:

> The essay intends to make clear this one principle: In matters upon which the protection of society depends, society has the right to control, coerce or compel the individual; in matters which concern

only the individual, society, although it may attempt to persuade him to his own good, has no right to use any sort of force. A man is sovereign over himself and what concerns only himself.

6) Here are four student summaries. Consider how far each is adequate. Examine each minutely.

I

This essay will assert that the only justification for compelling a man to do or refrain from doing a certain act is that you prevent harm to others. That you prevent him from harming himself in any way is insufficient. A man has absolute rule where he is the only one concerned.

2

The principle of this essay is that in our civilization no person can be rightfully punished for any act, unless it be harmful to other members of the society. He may be advised and reasoned with about what is best for him, but never compelled to do it. The individual is the sovereign over matters concerning himself only.

3

The principle asserted in this essay is: An individual has the right to do anything that he may choose to do as long as it does not molest others. You may argue with him and tell him how much better it would be for his own good to change, but you cannot compel him to do so. The only way he is amenable to society is by harming someone other than himself. The individual is the sole ruler of his own life.

4

The principle of this essay is that mankind are warranted, individually or collectively, in interfering with the action of any person only for self-protection. A man may be reasoned with but not forced to do what would be good for him, for he has final authority over himself and his own concerns. But society may rightfully control his conduct when it affects others.

7) You may find it easy to decide about the relative adequacy of another's writing. It is hard to judge one's own, because one is likely to read into his own writing his intention, whether or not what he has written actually states it. You will find it helpful to revise a summary a considerable time after you have written it, for objectivity will then be easier to obtain. You need to cultivate the ability to read your own writing objectively.

8) Can you tell in the summaries you consider inadequate where the failure was—in reading or in writing? You may think this an academic question, since a poor summary is a poor summary, no matter how willing we may be to assume that its writer has read well enough. But in your consideration of your own work the question is vital.

9) Oliver Wendell Holmes wrote this sentence in one of his opinions as Justice of the Supreme Court: "The liberty of the citizen to do as he likes so long as he does not interfere with the liberty of others to do the same, which has been a shibboleth for some well-known writers, is interfered with by the school laws, by the Post Office, by every state and munici-

pal institution which takes his money for purposes thought desirable, whether he likes it or not." Is Mill among the well-known writers who employ this shibboleth? (What is a "shibboleth"? A good dictionary will make this literary allusion clear to you.) Can you think of concrete examples of the interference with the principle by the school laws?

10) *On Liberty* was published in 1859. Do you think that since that time the sphere in which a man may be considered sovereign over himself has lessened? Why or why not?

_____

We consider now another passage from Mill's essay; it is perhaps a little more difficult than the first, for it concerns an abstraction, "truth." Read it carefully and do all you can to get control of it before you consider the questions.

[ii]

But, indeed, the dictum that truth always triumphs over persecution, is one of those pleasant falsehoods which men repeat after one another till they pass into commonplaces, but which all experience refutes. History teems with instances of truth put down by persecution. If not suppressed forever, it may be thrown back for centuries. . . . It is a piece of idle sentimentality that truth, merely as truth, has any inherent power denied to error, of prevailing against the dungeon and the stake. Men are not more zealous for truth than they often are for error, and a sufficient application of legal or even of social penalties will generally succeed in stopping the propagation of either. The real advantage which truth has, consists in this, that when an opinion is true, it may be extinguished once, twice, or many times, but in the course of ages there will generally be found persons to rediscover it, until some one of its reappearances falls on a time when from favourable circumstances it escapes persecution until it has made such head as to withstand all subsequent attempts to suppress it.

_____

1) Note the structure of this selection: it first of all denies an idea about the nature of truth; then it states what Mill believes to be the proper idea. The idea denied has been a common one, part of the faith of many liberals. Here is one expression of it, from William Cullen Bryant's "The Battle-Field":

> Truth, crushed to earth, shall rise again;
>   Th' eternal years of God are hers;
> But Error, wounded, writhes in pain,
>   And dies among his worshippers.

2) Now if Mill is denying that truth has in itself a power of victory or even of survival, what is the positive idea that arises in the passage?

3) Here is a summary by a student who thought the exercise an easy one:

> Both truth and evil may be suppressed by legal or social penalties, but truth has the advantage of coming up again and again until it reaches a point where it becomes unextinguishable.

But do you see what the student has done? He has come close to making Mill out as saying that truth *does* have an inherent power of survival, for the second clause suggests no human agency. How much better is the following?

> History and experience have proved that the dictum that truth always triumphs over persecution is untrue. However, though a truth may be extinguished many times or remain undiscovered for a long period of time, because it is truth it will eventually find a favorable condition in which it will be accepted.

4) The following seems an adequate summary:

> That truth has any power of survival in itself is, history shows us, a sentimental lie. Persecution has often suppressed a truth for years, and might suppress a truth forever. Nor do men fight harder for truth than they often do for error. But a truth does have this advantage: although it may be suppressed time after time, there will usually be someone who rediscovers it. And when it is rediscovered in a time in which it is subjected to little or no persecution, it will be established.

The procedure of summary writing you will have to learn, primarily, through example, by practice, and with the help of your instructor. But you will find the following check list of principles helpful:

1. Read the passage as many times as are necessary for you to feel that you have a control of it. Use your dictionary, and use other reference books if you need to identify a name or an allusion.

2. Make your own statement; do not patch together phrases from the passage. But do not strain to find synonyms; a summary is not a PARA-PHRASE. It is not at all necessary to avoid words used in the original passage when they are immediately clear, appropriate to ordinary workaday prose, and natural to your writing.

3. Alter the order of idea and fact in the original very little, if at all. Ideally, you should keep to the order of the original precisely.

4. Keep to the proportion of the original passage. If, for example, half of the passage were devoted to beliefs about witchcraft in England and half to parallel beliefs in New England, that proportion would be maintained in the summary.

5. Do not comment upon what is said in the passage; just restate it briefly.

6. Watch your sentence structure, for both clarity and proportion depend upon it. Try to write good, economical prose: make your nouns and verbs work hard; do not always be bolstering them with modifiers.

7. Be sure that you get a considerable condensation. Just how brief a summary should be depends, of course, on how packed the original passage is. Ordinarily a formal summary is no longer than one third of the length of the original; often it may be shorter than that.

8. Take this question as a test of a summary: "Would this summary give an ordinarily intelligent reader who has not read the original passage

a just and adequate understanding of what the original passage said?" That is not to ask whether your summary is clear to you—you have read the original. A summary must be clear in itself.

9. Take every legitimate opportunity to compare what you have done with the work of others in the class.

When you put these principles into practice, particularly when you are working on a passage of some length, you may find it well to do your work in three stages. At least give this method a trial: (1) Read the passage carefully. (2) Write a series of brief statements, carefully following the development of the passage. (3) Combine the series of brief statements into a coherent whole. When you are working in the third stage, do not look back at the original until you are ready to check your completed summary against it.

As exercises in which you may put these principles into practice, we shall take first two more passages from Mill's essay. The familiarity with Mill's style gained from your examination of the two passages above will give you a little start. The passages will take a considerable reduction, but every sentence of each will need attention.

[iii]

He who knows only his own side of the case, knows little of that. His reasons may be good, and no one may have been able to refute them. But if he is equally unable to refute the reasons on the opposite side; if he does not so much as know what they are, he has no ground for preferring either opinion. . . . Nor is it enough that he should hear the arguments of adversaries from his own teachers, presented as they state them, and accompanied by what they offer as refutations. This is not the way to do justice to the arguments, or bring them into real contact with his own mind. He must be able to hear them from persons who actually believe them; who defend them in earnest, and do their very utmost for them. He must know them in their most plausible and persuasive form; he must feel the whole force of the difficulty which the true view of the subject has to encounter and dispose of, else he will never really possess himself of the portion of truth which meets and removes that difficulty. . . . So essential is this discipline to a real understanding of moral and human subjects, that if opponents of all important truths do not exist, it is indispensable to imagine them and supply them with the strongest arguments which the most skillful devil's advocate can conjure up.

[iv]

In politics . . . it is almost a commonplace, that a party of order or stability, and a party of progress or reform, are both necessary elements of a healthy state of political life; until the one or the other shall have so enlarged its mental grasp as to be a party equally of order and of progress, knowing and distinguishing what is fit to be preserved from what ought to be swept away. Each of these modes of thinking derives its utility from the deficiencies of the other; but it is in a great measure the opposition of the other that keeps each within the limits of reason and sanity. Unless opinions favorable to democracy and to aristocracy, to property and to equality, to co-operation and to competition, to luxury and to abstinence, to sociality and individuality, to liberty and discipline, and all the other standing antagonisms of practical life, are expressed with equal freedom, and enforced and defended with equal talent and energy, there is no chance of both elements obtaining their due; one scale is sure to go up, and the other down. Truth, in the great practical concerns of life, is so much a question of the reconciling and combining of opposites, that very few have minds sufficiently capacious and impartial to make the adjustment with an approach to correctness, and it has to be made by the rough process of a struggle between combatants fighting under hostile banners. On any of the great open questions just enumerated, if either of the two opinions has a better claim than the other, not merely to be tolerated, but to be encouraged and countenanced, it is the one which happens at the particular time and place to be in a minority. That is the opinion which, for the time being, represents the neglected interests, the side of human well-being which is in danger of obtaining less than its share.

ii A COMPLETE ADDRESS FOR SUMMARY

Benjamin Franklin's last great service to his country was his work in the Constitutional Convention. In 1787 Franklin was eighty-one and unable to make his own address, although he was present when it was read for him. In at least one major matter Franklin's political thought was different from that incorporated in the Constitution, for he always favored a unicameral (one-house) legislature, as the other delegates to the convention well knew. Since he had given up what he most wanted, he could with grace and effectiveness ask the delegates to give up their individual preferences.

This address is presented for an exercise in summary writing, but it is followed by some questions that you should work over before you write your summary—they will help you gain control of the passage. You will probably prefer to write your summary in the third person, beginning "Franklin says . . ." You will not be able to reproduce the tone of the original, but at least you can avoid misleading your reader about the tone, and perhaps you can suggest it.

Speech in the Constitutional Convention at the Conclusion of Its Deliberations (1787)

BENJAMIN FRANKLIN

MR. PRESIDENT,

1 I confess, that I do not entirely approve of this Constitution at present; but, Sir, I am not sure I shall never approve it; for, having lived long, I have experienced many instances of being obliged, by better information

or fuller consideration, to change my opinions even on important subjects, which I once thought right, but found to be otherwise. It is therefore that, the older I grow, the more apt I am to doubt my own judgment of others. Most men, indeed, as well as most sects in religion, think themselves in possession of all truth, and that wherever others differ from them, it is so far error. Steele, a Protestant, in a dedication, tells the Pope, that the only difference between our two churches in their opinions of the certainty of their doctrine, is, the Romish Church is *infallible,* and the Church of England is *never in the wrong.* But, though many private Persons think almost as highly of their own infallibility as of that of their Sect, few express it so naturally as a certain French Lady, who, in a little dispute with her sister, said, "But I meet with nobody but myself that is *always* in the right." *"Je ne trouve que moi qui aie toujours raison."*

II In these sentiments, Sir, I agree to this Constitution, with all its faults,—if they are such; because I think a general Government necessary for us, and there is no *form* of government but what may be a blessing to the people, if well administered; and I believe, farther, that this is likely to be well administered for a course of years, and can only end in despotism, as other forms have done before it, when the people shall become so corrupted as to need despotic government, being incapable of any other. I doubt, too, whether any other Convention we can obtain, may be able to make a better constitution; for, when you assemble a number of men, to have the advantage of their joint wisdom, you inevitably assemble with those men all their prejudices, their passions, their errors of opinion, their local interests, and their selfish views. From such an assembly can a *perfect* production be expected? It therefore astonishes me, Sir, to find this system approaching so near to perfection as it does; and I think it will astonish our enemies, who are waiting with confidence to hear, that our councils are confounded like those of the builders of Babel, and that our States are on the point of separation, only to meet hereafter for the purpose of cutting one another's throats. Thus I consent, Sir, to this Constitution, because I expect no better, and because I am not sure that it is not the best. The opinions I have had of its *errors* I sacrifice to the public good. I have never whispered a syllable of them abroad. Within these walls they were born, and here they shall die. If every one of us, in returning to our Constituents, were to report the objections he has had to it, and endeavour to gain Partisans in support of them, we might prevent its being generally received, and thereby lose all the salutary effects and great advantages resulting naturally in our favour among foreign nations, as well as among ourselves, from our real or apparent unanimity. Much of the strength and efficiency of any government, in procuring and securing happiness to the people, depends on *opinion,* on the general opinion of the goodness of that government, as well as of the wisdom and integrity of its governors. I hope, therefore, for our own sakes, as a part of the people, and for the sake of our posterity, that we shall act heartily and unanimously in recommending this Constitution, wherever our Influence may extend, and turn our future thoughts and endeavours to the means of having it *well administered.*

III On the whole, Sir, I cannot help expressing a wish, that every member of the Convention who may still have objections to it, would with me on this occasion doubt a little of his own infallibility, and, to make *manifest* our *unanimity,* put his name to this Instrument.

---

1) The second paragraph of this address is longer than is common in writing today. If it were divided into two paragraphs, where would the division come? Might it be divided into more than two paragraphs? How?

2) We expect the last paragraph of a speech to be a conclusion. How is the last paragraph related in idea to the other two?

3) Franklin is asking, not just for adoption of the constitution by the convention, but for unanimous adoption. Why, according to the speech, is unanimity important in this matter?

4) What necessary evil does Franklin say accompanies the democratic process?

5) "Thus I consent, Sir, to this Constitution, because I expect no better, and because I am not sure that it is not the best." Say what you believe "best" to mean in this context, and make clear why you give it the meaning you do. ("Best" could conceivably mean "the best in the world," "the best in all history," "the best possible," "the best we can hope for," and a number of other things.)

6) The primary appeal here is to reason and experience, but perhaps no effective speech is directed only to reason and experience. What other means of persuasion does Franklin use here, and in what sentences are they to be identified?

7) A historian writing on Franklin says that his political thinking was primarily practical and concerned with immediate problems, and not much concerned with theory and ideal systems. Could the historian use this speech or parts of it in support of his judgment? How or why not?

iii   SUMMARY FOR COMPARISON

We have here a pair of selections that have some connection in idea. The first is by Jean-Jacques Rousseau, a prophet of modern democracy whose ideas have been much admired and much attacked. The second is by Ernst Rudolf Huber, a prominent contributor to the elaborate philosophical justification of the Nazi movement. The two writers are doing very different things. Rousseau wrote his *The Social Contract* (1762) to describe and to justify in theory what he thought would be the best sort of state. Huber, writing about 1939, intended to justify National Socialism after the fact as it was embodied in Hitler's Germany. But you will find in these particular passages some likeness in idea, as well as some differences.

The two selections are offered as materials for exercises in formal summary. But when you have summarized them, you should find that your effort to get the essence of each will help you to discriminate and to compare. Both passages are full statements and will take considerable reduction. The problem in the passage by Rousseau is to decide just what he means by "legislator" (notice that "Law-giver" is also used). The Huber passage, even excised as we have it, is often REDUNDANT—Nazi writing seems usually so. But that quality may require of you close attention if you are to decide what is really being said.

FROM *The Social Contract* (1762)

JEAN-JACQUES ROUSSEAU

Of the Legislator

I In order to discover what social regulations are best suited to nations, there is needed a superior intelligence which can survey all the passions of mankind, though itself exposed to none: an intelligence having no contact with our nature, yet knowing it to the full: an intelligence, the well-being of which is independent of our own, yet willing to be concerned with it: which, finally, viewing the long perspectives of time, and preparing for itself a day of glory as yet far distant, will labour in one century to reap its reward in another. In short, only Gods can give laws to men.

II The same argument which Caligula applied in practice Plato used in theory when, in his dialogue of *The Statesman* [*Politicus*], he sought to define the nature of the Civil or 'Royal' man. But if it be true that a great prince occurs but rarely, what shall be said of a great Law-giver? The first has but to follow the rules laid down by the latter. The Law-giver invents the machine, the prince merely operates it. 'When societies first come to birth,' says Montesquieu, 'it is the leaders who produce the institutions of the Republic. Later, it is the institutions which produce the leaders.'

III Whoso would undertake to give institutions to a People must work with full consciousness that he has set himself to change, as it were, the very stuff of human nature; to transform each individual who, in isolation, is a complete but solitary whole, into a part of something greater than himself, from which, in a sense, he derives his life and his being; to substitute a communal and moral existence for the purely physical and independent life with which we are all of us endowed by nature. His task, in short, is to take from a man his own proper powers, and to give him in exchange powers foreign to him as a person, which he can use only if he is helped by the rest of the community. The more complete the death and destruction of his natural powers, the greater and more durable will those be which he acquires, and the more solid and perfect will that community be of which he forms a part. So true is this that the citizen by himself is nothing, and can do nothing, save with the co-operation of his neighbours, and the power acquired by the whole is equal or superior to the sum of the powers possessed by its citizens regarded as natural men. When that result has been achieved, and only then, can we say that the art of legislation has reached the highest stage of perfection of which it is capable.

IV The Legislator must, in every way, be an extraordinary figure in the State. He is so by reason of his genius, and no less so by that of his office. He is neither magistrate nor sovereign. His function is to constitute the State, yet in its Constitution it has no part to play. It exists in isolation, and is superior to other functions, having nothing to do with the governance of men. For if it be true that he who commands men should not ordain laws, so, too, he who ordains laws should be no longer in a position to command men. Were it otherwise, the laws, mere ministers to his passions, would often do no more than perpetuate his acts of injustice, nor could he ever avoid the danger that his views as a man might detract from the sanctity of his work. . . .

V Whoso codifies the laws of a community, therefore, has not, or should not have, any legislative right, a right that is incommunicable, and one of which the People, even should they wish to do so, cannot divest themselves. For, by reason of the social compact, the general will alone can constrain the individual citizen: [1] nor is there any other way of making sure that the will of the individual is in conformity with the general will, save by submitting it to the free votes of the People.

FROM

Constitutional Law of the Greater German Reich
(1939)

ERNST RUDOLF HUBER

[The Führer Principle] [2]

1 The Führer-Reich of the [German] people is founded on the recognition that the true will of the people cannot be disclosed through parliamentary votes and plebiscites but that the will of the people in its pure and uncorrupted form can only be expressed through the Führer. Thus a distinction must be drawn between the supposed will of the people in a par-

[1 The concept of "the social compact" you understand from a discussion in Chapter III. "The general will," according to Rousseau, is the common interest, and may be quite different from the sum of individual wills, and even from a majority decision arrived at through the process of voting as we know it. But he believes, too, that in a vote taken under very carefully controlled conditions, individual selfishnesses will cancel one another out—that it is possible to elicit the general will. "The legislator," then, is the gifted individual who knows intuitively what the general will is; "the one sufficient proof of the legislator's mission," Rousseau says finally, "is his own greatness of soul."]

2 This selection from Huber's *Verfassungsrecht des grossdeutschen Reiches* (Hamburg, 1939) is reprinted as translated in *National Socialism*, United States Department of State Publication 1864 (1943).

liamentary democracy, which merely reflects the conflict of the various social interests, and the true will of the people in the Führer-state, in which
the collective will of the real political unit is manifested. . . .

II The Führer is the bearer of the people's will; he is independent of all
groups, associations, and interests, but he is bound by laws which are inherent in the nature of his people. In this twofold condition: independence
of all factional interests, but unconditional dependence on the people, is
reflected the true nature of the Führer principle. Thus the Führer has
nothing in common with the functionary, the agent, or the exponent who
exercises a mandate delegated to him and who is bound to the will of those
who appoint him. The Führer is no 'representative' of a particular group
whose wishes he must carry out. He is no 'organ' of the state in the sense
of a mere executive agent. He is rather himself the bearer of the collective
will of the people. In his will the will of the people is realized. He trans-
forms the mere feelings of the people into a conscious will. . . .

III But the Führer, even as the bearer of the people's will, is not arbitrary and free of all responsibility. His will is not the subjective, individual
will of a single man, but the collective national will is embodied within
him in all its objective, historical greatness. . . . The Führer principle
rests upon unlimited authority but not upon mere outward force. It has
often been said, but it must constantly be repeated, that the Führer principle has nothing in common with arbitrary bureaucracy and represents no
system of brutal force, but that it can only be maintained by mutual loyalty which must find its expression in a free relation. The Führer-order
depends upon the responsibility of the following, just as it counts on the
responsibility and loyalty of the Führer to his mission and his following. . . .

IV That the will of the people is embodied in the Führer does not exclude the possibility that the Führer can summon all members of the people to a plebiscite on a certain question. In this 'asking of the people' the
Führer does not, of course, surrender his decisive power to the voters. The
purpose of the plebiscite is not to let the people act in the Führer's place
or to replace the Führer's decision with the result of the plebiscite. Its purpose is rather to give the whole people an opportunity to demonstrate and
proclaim its support of an aim announced by the Führer. . . . This approval of the Führer's decision is even more clear and effective if the plebiscite is concerned with an aim which has already been realized rather
than with a mere intention. . . .

V The office of the Führer developed out of the National Socialist
movement. It was originally not a state office; this fact can never be dis-
regarded if one is to understand the present legal and political position of
the Führer. The office of the Führer first took root in the structure of the
Reich when the Führer took over the powers of the Chancellor, and then
when he assumed the position of the Chief of State. But his primary significance is always as leader of the movement. . . . We must speak not
of the state's authority but of the Führer's authority if we wish to designate
the character of the political authority within the Reich correctly. The

state does not hold political authority as an impersonal unit but receives it
from the Führer as the executor of the national will.

SUGGESTIONS FOR PAPERS

This section deals with a skill so important to you in your academic
work that you can hardly practice it too much. Besides the passages here
offered as practice material, a number of the selections in Chapters I–IV
are appropriate material for summary writing as your instructor may direct. Or he can find passages for you to use in subsequent chapters. But he
may feel that it would be good practice for you to write formal summaries
of passages from textbooks or assigned material in your other courses. And
you would do well to use the technique of summary, on your own initiative, whenever you particularly need full control of a difficult passage.

VI

Writer to Reader

Any piece of writing has its function and its life when someone reads
it. That is obvious enough—so obvious that students often forget it
when they are writing. Most writing is intended for a particular sort
of readers. Of course, if the intended readers include persons of many levels of education, experience, and ability—as in newspaper writing, for instance—then the writer must consider first of all the less capable, for if
they understand, the more capable certainly will. But often a writer may
direct his work more particularly than the newspaper writer does. When
you write a letter to a friend, you envisage him and adapt your writing to
him; the professional writer tries to envisage a sort of composite reader and
to adapt his writing to that reader.

Probably the greatest difference between the skillful writer and the unpracticed writer, given equal potential capability, is that the skillful writer
considers his readers. He knows that he can communicate with them only
through their knowledge and experience. He communicates through their
knowledge of the language, of course, and he must predict what words
they know and what associations they have with those words. But communication is not only a matter of vocabulary. Readers can gain new intellectual experience only through their old, and therefore good writers
carefully take into account what their readers are like and what they have
to start with. In this chapter we shall consider the assumptions some accomplished writers have made about their readers, and we shall try to discover what they have done to make sure that communication will be complete.

CONSIDERATION FOR THE READER

Our first selection is from George Lyman Kittredge's *Witchcraft in Old
and New England*. It is a part of the last chapter, "Witchcraft and the
Puritans," considerably excised. You can profit by careful attention to the
way in which ideas are developed in this selection, for Kittredge's style
has just the virtues that student writing commonly lacks.

The persistent fault of the typical student writer is that he requires the
reader to do what the writer himself ought to have done. That is, he puts

the burden of connecting ideas and of making transitions—even, perhaps, of fully developing ideas—onto the reader, to whom it does not belong. It is right to expect the reader to do his part, but the writer must then know what his own part is. Just here you can learn from Kittredge. You will see that, even though he is writing a scholarly book intended for highly literate and practiced readers, he takes every care that his statements shall be clear, connected, and developed far enough so that they really make an impression upon the reader's mind.

But Kittredge is assuming that his readers have some knowledge of English history and of the colonial history of New England—possibly more knowledge than you have. In order that we may get on with the matter in hand, there are editor's explanatory footnotes to some paragraphs. Use them your first time through the piece.

FROM *Witchcraft in Old and New England* (1929)

GEORGE LYMAN KITTREDGE

[Salem Witchcraft] [1]

1 The darkest page of New England history is, by common consent, that which is inscribed with the words Salem Witchcraft. The hand of the apologist trembles as it turns the leaf. The reactionary writer who prefers iconoclasm to hero-worship sharpens his pen and pours fresh gall into his inkpot when he comes to this sinister subject. Let us try to consider the matter, for a few minutes, unemotionally, and to that end let us pass in review a number of facts which may help us to look at the Witchcraft Delusion of 1692 in its due proportions,—not as an abnormal outbreak of fanaticism, not as an isolated tragedy, but as a mere incident, a brief and transitory episode in the biography of a terrible, but perfectly natural, superstition. [2]

II In the first place, we know that the New Englanders did not invent the belief in witchcraft. It is a universally human belief. No race or nation is exempt from it. Formerly, it was an article in the creed of everybody in

[1] Reprinted by permission of the publishers from George Lyman Kittredge, *Witchcraft in Old and New England*, Cambridge, Mass.: Harvard University Press; copyright, 1929, by The President and Fellows of Harvard College.

[2 The witchcraft trials came about sixty years after the founding of the Bay Colony, when the Puritan ideal seemed to be failing of achievement, and when the relationships of the colonists with England were unhappy. The Massachusetts Company Charter under which the Colony was founded had been revoked in 1684, and the new charter of 1691 made Massachusetts a royal province. You have probably heard people speak of the "witch-burnings" at Salem as evidence of a unique Puritan kind of superstition. The persons executed at Salem were hanged; and talk about "witch-burning" is a small indication of the general misconception of the Salem affair. Not every student of the period would agree that Kittredge's attitude is in all points right; but the contentions made in our selection are most carefully supported by documentary evidence in the text of *Witchcraft in Old and New England* and in the notes. You can find a brief account of witchcraft in New England under "Salem witchcraft trials" in the *Oxford Companion to American Literature*.]

the world, and it is still held, in some form or other, and to a greater or less extent, by a large majority of mankind.

III Further, our own attitude of mind toward witchcraft is a very modern attitude indeed. To us, one who asserts the existence, or even the possibility, of the crime of witchcraft staggers under a burden of proof which he cannot conceivably support. His thesis seems to us unreasonable, abnormal, monstrous; it can scarcely be stated in intelligible terms; it savors of madness. Now, before we can do any kind of justice to our forefathers,—a matter, be it remembered, of no moment to them, for they have gone to their reward, but, I take it, of considerable importance to us,—we must empty our heads of all such rationalistic ideas. To the contemporaries of William Stoughton and Samuel Sewall the existence of this crime was not merely an historical phenomenon, it was a fact of contemporary experience. Whoever denied the occurrence of witchcraft in the past, was an atheist; whoever refused to admit its actual possibility in the present, was either stubbornly incredulous, or destitute of the ability to draw an inference. Throughout the seventeenth century, very few persons could be found—not merely in New England, but in the whole world—who would have ventured to take so radical a position. That there had been witches and sorcerers in antiquity was beyond cavil. That there were, or might be, witches and sorcerers in the present was almost equally certain. The crime was recognized by the Bible, by all branches of the Church, by philosophy, by natural science, by the medical faculty, by the law of England. I do not offer these postulates as novelties. They are commonplaces. They will not be attacked by anybody who has even a slight acquaintance with the mass of testimony that might be adduced to establish them.[1]

IV It is a common practice to ascribe the tenets of the New Englanders in the matter of witchcraft to something peculiar about their religious opinions,—to what is loosely called their Puritan theology. This is a very serious error. The doctrines of our forefathers differed, in this regard, from the doctrines of the Roman and the Anglican Church in no essential,— one may safely add, in no particular. Lord Bacon was not a Puritan,—yet he has left his belief in sorcery recorded in a dozen places. James I was not a Puritan, but his Dæmonologie (1597) is a classic treatise, his zeal in prosecuting Scottish sorcerers is notorious, and the statute of 1604 was the act under which Matthew Hopkins, in the time of the Commonwealth, sent two hundred witches to the gallows in two years,—nearly ten times as many as perished in Massachusetts from the first settlement to the beginning of the eighteenth century. . . .

[1 William Stoughton presided at the Salem trials and Samuel Sewall was one of the judges. Sewall's confession of error (see x) was read by a clergyman in church, Sewall standing the while. It went in part: "Samuel Sewall . . . sensible that as to the Guilt contracted . . . he is, upon many counts, more concerned than any that he knows of, Desires to take the Blame and shame of it, Asking pardon of men, And especially desiring prayers that God, who has an Unlimited Authority, would pardon the sin. . . ." The recognition of the crime of witchcraft in the Bible is in such passages as Exodus 22:18 (quoted at the end of VII) and Deuteronomy 18:9–13. And see especially the striking story of Saul and the Witch of Endor, 1 Samuel 28.]

v The Salem outbreak was not due to Puritanism; it is not assignable to any peculiar temper on the part of our New England ancestors; it is no sign of exceptional bigotry or abnormal superstition. Our forefathers believed in witchcraft, not because they were Puritans, not because they were Colonials, not because they were New Englanders,—but because they were men of their time. They shared the feelings and beliefs of the best hearts and wisest heads of the seventeenth century. What more can be asked of them? . . .

vi Another point requires consideration if we would arrive at a just judgment on the Salem upheaval. It is frequently stated, and still oftener assumed, that the outbreak at Salem was peculiar in its virulence, or, at all events, in its intensity. This is a serious error, due, like other misapprehensions, to a neglect of the history of witchcraft as a whole. The fact is, the Salem excitement was the opposite of peculiar,—it was perfectly typical. The European belief in witchcraft, which our forefathers shared without exaggerating it, was a constant quantity. It was always present, and continuously fraught with direful possibilities. But it did not find expression in a steady and regular succession of witch-trials. On the contrary, it manifested itself at irregular intervals in spasmodic outbursts of prosecution. . . .

vii There was a very special reason why troubles with the powers of darkness were to be expected in New England,—a reason which does not hold good for Great Britain or, indeed, for any part of Western Europe. I refer, of course, to the presence of a considerable heathen population—the Indians. These were universally supposed to be devil-worshippers,—not only by the Colonists but by all the rest of the world,—for paganism was held to be nothing but Satanism. Cotton Mather [1] and the Jesuit fathers of Canada were at one on this point. The religious ceremonies of the Indians were, as we know, in large part an invocation of spirits, and their pow-waws, or medicine men, supposed themselves to be wizards,—*were* wizards, indeed, so far as sorcery is possible. The Colonial government showed itself singularly moderate, however, in its attitude toward Indian practices of a magical character. Powwawing was, of course, forbidden wherever the jurisdiction of the white men held sway, but it was punishable by fine only, nor was there any idea of inflicting the extreme penalty—although the offence undoubtedly came under the Mosaic law, so often quoted on the title-pages of books on witchcraft, "Thou shalt not suffer a witch to live."

viii The existence of all these devil-worshipping neighbors was a constant reminder of the possibility of danger from witchcraft. One is surprised, therefore, to find that there was no real outbreak until so late in the century. It argues an uncommon degree of steadiness and common sense among our forefathers that they held off the explosion so long. Yet even

[1 Cotton Mather was a great Puritan divine, the third in the "Mather Dynasty." He was an influential leader and writer, the author of (among many other works) *The Wonders of the Invisible World.* Some writers have held him largely responsible for the witch trials.]

this delay has been made to count against them, as if, by 1692, they ought to have known better, even if they might have been excusable some years before. In point of fact, the New Englanders, as we have seen, made an end of trying witches nearly twenty years earlier than their English fellow-citizens. . . .

IX Much has been written of the stupendous and criminal foolishness of our ancestors in admitting "spectral evidence" at the Salem trials. Nothing, of course, can be said in defence of such evidence in itself; but a great deal might be said in defence of our ancestors on this score. The fact is,— and it should never be lost sight of,—there was nothing strange in their admitting such evidence. It was a matter of course that they should admit it. To do so, indeed, was one of the best established of all legal principles. . . . On the other hand, it is much to their credit that they soon began to suspect it, and that, having taken advice, they decided, in 1693, to allow it no further weight. . . .[1]

X The most remarkable things about the New England prosecution were the rapid return of the community to its habitually sensible frame of mind and the frank public confession of error made by many of those who had been implicated. These two features, and especially the latter, are without a parallel in the history of witchcraft. It seems to be assumed by most writers that recantation and an appeal to heaven for pardon were the least that could have been expected of judge and jury. In fact, as I have just ventured to suggest, no action like Samuel Sewall's on the part of a judge and no document like that issued by the repentant Massachusetts jurymen have yet been discovered in the witch records of the world. . . .

----

1) What does "apologist" mean in 1? May Kittredge himself be considered an apologist in this sense? Find a definition of the word that will fit this context.

2) The last sentence in 1 is a statement of purpose for the whole selection; it makes clear that we are to consider Salem witchcraft in historical perspective. Point out in detail how this statement of purpose controls the structure of the selection—that is, how this sentence is developed part by part in the selection.

3) Consider II. A typical student writer would let the matter go with the first sentence, not staying with it long enough to enforce it. Notice that a short paragraph among longer ones is emphatic, and that short sentences are here used for emphasis. But you should remember in your own writing that short sentences and short paragraphs are effective devices for empha-

[1 The admission of "spectral evidence" means the use in court of such evidence as the following, recorded by Cotton Mather at the trial of Bridget Bishop: "Samuel Gray, testify'd, That about fourteen years ago, he wak'd on a Night, & saw the Room where he lay, full of Light; & that he then saw plainly a Woman between the Cradle, and the Bed-side, which look'd upon him. He Rose, and it vanished; tho' he found the Doors all fast. . . . He knew not Bishop nor her Name; but when he saw her after this, he knew by her Countenance, and Apparrel, and all Circumstances, that it was the Apparition of the *Bishop,* which had thus troubled him."]

sis only by contrast with sentences or paragraphs of normal length. And if you use them haphazardly, you may give emphasis to what you do not intend to emphasize.

4) Note how Kittredge uses restatement of the same idea in successive sentences to achieve force and clarity. But note also that the restatement is not simply repetition, that in sentences which repeat an idea previously stated there is always some further development of that idea. Where are examples?

5) You are probably familiar with the rhetorical principle of PARAL-LELISM; if you are not, your handbook will instruct you. Parallelism is not merely a grace that your instructor and your handbook writer think desirable; it is a way of helping your reader to realize the relationship between ideas. Point out sentences that are a series of parallel clauses. Do you find successive sentences parallel in construction?

6) Note Kittredge's use of negative statement as a means of emphasis and of fixing an idea in his reader's mind. The next-to-last sentence in vi illustrates the device. What are other examples?

7) Consider in v and vi how transition from sentence to sentence is provided: sometimes by transitional expressions—"the fact is" or "on the contrary"; sometimes by the reference of the subject of the sentence to the sentence before; only once by a simple conjunction. Similar analysis of other paragraphs in this selection would repay you.

8) Your handbook discusses all the rhetorical matters we have been observing, for good rhetoricians merely describe the practice of clear and forceful writers. And the practice of clear and forceful writers arises from their care for the reader, their desire to be sure the reader understands. They realize that unless adequate readers comprehend what they have written, it has failed in its purpose. Is Kittredge taking more care for his readers than you commonly take for yours in your writing?

9) Since this is a good structure, it is all one. But parts are separable for discussion, and we can consider paragraphs by themselves. Making a summary is a good way to test how closely knit a paragraph is. For instance, iii is so close-knit that it may be summarized in one long sentence:

> Although a belief in the actuality of witchcraft seems now impossible in any reasonable person, in justice to the Puritans we must remember that in the seventeenth century anyone who did not believe in the existence of witches in the past was considered an atheist, that anyone who denied the existence of witches in the present was considered to be willfully or stupidly denying experience, and that the crime of witchcraft was recognized by religious, scientific, and legal authority.

Perhaps we would not ordinarily write so long a sentence; the point is that we *can* get a summary of the paragraph into a single sentence.

10) But we have seen that paragraphs in good writing are not just blocks placed one after another, and we have here noted how the first, signpost, paragraph controls the whole. Now consider the relationship of vi, vii, and viii. Can they be thought of together as a portion of the main structure?

11) How about ix and x? Do they have a special relationship to one another?

12) In order to establish certain useful ways of thinking about communication, we have so far concerned ourselves with the rhetoric and structure of this piece. But rhetoric and structure do not exist for themselves; they exist for meaning. How good a control of the ideas do you have? We can test it. Read carefully the following passage from J. S. Bassett's *A Short History of the United States:*

> . . . New England Puritans believed thoroughly in the guidance of God. When, for example, their charter was threatened the council implored divine enlightenment and believed that God wished them to resist. For all that, the charter was lost. This but increased the despair of those who saw everywhere a relaxation of the pure faith of their fathers. The ravages of the Indians were not forgotten before this new calamity was upon them. To the stricter party it seemed that the anger of God was heavy on his people, and the natural consequence was a heightening of mysticism.
>
> Circumstances turned this tendency of the time so that it hit upon witchcraft. About 1680 a number of clergymen around Boston began to investigate the history of witchcraft in New England. A short time later Increase Mather, in a book called "Illustrious Providences," described the nature of witchcraft, and his pedantic son, Cotton Mather, desiring to study the subject experimentally, began to gather data for a book on "The Wonders of the Invisible World," a discussion of the "nature, number, and operations of the devils." In 1688 two children of Boston declared themselves bewitched by an Irish laundress, who was tried and executed. He took the two girls to his own house, observed their actions, and published his conclusions in 1689. Thus the public mind was made ready for the sad affair at Salem.[1]

Kittredge would have denied none of the facts here used. The questions are these: How exactly do emphasis and interpretation differ in the selection from Kittredge? Does this passage represent the interpretation of New England witchcraft that Kittredge is concerned to correct or modify? How far and in what way? What perspectives are used in the selection from Kittredge that are not used here?

ADAPTATION FOR A SPECIAL AUDIENCE   *ii*

Our next selection was originally designed for a kind of audience very different from that for which Kittredge wrote. It is from an address to workingmen, delivered in 1863 by Thomas Henry Huxley (1825–95). Huxley had a medical education and did some specifically scientific writing; but his fame rests upon his many addresses and publications, widely influential in his time, on the philosophical implications of nineteenth-century science. He was an interpreter and supporter of Darwinism, and he vigorously urged that a knowledge of science must be considered a necessary part of the equipment of an educated man.

Although our selection was originally part of an address, it has since been read by many thousands of persons. It is very often reprinted in books for freshman composition, and sometimes offered to students as an almost perfect example of a piece of explanation. You will have to decide about that. It is at any rate a famous piece of popularization. You will see at once that Huxley works from the familiar to the unfamiliar and intends to use experience that he can confidently predict his audience has in order to convey new knowledge to them. But there is more to it than that.

[Scientific Law] [1]

THOMAS HENRY HUXLEY

I [1] The method of scientific investigation is nothing but the expression of the necessary mode of working of the human mind. [2] It is simply the mode at which all phenomena are reasoned about, rendered precise and exact. [3] There is no more difference, but there is just the same kind of difference, between the mental operations of a man of science and those of an ordinary person as there is between the operations and methods of a baker or of a butcher weighing out his goods in common scales and the operations of a chemist in performing a difficult and complex analysis by means of his balance and finely graduated weights. [4] It is not that the action of the scales in the one case and the balance in the other differ in the principles of their construction or manner of working; but the beam of one is set on an infinitely finer axis than the other and of course turns by the addition of a much smaller weight.

II [1] You will understand this better, perhaps, if I give you some familiar example. [2] You have all heard it repeated, I dare say, that men of science work by means of induction and deduction, and that by the help of these operations they, in a sort of sense, wring from nature certain other things which are called natural laws and causes, and that out of these, by some cunning skill of their own, they build up hypotheses and theories. [3] And it is imagined by many that the operations of the common mind can be by no means compared with these processes, and that they have to be acquired by a sort of special apprenticeship to the craft. [4] To hear all these large words you would think that the mind of a man of science must be constituted differently from that of his fellow men; but if you will not be frightened by terms, you will discover that you are quite wrong and that all these terrible apparatus are being used by yourselves every day and every hour of your lives.

III [1] There is a well-known incident in one of Molière's plays where the author makes the hero express unbounded delight on being told that he

---

[1] The full title of the address is "The Method by Which the Causes of the Present and Past Conditions of Organic Nature Are to Be Discovered."

had been talking prose during the whole of his life. ² In the same way I trust that you will take comfort and be delighted with yourselves on the discovery that you have been acting on the principles of inductive and deductive philosophy during the same period. ³ Probably there is not one here who has not in the course of the day had occasion to set in motion a complex train of reasoning of the very same kind, though differing of course in degree, as that which a scientific man goes through in tracing the causes of natural phenomena.

IV ¹ A very trivial circumstance will serve to exemplify this. ² Suppose you go into a fruiterer's shop, wanting an apple. ³ You take up one, and on biting it you find it is sour; you look at it and see that it is hard and green. ⁴ You take up another one, and that too is hard, green, and sour. ⁵ The shopman offers you a third; but before biting it you examine it and find that it is hard and green, and you immediately say that you will not have it, as it must be sour like those that you have already tried.

V ¹ Nothing can be more simple than that, you think; but if you will take the trouble to analyze and trace out into its logical elements what has been done by the mind, you will be greatly surprised. ² In the first place you have performed the operation of induction. ³ You found that in two experiences hardness and greenness in apples go together with sourness. ⁴ It was so in the first case, and it was confirmed by the second. ⁵ True, it is a very small basis, but still it is enough to make an induction from; you generalize the facts, and you expect to find sourness in apples where you get hardness and greenness. ⁶ You found upon that a general law that all hard and green apples are sour; and that, so far as it goes, is a perfect induction. ⁷ Well, having got your natural law in this way, when you are offered another apple which you find is hard and green, you say, "All hard and green apples are sour; this apple is hard and green; therefore this apple is sour." ⁸ That train of reasoning is what logicians call a syllogism and has all its various parts and terms—its major premise, its minor premise, and its conclusion. ⁹ And by the help of further reasoning, which if drawn out would have to be exhibited in two or three other syllogisms, you arrive at your final determination, "I will not have that apple." ¹⁰ So that, you see, you have, in the first place, established a law by induction, and upon that you have founded a deduction and reasoned out the special conclusion of the particular case. ¹¹ Well now, suppose, having got your law, that at some time afterwards you are discussing the qualities of apples with a friend. ¹² You will say to him, "It is a very curious thing, but I find that all hard and green apples are sour!" ¹³ Your friend says to you, "But how do you know that?" ¹⁴ You at once reply, "Oh, because I have tried them over and over again and have always found them to be so." ¹⁵ Well, if we were talking science instead of common sense, we should call that an experimental verification. ¹⁶ And if still opposed you go further and say, "I have heard from the people in Somersetshire and Devonshire, where a large number of apples are grown, that they have observed the same thing. ¹⁷ It is also found to be the case in Normandy and in North America. ¹⁸ In short, I find it to be the universal experience of mankind wherever attention has been directed to the subject." [19] Whereupon, your friend, unless he is a very unreasonable man, agrees with you and is convinced that you are quite right in the conclusion you have drawn. [20] He believes, although perhaps he does not know he believes it, that the more extensive verifications are, that the more frequently experiments have been made and results of the same kind arrived at, that the more varied the conditions under which the same results have been attained, the more certain is the ultimate conclusion, and he disputes the question no further. [21] He sees that the experiment has been tried under all sorts of conditions as to time, place, and people with the same result; and he says with you, therefore, that the law you have laid down must be a good one and he must believe it.

VI [1] In science we do the same thing; the philosopher exercises precisely the same faculties, though in a much more delicate manner. [2] In scientific inquiry it becomes a matter of duty to expose a supposed law to every possible kind of verification, and to take care, moreover, that this is done intentionally and not left to mere accident as in the case of the apples. [3] And in science, as in common life, our confidence in a law is in exact proportion to the absence of variation in the result of our experimental verifications. [4] For instance, if you let go your grasp of an article you may have in your hand, it will immediately fall to the ground. [5] That is a very common verification of one of the best established laws of nature, that of gravitation. [6] The method by which men of science established the existence of that law is exactly the same as that by which we have established the trivial proposition about the sourness of hard and green apples. [7] But we believe it in such an extensive, thorough, and unhesitating manner because the universal experience of mankind verifies it, and we can verify it ourselves at any time; and that is the strongest possible foundation on which any natural law can rest.

VII [1] So much by way of proof that the method of establishing laws in science is exactly the same as that pursued in common life.

---

1) Before we consider how Huxley adapts his material to those he would inform—hearers in the first instance, but readers ultimately—we should make sure that the selection has been a successful piece of communication for us. One of its purposes is to make certain terms clear and familiar—to make the hearer or reader feel at home with them. See if you can explain them by examples of your own (not green apples). What is "a natural law"? How does one distinguish between inductive and deductive reasoning? Illustrate VI:3.

2) Does V:6–10 make clear to you what a syllogism is? Suppose that Mr. X is driving about town and hears over his car radio that a drop in temperature to 20 degrees Fahrenheit is forecast. He thereupon stops and has some antifreeze put in the radiator of his car. Can you express his reasoning in a syllogism or syllogisms?

3) Our selection starts with a sentence which states the idea around which it is organized. Notice how that initial statement is developed in the paragraph. Does 2 add anything to its restatement of 1? What is the rela-

tionship of 3–4 to 1–2? This address is the third in a series. Could Huxley have safely used "phenomena" in 2 if he had not made his hearers familiar with it previously? What does the word mean in this context?

4) In II Huxley introduces the terms that he will define. He introduces them in the sort of vague statement which his hearers might themselves be able to make. Then he at once assures his hearers that even if the terms are not fully a part of their experience, the mental activities the terms designate are. Huxley knows, as most teachers know, that hearers are likely to be dismayed by an unfamiliar term. Paragraphs II and III are more important in establishing a particular attitude in the hearer or reader than they are in informing him. Does III make any point or contention that has not been made in I?

5) Do you think that the tone and approach here are appropriate for any audience whatever that one might be addressing on this particular subject? Give reasons for your answer.

6) What characteristics of this piece of writing are determined by the fact that Huxley intends it for oral delivery?

7) In considering question 6, it may have occurred to you that there is no absolute distinction between the technique of writing for oral delivery and the technique of writing for readers. Generally speaking, we can say that writing for oral delivery should not have very long sentences, that transitions should be clear and strongly marked, and that ideas ought to be fully developed and sufficiently restated. But all these things may well be considered virtues in writing intended to be read in the first instance. Yet one thing should certainly be remembered when one writes for oral delivery: a reader who has not fully understood a passage or who has missed a transition may go back, but a hearer cannot do so. The writer of a piece for oral delivery will therefore restate each important idea, and he will make sure his transitions are unmistakable.

8) Perhaps our further consideration may be devoted to the means Huxley uses to be clear for hearer and reader alike. One is his constant effort to carry the reader along with him: notice the approach in II:4 or v:1. The little story about green apples might have been told with John Doe as the central figure. Why does Huxley use the pronoun "you"?

9) The transitions are clear and marked. But notice, too, that they do not hurry the reader, and that they announce what is coming. Huxley tells the reader in II:1 that explanation will be by way of a familiar example, but the example is not stated until IV. And notice how v:1 announces an analysis to come.

10) In VI we have the return to, and the restatement of, the central contention that scientific reasoning is not different in kind from the reasoning we all employ in common life. We have noted the close relationship of III to I. Now notice how VI repeats the contention of I and III and develops it a little further by a restatement of the concept of experimental verification introduced in the latter part of v. But even in this summary paragraph Huxley does not allow the discussion to become abstract—he returns twice to the example of "you" in the fruit store, and introduces a new one: our constant verification of the law of gravitation.

11) Certainly, as we have seen, there is much to be learned from this

piece; certainly for its purpose it is most efficient. But perhaps in considering question 5 you decided that for some readers the piece would have something of an air of condescension and even oversimplification—that in another time and place its success would not be complete. If you did so decide, you would only be recognizing that we ask about any piece of writing, *clear to whom? effective for whom?* and that we can reasonably demand no more than that it be clear and effective for its intended readers.

12) A single paragraph of Huxley's "On the Advisableness of Improving Natural Knowledge" will illustrate how Huxley's own style changes in relation to his audience. The paragraph is interesting, too, for its expression of the nineteenth-century faith in "the universality of a definite and predictable order and succession of events." Huxley has been giving examples of the way in which investigation for immediate and practical ends has often resulted in the formation of new principles and the discarding of old ones. He goes on:

> And how has it fared with "Physick" and Anatomy? Have the anatomist, the physiologist, or the physician, whose business it has been to devote themselves assiduously to that eminently practical and direct end, the alleviation of the sufferings of mankind,—have they been able to confine their vision more absolutely to the strictly useful? I fear they are the worst offenders of all. For if the astronomer has set before us the infinite magnitude of space, and the practical eternity of the duration of the universe; if the physical and chemical philosophers have demonstrated the infinite minuteness of its constituent parts, and the practical eternity of matter and of force; and if both have alike proclaimed the universality of a definite and predictable order and succession of events, the workers in biology have not only accepted all these, but have added more startling theses of their own. For, as the astronomers discover in the earth no centre of the universe, but an eccentric speck, so the naturalists find man to be no centre of the living world, but one amidst endless modifications of life; and as the astronomer observes the mark of practically endless time set upon the arrangements of the solar system, so the student of life finds the records of ancient forms of existence peopling the world for ages, which, in relation to human experience, are infinite.

How is this paragraph different in style and in approach to the reader from the selection we have called "Scientific Law"?

Our selection from Huxley's address is broken off at a major transition, and just before Huxley begins his discussion of "hypotheses," a term, you remember, introduced in 11. The selection has been so ended because an analysis of the rest of the address would involve certain conflicts in nineteenth-century thought and so distract us from our present purpose. But this term, undiscussed in the selection, will give you an opportunity to demonstrate the truth of the contention that a reader is not helpless in the face of an unexplained reference or term. First see what your dictionary says about "hypothesis"; and then whether it distinguishes it from "law" and "theory," and whether it has an entry for "nebular hypothesis." When you have done that, you may have a pretty clear idea of what a hypothesis is in science. But here is the entry for "nebular hypothesis" from *The Columbia Encyclopedia,* a work that is particularly useful for the simplicity and clarity of its accounts of matters that offer any kind of technical difficulty. This entry is an example of another kind of reader adaptation.

Nebular Hypothesis [1]

THE COLUMBIA ENCYCLOPEDIA

NEBULAR HYPOTHESIS, an attempt to explain the regularity of arrangement and motion exhibited by the planetary system. It originated in the 18th cent. and was propounded by Swedenborg and Kant before Laplace gave it scientific form. It was long accepted by astronomers, but is no longer tenable. The theory assumes that in its first state in the far remote past our solar system was a vast mass of rarefied matter—a nebula— slowly rotating and enormously hot. Gradually cooling because of the loss of heat by radiation, the mass contracted little by little; and as the volume grew less, the rotation was more and more rapid. Laplace assumed that in time there would come a stage when the centrifugal force at the equator, driving away from the center, must equal the pull of gravity, the attraction toward the center of the mass. Then a ring of gaseous matter would become separated from the outer rim. Equilibrium would be restored for the time by the detaching of the ring. Again contraction would bring about the balance of the two opposing forces, and again a ring would be left outside the further contracting central mass. The process would be repeated several times, until the diminished nebula at the center would be surrounded by a series of rings, all revolving, the smaller the more rapidly. Out of the material of each ring would in some way be formed a single great ball of gases, which by shrinking would eventually become a planet. The mass at the center of the whole system after condensation would form the sun. Modern studies in mechanics have pointed out objections to this hypothesis; these are chiefly that rings of material thrown off as postulated in this hypothesis would tend to form swarms of small bodies and not to condense into planets and that the angular momentum (momentum of rotation) of the planets is too great in proportion to that of the sun to make the theory plausible.

---

1) Of course in considering this piece we must keep in mind the limitations of space under which the writer for the small encyclopedia works. He also has advantages; here, for instance, he need not identify the three names in the second sentence, since there will be an entry for each of them in the encyclopedia.

2) All writers face this question: "How full a discussion is required by

[1] Reprinted from *The Columbia Encyclopedia,* Second Edition, by permission of the Columbia University Press. Copyright, 1950, by Columbia University Press.

my purpose and by the needs of my readers?" This material could have been treated for pages. On the other hand James R. Newman, in a general article on Laplace, describes the nebular hypothesis in two sentences: "Its gist is that the solar system evolved from a rotating mass of gas, which condensed to form the sun and later threw off a series of gaseous rings that became the planets. While still in the gaseous state the planets threw off rings which became satellites." [1] (Notice that the encyclopedia writer did not find space to mention the formation of satellites.)

3) What is the writer assuming about the average user of the encyclopedia? Is there evidence that he does not assume much scientific knowledge on the user's part? What? Is the nature of the modern objections to Laplace's hypothesis clear to you? Did the writer expect it to be? Do you think the writer made the right assumptions? Is this a good job of adapting difficult material to general readers?

iii   A PROBLEM IN APPROACH

We turn now to a selection from C. S. Lewis, doubtless the most effective Christian apologist of our time. Although the selection is in a quite different field from that of our selection from Huxley, it illustrates related, but more difficult, problems in writing. It was originally the first of a series of broadcast talks over BBC, and its intended audience would have ranged from the highly educated to, perhaps, the barely literate. And Mr. Lewis has a further problem. Huxley's audience probably had no very clear presuppositions about his subject; but about Mr. Lewis's subject everyone has some presuppositions and convictions.

FROM *Mere Christianity* (1952)

C. S. LEWIS

The Law of Human Nature [2]

I Every one has heard people quarrelling. Sometimes it sounds funny and sometimes it sounds merely unpleasant; but however it sounds, I believe we can learn something very important from listening to the kind of things they say. They say things like this: "How'd you like it if anyone did the same to you?"—"That's my seat, I was there first"—"Leave him alone, he isn't doing you any harm"—"Why should you shove in first?"—"Give me a bit of your orange, I gave you a bit of mine"—"Come on, you promised." People say things like that every day, educated people as well as uneducated, and children as well as grown-ups.

II Now what interests me about all these remarks is that the man who makes them is not merely saying that the other man's behaviour does not

[1] Reprinted with permission of *Scientific American*, June, 1954, Volume #190, No. 6.

[2] The selection from C. S. Lewis, *Mere Christianity*, copyright, 1943, 1945, 1952, by The Macmillan Company and used with their permission.

happen to please him. He is appealing to some kind of standard of behaviour which he expects the other man to know about. And the other man very seldom replies: "To hell with your standard." Nearly always he tries to make out that what he has been doing does not really go against the standard, or that if it does there is some special excuse. He pretends there is some special reason in this particular case why the person who took the seat first should not keep it, or that things were quite different when he was given the bit of orange, or that something has turned up which lets him off keeping his promise. It looks, in fact, very much as if both parties had in mind some kind of Law or Rule of fair play or decent behaviour or morality or whatever you like to call it, about which they really agreed. And they have. If they had not, they might, of course, fight like animals, but they could not *quarrel* in the human sense of the word. Quarrelling means trying to show that the other man is in the wrong. And there would be no sense in trying to do that unless you and he had some sort of agreement as to what Right and Wrong are; just as there would be no sense in saying that a footballer had committed a foul unless there was some agreement about the rules of football.

III Now this Law or Rule about Right and Wrong used to be called the Law of Nature. Nowadays, when we talk of the "laws of nature" we usually mean things like gravitation, or heredity, or the laws of chemistry. But when the older thinkers called the Law of Right and Wrong "the Law of Nature," they really meant the Law of *Human* Nature. The idea was that, just as all bodies are governed by the law of gravitation and organisms by biological laws, so the creature called man also had *his* law—with this great difference, that a body could not choose whether it obeyed the law of gravitation or not, but a man could choose either to obey the Law of Human Nature or to disobey it.

IV We may put this in another way. Each man is at every moment subjected to several different sets of law but there is only one of these which he is free to disobey. As a body, he is subjected to gravitation and cannot disobey it; if you leave him unsupported in mid-air, he has no more choice about falling than a stone has. As an organism, he is subjected to various biological laws which he cannot disobey any more than an animal can. That is, he cannot disobey those laws which he shares with other things; but the law which is peculiar to his human nature, the law he does not share with animals or vegetables or inorganic things, is the one he can disobey if he chooses.

V This law was called the Law of Nature because people thought that every one knew it by nature and did not need to be taught it. They did not mean, of course, that you might not find an odd individual here and there who did not know it, just as you find a few people who are colour-blind or have no ear for a tune. But taking the race as a whole, they thought that the human idea of decent behaviour was obvious to every one. And I believe they were right. If they were not, then all the things we said about the war were nonsense. What was the sense in saying the enemy were in the wrong unless Right is a real thing which the Nazis at bottom knew as well as we did and ought to have practised? If they had had no notion of what we mean by right, then, though we might still have had to fight them, we could no more have blamed them for that than for the colour of their hair.

VI I know that some people say the idea of a Law of Nature or decent behaviour known to all men is unsound, because different civilisations and different ages have had quite different moralities.

VII But this is not true. There have been differences between their moralities, but these have never amounted to anything like a total difference. If anyone will take the trouble to compare the moral teaching of, say, the ancient Egyptians, Babylonians, Hindus, Chinese, Greeks and Romans, what will really strike him will be how very like they are to each other and to our own. Some of the evidence for this I have put together in the appendix of another book called *The Abolition of Man;* but for our present purpose I need only ask the reader to think what a totally different morality would mean. Think of a country where people were admired for running away in battle, or where a man felt proud of double-crossing all the people who had been kindest to him. You might just as well try to imagine a country where two and two made five. Men have differed as regards what people you ought to be unselfish to—whether it was only your own family, or your fellow countrymen, or everyone. But they have always agreed that you ought not to put yourself first. Selfishness has never been admired. Men have differed as to whether you should have one wife or four. But they have always agreed that you must not simply have any woman you liked.

VIII But the most remarkable thing is this. Whenever you find a man who says he does not believe in a real Right and Wrong, you will find the same man going back on this a moment later. He may break his promise to you, but if you try breaking one to him he will be complaining "It's not fair" before you can say Jack Robinson. A nation may say treaties do not matter; but then, next minute, they spoil their case by saying that the particular treaty they want to break was an unfair one. But if treaties do not matter, and if there is no such thing as Right and Wrong—in other words, if there is no Law of Nature—what is the difference between a fair treaty and an unfair one? Have they not let the cat out of the bag and shown that, whatever they say, they really know the Law of Nature just like anyone else?

IX It seems, then, we are forced to believe in a real Right and Wrong. People may be sometimes mistaken about them, just as people sometimes get their sums wrong; but they are not a matter of mere taste and opinion any more than the multiplication table. Now if we are agreed about that, I go on to my next point, which is this. None of us are really keeping the Law of Nature. If there are any exceptions among you, I apologise to them. They had much better read some other work, for nothing I am going to say concerns them. And now, turning to the ordinary human beings who are left:

X I hope you will not misunderstand what I am going to say. I am not preaching, and Heaven knows I do not pretend to be better than anyone else. I am only trying to call attention to a fact; the fact that this year, or this month, or, more likely, this very day, we have failed to practise ourselves the kind of behaviour we expect from other people. There may be all sorts of excuses for us. That time you were so unfair to the children was when you were very tired. That slightly shady business about the money— the one you have almost forgotten—came when you were very hard up. And what you promised to do for old So-and-so and have never done— well, you never would have promised if you had known how frightfully busy you were going to be. And as for your behaviour to your wife (or husband) or sister (or brother) if I knew how irritating they could be, I would not wonder at it—and who the dickens am I, anyway? I am just the same. That is to say, I do not succeed in keeping the Law of Nature very well, and the moment anyone tells me I am not keeping it, there starts up in my mind a string of excuses as long as your arm. The question at the moment is not whether they are good excuses. The point is that they are one more proof of how deeply, whether we like it or not, we believe in the Law of Nature. If we do not believe in decent behaviour, why should we be so anxious to make excuses for not having behaved decently? The truth is, we believe in decency so much—we feel the Rule or Law pressing on us so— that we cannot bear to face the fact that we are breaking it, and consequently we try to shift the responsibility. For you notice that it is only for our bad behaviour that we find all these explanations. It is only our bad temper that we put down to being tired or worried or hungry; we put our good temper down to ourselves.

xi These, then, are the two points I wanted to make. First, that human beings, all over the earth, have this curious idea that they ought to behave in a certain way, and cannot really get rid of it. Secondly, that they do not in fact behave in that way. They know the Law of Nature; they break it. These two facts are the foundation of all clear thinking about ourselves and the universe we live in.

---

1) Perhaps we can use some of the terms we picked up in the Huxley selection. Does this selection by C. S. Lewis proceed inductively or deductively? Where do you find the first inductive generalization?

2) Of course the organization might have been the other way round: the principles stated in xi might have been stated first and then substantiated by example. But do you see why, considering Lewis's purpose and his hearers or readers, this structure is the better one?

3) As is pointed out in vi, not everyone agrees with the principles. You may indeed find that some of your textbooks take the idea of a morality relative to time and place further and speak as if an individual or a group could devise a moral standard that the rest of mankind would do well to accept. How would you have reacted if the statement of principles in xi had come first?

4) Lewis's generalization comes after the concrete instances in i. No reader is likely to deny that they are representative of human behavior nor that the interpretation of them in ii is sound. If Lewis can carry his reader

along with him thus far, do you think he is likely to lose his reader's assent later? Even if he does, what has he gained?

5) In III "laws of nature" means exactly what Huxley means by "natural laws"; but "law" in "the Law of Nature" as Lewis says the older writers used the term, and as he uses it, really has a different sense. You will find that your dictionary defines "law" in both of these senses, as well as in others. Find the definitions that fit here. For our discussion perhaps the best term for the moral law is "the Law of Human Nature," for it is just this recognition of Right and Wrong that gives man his peculiarly human interests and problems. Consider how the word "conscience" is made up—"con" plus "science." What seems to be its root meaning?

6) In the original broadcast talk, III and V were one paragraph, and IV did not appear at all. Why do you suppose Lewis thought it well to insert IV?

7) Do you see that the first two sentences in IX mean that Right and Wrong have a real existence outside our minds? The sentences deny Hamlet's remark that "there is nothing either good or bad but thinking makes it so," as indeed Hamlet denies it by his whole behavior in the play.

8) And do you see that the idea of completely relative moral standards, the idea noticed in VI, depends upon the assumption that moral laws are like natural laws—descriptive of what people do, as the laws about gases, for instance, are descriptive of the way gases behave? But the assumption hardly stands examination. There is a moral law that people ought to be just; but some people are unjust, some are usually just, and some are as often unjust as just. The moral law remains whether it is kept or violated.

9) We are likely to say that Lewis writes simply. But since we are trying to improve our skill in writing, we need always to be clear about what we mean by writing simply—to remember that what is easy to read was probably written, not with ease, but with painstaking care. Much of Lewis's care is for the reader who is not very much used to dealing with ideas in abstract statement.

10) But notice that the writer does not assume that his reader is unintelligent. The pattern of discussion allows the reader, on the basis of concrete instances, to come to conclusions as he goes along. Did not you find that you could predict where the discussion was tending as you read, and that, when the conclusion was stated, it was already in your mind? The effect is, of course, that the reader feels that the conclusion is *his* conclusion. It is Lewis's special skill that, even while he puts no difficulties in the way of his reader, he does keep his reader active.

11) Is there good reason that—for this subject matter—the approach should be personal and familiar? When Lewis revised the broadcast talk for *Mere Christianity,* he took out some things more appropriate to speech than to the printed page (like contractions) but he changed the tone very little. Notice his use of "I" and "you" and "we." Are they used in quite the same tone and way that Huxley used them?

12) Finally we should observe the sort of repetition in this selection. When an idea is restated, you will usually find, it is also a little further developed. The restatement is not just a matter of saying it over again; some new facet is added. For an instance, examine VIII. And notice the

parallel structure of sentences there and elsewhere in the selection. Point out a number of sentences that have parallel clauses. And point out passages that have a repetition of sentence pattern—one instance is in the last part of VII.

13) As we took a passage from Huxley to illustrate his style when he was assuming very capable readers, so we may take a passage from the book Lewis mentions in VII, *The Abolition of Man* (1947). Knowledge of our selection will help you understand it; the Law of Human Nature is *part* of what is here called the *Tao* (pronounce the word as if it were spelled "Dow").

> . . . The Chinese also speak of a great thing (the greatest thing) called the *Tao*. It is the reality beyond all predicates, the abyss that was before the Creator Himself. It is Nature, it is the Way, the Road. It is the Way in which the universe goes on, the Way in which things everlastingly emerge, stilly and tranquilly, into space and time. It is also the Way which every man should tread in imitation of that cosmic and supercosmic progression, conforming all activities to that great exemplar. 'In ritual,' say the Analects, 'it is harmony with Nature that is prized.' The ancient Jews likewise praise the Law as being 'true.'
>
> This conception in all its forms, Platonic, Aristotelian, Stoic, Christian, and Oriental alike, I shall henceforth refer to for brevity simply as 'the *Tao*.' Some of the accounts of it . . . will seem, perhaps, to many of you merely quaint or even magical. But what is common to them all is something we cannot neglect. It is the doctrine of objective value, the belief that certain attitudes are really true, and others really false, to the kind of thing the universe is and the kind of things we are. Those who know the *Tao* can hold that to call children delightful or old men venerable is not simply to record a psychological fact about our own parental or filial emotions at the moment, but to recognize a quality which *demands* a certain response from us whether we make it or not. . . .[1]

A PROBLEM FOR THE READER *iv*

So far in this section we have been concerned with writers who carefully consider their readers, and our main interest has been in what those writers did to carry their readers along with them. You may feel that in the following selection the writer puts an undue burden upon his readers, although you will see that he is aware of them and carefully calculates his effect upon them. But this time we shall have to be primarily concerned with what the reader must do to follow the writer.

Thorstein Veblen is an interesting and important writer, a realistic sort of economist whose work has had a permanent influence in both economics and sociology. In his writing we have an example of vital thought expressed in a manner not altogether fortunate. His terminology was in his time new and fresh, but he may have been influential in establishing the habit of

[1] From C. S. Lewis, *The Abolition of Man*, copyright, 1947, by The Macmillan Company and used with their permission.

jargon and unrelieved abstraction that disfigures much writing in economics, sociology, and educational theory. For the unpracticed reader, Veblen's continual abstraction and wordiness may obscure his thought.

Our selection comes from a chapter called "Conspicuous Consumption." Veblen believes that in civilized society the marks of prestige and power have been, first, the consumption of goods not from need but for display and, second, the ability to be at leisure. This leisure need not be inactivity; it may be an active cultivation of unproductive skills and tastes. "The basis on which good repute in any highly organized industrial community ultimately rests," Veblen says, "is pecuniary strength; and the means of showing pecuniary strength, and so of gaining or retaining a good name, are leisure and a conspicuous consumption of goods." Of course, some leisure is necessary to any elaborate conspicuous consumption.

Just before we pick up the chapter in our selection, Veblen has been speaking of the way in which the number of men-at-arms and, later in history, the number of liveried servants have manifested the prestige and position of the master. In our selection he discusses the role of the middle- and lower-class wife in conspicuous consumption.

F R O M   *The Theory of the Leisure Class*   (1899)

THORSTEIN VEBLEN

[The Middle-Class Wife]

I ¹ With the disappearance of servitude, the number of vicarious consumers attached to any one gentleman tends, on the whole, to decrease. ² The like is of course true, and perhaps in a still higher degree, of the number of dependents who perform vicarious leisure for him. ³ In a general way, though not wholly nor consistently, these two groups coincide. ⁴ The dependent who was first delegated for these duties was the wife, or the chief wife; and, as would be expected, in the later development of the institution, when the number of persons by whom these duties are customarily performed gradually narrows, the wife remains the last. ⁵ In the higher grades of society a large volume of both these kinds of service is required; and here the wife is of course still assisted in the work by a more or less numerous corps of menials. ⁶ But as we descend the social scale, the point is presently reached where the duties of vicarious leisure and consumption devolve upon the wife alone. ⁷ In the communities of the Western culture, this point is at present found among the lower middle class.

II ¹ And here occurs a curious inversion. ² It is a fact of common observation that in this lower middle class there is no pretence of leisure on the part of the head of the household. ³ Through force of circumstances it has fallen into disuse. ⁴ But the middle-class wife still carries on the business of

From *The Theory of the Leisure Class* by Thorstein Veblen, included in *The Portable Veblen*, edited by Max Lerner. Reprinted by permission of The Viking Press, Inc., New York.

vicarious leisure, for the good name of the household and its master. [5] In descending the social scale in any modern industrial community, the primary fact—the conspicuous leisure of the master of the household—disappears at a relatively high point. [6] The head of the middle-class household has been reduced by economic circumstances to turn his hand to gaining a livelihood by occupations which often partake largely of the character of industry, as in the case of the ordinary business man of today. [7] But the derivative fact—the vicarious leisure and consumption rendered by the wife, and the auxiliary vicarious performance of leisure by menials—remains in vogue as a conventionality which the demands of reputability will not suffer to be slighted. [8] It is by no means an uncommon spectacle to find a man applying himself to work with the utmost assiduity, in order that his wife may in due form render for him that degree of vicarious leisure which the common sense of the time demands.

III [1] The leisure rendered by the wife in such cases is, of course, not a simple manifestation of idleness or indolence. [2] It almost invariably occurs disguised under some form of work or household duties or social amenities, which prove on analysis to serve little or no ulterior end beyond showing that she does not and need not occupy herself with anything that is gainful or that is of substantial use. [3] As has already been noticed under the head of manners, the greater part of the customary round of domestic cares to which the middle-class housewife gives her time and effort is of this character. [4] Not that the results of her attention to household matters, of a decorative and mundificatory character, are not pleasing to the sense of men trained in middle-class proprieties; but the taste to which these effects of household adornment and tidiness appeal is a taste which has been formed under the selective guidance of a canon of propriety that demands just these evidences of wasted effort. [5] The effects are pleasing to us chiefly because we have been taught to find them pleasing. [6] There goes into these domestic duties much solicitude for a proper combination of form and colour, and for other ends that are to be classed as æsthetic in the proper sense of the term; and it is not denied that effects having some substantial æsthetic value are sometimes attained. [7] Pretty much all that is here insisted on is that, as regards these amenities of life, the housewife's efforts are under the guidance of traditions that have been shaped by the law of conspicuously wasteful expenditure of time and substance. [8] If beauty or comfort is achieved—and it is a more or less fortuitous circumstance if they are—they must be achieved by means and methods that commend themselves to the great economic law of wasted effort. [9] The more reputable, 'presentable' portion of middle-class household paraphernalia are, on the one hand, items of conspicuous consumption, and on the other hand, apparatus for putting in evidence the vicarious leisure rendered by the housewife.

IV [1] The requirement of vicarious consumption at the hands of the wife continues in force even at a lower point in the pecuniary scale than the requirement of vicarious leisure. [2] At a point below which little if any pretence of wasted effort, in ceremonial cleanness and the like, is observable, and where there is assuredly no conscious attempt at ostensible leisure, decency still requires the wife to consume some goods conspicuously for the reputability of the household and its head. ³ So that, as the latter-day outcome of this evolution of an archaic institution, the wife, who was at the outset the drudge and chattel of the man, both in fact and in theory—the producer of goods for him to consume—has become the ceremonial consumer of goods which he produces. ⁴ But she still quite unmistakably remains his chattel in theory; for the habitual rendering of vicarious leisure and consumption is the abiding mark of the un-free servant.

v ¹ This vicarious consumption practiced by the household of the middle and lower classes can not be counted as a direct expression of the leisure-class scheme of life, since the household of this pecuniary grade does not belong within the leisure class. ² It is rather that the leisure-class scheme of life here comes to an expression at the second remove. ³ The leisure class stands at the head of the social structure in point of reputability; and its manner of life and its standards of worth therefore afford the norm of reputability for the community. ⁴ The observance of these standards, in some degree of approximation, becomes incumbent upon all classes lower in the scale. ⁵ In modern civilized communities the lines of demarcation between the social classes have grown vague and transient, and wherever this happens the norm of reputability imposed by the upper class extends its coercive influence with but slight hindrance down through the social structure to the lowest strata. ⁶ The result is that the members of each stratum accept as their ideal of decency the scheme of life in vogue in the next higher stratum, and bend their energies to live up to that ideal. ⁷ On pain of forfeiting their good name and their self-respect in case of failure, they must conform to the accepted code, at least in appearance.

VI ¹ The basis on which good repute in any highly organized industrial community ultimately rests is pecuniary strength; and the means of showing pecuniary strength, and so of gaining or retaining a good name, are leisure and a conspicuous consumption of goods. ² Accordingly, both of these methods are in vogue as far down the scale as it remains possible; and in the lower strata in which the two methods are employed, both offices are in great part delegated to the wife and children of the household. ³ Lower still, where any degree of leisure, even ostensible, has become impracticable for the wife, the conspicuous consumption of goods remains and is carried on by the wife and children. ⁴ The man of the household also can do something in this direction, and, indeed, he commonly does; but with a still lower descent into the levels of indigence—along the margin of the slums—the man, and presently also the children, virtually cease to consume valuable goods for appearances, and the woman remains virtually the sole exponent of the household's pecuniary decency. ⁵ No class of society, not even the most abjectly poor, forgoes all customary conspicuous consumption. ⁶ The last items of this category of consumption are not given up except under the stress of the direst necessity. ⁷ Very much of squalor and discomfort will be endured before the last trinket or the last pretence of pecuniary decency is put away. ⁸ There is no class and no country that has yielded so abjectly before the pressure of physical want as to deny themselves all gratification of this higher or spiritual need.

---

1) What is difficult about reading this piece? Many students would answer at once that the difficulty is a great many words that they do not know. But if that were all, should we call the reading difficult? As long as you have a good dictionary, an unfamiliar word need remain unfamiliar but a minute or so. If you do not know, for instance, "fortuitous," or "assiduity," you have an immediate remedy. (But your desk dictionary may fail you for "mundificatory." The Latin adjective *mundus* means "neat" or "elegant." And does the second clause in the sentence help with a synonym?)

2) Yet there is a real difficulty in Veblen's diction, and it may be connected with words which seem entirely familiar to you, as well as with words which are unfamiliar. Veblen often uses words in senses that he fixes upon them, senses somewhat different from the senses the same words carry in ordinary use. He has what we may call a terminology of his own, or less politely, a jargon.

3) For example, the last clause in ii:8 is "which the common sense of the time demands." Now "common sense" is here used to mean something like "social customs"—if the reader does not consider context carefully enough, he will certainly find the expression confusing. Or take "canon of propriety." "Canon" in any of its more familiar senses does not fit; this "canon" is not a written set of rules or laws. A more complex example is the expression "perform vicarious leisure." Do you see that what makes this expression difficult is not the relatively unfamiliar "vicarious" but the special sense carried by the familiar "leisure"? What are other examples of Veblen's use of words a little apart from their ordinary senses?

4) Another characteristic of Veblen's style is a persistent abstraction. Take iii for instance. What exactly are the activities to which the middle-class wife devotes her conspicuous leisure? We are given no instance of them. Or in v:3–6, would not the discussion have been more effective for you had some example been given of the way in which the members of one class try to achieve the "norm of reputability" imposed by the class above them? For a reader who has thought much about social and economic matters, such abstract generalizations as Veblen's may be clear. But for a reader unused to the consideration of these matters, generalizations without concrete substantiation may seem for a moment vague, even meaningless. He must stop to think what would be a concrete example.

5) Veblen's diction and his abstraction may be partially justified, or at least explained, by his purpose and the readers he envisages. His habit of what your handbook may call "wordiness" can hardly be excused. He writes, in ii:8, for instance, "It is by no means an uncommon spectacle to find a man applying himself to work with the utmost assiduity. . . ." Has he said more than "We often see a man working hard . . ."? Or take ii:6; we have there the expression "to turn his hand to gaining a livelihood by occupations which often partake largely of the character of industry." See how much you can reduce ii:6 without loss of meaning. What are other examples of wordy sentences in the selection? Try reducing a few.

6) Now if these qualities of style were Veblen's alone, we should not need to consider them. But, as we have noted, some contemporary writing is likely to have a pretentious quality, and one can find in it a jargon much like Veblen's. Perhaps you can match some of Veblen's most wordy sentences in things you have been reading recently.

7) Yet there is a subtle effect of Veblen's style that we ought not to overlook. His elaborate ways of designating the weaknesses or the follies of men and women have an IRONIC quality. One suspects that Veblen had his tongue in his cheek while he was writing—at least part of the time. He *seems* to make no moral judgment; he *seems* removed, scientific. There are familiar terms for "conspicuous consumption" and for "the vicarious leisure rendered by the housewife," and moralists have long used them. But the sort of words we might expect the moralist to use were he discussing Veblen's subject—vanity, snobbishness, envious emulation—are quite absent. Perhaps the elaborate objectivity of Veblen's terminology jars us a little, and so helps us to see human folly freshly and to re-examine our own set of values.

8) We may not consider this selection a model of style; and yet Veblen, like many other writers whose style we find neither easy nor pleasant, has something of importance to say. His discussion of the middle-class wife in the late nineteenth century makes clear to us that we cannot represent all economic facts on graphs, that we do not understand economic activity without some consideration of human nature. And you can understand Veblen's contentions fully if you will take the trouble. If you believe that you do not now have a full control of the selection, go back over it and underline on its first appearance each word or expression that Veblen uses in a specialized sense. And as you underline, try to think of equivalent terms from your own active vocabulary—terms you commonly use.

9) Before you are through college your recognition vocabulary ought to increase enough so that you can read such writing as Veblen's without much trouble. But let us be clear about one matter in diction. The language could perhaps get along without "vicarious" or "fortuitous" or "ostensible," but not so well as with them. Though we ought to prefer the more common word when it serves as well as the less common, the most important thing is to say what we have to say with precision. If you will really consider, for instance, "vicarious," you will see that for some contexts there is no equivalent term. If one were writing for readers for whom the word is not available, then he would have to substitute for it a long expression. And he might not even then get the precision he could get for readers who know the word.

SUGGESTIONS FOR PAPERS

"I know not how it comes to pass," wrote Jonathan Swift, "that professors in most arts and sciences are generally the worst qualified to explain their meanings to those who are not of their tribe." Swift meant by "professors" those who profess specialized knowledge. Almost any writer, however, has occasion to explain things to readers who, by reason of age, education, or background, are not "of his tribe"; he needs to achieve "that simplicity without which no human performance can arrive to any great perfection."

The fault Swift remarks may often be the fault of professors in our modern sense of the word; it is also the besetting fault of student writers. In writing outside of schools, the very occasion for the writing may make the writer sufficiently aware of his readers. But if a student thinks of no occasion for writing but the due date of the paper, and of no reader but his instructor, he may not really direct his writing at all. One is tempted to say that some student writing is the only writing completely without purpose.

Indeed, we must recognize that there is a tendency toward artificiality in much college writing. In examinations, in term papers, and in reports a student's actual reader is his instructor. The student often reverses the ordinary writer and reader relationship, and writes for a reader who knows more about his subject than he does. The instructor's tendency is, naturally enough, to look for evidence of the student's knowledge and understanding and, if he finds it, not to consider matters of communication very closely. In this academic relationship it is quite possible for a student to pick up habits of writing that stand in his way when the writer-reader relationship is the ordinary one.

Of course the writing you do in a composition course is exercise writing and part of a discipline. But it will be profitable exercise only if you can assume a particular sort of readers, envisage them as a composite reader, and then adapt your writing to that composite reader. In your practice it will be well to assume usually that you are writing for a person of your own age and education, with experience like your own. But it is also very good practice in being clear to assume for some exercises a reader somewhat younger than yourself, or a reader whose experience or knowledge differs from yours in some important respect.

You can easily devise for yourself a profitable exercise toward this aim of really writing for readers and for a purpose. You know best what special interests and knowledge you have. But be sure you do assume a particular sort of readers; and in order to be sure, write a headnote for your paper indicating your intended readers—their age, education, background.

An equally profitable exercise in reader adaptation involves no sort of very specialized knowledge. What is most commonplace in your section of the United States, most typical of it, might be of most interest for readers in another section. For a paper discussing some sectional custom, activity, or condition, assume readers of your own age and level of education, but with little or no knowledge of your subject. Or discuss baseball or American football for English readers who have never seen it played. This exercise will require precision. Consider first how full a discussion is needed for your purpose and your readers.

Here are some suggestions for exercises closely related to the first three selections: (a) Restate the passage from Huxley quoted in question 12 following the Huxley selection for such readers as would find the original hard going. Of course you will have to be sure you understand it first. What, for instance, does Huxley mean by "For, as the astronomers discover in the earth no centre of the universe, but an eccentric speck . . ."? (b) Assume for your readers the present-day equivalent of the persons Huxley was addressing. Explain for them what a scientist does when he forms a hypothesis. Begin, as Huxley did in his discussion of scientific law, with an illustration from common life.[1] Then illustrate by reference to the nebular hypothesis. (c) Make question 12 following the selection from Kittredge into a written exercise. Assume as your reader a college freshman who has read and has before him the passage from Bassett's history, but who has no other information about New England witchcraft. Write an account of Kittredge's position. You need not be concerned to convince your reader, but merely to inform him. (d) Assume a reader who has come upon the passage from C. S. Lewis quoted in question 13 following the Lewis selection, and who says to you, "I still don't understand what is meant by the *Tao*." On the basis of your knowledge of our selection from *Mere Christianity* write a note that will help him understand.

And here is a suggestion for a paper generally related to the selection from *Witchcraft in Old and New England*. In his judgment of the witchcraft delusion, Kittredge is opposing opinions very widely received. You might try a paper intending to correct some prejudice or misapprehension. Choose some particular manifestation of racial prejudice—not the whole matter of racial prejudice nor even the prejudice against one race, but some one mistaken and unjust belief about a race. Or you might oppose some common slander of your own section of the country or some prejudice current in your section about another. Whatever subject you take, try to treat it with great clarity and simplicity—try to consider your readers as Kittredge considered his.

For an exercise in close connection with the selection from Veblen you might do a piece of restatement. Here is one suggestion: Write a formal summary, avoiding whenever you can Veblen's specialized diction. But some of the terms central to his contentions you will need to use—for instance, "conspicuous consumption" and "vicarious leisure." Treat them as Carl Becker treats the technical terms of Communism: put quotation marks around them on their first appearance in your summary, and see that the context makes them clear. You can get a considerable reduction. And perhaps you can do a piece of writing better adapted to some readers than the original is.

Or perhaps you would like to try a somewhat more interesting kind of restatement. You might assume that you are writing an article for one of

[1] Your illustration should be one in which a hypothesis is formed to cover and explain several phenomena. For instance, one might make up a little anecdote about a man who came home and found his ink spilled, books pulled from the lower shelves of his bookcases, and crayon marks on the walls, all less than three feet up. He would not *know* what had happened; his hypothesis might well be that his wife had left his little son unattended.

the women's magazines of mass circulation, an article with some such title as "Husbands and Wives in the Nineteenth Century." You have come to a portion of your article in which you wish to review Veblen's interpretation of the activities of the middle-class housewife in the late nineteenth century. Write an account of our selection to use as part of the article. You can do it in fewer than 500 words.

VII

Science for the General Reader

I n this chapter we concern ourselves with but one aspect of the writer and reader relationship we considered in the last. Even readers highly trained in one science cannot read highly technical writing in all the other sciences. The capable scientist who is also capable of writing for persons not specially trained in his field is a valuable person in our society; for the general understanding of science has by no means kept pace with its momentous developments.

i **ACCOUNTS OF WORK DONE**

A mediaeval writer, Alexander Neckam, tells a fable about a flying contest among the birds. The wren hid himself under the eagle's wing and, when the eagle had flown as high as he could, came forth and claimed the victory. Neckam goes on, "As the philosopher [Bernard of Chartres] says, 'We are all like dwarfs standing upon giants' shoulders.' We should therefore be careful to ascribe to our predecessors those things which we ought not to claim for our own glory, and not to follow the example of that wren which, with little or no effort of his own, claimed to have outdone the eagle."

One of the weaknesses of our education is that it leads those of us who are not scientists to think of science as something that belongs just to our generation. Of course we realize, when we consider, that most of what we know of ourselves and of our world has been brought together little by little by generations of our forebears. Here is a bit of scientific writing; you might, as you read it, guess at its date.

Truly the moon's orb is always whole and perfect, although it does not always shine equally. Every day the moon's light is waxing or waning four points through the sun's light. . . . We speak of the new moon according to the custom of men, but the moon is always the same, though its light often varies. . . . It happens sometimes when the moon runs on the same track that the sun runs, that its orb intercepts the sun's, so that the sun is all darkened and the stars appear as by night. This happens but seldom, and never but at new moons.

We have more information about the moon than this writer had, but this is a piece of scientific writing, a record of what has been observed and concluded—much modern scientific writing does what this tenth-century writer did.

Particularly the science textbook writer of our day resembles the writer of this tenth-century manual, who is abridging a work called *Of the Nature of Things* by the Venerable Bede (673–735). The writer of your science textbook gives you a summary account of the work of his predecessors—which may in itself be a great achievement. He intends that his readers become, at least in a limited fashion, geographers, say, or biologists. But you ought to keep remembering that you are reading an account of the work of many men—the most important may be mentioned incidentally—not in the order that they made their observations and formulated their principles, but in an order designed to relate the facts and principles to one another.

We use here an article of a different intention from that of the science textbook. It was first printed in an issue of the *Scientific American* devoted to reviewing the progress of science in the first half of our century. Like a textbook it is a summary account of previous work, but it has a historical order. And it intends, not to make its readers geneticists, but to make them understand what geneticists are, and what they have been doing. If you will use your dictionary, and if you will watch the technical terms as they are progressively defined in the article, you will have no difficulty.

Genetics (1950)

THEODOSIUS DOBZHANSKY

1 From the age of Galileo through the first half of the 20th century the scientific movement has been led by the physical sciences. These sciences still retain indisputable supremacy as wellsprings of technological progress. But in our age more and more of the intellectually and philosophically significant advances in knowledge appear in the realm of biology. Man's deepest urge, after all, is to understand himself and his place in the Universe—to fathom his own nature as a living organism and the interactions between heredity and environment that shape the development of his body and mind.

11 In this quest for self-understanding no investigation of the past 50 years has been more enlightening nor more dramatic than the study of heredity. The discovery of the basic laws of heredity is one of the major conquests of 20th-century science, and genetics has become a cornerstone of modern biology. Genetics, like nuclear physics, is peculiarly a science of our century. To be sure, its founder, the Austrian monk Gregor Mendel, reported his historic conclusions from his experiments with peas in 1865,

Reprinted with permission of *Scientific American*, September, 1950, Volume #183, No. 3.

but nobody then paid attention to them. It was in the year 1900 that Hugo de Vries in Holland, Karl Correns in Germany and E. von Tschermak in Austria rediscovered Mendel's findings and thereby initiated the growth of a new science. By then biology was prepared to appreciate the significance of Mendel's work, and from 1900 on the study of heredity developed very rapidly.

III Mendel's experiments were remarkably simple. He crossed varieties of peas that differed in clear-cut traits, such as the color or shape of their seeds, their flower colors and so on. He found that ancestral heredities do not mix or blend in the progeny, but reappear uncontaminated in the second generation of hybrids. When yellow peas were crossed with green peas, some of the descendants were yellow and some green, but none of a shade in between. Mendel concluded that heredity was controlled by discrete units or particles of living substance transmitted by both parents to their offspring and reassorted in each generation.

IV Later investigators named these units genes, from the Greek *genos,* meaning race or stock. But in 1900 it was far from clear that all heredity is transmitted by genes. There was, for instance, the case of mulattoes— hybrids whose skin color is intermediate between that of their Negro and white parents. Did this not argue for a blending of "bloods" rather than segregation of genes? Biologists found in nature all sorts of refractory cases whose inheritance seemed to defy explanation in terms of the gene theory. But one by one they were all explained. In the case of mulatto inheritance, the answer was that skin color is determined not by a single gene but by the interaction of many genes. In general every trait and tissue of the human organism develops under the joint influence of the whole constellation of genes and of the environment.

V If the organism was such a complicated product of heredity and environment, how could one even begin to distinguish between an individual's observable traits and his basic inheritance? In 1909 the Danish geneticist Wilhelm Johannsen proposed a distinction in terms which served to define the problem clearly. He suggested that the appearance and structure of an individual be called the phenotype, and that this be distinguished from the genotype, the endowment of genes inherited by the individual from his parents. The genotype determines how the developing individual will react to environment. The phenotype, say his size or stature, is the result of the interaction of the genotype with the environments the individual encounters during his lifetime.

VI The problem is to evaluate or measure the relative importance of genotype and environment in the formation of human phenotypes. This heredity *v.* environment question has fascinated biologists for half a century, but no generally convincing solution of the problem has yet emerged. The possibilities of experimentation with human beings obviously are severely limited. Almost the only way the question can be studied in the human realm is to observe the development of identical twins reared from early infancy in different environments. Horatio H. Newman of the University of Chicago and other investigators who have made studies of this kind have found that the normal environmental variations in an industrial civilization like that of the U. S. produce relatively little modification of physical traits, such as eye and hair colors, body build and the like. So we can conclude that variations in these traits are due mainly to genotypic differences. In the formation of psychic traits such as intelligence and temperament, however, environment plays a much more important role. We are still very far from understanding precisely how either heredity or environment influences these qualities, and during the next half-century genetics will certainly devote a great deal of attention to the problem—a problem of prime philosophical and sociological significance to mankind.

VII The investigation of the fundamental units of heredity—the genes —has made much greater progress; indeed these powerful particles have occupied the center of the geneticists' interest. The genes are extremely minute quantities of living matter, and they are transmitted from parents to offspring in sex cells which are themselves very small. The geneticist Hermann J. Muller, of Indiana University, has estimated that the egg cells from which the 2,200 million human beings now on the earth developed would about fit into a one-gallon pitcher, and the 2,200 million spermatozoa that fertilized them would occupy about the volume of an aspirin tablet. Within these cells the genes themselves—the bits of matter that account for the heredity of the entire human race—all together would make a small thimbleful. The powers of this hereditary substance are prodigious indeed!

VIII Almost from the start geneticists singled out the nuclei of sex cells for special study. As early as 1903 W. S. Sutton of Columbia University and Theodore Boveri in Germany concluded that the genes are carried in the chromosomes, the nuclear structures which are visible under the microscope and were already well known at that time. In 1911 Thomas Hunt Morgan, then at Columbia University, inferred that the genes are arranged in a linear file, or row, on the chromosomes. He set up this hypothesis in order to make sense of certain results of hybridization experiments which would otherwise have been incomprehensible. His hypothesis soon received further support. In genetics, as in science generally, one frequently learns more from the abnormal than from the normal—the exception often proves the rule. In this case the earliest validation of Morgan's theory came from studies of certain aberrant cases of inheritance in Drosophila flies that seemed to break all the rules. It was found that whenever a trait appeared to break the usual rules of inheritance, the chromosomes showed a deviation from their normal conformation or behavior that explained the seemingly irregular heredity. And *vice versa:* deviations in the chromosomes always forecast corresponding abnormalities in the phenotype.

IX As the result of experiments suggested by the linear hypothesis, Morgan and others were able to construct genetic "maps," showing the relative positions of the known genes, of the chromosomes of the fly *Drosophila melanogaster,* which became the organism most widely used for genetic research. More or less detailed maps of this sort now exist for several species of Drosophila flies, for corn and some other plants, for certain chromosomes of mice and poultry and for the sex chromosome in man.

x In 1933 and 1934 several investigators discovered a remarkably useful genetic material in the giant chromosomes in the salivary glands of the larvae of certain flies. Actually these chromosomes, like Mendel's laws, were a rediscovery: the extraordinary size of the salivary-gland chromosomes in a water midge, *Chironomus,* had been noticed by the Italian zoologist B. G. Balbiani as early as 1881. When, in the fullness of time, geneticists inspected the giant chromosomes closely under a microscope, they found them most revealing. In stained microscopic preparations these chromosomes appeared as cylinders or ribbons, composed of alternating dark and light disks. The patterns formed by these disks made it possible not only to distinguish the various chromosomes that a species possessed but also to recognize parts of the chromosomes. The linear arrangement of the disks suggested, and there now exists fairly convincing evidence to show, that each disk corresponds to a gene—though it would be incorrect to say that a disk *is* a gene.

xi Thus the gene was finally given a local habitation and a tangible existence—it was no longer some abstract unit of heredity; it was a material particle in a chromosome. . . .

xii Very early in the study of genetics biologists began to pay particular attention to the aberrations now known as mutations; this investigation was initiated by de Vries at the turn of the century and brilliantly developed by Morgan and his school from 1910 on. A gene, by definition, is a living particle that reproduces itself, and nearly always it does so exactly. But occasionally, probably under the influence of some outside agent, it forms an imperfect copy of itself. If this altered gene is able to reproduce itself in its new form, the result is a mutation, which is evidenced in a permanent change in some trait of the organism.

xiii Thus mutation is the antithesis of heredity. Heredity insures the basic continuity and coherence of the organic form; mutation creates a diversity of genes, and thereby is ultimately responsible for the great diversity of living beings on the earth. The mutation process, in short, supplies the building blocks of evolution. With this discovery, the biologists of the 20th century started to unravel the mechanisms of that evolutionary process which Jean Baptiste Lamarck, Charles Darwin and their successors of the 19th century had suggested but only dimly understood.

xiv The spontaneous mutations in nature that account for evolution occur relatively rarely. In 1927 Muller announced that the frequency of mutations could be greatly increased by exposing genes to X-rays. Since then it has been shown that the mutation rate can also be speeded up by other kinds of radiations, by high temperatures and by certain chemicals. But all these "mutagens" are nonspecific in their effects; they accelerate mutations in general, not exclusively in one particular gene or group of genes. Controlled mutation is a problem for the future.

xv Genetics is a fundamental or "theoretical" science; its value is before all else philosophical, in the sense that it strives to contribute toward man's understanding of the nature of life and of himself. Yet genetics will surely play a major role in the still infant technology of biological engineering. Already it has borne a huge harvest of "practical" results through improvements in breeds of food plants and animals. The development of hybrid corn in the U. S. has increased the average corn yield from 25.9 bushels per acre in 1932 to 36.5 bushels in 1946. In Sweden, with the aid of genetics, during the past half-century the average yield of winter wheat per hectare has been raised by 41 per cent, summer wheat 19 per cent, oats 9 per cent, barley 29 per cent and rye 19 per cent. In the field of medicine, the development of new strains of the mold *Penicillium* played a major part in making possible large-scale production of penicillin, and genetics steadily becomes more and more important as a tool for improvements in the prevention, diagnosis and treatment of many diseases.

xvi There remains the ultimate hope that genetics will point the way to improving the human species. Some of the early attempts to apply eugenics in the human realm were based more on enthusiasm than on understanding. But as our understanding of the genetics of human populations grows, the possibilities for useful application of our knowledge doubtless will multiply.

---

1) Is Professor Dobzhansky following Neckam's principle that we ought to ascribe to our predecessors what belongs to them? On what giant's shoulders do contemporary geneticists stand?

2) Here is an entry from *Webster's New Collegiate Dictionary:*

> *Mendel's law.* The law observed in the inheritance of many characters in animals and plants, discovered by Gregor J. Mendel (Austrian Augustinian abbot, 1822–84) in breeding experiments with peas. He showed that the height, color, and other characters depend on the presence of determining factors (*genes*) which behave as units, and that the second and later generations of crossbreeds exhibit these characters in all possible combinations, each combination in a definite proportion of individuals.[1]

Read the entry in connection with iii. Just what does iii do for the reader that the dictionary entry does not do? (We might here review a bit: exactly what does "law" mean in this context?)

3) How many scientific terms are defined in the course of paragraphs iv–vii? How many times did you have to use your dictionary? What is the derivation of "chromosome" (viii)?

4) Why would fruit flies be especially convenient and important in the work of the geneticist?

5) We have dealt with the term "hypothesis" before. How do you define it? Why is "inferred" in "inferred that the genes are arranged in a

---

[1] By permission. From *Webster's New Collegiate Dictionary,* copyright, 1949, 1951, 1953, by G. & C. Merriam Co.

linear file" a proper word to describe the mental process in a hypothesis? What does "support" for a hypothesis consist of?

6) What exactly does the first sentence in XIII mean? What is the derivation of "mutation"?

7) What dramatic and horrible possibilities of mutation have you heard about in connection with atomic explosions? If you are a science fiction addict you have read a number of stories about mutation (or perhaps better to say, the same story in a number of forms). Does this article make these stories (or this story) more or less convincing to you?

8) In xv both "theoretical" and "practical" appear in quotation marks. What implication is made by putting quotation marks around these words? What is the implication of the expression "the still infant technology of biological engineering"? (Note that the word "science" seems to be here avoided. Is some distinction implied?) Do you know any further instances of the "practical" value of genetics?

9) Consider the implications of the last paragraph. Do you think them altogether happy? If the findings of genetics are applied in the "human realm," who applies them? What questions, beyond specifically scientific questions, might arise?

10) Does not this article suggest a number of considerations about our intellectual history? It is clear that the importance of Gregor Mendel went unrecognized in his time. Is it probable that we recognize all the most important persons of ours? Do you know any instances in literary history in which the recognition of greatness was much delayed? (Two American writers whose work is used in this book, Melville and Thoreau, are instances, and there are others.)

11) A little thought about this article suggests that much of what has been commonly said about evolution, and about heredity and environment, has been said on the basis of doubtful assumptions. May we say that one index of an educated person is a certain caution about assumptions? How much knowledge of genetics ought a sociologist to have?

12) We come finally to the technique of writing in this article. One thing about it is so obvious that it may be easily overlooked: Professor Dobzhansky does not feel impelled to use all his knowledge at once. His special scientific interest is the relationship between genetics and the study of evolution—how much of this article is given to it? Students very often have to learn to use just the material that is appropriate to a present purpose.

13) And all of us know the writer or the teacher who, knowing his subject well, still partially fails to inform. How is this special subject matter adapted for general readers? One of the ways you have doubtless already observed: the skill with which definitions of new terms are tucked into a paragraph—sometimes into a sentence—without clogging it. Have you also noted a graceful handling of metaphor when metaphor is appropriate? There is, for instance, "the whole constellation of genes" in IV. What others do you find?

14) Then there is a consideration about the pattern of this article. The writer has to do two things: he must keep scientific relationships clear; he must show the progress of research and discovery. Notice the time tran-

sitions, which come within paragraphs as frequently as they do at the beginnings. (For instance, you find in the middle of x, "When, in the fullness of time, geneticists inspected . . ." What other such time transition
do you find?) The pattern is fundamentally narrative; the trick, of course,
is to prevent explanations from clogging the narrative. After the first, introductory, paragraph, is there any paragraph in which the "story" does
not move forward?

15) What do you infer about the writer's education—is it exclusively
scientific?

_____

For the writers in this section we really need a new term. As they function in our selections, they are perhaps "popular scientific writers," in so
far as they adapt their treatment of their subjects to persons with no training in them. But if the term has for you associations with the Sunday supplement and the mass magazine, it will be an inadequate and misleading
term. Our next selection is by Rachel Carson, a distinguished scientist and
an effective and much-read writer. As you read the selection you would do
well to consider what qualities of her writing account for the pleasure—
even the excitement—with which thousands of persons have read her
book.

FROM   *The Sea Around Us* (1951)

RACHEL L. CARSON

The Moving Tides

In every country the moon keeps ever the rule of alliance
with the sea which it once for all has agreed upon.

THE VENERABLE BEDE

I There is no drop of water in the ocean, not even in the deepest parts of
the abyss, that does not know and respond to the mysterious forces that
create the tide. No other force that affects the sea is so strong. Compared
with the tide the wind-created waves are surface movements felt, at most,
no more than a hundred fathoms below the surface. So, despite their impressive sweep, are the planetary currents, which seldom involve more
than the upper several hundred fathoms. The masses of water affected by
the tidal movement are enormous, as will be clear from one example. Into
one small bay on the east coast of North America—Passamaquoddy—2
billion tons of water are carried by the tidal currents twice each day; into
the whole Bay of Fundy, 100 billion tons.

II Here and there we find dramatic illustration of the fact that the tides
affect the whole ocean, from its surface to its floor. The meeting of opposing tidal currents in the Strait of Messina creates whirlpools (one of them

is Charybdis of classical fame) which so deeply stir the waters of the strait that fish bearing all the marks of abyssal existence, their eyes atrophied or abnormally large, their bodies studded with phosphorescent organs, frequently are cast up on the lighthouse beach, and the whole area yields a rich collection of deep-sea fauna for the Institute of Marine Biology at Messina.

III The tides are a response of the mobile waters of the ocean to the pull of the moon and the more distant sun. In theory, there is a gravitational attraction between every drop of sea water and even the outermost star of the universe. In practice, however, the pull of the remote stars is so slight as to be obliterated in the vaster movements by which the ocean yields to the moon and the sun. Anyone who has lived near tidewater knows that the moon, far more than the sun, controls the tides. He has noticed that, just as the moon rises later each day by fifty minutes, on the average, than the day before, so, in most places, the time of high tide is correspondingly later each day. And as the moon waxes and wanes in its monthly cycle, so the height of the tide varies. Twice each month, when the moon is a mere thread of silver in the sky, and again when it is full, we have the highest of the high tides, called the springs. At these times sun, moon, and earth are directly in line and the pull of the two heavenly bodies is added together to bring the water high on the beaches, and send its surf leaping upward against the sea cliffs, and draw a brimming tide into the harbors so that the boats float high beside their wharfs. And twice each month, at the quarters of the moon, when sun, moon, and earth lie at the apexes of a triangle, and the pull of sun and moon are opposed, we have the least tides of the lunar month, called the neaps.

IV That the sun, with a mass 27 million times that of the moon, should have less influence over the tides than a small satellite of the earth is at first surprising. But in the mechanics of the universe, nearness counts for more than distant mass, and when all the mathematical calculations have been made we find that the moon's power over the tides is more than twice that of the sun.

V The tides are enormously more complicated than all this would suggest. The influence of sun and moon is constantly changing, varying with the phases of the moon, with the distance of moon and sun from the earth, and with the position of each to north or south of the equator. They are complicated further by the fact that every body of water, whether natural or artificial, has its own period of oscillation. Disturb its waters and they will move with a seesaw or rocking motion, with the most pronounced movement at the ends of the container, the least motion at the center. Tidal scientists now believe that the ocean contains a number of 'basins,' each with its own period of oscillation determined by its length and depth. The disturbance that sets the water in motion is the attracting force of the moon and sun. But the kind of motion, that is, the period of the swing of the water, depends upon the physical dimensions of the basin. What this means in terms of actual tides we shall presently see.

VI The tides present a striking paradox, and the essence of it is this: the force that sets them in motion is cosmic, lying wholly outside the earth and presumably acting impartially on all parts of the globe, but the nature of the tide at any particular place is a local matter, with astonishing differences occurring within a very short geographic distance. When we spend a long summer holiday at the seashore we may become aware that the tide in our cove behaves very differently from that at a friend's place twenty miles up the coast, and is strikingly different from what we may have known in some other locality. If we are summering on Nantucket Island our boating and swimming will be little disturbed by the tides, for the range between high water and low is only about a foot or two. But if we choose to vacation near the upper part of the Bay of Fundy, we must accommodate ourselves to a rise and fall of 40 to 50 feet, although both places are included within the same body of water—the Gulf of Maine. Or if we spend our holiday on Chesapeake Bay we may find that the time of high water each day varies by as much as 12 hours in different places on the shores of the same bay.

VII The truth of the matter is that local topography is all-important in determining the features that to our minds make 'the tide.' The attractive force of the heavenly bodies sets the water in motion, but how, and how far, and how strongly it will rise depend on such things as the slope of the bottom, the depth of a channel, or the width of a bay's entrance.

VIII The United States Coast and Geodetic Survey has a remarkable, robotlike machine with which it can predict the time and height of the tide on any past or future date, for any part of the world, on one essential condition. This is that at some time local observations must have been made to show how the topographic features of the place modify and direct the tidal movements.

IX Perhaps the most striking differences are in the range of tide, which varies tremendously in different parts of the world, so that what the inhabitants of one place might consider disastrously high water might be regarded as no tide at all by coastal communities only a hundred miles distant. The highest tides in the world occur in the Bay of Fundy, with a rise of about 50 feet in Minas Basin near the head of the Bay at the spring tides. At least half a dozen other places scattered around the world have a tidal range of more than 30 feet—Puerto Gallegos in Argentina and Cook Inlet in Alaska, Frobisher Bay in Davis Strait, the Koksoak River emptying into Hudson Strait, and the Bay of St. Malo in France come to mind. At many other places 'high tide' may mean a rise of only a foot or so, perhaps only a few inches. The tides of Tahiti rise and fall in a gentle movement, with a difference of no more than a foot between high water and low. On most oceanic islands the range of the tide is slight. But it is never safe to generalize about the kinds of places that have high or low tides, because two areas that are not far apart may respond in very different ways to the tide-producing forces. At the eastern end of the Panama Canal the tidal range is not more than 1 or 2 feet, but at the Pacific end, only 40 miles away, the range is 12 to 16 feet. The Sea of Okhotsk is another example of the way the height of the tide varies. Throughout much of the Sea the tides are moderate—only about 2 feet—but in some parts of the Sea there is a

10-foot rise, and at the head of one of its arms—the Gulf of Penjinsk—the rise is 37 feet.

x What is it about one place that will bring 40 or 50 feet of water ri ing about its shores, while at another place, lying under the same moon an sun, the tide will rise only a few inches? What, for example, can be the explanation of the great tides on the Bay of Fundy, while only a few hundred miles away at Nantucket Island, on the shores of the same ocean, the tide range is little more than a foot?

xi The modern theory of tidal oscillation seems to offer the best explanation of such local differences—the rocking up and down of water in each natural basin about a central, virtually tideless node. Nantucket is located near the node of its basin, where there is little motion, hence a small tide range. Passing northeastward along the shores of this basin, we find the tides becoming progressively higher, with a 6-foot range at Nauset Harbor on Cape Cod, 8.9 feet at Gloucester, 15.7 feet at West Quoddy Head, 20.9 feet at St. John, and 39.4 feet at Folly Point. The Nova Scotia shore of the Bay of Fundy has somewhat higher tides than the corresponding points on the New Brunswick shore, and the highest tides of all are in Minas Basin at the head of the Bay. The immense movements of water in the Bay of Fundy result from a combination of circumstances. The Bay lies at the end of an oscillating basin. Furthermore, the natural period of oscillation of the basin is approximately 12 hours. This very nearly coincides with the period of the ocean tide. Therefore the water movement within the bay is sustained and enormously increased by the ocean tide. The narrowing and shallowing of the bay in its upper reaches, compelling the huge masses of water to crowd into a constantly diminishing area, also contribute to the great heights of the Fundy tides.

xii The tidal rhythms, as well as the range of tide, vary from ocean to ocean. Flood tide and ebb succeed each other around the world, as night follows day, but as to whether there shall be two high tides and two low in each lunar day, or only one, there is no unvarying rule. To those who know best the Atlantic Ocean—either its eastern or western shores—the rhythm of two high tides and two low tides in each day seems 'normal.' Here, on each flood tide, the water advances about as far as on the preceding high; and succeeding ebb tides fall about equally low. But in that great inland sea of the Atlantic, the Gulf of Mexico, a different rhythm prevails around most of its borders. At best the tidal rise here is but a slight movement, of no more than a foot or two. At certain places on the shores of the Gulf it is a long, deliberate undulation—one rise and one fall in the lunar day of 24 hours plus 50 minutes—resembling the untroubled breathing of that earth monster to whom the ancients attributed all tides. This 'diurnal rhythm' is found in scattered places about the earth—such as at Saint Michael, Alaska, and at Do Son in French Indo-China—as well as in the Gulf of Mexico. By far the greater part of the world's coasts—most of the Pacific basin and the shores of the Indian Ocean—display a mixture of the diurnal and semidiurnal types of tide. There are two high and two low tides in a day, but the succeeding floods may be so unequal that the second scarcely rises to mean sea level; or it may be the ebb tides that are of extreme inequality.

XIII There seems to be no simple explanation of why some parts of the ocean should respond to the pull of sun and moon with one rhythm and other parts with another, although the matter is perfectly clear to tidal scientists on the basis of mathematical calculations. To gain some inkling of the reasons, we must recall the many separate components of the tide-producing force, which in turn result from the changing relative positions of sun, moon, and earth. Depending on local geographic features, every part of earth and sea, while affected in some degree by each component, is more responsive to some than to others. Presumably the shape and depths of the Atlantic basin cause it to respond most strongly to the forces that produce a semidiurnal rhythm. The Pacific and Indian oceans, on the other hand, are affected by both the diurnal and semidiurnal forces, and a mixed tide results.

XIV The island of Tahiti is a classic example of the way even a small area may react to one of the tide-producing forces to the virtual exclusion of the others. On Tahiti, it is sometimes said, you can tell the time of day by looking out at the beach and noticing the stage of the tide. This is not strictly true, but the legend has a certain basis. With slight variations, high tide occurs at noon and at midnight; low water, at six o'clock morning and evening. The tides thus ignore the effect of the moon, which is to advance the time of the tides by 50 minutes each day. Why should the tides of Tahiti follow the sun instead of the moon? The most favored explanation is that the island lies at the axis or node of one of the basins set in oscillation by the moon. There is very little motion in response to the moon at this point, and the waters are therefore free to move in the rhythm induced by the sun.

XV If the history of the earth's tides should one day be written by some observer of the universe, it would no doubt be said that they reached their greatest grandeur and power in the younger days of Earth, and that they slowly grew feebler and less imposing until one day they ceased to be. For the tides were not always as they are today, and as with all that is earthly, their days are numbered.

XVI In the days when the earth was young, the coming in of the tide must have been a stupendous event. If the moon was, as we have supposed in an earlier chapter, formed by the tearing away of a part of the outer crust of the earth, it must have remained for a time very close to its parent. Its present position is the consequence of being pushed farther and farther away from the earth for some 2 billion years. When it was half its present distance from the earth, its power over the ocean tides was eight times as great as now, and the tidal range may even then have been several hundred feet on certain shores. But when the earth was only a few million years old, assuming that the deep ocean basins were then formed, the sweep of the tides must have been beyond all comprehension. Twice each day, the fury of the incoming waters would inundate all the margins of the continents. The range of the surf must have been enormously extended by the reach of the tides, so that the waves would batter the crests of high cliffs and sweep inland to erode the continents. The fury of such tides would contribute not a little to the general bleakness and grimness and un-inhabitability of the young earth.

XVII Under such conditions, no living thing could exist on the shores or pass beyond them, and, had conditions not changed, it is reasonable to suppose that life would have evolved no further than the fishes. But over the millions of years the moon has receded, driven away by the friction of the tides it creates. The very movement of the water over the bed of the ocean, over the shallow edges of the continents, and over the inland seas carries within itself the power that is slowly destroying the tides, for tidal friction is gradually slowing down the rotation of the earth. In those early days we have spoken of, it took the earth a much shorter time—perhaps only about 4 hours—to make a complete rotation on its axis. Since then, the spinning of the globe has been so greatly slowed that a rotation now re-quires, as everyone knows, about 24 hours. This retarding will continue, according to mathematicians, until the day is about 50 times as long as it is now.

XVIII And all the while the tidal friction will be exerting a second effect, pushing the moon farther away, just as it has already pushed it out more than 200,000 miles. As the moon recedes, it will, of course, have less power over the tides and they will grow weaker. It will also take the moon longer to complete its orbit around the earth. When finally the length of the day and of the month coincide, the moon will no longer rotate rela-tively to the earth, and there will be no lunar tides.

XIX All this, of course, will require time on a scale the mind finds it difficult to conceive, and before it happens it is quite probable that the hu-man race will have vanished from the earth. This may seem, then, like a Wellsian fantasy of a world so remote that we may dismiss it from our thoughts. But already, even in our alloted fraction of earthly time, we can see some of the effects of these cosmic processes. Our day is believed to be several seconds longer than that of Babylonian times. Britain's Astronomer Royal recently called the attention of the American Philosophical Society to the fact that the world will soon have to choose between two kinds of time. The tide-induced lengthening of the day has already complicated the problems of human systems of keeping time. Conventional clocks, geared to the earth's rotation, do not show the effect of the lengthening days. New atomic clocks now being constructed will show actual time and will differ from other clocks.

XX Although the tides have become tamer, and their range is now meas-ured in tens instead of hundreds of feet, mariners are nevertheless greatly concerned not only with the stages of the tide and the set of the tidal cur-rents, but with the many violent movements and disturbances of the sea that are indirectly related to the tides. Nothing the human mind has in-vented can tame a tide rip or control the rhythm of the water's ebb and flow, and the most modern instruments cannot carry a vessel over a shoal until the tide has brought a sufficient depth of water over it. Even the

Queen Mary waits for slack water to come to her pier in New York; otherwise the set of the tidal current might swing her against the pier with enough force to crush it. On the Bay of Fundy, because of the great range of tide, harbor activities follow a pattern as rhythmic as the tides themselves, for vessels can come to the docks to take on or discharge cargo during only a few hours on each tide, leaving promptly to avoid being stranded in mud at low water.

THE INVESTIGATIVE PROCESS   *ii*

In this section we turn to some pieces of scientific writing in which observations and ideas new at the time of writing are recorded. Our first selections are from a classic, perhaps in science, certainly in literature: Gilbert White's *The Natural History of Selborne* (1789). White, an English country clergyman, was a field naturalist, one of a number of important amateurs in the history of science. His book has had a curious interest for discriminating persons, even for persons with only a very moderate interest in his subjects. White is an excellent writer; he has none of the repellent sort of sentimentality of some "nature writers" and none of the professional dullness of some scholars. And his work will serve to remind us that all science starts with observation, that unless the observation is good, all else is useless. His observations were limited to a small field, the parish of Selborne, and he gave them the form of letters to two naturalist friends.[1]

FROM *The Natural History of Selborne* (1789)

GILBERT WHITE

[i]

[Bird Migration]

I If ever I saw anything like actual migration, it was last Michaelmas Day. I was travelling, and out early in the morning: at first there was a vast fog; but, by the time that I was got seven or eight miles from home towards the coast, the sun broke out into a delicate warm day. We were then on a large heath or common, and I could discern, as the mist began to break away, great numbers of swallows (*Hirundines rusticæ*) clustering on the stunted shrubs and bushes, as if they had roosted there all night. As soon as the air became clear and pleasant they were all on the wing at once; and, by a placid and easy flight, proceeded on southward towards the sea: after this I did not see any more flocks, only now and then a straggler.

II I cannot agree with those persons that assert that the swallow kind disappear some and some gradually, as they come, for the bulk of them seem to withdraw at once; only some stragglers stay behind a long while, and do never, there is the greatest reason to believe, leave this island. Swallows seem to lay themselves up, and to come forth in a warm day, as bats

[1] The selections here are these: from the letters to Thomas Pennant, part of XXIII; from the letters to Daines Barrington, XI, XXXV, and part of LVI.

do continually of a warm evening, after they have disappeared for weeks. For a very respectable gentleman assured me that, as he was walking with some friends under Merton wall on a remarkably hot noon, either in the last week in December or the first week in January, he espied three or four swallows huddled together on the moulding of one of the windows of that college. I have frequently remarked that swallows are seen later at Oxford than elsewhere; is it owing to the vast massy building of that place, to the many waters round it, or to what else?

III When I used to rise in the morning last autumn, and see the swallows and martins clustering on the chimneys and thatch of the neighbouring cottages, I could not help being touched with a secret delight, mixed with some degree of mortification: with delight, to observe with how much ardour and punctuality those poor little birds obeyed the strong impulse towards migration, or hiding, imprinted on their minds by their great Creator; and with some degree of mortification, when I reflected that, after all our pains and inquiries, we are yet not quite certain to what regions they do migrate; and are still farther embarrassed to find that some do not actually migrate at all.

[ii]

[The Flocking of Birds]

I When I ride about in the winter, and see such prodigious flocks of various kinds of birds, I cannot help admiring at these congregations, and wishing that it was in my power to account for those appearances almost peculiar to the season. The two great motives which regulate the proceedings of the brute creation are love and hunger; the former incites animals to perpetuate their kind; the latter induces them to preserve individuals: whether either of these should seem to be the ruling passion in the matter of congregating is to be considered. As to love, that is out of the question at a time of the year when that soft passion is not indulged: besides, during the amorous season, such a jealousy prevails between the male birds that they can hardly bear to be together in the same hedge or field. Most of the singing and elation of spirits of that time seem to me to be the effect of rivalry and emulation: and it is to this spirit of jealousy that I chiefly attribute the equal dispersion of birds in the spring over the face of the country.

II Now as to the business of food: as these animals are actuated by instinct to hunt for necessary food, they should not, one would suppose, crowd together in pursuit of sustenance at a time when it is most likely to fail; yet such associations do take place in hard weather chiefly, and thicken as the severity increases. As some kind of self-interest and self-defence is no doubt the motive for the proceeding, may it not arise from the helplessness of their state in such rigorous seasons; as men crowd together, when under great calamities, though they know not why? Perhaps approximation may dispel some degree of cold; and a crowd may make each individual appear safer from the ravages of birds of prey and other dangers.

III If I admire when I see how much congenerous birds love to congregate, I am the more struck when I see incongruous ones in such strict amity. If we do not much wonder to see a flock of rooks usually attended by a train of daws, yet it is strange that the former should so frequently have a flight of starlings for their satellites. Is it because rooks have a more discerning scent than their attendants, and can lead them to spots more productive of food? Anatomists say that rooks, by reason of two large nerves which run down between the eyes into the upper mandible, have a more delicate feeling in their beaks than other round-billed birds, and can grope for their meat when out of sight. Perhaps, then, their associates attend them on the motive of interest, as greyhounds wait on the motions of their finders; and as lions are said to do on the yelpings of jackals. Lapwings and starlings sometimes associate.

[iii]

[Earthworms]

1 Lands that are subject to frequent inundations are always poor; and probably the reason may be because the worms are drowned. The most insignificant insects and reptiles are of much more consequence, and have much more influence in the economy of Nature, than the incurious are aware of; and are mighty in their effect, from their minuteness, which renders them less an object of attention, and from their numbers and fecundity. Earthworms, though in appearance a small and despicable link in the chain of Nature, yet, if lost, would make a lamentable chasm. For to say nothing of half the birds, and some quadrupeds, which are almost entirely supported by them, worms seem to be the great promoters of vegetation, which would proceed but lamely without them, by boring, perforating, and loosening the soil, and rendering it pervious to rains and fibres of plants, by drawing straws and stalks of leaves and twigs into it; and, most of all, by throwing up such infinite numbers of lumps of earth called wormcasts, which, being their excrement, is a fine manure for grain and grass. Worms probably provide new soil for hills and slopes where the rain washes the earth away; and they affect slopes, probably to avoid being flooded. Gardeners and farmers express their detestation of worms; the former because they render their walks unsightly, and make them much work; and the latter because, as they think, worms eat their green corn. But these men would find that the earth without worms would soon become cold, hardbound, and void of fermentation, and consequently sterile; and besides, in favour of worms, it should be hinted that green corn, plants, and flowers, are not so much injured by them as by many species of *coleoptera* (scarabs), and *tipulæ* (long-legs) in their larva, or grub-state; and by unnoticed myriads of small shell-less snails, called slugs, which silently and imperceptibly make amazing havoc in the field and garden.[1]

[1] Farmer Young, of Norton Farm, says, that this spring (1777) about four acres of his wheat in one field were entirely destroyed by slugs, which swarmed on the blades of corn, and devoured it as fast as it sprang.

II These hints we think proper to throw out in order to set the inquisitive and discerning to work.

III A good monography of worms would afford much entertainment and information at the same time, and would open a large and new field in natural history. Worms work most in the spring; but by no means lie torpid in the dead months: are out every mild night in the winter, as any person may be convinced that will take the pains to examine his grassplots with a candle; are hermaphrodites, and much addicted to venery, and consequently very prolific.

[iv]
[Instinct]

I They who write on natural history cannot too frequently advert to instinct, that wonderful limited faculty, which in some instances raises the brute creation, as it were, above reason, and in others leaves them so far below it. Philosophers have defined instinct to be that secret influence by which every species is compelled naturally to pursue, at all times, the same way or track, without any teaching or example; whereas reason, without instruction, would often vary and do that by many methods which instinct effects by one alone. Now this maxim must be taken in a qualified sense; for there are instances in which instinct does vary and conform to the circumstances of place and convenience.

II It has been remarked that every species of bird has a mode of nidification peculiar to itself, so that a schoolboy would at once pronounce on the sort of nest before him. This is the case among fields and woods and wilds; but in the villages round London, where mosses and gossamer, and cotton from vegetables, are hardly to be found, the nest of the chaffinch has not that elegant finished appearance, nor is it so beautifully studded with lichens, as in a more rural district; and the wren is obliged to construct its house with straws and dry grasses, which do not give it that rotundity and compactness so remarkable in the edifices of that little architect. Again, the regular nest of the house-martin is hemispheric; but where a rafter, or a joist, or a cornice may happen to stand in the way, the nest is so contrived as to conform to the obstruction, and becomes flat, or compressed.

III In the following instances instinct is perfectly uniform and consistent. There are three creatures, the squirrel, the field-mouse and the bird called the nut-hatch (*Sitta Europœa*), which live much on hazel-nut; and yet they open them each in a different way. The first, after rasping off the small end, splits the shell in two with his long fore-teeth, as a man does with his knife; the second nibbles a hole with his teeth, so regular as if drilled with a wimble [gimlet], and yet so small that one could wonder how the kernel can be extracted through it; while the last picks an irregular ragged hole with its bill: but as this artist has no paws to hold the nut firm while he pierces it, like an adroit workman, he fixes it, as it were in a vice, in some cleft of a tree, or in some crevice; when, standing over it, he perforates the stubborn shell. We have often placed nuts in the chink of a gate-post, where nut-hatches have been known to haunt, and have always found that those birds have readily penetrated them. While at work they make a rapping noise that may be heard at a considerable distance.

---

1) One who thinks we "always knew" about the migration of birds may find what White says surprising, for he wrote in a time when most of the facts of migration were still in doubt. White tended to believe in migration; one of his correspondents had published an argument against it. Paragraph 11 of "Bird Migration" refers obliquely to a theory of hibernation of birds. The establishment of the facts of migration depended almost entirely upon observation. Would you have supposed that the matter was in doubt as late as the end of the eighteenth century?

2) An editor of *The Natural History of Selborne,* James Fisher, points out that both in the suggestion of psychological motives for the congregating of birds, and in the suggestion that birds hold territories, White predicts the direction of much later investigation. Fisher also points out that White was misled if he believed that rooks had a keener sense of smell than other birds.

3) For a long time after the work of Charles Darwin on evolution, men were preoccupied with the idea of the struggle for existence in nature. White's work sometimes reminds us of a more recent concern with cooperation and community in nature.

4) In "Earthworms," 11 and the first sentence of 111 have a curious sort of interest. Charles Darwin's *The Formation of Vegetable Mould, through the Action of Worms* was published a little more than a century after White wrote. It was the first thorough treatment of the matter. Fisher points out that, although Darwin did not quote the letter, he must have known it.

5) A relatively new science, ecology, deals with what White calls in 1 "the economy of Nature." It concerns itself with the relationships between organisms and their environment. Since man is always for his own purposes disturbing what is known as "the balance of nature"—often, as it turns out, to his own detriment—he needs to understand it.

6) The distinction between instinct and reason is still not a clear distinction. Notice that it is White's own observation that keeps him from accepting entirely the facile philosophical definition recorded in "Instinct."

7) Perhaps it was the minuteness of the observation that you found most striking when you read this passage. Yet White's observation has surely been equaled often; it is his writing that has preserved his work. You can distinguish two sorts of excellence here. One is economy of description. The other great excellence is in structure. You would do well to analyze the organization of the whole piece, and to consider the structure of sentences, especially the second in 11 and the third in 111.

8) You probably did not see any attempt on White's part at "originality" or "self-expression" in our selections. And yet you probably were quite aware of White as a person. There is a good deal of evidence that a fresh,

individual style does not come from trying for *it,* but rather from trying to say with great clarity just what one has to say.

Gilbert White, as we have seen, had some prophetic realization of the science of ecology. And in one of his letters he says:

A full history of noxious insects hurtful in the field, garden, and house, suggesting all the known and likely means of destroying them, would be allowed by the public to be a most useful and important work. What knowledge there is of this sort lies scattered, and wants to be collected; great improvements would soon follow of course. A knowledge of the properties, economy, propagation, and, in short, of the life and conservation of these animals, is a necessary step to lead us to some method of preventing their depredations.

Our next selection gives us some notion of the science of ecology, and suggests to us what the full history of an insect might be. As the writers say in the course of their article, it is impossible to study the ecological system entire. The article is important for its illustrative discussion of a particular problem as it is related to a general concept. There may well be readers for whom the particular problem is itself vitally interesting and important; nevertheless it is here presented as a specimen problem in ecological research.

Insect Control and the Balance of Nature (1954)

RAY F. SMITH and WILLIAM W. ALLEN

I The activities of man are continually making changes in what has so inappropriately been called "the balance of nature." He has cleared the forest, plowed the plain, changed the courses of rivers, bred new plants and animals, introduced plants and animals into new areas, protected some from competition and provided others with new foods on which to flourish. For instance, the Colorado potato beetle, once an insignificant insect feeding on wild herbs in the Rocky Mountain region, has grown abundant on the cultivated potato.

II Even in the absence of man, however, the balance of nature is a dynamic and ever-changing system. The relative numbers of the various kinds of plants and animals in the simplest natural community fluctuate constantly in accord with a complex web of interactions that ties them together. Under normal conditions the system as a whole tends to be self-regulating. Such factors as parasites, predators, disease, food supply and the competition for shelter keep any one organism from upsetting the balance. If man is to make a move that will shift the balance in his favor, he must understand all of the ramifications of the system.

Reprinted with permission of *Scientific American,* June, 1954, Volume #190, No. 6.

III Thus control of insect pests cannot be assured simply by inventing new and more potent insecticides. Our spectacular new chemical weapons have added immeasurably to the welfare of mankind. But they have also created new problems of their own; witness the phenomenal increase of destructive mites that has followed the slaughter of their insect enemies with DDT and other new insecticides, and the rise of new strains of insects resistant to the poisons. Chemical control is at best temporary. If we are to escape this ever tightening spiral of more complex problems and ever increasing costs of control, then we must integrate chemical control with the natural factors influencing populations.

IV For progress in this direction in recent years we are indebted to the science of ecology. This is the study of the interrelationships of organisms and their environment. We shall here recount such a study of an insect, carried out during the past 15 years in California, which will illustrate how complex these relationships can be. The insect is the orange alfalfa caterpillar, *Colias philodice eurytheme.*

V In its adult form the insect is the common orange and yellow butterfly seen flitting about alfalfa and clover fields in summer. In alfalfa-growing sections of the country the butterflies often are so abundant that they clog the radiator grills of automobiles. The female lays tiny, cigar-shaped eggs on the leaves of young alfalfa. In summer the eggs hatch in about three days; in cooler seasons they take up to 10 days or more. After hatching, the tiny caterpillar eats its eggshell and then begins to feed on young alfalfa leaves. Three days later it makes its first molt; it sheds its skin four times before it is fully grown. After each molt the caterpillar and its appetite increase in size. By the time it is full-grown it may consume more than a dozen leaves a day. After about 12 days (in hot weather) the caterpillar descends to the base of the plant to pupate. Five or six days later the beautiful butterfly emerges.

VI During the summer it has two peaks of activity each day. It spends the night near the base of the plant. After sunrise it crawls up the plant and turns its body to receive the maximum radiation from the sun. After its body temperature has warmed up to the necessary level, it takes off in flight. It feeds on flower nectar and stops from time to time to lay eggs. During the heat of midday it siestas in the cool alfalfa or on the moist soil. Then in the afternoon it goes forth again to flit about until the sun sinks.

VII The males spend most of their time seeking young females; the latter mate just after they have emerged from the pupal state. After mating, the female leaves the field in which it developed. To provide its young with proper food, it always lays its eggs on a young, succulent legume. This remarkable adaptation, originally evolved for survival on wild plants, stands the insect in excellent stead in alfalfa fields. Its eggs are laid only on very young alfalfa shoots; as a result the caterpillars can complete their development before the hay is cut.

VIII Because females concentrate for egg-laying in recently cut fields where a new crop is beginning to leaf out, alfalfa fields can be classified according to the stage of development of their caterpillars. First is the egg-laying stage, when the alfalfa is short; the field is populated mainly by egg-laying females. In the second stage, when the alfalfa is less than a third grown, its population is mainly tiny larvae. In the third, when the alfalfa is about half grown and the larvae are bigger, it becomes possible to predict how much damage the population will do and to decide on preventive measures. In the fourth stage, the larvae do much damage to the maturing alfalfa. In the fifth, when the alfalfa is mature or nearly so, the field is full of pupae and butterflies, about three fourths of which are males. Any caterpillars that have not become butterflies when the field is mowed are out of luck—they die in the hot sun.

ix The critical requirements of the alfalfa caterpillar probably are: (1) a sufficient concentration of suitable legumes, (2) a period of warm weather long enough for the development of at least one generation, and (3) suitable places for survival during the unfavorable times of the year. These broad requirements can be met in many different ways, and the alfalfa caterpillar is therefore widespread in the U. S. Its range changes with the seasons and the year-to-year fluctuations in the weather; for example, the butterflies migrate north in the spring and invade desert areas when rains produce legumes there. In the past few decades the alfalfa caterpillar has expanded tremendously in the Eastern U. S. since Eastern farmers began to lime the soil and grow alfalfa.

x A single female butterfly can lay as many as 1,500 eggs. We would soon be smothered by alfalfa caterpillars but for a complex of natural control factors which we do not yet completely understand. The abundance of this insect, like that of any other organism, depends on natality and mortality. These in turn are determined by a complex system of ecological relationships which we call an ecosystem. The ecosystem includes the influences and relationships of all the living and non-living parts of the environment, among which must be counted food supply, weather, natural enemies and the caterpillar population itself. Because of its great complexity it is difficult, if not impossible, to study an ecosystem per se. However, we can study a particular kind of organism in its relationships to the ecosystem. Such a study has revealed some of the factors influencing the abundance of the alfalfa caterpillar.

xi When the alfalfa caterpillar was first discovered in California about 1850, its population level was much lower than today. It lived on scattered native legumes such as lupine, clover, lotus and locoweed, which are most abundant during the late spring. In summer it was restricted to streams and rivers or the mountains. Now not only its range but its population density has been increased enormously by the growing of alfalfa—today covering more than a million and a half acres in California. Alfalfa and certain cultivated clovers supply it with an abundance of food throughout the year. Furthermore, the concentrated cultivation of alfalfa in fields close together favors the reproduction of the caterpillars. Since the fields are not likely to be in the same stage of growth, the butterflies emerging from one field have a good chance of finding a nearby field which is in the proper stage for egg-laying. Thus a moderate outbreak in one field can result in a severe outbreak in another. This explains why some fields are hard hit while others nearby may be undamaged.

XII Within a given field the extent of the outbreak and the damage done will, of course, depend upon the growth pattern of the alfalfa, which in turn is influenced by the type of soil, drainage, irrigation methods, rainfall, topography and cultivation. Cool weather greatly affects the egg-laying of the females, since, as cold-blooded animals, they need warmth to become active. The alfalfa caterpillar passes the severest part of the winter as a small larva. In the short summer of the northern parts of its range only one generation can mature; in mild southern climates there may be as many as seven in a year. In the hot Imperial Valley the population peaks in the spring and fall. In the cool coastal areas of California, where it takes more than 40 days for a larva to develop into a butterfly, the insects do not thrive; the alfalfa is not retarded as much as the caterpillars, hence the hay is cut before the butterflies can emerge. If growers were to change to cutting the alfalfa later, the caterpillars probably would become more abundant.

XIII California's San Joaquin Valley is highly favorable to caterpillars. But in that area the density of the caterpillar population itself provides a measure of control by bringing into play what the ecologist calls density-dependent factors. These are factors in which the intensity of effect increases as population density increases. Competition for food is such a factor, but it is not ordinarily important in the regulation of alfalfa caterpillar populations. Here the most important density-dependent factors are the insect's natural enemies. Among them are beetles, dragonflies, viruses and parasitic wasps. . . .

XIV The tiny wasp *Apanteles medicaginis* is one of the most important parasites on the caterpillar population. The female wasp lays an egg in the caterpillar when it is a small larva. When the egg itself hatches into a larva, it feeds in the caterpillar's interior and retards its growth. After about a week the wasp larva emerges from its host and spins a bright yellow or white silken cocoon on the alfalfa leaves. The attacked caterpillar dies. The larvae of this little parasitic wasp are to be found in caterpillars throughout the year. They become more numerous, however, during the summer months when caterpillars are most abundant.

XV Each year *Apanteles* saves thousands of acres of alfalfa from damage. It has its own requirements, however, which must be met if it is to help farmers. It needs nectar or aphid honeydew as food. Since the wasp, like the caterpillar, must leave the alfalfa fields when they are cut, it can be fully effective only in areas where other food sources are plentiful. Weeds in fence rows and along irrigation ditches can provide it with nourishment.

XVI If *Apanteles* fails to keep the caterpillar population at a low level, the population may be heavily attacked by a virus disease known to farmers as "wilt." The virus, harbored throughout the year in the soil and surface debris, infects the caterpillars only after it has contaminated the alfalfa. After the insects have fed on infected plants, they transmit the virus among themselves. An infected caterpillar soon stops feeding and dies. Then the body breaks down into a semiliquid mass, which contaminates the surrounding leaves. In this way small foci of wilt develop, and soon the virus becomes widespread in the population. The wilt disease may completely destroy a large population in a few days.

xvii Ordinarily an epizootic of this disease does not occur until the insects have badly damaged the alfalfa. However, one may be initiated artificially by spraying the alfalfa fields with virus when the caterpillars are small. Spraying with a certain bacillus which does not occur naturally in populations of the alfalfa caterpillar also is highly effective against the insect. In the application of these pathogens the proper timing is obviously important.

xviii Let us turn now to the problem of the alfalfa farmer who must decide what to do about the insect situation in his field. It should be apparent from our brief description of some of the many interacting factors that every alfalfa field is a special problem, and the situation must be judged in the light of a complex ecological picture. Farmers know that the infestations vary from field to field and from time to time, and that by the time they have discovered an infestation it is usually too late to do much about it. Furthermore, it does not pay to do general preventive spraying of hay crops. The farmer needs a way of predicting what will happen in his fields so that he can apply control measures only where necessary.

xix As an answer to the farmer's dilemma a supervised control system has been developed in California. The farmer, or a group of farmers, hires an entomologist to follow the insect populations in the fields. On the basis of the conditions peculiar to each field and of his knowledge of the ecology of the alfalfa caterpillar, the entomologist makes a prediction early in the growth of the crop as to whether or not economic damage will occur. If the crop is threatened, he may suggest in some situations that the alfalfa be mowed a few days early to avoid damage. The caterpillars on the cut hay will be destroyed by the sun, and the ratio of parasites to caterpillars in the area will be shifted in favor of the parasites. In other cases he may recommend an application of the virus or the bacillus or a combination of the two. Since the timing is critical, they should be applied under supervised control. In still other cases he may prescribe chemical spraying. The insecticide should be one which will not leave any harmful residue on the hay, will not injure the plants, will cause minimum harm to the parasites, and will control the caterpillars economically. Thus far we have no such perfect insecticide; the closest to meeting the requirements are methoxychlor and perthane. Fortunately chemicals harmful to the parasite are not altogether excluded, because they may be used in fields where the caterpillar population is relatively high and the parasite population relatively low. Perhaps not the least of the benefits of the supervised control program to the farmer is the peace of mind he has through the assurance that his fields are under the constant supervision of qualified personnel.

xx This has been the story of the application of ecological research to the alfalfa caterpillar problem in California. Research is continuing on this problem and further benefits will accrue. The same approach is being made to insect problems in other parts of the world. We have a long way to go to unravel all the strands of this ecosystem of which man is a part. However, we are now in a position to take more intelligent steps toward an integrated control program which will utilize all the resources of ecology and give us the most permanent, satisfactory and economical insect control that is possible.

_____

For a last selection in this section, here is an article that records the application of the scientific method to a human problem, the incidence of mental disease. You will see that the writers have used the inductive procedure with which all new scientific investigation must begin. We have here a record of careful observations of a small group, and of the inductive generalizations that are based upon the observations. The method used is more really like that of the physical and natural sciences than is the method of most studies of the problem, for here there is no dependence upon public records of questionable scientific value.

In connection with a piece of writing by Gilbert Highet we examined the rather arrogant notion that, if the scientific method were only consistently applied to human problems, they would all yield at once. Our writers are modest enough in their claims. They point out that their studies need to be complemented by genetic studies of the same group. And the very fact that the group here studied is unusually convenient for investigation points up the kind of difficulty that must be encountered in the study of larger and less integrated groups.

Quite apart from the particular scientific intent of the article, it is interesting as a record of one of the many small ethnic groups in America. In our relations with the larger ethnic groups, we often have had little to be proud of. We may well be gratified whenever we find that a group with values very different from those of the majority has survived and prospered in its chosen way of life.

For the purposes of this article, your dictionary will sufficiently inform you about the terms for mental states and disorders. Perhaps you had better use it even when you think you know the meaning of a term. Your instructor will probably confirm this observation: students are quite as likely to be wrong as right in their notions about the meaning of such medical terms as are used here.

The Mental Health of the Hutterites (1953)

JOSEPH W. EATON and ROBERT J. WEIL

1 Is modern life driving many people insane? Would insanity diminish or disappear if mankind could return to a simpler life? From Virgil to

Reprinted with permission of *Scientific American*, December, 1953, Volume #189, No. 6. The full findings of the authors' study of the Hutterites are to be found in *Culture and Mental Disorders* (Glencoe, Ill., 1955).

Thoreau the philosophers have had little doubt about the answer to these questions, and some modern anthropologists have offered data which seem to bear them out. They say they have found mental disorders rare among technologically primitive peoples. For instance, recent cursory studies of the people on Okinawa and of the natives of Kenya have suggested that these groups are virtually free of some psychoses. Contrasted with this picture is the civilized U. S., where some authorities have estimated that one person in 10 suffers an incapacitating mental illness at one time or another during his life.

II Whether a culture can cause psychoses is not easy to discover, but one way to get at the question is to examine the mental health of a secure, stable society. The Hutterites, an isolated Anabaptist religious sect who inhabit a section of the North American Middle West, provide an ideal social laboratory of this kind. These people live a simple, rural life, have a harmonious social order and provide every member with a high level of economic security from the womb to the tomb. They are a homogeneous group, free from many of the tensions of the American melting-pot culture. And they have long been considered almost immune to mental disorders. In a study during the 1930s Lee Emerson Deets said that psychoses were almost nonexistent among them. The Manitoba Provincial Legislature received in 1947 a report which said that the Hutterites "do not contribute to the overcrowding of mental hospitals, since the mental security derived from their system results in a complete absence of mental illness."

III Three years ago a research team consisting of the writers of this article—a sociologist and a psychiatrist—and the Harvard University clinical psychologists Bert Kaplan and Thomas Plant undertook a more intensive study of the Hutterites' mental health. The investigation was administered by Wayne University and financed largely by the National Institute for Mental Health. The Hutterite people cooperated generously. In the interest of science they opened their "family closets" and helped us to obtain a census of every person in their community who was then or had ever been mentally ill.

IV The Hutterites, whose origin as a sect goes back to 1528, are a closely knit group of German stock who had lived together in neighboring villages in Europe for a long time before they migrated to the U. S. from southern Russia between 1874 and 1877. The immigrants—101 married couples and their children—settled in eastern South Dakota. Their descendants have now spread over a wide area in the Dakotas, Montana and the prairie provinces of Canada. They live in 98 hamlets, which they call colonies. But they remain a remarkably cohesive group; each grownup is intimately acquainted with hundreds of other members in the settlements. The Hutterites believe it sinful to marry outside the sect, and all of the present descendants (8,542 in 1950) stem from the original 101 couples.

V Cardinal principles of the Hutterites are pacifism, adult baptism, the communal ownership of all property and simple living. Jewelry, art and overstuffed chairs are regarded as sinful luxuries. Radio sets and the movies are taboo. Children are the only possessions to which there is no limit: the average completed family has more than 10. The Hutterites cling to their own customs and are considered "different" by their neighbors. But they are not primitive in the ethnographic sense. They get a grammar-school education and speak English fluently. They read daily newspapers, have a telephone in most colonies and own trucks. Since their own members are not encouraged to seek formal education beyond the primary grades, there are no doctors or lawyers among them, but they utilize such professional services from outside. Each hamlet engages in a highly mechanized form of agriculture. Their business with the "outside world," as Hutterites are apt to refer to their neighbors, usually exceeds $100,000 per year per colony.

VI On the surface it seemed that the Hutterites did indeed enjoy extraordinary freedom from mental illness. We did not find a single Hutterite in a mental hospital. The 55 outside doctors patronized by these people said they showed fewer psychosomatic and nervous symptoms than their neighbors of other faiths. But this appearance of unusual mental health did not stand the test of an intensive screening of the inhabitants, carried out colony by colony. Among the 8,542 Hutterites we discovered a total of 199 (one in 43) who either had active symptoms of a mental disorder or had recovered from such an illness. Of these illnesses 53 were diagnosed as psychoses, all but five of them of a functional (non-organic) character.

VII In short, the Hutterite culture provides no immunity to mental disorders. The existence of these illnesses in so secure and stable a social order suggests that there may be genetic, organic or constitutional predispositions to psychosis which will cause breakdowns among individuals in any society, no matter how protective and well integrated.

VIII The distribution of symptoms among the Hutterites was quite unusual. There were few cases diagnosed as schizophrenia, although elsewhere this is the most common psychosis. Only nine Hutterites had ever manifested the pattern of delusions, hallucinations and other recognized symptoms of schizophrenia; the group lifetime rate was 2.1 per 1,000 persons aged 15 and over. On the other hand, the proportion of manic-depressive reactions among those with mental disorders was unusual; this disorder accounted for 39 of the 53 psychoses, and the rate was 9.3 per 1,000 aged 15 and over. The name of the disorder is misleading; manic-depressives often are not dangerous to other persons, and none of the Hutterite patients was. Their symptoms were predominantly depressive. There was much evidence of irrational guilt feelings, self-blame, withdrawal from normal social relations and marked slowing of mental and motor activities. Five of the patients had suicidal impulses. Two Hutterites had actually killed themselves.

IX The fact that in the Hutterite society manic-depression is more common than schizophrenia, reversing the situation in all other populations for whom comparable data have been obtained, suggests that cultural factors do have some influence on the manifestation of psychoses. A Johns Hopkins University team of researchers who recently made an extensive analysis of mental hospital statistics concluded that schizophrenic symptoms are most common among unskilled laborers, farmers, urban residents in rooming-house sections and other persons who are relatively isolated socially, while manic-depressive reactions are more prevalent among professional, socially prominent and religious persons, who have a stronger need to live up to social expectations. Our data fit this theory well. Religion is the focus of the Hutterite way of life. Their whole educational system, beginning with nursery school, orients the people to look for blame and guilt within themselves rather than in others. Physical aggression is taboo. Like the Catholic orders, Hutterites own everything in the name of their church. They eat in a common dining room, pay medical bills from the communal treasury and work at jobs assigned to them by managers elected by the males of the colony. The group, rather than the individual, comes first.

x In projective psychological tests the Hutterites, like other groups, show antisocial and aggressive impulses, but in their daily lives they repress these effectively. Their history showed no case of murder, arson, severe physical assault or sex crime. No individual warranted the diagnosis of psychopath. Divorce, desertion, separation or chronic marital discord were rare. Only five marriages were known to have gone on the rocks since 1875. Personal violence and childish or amoral forms of behavior among adults were uncommon, even in persons with psychotic episodes. There were no psychoses stemming from drug addiction, alcoholism or syphilis, although these disorders account for approximately 10 per cent of all first admissions to state mental hospitals in the U. S. In general our study tends to confirm the theory of many social scientists and public health officials that a favorable cultural setting can largely prevent these forms of social maladjustment.

xi All this does not entirely rule out the possibility that genetic factors play some part in the unusual proportions of manic-depression and schizophrenia symptoms among the Hutterites. There is some evidence that these disorders tend to run in families. The Hutterites are biologically inbred. Three surnames—Hofer, Waldner and Wipt—accounted for nearly half of all families in 1950. It is possible that the Hutterite group has a disproportionate number of persons genetically prone to becoming depressed—if there is such a predisposition. A team of Harvard University workers is planning to make a follow-up genetic study of the Hutterites.

xii The question of the relation of mental disorders to culture is difficult to investigate quantitatively. No country has a really complete record of mental disorders among its population. Censuses of patients in mental hospitals are almost worthless for this purpose; they leave out patients who have recovered and mentally ill persons who have never come to the attention of doctors.

xiii The Hutterite study attempted to track down every case of a mental disorder, past or present, hospitalized or not, in the whole living population. It probably succeeded in finding virtually all the cases of psychosis. Similar studies have been made of seven other communities in various parts of the world. . . .

xiv On this basis the Hutterites apparently rank second highest among the eight populations in the rate of psychosis, being exceeded only by an area in the north of Sweden. But there is considerable evidence that the count of mental disorders was less complete in the other seven groups; that is, in those studies many cases were missed because their illness was not a matter of public record, while the Hutterite population was thoroughly screened. It is probable that the psychosis rate among the Hutterites is actually low compared with that in other populations. It seems to be only one third as high as the rate in New York State, for instance, taking into consideration the common estimate that even in that State (where mental hospital facilities are among the most extensive) there is at least one undetected psychotic person for every one in an institution.

xv The statistical comparison of mental disorder rates has many limitations, but it does offer several promising leads to the puzzle that the problem of functional psychoses presents to modern science. Among the Hutterites, as in all the other populations, the frequency of psychoses increases rapidly with age. Among those who showed manic-depressive reactions, females predominated. The social biology of the aging process and of sex probably holds worthwhile clues to some of the problems of cause and treatment.

xvi Neuroses were more common than psychoses among the Hutterites, as elsewhere. Four fifths of the 69 discovered neurotics were female. Melancholy moods were regarded by teachers as the number one emotional problem of Hutterite school children. Hutterite neurotics showed the same tendency as psychotics to take out mental stress on themselves instead of on others. Self-blame and remorse were common, as were psychosomatic headaches, backaches and hysteric paralysis of a limb. There was little scapegoating or projection of hostile feelings by imputing them to others.

xvii There is no evidence of any unusual concentration of hereditary mental defects in the Hutterite population. A total of 51 persons was diagnosed as mentally deficient, and 20 normal persons had suffered epileptic attacks. These epilepsy and mental deficiency rates are not high in comparison with other groups.

xviii How does the Hutterite culture deal with mental illness? Although it does not prevent mental disorders, it provides a highly therapeutic atmosphere for their treatment. The onset of a symptom serves as a signal to the entire community to demonstrate support and love for the patient. Hutterites do not approve of the removal of any member to a "strange" hospital, except for short periods to try shock treatments. All patients are looked after by the immediate family. They are treated as ill rather than "crazy." They are encouraged to participate in the normal life of their family and community, and most are able to do some useful work. Most of the manic-depressive patients get well, but among neurotic patients recovery is less common. Most of the epileptics were either cured or took drugs which greatly relieved the condition. No permanent stigma is attached to patients after recovery. The traumatic social consequences which a mental disorder usually brings to the patient, his family and sometimes his community are kept to a minimum by the patience and tolerance with which most Hutterites regard these conditions. This finding supports the theory that at least some of the severely antisocial forms of behavior usually displayed by psychotic and disturbed patients are not an inherent attribute. They may be reflections of the impersonal manner of handling patients in most mental hospitals, of their emotional rejection by the family and of their stigmatization in the community.

XIX In the Hutterite social order people are exposed to a large number of common experiences. Their indoctrination begins in infancy and is continued by daily religious instruction and later by daily church-going. Hutterites spend their entire life within a small and stable group. Their homes consist only of bedrooms, all furnished in an almost identical manner. The women take turns cooking and baking for everybody. Everyone wears the same kind of clothes; the women, for example, all let their hair grow without cutting, part it in the middle and cover it with a black kerchief with white polka dots. The Hutterite religion provides definite answers for many of the problems that come up.

XX Despite this uniformity in the externals of living, Hutterites are not stereotyped personalities. Differences in genetic, organic and psychological factors seem to be sufficiently powerful to produce an infinite variety of behavior, even in a social order as rigid as this one. It appears that the nightmare of uniformity sketched in George Orwell's *Nineteen Eighty-four* is actually unachievable in a living society. At least our study in depth disclosed no simple standardization of personality structure among Hutterites.

XXI There is considerable objective evidence that the great majority of Hutterites have a high level of psychological adjustment. Their misfortunes and accidents are alleviated greatly by the group's system of mutual aid. The sick, the aged, the widows and orphans are well taken care of. In the last three decades only about 100 persons (most of them male) have left the community permanently. During World War II about one third of the men between the ages of 20 and 40 served in camps for conscientious objectors; more than 98 per cent of them ultimately returned to their colonies.

XXII There has not, however, been any rush of applicants from outside to join the Hutterite sect. Mental health involves value judgments and depends on what people want from life. Only 19 adults have joined the sect in America during the last few decades. The austere and puritanical customs of the sect impose restrictions which even the members, who learn to accept them, regard as a "narrow path." Their culture is therapeutic only for conformists. There are occasional rebels; the more able ones find a means of expressing themselves by becoming leaders, the less brilliant have difficulties.

XXIII The survival of this 16th-century peasant culture in the heart of the most 20th-century-minded continent is a vivid demonstration of the power of values and beliefs. Although our data on the Hutterites' mental disorders clearly demonstrate the inadequacy of a purely cultural approach to the problem of mental health, they do show that culture has a large influence in shaping personality. Psychiatrists who work exclusively in hospitals or clinics cannot see the whole patient as he functions in his total environment. Our findings lead us to conclude that the social relations of the patient and his culture, including the things in which he believes, deserve more attention from psychiatric researchers and clinicians than is commonly given to them.

SUGGESTIONS FOR PAPERS

The writing the student will wish to do will depend upon his own scientific interests. The following suggestions are in connection with the selections, and intended particularly for students who have done little work or reading in science.

Suggestions for summaries: (a) Write a careful formal summary of the first seven paragraphs of the selection by Rachel Carson. (b) Write an account, by means of selective summary, of the way of life of the Hutterites, an account that does not include any consideration of mental disease.

An exercise in connection with the Gilbert White selections might be this: Assume that you are writing for a small work of reference, and that you have written this paragraph:

White, Gilbert (1720–93), was born in Selborne in Hampshire and educated at Oxford. He spent most of his life as curate of Selborne, devoting himself to the study of natural history. His study was carried on for its own sake, but in the course of it he made the acquaintance of two distinguished naturalists, Thomas Pennant and the Hon. Daines Barrington. His correspondence with them was made into his *Natural History of Selborne* (1789).

Continue with another paragraph of 250 words, illustrating the nature of the book by reference to our selections, and perhaps by brief quotation. (This suggestion may be adapted for a longer paper. Then read a few more of the letters on whichever of White's various subjects interest you.)

The article about the Hutterites may suggest for some students an account of some small ethnic group that they have observed. And for other students "Insect Control" may suggest an account of some agricultural problem they know about.

A paper requiring a little further reading might be one of these: (a) Find out through reference books about the scientific work of the Venerable Bede and write a report for the class. (b) Starting with the information about Gregor Mendel in this chapter and gathering more from reference books, write for the class an account of Mendel's life and importance in the history of biology. (c) Read the review of *The Sea Around Us* in Chapter XV and choose the chapter you think will most interest you. Write a report of it for the class.

In the first chapter of this book we had an essay by Samuel Eliot Morison, discussing the way in which history ought to be written if it is to have a wide appeal. You might be interested in going over the selections in this chapter by twentieth-century writers, deciding what virtues they have in common, and writing a short essay which you may call "Scientific Writing as a Literary Art." You would need to quote some passages as examples.

VIII

Personal Experience in Retrospect

We all know that an account of personal experience by a friend or an acquaintance may be rather a bore. Your instructor will probably confess that he has found a good many student accounts of personal experience pretty dull reading. And yet we know that some accounts of personal experience are among the most interesting things we have ever read. How are we to account for the difference?

When we think over the interesting pieces, the experiences recounted may seem so various that at first we see no quality in common. But upon consideration a common quality does become apparent. The friend who tells his experience, or the student writing about what has happened to him, is likely, if he selects his material at all, to think only of what is memorable to himself. But if you will consider the records of personal experience in this section, or others you have especially enjoyed, you will find that they are not in one way quite "personal," that they are not concentrated on the self. Perhaps we may say that in them the "I" has an antecedent bigger than the writer's self. At any rate you see, when you begin to look, the representative quality of the experience.

A great writer may manage to make his "I" stand for mankind, and to make us as readers find ourselves in him. Indeed all good writers on human concerns have something of this quality. But the special distinction of the selections here grouped is that they show how a good writer can make his experience represent the experience of his contemporaries. The writers of our selections are "personal" enough, but you will find them using that portion of their experience that interprets for us human experience at one time and in one place.

MEMORIES IN PATTERNS

i

A Boy's Town is William Dean Howells's account of his own boyhood in Hamilton, Ohio, more than a century ago. As time passes, this account of boy life in a little community not far removed from frontier conditions grows in its importance as a document in social history. Moreover, Howells knew, before the sociologists discovered it, that whenever children have considerable freedom, they have their own community, independent of the adult community. In this community, laws, traditions, and folklore are transmitted from child to child.

A Boy's Town has a good deal of technical interest. In it Howells does not write in the first person; his central character he calls "my boy." "My boy" is of indeterminate age, but (except in the last chapter) under twelve. Howells is recognizing the feeling, common to many men, that the boy he was seems detached from the man he is, so that the boy can be viewed with a kind of objectivity. Moreover, "my boy" is often a specimen boy. For Howells this emphasis on representative quality is not just a literary approach; it is a matter of deepest conviction. He writes:

If you have anything in common with your fellow-creatures, it is something that God gave you; if you have anything that seems quite your own, it is from your silly self, and is a sort of perversion of what came to you from the Creator who made you out of himself, and had nothing else to make any one out of. There is not really any difference between you and your fellow-creatures; but only a seeming difference that flatters and cheats you with a sense of your strangeness, and makes you think you are a remarkable fellow.

Nor is the Boy's Town quite Hamilton, Ohio. It is rather the community of boys; the adult Hamilton is recorded only as it touches the boys' life and is understood or misunderstood by them. And the account of the Boy's Town does not have, for the most part, the ordinary structure of chronological narrative, since days and events are fused, as they would present themselves in memory.

FROM *A Boy's Town* (1890)

WILLIAM DEAN HOWELLS

[i]

The Hydraulic and Its Reservoirs

1 There were two branches of the Hydraulic: one followed the course of the Miami, from some unknown point to the northward, on the level of its high bank, and joined the other where it emptied into the river just above the bridge. This last came down what had been a street, and it must have been very pretty to have these two swift streams of clear water rushing through the little town, under the culverts, and between the stone walls of its banks. But what a boy mainly cares for in a thing is *use,* and the boys tried to make some use of the Hydraulic, since it was there to find what they could do with it. Of course they were aware of the mills dotted along its course, and they knew that it ran them; but I do not believe any of them thought that it was built merely to run flour-mills and saw-mills and cotton-mills. They did what they could to find out its real use, but they could make very little of it. The current was so rapid that it would not freeze in winter,

and in summer they could not go in swimming in it by day, because it was so public, and at night the Basin had more attractions. There was danger of cutting your feet on the broken glass and crockery which people threw into the Hydraulic, and though the edges of the culverts were good for jumping off of, the boys did not find them of much practical value. Sometimes you could catch sunfish in the Hydraulic, but it was generally too swift, and the only thing you could depend upon was catching crawfish. These abounded so that if you dropped a string with a bit of meat on it into the water anywhere, you could pull it up again with two or three crawfish hanging to it. The boys could not begin to use them all for bait, which was the only use their Creator seemed to have designed them for; but they had vaguely understood that people somewhere ate them, or something like them, though they had never known even the name of lobsters; and they always intended to get their mothers to have them cooked for them. None of them ever did.

II They could sometimes, under high favor of fortune, push a dog into the Hydraulic, or get him to jump in after a stick; and then have the excitement of following him from one culvert to another, till he found a foothold and scrambled out. Once my boy saw a chicken cock sailing serenely down the current; he was told that he had been given brandy, and that brandy would enable a chicken to swim; but probably this was not true. Another time, a tremendous time, a boy was standing at the brink of a culvert, when one of his mates dared another to push him in. In those days the boys attached peculiar ideas of dishonor to taking a dare. They said, and in some sort they believed, that a boy who would take a dare would steal sheep. I do not now see why this should follow. In this case, the high spirit who was challenged felt nothing base in running up behind his unsuspecting friend and popping him into the water, and I have no doubt the victim considered the affair in the right light when he found that it was a dare. He drifted under the culvert, and when he came out he swiftly scaled the wall below, and took after the boy who had pushed him in; of course this one had the start. No great harm was done; everybody could swim, and a boy's summer costume in that hot climate was made up of a shirt and trousers and a straw hat; no boy who had any regard for his social standing wore shoes or stockings, and as they were all pretty proud, they all went barefoot from April till October.

III The custom of going barefoot must have come from the South, where it used to be so common, and also from the primitive pioneer times which were so near my boy's time, fifty years ago. The South characterized the thinking and feeling of the Boy's Town, far more than the North. Most of the people were of Southern extraction, from Kentucky or Virginia, when they were not from Pennsylvania or New Jersey. There might have been other New England families, but the boys only knew of one—that of the blacksmith whose shop they liked to haunt. His children were heard to dispute about an animal they had seen, and one of them said, "Tell ye 'twa'n't a squeerrel; 'twas a maouse"; and the boys had that for a by-word. They despised Yankees as a mean-spirited race, who were stingy and would cheat, and would not hit you if you told them they lied. A person must always hit a person who told him he lied; but even if you called a Yankee a *fighting liar* (the worst form of this insult), he would not hit you, but just call you a liar back. My boy long accepted these ideas of New England as truly representative of the sectional character. Perhaps they were as fair as some ideas of the West which he afterwards found entertained in New England; but they were false and stupid all the same.

iv If the boys could do little with the Hydraulic, they were at no loss in regard to the Reservoirs, into which its feeding waters were gathered and held in reserve, I suppose, against a time of drought. There was the Little Reservoir first, and then a mile beyond it the Big Reservoir, and there was nearly always a large flat boat on each which was used for repairing the banks, but which the boys employed as a pleasure-barge. It seemed in some natural way to belong to them, and yet they had a feeling of something clandestine in pushing out on the Reservoir in it. Once they filled its broad, shallow hold with straw from a neighboring oatfield, and spent a long golden afternoon in simply lying under the hot September sun, in the middle of the Reservoir, and telling stories. My boy then learned, for the first time, that there was such a book as the "Arabian Nights"; one of the other boys told stories out of it, and he inferred that the sole copy in existence belonged to this boy. He knew that they all had school-books alike, but it did not occur to him that a book which was not a Reader or a Speller was ever duplicated. They did nothing with their boat except loll in it and tell stories, and as there was no current in the Reservoir, they must have remained pretty much in the same place; but they had a sense of the wildest adventure, which mounted to frenzy, when some men rose out of the earth on the shore, and shouted at them, "Hello, there! What are you doing with that boat?" They must have had an oar; at any rate, they got to the opposite bank, and, springing to land, fled somewhere into the vaguest past.

v The boys went in swimming in the Little Reservoir when they were not in the River or the Basin; and they fished in the Big Reservoir, where the sunfish bit eagerly. There were large trees standing in the hollow which became the bed of the Reservoir, and these died when the water was let in around them, and gave the stretch of quiet waters a strange, weird look; about their bases was the best kind of place for sunfish, and even for bass. Of course the boys never caught any bass; that honor was reserved for men. . . . It was several years before the catfish got in, and then they were mud-cats; but the boys had great luck with sunfish there and in the pools about the flood-gates, where there was always some leakage, and where my boy once caught a whole string of live fish which had got away from some other boy, perhaps weeks before; they were all swimming about, in a lively way, and the largest hungrily took his bait. The great pleasure of fishing in these pools was that the waters were so clear you could see the fat, gleaming fellows at the bottom, nosing round your hook, and going off and coming back several times before they made up their minds to bite. It seems now impossible that my boy could ever have taken pleasure in the capture of these poor creatures. I know that there are grown people, and very good, kind men, too, who defend and celebrate the sport, and value themselves on their skill in it; but I think it tolerable only in boys, who are cruel because they are thoughtless. It is not probable that any lower organism

> "In corporal sufferance feels a pang as great
> As when a giant dies," [1]

but still, I believe that even a fish knows a dumb agony from the barbs of the hook which would take somewhat from the captor's joy if he could but realize it.

vi There was, of course, a time when the Hydraulic and the Reservoirs were not where they afterwards appeared always to have been. My boy could dimly recall the day when the water was first let into the Hydraulic, and the little fellows ran along its sides to keep abreast of the current, as they easily could; and he could see more vividly the tumult which a break in the embankment of the Little Reservoir caused. The whole town rushed to the spot, or at least all the boys in it did, and a great force of men besides, with shovels and wheelbarrows, and bundles of brush and straw, and heavy logs, and heaped them into the crevasse, and piled earth on them. The men threw off their coats and all joined in the work; a great local politician led off in his shirt-sleeves; and it was as if my boy should now see the Emperor of Germany in his shirt-sleeves pushing a wheelbarrow, so high above all other men had that exalted Whig always been to him. But the Hydraulic, I believe, was a town work, and everybody felt himself an owner in it, and hoped to share in the prosperity which it should bring to all. It made the people so far one family, as every public work which they own in common always does; it made them brothers and equals, as private property never does.

vii Of course the boys rose to no such conception of the fact before their eyes. I suspect that in their secret hearts they would have been glad to have seen that whole embankment washed away, for the excitement's sake, and for the hope of catching the fish that would be left flopping at the bottom of the Reservoir when the waters were drained out. I think that these waters were brought somehow from Old River, but I am not sure how. Old River was very far away, and my boy was never there much, and knew little of the weird region it bounded. Once he went in swimming in it, but the still, clear waters were strangely cold, and not like those of the friendly Miami. Once, also, when the boys had gone into the vast woods of that measureless continent which they called the Island, for pawpaws or for hickory-nuts, or maybe buckeyes, they got lost; and while they ran about in terror, they heard the distant lowing and bellowing of cattle. They knew somehow, as boys know everything, that the leader of the herd, which ranged those woods in a half-savage freedom, was a vicious bull, and as the lowing and bellowing sounded nearer, they huddled together in the wildest dismay. Some were for running, some for getting over a fence near by; but they could not tell which side of the fence the herd was on. In the

[1 See Shakespeare's *Measure for Measure*, III, i, 72–79.]

primitive piety of childhood my boy suggested prayer as something that had served people in extremity, and he believed that it was the only hope left. Another boy laughed, and began to climb a tree; the rest, who had received my boy's suggestion favorably, instantly followed his example; in fact, he climbed a tree himself. The herd came slowly up, and when they reached the boys' refuge they behaved with all the fury that could have been expected—they trampled and tossed the bags that held the pawpaws or buckeyes or hickory-nuts; they gored the trees where the boys hung trembling; they pawed and tossed the soft earth below; and then they must have gone away, and given them up as hopeless. My boy never had the least notion how he got home; and I dare say he was very young when he began these excursions to the woods.

[ii]
Circuses and Shows

1 What every boy expected to do, some time or other, was to run off. He expected to do this because the scheme offered an unlimited field to the imagination, and because its fulfilment would give him the highest distinction among the other fellows. To run off was held to be the only way for a boy to right himself against the wrongs and hardships of a boy's life. As far as the Boy's Town was concerned, no boy had anything to complain of; the boys had the best time in the world there, and in a manner they knew it. But there were certain things that they felt no boy ought to stand, and these things were sometimes put upon them at school, but usually at home. In fact, nearly all the things that a fellow intended to run off for were done to him by those who ought to have been the kindest to him. Some boys' mothers had the habit of making them stop and do something for them just when they were going away with the fellows. Others would not let them go in swimming as often as they wanted, and, if they saw them with their shirts on wrong side out, would not believe that they could get turned in climbing a fence. Others made them split kindling and carry in wood, and even saw wood. None of these things, in a simple form, was enough to make a boy run off, but they prepared his mind for it, and when complicated with whipping they were just cause for it. Weeding the garden, though, was a thing that almost, in itself, was enough to make a fellow run off.

11 Not many of the boys really had to saw wood, though a good many of the fellows' fathers had saws and bucks in their wood-sheds. There were public sawyers who did most of the wood-sawing; and they came up with their bucks on their shoulders, and asked for the job almost as soon as the wood was unloaded before your door. The most popular one with the boys was a poor half-wit known among them as Morn; and he was a favorite with them because he had fits, and because, when he had a fit, he would seem to fly all over the wood-pile. The boys would leave anything to see Morn in a fit, and he always had a large crowd round him as soon as the cry went out that he was beginning to have one. They watched the hapless

creature with grave, unpitying, yet not unfriendly interest, too ignorant of the dark ills of life to know how deeply tragic was the spectacle that entertained them, and how awfully present in Morn's contortions was the mystery of God's ways with his children, some of whom he gives to happiness and some to misery. When Morn began to pick himself weakly up, with eyes of pathetic bewilderment, they helped him find his cap, and tried to engage him in conversation, for the pleasure of seeing him twist his mouth when he said, of a famous town drunkard whom he admired, "He's a strong man; he eats liquor." It was probably poor Morn's ambition to eat liquor himself, and the boys who followed that drunkard about to plague him had a vague respect for his lamentable appetite.

III None of the boys ever did run off, except the son of one of the preachers. He was a big boy, whom my boy remotely heard of, but never saw, for he lived in another part of the town; but his adventure was known to all the boys, and his heroism rated high among them. It took nothing from this, in their eyes, that he was found, homesick and crying in Cincinnati, and was glad to come back—the great fact was that he had run off; nothing could change or annul that. If he had made any mistake, it was in not running off with a circus, for that was the true way of running off. Then, if you were ever seen away from home, you were seen tumbling through a hoop and alighting on the crupper of a bare-backed piebald, and if you ever came home you came home in a gilded chariot, and you flashed upon the domestic circle in flesh-colored tights and spangled breech-cloth. As soon as the circus-bills began to be put up you began to hear that certain boys were going to run off with that circus, and the morning after it left town you heard they had gone, but they always turned up at school just the same. It was believed that the circus-men would take any boy who wanted to go with them, and would fight off his friends if they tried to get him away.

IV The boys made a very careful study of the circus-bills, and afterwards, when the circus came, they held the performance to a strict account for any difference between the feats and their representation. For a fortnight beforehand they worked themselves up for the arrival of the circus into a fever of fear and hope, for it was always a question with a great many whether they could get their fathers to give them the money to go in. The full price was two bits, and the half-price was a bit, or a Spanish *real,* then a commoner coin than the American dime in the West; and every boy, for that time only, wished to be little enough to look young enough to go in for a bit. Editors of newspapers had a free ticket for every member of their families; and my boy was sure of going to the circus from the first rumor of its coming. But he was none the less deeply thrilled by the coming event, and he was up early on the morning of the great day, to go out and meet the circus procession beyond the corporation line.

V I do not really know how boys live through the wonder and the glory of such a sight. Once there were two chariots—one held the band in red-and-blue uniforms, and was drawn by eighteen piebald horses; and the other was drawn by a troop of Shetland ponies, and carried in a vast mythical sea-shell little boys in spangled tights and little girls in the gauze skirts and wings of fairies. There was not a flaw in this splendor to the young eyes that gloated on it, and that followed it in rapture through every turn and winding of its course in the Boy's Town; nor in the magnificence of the actors and actresses, who came riding two by two in their circus-dresses after the chariots, and looking some haughty and contemptuous, and others quiet and even bored, as if it were nothing to be part of such a procession. The boys tried to make them out by the pictures and names on the bills: which was Rivers, the bare-back rider, and which was O'Dale, the champion tumbler; which was the India-rubber man, which the ring-master, which the clown. Covered with dust, gasping with the fatigue of a three hours' run beside the procession, but fresh at heart as in the beginning, they arrived with it on the Commons, where the tent-wagons were already drawn up, and the ring was made, and mighty men were driving the iron-headed tent-stakes, and stretching the ropes of the great skeleton of the pavilion which they were just going to clothe with canvas. The boys were not allowed to come anywhere near, except three or four who got leave to fetch water from a neighboring well, and thought themselves richly paid with half-price tickets. The other boys were proud to pass a word with them as they went by with their brimming buckets; fellows who had money to go in would have been glad to carry water just for the glory of coming close to the circus-men. They stood about in twos and threes, and lay upon the grass in groups debating whether a tanbark ring was better than a saw-dust ring; there were different opinions. They came as near the wagons as they dared, and looked at the circus-horses munching hay from the tail-boards, just like common horses. The wagons were left standing outside of the tent; but when it was up, the horses were taken into the dressing-room, and then the boys, with many a backward look at the wide spread of canvas, and the flags and streamers floating over it from the centre-pole (the centre-pole was revered almost like a distinguished personage), ran home to dinner so as to get back good and early, and be among the first to go in. All round, before the circus doors were open, the doorkeepers of the side-shows were inviting people to come in and see the giants and fat woman and boa-constrictors, and there were stands for peanuts and candy and lemonade; the vendors cried, "Ice-cold lemonade, from fifteen hundred miles under ground! Walk up, roll up, tumble up, any way to get up!" The boys thought this brilliant drolling, but they had no time to listen after the doors were open, and they had no money to spend on side-shows or dainties, anyway. Inside the tent, they found it dark and cool, and their hearts thumped in their throats with the wild joy of being there; they recognized one another with amaze, as if they had not met for years, and the excitement kept growing, as other fellows came in. It was lots of fun, too, watching the country-jakes, as the boys called the farmer-folk, and seeing how green they looked, and how some of them tried to act smart with the circus-men that came round with oranges to sell. But the great thing was to see whether fellows that said they were going to hook in really got in. The boys held it to be a high and creditable thing to hook into a show of any kind, but hooking into a circus was something that a fellow ought to be held in special honor for doing. He ran great risks, and if he escaped the vigilance of the massive circus-man who patrolled the outside of the tent with a cowhide and a bulldog, perhaps he merited the fame he was sure to win.

VI I do not know where boys get some of the notions of morality that govern them. These notions are like the sports and plays that a boy leaves off as he gets older to the boys that are younger. He outgrows them, and other boys grow into them, and then outgrow them as he did. Perhaps they come down to the boyhood of our time from the boyhood of the race, and the unwritten laws of conduct may have prevailed among the earliest Aryans on the plains of Asia that I now find so strange in a retrospect of the Boy's Town. The standard of honor there was, in a certain way, very high among the boys; they would have despised a thief as he deserved, and I cannot remember one of them who might not have been safely trusted. None of them would have taken an apple out of a market-wagon, or stolen a melon from a farmer who came to town with it; but they would all have thought it fun, if not right, to rob an orchard or hook a watermelon out of a patch. This would have been a foray into the enemy's country, and the fruit of the adventure would have been the same as the plunder of a city, or the capture of a vessel belonging to him on the high seas. In the same way, if one of the boys had seen a circus-man drop a quarter, he would have hurried to give it back to him, but he would only have been proud to hook into the circus-man's show, and the other fellows would have been proud of his exploit, too, as something that did honor to them all. As a person who enclosed bounds and forbade trespass, the circus-man constituted himself the enemy of every boy who respected himself, and challenged him to practise any sort of strategy. There was not a boy in the crowd that my boy went with who would have been allowed to hook into a circus by his parents; yet hooking in was an ideal that was cherished among them, that was talked of, and that was even sometimes attempted, though not often. Once, when a fellow really hooked in, and joined the crowd that had ignobly paid, one of the fellows could not stand it. He asked him just how and where he got in, and then he went to the door, and got back his money from the doorkeeper upon the plea that he did not feel well; and in five or ten minutes he was back among the boys, a hero of such moral grandeur as would be hard to describe. Not one of the fellows saw him as he really was—a little lying, thievish scoundrel. Not even my boy saw him so, though he had on some other points of personal honesty the most fantastic scruples.

[iii]

Pets

1 As there are no longer any Whig boys in the world, the coon can no longer be kept anywhere as a political emblem, I dare say. Even in my boy's time the boys kept coons just for the pleasure of it, and without meaning to elect Whig governors and presidents with them. I do not know how they

got them—they traded for them, perhaps, with fellows in the country that had caught them, or perhaps their fathers bought them in market; some people thought they were very good to eat, and, like poultry and other things for the table, they may have been brought alive to market. But, anyhow, when a boy had a coon, he had to have a store-box turned open side down to keep it in, behind the house; and he had to have a little door in the box to pull the coon out through when he wanted to show it to other boys, or to look at it himself, which he did forty or fifty times a day, when he first got it. He had to have a small collar for the coon, and a little chain, because the coon would gnaw through a string in a minute. The coon himself never seemed to take much interest in keeping a coon, or to see much fun or sense in it. He liked to stay inside his box, where he had a bed of hay, and whenever the boy pulled him out, he did his best to bite the boy. He had no tricks; his temper was bad; and there was nothing about him except the rings round his tail and his political principles that anybody could care for. He never did anything but bite, and try to get away, or else run back into his box, which smelt, pretty soon, like an animal-show; he would not even let a fellow see him eat.

II My boy's brother had a coon, which he kept a good while, at a time when there was no election, for the mere satisfaction of keeping a coon. During his captivity the coon bit his keeper repeatedly through the thumb, and upon the whole seemed to prefer him to any other food; I do not really know what coons eat in a wild state, but this captive coon tasted the blood of nearly that whole family of children. Besides biting and getting away, he never did the slightest thing worth remembering; as there was no election, he did not even take part in a Whig procession. He got away two or three times. The first thing his owner would know when he pulled the chain out was that there was no coon at the end of it, and then he would have to poke round the inside of the box pretty carefully with a stick, so as not to get bitten; after that he would have to see which tree the coon had gone up. It was usually the tall locust-tree in front of the house, and in about half a second all the boys in town would be there, telling the owner of the coon how to get him. Of course the only way was to climb for the coon, which would be out at the point of a high and slender limb, and would bite you awfully, even if the limb did not break under you, while the boys kept whooping and yelling and holloing out what to do, and Tip the dog just howled with excitement. I do not know how that coon was ever caught, but I know that the last time he got away he was not found during the day, but after nightfall he was discovered by moonlight in the locust-tree. His owner climbed for him, but the coon kept shifting about, and getting higher and higher, and at last he had to be left till morning. In the morning he was not there, nor anywhere.

III It had been expected, perhaps, that Tip would watch him, and grab him if he came down, and Tip would have done it probably if he had kept awake. He was a dog of the greatest courage, and he was especially fond of hunting. He had been bitten oftener by that coon than anybody but the coon's owner, but he did not care for biting. He was always getting bitten by rats, but he was the greatest dog for rats that there almost ever was. The boys hunted rats with him at night, when they came out of the stables that backed down to the Hydraulic, for water; and a dog who liked above all things to lie asleep on the back-step, by day, and would no more think of chasing a pig out of the garden than he would think of sitting up all night with a coon, would get frantic about rats, and would perfectly wear himself out hunting them on land and in the water, and keep on after the boys themselves were tired. He was so fond of hunting, anyway, that the sight of a gun would drive him about crazy; he would lick the barrel all over, and wag his tail so hard that it would lift his hind-legs off the ground.

iv I do not know how he came into that family, but I believe he was given to it full grown by somebody. It was some time after my boy failed to buy what he called a Confoundland dog, from a colored boy who had it for sale, a pretty puppy with white and black spots which he had quite set his heart on; but Tip more than consoled him. Tip was of no particular breed, and he had no personal beauty; he was of the color of a mouse or an elephant, and his tail was without the smallest grace; it was smooth and round, but it was so strong that he could pull a boy all over the town by it, and usually did; and he had the best, and kindest, and truest ugly old face in the world. He loved the whole human race, and as a watch-dog he was a failure through his trustful nature; he would no more have bitten a person than he would have bitten a pig; but where other dogs were concerned, he was a lion. He might be lying fast asleep in the back-yard, and he usually was, but if a dog passed the front of the house under a wagon, he would be up and after that dog before you knew what you were about. He seemed to want to fight country dogs the worst, but any strange dog would do. A good half the time he would come off best; but, however he came off, he returned to the back-yard with his tongue hanging out, and wagging his tail in good-humor with all the world. Nothing could stop him, however, where strange dogs were concerned. He was a Whig dog, of course, as any one could tell by his name, which was Tippecanoe in full, and was given him because it was the nickname of General Harrison, the great Whig who won the battle of Tippecanoe. The boys' Henry Clay Club used him to pull the little wagon that they went about in singing Whig songs, and he would pull five or six boys, guided simply by a stick which he held in his mouth, and which a boy held on either side of him. But if he caught sight of a dog that he did not know, he would drop that stick and start for that dog as far off as he could see him, spilling the Henry Clay Club out of the wagon piecemeal as he went, and never stopping till he mixed up the strange dog in a fight where it would have been hard to tell which was either champion and which was the club wagon. When the fight was over Tip would come smilingly back to the fragments of the Henry Clay Club, with pieces of the vehicle sticking about him, and profess himself, in a dog's way, ready to go on with the concert.

v Any crowd of boys could get Tip to go off with them, in swimming, or hunting, or simply running races. He was known through the whole town, and beloved for his many endearing qualities of heart. As to his

mind, it was perhaps not much to brag of, and he certainly had some defects of character. He was incurably lazy, and his laziness grew upon him
as he grew older, till hardly anything but the sight of a gun or a bone
would move him. He lost his interest in politics, and, though there is no
reason to suppose that he ever became indifferent to his principles, it is
certain that he no longer showed his early ardor. He joined the Free-Soil
movement in 1848, and supported Van Buren and Adams, but without the
zeal he had shown for Henry Clay. Once a year as long as the family lived
in the Boy's Town, the children were anxious about Tip when the dog-law
was put in force, and the constables went round shooting all the dogs that
were found running at large without muzzles. At this time, when Tip was
in danger of going mad and biting people, he showed a most unseasonable
activity, and could hardly be kept in bounds. A dog whose sole delight at
other moments was to bask in the summer sun, or dream by the winter fire,
would now rouse himself to an interest in everything that was going on in
the dangerous world, and make forays into it at all unguarded points. The
only thing to do was to muzzle him, and this was done by my boy's brother
with a piece of heavy twine, in such a manner as to interfere with Tip's
happiness as little as possible. It was a muzzle that need not be removed
for either eating, drinking, or fighting; but it satisfied the law, and Tip
always came safely through the dog-days, perhaps by favor or affection with
the officers who were so inexorable with some dogs.

vi My boy long remembered with horror and remorse his part in giving
up to justice an unconscious offender, and seeing him pay for his trans-
gression with his life. The boy was playing before his door, when a constable came by with his rifle on his shoulder, and asked him if he had seen
any unmuzzled dogs about; and partly from pride at being addressed by a
constable, partly from a nervous fear of refusing to answer, and partly from
a childish curiosity to see what would happen, he said, "Yes; one over there
by the pork-house." The constable whistled, and the poor little animal,
which had got lost from the farmer it had followed to town, came running
into sight round the corner of the pork-house, and sat up on its haunches
to look about. It was a small red dog, the size of a fox, and the boy always
saw it afterwards as it sat there in the gray afternoon, and fascinated him
with its deadly peril. The constable swung his rifle quickly to his shoulder;
the sharp, whiplike report came, and the dog dropped over, and its heart's
blood flowed upon the ground and lay there in a pool. The boy ran into the
house, with that picture forever printed in his memory. For him it was as
if he had seen a fellow-being slain, and had helped to bring him to his
death.

vii Whilst Tip was still in his prime the family of children was further
enriched by the possession of a goat; but this did not belong to the whole
family, or it was, at least nominally, the property of that eldest brother
they all looked up to. I do not know how they came by the goat, any more
than I know how they came by Tip; I only know that there came a time
when it was already in the family, and that before it was got rid of it was
a presence there was no mistaking. Nobody who has not kept a goat can

have any notion of how many different kinds of mischief a goat can get into, without seeming to try, either, but merely by following the impulses of its own goatishness. This one was a nanny-goat, and it answered to the name of Nanny with an intelligence that was otherwise wholly employed in making trouble. It went up and down stairs, from cellar to garret, and in and out of all the rooms, like anybody, with a faint, cynical indifference in the glance of its cold gray eyes that gave no hint of its purposes or performances. In the chambers it chewed the sheets and pillow-cases on the beds, and in the dining-room, if it found nothing else, it would do its best to eat the table-cloth. Washing-day was a perfect feast for it, for then it would banquet on the shirt-sleeves and stockings that dangled from the clothes-line, and simply glut itself with the family linen and cotton. In default of these dainties, Nanny would gladly eat a chip-hat; she was not proud; she would cat a split-basket, if there was nothing else at hand. Once she got up on the kitchen-table, and had a perfect orgy with a lot of fresh-baked pumpkin-pies she found there; she cleaned all the pumpkin so neatly out of the pastry shells that, if there had been any more pumpkin left, they could have been filled up again, and nobody could have told the difference. The grandmother, who was visiting in the house at the time, declared to the mother that it would serve the father and the boys just right if she did fill these very shells up and give them to the father and the boys to eat. But I believe this was not done, and it was only suggested in a moment of awful exasperation, and because it was the fathcr who was to blame for letting the boys keep the goat. The mother was always saying that the goat should not stay in the house another day, but she had not the heart to insist on its banishment, the children were so fond of it. I do not know why they were fond of it, for it never showed them the least affection, but was always taking the most unfair advantages of them, and it would butt them over whenever it got the chance. It would try to butt them into the well when they leaned down to pull up the bucket from the curb; and if it came out of the house, and saw a boy cracking nuts at the low flat stone the children had in the back-yard to crack nuts on, it would pretend that the boy was making motions to insult it, and before he knew what he was about it would fly at him and send him spinning head over heels. It was not of the least use in the world, and could not be, but the children were allowed to keep it till, one fatal day, when the mother had a number of other ladies to tea, as the fashion used to be in small towns, when they sat down to a comfortable gossip over dainty dishes of stewed chicken, hot biscuit, peach-preserves, sweet tomato-pickles, and pound-cake. That day they all laid off their bonnets on the hall-table, and the goat, after demurely waiting and watching with its faded eyes, which saw everything and seemed to see nothing, discerned a golden opportunity, and began to make such a supper of bonnet-ribbons as perhaps never fell to a goat's lot in life before. It was detected in its stolen joys just as it had chewed the ribbon of a best bonnet up to the bonnet, and was chased into the back-yard; but, as it had swallowed the ribbon without being able to swallow the bonnet, it carried that with it. The boy who specially owned the goat ran it down in a frenzy of horror and apprehension, and managed to unravel the ribbon from its throat, and get back the bonnet. Then he took the bonnet in and laid it carefully down on the table again, and decided that it would be best not to say anything about the affair. But such a thing as that could not be kept. The goat was known at once to have done the mischief; and this time it was really sent away. All the children mourned it, and the boy who owned it the most used to go to the house of the people who took it, and who had a high board fence round their yard, and try to catch sight of it through the cracks. When he called "Nanny!" it answered him instantly with a plaintive "Baa!" and then, after a vain interchange of lamentations, he had to come away, and console himself as he could with the pets that were left him.

[iv]

Fantasies and Superstitions

1 He used to talk to himself when he was little, but one day his mother said to him jokingly, "Don't you know that he who talks to himself has the devil for a listener?" and after that he never dared whisper above his breath when he was alone, though his father and mother had both taught him that there was no devil but his own evil will. He shuddered when he heard a dog howling in the night, for that was a sign that somebody was going to die. If he heard a hen crow, as a hen sometimes unnaturally would, he stoned her, because it was a sign of the worst kind of luck. He believed that warts came from playing with toads, but you could send them away by saying certain words over them; and he was sorry that he never had any warts, so that he could send them away, and see them go; but he never could bear to touch a toad, and so of course he could not have warts. Other boys played with toads just to show that they were not afraid of having warts; but every one knew that if you killed a toad, your cow would give bloody milk. I dare say the far forefathers of the race knew this too, when they first began to herd their kine in the birthplace of the Aryan peoples; and perhaps they learned then that if you killed a snake early in the day its tail would live till sundown. My boy killed every snake he could; he thought it somehow a duty; all the boys thought so; they dimly felt that they were making a just return to the serpent-tribe for the bad behavior of their ancestor in the Garden of Eden. Once, in a corn-field near the Little Reservoir, the boys found on a thawing day of early spring knots and bundles of snakes writhen and twisted together, in the torpor of their long winter sleep. It was a horrible sight, that afterwards haunted my boy's dreams. He had nightmares which remained as vivid in his thoughts as anything that happened to him by day. There were no poisonous snakes in the region of the Boy's Town, but there were some large blacksnakes, and the boys said that if a blacksnake got the chance he would run up your leg, and tie himself round your body so that you could not breathe. Nobody had ever seen a blacksnake do it, and nobody had ever seen a hoop-snake, but the boys believed there was such a snake, and that he would take his tail in his mouth, when he got after a person, and roll himself along swifter than the fastest

race-horse could run. He did not bite, but when he came up with you he would take the point of his tail out of his mouth and strike it into you. If he struck his tail into a tree, the tree would die. My boy had seen a boy who had been chased by a hoop-snake, but he had not seen the snake, though for the matter of that the boy who had been chased by it had not seen it either; he did not stop to see it. Another kind of snake that was very strange was a hair-snake. No one had ever seen it happen, but every one knew that if you put long horsehairs into a puddle of water and let them stay, they would turn into hair-snakes; and when you drank out of a spring you had to be careful not to swallow a hair-snake, or it would remain in your stomach and grow there.

  II When you saw a lizard, you had to keep your mouth tight shut, or else the lizard would run down your throat before you knew it. That was what all the boys said, and my boy believed it, though he had never heard of anybody that it happened to. He believed that if you gave a chicken-cock burnt brandy it could lay eggs, and that if you gave a boy burnt brandy it would stop his growing. That was the way the circus-men got their dwarfs, and the India-rubber man kept himself limber by rubbing his joints with rattlesnake oil.

  III A snake could charm a person, and when you saw a snake you had to kill it before it could get its eye on you or it would charm you. Snakes always charmed birds; and there were mysterious powers of the air and forces of nature that a boy had to be on his guard against, just as a bird had to look out for snakes. You must not kill a granddaddy-long-legs, or a lady-bug; it was bad luck. My boy believed, or was afraid he believed, that

> "What you dream Monday morning before daylight
> Will come true before Saturday night,"

but if it was something bad, you could keep it from coming true by not telling your dream till you had eaten breakfast. He governed his little, foolish, frightened life not only by the maxims he had learned out of his "Gesta Romanorum," but by common sayings of all sorts, such as

> "See a pin and leave it lay
> You'll have bad luck all the day,"

and if ever he tried to rebel against this slavery, and went by a pin in the path, his fears tormented him till he came back and picked it up. He would not put on his left stocking first, for that was bad luck; but besides these superstitions, which were common to all the boys, he invented superstitions of his own, with which he made his life a burden. He did not know why, but he would not step upon the cracks between the paving-stones, and some days he had to touch every tree or post along the sidewalk, as Doctor Johnson did in his time, though the boy had never heard of Doctor Johnson then.

  IV While he was yet a very little fellow, he had the distorted, mistaken piety of childhood. He had an abject terror of dying, but it seemed to him that if a person could die right in the centre aisle of the church—the

Methodist church where his mother used to go before she became finally a New Churchwoman—the chances of that person's going straight to heaven would be so uncommonly good that he need have very little anxiety about it. He asked his mother if she did not think so too, holding by her hand as they came out of church together, and he noticed the sort of gravity and even pain with which she and his father received this revelation of his darkling mind. They tried to teach him what they thought of such things; but though their doctrine caught his fancy and flattered his love of singularity, he was not proof against the crude superstitions of his mates. He thought for a time that there was a Bad Man, but this belief gave way when he heard his father laughing about a certain clergyman who believed in a personal devil.

v The boys said the world was going to be burned up some time, and my boy expected the end with his full share of the trouble that it must bring to every sinner. His fears were heightened by the fact that his grandfather believed this end was very near at hand, and was prepared for the second coming of Christ at any moment. Those were the days when the minds of many were stirred by this fear or hope; the believers had their ascension robes ready, and some gave away their earthly goods so as not to be cumbered with anything in their heavenward flight. At home, my boy heard his father jest at the crazy notion, and make fun of the believers; but abroad, among the boys, he took the tint of the prevailing gloom. One awful morning at school, it suddenly became so dark that the scholars could not see to study their lessons, and then the boys knew that the end of the world was coming. There were no clouds, as for a coming storm, but the air was blackened almost to the dusk of night; the school was dismissed, and my boy went home to find the candles lighted, and a strange gloom and silence on everything outside. He remembered entering into this awful time, but he no more remembered coming out of it than if the earth had really passed away in fire and smoke.

------

1) Howells is writing more than forty years after the experience recorded. Think how you might write of your life when you were nine. Would you write about it from your POINT OF VIEW now? Or would you —this would be harder—write about it from the point of view of a nine-year-old? Is Howells doing just the one, or just the other?

2) Do the points of view Howells is using conflict with one another? If they do, point out instances of the conflict. But if they do not, can you explain how Howells manages to avoid a conflict?

3) Perhaps we should push question 2 a bit further. Certain sentences are clearly written from Howells's point of view as an adult; the last two sentences of vi in "The Hydraulic and Its Reservoirs" are an example. What are other examples? But consider also this paragraph from a chapter not part of our selections:

It was thought a great thing in a kite to pull, and it was a favor to another boy to let him take hold of your string and feel how your kite pulled. If you wanted to play mumble-the-peg, or anything, while your kite was up, you tied it to a stake in the ground, or gave it to some other fellow to hold; there were always lots of fellows eager to hold it. But you had to be careful how you let a little fellow hold it; for, if it was a very powerful kite, it would take him up. It was not certain just how strong a kite had to be to take a small boy up, and nobody had ever seen a kite do it, but everybody expected to see it.

What are examples of passages in our selections written from a point of view like that of this passage? Just how will you describe the point of view in this passage and the others like it?

4) You must have concluded that point of view in part determines style. But be careful here. Are we going to say that, in such sentences as you have just pointed out, Howells writes exactly as a boy would write or speak? Does he limit himself in that fashion? Perhaps you have read Twain's *The Adventures of Huckleberry Finn* and can make a comparison. Now in that book Huck is the purported writer, and the effect is one of complete VERISIMILITUDE: we feel that Huck is writing the book, and the diction, the grammar, and the cadence seem just right. But if you will look back at the book you will find that the pattern of sentences and paragraphs is beyond the reach of anyone but a most accomplished writer.

5) The headnote remarks that the structure of *A Boy's Town* is not that of ordinary chronological narrative. In the selections called "Pets" and "Fantasies and Superstitions" consider the between-paragraph transition. How is it managed? If you find no specifically transitional expressions between paragraphs, does that mean that the paragraphs are quite unrelated?

6) "Circuses and Shows" begins with a discussion of "running off." How does Howells get to the subject matter announced by the title? Is there any time pattern in the selection? The last paragraph begins as an expository paragraph. How does Howells get back to narrative again? Has he violated his time pattern?

7) In "The Hydraulic and Its Reservoirs" the problem of structure seems a bit more complex. The title and the opening sentence suggest that the intention is description, and that the structure will be governed by the physical point of view—the way in which writer and reader view the system described. This physical point of view is somewhat modified, because to the boy's mind place and events go together, and to the man looking back they fuse in memory. But notice the first sentence in iv, and that the account moves in an orderly fashion from the Hydraulic to the Little Reservoir and thence to the Big Reservoir.

8) *A Boy's Town* was first printed in a magazine called *Harper's Young People*. Howells, as an accomplished professional writer, is of course quite aware of his readers and of the necessity of writing for *them*. Does he ever "write down" to them? This textbook started out with selections from two writers who insist that a writer ought to respect his readers. Does the principle hold here in a work written by a man past fifty for readers of, say, twelve?

9) Howells was the leader of the realistic movement in American fiction beginning after 1870, and he greatly influenced other American writ-

ers. When he is writing critical theory he seems sometimes almost to think of REALISM as fidelity to external reality—as a sort of scientific observation. But is realism here merely a truth to things and events? What kind of existence, for example, does the Boy's Town have?

10) Is the nature of boys as it is described and implied in our selections the nature of boys at all times and in all places? If your answer is the obvious one, "Yes, it is," you should be prepared to defend it. But consider whether in your time adults have not invaded the Boy's Town. If your instructor is a man whose hair is gray enough, he may remember a boys' sphere of existence more like the one described by Howells than the one you know. But Howells's Boy's Town was not far from the frontier.

ii   REMINISCENCE INTERPRETED

Our selections from Hamlin Garland's *A Son of the Middle Border* are intended to make a pattern of those portions of the book that deal with the Garland family's westward migration. Garland, in writing this account of his boyhood experience, is looking back thirty years and more. But there is a kind of interpretation in these selections beyond that of reminiscence. Garland sees his own experience through his knowledge of American history. You can make connections between these selections and other pieces we have read, and you can learn something more of the quality of the westward urge. You can see what our mobility of population meant to those who were moving. And you can sense something of the disillusionment that came at last from the equating of a finer future and a compass direction.

Garland's father was born and brought up in Massachusetts. The first move here described came when Garland, who was born in 1860, was a child, and soon after his father had returned from his service with the Union army. The last move of the Garland family westward came when Garland was a very young man just through with his schooling. Garland makes a fine use of this Midwestern material in his collection of short stories, *Main-Travelled Roads,* his one distinguished work of fiction.

FROM *A Son of the Middle Border* (1917)

HAMLIN GARLAND

[Westward with the Garlands]

[i]

1 Green's Coulee [Wisconsin] was a delightful place for boys. It offered hunting and coasting and many other engrossing sports, but my father, as the seasons went by, became thoroughly dissatisfied with its disadvantages.

More and more he resented the stumps and ridges which interrupted his plow. Much of his quarter-section remained unbroken. There were ditches to be dug in the marsh and young oaks to be uprooted from the forest, and he was obliged to toil with unremitting severity. There were times, of course, when field duties did not press, but never a day came when the necessity for twelve hours' labor did not exist.

II Furthermore, as he grubbed or reaped he remembered the glorious prairies he had crossed on his exploring trip into Minnesota before the war, and the oftener he thought of them the more bitterly he resented his up-tilted, horse-killing fields, and his complaining words sank so deep into the minds of his sons that for years thereafter they were unable to look upon any rise of ground as an object to be admired.

III It irked him beyond measure to force his reaper along a steep slope, and he loathed the irregular little patches running up the ravines behind the timbered knolls, and so at last like many another of his neighbors he began to look away to the west as a fairer field for conquest. He no more thought of going east than a liberated eagle dreams of returning to its narrow cage. He loved to talk of Boston, to boast of its splendor, but to live there, to earn his bread there, was unthinkable. Beneath the sunset lay the enchanted land of opportunity and his liberation came unexpectedly.

IV Sometime in the spring of 1868, a merchant from LaCrosse, a plump man who brought us candy and was very cordial and condescending, began negotiations for our farm, and in the discussion of plans which followed, my conception of the universe expanded. I began to understand that "Minnesota" was not a bluff but a wide land of romance, a prairie, peopled with red men, which lay far beyond the big river. And then, one day, I heard my father read to my mother a paragraph from the county paper which ran like this, "It is reported that Richard Garland has sold his farm in Green's Coulee to our popular grocer, Mr. Speer. Mr. Speer intends to make of it a model dairy farm."

V This intention seemed somehow to reflect a ray of glory upon us, though I fear it did not solace my mother, as she contemplated the loss of home and kindred. She was not by nature an emigrant,—few women are. She was content with the pleasant slopes, the kindly neighbors of Green's Coulee. Furthermore, most of her brothers and sisters still lived just across the ridge in the valley of the Neshonoc, and the thought of leaving them for a wild and unknown region was not pleasant.

VI To my father, on the contrary, change was alluring. Iowa was now the place of the rainbow, and the pot of gold. He was eager to push on toward it, confident of the outcome. His spirit was reflected in one of the songs which we children particularly enjoyed hearing our mother sing, a ballad which consisted of a dialogue between a husband and wife on this very subject of emigration. The words as well as its wailing melody still stir me deeply, for they lay hold of my sub-conscious memory—embodying admirably the debate which went on in our home as well as in the homes of other farmers in the valley,—only, alas! our mothers did not prevail. . . .

VII [Another] ballad which dates back to the conquest of the Allegheny mountains opens with a fine uplifting note,

> Cheer up, brothers, as we go
> O'er the mountains, westward ho,
> Where herds of deer and buffalo
> Furnish the fare.

and the refrain is at once a bugle call and a vision:

> Then o'er the hills in legions, boys,
> Fair freedom's star
> Points to the sunset regions, boys,
> Ha, ha, ha-ha!

and when my mother's clear voice rose on the notes of that exultant chorus, our hearts responded with a surge of emotion akin to that which sent the followers of Daniel Boone across the Blue Ridge, and lined the trails of Kentucky and Ohio with the canvas-covered wagons of the pioneers.

VIII A little farther on in the song came these words,

> When we've wood and prairie land,
> Won by our toil,
> We'll reign like kings in fairy land,
> Lords of the soil!

which always produced in my mind the picture of a noble farm-house in a park-like valley, just as the line, "We'll have our rifles ready, boys," expressed the boldness and self-reliance of an armed horseman.

IX The significance of this song in the lives of the McClintocks and the Garlands cannot be measured. It was the marching song of my grandfather's generation and undoubtedly profoundly influenced my father and my uncles in all that they did. It suggested shining mountains, and grassy vales, swarming with bear and elk. It called to green savannahs and endless flowery glades. It voiced as no other song did, the pioneer impulse throbbing deep in my father's blood. That its words will not bear close inspection today takes little from its power. Unquestionably it was a directing force in the lives of at least three generations of my pioneering race. Its strains will be found running through this book from first to last, for its pictures continued to allure my father on and on toward "the sunset regions," and its splendid faith carried him through many a dark vale of discontent.

[ii]

I Neighbors came in now and again to talk of our migration, and yet in spite of all that, in spite of our song, in spite of my father's preparation I had no definite premonition of coming change, and when the day of departure actually dawned, I was as surprised, as unprepared as though it had all happened without the slightest warning.

II So long as the kettle sang on the hearth and the clock ticked on its shelf, the idea of "moving" was pleasantly diverting, but when one raw winter day I saw the faithful clock stuffed with rags and laid on its back in a box, and the chairs and dishes being loaded into a big sleigh, I began to experience something very disturbing and very uncomfortable. "O'er the hills in legions, boys," did not sound so inspiring to me then. "The woods and prairie lands" of Iowa became of less account to me than the little cabin in which I had lived all my short life.

III Harriet and I wandered around, whining and shivering, our own misery augmented by the worried look on mother's face. It was February, and she very properly resented leaving her home for a long, cold ride into an unknown world, but as a dutiful wife she worked hard and silently in packing away her treasures, and clothing her children for the journey.

IV At last the great sleigh-load of bedding and furniture stood ready at the door, the stove, still warm with cheerful service, was lifted in, and the time for saying good-bye to our coulee home had come.

V "Forward march!" shouted father and led the way with the big bob-sled, followed by cousin Jim and our little herd of kine, while mother and the children brought up the rear in a "pung" drawn by old Josh, a flea-bit gray.—It is probable that at the moment the master himself was slightly regretful.

VI A couple of hours' march brought us to LaCrosse, the great city whose wonders I had longed to confront. It stood on the bank of a wide river and had all the value of a sea-port to me, for in summer-time great hoarsely bellowing steamboats came and went from its quay, and all about it rose high wooded hills. Halting there, we overlooked a wide expanse of snow-covered ice in the midst of which a dark, swift, threatening current of open water ran. Across this chasm stretching from one ice-field to another lay a flexible narrow bridge over which my father led the way toward hills of the western shore. There was something especially terrifying in the boiling heave of that black flood, and I shivered with terror as I passed it, having vividly in my mind certain grim stories of men whose teams had broken through and been swept beneath the ice never to reappear.

VII It was a long ride to my mother, for she too was in terror of the ice, but at last the Minnesota bank was reached, La Crescent was passed, and our guide entering a narrow valley began to climb the snowy hills. All that was familiar was put behind; all that was strange and dark, all that was wonderful and unknown, spread out before us, and as we crawled along that slippery, slanting road, it seemed that we were entering on a new and marvellous world.

VIII We lodged that night in Hokah, a little town in a deep valley. The tavern stood near a river which flowed over its dam with resounding roar and to its sound I slept. Next day at noon we reached Caledonia, a town high on the snowy prairie. Caledonia! For years that word was a poem in my ear, part of a marvellous and epic march. Actually it consisted of a few frame houses and a grocery store. But no matter. Its name shall ring like a peal of bells in this book.

IX It grew colder as we rose, and that night, the night of the second day, we reached Hesper and entered a long stretch of woods, and at last turned in towards a friendly light shining from a low house beneath a splendid oak.

x As we drew near my father raised a signal shout, "Hallo-o-o the House!" and a man in a long gray coat came out. "Is that thee, friend Richard?" he called, and my father replied, "Yea, neighbor Barley, here we are!"

xi I do not know how this stranger whose manner of speech was so peculiar, came to be there, but he was and in answer to my question, father replied, "Barley is a Quaker," an answer which explained nothing at that time. Being too sleepy to pursue the matter, or to remark upon anything connected with the exterior, I dumbly followed Harriet into the kitchen which was still in possession of good Mrs. Barley.

xii Having filled our stomachs with warm food mother put us to bed, and when we awoke late the next day the Barleys were gone, our own stove was in its place, and our faithful clock was ticking calmly on the shelf. So far as we knew, mother was again at home and entirely content.

xiii This farm, which was situated two miles west of the village of Hesper, immediately won our love. It was a glorious place for boys. Broadarmed white oaks stood about the yard, and to the east and north a deep forest invited to exploration. The house was of logs and for that reason was much more attractive to us than to our mother. It was, I suspect, both dark and cold. I know the roof was poor, for one morning I awoke to find a miniature peak of snow on the floor at my bedside. It was only a rude little frontier cabin, but it was perfectly satisfactory to me.

[iii]

i One day there came into our home a strange man who spoke in a fashion new to me. He was a middle-aged rather formal individual, dressed in a rough gray suit, and father alluded to him privately as "that English duke." I didn't know exactly what he meant by this, but our visitor's talk gave me a vague notion of "the old country."

ii "My home," he said, "is near Manchester. I have come to try farming in the American wilderness."

iii He was kindly, and did his best to be democratic, but we children stood away from him, wondering what he was doing in our house. My mother disliked him from the start for as he took his seat at our dinner table, he drew from his pocket a case in which he carried a silver fork and spoon and a silver-handled knife. Our cutlery was not good enough for him!

iv Every family that we knew at that time used three-tined steel forks and my mother naturally resented the implied criticism of her table ware. I heard her say to my father, "If our ways don't suit your English friend he'd better go somewhere else for his meals."

v This fastidious pioneer also carried a revolver, for he believed that having penetrated far into a dangerous country, he was in danger, and I am not at all sure but that he was right, for the Minnesota woods at this time were filled with horse-thieves and counterfeiters, and it was known that many of these landhunting Englishmen carried large sums of gold on their persons.

VI We resented our guest still more when we found that he was trying to buy our lovely farm and that father was already half-persuaded. We loved this farm. We loved the log house, and the oaks which sheltered it, and we especially valued the glorious spring and the plum trees which stood near it, but father was still dreaming of the free lands of the farther west, and early in March he sold to the Englishman and moved us all to a rented place some six miles directly west, in the township of Burr Oak.

VII This was but a temporary lodging, a kind of camping place, for no sooner were his fields seeded than he set forth once again with a covered wagon, eager to explore the open country to the north and west of us. The wood and prairie land of Winnishiek County did not satisfy him, although it seemed to me then, as it does now, the fulfillment of his vision, the realization of our song.

VIII For several weeks he travelled through southern Minnesota and northern Iowa, always in search of the perfect farm, and when he returned, just before harvest, he was able to report that he had purchased a quarter-section of "the best land in Mitchell County" [Iowa] and that after harvest we would all move again.

IX If my mother resented this third removal she made no comment which I can now recall. I suspect that she went rather willingly this time, for her brother David wrote that he had also located in Mitchell County, not two miles from the place my father had decided upon for our future home, and Samantha, her younger sister, had settled in Minnesota. The circle in Neshonoc seemed about to break up. A mighty spreading and shifting was going on all over the west, and no doubt my mother accepted her part in it without especial protest. . . .

X Late in August my father again loaded our household goods into wagons, and with our small herd of cattle following, set out toward the west, bound once again to overtake the actual line of the middle border.

XI This journey has an unforgettable epic charm as I look back upon it. Each mile took us farther and farther into the unsettled prairie until, in the afternoon of the second day, we came into a meadow so wide that its western rim touched the sky without revealing a sign of man's habitation other than the road in which we travelled.

XII The plain was covered with grass tall as ripe wheat and when my father stopped his team and came back to us and said, "Well, children, here we are on The Big Prairie," we looked about us with awe, so endless seemed this spread of wild oats and waving blue-joint.

XIII Far away dim clumps of trees showed, but no chimney was in sight, and no living thing moved save our own cattle and the hawks lazily wheeling in the air. My heart filled with awe as well as wonder. The majesty of this primeval world exalted me. I felt for the first time the poetry of the unplowed spaces. It seemed that the "herds of deer and buffalo" of our song might, at any moment, present themselves,—but they did not, and my father took no account even of the marsh fowl.

xiv "Forward march!" he shouted, and on we went.

xv Hour after hour he pushed into the west, the heads of his tired horses hanging ever lower, and on my mother's face the shadow deepened, but her chieftain's voice cheerily urging his team lost nothing of its clarion resolution. He was in his element. He loved this shelterless sweep of prairie. This westward march entranced him, I think he would have gladly kept on until the snowy wall of the Rocky Mountains met his eyes, for he was a natural explorer.

xvi Sunset came at last, but still he drove steadily on through the sparse settlements. Just at nightfall we came to a beautiful little stream, and stopped to let the horses drink. I heard its rippling, reassuring song on the pebbles. Thereafter all is dim and vague to me until my mother called out sharply, "Wake up, children! Here we are!"

xvii Struggling to my feet I looked about me. Nothing could be seen but the dim form of a small house.—On every side the land melted into blackness, silent and without boundary.

xviii Driving into the yard, father hastily unloaded one of the wagons and taking mother and Harriet and Jessie drove away to spend the night with Uncle David who had preceded us, as I now learned, and was living on a farm not far away. My brother and I were left to camp as best we could with the hired man.

xix Spreading a rude bed on the floor, he told us to "hop in" and in ten minutes we were all fast asleep.

xx The sound of a clattering poker awakened me next morning and when I opened my sleepy eyes and looked out a new world displayed itself before me.

xxi The cabin faced a level plain with no tree in sight. A mile away to the west stood a low stone house and immediately in front of us opened a half-section of unfenced sod. To the north, as far as I could see, the land billowed like a russet ocean, with scarcely a roof to fleck its lonely spread. —I cannot say that I liked or disliked it. I merely marvelled at it, and while I wandered about the yard, the hired man scorched some cornmeal mush in a skillet and this with some butter and gingerbread, made up my first breakfast in Mitchell County.

xxii An hour or two later father and mother and the girls returned and the work of setting up the stove and getting the furniture in place began. In a very short time the experienced clock was voicing its contentment on a new shelf, and the kettle was singing busily on its familiar stove. Once more . . . Belle Garland adjusted herself to a pioneer environment, comforted no doubt by the knowledge that David and Deborah were near and that her father was coming soon. No doubt she also congratulated herself on the fact that she had not been carried beyond the Missouri River—and that her house was not "surrounded by Indians who murder by night."

xxiii A few hours later, while my brother and I were on the roof of the house with intent to peer "over the edge of the prairie" something grandly significant happened. Upon a low hill to the west a herd of horses suddenly appeared running swiftly, led by a beautiful sorrel pony with shining white mane. On they came, like a platoon of cavalry rushing down across the open sod which lay before our door. The leader moved with lofty and graceful action, easily out-stretching all his fellows. Forward they swept, their long tails floating in the wind like banners,—on in a great curve as if scenting danger in the smoke of our fire. The thunder of their feet filled me with delight. Surely, next to a herd of buffalo this squadron of wild horses was the most satisfactory evidence of the wilderness into which we had been thrust.

xxiv Riding as if to intercept the leader, a solitary herder now appeared, mounted upon a horse which very evidently was the mate of the leader. He rode magnificently, and under him the lithe mare strove resolutely to overtake and head off the leader.—All to no purpose! The halterless steeds of the prairie snorted derisively at their former companion, bridled and saddled, and carrying the weight of a master. Swiftly they thundered across the sod, dropped into a ravine, and disappeared in a cloud of dust.

xxv Silently we watched the rider turn and ride slowly homeward. The plain had become our new domain, the horseman our ideal.

[iv]

i During the years '79 and '80, while Burton and I had been living our carefree jocund life at the Seminary, a series of crop failures had profoundly affected the county, producing a feeling of unrest and bitterness in the farmers which was to have a far-reaching effect on my fortunes as well as upon those of my fellows. For two years the crop had been almost wholly destroyed by chinch bugs. . . .

ii DAKOTA was the magic word. The "Jim River Valley" was now the "land of delight," where "herds of deer and buffalo" still "furnished the cheer." Once more the spirit of the explorer flamed up in the soldier's heart. Once more the sunset allured. Once more my mother sang the marching song of the McClintocks,

> O'er the hills in legions, boys,
> Fair freedom's star
> Points to the sunset regions, boys,
> Ha, ha, ha-ha!

and sometime, in May I think it was, father again set out—this time by train, to explore the Land of The Dakotas which had but recently been wrested from the control of Sitting Bull.

iii He was gone only two weeks, but on his return announced with triumphant smile that he had taken up a homestead in Ordway, Brown County, Dakota. His face was again alight with the hope of the borderman, and he had much to say of the region he had explored.

A COMPLEX USE OF REMINISCENCE *iii*

Perhaps you have read the following selection from Mark Twain's *Life on the Mississippi,* but no one minds reading Twain over again. The book is important as a record of the lost era when the Mississippi was the great artery of commerce in the United States. There are other records, of course, but without Twain we should hardly know how this life felt. And it is our great good fortune that Twain knew Horace Bixby. Bixby was important enough so that we should have known about him without Twain's record, but with it we feel that we know him.

Our selection is written retrospectively, but the point of view is complex. The questions that follow the selection are intended to help you be aware of some interesting technical matters about it. But you ought also to consider as you read it in what ways the point of view is different from any used in the foregoing selections.

FROM *Life on the Mississippi* (1875, 1883)

MARK TWAIN

A Cub-Pilot's Experience

What with lying on the rocks four days at Louisville, and some other delays, the poor old *Paul Jones* fooled away about two weeks in making the voyage from Cincinnati to New Orleans. This gave me a chance to get acquainted with one of the pilots, and he taught me how to steer the boat, and thus made the fascination of river life more potent than ever for me.

It also gave me a chance to get acquainted with a youth who had taken deck passage—more's the pity; for he easily borrowed six dollars of me on a promise to return to the boat and pay it back to me the day after we should arrive. But he probably died or forgot, for he never came. It was doubtless the former, since he had said his parents were wealthy, and he only traveled deck passage because it was cooler.[1]

I soon discovered two things. One was that a vessel would not be likely to sail for the mouth of the Amazon under ten or twelve years; and the other was that the nine or ten dollars still left in my pocket would not suffice for so impossible an exploration as I had planned, even if I could afford to wait for a ship. Therefore it followed that I must contrive a new career. The *Paul Jones* was now bound for St. Louis. I planned a siege against my pilot, and at the end of three hard days he surrendered. He agreed to teach me the Mississippi River from New Orleans to St. Louis for five hundred dollars, payable out of the first wages I should receive after graduating. I entered upon the small enterprise of "learning" twelve or thirteen hundred miles of the great Mississippi River with the easy confidence of my time of life. If I had really known what I was about to require of my faculties, I should not have had the courage to begin. I supposed that all a pilot had to do was to keep his boat in the river, and I did not consider that that could be much of a trick, since it was so wide.

The boat backed out from New Orleans at four in the afternoon, and it was "our watch" until eight. Mr. Bixby, my chief, "straightened her up,"

[1] "Deck" passage—*i.e.*, steerage passage.

plowed her along past the sterns of the other boats that lay at the Levee, and then said, "Here, take her; shave those steamships as close as you'd peel an apple." I took the wheel, and my heart-beat fluttered up into the hundreds; for it seemed to me that we were about to scrape the side off every ship in the line, we were so close. I held my breath and began to claw the boat away from the danger; and I had my own opinion of the pilot who had known no better than to get us into such peril, but I was too wise to express it. In half a minute I had a wide margin of safety intervening between the *Paul Jones* and the ships; and within ten seconds more I was set aside in disgrace, and Mr. Bixby was going into danger again and flaying me alive with abuse of my cowardice. I was stung, but I was obliged to admire the easy confidence with which my chief loafed from side to side of his wheel, and trimmed the ships so closely that disaster seemed ceaselessly imminent. When he had cooled a little he told me that the easy water was close ashore and the current outside, and therefore we must hug the bank, up-stream, to get the benefit of the former, and stay well out, down-stream, to take advantage of the latter. In my own mind I resolved to be a down-stream pilot and leave the up-streaming to people dead to prudence.

Now and then Mr. Bixby called my attention to certain things. Said he, "This is Six-Mile Point." I assented. It was pleasant enough information, but I could not see the bearing of it. I was not conscious that it was a matter of any interest to me. Another time he said, "This is Nine-Mile Point." Later he said, "This is Twelve-Mile Point." They were all about level with the water's edge; they all looked about alike to me; they were monotonously unpicturesque. I hoped Mr. Bixby would change the subject. But no; he would crowd up around a point, hugging the shore with affection, and then say: "The slack water ends here, abreast this bunch of China trees; now we cross over." So he crossed over. He gave me the wheel once or twice, but I had no luck. I either came near chipping off the edge of a sugar-plantation, or I yawed too far from shore, and so dropped back into disgrace again and got abused.

The watch was ended at last, and we took supper and went to bed. At midnight the glare of a lantern shone in my eyes, and the night watchman said:

"Come, turn out!"

And then he left. I could not understand this extraordinary procedure; so I presently gave up trying to, and dozed off to sleep. Pretty soon the watchman was back again, and this time he was gruff. I was annoyed. I said:

"What do you want to come bothering around here in the middle of the night for? Now, as like as not, I'll not get to sleep again to-night."

The watchman said:

"Well, if this ain't good, I'm blessed."

The "off-watch" was just turning in, and I heard some brutal laughter from them, and such remarks as "Hello, watchman! ain't the new cub turned out yet? He's delicate, likely. Give him some sugar in a rag, and send for the chambermaid to sing 'Rock-a-by Baby,' to him."

About this time Mr. Bixby appeared on the scene. Something like a minute later I was climbing the pilot-house steps with some of my clothes on and the rest in my arms. Mr. Bixby was close behind, commenting. Here was something fresh—this thing of getting up in the middle of the night to go to work. It was a detail in piloting that had never occurred to me at all. I knew that boats ran all night, but somehow I had never happened to reflect that somebody had to get up out of a warm bed to run them. I began to fear that piloting was not quite so romantic as I had imagined it was; there was something very real and worklike about this new phase of it.

It was a rather dingy night, although a fair number of stars were out. The big mate was at the wheel, and he had the old tub pointed at a star and was holding her straight up the middle of the river. The shores on either hand were not much more than half a mile apart, but they seemed wonderfully far away and ever so vague and indistinct. The mate said:

"We've got to land at Jones' plantation, sir."

The vengeful spirit in me exulted. I said to myself, "I wish you joy of your job, Mr. Bixby; you'll have a good time finding Mr. Jones' plantation such a night as this; and I hope you never *will* find it as long as you live."

Mr. Bixby said to the mate:

"Upper end of the plantation, or the lower?"

"Upper."

"I can't do it. The stumps there are out of water at this stage. It's no great distance to the lower, and you'll have to get along with that."

"All right, sir. If Jones don't like it, he'll have to lump it, I reckon."

And then the mate left. My exultation began to cool and my wonder to come up. Here was a man who not only proposed to find this plantation on such a night, but to find either end of it you preferred. I dreadfully wanted to ask a question, but I was carrying about as many short answers as my cargo-room would admit of, so I held my peace. All I desired to ask Mr. Bixby was the simple question whether he was ass enough to really imagine he was going to find that plantation on a night when all plantations were exactly alike and all of the same color. But I held in. I used to have fine inspirations of prudence in those days.

Mr. Bixby made for the shore and soon was scraping it, just the same as if it had been daylight. And not only that, but singing:

"Father in heaven, the day is declining," etc.

It seemed to me that I had put my life in the keeping of a peculiarly reckless outcast. Presently he turned on me and said:

"What's the name of the first point above New Orleans?"

I was gratified to be able to answer promptly, and I did. I said I didn't know.

"Don't *know?*"

This manner jolted me. I was down at the foot again, in a moment. But I had to say just what I had said before.

"Well, you're a smart one!" said Mr. Bixby. "What's the name of the *next* point?"

Once more I didn't know.

"Well, this beats anything. Tell me the name of *any* point or place I told you."

I studied a while and decided that I couldn't.

"Look here! What do you start out from, above Twelve-Mile Point, to cross over?"

"I—I—don't know."

"You—you—don't know?" mimicking my drawling manner of speech. "What *do* you know?"

"I—I—nothing, for certain."

"By the great Cæsar's ghost, I believe you! You're the stupidest dunderhead I ever saw or ever heard of, so help me Moses! The idea of *you* being a pilot—*you!* Why, you don't know enough to pilot a cow down a lane."

Oh, but his wrath was up! He was a nervous man, and he shuffled from one side of his wheel to the other as if the floor was hot. He would boil a while to himself, and then overflow and scald me again.

"Look here! What do you suppose I told you the names of those points for?"

I tremblingly considered a moment, and then the devil of temptation provoked me to say:

"Well to—to—be entertaining, I thought."

This was a red rag to the bull. He raged and stormed so (he was crossing the river at the time) that I judged it made him blind, because he ran over the steering-oar of a trading-scow. Of course the traders sent up a volley of red-hot profanity. Never was a man so grateful as Mr. Bixby was; because he was brimful, and here were subjects who could *talk back.* He threw open a window, thrust his head out, and such an irruption followed as I never had heard before. The fainter and farther away the scowmen's curses drifted, the higher Mr. Bixby lifted his voice and the weightier his adjectives grew. When he closed the window he was empty. You could have drawn a seine through his system and not caught curses enough to disturb your mother with. Presently he said to me in the gentlest way:

"My boy, you must get a little memorandum-book; and every time I tell you a thing, put it down right away. There's only one way to be a pilot, and that is to get this entire river by heart. You have to know it just like A B C."

That was a dismal revelation to me; for my memory was never loaded with anything but blank cartridges. However, I did not feel discouraged long. I judged that it was best to make some allowances, for doubtless Mr. Bixby was "stretching." Presently he pulled a rope and struck a few strokes on the big bell. The stars were all gone now, and the night was as black as ink. I could hear the wheels churn along the bank, but I was not entirely certain that I could see the shore. The voice of the invisible watchman called up from the hurricane-deck:

"What's this, sir?"

"Jones' plantation."

I said to myself, "I wish I might venture to offer a small bet that it isn't." But I did not chirp. I only waited to see. Mr. Bixby handled the engine-bells, and in due time the boat's nose came to the land, a torch glowed from the forecastle, a man skipped ashore, a darkey's voice on the bank said: "Gimme de k'yarpet-bag, Mass' Jones," and the next moment we were standing up the river again, all serene. I reflected deeply awhile, and then said—but not aloud—"Well, the finding of that plantation was the luckiest accident that ever happened; but it couldn't happen again in a hundred years." And I fully believed it *was* an accident, too.

By the time we had gone seven or eight hundred miles up the river, I had learned to be a tolerably plucky up-stream steersman, in daylight; and before we reached St. Louis I had made a trifle of progress in night-work, but only a trifle. I had a note-book that fairly bristled with the names of towns, "points," bars, islands, bends, reaches, etc.; but the information was to be found only in the note-book—none of it was in my head. It made my heart ache to think I had only got half of the river set down; for as our watch was four hours off and four hours on, day and night, there was a long four-hour gap in my book for every time I had slept since the voyage began.

My chief was presently hired to go on a big New Orleans boat, and I packed my satchel and went with him. She was a grand affair. When I stood in her pilot-house I was so far above the water that I seemed perched on a mountain; and her decks stretched so far away, fore and aft, below me, that I wondered how I could ever have considered the little *Paul Jones* a large craft. There were other differences, too. The *Paul Jones'* pilot-house was a cheap, dingy, battered rattletrap, cramped for room; but here was a sumptuous glass temple; room enough to have a dance in; showy red and gold window-curtains; an imposing sofa; leather cushions and a back to the high bench where visiting pilots sit, to spin yarns and "look at the river"; bright, fanciful "cuspadores," instead of a broad wooden box filled with sawdust; nice new oilcloth on the floor; a hospitable big stove for winter; a wheel as high as my head, costly with inlaid work; a wire tiller-rope; bright brass knobs for the bells; and a tidy, white-aproned, black "texas-tender," to bring up tarts and ices and coffee during mid-watch, day and night. Now this was "something like"; and so I began to take heart once more to believe that piloting was a romantic sort of occupation after all. The moment we were under way I began to prowl about the great steamer and fill myself with joy. She was as clean and as dainty as a drawing-room; when I looked down her long, gilded saloon, it was like gazing through a splendid tunnel; she had an oil-picture, by some gifted sign-painter, on every stateroom door; she glittered with no end of prism-fringed chandeliers; the clerk's office was elegant, the bar was marvelous, and the bar-keeper had been barbered and upholstered at incredible cost. The boiler-deck (*i.e.*, the second story of the boat, so to speak) was as spacious as a church, it seemed to me; so with the forecastle; and there was no pitiful handful of deck-hands, firemen, and roustabouts down there, but a whole battalion of men. The fires were fiercely glaring from a long row of furnaces, and over them were eight huge boilers! This was unutterable pomp.

The mighty engines—but enough of this. I had never felt so fine before. And when I found that the regiment of natty servants respectfully "sir'd" me, my satisfaction was complete.

A Daring Deed

When I returned to the pilot-house St. Louis was gone, and I was lost. Here was a piece of river which was all down in my book, but I could make neither head nor tail of it: you understand, it was turned around. I had seen it when coming up-stream, but I had never faced about to see how it looked when it was behind me. My heart broke again, for it was plain that I had got to learn this troublesome river *both ways*.

The pilot-house was full of pilots, going down to "look at the river." What is called the "upper river" (the two hundred miles between St. Louis and Cairo, where the Ohio comes in) was low; and the Mississippi changes its channel so constantly that the pilots used to always find it necessary to run down to Cairo to take a fresh look, when their boats were to lie in port a week; that is, when the water was at a low stage. A deal of this "looking at the river" was done by poor fellows who seldom had a berth, and whose only hope of getting one lay in their being always freshly posted and therefore ready to drop into the shoes of some reputable pilot, for a single trip, on account of such pilot's sudden illness, or some other necessity. And a good many of them constantly ran up and down inspecting the river, not because they ever really hoped to get a berth, but because (they being guests of the boat) it was cheaper to "look at the river" than stay ashore and pay board. In time these fellows grew dainty in their tastes, and only infested boats that had an established reputation for setting good tables. All visiting pilots were useful, for they were always ready and willing, winter or summer, night or day, to go out in the yawl and help buoy the channel or assist the boat's pilots in any way they could. They were likewise welcomed because all pilots are tireless talkers, when gathered together, and as they talk only about the river they are always understood and are always interesting. Your true pilot cares nothing about anything on earth but the river, and his pride in his occupation surpasses the pride of kings.

We had a fine company of these river inspectors along this trip. There were eight or ten, and there was abundance of room for them in our great pilot-house. Two or three of them wore polished silk hats, elaborate shirt-fronts, diamond breastpins, kid gloves, and patent-leather boots. They were choice in their English, and bore themselves with a dignity proper to men of solid means and prodigious reputation as pilots. The others were more or less loosely clad, and wore upon their heads tall felt cones that were suggestive of the days of the Commonwealth.

I was a cipher in this august company, and felt subdued, not to say torpid. I was not even of sufficient consequence to assist at the wheel when it was necessary to put the tiller hard down in a hurry; the guest that stood nearest did that when occasion required—and this was pretty much all the time, because of the crookedness of the channel and the scant water. I stood in a corner; and the talk I listened to took the hope all out of me. One visitor said to another:

"Jim, how did you run Plum Point, coming up?"

"It was in the night, there, and I ran it the way one of the boys on the *Diana* told me; started out about fifty yards above the wood-pile on the false point, and held on the cabin under Plum Point till I raised the reef— quarter less twain—then straightened up for the middle bar till I got well abreast the old one-limbed cottonwood in the bend, then got my stern on the cottonwood, and head on the low place above the point, and came through a-booming—nine and a half."

"Pretty square crossing, an't it!"

"Yes, but the upper bar's working down fast."

Another pilot spoke up and said:

"I had better water than that, and ran it lower down; started out from the false point—mark twain—raised the second reef abreast the big snag in the bend, and had quarter less twain."

One of the gorgeous ones remarked:

"I don't want to find fault with your leadsmen, but that's a good deal of water for Plum Point, it seems to me."

There was an approving nod all around as this quiet snub dropped on the boaster and "settled" him. And so they went on talk-talk-talking. Meantime, the thing that was running in my mind was, "Now, if my ears hear aright, I have not only to get the names of all the towns and islands and bends, and so on, by heart, but I must even get up a warm personal acquaintanceship with every old snag and one-limbed cottonwood and obscure wood-pile that ornaments the banks of this river for twelve hundred miles; and more than that, I must actually know where these things are in the dark, unless these guests are gifted with eyes that can pierce through two miles of solid blackness. I wish the piloting business was in Jericho and I had never thought of it."

At dusk Mr. Bixby tapped the big bell three times (the signal to land), and the captain emerged from his drawing-room in the forward end of the "texas," and looked up inquiringly. Mr. Bixby said:

"We will lay up here all night, captain."

"Very well, sir."

That was all. The boat came to shore and was tied up for the night. It seemed to me a fine thing that the pilot could do as he pleased, without asking so grand a captain's permission. I took my supper and went immediately to bed, discouraged by my day's observations and experiences. My late voyage's note-booking was but a confusion of meaningless names. It had tangled me all up in a knot every time I had looked at it in the daytime. I now hoped for respite in sleep; but no, it reveled all through my head till sunrise again, a frantic and tireless nightmare.

Next morning I felt pretty rusty and low-spirited. We went booming along, taking a good many chances, for we were anxious to "get out of the river" (as getting out to Cairo was called) before night should overtake us.

But Mr. Bixby's partner, the other pilot, presently grounded the boat, and we lost so much time getting her off that it was plain the darkness would overtake us a good long way above the mouth. This was a great misfortune, especially to certain of our visiting pilots, whose boats would have to wait for their return, no matter how long that might be. It sobered the pilot-house talk a good deal. Coming up-stream, pilots did not mind low water or any kind of darkness; nothing stopped them but fog. But down-stream work was different; a boat was too nearly helpless, with a stiff current pushing behind her; so it was not customary to run down-stream at night in low water.

There seemed to be one small hope, however: if we could get through the intricate and dangerous Hat Island crossing before night, we could venture the rest, for we would have plainer sailing and better water. But it would be insanity to attempt Hat Island at night. So there was a deal of looking at watches all the rest of the day, and a constant ciphering upon the speed we were making; Hat Island was the eternal subject; sometimes hope was high and sometimes we were delayed in a bad crossing, and down it went again. For hours all hands lay under the burden of this suppressed excitement; it was even communicated to me, and I got to feeling so solicitous about Hat Island, and under such an awful pressure of responsibility, that I wished I might have five minutes on shore to draw a good, full, relieving breath, and start over again. We were standing no regular watches. Each of our pilots ran such portions of the river as he had run when coming up-stream, because of his greater familiarity with it; but both remained in the pilot-house constantly.

An hour before sunset Mr. Bixby took the wheel, and Mr. W. stepped aside. For the next thirty minutes every man held his watch in his hand and was restless, silent, and uneasy. At last somebody said, with a doomful sigh:

"Well, yonder's Hat Island—and we can't make it."

All the watches closed with a snap, everybody sighed and muttered something about its being "too bad, too bad—ah, if we could *only* have got here half an hour sooner!" and the place was thick with the atmosphere of disappointment. Some started to go out, but loitered, hearing no bell-tap to land. The sun dipped behind the horizon, the boat went on. Inquiring looks passed from one guest to another; and one who had his hand on the door-knob and had turned it, waited, then presently took away his hand and let the knob turn back again. We bore steadily down the bend. More looks were exchanged, and nods of surprised admiration—but no words. Insensibly the men drew together behind Mr. Bixby, as the sky darkened and one or two dim stars came out. The dead silence and sense of waiting became oppressive. Mr. Bixby pulled the cord, and two deep, mellow notes from the big bell floated off on the night. Then a pause, and one more note was struck. The watchman's voice followed, from the hurricane deck:

"Labboard lead, there! Stabboard lead!"

The cries of the leadsmen began to rise out of the distance, and were gruffly repeated by the word-passers on the hurricane deck.

"M-a-r-k three! M-a-r-k three! Quarter-less-three! Half twain! Quarter twain! M-a-r-k twain! Quarter-less——"

Mr. Bixby pulled two bell-ropes, and was answered by faint jinglings far below in the engine-room, and our speed slackened. The steam began to whistle through the gauge-cocks. The cries of the leadsmen went on— and it is a weird sound, always, in the night. Every pilot in the lot was watching now, with fixed eyes, and talking under his breath. Nobody was calm and easy but Mr. Bixby. He would put his wheel down and stand on a spoke, and as the steamer swung into her (to me) utterly invisible marks—for we seemed to be in the midst of a wide and gloomy sea—he would meet and fasten her there. Out of the murmur of half-audible talk, one caught a coherent sentence now and then—such as:

"There; she's over the first reef all right!"

After a pause, another subdued voice:

"Her stern's coming down just *exactly* right, by *George!*"

"Now she's in the marks; over she goes!"

Somebody else muttered:

"Oh, it was done beautiful—*beautiful!*"

Now the engines were stopped altogether, and we drifted with the current. Not that I could see the boat drift, for I could not, the stars being all gone by this time. This drifting was the dismalest work; it held one's heart still. Presently I discovered a blacker gloom than that which surrounded us. It was the head of the island. We were closing right down upon it. We entered its deeper shadow, and so imminent seemed the peril that I was likely to suffocate; and I had the strongest impulse to do *something,* anything, to save the vessel. But still Mr. Bixby stood by his wheel, silent, intent as a cat, and all the pilots stood shoulder to shoulder at his back.

"She'll not make it!" somebody whispered.

The water grew shoaler and shoaler, by the leadsman's cries, till it was down to:

"Eight-and-a-half! E-i-g-h-t feet! E-i-g-h-t feet! Seven-and——"

Mr. Bixby said warningly through his speaking-tube to the engineer:

"Stand by, now!"

"Ay, ay, sir!"

"Seven-and-a-half! Seven feet! *Six*-and——"

We touched bottom! Instantly Mr. Bixby set a lot of bells ringing, shouted through the tube, "*Now,* let her have it—every ounce you've got!" then to his partner, "Put her hard down! snatch her! snatch her!" The boat rasped and ground her way through the sand, hung upon the apex of disaster a single tremendous instant, and then over she went! And such a shout as went up at Mr. Bixby's back never loosened the roof of a pilot-house before!

There was no more trouble after that. Mr. Bixby was a hero that night; and it was some little time, too, before his exploit ceased to be talked about by river men.

Fully to realize the marvelous precision required in laying the great steamer in her marks in that murky waste of water, one should know that not only must she pick her intricate way through snags and blind reefs, and then shave the head of the island so closely as to brush the overhanging foliage with her stern, but at one place she must pass almost within arm's reach of a sunken and invisible wreck that would snatch the hull timbers from under her if she should strike it, and destroy a quarter of a million dollars' worth of steamboat and cargo in five minutes, and maybe a hundred and fifty human lives into the bargain.

The last remark I heard that night was a compliment to Mr. Bixby, uttered in soliloquy and with unction by one of our guests. He said:

"By the Shadow of Death, but he's a lightning pilot!"

------

1) Twain became an apprentice pilot about a century ago. Does he seem further removed from you than the magazine writer you read last week? Can you account for the immediacy of effect?

2) Do you suppose that Twain's account of his reception of Mr. Bixby's first instruction is wholly factual? (Twain was brought up on the river and as a young man surely knew in a general way what a pilot's function was.) Is he justified in departing from the facts? Does the departure serve a purpose?

3) Twain advised the young Kipling first to get his facts and then to distort them as he liked. Twain's poor work—have you read some of it?—shows how thin humorous writing without this core of fact may be. A beginning writer need never fear that facts about human experience, if they are made clear, will be uninteresting.

4) Twain has a little trick of ELLIPSIS in narrative, pleasing to the reader because it requires imaginative activity from him. Consider this: "About this time Mr. Bixby appeared on the scene. Something like a minute later I was climbing the pilot-house steps. . . ." This trick belongs to any writer who can work it.

5) What is Twain doing with his ANECDOTE about the finding of Jones's plantation in the dark? Are his mistaken notions the important thing? What about the description of the "big New Orleans boat"? (Can you suggest any reason why we are not told her name?)

6) "A Daring Deed" is centered on a single anecdote about Bixby's negotiation of the Hat Island crossing. Is the intention in this anecdote parallel to that in the anecdote about finding Jones's plantation?

7) Our selection is built around illustrative anecdotes. How does Twain manage his continuity? Point out a passage of summary narrative.

8) There must often be an admixture of exposition in narrative; Twain gets along with a minimum here. Notice the treatment of the expository paragraph almost at the end of the second chapter in our selection. But not at the end—why not?

9) Notice that here the expository general statement arises from the concrete anecdote. In ordinary exposition we do the opposite thing; we try to back up and illustrate some, at least, of our generalizations with concrete illustration. But, as we shall see, an accomplished writer of exposition may use this pattern, too.

10) One may count as many as five capital I's in two lines in this selection; but surely you have realized that the "I" is standing for a point of view, a point of view with which we can easily identify ourselves since we, too, know little of the river. But is that point of view Twain's in the year in which he wrote these chapters, some eighteen years after the experience they record? Would Twain then have admired the "red and gold window-curtains" and the stateroom door oil paintings he describes as part of the splendor of the New Orleans boat? Consider point of view throughout the selection. You will find it consistently maintained down to detail: the "I" always speaks, for instance, of "Mr. Bixby"—as the awed apprentice pilot would always have thought of him.

11) We come finally to the matter of selection. We cannot say precisely what Twain left out of his record of experience; we can be sure that he left out far more than he put in. There is an amusing character in *Life on the Mississippi,* a pilot named Brown, who has what is called sometimes "the curse of total recall." Not many students are so cursed; yet all of us may recall more details of an experience than we can make literary use of. Twain somewhere speaks of a selective memory as the chief asset of a novelist, but most of us will have to accomplish our selection consciously. At least you can ask, "Is this event, or person, or detail, significant for my reader as well as for me?" You will find it instructive to consider the reason for certain obvious suppressions of detail in our selection. A river boat had two pilots—what do we know of Mr. Bixby's partner, and why do we not know more? Why are not the guest pilots "looking at the river" separated and named? Is anything accomplished by having them a sort of chorus? (Do not answer that Twain cannot remember all the detail; he can remember, or purport to remember, the hymn Mr. Bixby was singing at a particular trick at the wheel. In his latter years Twain wrote, "When I was younger I could remember anything, whether it happened or not. . . .")

12) Go back to question 1 for a minute. Can you answer it more fully now?

SUGGESTIONS FOR PAPERS

Exercises directly connected with the selections might be pieces of narrative summary. Each of the three writers offers special problems. If, however, you would like a little more precisely defined exercise, here are two suggestions:

You might assume that you are writing a paper on the development of the Middle West and that you wish to use the selection from *A Son of the Middle Border* as illustrative material. Assume further that you have written this sentence as the first sentence in a paragraph: "The experience of Hamlin Garland must have been typical of that of many a Middle Western boy." Then develop the sentence in a substantial paragraph. It will take careful selection and economy of statement.

Or you may prefer this assumption: You are writing an entry on Horace Bixby for a reference book devoted to American history and literature, and you have written these sentences:

Bixby, Horace (1826–1912), a Mississippi River pilot and steamboat captain, famous for a remarkable knowledge of the river. In the War between the States, Bixby piloted a gunboat and was afterward chief of the Union River Service. He was later captain of the *City of Baton Rouge,* a famous steamer on the St. Louis–New Orleans run; and was active on the river until his death. Mark Twain . . .

Continue this entry for five or six sentences to give a reader as clear an idea of Twain's treatment of Bixby as is possible in so limited a scope.

The selections, perhaps particularly those from *A Boy's Town,* will suggest any number of papers using personal experience. Now students should not be given so much advice about using their own experience in papers that they are straitened by it. One piece of negative advice seems indicated: ordinarily the student who writes about a recent trip, vacation, or the like does not write a good paper. If you will remember the times that you have been bored by your friends' oral accounts of such material, you will agree that failure with it is likely. What will work better is material with which you have a continuing experience. And remember this: just the experience that is most commonplace to you may be what is most interesting to your reader.

Students often succeed well with records of group activities: the business meeting of a club, a choir rehearsal, a day with a corn-detasseling gang, a day on a fishing boat, a rush period for the employees of a chain store—the list is endless. In such a paper the function of the "I" is clear; he is at once part of the group and the observer. Pick a particular, typical period in the group life; and pay attention to timing in your paper, so that the paper does not sprawl.

Just as often, students do well with accounts of the experiences of their families. Has your family continued the tradition of American mobility? Were your grandparents immigrants and does your family have a history of making its way in a new country? Can you write an account of the place of a family of minority race or religion in American society? How have the wars of the twentieth century affected your family and you? Social historians point out that rapid shifts in financial status from generation to generation are typical of American life. Does your family history illustrate that? But you see where these questions are tending. Look for what is representative in your family's experience.

The selections in this chapter offer opportunities for comparative critical studies of no very great difficulty. You might, for instance, read part or all of Thomas Bailey Aldrich's *The Story of a Bad Boy* (1870), an excellent account of boy experience in New England in the same years that Howells was a boy in Ohio. You would find it interesting to consider the likenesses—since boys will be boys—and the differences accounted for by place.

Both Garland and Twain have used the experiences recorded in our selections as backgrounds for works of fiction. A comparative paper using the selection from Garland and one of the stories from *Main-Travelled*

Roads—perhaps "Under the Lion's Paw"—would require but little extra reading. And if you have read *The Adventures of Huckleberry Finn* you will be able to discuss the river lore in that book in reference to the river lore in our two chapters of *Life on the Mississippi*. The first part of *Life on the Mississippi* and *Huck Finn* are the result of the same literary impulse; for instance, at one point when Twain wanted some illustrative material for *Life on the Mississippi*, he simply took a chapter he had prepared for *Huck Finn* and made it into his third chapter (which, if you choose this suggestion for a paper, be sure to read).

IX

Reporting

The day-by-day writing of good reporters on newspapers and news-magazines requires a degree of skill and discipline that would astonish students who suppose that "just giving the facts" is an easy matter. Such pieces of current reporting are well worth your study; but since examples are readily available, we shall not use our space in this chapter for them. Instead we shall take here selections that have rather more literary intention than does most newspaper and magazine reporting. The excellence in our selections, like excellence in all reporting, begins with the writer's firm control of the facts. But these pieces will also give us special opportunities to consider some technical problems of selection, organization, and point of view.

THE REPORT BY A PARTICIPANT   *i*

The writer is John William De Forest, and the report is his *A Volunteer's Adventures.* De Forest was a novelist who became a volunteer officer in the Union army in the War between the States. But he is not here a writer of fiction (although some of this material was used in his *Miss Ravenel's Conversion from Secession to Loyalty,* a novel you might enjoy). *A Volunteer's Adventures* is a remarkable work; few of the best writers of the time had war experience, and none of them made so distinguished a use of it. De Forest was a sensitive, highly articulate man undergoing experience like that of thousands of his fellow countrymen. His experience is important because it is representative; his record is perceptive and skillful.

William Dean Howells once wrote that De Forest's novels were "of an advanced realism before realism was known by that name"; and to some of his first readers his novels were rather too much like life. You can see something of his honesty of mind in our selections: he does not make his experience heroic; neither does he exploit its squalor and pain. Our selections represent three kinds of war experience, each recorded close to the fact. (The date given for the book is the date of first publication in book form; most of our material was first published in magazines between 1864 and 1868.)

FROM *A Volunteer's Adventures* (1946)

JOHN WILLIAM DE FOREST

[i]

Camp Life in Louisiana [1862]

I Since we have been here regiment after regiment has arrived from below and sailed up the river. Where they go the general does not bother himself to inform us; but we learn that there are troops at Baton Rouge and
that others are said to have started for Vicksburg. It would seem that we
of the Twelfth Connecticut, one of the healthiest, largest and best drilled
regiments in the division, are destined to stay in peaceful possession of this
earthwork, guarding New Orleans against a foe which cannot get near it.
I begin to despair of finding a chance to fight unless there is another war
after this one.

II Singular as it may seem, this is a disappointment. Nearly every officer and the majority of the men would prefer to go up the river, taking
the certainty of hard fare and hard times generally, with a fair likelihood
of being killed or wounded, rather than stay here drilling and guard
mounting in peace. When the long roll beat for the Seventh Vermont to
start foeward, they hurrahed for ten minutes while we sulked over their
luck and their exultation, not even giving them a cheer as they marched by
us to embark. Meanwhile we sniff at the Thirteenth Connecticut as a
dandy corps which has never lived out of doors and is only fit to stand
guard around General Butler. We believe that we could whip it in a fight,
and we know that we could beat it in battalion drill. And so on, through a
series of grumblings and snarlings, all illustrative of human nature.

III The colonel of the Thirteenth met me lately in the city and asked
me to dinner. You would have considered it a decent meal, and I marvelled
at it as a luxurious one. Just think of claret; also of sparkling Isabella,
served in coffee cups for lack of glasses; also wine sauce on the pudding,
and *café noir* as a final. The Thirteenth is a terrible regiment in the way
of spoiling the Egyptians and letting the oppressed go free. General Butler
pets it because of its fine clothes, its bright outfit of Springfield and Sharpe
rifles, and its dandy officers whose uniforms are as yet unsoiled by field
service.

IV But it worries him much (or so he makes believe) by its hostility to
the patriarchal institution. It has forty Negro laundresses, all belonging to
men whom he is trying to pacificate. The owners go to the general and beg
for their ebony chattels. The general sends for the captains of the Thirteenth and requests them to let the people go. The captains argue that the
girls want to wash and get paid for it, and that the regulations allow forty
washerwomen to a battalion of ten companies. There the matter invariably

ends, as the story is told to me. Meantime the quartermaster has seventy Negro men, regularly enrolled and rationed, who clean and repair the customhouse, which is the regimental barrack.

v The Twelfth also has contrabands, fully sixty in number, some of them nurses and laborers at the hospital, others servants to officers, the remainder company cooks. Two of them carry my written protections in their pockets. Who said John Brown was dead? There are six hundred thousand John Browns now in the South. The old enthusiast is terribly avenged. The rotten post of slavery is getting a rousing shake.

vi The officer of the guard tells me that outside of his picket there is a camp, or rather bivouac, of one hundred and fifty Negroes, lately arrived from the other bank of the river. Their owner (a thousand-hogshead man) got into a rage about something, perhaps their insubordination, ordered them off the plantation and bade them go to the devil. Also there is a great floating population of blacks; men and women and pickaninnies streaming daily into the camp and sticking there until they are expelled as "unemployed persons"; a burden to the soul of our brigade provost marshal and a subject of intense commiseration to our general.

vii We have at last established an officers' mess. We dine in a small house inside camp limits, waited on at table by our own servants, and cooked for by artists borrowed from neighboring plantations. Our crockery we were also obliged to borrow from the deserted dwelling of a gentleman who is absent as captain in the Rebel army. As the paymaster has not yet arrived we cannot indulge in luxuries; but our steward draws army stores on our account from the regimental commissary and barters them for fish, chickens, eggs, and vegetables; these delicacies being mostly brought in by nocturnal darkies who perhaps stole them from "Masr." The living is not exceptionally fine, but is far above our former barbarous style.

. . . .

viii Last evening I thought that Breckinridge had come, and that the Twelfth was about to fight its first battle. About nine o'clock scattering musket shots broke out on the picket line, running along the front from the river to the cypress swamp. Then, before I could buckle on sword and revolver, there was a yell from the sergeants of "Fall in!" followed by the long roll of all the regiments roaring sullenly through the damp night.

ix The rain had poured nearly all day, and the camp was a slop of mud and puddles. My men splashed through the sludge and halted on the little company parade, jabbering, reeling, and scuffling. I saw at once what was the matter: payday had worked its usual mischief: one third of them were as drunk as pipers. In my rage at their condition I forgot all about the enemy. I pushed and flung them into their places, and called them sots, and used other bad language.

x "If I was the angel Gabriel," said my second lieutenant, "I should take my trumpet out of my mouth to swear."

xi The company had scarcely counted off when there came a yell from the piercing voice of the lieutenant colonel: "Battalion! load at will;

load!"—When the rattle and thud of the ramrods ceased he added, "To the parapet!—double quick; mar—ch!"

XII Through the mud we trotted, jumping the ditches which pretend to drain the camp, and forming battalion-line along the base of our earth-work. Ten minutes of silence followed, and then came an order from the general to return to quarters, the alarm having been a false one, perhaps for practice. Now ensued a real fight among my bacchanals, which I qui-eted by sending one man to the guardhouse, pushing others into their tents, and ordering lights out.

XIII To comprehend this drunkenness you must understand that many of my men are city toughs, in part Irish; also that they are desperate with malaria, with the monotony of their life, and with incessant discomforts; finally, that intoxication in itself is not a military offence and not punish-able. If you could look into our tents you would not wonder that consola-tion is sought for in whiskey. The never-ceasing rain streams at will through numerous rents and holes in the mouldy, rotten canvas. Nearly every night half the men are wet through while asleep unless they wake up, stack their clothing in the darkness, and sit on it with their rubber blankets over their heads, something not easy to do when they are so crowded that they can hardly move.

XIV It must be added in fairness that intoxication is not confined to the soldiers. The officers are nearly as miserable, and are tempted to seek the same consolation. Lately a lieutenant reeled into my tent, dropped heavily on a bed, stared at me for a minute as if to locate me, and said in a thick voice, "Capm, everybody's drunk today. Capm, the brigade's drunk."

.   .   .   .

XV The court-martial has closed, and I am again on company duty. We have settled down into a new station and are brigaded under Weitzel, a young regular officer who has lately been made general.

XVI Do you fancy the idea of my applying for the colonelcy of a colored regiment? Important people here advise it and promise to help me with recommendations. It would be a comfortable position, I suppose; but there are some obvious serious disadvantages. The colored troops will probably be kept near here and used to garrison unhealthy positions; they will be called on for fatigue duty, such as making roads, building bridges and draining marshes; they will be seldom put into battle, and will afford small chance of distinction.

XVII Since writing the above I have talked on the subject with Colonel Deming, who is acting mayor of New Orleans and well informed concern-ing affairs at headquarters. I had decided to apply for a black regiment, and I wrote to him for an introduction to General Butler. Thereupon he sent for me, treated me to a fine dinner and gave me his views.

XVIII "I advise you," said he, "not to make your proposed application, for fear it might be successful."

XIX Then he went into details concerning the character of the officers who would be associated with me, and the nature of the service that will be assigned to the Negro troops, which details I do not feel free to repeat. In short, he counselled me so urgently against the step that I have given it up and decided to fight my way on in the Twelfth, if it is ever to have any fighting.

xx I must tell you of an adventure of mine with one of the heroines of secession. On my way down to the city in the crowded, dirty cars, I saw behind me, standing, a lady in half-mourning, a pallid and meagre young woman, with compressed thin lips, sharp grey eyes and a waspish expression. Much doubting whether my civility would be well received, I rose and offered her my seat. She would not look at me; she just conceded me a quick shake of the head and a petulant shrug of the shoulders; then, pinching her pale lips, she stood glaring straight before her.

xxi After waiting her pleasure a moment I resumed my seat. Presently a rather pretty lady opposite me (a young mother with kindly eyes and a cultured expression) took her little girl into her lap and beckoned the scowling heroine to the vacant place. She accepted it with lavish thanks, adding in a loud, ostentatious tone, "I wasn't going to take a seat from a Yankee. These cars used to be a fit place for ladies. Now niggers and Yankees crowd decent people out."

xxii The lady with the kindly eyes threw me an apologetic glance which seemed to say, "I hope you did not hear." There ended the comedy; or was it a tragedy?

[ii]
The First Time under Fire

[De Forest's first experience under fire was at the engagement at Georgia Landing in western Louisiana. The Weitzel who addresses De Forest's men is Brigadier General Godfrey Weitzel. The engagement is with a part of the Confederate forces commanded by Brigadier General Alfred C. Mouton.]

i This day (Monday, October 27, 1862) the Eighth New Hampshire and Perkins' troop of cavalry held the right bank of the bayou, parallel with the head of the main column. It was prudent to keep our principal force on the western bank because that furnished the easiest line of retreat in case of a repulse. The troops marched like greenhorns, straggling about the road, the levee, and the fields, and taking advantage of every discoverable cut-off. A few months later we would have been ashamed to exhibit such a spectacle of disorder. We passed pretty residences, flourishing plantations and endless flats of waving cane. But the owners of this comfort and wealth were not visible; not a vehicle, nor even an equestrian, appeared on the highways. The only planter discoverable was a tall, cadaverous man with lank iron-grey hair and the voice of a camp-meeting preacher, who shouted lugubrious warnings to us.

ii "Ah boys! boys! you don't know what awaits you. You are going to defeat and rout and slaughter. Better turn back while you can! Better turn back!"

III Some of the youngsters yelled impertinences to him, and he stalked solemnly into his house, leaving our impenitent array to its fate.

IV While the whites evaded us, or perhaps had already quitted the region, the Negroes swarmed about us with acclamations of joy. "God bless you, massas!" they cried.—"Oh, de Lawd's name be praised!—We knowed you'd come.—Ise a gwine 'long with you."

V And go with us they did by hundreds, ready to do anything for their deliverers and submitting unmurmuringly to the tricks and robberies which were practiced upon them by our jokers and scapegraces. Nowhere in the South did I ever find or hear of one Negro who was hostile to us. But meanwhile they were not vindictive toward their masters, at least not to the extent of insurrection, or massacre, or murder.

. . . .

VI . . . With drums beating, fifes screaming and banners flying we tramped along, listening to the slow *pumming* of artillery two miles away. I was anxious, but thus far only for my men, not knowing how they would behave in this their first battle. I commenced joking with them, not because I was gay, but because I wanted them to be gay. I have forgotten what I said; it was poor, coarse fun enough probably; but it answered the purpose. The cheerful yet steady countenance of the company, and of the whole regiment as well, was all that one could desire.

VII We found the bridge in place, and the two sentinel howitzers barking at intervals, while an invisible Rebel battery responded with similar deliberation. Here we first came under fire, and here I first beheld a wounded man. In a country carriage, upheld by two Negroes, was a ghastly sufferer, his knee crushed by a shot, his torn trousers soaked with a dirty crimson, his eyes full of the agony of death. I did not want my men to see the dismaying spectacle and called their attention to something, I have forgotten what, on the other side of the bayou.

VIII As we trotted down the inner slope of the levee a surprisingly loud, harsh scream passed over us, ending in a sharp explosion and a splashing in the muddy water. I was not alarmed, but rather relieved and gratified. If they can't aim better than that they are welcome to fire all day, I innocently thought. Then came another shell, striking close to the crowded bridge and spattering some of the men, but without deterring the thirsty ones from stopping to fill their canteens. It was very good practice, considering that the guns were behind the levee half a mile downstream, where the fellows who worked them could not see us. But I did not believe that they could hit me, and my chief anxiety was lest I should wet my feet in the sloppy bottom of the boat.

IX In general, the terror of battle is not an abiding impression, but comes and goes like throbs of pain; and this is especially the case with veterans who have learned to know when there is pressing danger and when not; the moment a peril has passed they are as tranquil as if it had never come near. On the present occasion I was not as yet conscious of any emotion which could be called fear. I was still ignorant of the great horrors of battle, and buoyed up by the excitement of a rapid advance. A regiment of well-drilled greenhorns, if neatly brought into action, can charge as brilliantly as veterans.

·   ·   ·   ·

x Now occurred a curious incident which might have brought disaster, had I not happened to be at the right of my company, near the color guard. We had two flags, the United States flag borne by a sergeant named Edwards and the Connecticut flag borne by a sergeant whom I forbear to name. This last man, on hearing the Rebel bullets, faced about and started rearward. I never saw anything done more naturally and promptly. He did not look wild with fright; he simply looked alarmed and resolved to get out of danger; it was the simplest and most persuaded expression of countenance imaginable. He was not a thorough coward, and never afterward turned tail that I know of; but he was confounded by the peril of the moment and thought of nothing but getting away from it.

xi It would have been lawful and right to pistol him, for he ran a risk of guiding the regiment rearward and bringing about defeat. In a great rage and with sabre uplifted, I pounced upon him as he was struggling through the color corporals, all of whom were pushing forward eagerly and gallantly. "Forward, or I'll split your head open," I shouted, catching him by the shoulder and facing him about. He obeyed in silence, with a curious dazed expression, and I pushed him into his place in the front rank of the color guard. We got two volleys after that; and at each one this man fell back a pace with a nervous start; but each time I howled "Forward!" in his ear and sent him on again.

xii There were plenty of other incidents, very interesting to raw soldiers. The first lieutenant of Company D saw with astonishment two of his men fall and roll over each other. To his mind they each seemed to be struggling to squirm undermost in order to escape the bullets. "Get into the ranks!" he ordered, hitting the uppermost with the flat of his sabre. One of them pointed to a bloody hole in his trousers and lay still; the other rose with a mazed air, picked up his rifle and ran after the company. A bullet had struck this man's gun barrel with such force as to knock him down, and then had glanced through the thigh of his rear-rank comrade, both falling in a heap.

·   ·   ·   ·

xiii All this time we were exposed to both cannon and musketry without being allowed to reply. "Oh dear! when shall *we* fire?" I heard one of the color corporals exclaim. I looked at the youngster; he was not a coward; his color was good. But to be boomed at and volleyed at without answering is one the most serious trials of battle. There was a general feeling of relief, near akin to delight, when the lieutenant colonel's clear, metallic voice pealed out, "Halt! Fire by file! Commence firing!"

xiv The men could not wait to fire by file, which is a graduated discharge running from right to left of each company; they leveled those five hundred rifles together and sent a grand, crashing volley into the hostile line of smoke which confronted them; for as yet we could see no other sign of an enemy. In the next second every one was loading his piece as if his life depended on the speed of the operation. Then of a sudden, to my utter amazement, the two centre companies fell on their faces. Turning upon the man nearest me, I threatened to kill him if he did not get up. "We were ordered to lie down," he explained, and my second lieutenant added, "That is so, Captain."

xv "It can't be," I replied. "The right of the regiment is advancing, and the colonel with it."

xvi The men promptly rose, and firing had already recommenced, when I and others near me distinctly heard an order to lie down. Of course we obeyed, all the more smartly because just then a shell flew between the colors, screeching like a mad panther. I laughed at the haste of my plunge, and saw one of my soldiers laughing also, probably at his own undignified hurry. I never could learn positively who uttered that stentorian cry of "Lie down." One story was that it came from the Thirteenth Connecticut which was just then close in rear of us as a support. Afterwards, when I could think of it at leisure, it reminded me of those godlike voices which resounded in ancient battles, giving encouragement or spreading panic. It certainly was not uttered by our commander, for we presently heard him yelling, "Forward, Twelfth!"

xvii In great haste we of the centre sprang up and recovered our place in line. It was the last stop or pause in our advance. We had been drilled long enough under fire, and we broke away from the lieutenant colonel. Once he tried his utmost to make us halt, dress the line and give a volley, as regulars are said to do in battle. But he might as well have ordered a regiment of screeching devils to halt. On we swept in the teeth of canister and musketry, every man loading and firing as fast as possible. There was such a pressure inward toward the colors that some of my lightweights were crowded out of their places, and we were three ranks deep instead of two. Little Sweeny, who belonged on the left of the company, fidgeted along the rear in search of a crack to poke his gun through until my second lieutenant dragged him back to his post and roared at him, "What in h—ll are you doing on the right?"

xviii "Liftenant, I'm purtectin' thim colors," yelped Sweeny, and then sent a bullet over Mouton's rear guard.

xix The swearing mania was irrepressible. In the excitement of the charge it seemed as if every extremity of language was excusable, providing it would help towards victory. Did I think of the other world, which was so near? Not once. I was anxious for nothing but to keep a steady line, and to reach the enemy quickly. I did not exhort my soldiers to fight gallantly and fire coolly. They were fighting the best they knew how, and aiming as well as the quick-step would permit. Nearly all that I said might be summed up as repetitions of the two orders, "Close up" and "Guide right."

. . . .

xx Just then a stunning volley, the voice of the Thirteenth coming into action, rang out on our left. It was given without orders from Colonel

Birge, but the sight of the escaping enemy was an irresistible temptation. Forward trampled both regiments, smack up to the cypress fence, yelling with delight and blazing away at the woods, although the enemy had vanished like a dream. It was all that the officers could do to halt the excited men and put an end to their riotous shouting. I was amazed at the feebleness of the Southern resistance and could not imagine that we had already won the battle.

xxi "Can't this firing be stopped?" I said to the lieutenant colonel. "Are we not wasting ammunition on a mere party of skirmishers?"

xxii "Cease firing!" he ordered, riding down the line; and with no little difficulty quiet was restored.

xxiii "Can't the regiment push into the woods?" I now queried. "The enemy may reform there and drive us back."

xxiv The lieutenant colonel improved on my suggestion; he ordered out two companies to search the wood. Meantime the captains of the remaining companies reformed ranks, counted off their men and had the roll called. We had scarcely got into shape when we heard a cheer on our left and saw that Weitzel was making a speech to the Thirteenth. What he said to our comrades in victory I could not hear, but his address to us was an admirable bit of practical instruction.

xxv "Twelfth Connecticut, you have done well. That is the way to do it. Never stop, and the enemy won't stay."

xxvi "That is the best speech I ever heard," commented one of my men.

[iii]

Forced Marches

[De Forest here writes in special reference to a forced march in pursuit of Confederate forces in April, 1863. The scene of the action is Louisiana, west of New Orleans. The Confederate forces were commanded by Brigadier General Alfred C. Mouton, the Union forces by Major General Nathaniel P. Banks. The pursuit was unsuccessful.]

i About five o'clock an order arrived to move out of range of fire. The skirmishers came in; the men rose and took their places in line; and we marched slowly back to our position of the morning. During the night we fought mosquitoes, not with the idea of amusing them, but in deadly earnest. During the night, also, the colonel in charge of the pickets, a greenhorn of some nine-months' regiment, distinguished himself by an exhibition of the minimum of native military genius. Early in the morning he reported to Weitzel that the enemy had vacated their position.

ii "How do you know?" demanded the startled general.

iii "I heard their artillery going off about two o'clock."

iv "Good God, sir! why didn't you inform me of it immediately?"

v "Why, General, I thought you wanted them to clear out; and I didn't like to disturb you after such a hard day's work."

vi Thus collapsed the plan by which we were to stick like a burr to the enemy and pitch into his rear whenever he should attempt to force his way

through Grover. Sling blankets and shoulder arms was the order now, and
we set off on our long chase to Alexandria. Mouton had gained five or six
hours the start of us, and Texans on horseback can travel faster than Yankees on foot, so that, although we marched furiously that hot day, making
twenty-four miles before nightfall, Grover had finished his battle long before we reached him. Unacquainted with the country and ordered to the
wrong place, he had gone to the wrong place. He had posted himself on
one of two parallel roads, instead of where the two met in one, affording
him a chance to fight decisively. The consequence was a sidelong battle,
both sides suffering, but the enemy escaping.

VII Forward at full speed the next day and the day after, scurrying and
popping of cavalry in the front, as our van skirmished with their rear. At
times a great distant dust, showing how close we were upon the Rebel
flight. It is a solemn and menacing phenomenon, the dust of a marching
enemy, but more particularly so, of course, when it is advancing upon you.
The smoke of burning cotton streaked the day, and the flare of it luridly
starred the night; for even in his haste Mouton was determined that no
fraction of the financial king should fall to the Yankees. Stragglers in grey
and butternut dropped back among us with pacific waving of caps and
handkerchiefs; for although we could not catch the Texan horsemen, we
were marching the Louisiana infantry to tatters. It seemed like meeting
old friends to come across the fellows of the Crescent regiment, whom we
had encountered six months before at Labadieville, or Georgia Landing.
Shouts of recognition took place, gayer on our side than on theirs. They
told us that their officers were driving the men on with drawn sabres, or
the whole force would have gone to pieces under the exhaustion of the retreat. Mightily encouraged by these statements, we blistered our soles with
renewed energy.

VIII Oh, the horrors of marching on blistered feet! It is an incessant
bastinado applied by one's own self, from morning to night. I do not mean
a single blister, as big as a pea, but a series of blisters, each as large as a
dollar, or, to judge by one's sensations, as large as a cartwheel. I have had
them one under the other, on the heel, behind the heel, on the ball of the
foot, on every toe, a network, a labyrinth, an archipelago of agony. Heat,
hunger, thirst, and fatigue are nothing compared with this torment. When
you stand, you seem to be on red-hot iron plates; when you walk, you
make grimaces at every step. In the morning the whole regiment starts
limping, and by noon the best soldiers become nearly mutinous with suffering. They snarl and swear at each other; they curse the general for ordering such marching; they curse the enemy for running away instead of
fighting; they fling themselves down in the dust, refusing to move a step
further. Fevered with fatigue and pain, they are actually not themselves.
Meantime, the company officers, as sore-footed as anyone, must run about
from straggler to straggler, coaxing, arguing, ordering, and, perhaps, using
the flat of the sabre. Instead of marching in front of my company, I followed immediately in the rear, so that I could see and at once pounce upon
everyone who fell out.

IX It was curious to note how cheerful everyone became if cannon in front told of the proximity of the enemy. We were ready to fight the bloodiest of combats rather than march a mile further. We filed into line of battle delighted, and then resumed our pursuit heartsick.

X It will be asked, perhaps, whether I, an officer and claiming, of course, to be a patriot, preserved my staunchness under these trials. I must confess, and I do it without great shame, conscious of being no more than human, that in my inmost soul I was as insubordinate as the worst men were in speech and behavior. In my unspeakable heart I groaned and raved. I wished the bridges would break down—I wished the regiment would refuse to take another step—it seemed to me that I should have been silent in the face of mutiny. But nothing of all this passed my lips, and none could suspect it from my actions.

XI When we bivouacked at night came the severest trial. Our regiment was on the left of the brigade, and as we always slept in line of battle, this threw us half a mile from the bayou, along which we marched, and which was our only source of water. It was necessary to order a squad of the blistered and bloody-footed men to bring water for the company's coffee. The first sergeant takes out his book and reads off the fatigue detail: "Corporal Smith, Privates Brown, Jones, Robinson, and Brown second, fall in with canteens to get water."

XII Now ensues a piteous groaning, pleading, and showing of bloody heels or blistered soles, on the part of the most fagged or least manly of the victims of rotation in labor. The first sergeant feels that he has no discretion in the matter, and he knows, moreover, that the other men are fully as incapable of marching as these. He stands firm on his detail, and the opposition grumblingly yields. Slowly and sadly Messrs. Brown, Jones, Robinson, and Brown second take up the canteens of the company, each backing six or eight, and limp away to the river, returning, an hour later, wet, muddy, dragged out, and savage.

XIII Somewhat similar scenes happened on the march. Aides passed down the length of the trailing column with the order, "Water half a mile in front; details will be sent forward with canteens." Under these circumstances, roguish soldiers would sometimes use the chance to forage, falling in an hour later with a load of chickens as well as of fluid.

XIV Having tried various alleviations for the hardships of marching, without much benefit, I conclude that man was not made to foot it at the rate of thirty miles a day. Soaping the inside of the stockings does some good, by diminishing the friction and, as a consequence, the blistering. It is also advisable to wash the feet before starting, always providing you have sufficient time and water. Beware of washing them at night; it cracks the heated skin and increases the misery. Beware, too, of trying to march on the strength of whiskey; you go better for a few minutes, and then you are worse off than ever. Opium is far superior as a temporary tonic, if I may judge by a single day's experience. I started out sick, took four grains of opium, marched better and better every hour, and at the end of twenty-two miles came in as fresh as a lark.

xv It must be understood by the non-military reader that company officers of infantry are not permitted to mount horses, whether by borrowing or stealing, but must foot it alongside of their men, for the double purpose of keeping them in order and of setting them an example of hardihood. On this march, General Banks impounded, at a certain point on the road, more than a dozen infantry officers who were found astride of animals, causing each to rejoin his command as it passed, placing some under arrest and summarily dismissing one from the service. They looked exceedingly crestfallen as they stood there, cooped up in a barnyard under charge of the provost guard. The passing soldiers grinned at them, hooted a little, and marched on, much cheered by the spectacle.

xvi If it had not been for the counter irritant of blistered feet, we should have heard a mutinous deal of grumbling on account of thirst. A man strapped up as a soldier is, and weighted with forty rounds of ammunition, knapsack, three days' rations, canteen containing three pints, and rifle, perspires profusely. I have seen the sweat standing on the woolly fibres of their flannel sacks like dew. To supply this waste of moisture they pour down the warm water of their canteens, and are soon begging for leave to fall out of the ranks in search of incredibly situated springs and rivulets. It will not do to accede to the request, for if one man goes, all have a right to go, and, moreover, the absence would probably terminate in a course of foraging or pillaging. Mindful of his duty and the orders of his superiors, the captain grimly responds, "Keep your place, sir," and trudges sufferingly on, cursing inwardly the heat, the dust, the pace and, perhaps, the orders. He knows that if his fellows are caught a mile to the rear wringing the necks of chickens, he may be sent after them; and, in view of his blisters and the fifteen miles already marched and the indefinite miles yet to go, he has no fancy for such an expedition. . . .

xvii In describing the miseries of marching, I must not forget the dust. The movement of so many thousands of feet throws up such dense and prodigious clouds that one who has not witnessed the phenomenon will find it difficult to imagine it in all its vastness and nuisance. The officers dodge from side to side of the road to escape the pulverous suffocation; and the men, bound to their fours, choke desperately along in the midst of it. The faces become grimed out of all human semblance; the eyelashes are loaded, the hair discolored, and the uniform turns to the color of the earth. It frequently happens that you cannot see the length of your regiment, and it has occurred to me that I have been unable to see the length of my own company of perhaps twenty files. Of course, this annoyance varies greatly in magnitude, according to the nature of the earth.

xviii Rain is good or bad, according to circumstances. In hot weather it cools the skin, invigorates the muscles, and is a positive comfort, except in so far as it spoils the footing. On the second day of this advance we had a pelting shower, which soaked everybody, including General Banks—which last circumstance was a source of unmixed satisfaction to the soldiers. Enlisted men like to see officers bear their share of the troubles of war; and, moreover, our fellows held the general responsible for the tearing speed at which we were going. But rain, although pleasant to the skin in warm weather, will reach the earth and make puddles; and to infantry in march a puddle in the road is a greater nuisance than people in carriages would imagine. No man, however wet he may be, wants to step into it; he crowds his next comrade, and so gets into a growling bout; or he hangs back, and so checks the succeeding files. A large puddle always produces a tailing-off of the regiment, which must be made up presently by double-quicking, much to the fatigue and wrath of the rearmost. Oh, miserable left of the column! how many times a day it has to run in order to catch up with the right! and how heartily it hates the right in consequence! Put a regiment or a brigade "left in front," and see how it will go. The men who usually march in the rear are now in the lead, and they are sure to give the fellows at the other end of the line a race. This opening out of the column of march is a constant evil, and one which officers soon learn to struggle against with incessant watchfulness. I believe that I used to shout, "Close up, men," at least a hundred times a day, in every conceivable tone of authority, impatience, and entreaty.

xix But are there no comforts, no pleasures, in forced marching? Just one: stopping it. Yes, compared with the incessant anguish of going, there was a keen luxury in the act of throwing one's self at full length and remaining motionless. It was a beast's heaven; but it was better than a beast's hell—insupportable fatigue and pain. The march done, the fevered feet bare to the evening breeze, the aching limbs outstretched, the head laid on the blanket roll which had been such a burden through the day, the pipe in mouth, nature revived a little and found that life retained some sweetness. Delicious dreams, too—dreams wonderfully distinct and consecutive—made slumber a conscious pleasure. All night I was at home surrounded by loving faces. No visions of war or troubles; no calling up of the sufferings of the day, nor anticipation of those of the morrow; nothing but home, peace, and friends. I do not know why this should be, but I have always found it so when quite worn out with fatigue, and I have heard others say that it was their experience.

---

1) We shall need but few questions here; perhaps those few will suggest ways of thinking about the relationship of the "I" to the narrative— the point of view—and about the closely connected matter of literary selection. To begin with, consider the first part of "Camp Life in Louisiana." How fully is De Forest included in the "we" that is the most frequently used pronoun?

2) The third paragraph of the selection seems personal. Is it an intrusion in a generalized description—is there any general interest in what De Forest drank at a particular meal?

3) Why, later in the selection, does De Forest record in so much detail what happened on a horse car?

4) Do you see in "Camp Life in Louisiana" any indication of De Forest's training as a professional writer? Think of it this way: Had you not

known that De Forest was a novelist of some distinction, what in this selection would have led you to suspect that he might be?

5) The "I" pronoun is much more in evidence in "The First Time under Fire" than it is in "Camp Life in Louisiana." Does that mean that "The
First Time under Fire" is more personal? What would you say is De Forest's primary intention in describing this engagement?

6) Can you see De Forest using and distinguishing two points of view
in this battle-piece? Comment on his remark after the mysterious shouted
order "Lie down": "Afterwards, when I could think of it at leisure, it reminded me of those godlike voices which resounded in ancient battles, giving encouragement and spreading panic." Do you find other instances of
the same sort of thing?

7) Does it seem to you that De Forest writes much more emotionally
about blisters than he does about battles? How do you account for that?

8) Often in "Forced Marches" De Forest writes in the first person.
Once he writes of what "the captain" does (De Forest was a captain).
Sometimes he uses the pronoun of direct address: "When you stand, you
seem to be on red-hot iron plates; when you walk, . . ." Are these shifts
in point of view?

9) As you know, a writer, even if he wanted to, could not use all his
material in any record of personal or observed experience: he would have
more detail than the reader would tolerate and perhaps more than he could
get into any feasible space. He must make some selection, the more discriminating the better. Now when a writer is working a long time after the
fact, some of his selection may be unconscious; he uses part of what presents itself to him through the mysterious processes of memory. But De
Forest is writing close to his experience and observation. Is it possible to
say, at least in a general way, what principles of selection he is using?

10) Howells once remarked that many of the novels about the War between the States were written as if it had been fought by young ladies.
How clear a notion of the private soldier do you get from De Forest? Of
the officer?

11) Assuming that our selections from *A Volunteer's Adventures* are
representative of the whole, what would you say is the primary intention of
the book?

ii   THE REPORTER OUTSIDE THE EVENTS

De Forest writes a first-person report of events in which he was an
active participant. In Berton Roueché's account of a toxic fog, we have a
piece of reporting based on investigation and interviews after the event,
by a writer who never permits himself an appearance in the narrative. Yet
Mr. Roueché, like De Forest, intends to do a good deal more than just to
inform readers about what happened; he intends to give readers an imaginative realization of what happened. Stating a fact so that the intellect
recognizes it as a fact takes no small skill; stating a fact so that the intellect
and the imagination realize it needs a high skill.

You need some of the information Mr. Roueché gave in the first part of his article, here omitted. We are told that Donora, an industrial town in southwestern Pennsylvania on the Monongahela River, has a population of some 12,000. The smoke of its mills tends to linger in Donora, since there are hills and bluffs about; and in the autumn it has persistent fogs. The smoke-contaminated fog in Donora at the end of October, 1948, reached a toxic density; it killed twenty persons and made nearly six thousand ill.

FROM *The Fog* (1950)

BERTON ROUECHÉ

[i]

1 The fog closed over Donora on the morning of Tuesday, October 26th. The weather was raw, cloudy, and dead calm, and it stayed that way as the fog piled up all that day and the next. By Thursday, it had stiffened adhesively into a motionless clot of smoke. That afternoon, it was just possible to see across the street, and, except for the stacks, the mills had vanished. The air began to have a sickening smell, almost a taste. It was the bittersweet reek of sulphur dioxide. Everyone who was out that day remarked on it, but no one was much concerned. The smell of sulphur dioxide, a scratchy gas given off by burning coal and melting ore, is a normal concomitant of any durable fog in Donora. This time, it merely seemed more penetrating than usual.

[ii]

1 Dr. Ralph W. Koehler, a tense, stocky man of forty-eight . . . , and an associate, Dr. Edward Roth, who is big, heavyset, and in his middle forties, share an office on the second floor of a brownstone building one block up from the mills, on McKean Avenue, the town's main street. They have one employee, a young woman named Helen Stack, in whom are combined an attractive receptionist, an efficient secretary, and a capable nurse. Miss Stack was the first to reach the office that [Friday] morning. Like Dr. Koehler and many other Donorans, she was in uncertain spirits. The fog was beginning to get on her nerves, and she had awakened with a sore throat and a cough and supposed that she was coming down with a cold. The appearance of the office deepened her depression. Everything in it was smeared with a kind of dust. "It wasn't just ordinary soot and grit," she says. "There was something white and scummy mixed up in it. It was just wet ash from the mills, but I didn't know that then. I almost hated to touch it, it was so nasty-looking. But it had to be cleaned up, so I got out a cloth and went to work." When Miss Stack had finished, she lighted a cigarette and sat down at her desk to go through the mail. It struck her that the cigarette had a very peculiar taste. She held it up and sniffed at the smoke. Then she raised it to her lips, took another puff, and doubled up in a paroxysm of coughing. For an instant, she thought she was going to be

sick. "I'll never forget that taste," she says. "Oh, it was awful! It was sweet and horrible, like something rotten. It tasted the way the fog smelled, only ten times worse. I got rid of the cigarette as fast as I could and drank a glass of water, and then I felt better. What puzzled me was I'd smoked a cigarette at home after breakfast and it had tasted all right. I didn't know what to think, except that maybe it was because the fog wasn't quite as bad up the hill as here downstreet. I guess I thought my cold was probably partly to blame. I wasn't really uneasy. The big Halloween parade the Chamber of Commerce puts on every year was to be held that night, and I could hear the workmen down in the street putting up the decorations. I knew the committee wouldn't be going ahead with the parade if they thought anything was wrong. So I went on with my work, and pretty soon the Doctors came in from their early calls and it was just like any other morning."

[iii]

I Among the several organizations that participated in the parade was the Donora Fire Department. The force consists of about thirty volunteers and two full-time men. The latter, who live at the firehouse, are the chief, John Volk, a wiry man in his fifties, and his assistant and driver, a hard, round-faced young man named Russell Davis. Immediately after the parade, they returned to the firehouse. "As a rule," Chief Volk says, "I like a parade. We've got some nice equipment here, and I don't mind showing it off. But I didn't get much pleasure out of that one. Nobody could see us, hardly, and we couldn't see them. That fog was black as a derby hat. It had us all coughing. It was a relief to head for home. We hadn't much more than got back to the station, though, and got the trucks put away and said good night to the fellows than the phone rang. Russ and I were just sitting down to drink some coffee. I dreaded to answer it. On a night like that, a fire could have been real mean. But it wasn't any fire. It was a fellow up the street, and the fog had got him. He said he was choking to death and couldn't get a doctor, and what he wanted was our inhalator. He needed air. Russ says I just stood there with my mouth hanging open. I don't remember what I thought. I guess I was trying to think what to do as much as anything else. I didn't disbelieve him—he sounded half dead already—but, naturally, we're not supposed to go running around treating the sick. But what the hell, you can't let a man die! So I told him O.K. I told Russ to take the car and go. The way it turned out, I figure we did the right thing. I've never heard anybody say different."

II "That guy was only the first," Davis says. "From then on, it was one emergency call after another. I didn't get to bed until Sunday. Neither did John. I don't know how many calls we had, but I do know this: We had around eight hundred cubic feet of oxygen on hand when I started out Friday night, and we ended up by borrowing from McKeesport and Monessen and Monongahela and Charleroi and everywhere around here. I never want to go through a thing like that again. I was laid up for a week after. There never was such a fog. You couldn't see your hand in front of your face, day or night. Hell, even inside the station the air was blue. I drove on the left side of the street with my head out the window, steering by scraping the curb. We've had bad fogs here before. A guy lost his car in one. He'd come to a fork in the road and didn't know where he was, and got out to try and tell which way to go. When he turned back to his car, he couldn't find it. He had no idea where it was until, finally, he stopped and listened and heard the engine. That guided him back. Well, by God, this fog was so bad you couldn't even get a car to idle. I'd take my foot off the accelerator and—bango!—the engine would stall. There just wasn't any oxygen in the air. I don't know how I kept breathing. I don't know how anybody did. I found people laying in bed and laying on the floor. Some of them were laying there and they didn't give a damn whether they died or not. I found some down in the basement with the furnace draft open and their head stuck inside, trying to get air that way. What I did when I got to a place was throw a sheet or a blanket over the patient and stick a cylinder of oxygen underneath and crack the valves for fifteen minutes or so. By God, that rallied them! I didn't take any myself. What I did every time I came back to the station was have a little shot of whiskey. That seemed to help. It eased my throat. There was one funny thing about the whole thing. Nobody seemed to realize what was going on. Everybody seemed to think he was the only sick man in town. I don't know what they figured was keeping the doctors so busy. I guess everybody was so miserable they just didn't think."

III Toward midnight, Dr. Roth abandoned his car and continued his rounds on foot. He found not only that walking was less of a strain but that he made better time. He walked the streets all night, but he was seldom lonely. Often, as he entered or left a house, he encountered a colleague. "We all had practically the same calls," Dr. M. J. Hannigan, the president of the Donora Medical Association, says. "Some people called every doctor in town. It was pretty discouraging to finally get someplace and drag yourself up the steps and then be told that Dr. So-and-So had just been there. Not that I blame them, though. Far from it. There were a couple of times when I was about ready to call for help myself. Frankly, I don't know how any of us doctors managed to hold out and keep going that night."

IV Not all of them did. Dr. Koehler made his last call that night at one o'clock. "I had to go home," he says. "God knows I didn't want to. I'd hardly made a dent in my list. Every time I called home or the Physicians' Exchange, it doubled. But my heart gave out. I couldn't go on any longer without some rest. The last thing I heard as I got into bed was my wife answering the phone. And the phone was the first thing I heard in the morning. It was as though I hadn't been to sleep at all." While Dr. Koehler was bolting a cup of coffee, the telephone rang again. This time, it was Miss Stack. They conferred briefly about the patients he had seen during the night and those he planned to see that morning. Among the latter was a sixty-four-year-old steelworker named Ignatz Hollowitti. "One of the Hollowitti girls, Dorothy, is a good friend of mine," Miss Stack says. "So as soon as I finished talking to Dr. Koehler, I called her to tell her that Doctor would be right over. I wanted to relieve her mind. Dorothy was crying when she answered the phone. I'll never forget what she said. She said, 'Oh, Helen—my dad just died! He's dead!' I don't remember what I said. I was simply stunned. I suppose I said what people say. I must have. But all I could think was, My gosh, if people are dying—why, this is tragic! Nothing like this has ever happened before!"

v Mr. Hollowitti was not the first victim of the fog. He was the sixth. The first was a retired steelworker of seventy named Ivan Ceh. According to the records of the undertaker who was called in—Rudolph Schwerha, whose establishment is the largest in Donora—Mr. Ceh died at one-thirty Saturday morning. "I was notified at two," Mr. Schwerha says. "There is a note to such effect in my book. I thought nothing, of course. The call awakened me from sleep, but in my profession anything is to be expected. I reassured the bereaved and called my driver and sent him for the body. He was gone forever. The fog that night was impossible. It was a neighborhood case—only two blocks to go, and my driver works quick—but it was thirty minutes by the clock before I heard the service car in the drive. At that moment, again the phone rang. Another case. Now I was surprised. Two different cases so soon together in this size town doesn't happen every day. But there was no time then for thinking. There was work to do. I must go with my driver for the second body. It was in the Sunnyside section, north of town, too far in such weather for one man alone. The fog, when we got down by the mills, was unbelievable. Nothing could be seen. It was like a blanket. Our fog lights were useless, and even with the fog spotlight on, the white line in the street was invisible. I began to worry. What if we should bump a parked car? What if we should fall off the road? Finally, I told my driver, 'Stop! I'll take the wheel. You walk in front and show the way.' So we did that for two miles. Then we were in the country. I know that section like my hand, but we had missed the house. So we had to turn around and go back. That was an awful time. We were on the side of a hill, with a terrible drop on one side and no fence. I was afraid every minute. But we made it, moving by inches, and pretty soon I found the house. The case was an old man and he had died all of a sudden. Acute cardiac dilation. When we were ready, we started back. Then I began to feel sick. The fog was getting me. There was an awful tickle in my throat. I was coughing and ready to vomit. I called to my driver that I had to stop and get out. He was ready to stop, I guess. Already he had walked four or five miles. But I envied him. He was well and I was awful sick. I leaned against the car, coughing and gagging, and at last I riffled a few times. Then I was much better. I could drive. So we went on, and finally we were home. My wife was standing at the door. Before she spoke, I knew what she would say. I thought, Oh, my God—another! I knew it by her face. And after that came another. Then another. There seemed to be no end. By ten o'clock in the morning, I had nine bodies waiting here. Then I heard that DeRienzo and Lawson, the other morticians, each had one.

Eleven people dead! My driver and I kept looking at each other. What was happening? We didn't know. I thought probably the fog was the reason. It had the smell of poison. But we didn't know."

[iv]

I The emergency-aid station, generously staffed and abundantly supplied with drugs and oxygen inhalators, opened at eight o'clock Saturday night. "We were ready for anything and prepared for the worst," Mrs. Vernon [the Red Cross director] says. "We even had an ambulance at our disposal. Phillip DeRienzo, the undertaker, loaned it to us. But almost nothing happened. Altogether, we brought in just eight patients. Seven, to be exact. One was dead when the car arrived. Three were very bad and we sent them to the hospital in Charleroi. The others we just treated and sent home. It was really very queer. The fog was as black and nasty as ever that night, or worse, but all of a sudden the calls for a doctor just seemed to trickle out and stop. It was as though everybody was sick who was going to be sick. I don't believe we had a call after midnight. I knew then that we'd seen the worst of it."

II Dr. Roth had reached that conclusion, though on more slender evidence, several hours before. "I'd had a call about noon from a woman who said two men roomers in her house were in bad shape," he says. "It was nine or nine-thirty by the time I finally got around to seeing them. Only, I never saw them. The landlady yelled up to them that I was there, and they yelled right back, 'Tell him never mind. We're O.K. now.' Well, that was good enough for me. I decided things must be letting up. I picked up my grip and walked home and fell into bed. I was dead-beat."

III There was no visible indication that the fog was beginning to relax its smothering grip when the group summoned by Burgess Chambon assembled at the Borough Building the next morning to discuss the calamity. It was another soggy, silent, midnight day. "That morning was the worst," the Burgess says. "It wasn't just that the fog was still hanging on. We'd begun to get some true facts. We didn't have any real idea how many people were sick. That didn't come out for months. We thought a few hundred. But we did have the number of deaths. It took the heart out of you. The rumors hadn't come close to it. It was eighteen. I guess we talked about that first. Then the question of the mills came up. The smoke. L. J. Westhaver, who was general superintendent of the steel and wire works then, was there, and so was the head of the zinc plant, M. M. Neale. I asked them to shut down for the duration. They said they already had. They had started banking the fires at six that morning. They went on to say, though, that they were sure the mills had nothing to do with the trouble. We didn't know what to think. Everybody was at a loss to point the finger at anything in particular. There just didn't seem to be any explanation. We had another meeting that afternoon. It was the same thing all over again. We talked and we wondered and we worried. We couldn't think of anything to do that hadn't already been done. I think we heard about the nineteenth death before we broke up. We thought for a week that was the last. Then one more finally died. I don't remember exactly what all we did or said that afternoon. What I remember is after we broke up. When we came out of the building, it was raining. Maybe it was only drizzling then—I guess the real rain didn't set in until evening—but, even so, there was a hell of a difference. The air was different. It didn't get you any more. You could breathe."

[v]

I The investigation of the disaster lasted almost a year. It was not only the world's first full-blooded examination of the general problem of air pollution but one of the most exhaustive inquiries of any kind ever made in the field of public health. Its course was directed jointly by Dr. Joseph Shilen, director of the Bureau of Industrial Hygiene of the Pennsylvania Department of Health, and Dr. J. G. Townsend, chief of the Division of Industrial Hygiene of the United States Public Health Service, and at times it involved the entire technical personnel of both agencies. The Public Health Service assigned to the case nine engineers, seven physicians, six nurses, five chemists, three statisticians, two meteorologists, two dentists, and a veterinarian. The force under the immediate direction of Dr. Shilen, though necessarily somewhat smaller, was similarly composed.

II The investigation followed three main lines, embracing the clinical, the environmental, and the meteorological aspects of the occurrence. Of these, the meteorological inquiry was the most nearly conclusive. It was also the most reassuring. It indicated that while the situation of Donora is unwholesomely conducive to the accumulation of smoke and fog, the immediate cause of the October, 1948, visitation was a freak of nature known to meteorologists as a temperature inversion. This phenomenon is, as its name suggests, characterized by a temporary, and usually brief, reversal of the normal atmospheric conditions, in which the air near the earth is warmer than the air higher up. Its result is a more or less complete immobilization of the convection currents in the lower air by which gases and fumes are ordinarily carried upward, away from the earth.

III The clinical findings, with one or two exceptions, were more confirmatory than illuminating. One of the revelations, which was gleaned from several months of tireless interviewing, was that thousands, rather than just hundreds, had been ill during the fog. For the most part, the findings demonstrated, to the surprise of neither the investigators nor the Donora physicians, that the affection was essentially an irritation of the respiratory tract, that its severity increased in proportion to the age of the victim and his predisposition to cardio-respiratory ailments, and that the ultimate cause of death was suffocation.

IV The environmental study, the major phase of which was an analysis of the multiplicity of gases emitted by the mills, boats, and trains, was, in a positive sense, almost wholly unrewarding. It failed to determine the direct causative agent. Still, its results, though negative, were not without value. They showed, contrary to expectation, that no one of the several stack gases known to be irritant—among them fluoride, chloride, hydrogen sulphide, cadmium oxide, and sulphur dioxide—could have been present in the air in sufficient concentration to produce serious illness. "It seems reasonable to state," Dr. Helmuth H. Schrenk, chief of the Environmental Investigations Branch of the Public Health Service's Division of Industrial Hygiene, has written of this phase of the inquiry, "that while no single substance was responsible for the . . . episode, the syndrome could have been produced by a combination, or summation of the action, of two or more of the contaminants. Sulphur dioxide and its oxidation products, together with particulate matter [soot and fly ash], are considered significant contaminants. However, the significance of the other irritants as important adjuvants to the biological effects cannot be finally estimated on the basis of present knowledge. It is important to emphasize that information available on the toxicological effects of mixed irritant gases is meagre and data on possible enhanced action due to adsorption of gases on particulate matter is limited." To this, Dr. Leonard A. Scheele, Surgeon General of the Service, has added, "One of the most important results of the study is to show us what we do not know."

[vi]

1 Funeral services for most of the victims of the fog were held on Tuesday, November 2nd. Monday had been a day of battering rain, but the weather cleared in the night, and Tuesday was fine. "It was like a day in spring," Mr. Schwerha says. "I think I have never seen such a beautiful blue sky or such a shining sun or such pretty white clouds. Even the trees in the cemetery seemed to have color. I kept looking up all day."

---

1) What is here called "smoke-contaminated fog" you probably call "smog." "Smog" is a BLEND WORD or "portmanteau word" (why portmanteau?) like, for instance, "chortle." Why do you suppose Mr. Roueché avoids it? Does your dictionary recognize it as a word in good use?

2) What qualities of this writing explain its effectiveness? In answering this question you may answer some of the questions that follow; at any rate see how far you can go with it.

3) So far as you can tell from the report itself, what are the sources of the writer's information and the means which he took to gather it?

4) Do you think that the stories of the persons who speak at some length—the fire chief or the undertaker, say—are stenographic reports of continuous statements, or that they have been elicited by questions and organized by the writer?

5) How much selection from the accounts of persons he interviewed do you think Mr. Roueché exercised? How do the persons you know tell what happened to them—in an orderly manner and without much repetition?

6) When the writer had done his investigation and was ready to write his article, he must have had a number of separate documents. How do you suppose he began to organize his materials into a coherent account of the experience of the community?

7) The persons who give us information are all briefly characterized—but very briefly. For instance, there are two full-time firemen: "the chief, John Volk, a wiry man in his fifties, and his assistant and driver, a hard, round-faced young man named Russell Davis." Is this description sufficient for you to have an image of each? When you have read the account the several persons give of their experience, how completely do you imagine them? Are they less vivid than the persons in most fiction?

8) What means has the writer taken to give his report continuity and narrative pattern? Do you see a special problem? The experiences of these persons were simultaneous; the accounts of the experiences must be consecutive. How does the writer go about making the reader feel the experience as the experience of the community? Notice that this problem is one that the writer of a history faces—although for him the problem may be greater. In human experience a number of things happen at once—but the very words in one's sentence come in a time sequence. For the writer of "The Fog" and for the historian, what we ordinarily call transition must bear a special burden.

9) If the point of view of a single observer had been used—that might have been done with some success—which of the several persons would have been most useful as the writer's observer?

10) Is the style of the account of the scientific investigation (the fifth part of the selection) like the style of the rest? Should it be?

11) What is the signpost sentence for this account? Point out how it controls the rest.

12) Compare the style of the statement by Dr. Schrenk quoted by Mr. Roueché with Mr. Roueché's own style in the fifth part of the selection. How do the two styles differ?

13) Consider the effect of the last paragraph. Here, for comparison, is a paragraph from Bret Harte's story, "Tennessee's Partner," a description of the day on which Tennessee is hanged:

> How he met it, how cool he was, how he refused to say anything, how perfect were the arrangements of the committee, were all duly reported, with the addition of a warning moral and example to all future evil-doers, in the Red Dog *Clarion*, by its editor, who was present, and to whose vigorous English I cheerfully refer the reader. But the beauty of that midsummer morning, the blessed amity of earth and air and sky, the awakened life of the free woods and hills, the joyous renewal and promise of Nature, and, above all, the infinite serenity that thrilled through each, was not reported, as not being a part of the social lesson. And yet, when the weak and foolish deed was done, and a life, with its possibilities and responsibilities, had passed out of the misshapen thing that dangled between earth and sky, the birds sang, the flowers bloomed, the sun shone, as cheerily as before; and possibly the Red Dog *Clarion* was right.

What comparable effect is intended in both passages? Which achieves its intended effect best? Which seems to work hardest for it? What is the implication of the last sentence quoted from Mr. Schwerha?

14) What kinds of interest and value has this article? In what fields of inquiry might it be instructive? Should you now return to question 2 for reconsideration?

THE REPORTER AS NARRATOR *iii*

Our two selections here are somewhat more personal than "The Fog"; at least in each of them there is an "I" who moves through the account, gathering material from his informants and recording observations of his own. This movement of the "I" observer-narrator establishes the continuity. The student who purposes trying his own hand at reporting may find this pattern particularly useful.

Whatever is real *and* told so that it seems real will interest intelligent readers. Both of these pieces first appeared in *The New Yorker*. Now the readers of *The New Yorker* are in large part city folk; they have no special initial interest in either Connecticut agriculture or the zoology of the Green Bay region in Wisconsin. The editors of *The New Yorker* must believe that a good account of experience is interesting in and for itself. Notice that no straining on the part of either writer is apparent; one does not find either being "colorful" here or "striking" there.

FROM *Things of the Past* (1953)

CHRISTOPHER RAND

SALISBURY, CONNECTICUT

1 Over the past few years, I have seen change and decay attack this countryside in northwest Connecticut, where my father had a farm and where I grew up. I spent my teens here in the nineteen-twenties, and in the early thirties I worked a few summers on the farm. As I look back on those times when the farm was my home, I get a picture of a steady, solid country life, with cows, horses, men, and crops following their rounds unswervingly. I was far away from New England during the decade that ended with V–J Day, and when I then returned to Salisbury for a brief stay, I began to notice that things were getting off the track. The most striking manifestation of this was the abandonment to brush of rocky or hilly meadows, with which our part of Connecticut had long been well blessed. Though hard to work, such fields had been a part of nearly every New England landscape—open spaces one encountered on walks from certain points to certain other points—and to me they had seemed timeless as the hills. Now they were no longer mowed and were going first into weeds, then into sumac and birch. The change was gloomily plain if you walked much, because second growth is so nasty to get through, and I hardly escaped it for as much as a day of that visit. I also learned, then and on later trips, that berrypicking had almost ended in our region, and that

haycocks and oat shocks were rarely to be seen in the summer fields any more.

II My awakening to the change continued intermittently on subsequent visits. Last fall, I came back to Salisbury for a more protracted stay than usual and was told that the bobolinks had left their good lowland meadows and that the shape of barn roofs was being altered, because of new farming ways. At that time, a local dairy farmer, George Miner, told me there was no longer any team of work horses nearer to his farm than the south side of Canaan Mountain, perhaps five miles away. Later, my brother Jake, who is also a dairyman, said that this was wrong—that he himself knew of a team just over the state line in Millerton, New York, which would be some two miles closer. Further study has led Mr. Miner to revise his figures, and he now reports two teams of horses and one of mules within his original radius, but his findings hardly change the general outlook, for before the war there must have been two or three teams for every arable square mile of Salisbury Township. Mulling over these and other fragments of information and observation, I discerned the outlines of a revolution, and I decided to look deeper into it, right down to and including the bobolinks.

III We are a dairying country, producing milk for New York City, for urban sections of Connecticut, and for several boarding schools in our midst. Dairying is a profession that entails two main jobs—the direct care of cows and the growing of their food. Both jobs have been notably affected by the revolution, an event whose principal elements appear to be the spread of knowledge, the rise of the machine, and the near disappearance of hand labor. In the matter of food raising, most of the changes are a result in one way or another of a new technique called grassland farming. When I was a boy, the farmers here would grow at least four crops each year—corn, oats, clover, and timothy, all different in nature and standing in separate fields—and set other fields aside for pasture. This variety, with its shadings of greens and yellows, changing as the summer went on, made up the familiar old patchwork of farm-country landscape. Nowadays, as I hear from the neighbors and to some extent can see for myself, the patchwork is starting to blur, its lines being gradually erased by a tendency to plant all one's acreage to the same crop—a heavy, lush mixture of grasses (dominated as a rule by something called Ladino clover) that can be mowed as hay, chopped for ensilage, or grazed as pasture. This mixture has already gone far toward driving out timothy, which used to put the light gray-green into July fields. Corn, it seems, will be the next to go. My brother, who started a small farm here in 1946 (my father's farm having been sold), has never had a cornfield or a silo on it; he says that as late as the mid-thirties it would have been all but impossible to do without either. He gets along without ensilage by raising more nourishing hay and by buying modern extras like beet pulp. "The whole idea now is to get the most milk per acre," Jake says. "So you don't use poor fields any more." The new grasslands yield three crops a year, and often the cows are turned right out into the second and third of these. The cows are apt to be grazed on one small patch at a time, to which they are confined by movable electric fences—a big difference from ten years ago, when they were turned out daily, all summer long, into the same large fixed pasture, which was used for nothing else. There was a contrast in texture between hayfields and pastures then. Hayfields after mowing were stubbly but even; pastures were more closely cropped, down to a fraction of an inch in places, but there were always bumps in them, perhaps of thistles or milkweed. It was rather like the distinction between plush laid on a flat surface and velvet on a lumpy one. Now the contrast is fading, and in among the stubble one finds carefully planted rich red clover blossoms side by side with hoofmarks and manure, signifying that the cows have been in the hay, a state of affairs once thought intolerable. And here and there a sketchy electric fence threads its way on spindly, impermanent stakes, a sign of flux and the withering of established barriers. . . .

IV Cows themselves, in the words of George Miner, are so damn high-toned now it's awful. "They're particular as hell," he told me. "You have to cater to them all the time. Have to curry them. Wash their tails. You remember we didn't bother with them too much in the old days? Now if you try to make a living off cows you've got to be with them all the time. Scratch their necks. 'Cater to them' is the only way I can put it." Jake agrees. He says cows are tamer and get closer attention, especially as young stock, than formerly. In our boyhood, cows ready to calve were frequently turned out behind my father's farm onto a wild expanse called Butterly— one or two hundred acres of hilly woodland that opened now and then into pasture. They would have their calves and would often run loose with them for a time. Afterward, they would tend to jump fences, kick over pails, and play other jokes—becoming "characters." Such cows don't get by today, Jake says. To give much milk, it has been established, cows must be kept well in hand. So cows ready to calve are put in the barn or near it, and grazing herds are usually turned out in small fields close to the barn that are planted with the new grassland clover or that have been converted into "improved pasture"—fertilized, that is, and with the early-growing weeds mowed off. Such young stock as are still pastured on the old rough lots are given salt just inside the near fence, so that they can be checked on daily and petted. Calves in pasture are also fed grain—a new thing. Jake says the feet of his cattle must be trimmed more often now than of old, because they don't wear down so fast. He also says cows puff more when going up hills. In our youth, pastures were far off and we didn't think it hurt a cow to walk. Hay meadows were close because wagons were slow. Now the idea is to reverse this. Lester Simonton, one of the best dairymen in our township, whose cows were once pastured so far away from the barn that he rode a horse to get them, now tries to arrange things so they can have eaten their fill and be lying down with their cud within an hour after they have left the barn. (He uses electric fences a lot. He says grown cows get so broken to them that half the time the current can be left off, but this doesn't work with young stock.)

V The value of cows and the amount of milk they give have shot up along with everything else. Twenty years ago, a good grade cow cost around seventy-five dollars in these parts. Now the price is four or five hundred. The cow puts out a third or a half again as much milk as it used to—the result of better breeding, feeding, and care. My brother has eighteen milking cows, and they give more than half as much milk as the forty-five at my father's did, and, because of high prices, my brother gets just about as much cash income. He pays two men where my father paid at least five, but he says he is making no more profit. Farmers here talk poor, now as always.

vi George Miner thinks cows get tired of the fancy stuff they are fed today. "They hanker for some of that old kind of grass," he says. "They like variety. You know when you go out to a restaurant you will go now to an Italian one, now to a Swedish one, and so on. It's the same with cows. Sometimes when you mow a pasture, and cut off the old, dead tops of weeds, the cows will come in and eat their fill of tender green grass. And then, just for the heck of it, they will pick up some of the old, dry cut stuff and lie down and chew it." . . .

vii Among human beings, the great vanished race with us is the teamsters. In my boyhood, teamsters grew locally or came down from the north—from Maine, New Hampshire, and Vermont, where wages were lower. These men were close to nature and could do things like carve better axe handles than you could buy. As a rule, teamsters did a vast amount of work in a day, at a deliberate but lasting pace. One afternoon, I was working in the hayloft with a teamster, a portly Maine man, temporarily detached from his horses. I used to chew tobacco then—it was a manly way to take on nicotine without burning the barn down—and I got out my plug and offered him some, for I knew he liked it. He thanked me but said he thought he wouldn't take any right then. He had had some greens for lunch, he said, and had put a great deal of salt on them ("greddeal" was the way he pronounced it). This had made him thirsty and dry, and so he had taken his teeth out, and he didn't think he would chew for the present, though he might later. The whole response took considerable time, and as he spoke he stowed big forkfuls of hay under the roof beams, slowly and methodically. And slowly and methodically he went on with us for ten years, occasionally having trouble with his back, but now he has disappeared and neither Jake nor I know where he is. It also might be noted that tobacco chewing has faded, along with the other things. The Salisbury Pharmacy sells but a quarter of its old volume, according to Sam Whitbeck, the owner.

viii Teamsters got up early, though not so early as cow-barn men, and spent much time currying their horses and cleaning the stalls. Then, after breakfast, they went forth to the haying or whatever other outside job presented itself. They had little traffic with the cows. Jake says this is one reason they have gone—they and their horses couldn't qualify as cash earners in the eyes of modern cost accounting. The cows were the breadwinners and the horses and teamsters their servants, and, of course, servants have been vanishing all over. The number of men on a farm now, Jake says, is determined by the number of cows that must be milked. All hands milk every morning and evening. Between milkings, the men skip off to the fields with their machines. So there is no room for teamsters, and teams in our country that haven't died off have mostly been sent elsewhere. George Miner says the last team he remembers leaving was given by his neighbor Paul Cleaveland to a farmer in New Hampshire who was known to be kind. The horses went off one day looking out noncommittally from the back of a truck.

ix In winter, when the fields were frozen and perhaps covered with snow, the teamsters would get the ice in or spread manure or cut wood. These jobs have mainly disappeared, too. My father got his ice from Lake Wononscopomuc, perhaps three miles away, and each year a month was given to the job. The teams and sleighs took a half day for the round trip, and when we were little, we used to bob behind them, tying a Flexible Flyer to a back runner. The pace wasn't much, but we could swerve sidewise, tip over, and play other tricks, and the snow and cold were bracing. Hard snow bordering the ruts cut our fingers on the handle bars. Now the roads are scraped too thin for sleighs, and no ice is harvested anyway. The lake didn't even freeze over this year, for the first time in anybody's memory. The icehouses of our neighborhood have become tool houses, playhouses, or additional places to put hay bales. There is no extra supply of manure to spread in the winter, because it is no longer saved and piled up through the summer, and little wood is cut, for although logs are still burned in fireplaces, they aren't used much for cooking or basic heating. Farmhands must still be prepared to cut fence posts, Jake says, and put them up, but there has been a change even in this. Posts are no longer sunk properly by the old lights—that is, planted in specially dug holes—but are sharpened and driven in like stakes. And often the sharpening is done with a buzz saw, Jake says, rather than with an axe. Before the war, practices such as these would have been considered shiftless and against nature. As a boy, I read or heard that fences should be "bull strong, horse high, and hog tight." I don't suppose they often were. The phrase represented an ideal; perhaps it was a slogan I saw in a catalogue. But at least the fences stood up straight. Now labor and wire are so costly (most of the nation's barbed wire is in Korea, farmers here think) that little is done in the way of repairs. Some stretches of fence sag or lean morosely, some are haphazardly patched, as if by string-saving old ladies. Frequently, when a farmer's fences get too bad now, he just puts in electric fencing and lets the old stuff go. This adds to the air of decay. It should be noted, though, that the decay isn't all-pervading. Our community isn't like sweet Auburn, loveliest village of the plain. The farms and farmers are still here. It is only that the farmers are working in another way now—less extensively so far as space is concerned—and have let hundreds of acres slip back to woods.

x On some farms, there are workshops that are heated in winter, so that machines can be overhauled there. On the rest, the men get more leisure during the cold months. No matter what the time of year, leisure, naturally, is used differently now. Most farmhands' houses have television—the smaller the house, it seems, the bigger the antenna. The decline in berrypicking tells something about the use of leisure. Our mountains grow fine huckleberries, and each August in my childhood much of the population too old or too young for farming turned to them, devoting its spare time to picking for sale or use. One father and his daughter used to walk up Mount Riga—a two-mile climb—every day of the season, and walk down again carrying two twelve- or fourteen-quart pails of berries apiece. Berries were so cheap that, while they lasted, each of my brothers and I had a soup plate full of them every morning for breakfast, with pilot biscuit broken over them and milk and sugar poured on. Today, one can drive a car right up near the berry fields, but they are little disturbed. Most huckleberries now at our market, I am told, come from truck gardens in New Jersey; the price is high and we have no more Bourbon breakfasts.

xi For outdoor sports, the men of the village lean toward golf and skiing now, which are city men's sports, too. They do a good deal of fishing, but in our parts fishing has also taken on a weekend Abercrombie & Fitch aspect. The lakes and streams are thickly stocked, and on them trippers from afar mix indistinguishably with the local men. There is less of the old-time hunting with hound-dogs here, less gathering of nuts, less of other country pastimes.

xii There seems to be much gain in all this—more freedom from heat and cold and heavy things to lift. In exchange, part of man's former closeness to nature has been given up. Some here call the change progress. Some think it a further fall from Paradise. Some do not judge but take it as it is.

FROM *A Carnival of Frogs* (1953)

ELI WALDRON

1 However fateful, sad, and uncertain the year 1952 may have been for the human race, it was a perfect year for frogs. At least it was in Oconto County, Wisconsin, which is on the western shore of Green Bay, which, in turn, is a long arm of Lake Michigan, reaching southwestward into the state. The lower, or fenny, half of this shoreline lies in Oconto County, and the other half extends along the Upper Peninsula of Michigan, where the land is higher and less hospitable to frogs. Last July, a determined, green froggy army, searching for food, came pouring out of the wild wet world between Pensaukee and Peshtigo Harbors, a soggy strip about twenty-five miles long and two or three miles wide, and descended on Oconto, the county seat, which is in the middle of the strip. This is my home town. The frogs established themselves strongly in all the gardens and on all the lawns, and swarmed on the streets and sidewalks at night like creatures in a very strange, disorderly dream. Frogs are difficult to count, but scientists and the county officials in Oconto made a stab at it, and estimated that there were a hundred and seventy-five million of them in the area. (The human population of Oconto is 5,030.) Nobody there

had ever seen so many frogs, and it began to look as if the balance of nature had been upset in an extremely serious way. Everyone said it was probably the greatest frog uprising since the days of Moses, and some of the more God-fearing of the marsh dwellers declared that it heralded the end of the world. They cited Exodus and Revelation [1] to prove it, particularly Exodus 8:3: *And the river shall bring forth frogs abundantly, which shall go up and come into thine house, and into thy bedchamber, and upon thy bed, and into the house of thy servants, and upon thy people, and into thine ovens, and into thy kneading-troughs.*

II After the first wave of apprehension, Oconto was inclined for the most part to regard the visitation rationally—as a curious and even wonderful example of the vagrant explosiveness of nature. The people learned to live with the frogs, the frogs learned to live with the people, and community life, with the addition of this new amphibious element, which gradually diminished as the summer wore on, returned to normal. I bring all this up now because the 1953 frog season is just beginning and it may well be even more fruitful and astonishing than last season was. If it is, there will be hell to pay. For the present, everything hinges on the wind and the weather.

III In normal years, the frog population around Oconto is of modest size. Frogs have their ups and downs, like the fish in the bay and the people in the town, but by and large the area is well adjusted ecologically. Oconto, once a thriving lumber center, with a busy port, is now dependent on a hardwood-flooring mill and a pickle factory. The logs for the mill are trucked in from the north, and the cucumbers for the pickles grow nearby, where the forest used to be before the lumbermen cut it down. The pickle factory is the up-and-coming industry, busily canning dill pickles and sweet pickles and sliced pickles and sending them all over the country. Although pickles and flooring are the principal sources of employment, the bay supports a sizable fishing industry, and the strip of marshland, with its frogs, has always been there to take up the slack when there weren't enough jobs to go around. Oconto's frogs have never been hunted for the market in any large-scale way, but they've always been around for the taking, and the taking of frogs has, for a good many families, often meant the difference between having a little money and having none. The frogs that overran the place last year were mostly young frogs, however, that won't reach marketable size until year after next, so nobody struck it rich on them. And, as far as I know, nobody plans to set up a local frog market and try to take commercial advantage of last year's bumper crop when it grows up. Perhaps someone will if there is another bumper crop this year, but the feeling around Oconto is that you can't count on frogs—they're too unpredictable.

IV I was working in Chicago at the time of the frogs' invasion in Oconto. Someone sent me a newspaper clipping about it, and a few days later someone else wrote me of the prophetic utterances that had come up out of the swamp, out of Revelation and Exodus. I couldn't get home just

[1 See Revelation 16:13–14.]

then; in fact, I didn't get there until September. By that time, the worst was over. Most of the frogs had receded into the marsh, and the excitement in town had pretty well subsided, but my friends were eager to tell me what had happened.

v The hungry young frogs had come out of the marsh and in two days had practically enveloped the town. The explosions of amphibians beneath the wheels of automobiles at night sounded like rifle fire. People mowing their lawns did so in a storm of flying frog legs and truncated frog bodies. At night, you could hear frogs swishing and skittering in the grass and hear them croaking everywhere. In the daytime, the croaking stopped, but it was replaced by the yelping and barking of dogs, who were almost driven out of their minds. They ran around in circles, usually clockwise, then counterclockwise, and then stood still and barked, in a crazed and delighted way, as boys would bark if boys were dogs. There were so many frogs that they piled up on one another, and they seemed so purposeful that a man I know said they had besieged his house one night in what he swore was a highly organized way. He had gone out on his front lawn to have a look around with his flashlight and had been confronted by a million shining little eyes. He started toward the back yard and found that he had been outflanked. He swung the light around and discovered that the whole house was encircled. It was a scary thing to see, he said. It made the hair bristle on the back of his neck. But the plan of attack, if there had been a plan, didn't work out. Sometime during the night, the besiegers departed, he told me, leaving a great many of their comrades behind, trapped in the sunken boxes around the basement windows. He scooped more than two bushels of frogs out of the boxes with a shovel the following morning.

vi These were leopard frogs, the kind you see most often around Oconto. In the market, they are known as "grass frogs." Elsewhere, they are called "meadow frogs" or "shad frogs" or "herring hoppers" or "spotted frogs," but "leopard frog" is probably the most descriptive name for them. In any event, the leopard frog is the common and familiar frog, widespread over most of North America—the frog of pool, puddle, biology class, pregnancy test, and frying pan. The *other* familiar frog is, of course, the bullfrog, and this is the frog of song, fable, and also, sadly enough, the frying pan. He gets his name from his bellowing and his husky build.

vii As soon as I could after I reached Oconto, I drove out to the marsh, which I have always loved, and there I got a good idea of what things must have been like in town. As I said, the excitement in town had died down, but it hadn't in the marshes. There, with the water at an accommodating height, the frogs had made no compromise with civilization, with lawnmowers and automobiles, and they were everywhere in the ascendant, in the various colors young leopard frogs display. There were green frogs, bronze frogs, big ones, little ones, leaping and glistening in the sunlight, diving into pools and puddles, streaking through the grass. It was a fantastic carnival of frogs—as though they were rejoicing at last in the total triumph of frogism. And so it must have been for the first few happy days in town, before they had been subdued and chastened by the superior weight, reach, experience, and diabolic inventions of a larger and in some ways less jumpy creature.

VIII There was, of course, a somewhat different *kind* of excitement in the marsh. Here the frogs had their natural enemies to contend with, and these enemies had also increased marvellously during the summer, attracted by the huge new food supply. Almost anywhere you looked, you would see a heron stalking a frog or a bittern digesting one—sitting motionless on a log or a stone, looking solemnly down his long nose into the water. Far out, at the edge of the bay, the gulls were screaming, and among them white egrets soared and dipped. Practically everything and everybody likes to eat frogs (including frogs themselves at times). A friend of mine once told me that he had seen crows carrying them off to the young in their nests.

IX The marsh was a noisy, enchanting land during those days of early September, and I spent as much time there as I could. The autumnal transfiguration had just begun; the smell of autumn was in the air, and the look of autumn in the brown, wind-swept marsh grass. Teal rocketed over the treetops, and flocking blackbirds swirled across the pale-blue curve of the sky. Ducks and terns, sandpipers and kingfishers and killdeers—the whole marsh was bursting with activity, and dominating it all was the wild, possessive screaming of the gulls, and at the bottom of it all was the gay and leaping community of frogs, making the most of the days left to them before the first freeze came and they would go to sleep for the winter.

X The friend who sent me the newspaper clipping was Carl Richter, and he was also the one who told me about the crows carrying young frogs to their nests. Carl is a quiet, good-natured man of fifty, whose hobby is oölogy. For some forty-five of his fifty years, he has devoted every leisure moment to an impassioned study of the home-building habits of birds, and he is one of the few people in the state who are licensed to take eggs and nests. A charter member of the Wisconsin Society for Ornithology, he is an authority on the yellow rail, a bird that has some of the same shyness and contentment that Carl has. Carl is a storekeeper in the Oconto warehouse of the Wisconsin Public Service Corporation, a light and power company, and spends his weekends and holidays on the marsh. Perhaps his only regret is that he can't give all his time to his studies of nesting, but he gets away now and then, when he has saved up enough money, and makes a trip to Louisiana or the Dakotas, to look at nests there. I hunted him up right away, and over a cup of coffee in Porter's Restaurant, he explained what had caused the remarkable emergence of frogs.

XI I probably remembered, he said, that the bay had a habit of flooding in early spring and then slowly receding as the season progressed. Well, this year it had flooded and had remained in flood the whole summer long. It was pretty bad for a while. Some families had been forced out of their homes, the shoreline roads had melted away, and every time the wind blew from the northeast, more water came rolling in. The Great Lakes were full and Green Bay was brimming, and all it took was a little wind to set the water running over the marsh. It had finally eased off a bit—

enough, at least, so that Oconto itself was no longer threatened. As I could see for myself, though, there was still enough water in the lowlands to be troublesome when the wind was wrong.

xii As far as the frogs were concerned, however, Carl said, the winds had behaved beautifully. The frogs laid their eggs in the shallow water, when the flood was at its height, and lost very few of them to the sun and wind. Ordinarily, the water recedes, and eggs and tadpoles die by the million, but not this year. This time, the water, instead of ebbing away and leaving eggs and tadpoles stranded, had stayed on, and the result was an optimum hatch and optimum survival—maybe four per cent, maybe six per cent, instead of the usual one per cent or one-half of one per cent. Whatever the percentage was, it had added up to a lot of frogs, Carl said. If you figured, as some people did, that there were a hundred and seventy-five million frogs in the vicinity, that meant that there were as many frogs in this one marsh as there were people in the entire country.

xiii It was a nine days' wonder, he told me. The frogs—new ones and old ones alike, and all hungry—had come hopping in and had taken over; everywhere you looked there was a frog grinning at you. And there wasn't anything you could do about it except get used to the idea. There had been some talk about calling out the local company of the National Guard, but that was joking talk, mostly. It was just a crazy kind of situation and you had to accept it, and at least you could be thankful that the frogs had cleaned out nearly all the mosquitoes.

xiv Had I read the papers? The same kind of thing had been happening at about the same time in other parts of the country. Army worms had invaded the southwest part of Wisconsin, and tent caterpillars had overrun Minnesota. And the suburbs of Chicago had been crawling with crickets.

xv "It's biological warfare," Carl said. "The animal kingdom is taking over.". . .

SUGGESTIONS FOR PAPERS

A number of short exercises in direct connection with the pieces in this section are feasible; you will easily think of topics and approaches beyond those suggested here. For the selections from De Forest: (a) Assume that you are a historian writing a chapter on the citizen-soldier in the War between the States. Draw an illustrative paragraph from De Forest, making proper acknowledgment. (b) Assume that you are writing a paper for a course in American literature, a paper in which you are discussing *Miss Ravenel's Conversion from Secession to Loyalty*. You have come to a consideration of the hero, Colburne, a volunteer officer in the Union army, and you have written, "De Forest knew at first hand the difficulties and the responsibilities of an officer." Develop the sentence in a substantial paragraph. For "The Fog": (a) Assume a term paper of a technical sort on smoke control. You wish in the introductory portion to show its necessity. Draw a paragraph from the article, making proper acknowledgment.

(b) Write a formal summary of part v of our selection. (c) Write an editorial for a newspaper recommending that smoke control measures be taken in a particular community. Refer to the article with proper acknowledgment.

Here are suggestions for papers that will require further reading: (a) Write an account of one of the several "Annals of Medicine" articles that have appeared in *The New Yorker*.[1] Assume that the members of the class are your readers. (b) Write an account of Daniel Defoe's *Journal of the Plague Year* (1722) or such part of it as is reprinted in a textbook anthology of eighteenth-century English literature. (The *Journal* is an imaginative reconstruction of the horrors of the Great Plague in London in 1665.) Direct your account to the class, and consider manner as well as matter. (c) Write, for the class, an account of John Hersey's *Hiroshima* (1946). You might consider, among other things, how Mr. Hersey's very effective organization is achieved.

Our selections may give some students a start on pieces of reporting of their own. The selections from De Forest, for instance, may show veterans ways of handling their own military experience. And since American farming in every section of the country has changed remarkably in the past few years, "Things of the Past" may help some students to see usable material in their own experience and observation.

A list of specific topics for reports, however, would be more misleading than helpful. You will have to canvass your own experience to see what you have to report on—there is surely something there. But some advice about scope and focus may be of help. Such reports as our selections exemplify are space-consuming, and it may be that in order to try a piece of reporting you will have to find some narrow frame to work in. You might, for instance, take your own experience in some set of events in your community and report upon it as if it were the experience of someone else. Or, taking a little larger frame, you might report your family's experience in the same set of events.

If your instructor wants a paper of some length, try a report of some set of events (not necessarily catastrophic) as it affected a community or a group. You may write in the third person or in the first—but if you write in the first, remember that the "I" is, this time, reporter.

Whatever the scope of your paper, remember that almost any experience—toxic fog, agricultural change, a plague of frogs, or what you know about—is interesting to a reader in the degree it is made to seem real to him. You do not have to "sell" the reader your subject matter. The effect of reality will be enough, and it will depend upon concreteness and selection. You will not have space enough to get everything down; you must keep asking yourself what parts of the experience best represent the whole.

[1] Or use Berton Roueché, *Eleven Blue Men, and Other Narratives of Medical Detection*, Little, Brown and Company, 1954.

X

Definition

To define does not mean just to describe, or to explain, or to identify —although description, explanation, or identification may be necessary parts of some definitions. "To define" comes from the Latin *definire,* to limit; and when one defines he attempts to set forth the precise limits of the application of a word or term, to make clear what that word or term includes and what it excludes. Definition is not easy; writers often fail to define, and readers often fail fully to comprehend even the most careful definition.

Definition is, moreover, a serious matter. Much discussion is wasted because terms needing definition go undefined; much controversy arises not from real disagreement but from misunderstood terms. As a writer you have a duty to make your essential terms clear. And of course the writers you read have likewise a duty to make their essential terms clear. If they do not do so, you have a right to question their skill—only be sure the fault is in them and not in you.

The problem is not only intellectual; it is moral too. If a writer uses complex and emotion-laden terms and does not make clear, either by context or by definition, the meaning he would have them carry, you have a right to suspect the sincerity of his intent. If a man writes of "education for democracy," for instance, you ought to know what he means by both "education" and "democracy" before you allow yourself to be influenced by him. And equally you have a duty to make the complex and emotion-laden terms you have occasion to use clear to the reader in the sense you honestly intend them.

i THE PROBLEMS OF DEFINITION

A definition may be a single sentence or, if need be, a definition may be extended for several pages. Yet the really difficult problems of definition may arise within a sentence definition and with quite familiar terms. Since a definition must make clear what a term includes and what it excludes, we need to keep remembering that a true statement about a term is by no means necessarily a definition of it. Suppose you encounter this definition: "A textbook is a book used in the preparation of a school lesson." You will agree with the sentence as a statement. But the moment you begin to examine it as a definition, it will occur to you that textbooks are used outside of schools, and that books no one calls textbooks are used in the preparation of lessons in schools. You will say that there is here no definition.

Now a great many statements offered as definitions are really not definitions at all. You may very well have learned some such definition as this: "A sentence is a group of words that expresses a complete, independent thought or a group of closely related thoughts." But can you, or can anyone, tell where "a thought" begins or ends? When, or how, is a thought independent of another thought? Does that addition of "or a group of closely related thoughts" really help? This example suggests one simple test of the adequacy of a definition. One may ask this: Is there another term, not synonymous with the defined term, that the definition seems to cover about as well as it does the defined term? Suppose we substitute "paragraph" for "sentence" in our example definition. Have we not discovered something about the adequacy of the definition?

I. *Logical Definition.* In order to think clearly about a definition, we need to consider its form. The way of definition of nouns or of noun terms most familiar to you from your use of the dictionary is called LOGICAL DEFINITION. It is more than a sentence form—poor definitions like those above may have the sentence form of a logical definition. Properly understood, logical definition is a way of ordering the writer's thought and, therefore, that of the reader, too.

In a logical definition, a writer defines a term by first putting it into the class of things to which it belongs—the *genus*—and then proceeding to distinguish it from other things of the same class—we say he gives its *differentia* (plural, *differentiae*). A logical definition of "lead pencil" (in its most usual sense) might be this: *A lead pencil* (term) *is* (linking verb) *an instrument for writing or drawing* (genus) *consisting of a strip of graphite incased in a cylinder of wood* (differentia). A lead pencil has been differentiated from other writing or drawing instruments—crayons, chalk, pens.

You can learn much about logical definitions by studying them in your dictionary; for instance, *Webster's New Collegiate* defines "tornado" as "a whirling wind accompanied by a funnel-shaped cloud, very violent and destructive in a narrow path often for many miles over the land." [1] "Wind" is the genus, reduced by the adjective "whirling"; the modifiers following the genus differentiate a tornado from other whirling windstorms. This instance and any number of others you can find will show you how much defining information may be packed into a single sentence written as a logical definition (in dictionary definitions "is" is understood). You will find that almost all the definitions in your science texts are logical definitions, and that the form is frequently used in history, political science, and discussions of literature. You will discover, too, that in the extended defi-

[1] By permission. From *Webster's New Collegiate Dictionary*, copyright, 1949, 1951, 1953, by G. & C. Merriam Co.

nitions in the latter part of this chapter, some crucial sentences are logical definitions.

II. *A definition and its readers.* A description of the form of logical definition does not take into account the particular readers of a definition. A definition is, of course, intended for readers who do not know the meaning of the term defined, or who are not quite clear about it. Since a writer of a definition is not talking to himself, he ought to consider continually what information his readers have, for it is their information that he uses to make the new term clear. For instance, a general definition of "whale" might use for its genus "marine mammal." But if the definition were intended for children who do not know the word "mammal," the genus might better be "animal," even though it is larger and less convenient. On the other hand, a writer of a textbook in biology could find a smaller and a more precise genus than "mammal" for his definition of "whale." Common sense gives us the principle: Since the purpose of definition is ordinarily to remove a difficulty, a good definition adds no difficulty in the process of defining. But you know from your own experience that even well-intentioned, careful writers do not always perfectly exemplify the principle.

Preciseness, then, is not the only consideration in definition; a definition may be precise and yet unintelligible to those for whom it is intended. Here is a definition from an elementary book on poetry: "A quatrain is a poem of four verses." This is a precise definition in a strict sense. Is it a good definition for you? It is not if you are like many students and mistakenly use the words "stanza" and "verse" interchangeably. If you need a definition of "quatrain," a writer ought not to assume you know another technical term in the same field. He might better write: "A quatrain is a poem of four lines," and add that he has defined in a strict sense, and that the word commonly means a four-line stanza. Even dictionaries sometimes include pretty useless definitions; a notorious example is Dr. Samuel Johnson's definition of "network": "anything reticulated or decussated at equal distances, with interstices between the intersections."

A very careful writer will sometimes predict a possible confusion on his reader's part and guard against it by the making of a distinction. If, for instance, someone were defining "myth" for you, would you not like him, as part of the definition, to distinguish "myth" from "legend"? (Does your dictionary make the distinction? Must you look up both words to get it?) And in noun terms made up of two or more words especial care in the prediction of possible confusion may be necessary. Very often a combination of the literal meanings of two familiar words is by no means a definition of the term they make up. "Middle West" and "Old South" are instances, for they have meanings controlled by our history, and far different senses than one could arrive at merely by a knowledge of the literal senses of the words that have been combined to form them. Or, in another instance, "marginal land" deceives readers who know the literal but not the technical sense of "marginal." In such terms the definer needs to take care that the reader is made really aware of what has happened when two familiar words are combined to make up one term.

III. *The adequate development of a definition.* Since students find their dictionaries so useful, they are likely to think of dictionary definitions as standards of adequacy. But a dictionary, and particularly a desk dictionary, has little space either for development or reservation. For instance, your dictionary will probably define the literary term "local color" something like this: "the distinctive features of a region or an era as they are presented in literature." Now perhaps that definition would enable a reader previously unfamiliar with the term to understand its meaning in the context he had found it. But it might well lead him to apply the term where it really does not fit. What his dictionary did not tell him is that the term is generally applied only to work in which a particular setting and the customs and manners peculiar to it are the chief interest and distinction of the work—its reason for being. In other words, the dictionary definition may make clear to a reader the meaning of "local color" used in the context of a discussion of the work of Bret Harte. But it might also mislead him into supposing that he should use "local color" in a discussion of the work of Nathaniel Hawthorne, whose work is valued for its representation of place, era, customs, and manners, but for much else, too.

Now of course a one-sentence logical definition of "local color" might contain more information about the term than the definition above does. Some dictionary definitions pack in a great deal of defining information; the dictionary definition of "communism" quoted in Chapter II, for instance, is a masterpiece of compression. But good writers consider that an overcrowded sentence in general writing will defeat its own purpose. A writer needing to define "transitional paragraph" could put his definition into a single sentence, probably without much trouble. But if he is careful for his reader's convenience, he will design a short logical definition that is capable of being developed. Here is one: "A transitional paragraph is a paragraph used to connect parts of a piece of writing and to indicate the relationship between them." That sentence is developed by a second sentence: "Ordinarily it makes reference to what has gone before, often by means of a summary statement, and announces the discussion to follow."

Indeed, one kind of development of a definition is almost always required. A reader has reason to be discontented with the writer who defines but does not tell him how the definition applies. A definition is by its very nature a generalization, for the term defined covers a number of particulars. Precious as space is in a desk dictionary, the use of some words is illustrated. And a careful writer usually finds space for two or three sentences of illustration when his generalized definition of a term requires them. Here is a definition of a literary term briefly developed:

Objective narration is a narrative method in which the narrator records what characters do and say, without comment or interpretation or any assumption of insight into their minds and hearts. Ernest Hemingway's "The Killers" is a contemporary example of objective narration, for the story proceeds as if there were an invisible observer and listener recording the action in the lunchroom and the visit to Andreson. But the method is very old, and the story of Ruth in the Bible is also an example.

The writer has apparently assumed that the reader of his definition has read "The Killers," a reasonable assumption, since the story is well known. But his sentence in reference to it is full enough so that it is of service to a reader who does not know the story. And the two examples very far apart in time and temper have a definitive significance, since they show that the method defined is not limited to any one period, or to one kind of material.

But with some terms of special difficulty, the appropriate initial development may be comment on the use of the term. A writer beginning an essay on some social developments on the frontier in the middle nineteenth century needs to be sure first of all that his readers have control of the complex term "frontier." He might write, correctly enough, "In American history, 'the frontier' is the line of settlement that is farthest westward." But that definition does not cover a number of the ways in which the term is actually used, and any attempt to cover them in a single sentence would sadly overcomplicate it. The solution is a simple, and in itself inadequate, definition, developed by comment:

In American history, "the frontier" is the line of settlement that is farthest westward. But the term offers some difficulties in use. A writer using it may be thinking, not precisely of the edge of settlement, but of a strip of new settlement. And no frontier was long fixed: a strip of land was wilderness, then a frontier, then settled country. Moreover writers speak of kinds of frontiers; a farming frontier, for instance, may have been long preceded by a trading frontier.

For some purposes, a considerable development of logical definitions is appropriate, so considerable that we may call the developed definitions extended definitions. If you look up in *Webster's New Collegiate Dictionary* the term "witches' Sabbath," you will find this definition: "In medieval demonology, a midnight assembly in which demons, sorcerers, and witches were thought to celebrate their orgies." [1] Now a desk dictionary has to stop there; no more can be done without doing much more (some desk dictionaries do not include the term at all). But what is left entirely undeveloped in the dictionary definition a reader needs to know in order to understand the term: he is left asking "How did they celebrate what orgies?" In the following selection, you will see that the writer starts with a one-sentence logical definition which functions as a topic sentence for his paragraph. And you will see that the paragraph develops just what was left undeveloped by the dictionary definition.

[1] By permission. From *Webster's New Collegiate Dictionary,* copyright, 1949, 1951, 1953, by G. & C. Merriam Co.

FROM *Witchcraft in Old and New England* (1929)

GEORGE LYMAN KITTREDGE

[Witches' Sabbath] [1]

The Witches' Sabbath in its developed form is a combined religious service and business meeting followed by a debauch of feasting, dancing, and wild lust. Satan is visibly present—as man, or monster, or huge demonic goat,—to receive homage as a feudal lord and worship as a deity. The rites are in elaborate profanation of Christian ceremonies, which they reverse or parody or burlesque. Proselytes are brought in, to make or confirm their formal compact with the devil: they renounce their baptism and all "seals and symbols of redeemèd sin," abandon their faith in God and in his Church, and abjure their redemption through Christ. Satan, for his part, promises them riches and pleasure so long as they live and happiness in the world to come. To each is assigned a familiar demon, who shall come at call to serve as operating agent in every malefic design. To and from the Sabbath the worshippers are swiftly transported through the air, often for long distances, riding on staffs or broomsticks, or on fiends in bestial form; or they may fly thither and home again by virtue of a magic ointment with which they smear themselves. This ointment, which has other occult properties, is sometimes prepared at the meetings from the fat and marrow of stolen infants who are sacrificed to Satan or of buried infants whom the hags have clawed up from their graves. Such were the orgies of the Witches' Sabbath as systematized in the fourteenth and fifteenth centuries by the scholastic ingenuity of devout theologians and described in confessions innumerable wrung by torture from ignorant and superstitious defendants in response to leading questions framed by inquisitors who had the whole system in mind before the trial began.

The nature of the term will usually suggest the appropriate means of extending a logical definition. Suppose we have a local term, "lagniappe." *Webster's New Collegiate Dictionary* defines it: "In Louisiana, a trifling present given to customers by tradesmen." [2] That definition would probably enable a reader to fit the word into most of the contexts in which he might find it—perhaps not all. But a definer may wish to do more for a reader; he may wish to make a reader feel thoroughly familiar with a word, to give it to him as a possession. It is easy to think of the following definition by Mark Twain as simply an extension of the dictionary's logical

[1] Reprinted by permission of the publishers from George Lyman Kittredge, *Witchcraft in Old and New England,* Cambridge, Mass.: Harvard University Press; copyright, 1929, by The President and Fellows of Harvard College.

[2] By permission. From *Webster's New Collegiate Dictionary,* copyright, 1949, 1951, 1953, by G. & C. Merriam Co.

definition of "lagniappe." From it you can learn an important means of extending a definition: the use of a term in typical contexts.

FROM *Life on the Mississippi*   (1875, 1883)

MARK TWAIN

[Lagniappe]

I We picked up one excellent word—a word worth travelling to New Orleans to get; a nice limber, expressive, handy word—"Lagniappe." They pronounce it lanny-*yap*. It is Spanish—so they said. We discovered it at the head of a column of odds and ends in the *Picayune* the first day; heard twenty people use it the second; inquired what it meant the third; adopted it and got facility in swinging it the fourth. It has a restricted meaning, but I think the people spread it out a little when they choose. It is the equivalent of the thirteenth roll in a "baker's dozen." It is something thrown in, gratis, for good measure. The custom originated in the Spanish quarter of the city. When a child or a servant buys something in a shop— or even the mayor or the governor, for aught I know—he finishes the operation by saying:

II "Give me something for lagniappe."

III The shopman always responds; gives the child a bit of licorice-root, gives the servant a cheap cigar or a spool of thread, gives the governor—I don't know what he gives the governor; support, likely.

IV When you are invited to drink—and this does occur now and then in New Orleans—and you say, "What, again?—no, I've had enough," the other party says, "But just this one time more—this is for lagniappe." When the beau perceives that he is stacking his compliments a trifle too high, and sees by the young lady's countenance that the edifice would have been better with the top compliment left off, he puts his "I beg pardon, no harm intended," into the briefer form of "Oh, that's for lagniappe." If the waiter in the restaurant stumbles and spills a gill of coffee down the back of your neck, he says, "F'r lagniappe, sah," and gets you another cup without extra charge.

The next selection seems a piece of informal reminiscence. But you will be able to distinguish three logical definitions, each briefly extended.

FROM *The Country Weekly Then*

I The country newspaper in the first decades of this century was dependent for much of its content on a newspaper service. I suppose that now, when even the smallest paper has a linotype, a country weekly may get along without boiler-plate, type-high, and ready-print. They were necessary enough to us.

ii Both boiler-plate and type-high were forms of lead printing plates made by a stereotyping process for use on flat bed presses. They were shipped to the country weekly in wooden boxes and, when they had been used, returned to the newspaper service in the same boxes to be melted up and made into new stereotypes. Boiler-plate was stereotypes in column lengths, designed to fit on metal bases and to be locked into the form along with columns of hand-set type. Boiler-plate had to be usable at any time; whatever was said in a column of boiler-plate could not be really news or even narrowly topical. One did not plan to use boiler-plate; one used it whenever he chanced to have a column to fill. Self-respecting country weeklies did not use it on the first page; or, if they did, they felt temporarily disgraced.

iii We of the *Leader,* however, were more dependent upon type-high than we were upon boiler-plate. A piece of type-high was a small stereotype cast, as the name indicates, in one piece on its own base. It came in assorted lengths—from about three column inches down to three lines—and was used to fill odd spaces, say at the bottoms of columns. Generally the matter of a piece of type-high was an isolated fact or a bit of useless statistical information: a plague of locusts in Ubangi, perhaps, or the average number of babies required to wear out a baby carriage. When, in making up the paper, one had a hole to fill, he scrabbled about in the type-high box until he found a piece the right size. But the type-high assortment never had enough very short pieces. I remember that at the bottom of a column of "business cards" of real-estate men, auctioneers, and the like, we ran the same piece of type-high for months, until it would print no longer.

iv Boiler-plate and type-high were auxiliaries. The ready-print (or "patent insides" or "the patent") was fundamental. Ready-print was a set of printed newspaper pages bought from a newspaper service and used for the inside pages of a country weekly. Instead of buying plain newsprint, country weeklies bought their newsprint—flat, of course—with two or four pages printed. (The number of pages printed depended upon the amount of advertising a weekly had in a particular week.) The other four or six pages they printed themselves. Only at Christmas time, when advertising was heavy, did we expect to print the full eight pages ourselves. Then the ready-print took the form of an insert which we folded in.

v The content of the ready-print was a masterpiece of the innocuous. It was designed not to offend any subscriber of any country paper. It had some columns set up like news stories. In addition there were commonly a housewives' department, some agricultural material, and a comic strip or two. There was always a serial (usually a Western). We used to get advance proofs of the serials, and as a kid I treasured them. But no one else connected with the *Leader* paid any attention to any of the content of the ready-print. Infrequently some subscriber remarked on something in it; it must sometimes have been read. But I think that the future researcher on the influence of ready-print on American culture will have a hard time finding his material.

vi The ready-print came in bundles by express. One hot day in August some expressman put his hook quite through our bundle, making such a hole in the sheets that we could not get them through the press. That was a time of crisis, for we had to print the whole eight pages ourselves. I can't think how we did it. We must have given ourselves a full-page ad, but even then we would have had three pages to fill with something. We may have had eighteen columns of new boiler-plate in stock, but that seems unlikely. I suspect that we eked out with boiler-plate and type-high that we had used before but had not yet returned to the newspaper service.

ii   EXTENDED DEFINITION

Sometimes a term is so complex, or of so disputed a meaning, that it must have extended definition. Professor Samuel Eliot Morison's definition of puritanism [1] exemplifies a sort of definition often necessary. It is not because the word is new to his readers that it needs careful definition. Quite the contrary. "Puritanism" has so often been used in senses limited by the attitudes of writers—perhaps by their prejudices and even by their ignorance—that a usable meaning for it must be fixed. The historian finds it necessary to make fully clear to his readers how he understands the term, and how they, for the purposes of his book, are to understand it. For similar reasons, Carl Becker finds it necessary to begin a book with an extended definition of "democracy," remarking that the term is "a kind of conceptual Gladstone bag which, with a little manipulation, can be made to accommodate almost any collection of social facts we may wish to carry about in it." Indeed, a good many abstract terms have been so manipulated that it is necessary to define them before they can be used intelligibly in discussion.

FROM *Builders of the Bay Colony* (1930)

SAMUEL ELIOT MORISON

[Puritanism] [2]

I [1] The time has come, the Walrus said, to talk of puritanism and the puritans. [2] I had hoped to get through this book without that disagreeable task of definition; but it cannot be done. [3] What then is meant by puritanism, and who were the puritans?

II [1] Puritanism was a way of life based on the belief that the Bible was the word of God, and the whole word of God. [2] Puritans were the Englishmen who endeavored to live according to that light. [3] Having been so round, I must shade off, for puritanism has had various meanings at different times. [4] Originally a nickname (*οἱ καθαροί, puritani*) flung about on

---

[1] In the sense in which the word is here used, "puritanism" is often capitalized; in this section Professor Morison's practice is followed.

[2] Reprinted from *Builders of the Bay Colony* by Samuel Eliot Morison, by permission of Houghton Mifflin Company. Copyright, 1930, by Samuel Eliot Morison.

the theological controversies of the late Roman Empire, it was revived in Queen Elizabeth's reign to describe that party of English Protestants who wished to carry out the Reformation to its logical conclusion, and purge the Anglican Church of forms and ceremonies for which there was no warrant in the Bible; or, to use a phrase of Cartwright which became a watchword for one party and a jest for their opponents, to restore the Christian Church 'pure and unspotted.' [5] At first it was applied only to persons within the Church of England; but by 1630, the term puritan had been stretched to include separatists like the Pilgrims who obtained purity outside the Anglican communion, and even the Scots Presbyterians, who had a different organization. [6] Further, the Church of England puritans were divided into non-conformists, who disobeyed the law rather than compromise with conscience, and the conformable puritans like John White and John Winthrop who performed or attended the prescribed services according to the Book of Common Prayer, while hoping for better things.

III [1] Beside this purely religious meaning of puritanism, there was a moral aspect. [2] Persons who read the Bible and sincerely believed in it, adopted or attempted a very exacting code of morals; and as they believed that this code was gospel ordinance, they endeavored to enforce it on others. [3] Such persons were originally called precisians, and were not necessarily puritans in a religious sense. [4] The most thoroughly puritanic diary I have ever read, full of moans and groans over the mildest peccadilloes of himself and others, is that of Samuel Ward, master of Sidney Sussex College, a stout Royalist and Anglican who was expelled by Cromwell. [5] We mean this moral preciseness when we use the term puritanism to-day; yet moral puritanism is by no means confined to the Protestant or English-speaking churches. [6] The Catholic counter-reformation of the sixteenth century was quite as puritanic in a moral sense as the Protestant reformation. [7] Jansenism was a puritanical movement within the Gallican Church in France; and no sect within the last century has been more puritanical in a moral sense than the Catholic Church in Ireland. [8] In England there was what we might call high church puritanism, of which the 'divine Herbert' was the highest example. [9] King Charles and Bishop Laud were both persons of high moral standards. [10] Laud's ecclesiastical courts were as zealous to punish immorality as to enforce conformity; and the reforms that he began in the University of Oxford were continued by its later puritan rulers. [11] If Bishop and King had not attempted religious innovations in the direction of Rome, if they had respected the ritual and doctrine of the Church as Elizabeth or even Archbishop Bancroft had left them, the puritans might never have become associated with radicalism and democracy.

IV [1] And what of the political side of puritanism? [2] Charles Borgeaud, and other political scientists, have traced democracy to puritanism. [3] I do not think that this theory will hold water, although there is something in it. [4] The Englishman of 1630 was politically mature, compared with other Europeans. [5] He was beginning to feel his way toward popular government, and during the Interregnum he went far on that road. [6] As we have seen in the case of the Salem Church, the congregational polity which one branch of the puritans favored, made laymen the governing body of the church. [7] But the connection between puritanism and political liberalism was fortuitous. [8] English puritans in 1630 rallied to representative government and traditional English liberty because that was their only refuge against innovating Bishops and a high church King; but in New England where they had things their own way, their political spirit was conservative and their temper autocratic. [9] If American democracy came out of puritan New England (and it may equally well be traced to Virginia), it came from the English and not the puritan in our ancestors, and from the newness not the puritanism of New England.

v [1] We would do well then to remember that puritanism in the seventeenth century had a purely religious connotation. [2] I will not detain my readers here with a summary of their beliefs and practices; these will appear as the lives of those commonwealth builders, puritans all, unfold. [3] Yet pardon me if I caution you against certain current delusions about the early puritans upon which historians have placed the stamp of authority. [4] The one is that they were mainly preoccupied with hell and damnation. [5] On the contrary, fire-and-brimstone sermons, and poems such as Wigglesworth's 'Day of Doom,' belong to a later generation or to the eighteenth century, when puritan pastors tried to frighten their backsliding congregations into good behavior. [6] The second delusion is that puritanism is synonymous with Calvinism. [7] Broadly speaking the English puritan theologians were Calvinist in their theology rather than Lutheran or Arminian; but being learned in the ancient tongues they derived their ideas mainly from the Bible and the Fathers. [8] Calvin's 'Institutes' was never to them a sacred book, and I have found Calvin less frequently quoted in their writings than English theologians like Ames, Perkins, and Whitaker. [9] A third delusion is that puritans were prohibitionists, or indirectly responsible for prohibition. [10] Their faith put more stress on the joys of the inner life than on those of the senses, but they made no attempt to proscribe one of God's good creatures, whose temperate use was sanctioned by the Bible, and by our Lord's example. [11] Finally, readers of New England history must be cautioned against ascribing to puritanism alone a coarseness that was common to the age, and a bigotry that was common to all Christian sects, and still is far too common. [12] We will not often find breadth of mind among the English puritans; but we will find a spiritual depth that belongs only to the great ages of religious experience.

vi [1] John Winthrop was happy to have lived in the golden age of English puritanism, when some of its early fanaticism had been sloughed off, without losing the bloom of youth. [2] It had not altogether broken with the stately and cadenced ritual of the Book of Common Prayer; it had grasped firm hold of the evangelistic principle, the 'tidings of great joy' that our Saviour brought to men. [3] Whatever puritanism may have come to mean in later ages—and I will freely admit that its more recent manifestations have been negative, narrow, and altogether unlovely—it meant three hundred years ago, a high sincerity of purpose, an integrity of life, and an eager searching for the voice of God. [4] The intellectual strength of the puritan was his knowledge of the Bible; the moral strength of the puritan was his direct approach to God. [5] No puritan ever said, as did the children of Israel when they heard the thunder and the trumpet blasts on Mount Sinai, 'Let not God speak to us, lest we die.' [6] His home, his study, his meeting-house, were filled with the reverberations of the awful and gracious voice for which he listened. [7] If he rejected the intercession of the saints, it was because he would meet God face to face. [8] If he despised the ancient pageantry of worship, it was because he would have no false and sensual symbols between him and his Redeemer. [9] Often, like the ancient Hebrews, he misunderstood the voice of God. [10] Often he mistook for it the echo of his own wants and passions. [11] But the desire to hear it, the sense that life consisted in hearing and obeying it, never left him.

---

1) Before we concern ourselves with the technique of extended definition, we ought to make sure that our example of extended definition has been well read. Define in context: "non-conformists" (II:6), "Jansenism" (III:7), "Interregnum" and "polity" (IV:5–6), and "Arminian" (V:7). "Peccadillo" (III:4) is a Spanish word taken into English—what is a literal translation of it? Restate VI:1 without using any metaphor. Explain the full meaning of IV:7.

2) Discuss the kinds of knowledge on the part of the reader that are here presupposed by the writer. For example, do you know on what occasion the children of Israel heard thunder and trumpet blasts on Mount Sinai? (If you do not, see Exodus 19:16–25.) Or consider such sentences as III:8. If "the 'divine Herbert' was the highest example" means nothing to a reader, how will he go about finding out something of George Herbert? What does "high church" mean? Do you see that the *ideal* reader for this sentence would know something about Herbert's poems?

3) *The American College Dictionary* has for its first definition of "Puritanism": "the principles and practices of the Puritans"; and for its first definition of "Puritan": "one of a class of Protestants who arose in the 16th century within the Church of England, demanding further reforms in doctrine and worship, and greater strictness in religious discipline, and during part of the 17th century constituting a powerful political party." Its second definition of "Puritan" is "(*l.c.*) one who affects great purity or strictness of life and religious principles." The definition gives the word a derogatory sense (for "one who affects" means usually "one who makes a show of"). The same dictionary's definition of "puritanical" recognizes the implied disapproval which frequently accompanies the use of the word by defining it as "excessively strict, rigid, or austere." [1]

4) Quite properly these dictionary definitions reflect current usage. But you can see why a writer using "puritanism" in reference to the American puritans of the fourth decade of the seventeenth century will find it necessary to dislodge the derogatory implications which have gathered themselves to the term in certain extensions of it. Moreover—and just as

[1] The definitions in this paragraph are reprinted by courtesy of the publishers from *The American College Dictionary*, copyright, 1947, by Random House, Inc. (textbook edition by Harper & Brothers).

important—there is real disagreement among scholars about what puritanism in the early history of the colonies was like.

5) What is the initial one-sentence definition of "puritanism" in our selection? What is the one-sentence definition of "puritans"? A dictionary would probably not use the metaphorical "light" in a definition. What does "that light" mean here? Do you find a one-sentence definition of "puritanism" late in the selection?

6) One help in understanding the meaning of a word is knowing its source. We have in II:4 the Latin *puritani,* those who would purify. The puritans in England and America were at first those who would purify the Anglican church according to their idea of what was right belief and ritual. The Greek expression is parallel, connected with our "cathartic," a purge. In II:4–6 we have a historical account of the use of the term from the reign of Elizabeth to 1630. Notice that the term extends in meaning: do you see that if, for instance, "puritans" comes to include "separatists," the term is then much more general than it was in its original use? You would find it interesting and illuminating to look up "puritan" and "puritanism" in the *Oxford New English Dictionary.*

7) Paragraphs III and IV deal with the ways in which "puritanism" has been extended and then specialized in meaning. What is the chief purpose of III? Why does the historian need to make clear that the moral attitude we are likely to designate as puritan was not more characteristic of puritans than it was of some other religious persons and groups? Note the transition between III and IV.

8) In IV the writer is discussing a logical fallacy of a sort into which anyone is liable to fall. It is easy to assume that what comes after one set of ideas and attitudes has developed out of them. We attribute, then, to the former thing the characteristics of the later; we read history backward.

9) Note carefully the structure of v. How is transition between IV and v accomplished? What sentence controls the organization of v? This paragraph, as is often necessary in the definition of a difficult or doubtful term, concerns itself with NEGATIVE DEFINITION, that is, it states what the puritans were not. Extended definitions often start with negative definition, eliminating definitions that are mistaken or beside the writer's purpose. Indeed, the structure of an extended definition may be the reverse of the structure of our example, developing toward, instead of from, the sentence definition the writer wishes to establish.

10) VI brings the definition to concrete terms. Puritanism was initially defined as a way of life; this last paragraph deals with the puritan and his conduct. Notice how VI:3 defines "puritanism" with the qualities of the individual puritan. And notice how the sentence structure—the balanced sentences and the successive parallel sentences—is used to point up the relationship of ideas.

The next two selections are both by Carl Becker, a writer with an especial skill in the extended definition used as a point of departure for an address or an essay. Notice in the first that, although its purpose is like that of our definition of "puritanism," the development is toward, instead of from, the sentence definition the writer wishes to fix as adequate for his purposes.

FROM *Modern Democracy* (1941)

CARL L. BECKER

[A Definition of Democracy]

I Democracy, like liberty or science or progress, is a word with which we are all so familiar that we rarely take the trouble to ask what we mean by it. It is a term, as the devotees of semantics say, which has no "referent" —there is no precise or palpable thing or object which we all think of when the word is pronounced. On the contrary, it is a word which connotes different things to different people, a kind of conceptual Gladstone bag which, with a little manipulation, can be made to accommodate almost any collection of social facts we may wish to carry about in it. In it we can as easily pack a dictatorship as any other form of government. We have only to stretch the concept to include any form of government supported by a majority of the people, for whatever reasons and by whatever means of ex- pressing assent, and before we know it the empire of Napoleon, the Soviet regime of Stalin, and the Fascist systems of Mussolini and Hitler are all safely in the bag. But if this is what we mean by democracy, then virtually all forms of government are democratic, since virtually all governments, except in times of revolution, rest upon the explicit or implicit consent of the people. In order to discuss democracy intelligently it will be necessary, therefore, to define it, to attach to the word a sufficiently precise meaning to avoid the confusion which is not infrequently the chief result of such discussions.

II All human institutions, we are told, have their ideal forms laid away in heaven, and we do not need to be told that the actual institutions con- form but indifferently to these ideal counterparts. It would be possible then to define democracy either in terms of the ideal or in terms of the real form —to define it as government of the people, by the people, for the people; or to define it as government of the people, by the politicians, for whatever pressure groups can get their interests taken care of. But as a historian I am naturally disposed to be satisfied with the meaning which, in the history of politics, men have commonly attributed to the word—a meaning, needless to say, which derives partly from the experience and partly from the aspira- tions of mankind. So regarded, the term democracy refers primarily to a form of government by the many as opposed to government by the one— government by the people as opposed to government by a tyrant, a dictator, or an absolute monarch. This is the most general meaning of the word as men have commonly understood it.

III In this antithesis there are, however, certain implications, always tacitly understood, which give a more precise meaning to the term. Peisistratus, for example, was supported by a majority of the people, but his government was never regarded as a democracy for all that. Caesar's power derived from a popular mandate, conveyed through established republican forms, but that did not make his government any the less a dictatorship. Napoleon called his government a democratic empire, but no one, least of all Napoleon himself, doubted that he had destroyed the last vestiges of the democratic republic. Since the Greeks first used the term, the essential test of democratic government has always been this: the source of political authority must be and remain in the people and not in the ruler. A democratic government has always meant one in which the citizens, or a sufficient number of them to represent more or less effectively the common will, freely act from time to time, and according to established forms, to appoint or recall the magistrates and to enact or revoke the laws by which the community is governed. This I take to be the meaning which history has impressed upon the term democracy as a form of government.

The groupings of subject matters in college study, and the terms for those groupings, are both unsatisfactory. A college catalogue may seem to say that an instructor in American literature is a teacher of humanities and an instructor in American history is a social scientist; it thereby suggests a kind of difference in interest and intent that does not—or at least should not—exist. However, Becker in the selection below is not concerned with finding better terms than those that have become standard. He is concerned with giving the term "social science" a usable meaning. The selection is technically interesting and worthy of study for its careful set of distinctions.

FROM *The Function of the Social Sciences* (1942)

CARL L. BECKER

[The Natural and the Social Sciences]

I In any discussion of the social sciences there arises, of course, the inevitable first question, or pair of questions: is history one of the social sciences, and in any case are the social sciences really sciences. I shall not attempt to answer these questions further than to suggest that the answer depends a good deal upon definitions and points of view.

II Science may be defined, in the original sense of the term, as a systematic body of demonstrable knowledge. The particular methods of ascertaining knowledge will depend upon the nature of the subject matter about which knowledge is desired; and the methods that are found suitable to the several branches of science are in fact so varied that it is difficult to say with much precision what "the scientific method" really is. The one thing that all scientists have in common is not a special technique, but a special attitude of mind towards their several enterprises. This attitude is simply the desire to know, in respect to the particular matter in hand, what is true about it, irrespective of any practical or esthetic or moral implications that may be involved in the truth that turns up. This does not mean that the scientist in any branch of learning is indifferent to these implications, but only that for the purpose of his inquiry he must disregard them. If one asks how he can afford to disregard them, the answer is that his enterprise proceeds upon the fundamental assumption that knowing what is true is itself a primary value upon which all other values must in the long run depend. In this sense history and the social studies are branches of science—that is to say, the pursuit of knowledge for its own sake.

III There are, nevertheless, two important differences between the natural sciences and the social studies which make it desirable (for the purpose of this essay, at least) to separate them into two categories, which we may label respectively science and history (including in history the other social studies). One of these differences has to do with the nature of the subject matter, the other with the method of apprehending it.

IV The natural sciences are primarily concerned with the material world (including living organisms in so far as they are parts of the material world), and their aim is to disclose the structure and behavior of material things in generalized terms (in terms of mathematics so far as possible) which will be true irrespective of variable conditions of time and place. In dealing with his subject matter the work of the natural scientist is greatly facilitated by the fact that he is not emotionally entangled with it: he does not care how his subject matter behaves, his subject matter is indifferent to what he does to it, and ignorant of what he has learned about it. Fortunately for the physicist, the atom cannot acquire a knowledge of physics. The physicist can, therefore, proceed on the assumption that any knowledge he may acquire about the behavior of the atom will not modify its behavior and thereby invalidate conclusions based upon its behavior up to date. The social scientist cannot make this assumption, at least not without important qualifications. For his subject matter is the behavior of men in the world of human relations; and men are not, like the atom, indifferent to what is done to them or ignorant of what is learned about them. On the contrary, the subject matter of the social scientist can find out what he has learned about its behavior in the past, and as a result of that knowledge behave differently in the future. This is the fundamental difference between the natural sciences and the social studies; whereas the behavior of material things remains the same whatever men learn about it, the behavior of men is always conditioned by what they know about themselves and the world in which they live.

V This difference between the natural sciences and the social studies in respect to subject matter gives rise to a corresponding difference in respect to the method of apprehending the subject matter—a difference between what may be called the scientific and the historical approach to knowledge. Generally speaking, the natural scientist is disposed to ask of any situation how it functions in a general or a universal context, the social scientist how it has developed in a time sequence. The statement needs to be qualified, no doubt. The social scientist is not always exclusively concerned with development in a time sequence, nor is the natural scientist always indifferent to it. It is well known that the geologist gives us the history of the earth, the biologist describes the evolution of plant and animal life, on a time scale that dwarfs the historian's temporal span to the measure of a passing moment. Even physics, according to Whitehead, cannot be properly understood without taking account of the history of physical concepts. Obviously, since everything is related to something else, anything can be apprehended in terms of its behavior in a general context; and since everything has a history, anything can be apprehended in terms of its transformation in a time sequence.

VI Everything has a history—true enough in one sense. But in another sense only man has a history. The earth has a history in the sense that certain things have happened to it as an object in time and space; but knowledge of that history, not being a possession of the earth but only of the geologist, plays no part in shaping that history. Man is not thus limited. Man is the only organism that is aware that it and all things have a history, the only organism, therefore, that can acquire some systematic and enduring knowledge of what that history is, the only organism, accordingly, whose activities are modified by that knowledge. Only man has a history in the sense that his own knowledge (or what he accepts as knowledge) of the history of all things, including himself, is an essential factor in determining what his own objective history has been and will be.

VII The social studies are concerned with the history of man in this sense. They are primarily concerned with man as a social animal, that is to say, with his social activities as conditioned by intelligence and inspired by conscious purpose. They aim to disclose not only what man has done in the world, but also what he has thought about the world and his doings in it. The subject matter of the social studies therefore includes the history of the social sciences. It includes equally the history of the natural sciences. The social studies and the natural sciences have each a long history, and at every stage the history of the one is closely related to the history of the other. A brief survey of certain aspects of that history and that relation, as manifested in western civilization, may throw some light on the essential function of the social studies in the life of man.

The three extended definitions we have considered thus far have this in common: they are all initial, points of departure for discussions of some length to follow. But of course each one of them is something besides definition; Morison's definition of "puritanism," for instance, stands quite well by itself as a brief essay. And we sometimes find a discussion, standing by itself or placed within a larger whole, proceeding by successive definition. Our next selection is interesting for its extraordinary precision in definition, and for the skill with which an analytical argument is developed by successive definitions and distinctions. It is from a lecture by Cardinal Newman called "Knowledge Viewed in Relation to Religious Duty." Newman is concerned to make clear the difference between certain Christian virtues and their secular complements, and to define the secular ideal of character.

The last paragraph of our selection—the definition of a gentleman—has sometimes been used in textbooks by itself as an example of extended definition. Yet reading it by itself may be misleading. The gentleman Newman defines is not a whole man, nor an ideal man; he is merely the product, at his best, of the training of the intellect, at its best. But the trained intellect is not, Newman believes, all-sufficient. "Quarry the granite rock with razors, or moor the vessel with a thread of silk"; he says, "then may you hope with such keen and delicate instruments as human knowledge and human reason to contend against those giants, the passion and the pride of man."

In the first sentence of the selection you will come upon the term "philosophical morality." Newman has been using "philosophy" to mean the training of the intellect in and for itself. This intellectual discipline has its morality—its results in conduct—a morality which is, though limited, attractive and useful to civilization.

FROM *The Idea of a University* (1852)

JOHN HENRY NEWMAN

[Secular and Christian Virtue]

1 [The] embellishment of the exterior is almost the beginning and the end of philosophical morality. This is why it aims at being modest rather than humble; this is how it can be proud at the very time that it is unassuming. To humility indeed it does not even aspire; humility is one of the most difficult of virtues both to attain and to ascertain. It lies close upon the heart itself, and its tests are exceedingly delicate and subtle. Its counterfeits abound; however, we are little concerned with them here, for, I repeat, it is hardly professed even by name in the code of ethics which we are reviewing. As has been often observed, ancient civilization had not the idea, and had no word to express it: or rather, it had the idea, and considered it a defect of mind, not a virtue, so that the word which denoted it conveyed a reproach. As to the modern world, you may gather its ignorance of it by its perversion of the somewhat parallel term 'condescension.' Humility or condescension, viewed as a virtue of conduct, may be said to consist, as in other things, so in our placing ourselves in our thoughts on a level with our inferiors; it is not only a voluntary relinquishment of the privileges of our own station, but an actual participation or assumption of the

condition of those to whom we stoop. This is true humility, to feel and to behave as if we were low; not, to cherish a notion of our importance, while we affect a low position. Such was St. Paul's humility, when he called himself 'the least of the saints'; such the humility of those many holy men who have considered themselves the greatest of sinners. It is an abdication, as far as their own thoughts are concerned, of those prerogatives or privileges to which others deem them entitled. Now it is not a little instructive to contrast with this idea,—with this theological meaning of the word 'condescension,'—its proper English sense; put them in juxta-position, and you will at once see the difference between the world's humility and the humility of the Gospel. As the world uses the word, 'condescension' is a stooping indeed of the person, but a bending forward, unattended with any the slightest effort to leave by a single inch the seat in which it is so firmly established. It is the act of a superior, who protests to himself, while he commits it, that he is superior still, and that he is doing nothing else but an act of grace towards those on whose level, in theory, he is placing himself. And this is the nearest idea which the philosopher can form of the virtue of self-abasement; to do more than this is to his mind a meanness or an hypocrisy, and at once excites his suspicion and disgust. What the world is, such it has ever been; we know the contempt which the educated pagans had for the martyrs and confessors of the Church; and it is shared by the anti-Catholic bodies of this day.

II Such are the ethics of Philosophy, when faithfully represented; but an age like this, not pagan, but professedly Christian, cannot venture to reprobate humility in set terms, or to make a boast of pride. Accordingly, it looks out for some expedient by which it may blind itself to the real state of the case. Humility, with its grave and self-denying attributes, it cannot love; but what is more beautiful, what more winning, than modesty? what virtue, at first sight, simulates humility so well? though what in fact is more radically distinct from it? In truth, great as is its charm, modesty is not the deepest or the most religious of virtues. Rather it is the advanced guard or sentinel of the soul militant, and watches continually over its nascent intercourse with the world about it. It goes the round of the senses; it mounts up into the countenance; it protects the eye and ear; it reigns in the voice and gesture. Its province is the outward deportment, as other virtues have relation to matters theological, others to society, and others to the mind itself. And being more superficial than other virtues, it is more easily disjoined from their company; it admits of being associated with principles or qualities naturally foreign to it, and is often made the cloak of feelings or ends for which it was never given to us. So little is it the necessary index of humility, that it is even compatible with pride. The better for the purpose of Philosophy; humble it cannot be, so forthwith modesty becomes its humility.

III Pride, under such training, instead of running to waste in the education of the mind, is turned to account; it gets a new name; it is called self-respect; and ceases to be the disagreeable, uncompanionable quality which it is in itself. Though it be the motive principle of the soul, it seldom comes to view; and when it shows itself, then delicacy and gentleness are its attire, and good sense and sense of honour direct its motions. It is no longer a restless agent, without definite aim; it has a large field of exertion assigned to it, and it subserves those social interests which it would naturally trouble. It is directed into the channel of industry, frugality, honesty, and obedience; and it becomes the very staple of the religion and morality held in honour in a day like our own. It becomes the safeguard of chastity, the guarantee of veracity, in high and low; it is the very household god of society, as at present constituted, inspiring neatness and decency in the servant girl, propriety of carriage and refined manners in her mistress, uprightness, manliness, and generosity in the head of the family. It diffuses a light over town and country; it covers the soil with handsome edifices and smiling gardens; it tills the field, it stocks and embellishes the shop. It is the stimulating principle of providence on the one hand, and of free expenditure on the other; of an honourable ambition, and of elegant enjoyment. It breathes upon the face of the community, and the hollow sepulchre is forthwith beautiful to look upon.

iv Refined by the civilization which has brought it into activity, this self-respect infuses into the mind an intense horror of exposure, and a keen sensitiveness of notoriety and ridicule. It becomes the enemy of extravagances of any kind; it shrinks from what are called scenes; it has no mercy on the mock-heroic, on pretence or egotism, on verbosity in language, or what is called prosiness in conversation. It detects gross adulation; not that it tends at all to the eradication of the appetite to which the flatterer ministers, but it sees the absurdity of indulging it, it understands the annoyance thereby given to others, and if a tribute must be paid to the wealthy or the powerful, it demands greater subtlety and art in the preparation. Thus vanity is changed into a more dangerous self-conceit, as being checked in its natural eruption. It teaches men to suppress their feelings, and to control their tempers, and to mitigate both the severity and the tone of their judgments. As Lord Shaftesbury would desire, it prefers playful wit and satire in putting down what is objectionable, as a more refined and good-natured, as well as a more effectual method, than the expedient which is natural to uneducated minds. It is from this impatience of the tragic and the bombastic that it is now quietly but energetically opposing itself to the unchristian practice of duelling, which it brands as simply out of taste, and as the remnant of a barbarous age; and certainly it seems likely to effect what Religion has aimed at abolishing in vain.

v Hence it is that it is almost a definition of a gentleman to say he is one who never inflicts pain. This description is both refined and, as far as it goes, accurate. He is mainly occupied in merely removing the obstacles which hinder the free and unembarrassed action of those about him; and he concurs with their movements rather than takes the initiative himself. His benefits may be considered as parallel to what are called comforts or conveniences in arrangements of a personal nature: like an easy chair or a good fire, which do their part in dispelling cold and fatigue, though nature provides both means of rest and animal heat without them. The true gentleman in like manner carefully avoids whatever may cause a jar or a jolt in the minds of those with whom he is cast;—all clashing of opinion, or collision of feeling, all restraint, or suspicion, or gloom, or resentment; his great concern being to make every one at their ease and at home. He has his eyes on all his company; he is tender towards the bashful, gentle towards the distant, and merciful towards the absurd; he can recollect to whom he is speaking; he guards against unseasonable allusions, or topics which may irritate; he is seldom prominent in conversation, and never wearisome. He makes light of favours while he does them, and seems to be receiving when he is conferring. He never speaks of himself except when compelled, never defends himself by a mere retort, he has no ears for slander or gossip, is scrupulous in imputing motives to those who interfere with him, and interprets every thing for the best. He is never mean or little in his disputes, never takes unfair advantage, never mistakes personalities or sharp sayings for arguments, or insinuates evil which he dare not say out. From a long-sighted prudence, he observes the maxim of the ancient sage, that we should ever conduct ourselves towards our enemy as if he were one day to be our friend. He has too much good sense to be affronted at insults, he is too well employed to remember injuries, and too indolent to bear malice. He is patient, forbearing, and resigned, on philosophical principles; he submits to pain, because it is inevitable, to bereavement, because it is irreparable, and to death, because it is his destiny. If he engages in controversy of any kind, his disciplined intellect preserves him from the blundering discourtesy of better, perhaps, but less educated minds; who, like blunt weapons, tear and hack instead of cutting clean, who mistake the point in argument, waste their strength on trifles, misconceive their adversary, and leave the question more involved than they find it. He may be right or wrong in his opinion, but he is too clear-headed to be unjust; he is as simple as he is forcible, and as brief as he is decisive. Nowhere shall we find greater candour, consideration, indulgence: he throws himself into the minds of his opponents, he accounts for their mistakes. He knows the weakness of human reason as well as its strength, its province and its limits. If he be an unbeliever, he will be too profound and large-minded to ridicule religion or to act against it; he is too wise to be a dogmatist or fanatic in his infidelity. He respects piety and devotion; he even supports institutions as venerable, beautiful, or useful, to which he does not assent; he honours the ministers of religion, and it contents him to decline its mysteries without assailing or denouncing them. He is a friend of religious toleration, and that, not only because his philosophy has taught him to look on all forms of faith with an impartial eye, but also from the gentleness and effeminacy of feeling, which is the attendant on civilization.

---

1) If you are to understand what Newman here says, you will have to supply concrete instance from your own observation; in I–IV Newman deals with certain virtues, not as qualities of persons, but in themselves, as abstractions. And you may have to watch out that certain of your habits of

mind do not get in the way of your following the discussion. If Newman makes distinctions between terms you are used to considering synonymous, then those distinctions must be granted while you are in the process of reading him. What, for instance, is the distinction he maintains between "humble" and "modest"?

2) According to Newman, does it make sense to say that a person is at the same time proud and modest? Why? Do you know any such person?

3) What exactly is Newman's point about the word "condescension"? Think about the way in which the word "condescend" is made up: "con" ("together with") plus "descend." What does he mean by speaking of the modern world's perversion of the word?

4) What does the last sentence in II mean in its context? Do you see that the quality for which modesty is an outward manifestation is not necessarily admirable? A person who likes praise and admiration may be vain; but there is a worse state, a state of contempt for the attitudes of one's fellows. And in this state one could be quite modest.

5) Now consider III. Do you see what Newman is saying in it? One thing he is saying is that, although the secular virtues may make little change in the human heart, they have their uses in civilization. "Philosophy" disciplines pride, softens its effects, even makes it socially useful.

6) Paragraphs III and IV have to be considered together. In III Newman speaks almost as if this disciplined pride, this self-respect, were completely a virtue. It does of course accomplish civilized ends: it will probably keep a man from financial dishonesty and out of bawdy houses and low barrooms; it may even make him a good citizen. It is likely, too, as we see in IV, to turn a man toward respectability, to lead him to tolerate injustice and to avoid unpleasantness. When it does not make evil less, it makes it less apparent.

7) But Newman has not here defined "pride," and has assumed an agreed-on meaning for it. Do you see that the sense here is very different from "vanity" and even from some of the familiar senses of "pride"? St. Thomas Aquinas says that pride in its essence scorns subjection to God, and "in consequence it scorns to be subject to a creature for God's sake." It is the evil effects of pride in a man's relations with his fellows that are partly lessened and partly disguised in the secular virtue of self-respect.

8) In V we come to the famous definition of a gentleman. Newman describes one in whom all the secular virtues have reached their perfection. This is the ultimate excellence that "philosophical morality" might produce in character. Of course we understand that Newman would agree that this perfection of urbanity and restraint will not be found completely exemplified in any one person.

9) We do not have the same attitude toward the word "gentleman" that the mid-nineteenth century had. Is the word meaningful in Newman's handling of it? Can you suggest another term to designate the product— in ideal perfection—of secular morality? Is the term you have suggested a better term for the purpose?

10) Does it seem to you that there is, here and there, in this long paragraph a suggestion of SATIRE—a touch of subtle ridicule of the gentleman? Perhaps that effect arises for us only because we can hardly help thinking

about how far short of this perfection fall the liberally educated persons of our acquaintance. But whether or not you think there is any satirical intention, you will see that Newman is describing only the perfection of "philosophical morality."

11) In the character of the gentleman Newman describes, what virtues and excellencies are left out?

12) Our selection from Newman, and indeed the foregoing selections too, are illustrations of a point in the ethics of writing. All of these definitions have a purpose as a means of discussion. Now definition in some of its uses should be entirely objective, quite without argumentative purpose (for instance, in dictionaries, in reference books, and in many textbook contexts).[1] When, therefore, a writer advances an opinion or states a belief in the form of a definition, he ought to make it clear to the reader that he is doing so. You will probably agree that in each of our selections the intention is made clear. But perhaps a simple illustration from academic life will enforce the principle. A professor of education, a teacher of history, and a student might each have an occasion to write on objective tests, and each might be writing for readers who had given or taken many such tests. Each might legitimately and effectively use a definition of the term "objective test" within the first paragraph of his discussion. We would, to be sure, expect the three definitions to be somewhat different. But one thing we would require of each: that it be quite clear—by context or by explicit statement—that the definition *is* for the purposes of discussion, that it states an opinion or an attitude. And so we require in all writing.

SUGGESTIONS FOR PAPERS

If your instructor wishes you to practice the writing of one-sentence logical definitions, you will find the following set of principles helpful. And even if you start with an extended definition, it will probably be organized around a logical definition. Classroom experience shows that a student needs to consider all of these principles for each logical definition he writes.

1. The genus should be the smallest class to which the term may be conveniently assigned—but the writer considers the reader's convenience as well as his own. Sometimes a part of the term may be used as genus: "A multiple-choice test is a test so set up that . . ."; "The Prime Meridian is that meridian . . . ." But then the writer must be sure the reader knows the part of the term used as genus.

2. The differentia should be so chosen that the term defined is distinguished from all others with which it is liable to be confused. The writer

---

[1] Dr. Samuel Johnson's occasional violations of this principle in his *Dictionary* have amused readers for two hundred years. Here, as instances, are four of his definitions: "*excise:* a hateful tax levied upon commodities, and adjudged, not by the common judges of property, but wretches hired by those to whom excise is paid. . . . *oats:* a grain which in England is generally given to horses, but in Scotland supports the people. . . . *patron:* commonly a wretch who supports with insolence, and is paid with flattery. . . . *pension:* an allowance made to anyone without an equivalent. In England it is generally understood to mean pay given to a State hireling for treason to his country." You might also be amused by Ambrose Bierce's *The Devil's Dictionary* (1911), a collection of cynical definitions in dictionary style.

needs to be sure that he has done more than write a true statement about a term. He needs to separate it from all other terms.

3. Since a word may have several senses, some of them highly special-ized, it may often be necessary to make clear at the outset the sense or the application with which one is concerned (a dictionary does this by a sys-tem of labeling). For example, the word "town" has a different sense in New England from its ordinary sense in the Midwest; one might need to begin a definition, "In New England, a town is . . . ."

4. The term and the genus must be parallel; the term being a noun, the genus is also a noun. Therefore one does not write or say "A touch-down is when . . ." or "A majority is where you have . . ." or "Natural-ization is how . . . ." If one finds that the form of logical definition is awkward for a particular term, the sensible thing is of course to abandon the form; for instance, "stymie" may be perhaps more easily defined in an-other way: "In golf, a stymie occurs when . . . ."

5. The method of logical definition may be adapted to the definition of verbs (students have little or no occasion to define any words but nouns or verbs). Verbs are defined in the infinitive. If, for example, a writer has the sentence, "He outlined the early history of the village," and wishes to define "to outline," he may write "To outline is to indicate briefly the main features of a subject." "To indicate" has a more inclusive meaning than "to outline," but he has limited it to the sense he wants by the modifier "briefly" and the object "the main features of a subject."

For obvious reasons, the best terms for out-of-class practice in logical definition are terms not included in dictionaries or textbooks. They may be terms connected with campus buildings or institutions; or terms connected with particular localities, for every locality has some activities, traditions, groups, and places quite its own. Or the terms may be terms belonging to particular occupations. Here is an example, a definition of a whaler's term by Herman Melville, which he writes as if he were a dictionary maker:

GAM. Noun—A social meeting of two (or more) Whaleships, generally on a cruising-ground; when, after exchanging hails, they exchange visits by boats' crews: the two captains remaining, for the time, on board of one ship, and the two chief mates on the other.

Further exercises in logical definition may be definitions of terms that have appeared so far in our reading. For example, you might write one-sentence logical definitions of the following, *in the sense in which the in-dicated writers use them:* a volcanic island (Carson); a natural law (Hux-ley); the Law of Nature (Lewis); a social revolution (according to Marx, in the Becker selection, Chapter II); vicarious leisure (Veblen); canon of propriety (Veblen).

Such exercises in logical definition are most valuable when there is classroom opportunity for students to consider one another's definitions. A critical examination of a number of student definitions will often make plain certain pitfalls and help students to avoid them in their subsequent work. In estimating the adequacy of a definition, you must keep remembering that any definition must be judged upon its relative usefulness to one who does not know the term defined.

As an exercise preliminary to writing original extended definitions, you might write a reduced statement (250–300 words) of Morison's definition of puritanism. So short a piece will be a highly selected restatement, with definitiveness the basis of selection. The Becker selection on the social sciences may be used for the same sort of exercise.

For a first exercise in extended definition, try the sort exemplified by Twain's definition of "lagniappe." Take a term familiar to you from your general experience—not one you know through a printed source. And take a term that you can reasonably assume is unknown to some group of intelligent readers, so that there can be a motive for defining it. Sports terms, for instance, or terms identified with particular trades, professions, and activities are appropriate, because such terms, however familiar they are to the groups that use them constantly, are unknown to many others. The terms for persons with special functions in churches serve well for this exercise, since members of one religious group commonly do not know the terminology of others. (But very few students can handle theological terms.) Perhaps most interesting of all are local terms such as Twain's "lagniappe."

Your extended definition should have a logical definition at or near the beginning, or at the end. Make use of whatever means of extension are appropriate to your term. For most extended definitions, use in typical contexts is an important means. Some (probably not all) of the following will be also appropriate to your definition: negative definition and discrimination of senses (both illustrated by the selection from Morison), discussion of the etymology or the origin of the term,[1] discussion of the history of its use, brief anecdote illustrating its use, description (if the term designates an object), and examples of approximate synonyms.

A particularly interesting exercise in extended definition is the definition of the same term for readers of very different backgrounds. You might try defining some academic term for three readers. Define it first for a contemporary of yours who goes to another college. Your intention will be to make the use of the term clear as you know it, so that he can see whether or not his school uses it in the same way. Then define the term for a reader much younger than yourself, your curious eleven-year-old brother, perhaps. Finally define the term for a reader in England, one quite unacquainted with American schools.

[1] Often a knowledge of the origin of a word is a great aid in defining it. Of course it would be a piece of pedantry to discuss the origin of a word unless such discussion really helps to make its meaning clear. A discussion of the origin of the word "sophistication" probably would help in defining it and in making clear why it may (and, if carefully used, does) imply disapproval. (You may need to go back to "sophism" and "Sophist" in your dictionary.) And with many other words—with "panic," "denouement," and "maverick," to take but three instances—the derivations really help to define. But do not forget, as too many writers and speakers do forget, that a modern sense of a word may be very far from its root meaning. When you say you are fond of Jane, you do not mean you are silly or foolish about her. Or, as we noted in the discussion of the selection from Newman, "condescension" does not now have its root meaning.

For a somewhat longer paper, you might try a definition like Morison's in intent. You would then assume readers familiar with the term, and, of course, choose a term of difficult or disputed meaning. But do not take a more complex term than you can handle. Although you will do best with a term of your own selection, here are some examples of the sort of term that may be used for the exercise: "a high school education," "athletic scholarship," "amateur athlete," "overemphasis on athletics," "vocational education," "objective test," "racial equality," "comic book," "the independent in politics," "public relations," "socialism," "subversive," and "church-connected college."

The selection from Newman suggests an exercise in the making of a difficult distinction. You might discuss a pair of terms, possibly one of these: sympathy and pity; caution and timidity; tolerance and acceptance; individualism and selfishness; principle and prejudice; goodness and respectability. If you deal with terms for human conduct, distinction between them need be neither trivial nor abstract. Indeed, you cannot make the distinction clear unless you show how these qualities are represented in what people do.

XI

Some Patterns of Analysis

The problem of analysis is not new to us. One cannot try to read well, much less to write well, without being concerned with the division of subjects for orderly discussion. Your experience has taught you that material cannot be arbitrarily divided, that something of the pattern of discussion inheres in the subject matter itself. But, although every piece of writing worth doing offers its own problems, the problems are not, fortunately, always new kinds of problems. There are ways of approach, ways of discovering what the constituent parts of particular subject matters are. We could, indeed, distinguish more varieties of analysis than it would be feasible to illustrate or describe. The few we shall consider are useful to writers in general, and perhaps particularly to students.

i   PROCESS

We start with some accounts of processes. Since a process goes on in time, an account of a process will be a piece of narrative. But unless that narrative is precisely organized, the reader will not understand the relationship of the parts to each other and to the whole. Often the narrative will be divided into stages. The chronology—the order in time—will be kept clear for the reader. But that may not be the only problem. When a good deal of incidental explanation is necessary, it must come in where it will be useful, but it ought not to clog the account nor to confuse the chronology.

The structure of a process analysis, then, is largely determined by the process itself. But it is also determined by the intention of the analysis, by the sort of design the writer has upon his reader. How much does the reader need to know? He may need to learn to carry on the process itself, or to understand it thoroughly and in detail. The technical writing that answers these needs has to be judged on technical criteria as well as on the ordinary principles of exposition. You could probably tell whether or not a technical account of a casting process was well-paragraphed and orderly; unless you happen to know a good deal about foundry work, you could hardly estimate its success. The study of what is properly called technical writing is not in our province.

The non-technical writer is most often concerned with the account of a process for a reader who needs to understand it in a general way. Often such a writer's problems are decisions about what to leave out. Our first example is from an advertising pamphlet—good writing, like gold, is where you find it.

The Making of Shipping Containers (1953) [1]

I In theory at least, the manufacture of corrugated board is simple. A sheet of paperboard known as corrugating material is run between two heavy rollers, each lengthwise deeply grooved and fitting together like a wide pair of gears, so that the paperboard which went in flat comes out fluted. Then two other flat sheets, known as kraft liners, are passed over and under the fluted corrugated sheet and glued into position, to make a sort of corrugated sandwich which passes between steam-heated plates and heavy cotton blankets until it is thoroughly dried. These machines can be set to make double-decker corrugated sandwiches for extra strength, with two layers of fluted paper between three binding liners.

II The arch construction of the corrugated sheet, held firmly by the top and bottom liners, gives remarkable strength and resilience to withstand hard knocks and rough handling. Its lightness and economy in both shipping space and cost are added qualities which have wrought a fundamental change in the transportation of goods.

III The simplicity of the theory of making corrugated sheets and boxes is perversely belied by the complexity of the huge machines which make them. For instance, an observer may stand beside a machine 294 feet long—as long as a football field—and watch it roll out each hour enough corrugated sheets to carpet a football field twice over. Though technically intricate, production is very rapid. The big corrugators can transform the giant rolls of kraft liners and corrugating material into corrugated sheets at the rate of 500 linear feet a minute.

IV In some plants, the corrugated sheet moves on through other machines which cut and crease it into tailor-made shapes to make folding shipping containers particularly suited to the special conditions they will meet in transit and to the goods they will carry. These go on to presses which print the customer-company's name and advertising design, then through other machines which fasten the blanks with staples, glue or tape into boxes that, shipped flat, can be instantly opened into containers.

---

1) This piece has a nice economy. Notice the second sentence in I, in which a mechanical principle is explained even while the narration of the process goes on. In the third and fourth sentences, notice how useful the obvious analogy to a sandwich is. Point out especially economical sentences in II and IV.

[1] Reprinted from *Gair Today* by permission of the Robert Gair Company, Inc. Copyright, 1953, Robert Gair Company, Inc.

2) In II the discussion of the reason for the construction of corrugated board is, for clarity, separated from the account of the process; the first sentence in III ties it to I.

3) How many stages are there in the process described in I? Why are they not separated from one another in a more decided fashion?

4) Do you see the importance of the comparison "as long as a football field"? Most student writers are perfectly content if they can give their readers an exact dimension. Yet for most people—for everyone who does not ordinarily deal with measurements—294 feet is just a number. Notice that the comparison is used twice in the same sentence. The reader does not so much need a comparison for 500 linear feet, for a scale has already been established in his imagination. Why is nothing said about workmen?

5) In the pamphlet in which this piece first appeared, there was a picture of a big corrugating machine, and text and picture were designed to complement one another. How much do you miss the picture? Do satisfactory images arise for you?

6) This little piece gives a reader a clear idea of the essentials of a complicated process without losing the principle in the detail. We may say that it is "simple," but we should recognize that the effect of simplicity is the result of careful plan.

Mark Twain's account of taking soundings on the river has an intention similar to that of the piece above. Twain wants to make his reader understand the principle and envisage the process. Out of the many details he might conceivably have used, he takes those which will accomplish his intention.

FROM *Life on the Mississippi*   (1875, 1883)

MARK TWAIN

Sounding

I When the river is very low, and one's steamboat is "drawing all the water" there is in the channel—or a few inches more, as was often the case in the old times—one must be painfully circumspect in his piloting. We used to have to "sound" a number of particularly bad places almost every trip when the river was at a very low stage.

II Sounding is done in this way: The boat ties up at the shore, just above the shoal crossing; the pilot not on watch takes his "cub" or steersman and a picked crew of men (sometimes an officer also), and goes out in the yawl—provided the boat has not that rare and sumptuous luxury, a regularly devised "sounding-boat"—and proceeds to hunt for the best water, the pilot on duty watching his movements through a spy-glass, meantime, and in some instances assisting by signals of the boat's whistle, signifying "try higher up" or "try lower down"; for the surface of the water, like an oil-painting, is more expressive and intelligible when inspected from a lit-

tle distance than very close at hand. The whistle signals are seldom necessary, however; never, perhaps, except when the wind confuses the significant ripples upon the water's surface. When the yawl has reached the shoal
place, the speed is slackened, the pilot begins to sound the depth with a
pole ten or twelve feet long, and the steersman at the tiller obeys the order
to "hold her up to starboard"; or "let her fall off to larboard"; [1] or "steady—
steady as you go."

III When the measurements indicate that the yawl is approaching the
shoalest part of the reef, the command is given to "Ease all!" Then the
men stop rowing and the yawl drifts with the current. The next order is,
"Stand by with the buoy!" The moment the shallowest point is reached, the
pilot delivers the order, "Let go the buoy!" and over she goes. If the pilot
is not satisfied, he sounds the place again; if he finds better water higher
up or lower down, he removes the buoy to that place. Being finally satisfied, he gives the order, and all the men stand their oars straight up in the
air, in line; a blast from the boat's whistle indicates that the signal has been
seen; then the men "give way" on their oars and lay the yawl alongside the
buoy; the steamer comes creeping carefully down, is pointed straight at the
buoy, husbands her power for the coming struggle, and presently, at the
critical moment, turns on all her steam and goes grinding and wallowing
over the buoy and the sand, and gains the deep water beyond. Or maybe she
doesn't; maybe she "strikes and swings." Then she has to while away several hours (or days) sparring herself off.

IV Sometimes a buoy is not laid at all, but the yawl goes ahead, hunting
the best water, and the steamer follows along in its wake. Often there is a
deal of fun and excitement about sounding, especially if it is a glorious
summer day, or a blustering night. But in winter the cold and the peril take
most of the fun out of it.

V A buoy is nothing but a board four or five feet long, with one end
turned up; it is a reversed schoolhouse bench, with one of the supports left
and the other removed. It is anchored on the shoalest part of the reef by a
rope with a heavy stone made fast to the end of it. But for the resistance of
the turned-up end of the reversed bench, the current would pull the buoy
under water. At night, a paper lantern with a candle in it is fastened on
top of the buoy, and this can be seen a mile or more, a little glimmering
spark in the waste of blackness.

---

1) You might consider the first sentence in II. We are told by an expert in clear writing that writing with an average sentence length of
twenty-nine words or more is very difficult, hardly to be read at all but by
the highly literate. Did Twain's sentence stop you? Did you notice at all its
excessive length? It is about 120 words long. The expert has a point, of
course. But difficulty is not a mere matter of length; and Twain's careful
punctuation guides us safely through the sentence. There may be, indeed,

[1] The term "larboard" is never used at sea, now, to signify the left hand; but was always used on the river in my time.

some real advantage in the length of the sentence, for its pattern seems to represent the continuity of the process. Twain was proud of his grammar, syntax, and punctuation; and the punctuation of this sentence, which uses most of the available marks, is worth your study.

2) Notice the position of the description of a buoy. Perhaps in a technical account of the process, it would have come first so that the reader would fully understand the first reference to it in the account of the process itself. But, no matter what the intention of the account, the description of the buoy should not clog the narrative of the process. Twain apparently puts the description last because the buoy is the last thing the observer sees. Twain's shape comparison, though doubtless useful to his first readers, is not a very useful one to us.

3) A process goes on in time, and a good account will always have a narrative quality. Go over this piece and mark the time words, not only connectives ("when" or "then") and adverbs ("finally") but the verbs that indicate elapsing time ("proceeds to hunt"). The long sentence in III beginning "Being finally satisfied . . ." is particularly interesting for its timing.

4) A process, moreover, is often carried on by persons. Now students have a tendency to write an account of what is being done as if there were no one doing it. The tendency may come from habits gained in the conventional writing of laboratory reports, impersonally and in the passive voice ("the mixture was heated slowly" or "then all results were tabulated"). Perhaps that is the best way to write up an experiment; even if we do not think so, there is not much we can do about it. But in our writing in general we can surely avoid the intangibility and occasional absurdity of the over-use of the passive. If, for instance, you are writing on table manners, you do not need to write as if eating were a non-human process; you do not need to write "the knife and fork are laid across the plate; the napkin is left unfolded." If you are giving directions, address your reader as "you" just as you would if you were speaking; if you write an account of what persons are doing, bring them into it by use of the active voice. Notice that, although Twain here uses the passive when appropriate, he uses the active voice often enough so that we have a sense of the people who are part of the process—we know even some of the things that they say.

5) You will have noticed that II and III are of considerable and approximately equal length. They mark out the process in two stages: (1) the search for the shoal place, and (2) the marking of it with the buoy and the steamboat's negotiation of it. Now if Twain had been writing a handbook for apprentice pilots, how do you think he would have handled this material?

6) It is obvious—is it not?—that a large number of details of the process are grouped in two stages for the convenience of just such readers as we are. The organization makes it possible for us to watch the yawl as it moves away from the boat and carries on the sounding; and then to connect the placing of the buoy and the boat's response. We are not likely to lose either our understanding of the purpose of the whole process or our sense of the whole scene. Twain has been careful not only to keep the chronology clear but to collect the images in an imaginatively comprehensible group.

7) Do you see, then, that Twain, familiar as he was with the process, must have had to think it through for a new purpose? His structure is in accord with the process; but more than that, it is carefully adapted to the needs and interests of the readers he has envisaged.

Often an account of a process is part of a larger whole, and it is well for us to examine one in a context. In the following selection from an article about excavations at Jericho, the account of the archaeologist's process called "stratigraphy" comes in paragraphs vi through ix. But that account depends, even for some of its terms, upon the preceding paragraphs; and the last three paragraphs of the selection illustrate stratigraphy in practice at Jericho. Although upon examination we can separate these three sections of the whole, transitions are so smooth and gradual that we would not ordinarily be aware of any sectioning. Notice also that, although vi–ix are written impersonally and with a number of constructions in the passive voice, the passive is not used persistently enough to lend its air of unreality. And we are kept aware that a person devised the method, and that persons carry it out.

FROM *Ancient Jericho* (1954) [1]

KATHLEEN M. KENYON

I Jericho fell to Joshua and the Israelites sometime between 1400 and 1250 B.C. It had had a long, long history before that. Modern archaeologists are greatly interested in the site of this ancient city, for in addition to the romantic attraction of the Biblical story,[2] the site has other claims to importance. There is reason to believe that Jericho may be the oldest town in the world, and we are finding there a wealth of material evidences of man's first steps toward civilization some 7,000 years ago.

II The site of ancient Jericho today is a great mound—a heap entombing dead towns. It contains a series of cities, each built on the ruins of those that went before. The Arabian name for a mound formed of the accumulated remains of human occupation is *tell*. The Jericho tell has a great deal to say indeed; its lowest levels go back to Neolithic times—the late stone-age period when man first took the revolutionary step from a nomadic life of hunting to the settled life of agriculture and community building. From that step has sprung all human progress: the beginning of architecture, arts, crafts and manufacture, community organization, religion, laws, the invention of writing and ultimately civilization.

III Although archaeologists have long been convinced that the Near East is the region where man first made the transition from a wandering to a settled life, the early stages of this transition have been shrouded in the mists of time. There are plenty of human artifacts from the Early

[1] Reprinted with permission of *Scientific American*, April, 1954, Volume #190, No. 4.

[2 In Joshua 6.]

Bronze Age in the Near East, but very few from the Neolithic period that preceded it. When, during the latter part of the 19th century and the early years of the 20th, archaeological expeditions began to explore the site of ancient Jericho, there was no suspicion that a prehistoric period lay beneath their spades. Their object was primarily to investigate the story of the capture of Jericho by Joshua's people, to date that event and thereby to throw light on the date of the first Israelite settlement in Palestine.

IV Between 1930 and 1936 the archaeologist John Garstang, of Liverpool University, carried out a series of deeper and more thorough excavations at Jericho. Far down in the mound, beneath the debris of Early Bronze Age cities, he found some flints and building remains which showed that men had occupied the site in the Neolithic age. His discoveries aroused in some archaeologists a keen desire to investigate the deep Jericho levels further.

V The Second World War delayed this investigation. . . . [Finally] in January, 1952, a joint Anglo-American expedition of some 20 workers, with myself as director and A. Douglas Tushingham of the American School as assistant director, camped at the Jericho tell and went to work.

VI The ancient mound is a mile from the modern town of Jericho on the left bank of the River Jordan. It lies in a flat plain 840 feet below sea level. What has made it habitable through all these thousands of years is a never-failing supply of fresh water gushing from Elisha's Fountain.[1] We began systematically to uncover the ancient Jerichos, layer by layer. Modern archaeological research is built upon foundations laid by the great 19th-century archaeologist Sir Flinders Petrie, a pioneer far ahead of his time. The dating of ancient cultures must depend, when inscriptions are lacking, upon the evolution of artifacts, especially pottery. Petrie showed that each stage of human history in the East had a distinctive pottery, and that one could establish a pottery sequence, some stages of which could be linked with inscriptions of known date in Egypt or Mesopotamia. On the foundations created by Petrie this sequence has now been built up, period by period, so that it is now possible for an archaeologist to date finds with considerable accuracy as far back as the beginning of the Early Bronze Age, about 3000 B.C.

VII The basic method of stratigraphy, as Petrie enunciated it in 1890, is to establish a fixed reference point and record the level of each find (in number of feet) above that point. This technique has its limitations, because an archaeological layer may slope instead of being horizontal or may have been cut into by later occupants. Since Petrie's time the method has been considerably refined. Each layer of soil is now traced through and treated as an entity; the finds discovered in that structure (e.g., a floor level) are then dated by it.

VIII Obviously such work requires close supervision by experts, for the workmen doing the digging cannot be expected to identify or understand the significance of the layers. Each small gang works under the direct su-

[1 See 2 Kings 2:18–22.]

pervision of a field assistant, who records the layers in a notebook and labels the finds. Drawings are made, so that we have a permanent record of the structures excavated.

ix The process of excavation is a process of dissection. The archaeologist breaks down the history of the site by peeling off the layers one by one; he traces the history backward from the top down. At Jericho we have found that the surviving deposits go down in some places to depths of about 70 feet. Excavations are still in progress, and only in a very few places have we reached the earliest layers, but we have enough to tell something of a consecutive story of the site.

x Garstang had discovered the Neolithic levels at the northwest end of the tell. The depth of deposit is so great there that he sounded the lowest levels only with a relatively narrow shaft. The present expedition is continuing the clearance of the levels he sounded. One of our first surprises was the discovery of Neolithic artifacts at a place on the west side of the tell some distance from where Garstang had found his. The Stone Age remains here were only about four feet below the surface, presumably because later levels in this place have been eroded or quarried away. What was remarkable about this discovery was that it showed that even in Neolithic times the settlement already covered a considerable area and had grown beyond the dimensions of a mere village.

xi In this area on the west side of the tell excavation has reached bedrock in some places. Just above the rock we have found rude huts which may be the Jericho settlers' earliest experiments in architecture. They are mud-brick structures with curved walls, and they look like a translation of the round tents and temporary structures of nomadic hunters into a more permanent material. This phase appears to have been short. The next stage (represented by a type of house discovered by Garstang at the north end) was a very big advance. These houses were rectangular, with solidly built walls, wide doorways and rooms grouped around courtyards. Most striking of all is the fact that the walls and floors were finished with highly burnished coats of fine plaster, giving a most sophisticated appearance. These houses belonged to a firmly established community, and moreover a well-organized one, for at this stage the settlement apparently was surrounded by a massive town wall.

xii These Stone Age people still had no pottery—a fact which underlines how close we are here to the beginnings of settled life, for pots and pans, a primary necessity, are one of the first technical inventions of settled man. No doubt the reason men settled here lies in the natural advantages of the site. The copious stream that emerges from the rock beside the settlement made the soil of the Jordan Valley, with its tropical climate, exceedingly fertile; the modern Jericho is still a brilliant green oasis in this arid land. The inhabitants of Jericho could be assured of success in their first experiments in agriculture, and the settlement could become truly permanent. . . .[1]

[1 Professor Kenyon and her associates found remains of a settlement that may have been as early as 5000 B.C., and they were able to trace something of what happened

ii   HISTORICAL PROCESS

"Process," your dictionary will tell you, may mean a series of events conducing to an end. A common sort of analysis is the division of a consecutive series of events, or of the development of a set of ideas, into stages. It is sometimes called CHRONOLOGICAL ANALYSIS. A writer may need the method whenever an ordinary narrative treatment would be too long for his purpose, or when it would not easily make clear the relationship of one part of a development to another.

The next selection—a shrewd piece of observation and interpretation—deserves to be better known than it is. It divides a consecutive set of events, the settlement of western Pennsylvania, into stages.

FROM *Essays* (1793)

BENJAMIN RUSH

[Three Settlers]

Dear Sir,

I Whatever tends to unfold *facts* in the history of the human species, must be interesting to a curious enquirer.—The manner of settling a new country exhibits a view of the human mind so foreign to the views of it which have been taken for many centuries in Europe, that I flatter myself the following account of the progress of population, agriculture, manners, and government in Pennsylvania will be acceptable to you. I have chosen to confine myself in the present letter to Pennsylvania only, that all the information I shall give you may be derived from my own knowledge and observations.

II The *first* settler in the woods is generally a man who has outlived his credit or fortune in the cultivated parts of the State. His time for migrating is in the month of April. His first object is to build a small cabbin of rough logs for himself and family. The floor of this cabbin is of earth, the roof is of split logs—the light is received through the door, and, in some instances, through a small window made of greased paper. A coarser building adjoining this cabbin affords a shelter to a cow and a pair of poor horses. The labor of erecting these buildings is succeeded by killing the trees on a few acres of ground near his cabbin; this is done by cutting a circle round the trees, two or three feet from the ground. The ground around these trees is then ploughed and Indian-corn planted in it. . . . For the first year he endures a great deal of distress from hunger—cold—and a variety of accidental causes, but he seldom complains or sinks under them. As he lives in the neighbourhood of Indians, he soon acquires a

---

on the site of Jericho down to about 1560 B.C. There, she tells us, "most of the archaeological history comes to an end . . . [for] over the rest of the mound erosion and human depredations have removed all traces of the Jericho after the 16th century B.C. No sign of the walls attacked by Joshua has been found."]

strong tincture of their manners. His exertions, while they continue, are violent; but they are succeeded by long intervals of rest. His pleasures consist chiefly in fishing and hunting. He loves spirituous liquors, and he eats, drinks and sleeps in dirt and rags in his little cabbin. . . . In this situation he passes two or three years. In proportion as population increases around him, he becomes uneasy and dissatisfied. . . . Above all, he revolts against the operation of laws. He cannot bear to surrender up a single natural right for all the benefits of government,—and therefore he abandons his little settlement, and seeks a retreat in the woods, where he again submits to all the toils which have been mentioned. There are instances of many men who have broken ground on bare creation, not less than four different times in this way, in different and more advanced parts of the State. It has been remarked, that the flight of this class of people is always increased by the preaching of the gospel. This will not surprise us when we consider how opposite its precepts are to their licentious manner of living. If our first settler was the owner of the spot of land which he began to cultivate, he sells it at a considerable profit to his successor; but if (as is oftener the case) he was a tenant to some rich landholder, he abandons it in debt; however, the small improvements he leaves behind him, generally make it an object of immediate demand to a *second* species of settler.

III This species of settler is generally a man of some property,—he pays one-third or one-fourth part in cash for his plantation, which consists of three or four hundred acres, and the rest in gales or instalments, as it is called here; that is, a certain sum yearly, without interest, 'till the whole is paid. The first object of this settler is to build an addition to his cabbin; this is done with hewed logs: and as sawmills generally follow settlements, his floors are made of boards; his roof is made of what are called clapboards, which are a kind of coarse shingles, split out of short oak logs. This house is divided by two floors, on each of which are two rooms: under the whole is a cellar walled with stone. The cabbin serves as kitchen to this house. His next object is to clear a little meadow ground, and plant an orchard of two or three hundred apple trees. His stable is likewise enlarged; and, in the course of a year or two, he builds a large log barn, the roof of which is commonly thatched with rye straw: he moreover encreases the quantity of his arable land; and, instead of cultivating Indian-corn alone, he raises a quantity of wheat and rye: the latter is cultivated chiefly for the purpose of being distilled into whiskey. This species of settler by no means extracts all from the earth, which it is capable of giving. . . . This species of settler is seldom a good member of civil or religious society: with a large portion of a hereditary mechanical kind of religion, he neglects to contribute sufficiently towards building a church, or maintaining a regular administration of the ordinances of the gospel: he is equally indisposed to support civil government: with high ideas of liberty, he refuses to bear his proportion of the debt contracted by its establishment in our country: he delights chiefly in company—sometimes drinks spirituous liquors to excess—will spend a day or two in every week, in attending political meetings; and, thus, he contracts debts which (if he cannot discharge in a depreciated paper currency) compel him to sell his plantation, generally in the course of a few years, to the *third* and last species of settler.

iv This species of settler is commonly a man of property and good character—sometimes he is the son of a wealthy farmer in one of the interior and ancient counties of the state. His first object is to convert every spot of ground, over which he is able to draw water, into meadow: where this cannot be done, he selects the most fertile spot on the farm, and devotes it by manure to that purpose. His next object is to build a barn, which he prefers of stone. This building is, in some instances, 100 feet in front, and 40 in depth: it is made very compact, so as to shut out the cold in winter; for our farmers find that their horses and cattle, when kept warm, do not require near as much food, as when they are exposed to the cold. He uses œconomy, likewise, in the consumption of his wood. Hence he keeps himself warm in winter, by means of stoves, which save an immense deal of labour to himself and his horses, in cutting and hawling wood in cold and wet weather. His fences are every where repaired, so as to secure his grain from his own and his neighbour's cattle. But further, he increases the number of the articles of his cultivation, and, instead of raising corn, wheat and rye alone, he raises oats, buckwheat, . . . and spelts. Near his house, he allots an acre or two of ground for a garden, in which he raises a large quantity of cabbage and potatoes. . . . The last object of his industry is to build a dwelling-house. This business is sometimes effected in the course of his life, but is oftener bequeathed to his son, or the inheritor of his plantation: and hence we have a common saying among our best farmers, "that a son should always begin where his father left off"; that is, he should begin his improvements, by building a commodious dwelling-house, suited to the improvements and value of the plantation. This dwelling-house is generally built of stone—it is large, convenient, and filled with useful and substantial furniture. . . . In proportion as he increases in wealth, he values the protection of laws: hence he punctually pays his taxes towards the support of government. Schools and churches likewise, as the means of promoting order and happiness in society, derive a due support from him: for benevolence and public spirit, as to these objects, are the natural offspring of affluence and independence. Of this class of settlers are twothirds of the farmers of Pennsylvania. These are the men to whom Pennsylvania owes her ancient fame and consequence. If they possess less refinement than their southern neighbours, who cultivate their land with slaves, they possess more republican virtue. . . .

v From a review of the three different species of settlers, it appears that there are certain regular stages which mark the progress from the savage to civilized life. The first settler is nearly related to an Indian in his manners—In the second, the Indian manners are more diluted: It is in the third species of settlers only, that we behold civilization completed— It is to the third species of settlers only, that it is proper to apply the term of *farmers*. While we record the vices of the first and second settlers, it is but just to mention their virtues likewise.—Their mutual wants produce mutual dependence: hence they are kind and friendly to each other—their solitary situation makes visitors agreeable to them;—hence they are hospitable to strangers: their want of money (for they raise but little more than is necessary to support their families) has made it necessary for them to associate for the purposes of building houseˢ, cutting their grain, and the like:—This they do in turns for each other, without any other pay than the pleasures which usually attend a country frolic—Perhaps what I have called virtues are rather *qualities,* arising from necessity, and the peculiar state of society in which these people live.—Virtue should, in all cases, be the offspring of principle.

vɪ I do not pretend to say, that this mode of settling farms in Pennsylvania is universal—I have known some instances where the first settler has performed the improvements of the second, and yielded to the third. I have known a few instances likewise, of men of enterprizing spirits, who have settled in the wilderness, and who, in the course of a single life, have advanced through all the intermediate stages of improvement that I have mentioned and produced all those conveniences which have been ascribed to the third species of settlers; thereby resembling, in their exploits, not only the pioneers and light-infantry, but the main body of an army. There are instances likewise, where the first settlement has been improved by the same family, in hereditary succession, 'till it has reached the third stage of cultivation.

---

1) Write a signpost paragraph such as might be inserted after ɪ, a signpost which will predict and seem to control the material to come.

2) The second paragraph begins "The *first* settler in the woods . . ." But the between-paragraph transition for ɪɪ and ɪɪɪ, and for ɪɪɪ and ɪᴠ, is handled by sentences at the ends of paragraphs. Do you think this a good way? Would it have worked less well if Rush had used more than one paragraph for the discussion of each species of settler? Why?

3) Notice that ɪɪ, ɪɪɪ, and ɪᴠ are parallel paragraphs. Discuss in some detail the parallelism in structure, material, and order of material.

4) What is accomplished in ᴠ? How about the second part of the paragraph—should its material have been included in ɪɪ and in ɪɪɪ? Do the reservations in ᴠɪ make Rush's discussion more or less convincing to you?

5) About how long a time would usually have been taken up in these three stages of settlement—from, let us say, the time the first settler builds his cabin until the time the third settler builds a stone dwelling house?

6) Rush uses the same tense to describe all three settlers. Can we then consider it an ordinary present indicative?

7) The three stages of settlement might have had one of several sorts of representation. Rush chooses to generalize a typical settler to represent each. We have, then, a sort of synthesis used within an analysis structure—an interesting combination of methods. What is gained thereby? Has Rush's essay reminded you of Crèvecoeur's "What Is an American?" (Chapter IV)?

8) Here are two passages from Frederick Jackson Turner's *The Significance of the Frontier in American History* (1893):

I

. . . at the frontier the environment is at first too strong for the man. He must accept the conditions which it furnishes, or perish, and so he fits himself into the Indian clearings and follows the Indian trails.

2

So long as free land exists, the opportunity for a competency exists, and economic power secures political power. But the democracy born of free land, strong in selfishness and individualism, intolerant of administrative experience and education, and pressing individual liberty beyond its proper bounds, has its dangers as well as its benefits.[1]

How far does Rush's account of Pennsylvania settlement substantiate these passages? Consider, too, the passage from Turner in Chapter IV, a passage that is part of his conclusion. Can you find a basis for some of Turner's generalizations in Rush?

9) Crèvecoeur concludes a description of the settlers on the "extended line of frontiers where the last settlers dwell" by saying this:

Thus are our first steps trod, thus are our first trees felled, in general, by the most vicious of our people; and thus the path is opened for the arrival of a second and better class, the true American freeholders; the most respectable set of people in this part of the world: . . .

Now Rush distinguishes three stages of settlement, and synthesizes a settler to represent each. Can what Crèvecoeur says be reconciled with what Rush says?

In the chapter on summary we have worked with four passages from Mill's *On Liberty;* now we take the first pages of the essay. In them Mill is writing a chronological analysis of the historical development of a problem, the problem of "the fitting adjustment between individual independence and social control." The scope is much greater than that of Rush's essay, and Mill is dealing with ideas as well as events. The selection will require careful reading.

FROM *On Liberty* (1859)

JOHN STUART MILL

1 The subject of this Essay is not the so-called Liberty of the Will, so unfortunately opposed to the misnamed doctrine of Philosophical Necessity; but Civil, or Social Liberty: the nature and limits of the power which

[1] From *The Frontier in American History.* Copyright, 1920, by Frederick J. Turner. Copyright, 1948, by Caroline Mae S. Turner. Used by permission of the publishers, Henry Holt and Company.

can be legitimately exercised by society over the individual. A question seldom stated, and hardly ever discussed, in general terms, but which profoundly influences the practical controversies of the age by its latent presence, and is likely soon to make itself recognized as the vital question of the future. It is so far from being new, that, in a certain sense, it has divided mankind, almost from the remotest ages; but in the stage of progress into which the more civilized portions of the species have now entered, it presents itself under new conditions, and requires a different and more fundamental treatment.

II The struggle between Liberty and Authority is the most conspicuous feature in the portions of history with which we are earliest familiar, particularly in that of Greece, Rome, and England. But in old times this contest was between subjects, or some classes of subjects, and the government. By liberty, was meant protection against the tyranny of the political rulers. The rulers were conceived (except in some of the popular governments of Greece) as in a necessarily antagonistic position to the people whom they ruled. They consisted of a governing One, or a governing tribe or caste, who derived their authority from inheritance or conquest; who, at all events, did not hold it at the pleasure of the governed, and whose supremacy men did not venture, perhaps did not desire, to contest, whatever precautions might be taken against its oppressive exercise. Their power was regarded as necessary, but also as highly dangerous; as a weapon which they would attempt to use against their subjects, no less than against external enemies. To prevent the weaker members of the community from being preyed upon by innumerable vultures, it was needful that there should be an animal of prey stronger than the rest, commissioned to keep them down. But as the king of the vultures would be no less bent upon preying on the flock than any of the minor harpies, it was indispensable to be in a perpetual attitude of defence against his beak and claws. The aim, therefore, of patriots, was to set limits to the power which the ruler should be suffered to exercise over the community; and this limitation was what they meant by liberty. It was attempted in two ways. First, by obtaining a recognition of certain immunities, called political liberties or rights, which it was to be regarded as a breach of duty in the ruler to infringe, and which, if he did infringe, specific resistance, or general rebellion, was held to be justifiable. A second, and generally a later expedient, was the establishment of constitutional checks; by which the consent of the community, or of a body of some sort supposed to represent its interests, was made a necessary condition to some of the more important acts of the governing power. To the first of these modes of limitation, the ruling power, in most European countries, was compelled, more or less, to submit. It was not so with the second; and to attain this, or when already in some degree possessed, to attain it more completely, became everywhere the principal object of the lovers of liberty. And so long as mankind were content to combat one enemy by another, and to be ruled by a master, on condition of being guaranteed more or less efficaciously against his tyranny, they did not carry their aspirations beyond this point.

III A time, however, came, in the progress of human affairs, when men ceased to think it a necessity of nature that their governors should be an independent power, opposed in interest to themselves. It appeared to them much better that the various magistrates of the State should be their tenants or delegates, revocable at their pleasure. In that way alone, it seemed, could they have complete security that the powers of government would never be abused to their disadvantage. By degrees, this new demand for elective and temporary rulers became the prominent object of the exertions of the popular party, wherever any such party existed; and superseded, to a considerable extent, the previous efforts to limit the power of rulers. As the struggle proceeded for making the ruling power emanate from the periodical choice of the ruled, some persons began to think that too much importance had been attached to the limitation of the power itself. *That* (it might seem) was a resource against rulers whose interests were habitually opposed to those of the people. What was now wanted was, that the rulers should be identified with the people; that their interest and will should be the interest and will of the nation. The nation did not need to be protected against its own will. There was no fear of its tyrannizing over itself. Let the rulers be effectually responsible to it, promptly removable by it, and it could afford to trust them with power of which it could itself dictate the use to be made. Their power was but the nation's own power, concentrated, and in a form convenient for exercise. This mode of thought, or rather perhaps of feeling, was common among the last generation of European liberalism, in the Continental section of which, it still apparently predominates. Those who admit any limit to what a government may do, except in the case of such governments as they think ought not to exist, stand out as brilliant exceptions among the political thinkers of the Continent. A similar tone of sentiment might by this time have been prevalent in our own country, if the circumstances which for a time encouraged it had continued unaltered.

IV But, in political and philosophical theories, as well as in persons, success discloses faults and infirmities which failure might have concealed from observation. The notion, that the people have no need to limit their power over themselves, might seem axiomatic, when popular government was a thing only dreamed about, or read of as having existed at some distant period of the past. Neither was that notion necessarily disturbed by such temporary aberrations as those of the French Revolution, the worst of which were the work of an usurping few, and which, in any case, belonged, not to the permanent working of popular institutions, but to a sudden and convulsive outbreak against monarchical and aristocratic despotism. In time, however, a democratic republic came to occupy a large portion of the earth's surface, and made itself felt as one of the most powerful members of the community of nations; and elective and responsible government became subject to the observations and criticisms which wait upon a great existing fact. It was now perceived that such phrases as 'self-government,' and 'the power of the people over themselves,' do not express the true state of the case. The 'people' who exercise the power, are not always the same people with those over whom it is exercised; and the self-government spoken of, is not the government of each by himself, but of each by all the rest. The will of the people, moreover, practically means, the will of the most numerous or the most active *part* of the people; the majority, or those who succeed in making themselves accepted as the majority: the people, consequently, *may* desire to oppress a part of their number; and precautions are as much needed against this, as against any other abuse of power. The limitation, therefore, of the power of government over individuals, loses none of its importance when the holders of power are regularly accountable to the community, that is, to the strongest party therein. This view of things, recommending itself equally to the intelligence of thinkers and to the inclination of those important classes in European society to whose real or supposed interests democracy is adverse, has had no difficulty in establishing itself; and in political speculations 'the tyranny of the majority' is now generally included among the evils against which society requires to be on its guard.

v Like other tyrannies, the tyranny of the majority was at first, and is still vulgarly, held in dread, chiefly as operating through the acts of the public authorities. But reflecting persons perceived that when society is itself the tyrant—society collectively, over the separate individuals who compose it—its means of tyrannizing are not restricted to the acts which it may do by the hands of its political functionaries. Society can and does execute its own mandates: and if it issues wrong mandates instead of right, or any mandates at all in things with which it ought not to meddle, it practises a social tyranny more formidable than many kinds of political oppression, since, though not usually upheld by such extreme penalties, it leaves fewer means of escape, penetrating much more deeply into the details of life, and enslaving the soul itself. Protection, therefore, against the tyranny of the magistrate is not enough; there needs protection also against the tyranny of the prevailing opinion and feeling; against the tendency of society to impose, by other means than civil penalties, its own ideas and practices as rules of conduct on those who dissent from them; to fetter the development, and, if possible, prevent the formation, of any individuality not in harmony with its ways, and compel all characters to fashion themselves upon the model of its own. There is a limit to the legitimate interference of collective opinion with individual independence; and to find that limit, and maintain it against encroachment, is as indispensable to a good condition of human affairs, as protection against political despotism.

----

1) We have here the first five paragraphs of a long essay. Since Mill is writing an essay in political theory, not a history, he can give only a limited space to the historical development of the problem he is considering. Yet if the problem itself is to be clear to the reader, that reader must know how it took shape. Mill must cover a long time span and a great deal of material in a very few pages. In order to do so he employs the method of chronological analysis.

2) Mill assumes that the reader himself can and will supply concrete

examples for many generalizations. He asks of the reader both knowledge and activity. Students sometimes complain that the demand is too great. But you will probably find that you *do* have historical knowledge enough to substantiate the generalizations, *if* you are willing to read actively enough. The next five questions are designed to suggest to you how knowledge you do have fits in.

3) In II Mill says that an early attempt to limit the power of the ruler over the community was "by obtaining a recognition of certain immunities, called political liberties or rights. . . ." What is a striking example from English history of this attempt? (If you find that here your education has been neglected, look up the reign of King John (1199–1216), perhaps in the *Encyclopedia of World History*, edited by William L. Langer.)

4) In III Mill points out that in Continental Europe as late as the 1850's political thinkers assumed that citizens did not need to be protected against a people's government. What in our own Constitution is clear evidence that, early in our history as a nation, Americans realized that the power of government over the citizens needed limiting—even in a republic?

5) Why would not the French Revolution seem to political thinkers a case in point when they were developing theories about popular government? What "democratic republic" made the real nature of the problem clear? Why do you think Mill may have used the term "democratic republic" instead of "democracy"?

6) How, exactly, is Mill defining a majority? Does that definition conform to your observation? Do you know any instance in which it has been contended that "the tyranny of the majority" operated "through the acts of the public authorities"—that is, that a particular governmental activity invaded the rights of citizens? Have you agreed with the contention?

7) What instances do you know of "the tyranny of the prevailing opinion and feeling" (v)? Can you find them within the small community of a college or university?

8) Now we may turn to the structure of this analysis. Highly generalized as this writing is, its pattern within paragraphs is fundamentally a narrative pattern. You will see that most clearly in an examination of III. Notice how often the within-paragraph transition indicates the progress of time.

9) But the paragraph structure is not determined primarily by considerations of elapsed time; instead it is determined by the stages of the development of the problem. The time span covered by II is far longer than the time span covered by III–IV; and v describes a stage contemporary with the essay.

10) Mill's paragraphs are rather long, but they are carefully constructed as units to hold together the discussion of the stages of the problem. No one of them could well be broken. How would you name the four stages represented by the four paragraphs?

11) In this sort of analysis, obviously, transition will have a special importance. It will be not only a matter of structure; it must succeed in representing historical transition. Notice that in IV, the first, second, and fourth sentences all have a transitional function. How about v?

12) Mill's chronological analysis of the development of the problem of the relationship between society and the individual is complete with v. Mill states the principle he believes should govern all discussions and determinations of the problem in a paragraph we have read. It is the first Mill passage in Chapter V. Turn back and reread it.

13) Mill's chief concern is, of course, with the problem as it presents itself in the middle nineteenth century, but he allows himself to prophesy that the problem will grow more formidable. "The tendency of all the changes taking place in the world," he writes, "is to strengthen society, and diminish the power of the individual." Is Mill a good prophet? Do you think that if he were writing his *On Liberty* today his chronological analysis of the development of the problem might include a fifth stage? What would that fifth stage be?

DIVISION AND CLASSIFICATION *iii*

In the first two sections of this chapter, we have been concerned with analysis in which the pattern is chronological. We turn now to another very common kind of writing problem, to analysis that is not handled in a time pattern. You are of course familiar with such analysis in both your reading and your writing, but it will be well to examine its problems somewhat more closely than we have had opportunity to do.

Rhetoric books have portentous names for patterns of analysis, but some of those patterns an orderly minded student may use without knowing they have any names. A student purposing to write a general (as distinguished from a scientific) discussion of an oak tree may separate roots, trunk, branches, and foliage, and devote a paragraph to each. A student writing about a golf club is likely to discuss separately the grip, the shaft, and the head. Another student about to discuss the external form of a business letter will remember that he has been taught that it has six parts and organize his discussion accordingly. Each of these students will have written an example of ANALYSIS BY PARTITION.

If any one of these students wants to be formal and precise, he may begin with a signpost sentence; for instance, the analysis of the golf club may start: "A driver, like any other golf club, has three parts: the grip, the shaft, and the head." Such a signpost is convenient for the reader (and good for the writer, since it insures he has a plan). In an extended discussion of a complex subject, the signpost is likely to be more elaborate.

Victor Hugo, in *Notre Dame de Paris* (1831), begins a discussion of fifteenth-century Paris with this paragraph:

In the fifteenth century Paris was still divided into three totally distinct and separate cities, each having its own physiognomy, individuality, manners, customs, privileges, and history: the Cité, the Université, and the Ville. The Cité, which occupied the island, was the mother of the two others, and cooped up between them, like—reader, forgive the comparison— like a little old woman between two handsome strapping daughters. The Université covered the left bank of the Seine from the Tournelle to the Tour de Nesle, points corresponding the one with the Halle aux Vins, and the other with the Mint, of modern Paris. Its enclosure encroached considerably upon the plain where Julian had built his baths. It included the hill of Sainte-Geneviève. The highest point of this curve of walls was the Papal Gate, which stood nearly upon the site of the present Panthéon. The Ville, the most extensive of the three divisions, stretched along the right bank. Its quay ran, with several interruptions indeed, along the Seine, from the Tour de Billy to the Tour du Bois, that is to say, from the spot where the Grenier d'Abondance now stands to that occupied by the Tuileries. These four points at which the Seine intersected the enclosure of the capital, the Tournelle and the Tour de Nesle on the left, and the Tour de Billy and the Tour du Bois on the right, were called by way of eminence "the four towers of Paris." The Ville penetrated still farther into the fields than the Université. The culminating point of the enclosure of the Ville was at the gates of Saint-Denis and Saint-Martin, the sites of which remain unchanged to this day.

Hugo has made a sort of contract with his readers to discuss fifteenth-century Paris with these partitions and in the order in which he has set them down. This contract he carries out elaborately and for some fourteen pages. But his way of organization is not essentially different from that of the college student whose paper on his home town begins with this paragraph:

Millville has three fairly well defined sections: a central business district with adjacent "bedroom" streets, a residential west side, and an industrial and residential east side. Expansion of the city will probably give Millville a north side and a south side, but as yet the residents do not use these designations.

Of course you understand that this signpost paragraph represents a late stage in the planning and perhaps even in the writing of the paper. The student could not have written it until he had thought over his subject carefully and decided how the subject was in itself partitioned. Having arrived at this paragraph, his plan is fixed. The great advantage of his plan, to him and to his reader, is that it will make transition easy and unmistakable. The paper will fall into four parts or sections (or, for quite a short paper, into four paragraphs). The four parts might begin in this fashion:

The central business district of Millville seems older than one might expect in a Midwest city. Most of the business places were built in the 1880's during a period of rapid growth. Originally built in the unfortunate style of the period, most of them have been remodeled on the street level in an equally unfortunate "modern" style . . .

The residential west side is somewhat dilapidated nearest the business section. The newer portion a few blocks west is made up, for the most part, of pleasant, modest homes on tree-lined streets . . .

The industrial and residential east side has grown very rapidly in the past quarter-century. Little planning was done, so that now many families live in very smoky neighborhoods, and traffic on some residential streets is heavy . . .

Expansion north and south has resulted in a number of diverse neigh-borhoods which seem to be the result of the whims of subdividers. Such unplanned expansion has had a number of unfortunate results. The most obvious one is the difficulty of locating schools . . .

Notice that since these parts begin by picking up the elements of the sign-post listing, no specifically transitional expressions are necessary.

Now so far we have considered the sort of subject to which the term par-tition applies best. Natural objects or organisms have their parts inherently. The physical works of man such as cities, implements, and machines are likewise in themselves partitioned. Moreover the relationships between parts are *there* in the subjects. An analysis by partition depends, then, upon observation of the subject, upon what one finds there. Of course a writer may for particular purposes neglect to discuss minor parts, or decide to discuss two or more together. Nevertheless he has found his organiza-tion instead of devising it. The problem of partitioning a subject is simply the analysis of a unit into the parts that make it up.

But a good many subjects which may be considered units do not have inherent or necessary partitions. Moreover, some plural subjects cannot well be handled by the technique of classification that, as we shall see, works efficiently for others. Yet all subjects need an orderly treatment; in all a writer must discuss one thing or group or idea at a time. We may not be able to call his procedure by any term less general than "division"; and that is especially likely if he is discussing concepts. Yet even then some-thing of the pattern of discussion inheres in the subject matter itself, al-though perhaps not objectively (as we know objectively that a golf club has three parts). The significance is in the subject; the writer, considering his readers on the one hand and his subject on the other, tries to achieve the division of his subject that will make its significance clear.

Of course you have been aware of this problem of division in a good number of our selections. But it is well for us to consider one example while the matter of pattern of analysis is especially in our minds. We shall ex-amine a piece by a skillful writer to see how he has gone about his problem. It is from a discussion of free speech, one designed for general readers. The writer has just referred to Plato and Athens.

FROM *Freedom of Speech and Press* (1955)

ZECHARIAH CHAFEE, JR.

Free Speech in the Bible

1 From another part of the ancient world came the Bible, the book the American colonists knew best. Although it had much less than the classics

Reprinted from *Freedom of Speech and Press* by Zechariah Chafee, Jr. by permis-sion of Carrie Chapman Catt Memorial Fund, Inc. Copyright, 1955, Carrie Chap-man Catt Memorial Fund, Inc.

to tell them about freedom of speech, it probably shaped their ideas on that subject in several ways.

II The Bible has one significant passage about the proper attitude of authorities toward distasteful talk. When the chief priests were inclined to have St. Peter and the other apostles executed, they were persuaded to set them free by a Pharisee named Gamaliel, "a doctor of the law, had in reputation among all the people," who was grandson of the wise Hillel and probably the teacher of St. Paul. Gamaliel stood up in the council and said to them:

> Ye men of Israel, take heed to yourselves what ye intend to do as touching these men. . . . Refrain from these men and let them alone: for if this counsel or this work be of men, it will come to nought: but if it be of God, ye cannot overthrow it; lest haply ye be found even to fight against God.[1]

III In the next place, the Bible shows the importance of procedure when men are called to account for objectionable speech. The proceedings of the Jewish leaders against Jesus and his followers resemble some sedition trials since 1600 in the use of false witnesses and in the vagueness of the charges brought. Contrast the insistence of the Roman officials in Palestine upon having specific charges made against St. Paul, who had the rights of a Roman citizen. Much later, the American colonists read Coke and Blackstone thoroughly, and knew that both of these English lawyers were much impressed by the words of Festus, the Roman governor of Judaea, "For it seemeth to me unreasonable to send a prisoner, and not withal to signify the crimes laid against him." Moreover, when the priests and elders were clamoring for quick condemnation of St. Paul, Festus had upheld other requirements of a fair trial:

> It is not the manner of the Romans to deliver any man to die, before that he which is accused have the accuser face to face and have license to answer for himself concerning the crime laid against him.[2]

IV Finally, the most notable contribution of the Bible to the cause of freedom of speech is its portrayal of prophets and apostles who spoke out the truth that was in them without fear of consequences. Many an English and American agitator forced to face judges and officials has been deterred from timidity and capitulation by remembering Nathan excoriating David for putting Uriah the Hittite in the forefront of the battle, Elijah hunting out Ahab to denounce the lawless seizure of Naboth's vineyard, and St. Paul speaking before Agrippa.[3] Like these men of old, dissenters have gone on talking and writing because they would rather be in prison or die than fail in their duty by keeping silent.

[1 See Acts 5:17–40.]
[2 See Acts 25.]
[3 See 2 Samuel 12:1–14; 1 Kings 21; Acts 26.]

v Most judges presiding over sedition trials have received such scriptural allusions stolidly. A few have treated them with scorn:

Scotch Political Prisoner: All great men have been reformers, even our Saviour himself.
Lord Braxfield: Muckle he made o' that, he was hanget.

Still, more than one thoughtful man on the bench must have compared the prisoner's courageous independence with his own state of mind and struggled against the uncomfortable suspicion that he himself was playing the part of Pontius Pilate.

---

1) Since you have read this selection with the problem of analysis in mind, perhaps it has occurred to you that Mr. Chafee must have considered and rejected one pattern of analysis. The order of the books in the Bible is generally chronological, and the material here might have been ordered chronologically. Why do you suppose Chafee rejected a chronological pattern?

2) Is there perhaps some objection to Chafee's order? For instance, two events in St. Paul's life—his hearing before Festus and his hearing before Agrippa—are separated, the one coming in iii and the other in iv.

3) How shall we say that Chafee is dividing his subject? Why had we better not say that he is partitioning it?

4) We can at least find designations for each of the three divisions. All are concerned with free speech in the Bible; what particular matter is each discussing?

5) Do you think Chafee found his divisions in a consideration of his general subject, free speech? Or do you think he found his divisions in a consideration of the particular subject matter of this little section? Might both considerations have entered into his decision? And might he have had other considerations?

6) But we must think of order as well as of division. Since Chafee begins iv with "Finally, the most notable contribution . . . ," we know why the references to the prophets and St. Paul come last—he wants the emphasis of the final position for this material. Is the order of the whole CLIMACTIC, with the paragraphs ii, iii, and iv so arranged that each succeeding one rises above its predecessor in force? Or could another consideration affect the order of ii and iii?

7) Chafee uses overt transition ("In the next place . . . ," "Finally . . .") but he does not use a signpost listing. See if you can construct a signpost sentence (or signpost sentences) to add to 1 which will announce and contract for the discussion to follow. Be sure to write a signpost that would not make necessary any change in the beginnings of ii, iii, and iv.

8) Chafee's teaching and writing for many years have been devoted to free speech and related matters. And we can be sure he knows the Bible well. Granting then that his material and ideas were easily available to him as he came to write, do you still see evidence of great care in every detail of structure?

9) Did you notice the care with which quotations are introduced and given an intelligible context? Most students have to learn to do that.

Chafee's problem of organization in "Free Speech in the Bible" was to deal with a concept (free speech) as it is embodied in particular documents (some of the books of the Bible). In course papers, students often have problems of division rather like Chafee's, and as upperclassmen they face those problems in extended papers. Let us take for an example such a problem as you may face as an upperclassman: A student in an honors course is to write on the demand for a national literature in the United States between 1815 and 1835, and he is to work with primary sources. He must deal, then, with the concept called "literary nationalism" as it is embodied in a number of documents. Even though he considers but a twenty-year span, he finds that he has a good deal of rather diverse material. And he believes that it will be difficult for him to handle the structure of a paper of the considerable length his instructor asks.

The student is wise enough to spend sufficient time in considering just how his material will best divide. He realizes that if he can find a three- or four-part treatment, he will not have to attempt a very complex, extended structure. He can, instead, devise a structure for each part, trying to keep the parts as closely parallel as his material allows. He decides that his material makes for a three-part treatment. He has a number of articles in the *North American Review,* written by critics important in their time. Then most of the major writers of the period made statements of intention. And, of course, he must illustrate the effect of the demand for a national literature upon creative work.

Since a course paper should announce its intention specifically and unmistakably, our student decides to have a signpost paragraph. As soon as he has determined upon his three sections, he sets down a brief, tentative signpost for his own use. After he has blocked out his entire paper and written a good part of it, he puts his signpost in final form. It turns out to be this:

In the first part of our literary history, literary discussion was primarily concerned with the necessity of a peculiarly American literature, and with the availability of American backgrounds and experience as literary material. The discussion was, in fact, a dispute, for many writers asserted that American materials were insufficient or inappropriate for literary use. But more writers were convinced that it was both a duty and a privilege to use American materials. The present purpose is to study, first, the magazine criticism which voiced the persistent demand for a distinctively American literature; second, the critical writing of the major writers who define their own intentions concerning a national literature; and, finally, some of the stories of Cooper, Irving, and Hawthorne as they illustrate the influence of the demand for a national literature on creative work.

Now what has been accomplished? The student has started at once, without the sort of purposeless "introduction" that disfigures many course papers. The first sentence announces the field of inquiry. The second and third sentences make clear that this paper is concerned only with the positive side of the discussion. The last, signpost, sentence is an elaborate one, but it clearly announces the concern of each of the three sections, and it will make between-section transition easy. In the following indications of the beginnings of sections, notice how the signpost listing is picked up:

i

From its beginning, the *North American Review* carried articles and addresses in which . . .

ii

But the demand for a national literature was not only a subject for magazine articles. Most of the major writers were concerned to define their own intentions . . .

iii

The writers of our early literature, then, were clear enough in their beliefs about a national literature. And very often we can see the influence of those beliefs on their work . . .

Thus far in this section we have considered only the sort of subjects that may be thought of as singular. Perhaps an analysis technique is the more necessary with plural subjects. Rhetoric books call a technique for handling plural subjects ANALYSIS BY CLASSIFICATION, that is, the systematic division of a plural subject into the kinds of members that make it up. You are familiar enough with the technique. A newspaper feature story about the behavior of parkers in a small city might well begin "Downtown Millville has three kinds of parkers: double, short-time, and all-day." Since the reporter cannot discuss individually all the parkers he knows about, he has divided them into kinds. You would expect him to proceed, if the story is short, by giving a paragraph to each of his three kinds in the order he has listed them. And you might expect him to represent each kind by an account of a parker typical of it.

But perhaps you are most familiar with analysis by classification in your reading in science. Here is a signpost paragraph that you will recognize as typical in textbooks:

As a practical approach to this subject a major division of plains is made in the following pages upon the basis of the dominant agents and processes concerned in their origin. These processes are (*a*) stream erosion, (*b*) stream deposition, (*c*) the work of glaciers, and (*d*) the work of wind.[1]

We may call this paragraph a full signpost. It indicates the logical process to be carried out. A full signpost (whether one or more sentences) for an analysis by classification (1) makes clear the plural subject to be discussed, (2) states the basis of division to be used, and (3) lists the divisions in the order they are to come. The quoted paragraph does just these

[1] By permission from *Elements of Geography* by Vernor C. Finch and Glenn T. Trewartha. Copyright, 1936, 1942, 1949, McGraw-Hill Book Company, Inc.

three things. The writers of it, therefore, have made a sort of contract with their readers; this, they promise, is the structure to be used. But whether or not a writer sets down his contract fully at the beginning of his analysis by classification, he has it in his mind.

"Analysis by classification" is a term not only for a structure but also for the process by which the mind deals with a multitude of similar entities. You will have recognized that some kinds of scientific writing could hardly proceed without it. But its usefulness is by no means limited to scientific writing.

A professional writer, let us say, has received a commission from a men's wear journal to do an article on men's hats—the journal wants it called "The Products of the Hatter's Art." Now the writer cannot deal with all varieties of men's hats; he would come out with a dull list for which he would not have space. But he may classify men's hats by their materials, for instance, or by the occasions upon which they are to be worn. He may have to think hard in deciding what basis of classification will allow him to fulfill his intention and to use his materials to advantage, for once he has chosen his basis of classification he must stick to it.

A writer with quite a different sort of plural subject may carry on much the same logical process. If a literary critic purposed a study of mystery stories, he would need some basis of classification, some clear and consistent way of dividing his discussion. He might classify them by appeal, and arrive at such kinds as stories of logical deduction, stories of atmosphere, and stories of violence. He must not then introduce some other basis of classification, and come up with, say, a grouping of mystery stories by English writers.

When any writer plans an analysis by classification, he has two important questions to ask: "Have I planned my divisions on some consistent basis?" and "Can I carry out this plan and still use the material I wish to?" It may be that a consideration of the second question will lead him to seek some new basis of classification. Of course there are only a limited number of possible bases of classification for a given plural subject, and they are inherent in the subject itself. But often a writer may choose the basis useful for a particular intention.

Since we are likely to associate an analysis by classification with textbooks, you may think of the technique as a modern one. It is not so particularly; here is an analysis by classification written a long time ago.

FROM *The Holy State and the Profane State* (1642)

THOMAS FULLER

[The Good Schoolmaster on Schoolboys]

[The good schoolmaster] studieth his scholars' natures as carefully as they their books; and ranks their dispositions into several forms. And though it may seem difficult for him in a great school to descend to all particulars, yet experienced schoolmasters may quickly make a grammar of boys' natures, and reduce them all, saving some few exceptions, to these general rules:

(a) Those that are ingenious and industrious. The conjunction of two such planets in a youth presage much good unto him. To such a lad a frown may be a whipping, and a whipping a death; yea, where their master whips them once, shame whips them all the week after. Such natures he useth with all gentleness.

(b) Those that are ingenious and idle. These think, with the hare in the fable, that, running with snails (so they count the rest of their schoolfellows), they shall come soon enough to the post, though sleeping a good while before their starting. Oh, a good rod would finely take them napping!

(c) Those that are dull and diligent. Wines, the stronger they be, the more lees they have when they are new. Many boys are muddy-headed till they be clarified with age, and such afterwards prove the best. Bristol diamonds are both bright, and squared and pointed by nature, and yet are soft and worthless; whereas orient ones in India are rough and rugged naturally. Hard, rugged, and dull natures of youth acquit themselves afterwards the jewels of the country, and therefore their dullness at first is to be borne with, if they be diligent. That schoolmaster deserves to be beaten himself, who beats nature in a boy for a fault. And I question whether all the whipping in the world can make their parts, which are naturally sluggish, rise one minute before the hour nature hath appointed.

(d) Those that are invincibly dull and negligent also. Correction may reform the latter, not amend the former. All the whetting in the world can never set a razor's edge on that which hath no steel in it. Such boys he consigneth over to other professions. Shipwrights and boatmakers will choose those crooked pieces of timber which other carpenters refuse. Those may make excellent merchants and mechanics who will not serve for scholars.

---

1) When students of Fuller use the term "wit"—in the sense it had in his day—to describe his style, they are thinking of his elaborate metaphor, proverbial allusion, and carefully balanced sentences. What do you think of the style? Is it mere artifice? Or does Fuller get something clearly and vividly said by means of it?

2) The metaphor in the second sentence in (a) may need explanation: in astrology it was believed that the conjunction of planets at the time of one's birth foretold one's future. Interpret the metaphor "a grammar of boys' natures."

3) Has this piece any purpose beyond putting schoolboys into classes? What purpose?

4) A modern educationalist writing on this subject would be likely to use such terms as "well-adjusted individuals," "intelligence quotients," "motivations," and "outcomes." Some of these terms filter down to students through their teachers. Do you think they mean more than Fuller's terms? How much more is there to be said of the nature of schoolboys? Do you recognize Fuller's classes?

5) Is there a clear and consistent basis of classification here, even though it is not specified in the first paragraph? What is it?

6) Make the first paragraph a full signpost by writing an additional sentence that makes clear the basis of classification to be used and that lists the classes in the order they are to be discussed.

7) Notice that the paragraphs that develop the signpost are designed to be parallel with one another. What is gained by the parallelism? In what other selections have you noted parallel paragraphs?

iv   THE ANALYSIS OF A PROBLEM

The selections here illustrate the application of analysis to a particular use—the clarification of a problem. The writers of these analyses are especially concerned to find the clearest possible distinctions of the components of their problems, without so separating those components that their relationships to one another are obscured.

The analysis of a problem usually starts with a definition of the problem. If its writer intends to persuade readers to a course of action or to an opinion, the analysis will include or become argument. But a writer may intend to show his readers the problem in and for itself, and our first two examples make no contentions about solving the problem. Since most of us are prone to contend for particular solutions before we have really understood problems, the technique of the analysis of problems has something more than a rhetorical importance.

Our first selection is taken from a textbook in political science, and from a section of that work carrying the title: "Restrictions under Which Legislatures Work."

FROM *Introduction to American Government* (1951)

FREDERIC A. OGG and P. ORMAN RAY

[Special Legislation by State Legislatures]

1 Another group of restrictions [upon the lawmaking power of state legislatures] has to do with "class legislation" and with local, special, or private laws, *i.e.*, laws applying to, or for the benefit of, some particular person, corporation, or locality, or which are not of general and uniform application throughout the state, or which do not apply to all persons or corporations included in some authorized classification. As a result of favoritism, corruption, waste of legislative time, and other abuses arising from this source, most constitutions (with exceptions chiefly in New Eng-

land and the South) now contain provisions designed to prevent such legislation altogether, or at all events to restrict the number and variety of special or local laws that may be enacted.

11 The most common ways of dealing with the problem are (1) to prohibit special, local, or private laws on any matters and in all situations which can be covered by a general law, with determination of the point commonly left to the legislature itself, although this often seriously weakens the force of the regulation; and (2) to enumerate in the constitution matters which may not be dealt with in special or local laws, *e.g.*, in the constitution of Illinois a list of 23 and in that of Indiana 17. Thus we find legislatures expressly forbidden to pass special laws granting divorces; locating or changing county seats; regulating county and township affairs; granting or amending city charters; and conferring on any corporation, association, or individual any special or exclusive privilege, immunity, or franchise. In many instances, such restrictions have had a salutary effect. Much special legislation nevertheless continues to be enacted (especially in some Southern states); for pressures exerted by localities and interests often prove irresistible, and ingenious ways of evading the supposed restraints have been found. Cities and counties, for example, can be thrown into classes according to population, with perhaps in some instances only a single one falling within a given class. According to the courts, legislation for a class, if applied uniformly, is "general." Manifestly, however, if only one city or county belongs to a given class, legislation for that "class" is to all intents and purposes "special." The only safeguard lies in judicial determination of the reasonableness of classifications; and more than one classification has been invalidated where palpably employed as a mere cloak for special legislation.

---

1) In this analysis, as in the analysis of any problem of long standing, attempts to solve or to deal with the problem become, for practical purposes, part of the problem. The structure of this selection is a generally useful one which might be adapted to any number of legal, political, and social problems. You will have noted that it moves from a definition of the problem to a statement of what has been done to solve the problem, and thence to a consideration of the relative success of the attempted solutions. It has then three parts.

2) The paragraphing in our selection is of course determined by the pattern of the section from which it comes. If the passage were designed to stand alone, the paragraphing might well be revised. What paragraph plan would make the analysis structure clear?

3) These textbook writers are of course strictly limited in the space that they can give to the analysis of the problem. Yet they do find room for some concrete examples. If they were to expand this piece for another purpose—say a magazine article on the improvement of state legislatures—what generalizations might get concrete illustration?

4) Notice the metaphors in the last sentence, good examples of the place of metaphor in workaday prose.

We turn from a political problem to a scientific one. But you will see that the structure of the analysis is not greatly different from that of the foregoing example. This analysis of a problem serves in its original context as an introduction to an account of the writer's own researches. Such an introductory analysis of a problem is as appropriate to a literary study, for instance, as it is to a scientific study. One of the things we can learn from the scientific writer is the way to define what our problems really are.

FROM *The Mystery of Corn* (1950)

PAUL C. MANGELSDORF

I The most important plant in America is corn. It is grown in every state and on three-fourths of all the farms of the U. S. Corn is the backbone of our agriculture. It is the most efficient plant that we Americans have for trapping the energy of the sun and converting it into food. True, we consume only small amounts of corn directly, but transformed into meat, milk, eggs and other animal products, it is the basic food plant of our civilization.

II Yet corn is also a mystery—a botanical mystery as baffling and intriguing as any in the pages of fiction. The plant has become so highly domesticated that it is no longer capable of reproducing itself without man's intervention. A grass, it differs from all other grasses, wild or cultivated, in the nature of its seed-bearing organ: the ear. This is a highly specialized inflorescence, or flower cluster, enclosed in husks, which when mature bears several hundred or more naked seeds upon a rigid cob. The pollen-bearing inflorescence, the tassel, occurs separately on the same plant. The ear of corn has no counterpart anywhere else in the plant kingdom, either in nature or among other cultivated plants. It is superbly constructed for producing grain under man's protection, but it has a low survival value in nature, for it lacks a mechanism of seed dispersal. When an ear of corn drops to the ground, scores of seedlings emerge, creating such fierce competition among themselves for moisture and soil nutrients that usually all die and none reaches the reproductive stage.

III What could have been the nature of the wild or primitive corn from which this pampered cereal has developed? Where, when and how was a species, once so hardy that it could survive in the wild, converted to a cultivated plant so specialized and so dependent upon man's ministrations that it would soon become extinct if deprived of man's help? These are questions that have puzzled botanists and anthropologists for more than a century. Now, as a result of research in botany, genetics, archaeology and history, the answers are a little nearer. The mystery has not been

Reprinted with permission of *Scientific American,* July, 1950, Volume #183, No. 1.

solved, but the web of circumstantial evidence is drawing tighter and the final solution is almost in sight.

IV The first reference to corn in recorded history occurs on November 5, 1492. On that day two Spaniards, whom Christopher Columbus had delegated to explore the interior of Cuba, returned with a report of "a sort of grain they call maiz which was well tasted, bak'd, dry'd and made into flour." Later explorers to the New World found corn being grown by Indians in all parts of America, from Canada to Chile. Corn proved to be as ubiquitous in the New World as it was unknown in the Old. There was a great diversity of corn varieties; all of the principal types we recognize to-day—dent corn, flint corn, flour corn, sweet corn and pop corn—were already in existence when America was discovered.

V The evidence that corn originated in America is so overwhelming that it seems sensible to concentrate, if not to confine, our search for its wild ancestor to the Western Hemisphere. In America corn has obviously had an ancient history. The seminomadic hunting and fishing Indians in both North and South America augmented their diet of fish and game with corn from cultivated fields. The more advanced Mound Builders of the Mississippi Valley and the Cliff Dwellers of the Southwest were corn-growing and corn-eating peoples. The highly civilized Mayas of Central America, the warlike and energetic Aztecs of Mexico and the fabulous Incas of Peru and Bolivia all looked to corn for their daily bread.

VI This universal reliance of the pre-Columbian cultures on corn as the basic food plant, and its great diversity of varieties, greater than that of any other cereal, bespeak a long period of domestication. How old is corn as a cultivated plant? Fortunately this investigation is no longer wholly a matter of guesswork. Radio-carbon dating of corncobs and kernels found in various ancient sites bears out previous archaeological and geological estimates that the oldest corn yet found in South America goes back to about 1000 B.C., and the oldest in North America to not earlier than 2000 B.C. The oldest prehistoric ears in both North and South America are small and primitive; they differ decidedly in several characteristics from the modern varieties of the Corn Belt. Yet almost any American farm boy would recognize them instantly as corn. So some 4,000 years ago corn was already well on the road to becoming the unique cereal it is now.

VII In what part of America did corn originate? And what kind of wild grass was it that gave rise to the multitude of present-day varieties of corn?

VIII One theory has corn originating from a plant called by the Aztecs *teocintle* (now Anglicized to teosinte). Teosinte is undoubtedly the closest wild relative of cultivated corn. Like corn, it has tassels and ears borne separately, although its "ears" contain only five or six seeds, each enclosed in a hard, bony shell—characteristics that make teosinte a most unpromising food plant. Also like corn, it has 10 chromosomes, indicating that it is a closely related species. Teosinte can readily be crossed with corn to produce hybrids that are completely fertile or almost so. If corn came from teosinte, as many botanists have supposed, it must have originated in Guatemala or Mexico, for teosinte is found only in those two areas.

ix The second principal theory is that corn originated in South America from a peculiar primitive plant called "pod" corn. Primitive pod corn
today has virtually vanished; it is no longer found in pure form but as an
admixture in modern varieties. As described in early references, and as
obtained by inbreeding from present-day mixtures, pod corn has its kernels
enclosed in a pod or chaffy shell similar to that found in all other cereals
—a condition which almost certainly was characteristic of wild corn.

x Which, if either, of these two theories is more likely to be correct?
Botanists, in attempting to determine the place of origin of a cultivated
plant, place considerable reliance upon two criteria. One is the occurrence
of wild relatives of the plant in question; the other is diversity in the cultivated species itself. It is assumed that other things being equal, the region
of maximum diversity should coincide with the center of origin, since di-
versification has progressed longer at the center than at the periphery of
the plant's present range. In the case of corn the two clues point in opposite directions: the wild-relative clue points to Guatemala and Mexico,
where teosinte, corn's closest relative, grows; the diversity clue points to
South America, where, on the eastern slopes of the Andes, occurs the
greatest diversity of corn varieties found anywhere in America in a region
of comparable size.[1]

---

1) When the writer speaks of corn as a "unique cereal," is he using the
word "unique" in its strict sense and, if he is, what is unique about corn?
When Joseph's brethren went to Egypt to buy corn, what did they bring
home? Why do we in this country understand the word differently from
the English? If corn was ubiquitous in the New World, does that explain
the special interest of American anthropologists in corn?

2) Increasingly modern science combines different kinds of knowledge
in a single piece of research. How many kinds contribute to the solving of
the problem of the origin of corn? What particular evidence is contributed
by each? (A new technique mentioned here is radio-carbon dating. The
amount of radioactive carbon a piece of plant material possessed when the
plant was alive is known, and the rate of its radioactive disintegration is
known. When its present radioactivity is measured, its age can be computed. Radio-carbon dating is useful for the approximate dating of very
old materials. For instance, radio-carbon dating determined that a recently
discovered manuscript of the Old Testament book of Isaiah was not, as
some scholars thought, a mediaeval forgery; but it could not determine
whether the manuscript was written a century or two before Christ, or a
century after.)

3) Most of the readers of the *Scientific American,* where this piece was
first printed, have some scientific training, but many of them have no special knowledge of botany or related sciences. Do you see any evidence that
the writer has been careful to adapt his work to general readers—such evidence as the definition of technical terms, or the explanation of matters

[1 Mangelsdorf's investigations indicate that teosinte was not the progenitor of corn.
Mangelsdorf believes that the progenitor was both a pod corn and a pop corn, and
that its place of origin is still an open question.]

likely to be perfectly familiar to botanists? When you did have to consult your dictionary, did you find the definitions sufficient for the purposes of this piece?

4) It will not take you long to see that the first paragraph is introductory, that the second paragraph defines the problem in general terms, and that the third states the specific questions that make up the problem. Where—later in the piece—is the problem somewhat narrowed?

5) You will also find that, after the third paragraph, the selection is divided into two sections, one dealing with the historical evidence about the problem, the other dealing with the principal theories about it. But you had better make an outline of the piece to make its structure clear to you and to show the relationship of paragraphing to structure.

The two analyses of problems above are dispassionate and objective. But of course the writer of an analysis of a problem may intend to make his reader concerned about the problem. He can do that without sacrificing precision or clarity. The following analysis of the problem of congestion in New York City is not so formally organized as the pieces we have just considered, but one can distinguish and list the components of the problem. Perhaps you should do so. Notice also that, just as in the selection from the political science textbook, efforts to deal with the problem have become, for practical purposes, part of the problem.

The first sentence in our selection is a transition from a previous article, which discussed building in New York and particularly proposals for two new super-skyscrapers.

FROM *The Roaring Traffic's Boom* (1955)

LEWIS MUMFORD

1 What happens in New York to the art of building is bound up with what happens to the city as a place to work and live in. If it ceases to be a milieu in which people can exist in reasonable contentment instead of as prisoners perpetually plotting to escape a concentration camp, it will be unprofitable to discuss its architectural achievements—buildings that occasionally cause people to hold their breath for a stabbing moment or that restore them to equilibrium by offering them a prospect of space and form joyfully mastered. For a whole generation, New York has become steadily more frustrating and tedious to move around in, more expensive to do business in, more unsatisfactory to raise children in, and more difficult to escape from for a holiday in the country. The subway rides grow longer and the commuting trains carry their passengers from more distant suburbs, until as much time is spent in transporting the human carcass as is gained by diminishing the work week. Because urban surface transporta-

tion often comes almost to a standstill, the cost of delivering anything to anyone is rising steeply and the futility of owning a car for any purpose but fleeing the city over the weekend is becoming clearer and clearer. Meanwhile, the distant dormitory areas of New York describe ever wider arcs. By 1975, the Regional Plan Association's experts calculate, more people will be living in the suburbs within fifty miles of New York than will live in the city itself. When that happens, it will be impossible to build enough highways to accommodate the weekend exodus, just as it is already impossible to provide enough internal traffic arteries to handle Manhattan's present congestion. And obviously, even if people could escape, they would then have no place within easy distance to go, since there would be no choice for recreation but metropolitan jam or suburban jelly.

II Fifty years ago, the upper-income groups here, as in most other big towns, began to move out of the city along the railroad lines, to provide their families with peace and quiet, open spaces and gardens, and tree-lined roads that brought them quickly into the country for a walk or a picnic. "Life with Father" took on a rural tinge, though Father rarely got home in time to do more than say good night to the children. Since then, the desire to escape the city has filtered down into every other economic group, and as a result of the suburb's popularity in satisfying this desire, that haven of refuge is itself filling up. Despite village zoning laws, skyscraper apartments overtop the trees in regions that were rural only yesterday, and the load of metropolitan traffic on the parks and highways around New York, abetted by the subdivider busily turning farms into building lots, has enormously cut down the open spaces that gave the suburb, despite its inconveniences, an edge over the city.

III Were the eruption of vehicles and buildings in and around New York a natural phenomenon, like Vesuvius, there would be little use discussing it; lava inexorably carves its own channels through the landscape. But the things that spoil life in New York and its environs were all made by men, and can be changed by men as soon as they are willing to change their minds. Most of our contributions to planned chaos are caused by private greed and public miscalculation rather than irrational willfulness. During the nineteenth century, when more cities were built than ever before, the business of assembling them was entirely in the hands of those who were thinking only of their immediate needs or their immediate profit. "Officers and all do seek their own gain, but for the wealth of the Commons not one taketh pain," a late-medieval poet commented at the very beginning of this urban breakdown. By now, hundreds of millions of dollars are poured every year into clearly obsolete and ineffectual efforts to overcome the ensuing congestion—street widenings, double-deck bridges, cloverleaf intersections, subways, garages—and the sole result of these improvements is to accelerate the disorder they are supposed to alleviate. Manhattan will soon be in the same predicament as imperial Rome; it will have to banish private wheeled traffic from the midtown area in daytime, as Julius Caesar did in Rome, to permit a modicum of public transportation and pedestrian movement. This will mean, as in Rome, the delivery of goods by night. That may temporarily relieve the congestion, but it will permanently increase insomnia, as Juvenal sardonically noted after Caesar issued his traffic ordinance.

IV I have put the whole urban picture within this ample frame to counteract the current habit of looking at one small corner of the problem—congestion at the Jersey end of the George Washington Bridge at 8:45 A.M. or at the intersection of Seventh Avenue and Thirty-fifth Street at 3 P.M. —and attempting to solve that. Perhaps the wisest words on the complexity of the traffic problem were uttered long ago by Benton MacKaye, who fathered the Appalachian Trail. To relieve the congestion of traffic in Times Square, he remarked, it might be necessary to reroute the flow of wheat through the Atlantic ports. But our one-eyed specialists continue to concoct grandiose plans for highway development, as if motor transportation existed in a social vacuum, and as if New York were a mere passageway or terminal for vehicles, with no good reasons of its own for existence. To these experts, a successful solution of the traffic problem consists of building more roads, bridges, and tunnels so that more motorcars may travel more quickly to more remote destinations in more chaotic communities, from which more roads will be built so that more motorists may escape from these newly soiled and clotted environments. If these planners had realized that it is as much the concern of good planning to prevent traffic from going into areas that should remain secluded and stable as it is to bring new traffic into areas that should be developed, they would never have offered their recent proposal for undermining what is left of rural Long Island. About that particular outrage, I shall have more to say in a later article.

V The fact is that motor transportation is the sacred cow of the American religion of technology, and in the service of this curious religion no sacrifice in daily living, no extravagance of public expenditure, appears too great. Motor transportation is not merely an object of public worship; it has succeeded the railroad as the most powerful tool for either distributing or congesting the population—and it currently does both. Like any other tool, it must be used for some human purpose beyond the employment of the tool itself, and that further purpose represents the difference between carving and mere whittling. Our transportation experts are only expert whittlers, and the proof of it is that their end product is not a new urban form but a scattered mass of human shavings. Instead of curing congestion, they widen chaos. . . .

SUGGESTIONS FOR PAPERS

The selections from Mangelsdorf, Rush, and Mill are all three excellent material for practice in formal summary. The Rush selection may be used for a technical problem, a very brief summary (say 300 words) making clear Rush's interpretation of the movement of frontier population. The selection from Mill offers a real test of a student's ability. If he can write a good formal summary of it, reducing it to something less than a third of its length, and keeping the essential ideas and relationships clear, he has good evidence of his competence for most college work.

You may not have time to practice all the varieties of analysis illustrated in this chapter; the order of suggestion here is not a necessary order, or even particularly significant. Your instructor may wish you to start with, say, an analysis by partition. If so, you might take as your subject a bicycle, a single-shot rifle, a pressure cooker, a steam iron, the format of a book— something of no very great complexity.

For an analysis by classification, find a subject you know about from your general experience or observation. Your own home town will furnish a number of subjects, your campus as many more. Can the population of your town be classified in any significant way? Can students preparing for teaching be classified by their motives in choosing the occupation? Does the piece by Fuller suggest a way of handling some fairly large group of persons you know about? Ask yourself such questions as these. A subject you have recently been reading about is not desirable—you need one in which the whole burden of organization falls upon you. You will need a complete plan before you can write your signpost sentence.

A good subject for analysis is a mass magazine. Assume that you are writing a report for a foundation that is making a study of the influence of mass magazines on American culture. Choose a particular magazine, one that you have some familiarity with, and pick out a representative issue. Write first an objective analysis of its content. Then go on to discuss what appeals it makes to its readers and, therefore, what it shows about them. Consider carefully your pattern of analysis, designing it for the efficient discussion of the magazine you have in hand.

An account of a process may be a short paper or a paper of some length. Length will depend upon the process, of course, but it will also depend upon what you mean to do for your reader. You will know better than anyone else what process you can write about. Whatever you take, consider first what your intention is. What are the needs and the interests of the reader you envisage? How thoroughly ought you to inform him? Then consider the process well, and let its structure determine the structure of your paper. If necessary definitions or secondary explanations are too long to be tucked into the account without clogging it, then perhaps you can handle them first.

The method of chronological analysis may be used with a number of kinds of material. Find the sort of material you will be interested in writing about. Can the history of the water supply of your community be treated by the method of chronological analysis? Does the growth of population in your city fall into stages that can be separated and described? What has happened to farm ownership in your section of the country? Can the history of some organization you know about be treated by chronological analysis? Can you trace three stages in the thinking about race relationships in your community or section? How about the history of your own family?

Analysis of a problem often proves interesting to student writers. In your first attempt, take a problem of no very great complexity and deal with it in and for itself. Is there a problem about athletic scholarships on your campus? Has there been discussion about the place of fraternities in college life? Does your community or your church face some particular difficulty? Be sure to keep to a concrete and particular problem. (As you know if you think about the matter, terms like "juvenile delinquency" are often used as generalizations through which people may escape from the real consideration of problems.) Then, when you have defined a problem belonging to a particular place, time, and group of persons, decide what its components are. You will need to distinguish them for your reader, but you will want him to see their relationship too.

XII

Argument

The term "argument" as we shall here use it means discourse designed to convince readers of a truth or to persuade them to a course of conduct, or to do both. The particular conditions of an argument are these: (1) Its subject is a matter on which differences of opinion or of belief are probable. (2) Some reasonable proportion of its readers are undecided about the subject or hold views different from those of the writer. Of course, one might have something vaguely like an argument without these conditions—he might "argue" that arson is undesirable—but unless he has an intention to convince some possible reader, his argument is hardly worth the writing.

An argument, therefore, usually is written and read in a context of discussion and disagreement. It must make a clear contention or set of contentions—student writers often fail to make clear just what they are contending that the reader ought to think or to do. (The root meaning of "argue" is "make clear.") And the contention must be supported. That support, for most contentions, will hardly be "proof" in any strict sense of the word, but it will be reasoning and evidence, of whatever kind, that give grounds for belief or for action. The reader of argument needs constantly to ask, "Are these reasons cogent—do they really direct the mind to acceptance of the contention?" And the question is just as necessary for the writer.

The writer of an argument, then, has a design upon his reader. And since he has, he needs to be sure, not only that his purpose is honest, but that in carrying it out he is not led to use dishonest means of persuasion. Since the reader of an argument wants to know why he accepts or rejects a contention, he needs to be clear, not only about what the writer is contending, but about the means of persuasion the writer uses. For both writer and reader there will be questions of honesty of purpose and of honesty of means.

Moreover, the writer has a problem of tact. Now, that is not to say that he should not be fully concerned for what he believes to be true. It is to say, however, that the surest way a writer may defeat his own purpose is so to offend his reader that the reader will not, cannot, attend to what is being said. In practice, tact in argument may often require that the writer give up some resounding phrase, some striking epithet, some clever stroke. If the writer is willing to make this suppression of self, the reader owes him an open-minded attention in return. But these difficult matters are best realized in the examination of particular arguments. We shall use arguments on questions connected with academic life.

AN ARGUMENT ON TEACHING   *i*

We shall start with an argument within your immediate experience. You know the context of discussion and disagreement into which it fits. Although its writer assumes college teachers as his readers, you are also adequate readers for it, because students and teachers are engaged in the same activity. You will of course judge the article in the light of your experience, but do consider its structure and its technique as argument, too. The title is a punning allusion to James Hilton's *Good-bye, Mr. Chips,* a well-known story of a kindly English schoolmaster.

Let Mr. Chips Fall Where He May (1952)

JOHN S. DIEKHOFF

I It is a commonplace of pedagogy that teachers should teach students, not subjects. It does not follow from this half-truth that students study teachers, not subjects. Yet this, too, is a frequent assumption. Donald J. Cowling, former president of Carleton College, and Carter Davidson, president of Union College, observe—without italics—in *Colleges for Freedom* (New York: Harper, 1947), that "The opportunity that a college gives to each of its students to come into *individual relations with unusually significant personalities* and to have the benefit of their instruction and inspiration is the most precious gift these institutions have to offer."

II "Unusually significant personalities" are unusual. "Every college probably has at least one outstanding teacher, the persistent topic of conversation among undergraduates and the alumni, beloved of many, and a continuing influence in their lives long after graduation. Those colleges with two or more are indeed fortunate." From these observations it follows that "in selecting new members of the faculty, the college president or dean or committee should be concerned primarily as to whether the candidate gives promise of developing into such a center of influence."

III This is a conventional view, and it is the despair of teachers. The statement implies that college teachers should be great personalities and that they should establish "individual relations" with each student. But it says explicitly that only one or two in each faculty may hope to become what they ought to be. The rest of us are mistakes made by the personnel officer or appointments committee. But if only two in a faculty of one hundred are persistent topics of conversation, the ninety-eight hewers of wood

Reprinted from *The American Scholar,* Summer, 1952, by permission of the publishers, United Chapters of Phi Beta Kappa.

and drawers of water who complete the staff are also useful in their humble ways. And their professional skills and more modest personal qualities are also important. Every prima donna needs a supporting cast.

IV The notion that a teacher must be great or nothing, and the notion that the effectiveness of teaching varies directly with the personality quotient of the instructor, spring from a misconception of the relationship between teacher and student. These notions are based on the assumption that good teaching always depends on an intimate personal relationship between teacher and student. This assumption seems to be based, in turn, on another one: that the teacher is what the student studies—almost as though the teacher's function were to rear the youth of the nation in his own image.

V The common view that the tutorial method is, in almost all circumstances, the ideal teaching method follows from these concepts and illustrates them. If the teacher-student relationship must be intimate and personal, and if the teacher is the object of study, the ideal teaching situation will, of course, seem to be that of a wise father with a dutiful son. The conversation of a wise and learned tutor with a single student is the academic approximation of this situation. Its peculiar value lies in the intimacy of the personal relationship between teacher and student, tutor and pupil.

VI As the personal relationship is weakened, teaching is presumed to become less effective. Accordingly, in our colleges we often claim to approximate the ideal tutor-pupil relationship by pretending to keep our classes as small as possible. The ratio of faculty to students (which is thought to reflect the size of classes) is a standard measure of the quality of a college.

VII Intramurally, we use a different standard, for the reputation of a particular instructor is often based on the number of students who "elect" his courses: the more the better. An instructor who can build an elective course from ten students to a hundred students is regarded as a successful teacher, in spite of his apparent willingness to sacrifice his "personal" relationship with his students. At least one college which claims to stress the "discussion" method of instruction, which boasts of its high ratio of teachers to students, and which sets up parallel sections of each of its required courses in order to keep classes small, allows students to attend any sections they please, if they please. The effectiveness of an instructor is inevitably judged by college administrators in part by counting the students he attracts. Students make the judgment that it is better to be in a class of one hundred six conducted by Professor Ampersand than in a class of six conducted by Professor Asterisk, not because the class is large, but because Professor Ampersand is knowing and skillful.

VIII Sometimes they will be right. Perhaps more often than not they will be right. Aristotle was remarkable (and remarkably successful) as tutor to Alexander; but it was not as tutor to Alexander that he won his reputation as a teacher, and there have been less successful tutors: George III of England was also educated by tutors. Good teachers from Abelard to

George Lyman Kittredge have been remarkable for the large number of students attracted to their classes. Students will travel from the corners of the world to study with a Sievers or an Osler; they do not insist on monopolizing the man with whom they study. Great teachers are great teachers because they are wise, learned and skillful men of good will—not because they have few students, and not because they have an intimate acquaintance with each student.

ix When it is insisted that the instructor must know each of his students "as an individual," the object is often something called "individualized instruction." Presumably, this means that the instructor will teach differently for students of different backgrounds, interests or capacities. To teach well, he must know which student is the daughter of a laundryman, which the son of a lawyer, and which are the twin children of a pharmacist. Presumably, he must know their family incomes, what their hobbies are, what they have read or not read, what effect television has had on their study habits, whether or not they go to church, and to what church, what their vocational objectives are, whether they have brothers and sisters, and what their personal tastes are. He must know what tensions exist between sibling and sibling, parent and child.

x Let us suppose a class of twenty students. Let us suppose an instructor who has so invaded the privacy of his students that he knows such things about each of them. Let us suppose further than he "knows" his students as one knows one's friends: a much subtler apprehension of personality or character, and one which does not depend upon the accumulation of personal (or personnel) data. Indeed, let us suppose that he is a friend to each student, and that being a friend means not only that he is well-intended toward each of them, but also that he has achieved some such apprehension of their personalities. Having established this relationship, when the instructor faces his heterogeneous class of unique human beings, what particularly does he do that he would not have done anyway? Does he give twenty different assignments? Set twenty different examinations? Choose or write twenty different textbooks? Must the teacher be a psychiatrist, giving each assignment as part of his therapy? If so, he must disband his class and conduct twenty different tutorials, replacing the furnishings of the classroom with the analyst's couch.

xi We need not pursue this further. When we ask what the instructor does differently when he comes to know his students, it becomes apparent that there is little that he can do differently. It is not necessary to his teaching that he "know" each student well "as an individual." He needs to know young men and women, not Henry and Susie; it is to their common humanity that he makes his appeal, not to their personal idiosyncrasies. More particularly, he needs to know the relevance to men and women in the modern world of the subject or skill that he teaches. For his object is not to acquaint his students with his own philosophy or his own eccentricities, or even with himself. His object is to assist them in the mastery of specific skills or the acquisition of specific knowledge. The obtrusion of his own personality may hinder rather than help. A wise teacher once observed that he was less distressed by what his students forgot than by what they remembered. And another wise teacher, George Herbert Palmer, insisted that "the teacher must keep himself entirely out of the way, fixing young attention on the proffered knowledge and not on anything so small as the one who brings it."

XII Two distinguished teachers, I. A. Richards and Gilbert Highet, have recently expressed this view, so old-fashioned that it is new again and needs iteration. In a lecture on "The Teaching Process," Mr. Richards spoke as follows:

My topic is the relation of the teacher to the pupil—or shall I say student? —the person addressed, the audience, the recipient. And I've only one solid piece of advice to give on that, which is: "Don't have a relation. Don't have one; don't."

XIII In the same lecture, Mr. Richards says:

. . . I have known superb teachers who to the end of their days couldn't tell one student from another, orally, optically, or even intellectually. That is very disturbing, but I think such teachers are speaking to the "all in each of all men," to use a phrase of Coleridge's. I have often suspected that Coleridge himself was talking most of his life to this "all in each." And there have not been many more influential teachers.[1]

XIV Gilbert Highet makes the same point in his recent book, *The Art of Teaching:*

The teacher, then, must know the young as such. Next, he must know the names and faces of his pupils. . . . But the teacher will find that, beyond that, it is seldom feasible to treat all his pupils as individuals. Even if it were possible, it would be unwise. For it would mean that the problem presented by each young man or girl would have to be approached as though it were unique. This would make it very difficult to solve, would be exhausting for the teacher, and would waste the profits of experience. The art of teaching, like the art of healing, consists partly in recognizing, within each individual, a particular type or combination of types.[2]

XV Even when the relationship of the teacher to his student is relatively impersonal, as Mr. Richards and Mr. Highet recommend, the relationship of a student to his teacher may be very personal. The more personal it is, the greater the impression made by the teacher upon the mind and character of the student—for good or ill. We may only hope that the teacher measures up to his responsibility. During an informal meeting of a small seminar at one American college, a famous novelist and playwright, doubling as professor of English, spilled beer on a student's best dress. The

[1] Reprinted by permission of the publishers from *A Handbook for College Teachers,* edited by Bernice Brown Cronkhite, Cambridge: Harvard University Press, 1950.
[2] Reprinted by permission of the publishers from *The Art of Teaching,* by Gilbert Highet, New York: Alfred A. Knopf, 1950.

dress was retired from service, instead of going to be cleaned, because the stain was more precious than the dress. The anecdote illustrates how very personal the relationship of student to teacher may be. But it is a one-way relationship; if the student had spilled beer on the novelist, his response would have been different. And if he also left an unexpunged mark on the student's mind, it was not merely because he got close enough to spill on it. Moreover, the student's emotional involvement probably interfered with her learning. Her attitude toward literature would be a better measure of the instructor's success than her attitude toward the instructor.

xvi We agree, of course, that the student's attitude toward the instructor is important, but the desirable attitude does not necessarily depend on the intimacy of a tête-à-tête, or even on the intimacy of small classes. The relationship of the bobby soxer to Frank Sinatra is a personal relationship —although Sinatra, again like the professor, need not reciprocate the emotion of each bobby soxer. Neither does he need to know each "as an individual" to exercise the peculiar influence which is the mark of his success.

xvii The kinship of teacher and entertainer is real. Teacher and orator are still closer kin. The success of the orator depends on the establishment of a somewhat personal one-way relationship between the members of the audience and himself. So does the success of the teacher. If the student is to do more than absorb, like a blotter, the factual information spilled on him, he must take an active part in the enterprise in which he is jointly engaged with his instructor. Unless the student regards the instructor at least with respect, the enterprise is difficult for them to manage jointly. If something like affection is added to respect, communication becomes easier and more meaningful. This is a principle recognized in ancient rhetoric. Aristotle (as translated by Lane Cooper) points out that:

. . . the speaker must not merely see to it that his speech . . . shall be convincing and persuasive, but he must . . . give the right impression of himself, and get his judge . . . into the right state of mind . . . for in conducing to persuasion it is highly important that the speaker should evince a certain character, and that the judges should conceive him to be disposed towards them in a certain way, and further, if possible, that the judges themselves should have a certain attitude towards him. . . . The same thing does not appear the same to men when they are friendly and when they hate, nor when they are angry and when they are in gentle mood. . . .

xviii Aristotle goes on to identify the three qualities in a speaker which will ensure him the confidence of his audience:

As for speakers themselves, the sources of our trust in them are three, for apart from arguments there are three things that gain our belief, namely, intelligence, character and good will.

xix The teacher's proper task of persuasion differs from the orator's, of course, and his techniques differ accordingly. He wishes to persuade the student to study or practice, to foster in the student an attitude toward the knowledge or skill which he seeks to master. The greater part of his task, however, is not to persuade at all. It is to expedite learning. Despite this difference, the qualities Aristotle lists are as important to the teacher as to the orator.

xx An orator, according to Quintilian, is a good man skilled in speech. A poet, according to Milton, is a good man skilled in poetry. These definitions assume that speaker and poet have something to say worth saying— their virtue includes knowledge. Making the same assumption, we may define the teacher as a good man possessed of knowledge and skilled in pedagogy. Unless the teacher has qualities which will command the respect of the student—intelligence, character and good will—the relationship which will best enable the student to learn from him is not likely to be established. Perhaps great teachers, under whose guidance students learn best, are great men skilled in pedagogy—men of great wisdom, great learning, great skill and great good will. Of course such men are rare.

xxi Fortunately, men of intelligence, character and good will, unqualified by the adjective *great,* are less rare; and fortunately, we may use something less than the best. Most of our college teaching—and so far as we can tell, much of it is acceptable—is done by men and women not very remarkable for their wisdom. Students may respect something less than superlative wisdom, may feel affection for something less than a great personality, and may learn from something less than profound scholarship.

xxii We shall guide their learning better still if we convince ourselves that the teacher is not what the student studies, and that we have overestimated the importance of intimacy in the personal relationship between teacher and student. For we shall then be able to recognize that in a college, however important the individual faculty member may be, teaching is a cooperative enterprise; and we may organize our colleges so as to encourage cooperation instead of pretending that there is no room for cooperative effort in teaching. If the entire education of a student were entrusted to a single tutor, and if the teacher were the proper object of the student's study, we should insist on greatness in our teachers. These are not the facts. In a college, the student studies a curriculum, not a man, and not a group of men. No single faculty member is responsible for the entire education of any single student. On the contrary, one hundred faculty members with different gifts and accomplishments may be jointly responsible for the education of fifteen hundred students. One of the reasons for the existence of a school is that it can educate many students at a time—more students than its staff members could educate working separately. Another reason is that a school can do it for less.

xxiii The final and conclusive reason is that a school can do it better. We need not argue the point. There are many colleges to which a conscientious parent may entrust the advanced schooling of his children with some confidence, but there are not many individuals to whom a conscientious parent could confidently entrust the entire advanced education of his children. There are not enough to go around, and only those with the resources and prestige of Philip of Macedon could secure such tutors for their children. If we put proper value on the hewers of academic wood, upon teachers who are competent if not great, and if we organize our colleges to exploit the competence they possess, we may keep our confidence in our colleges. When ideas, rather than faculty personalities, become the persistent topics of student conversation, students, teachers, and education in general will be greatly benefited.

---

1) This piece of argument is in part refutation, as arguments written about real issues must often be. The quotation in I from *Colleges for Freedom* does not, of course, indicate that Professor Diekhoff is contending against its authors particularly. He has found their statement a convenient way of representing the position he opposes. Can you see why it may be good practice to use such a quotation at the outset in an argument that is part of a controversy?

2) Most of the references here will be clear to you. In III "prima donna" is college teacher slang for a certain sort of faculty member, usually male. Your dictionary will identify the names of the famous teachers in VIII. Do our selections from Kittredge suggest to you what qualities made him a great teacher?

3) Perhaps your instructor will see the implication of the next-to-last sentence in XI more easily than you do. Many literature teachers have found with great dismay that students writing examinations have ascribed *their* by-the-way remarks to the writers being studied. Are there other instances in which you suspect implications that may not be clear to the general reader?

4) On the basis of the first few paragraphs, make a summary statement of the position about college teaching that this article is designed to refute. According to your observation is this position really held? Do you think the article states fairly the ideas it opposes? (Sometimes a writer will so state the position he opposes that his statement is, in effect, an argument against it. We can hardly expect him to state it sympathetically; but we may well consider whether he distorts it.)

5) The statements made in VI and VII, considered together, seem paradoxical. (What is a PARADOX?) Could the paradox be illustrated on your campus?

6) From the beginning through part of XI, the argument has been refutation, concerned primarily to show that the views being opposed are not in practice very consistently maintained. At what point in XI does a positive argument begin?

7) Paragraphs XII–XIV constitute what is called an ARGUMENT BY AUTHORITY. From one of our selections, you know something of Gilbert Highet; I. A. Richards, an Englishman, is a distinguished student of language. His name has been associated with that of C. K. Ogden in the promotion of Basic English.

8) An argument by authority may be merely a reference to some imposing name or names. But if it includes effective quotation, it may become an integral part of the main argument. Do these quotations serve in

that way? Does Professor Diekhoff go quite so far in insisting that the relationship of teacher to student must be impersonal as these quoted writers do?

9) It is clear that this article refutes the position that the most important thing a college offers is the students' "individual relations with unusually significant personalities." What sort of relationship do paragraphs XI–XXI describe? You had better write a short summary statement.

10) What is being done in XXI–XXIII? In any piece of writing we try to make our last chance at the reader count. Do these paragraphs really count? In what way?

11) If some teacher were persuaded by this argument, how might his conduct and procedure be affected? How about the student who may be persuaded? He can do little about the teaching in his college. Will his own practice be affected?

12) Does the argument apply without differentiation to all teachers, to the teacher of English literature as well as the teacher of chemistry? In many colleges there have been popular teachers of Shakespeare, and upperclassmen who advised their friends to be sure to take Dicky Volatile's Shakespeare. What may the remark reveal about Professor Volatile—and the upperclassmen?

13) Is the reasoning in this piece of argument generally inductive or generally deductive?

14) If we were to state briefly the argument here opposed, we could say that it has for its PREMISE: "The important function of a teacher is in his direct and personal influence upon individual students." And we could say that it has for its conclusion: "Therefore the aim of educational procedure and organization ought to be to allow the greatest opportunity for that influence." Can you make a statement of the premise and conclusion that are the center of Professor Diekhoff's argument?

15) In almost any discussion there will be some assumptions, some principles taken for granted without explicit statement, for without some community of opinion, even argument is almost impossible. Yet often a reader needs to stop and ask what they are. A writer may be making assumptions that, on examination, the reader will not accept. But all the assumptions here seem general and acceptable. One is that knowledge is a good in itself. Another is that American colleges really intend to be educational institutions. Without these two assumptions on the part of both writer and reader, communication in this argument could hardly take place.

16) Is this a tactful piece of argument? At least three sorts of readers would come to it with opinions different from the writer's: 1. Students who have valued the influence of particular teachers; 2. Teachers who feel themselves very successful in their personal relationships with students; 3. Educational theorists committed to another opinion. Will the article anywhere offend a representative of any one of these groups so that he cannot attend to the argument? For instance, might a reader from group 2 reading XVI resent an implied comparison to a crooner (or students feel they were being called bobby soxers)?

17) In many human relationships scientific proof or even full logical

demonstration of a contention is unlikely or impossible. Then we must judge the clarity of the contentions, and ask whether they have been stated with enough concreteness so that we realize them as they apply to persons and practice. If one asks whether this is a successful argument or not, he cannot answer by saying that he is convinced, or not convinced, or by taking a poll of readers. The most skillful of writers do not convince everyone, particularly when, as in this instance, presuppositions are strong. If the argument clarifies the reader's ideas, it has some success. Perhaps you will, in this regard, go back and read again a passage from John Stuart Mill in Chapter V, the passage that begins, "He who knows only his own side of the case, knows little of that."

THE QUESTION OF INTELLECTUAL FREEDOM   *ii*

In our time the question of intellectual freedom is a pressing one. But it is by no means a new one. We start with a selection that makes a set of contentions about intellectual freedom in the United States about 120 years ago. Alexis de Tocqueville (1805–59) came to the United States as a young man to make a report on prisons for the French government. He recorded his conclusions about the young nation in his *De la Démocratie en Amérique* (1835). Although you may feel that in our selection Tocqueville is censorious, he was in general a sympathetic and detached observer, and his is the first important estimate of American democracy. Readers today are often impressed by the way in which his judgments keep their pertinence; one comes upon passages that might have been written yesterday.

FROM *Democracy in America* (1835)

ALEXIS DE TOCQUEVILLE

[Majority Opinion and the American Character]

1 It is in the examination of the exercise of thought in the United States that we clearly perceive how far the power of the majority surpasses all the powers with which we are acquainted in Europe. Thought is an invisible and subtle power that mocks all the efforts of tyranny. At the present time the most absolute monarchs in Europe cannot prevent certain opinions hostile to their authority from circulating in secret through their dominions and even in their courts. It is not so in America; as long as the majority is still undecided, discussion is carried on; but as soon as its decision is irrevocably pronounced, everyone is silent, and the friends as well as the opponents of the measure unite in assenting to its propriety. The reason for this is perfectly clear: no monarch is so absolute as to combine all the powers of society in his own hands and to conquer all opposition, as a majority is able to do, which has the right both of making and of executing the laws.

II The authority of a king is physical and controls the actions of men without subduing their will. But the majority possesses a power that is physical and moral at the same time, which acts upon the will as much as upon the actions and represses not only all contest, but all controversy.

III I know of no country in which there is so little independence of mind and real freedom of discussion as in America. In any constitutional state of Europe every sort of religious and political theory may be freely preached and disseminated; for there is no country in Europe so subdued by any single authority as not to protect the man who raises his voice in the cause of truth from the consequences of his hardihood. If he is unfortunate enough to live under an absolute government, the people are often on his side; if he inhabits a free country, he can, if necessary, find a shelter behind the throne. The aristocratic part of society supports him in some countries, and the democracy in others. But in a nation where democratic institutions exist, organized like those of the United States, there is but one authority, one element of strength and success, with nothing beyond it.

IV In America the majority raises formidable barriers around the liberty of opinion; within these barriers an author may write what he pleases, but woe to him if he goes beyond them. Not that he is in danger of an auto-dafé, but he is exposed to continued obloquy and persecution. His political career is closed forever, since he has offended the only authority that is able to open it. Every sort of compensation, even that of celebrity, is refused to him. Before making public his opinions he thought he had sympathizers; now it seems to him that he has none any more since he has revealed himself to everyone; then those who blame him criticize loudly and those who think as he does keep quiet and move away without courage. He yields at length, overcome by the daily effort which he has to make, and subsides into silence, as if he felt remorse for having spoken the truth.

V Fetters and headsmen were the coarse instruments that tyranny formerly employed; but the civilization of our age has perfected despotism itself, though it seemed to have nothing to learn. Monarchs had, so to speak, materialized oppression; the democratic republics of the present day have rendered it as entirely an affair of the mind as the will which it is intended to coerce. Under the absolute sway of one man the body was attacked in order to subdue the soul; but the soul escaped the blows which were directed against it and rose proudly superior. Such is not the course adopted by tyranny in democratic republics; there the body is left free, and the soul is enslaved. The master no longer says: "You shall think as I do or you shall die"; but he says: "You are free to think differently from me and to retain your life, your property, and all that you possess; but you are henceforth a stranger among your people. You may retain your civil rights, but they will be useless to you, for you will never be chosen by your fellow citizens if you solicit their votes; and they will affect to scorn you if you ask for their esteem. You will remain among men, but you will be deprived of the rights of mankind. Your fellow creatures will shun you like an impure being; and even those who believe in your innocence will abandon you, lest they should be shunned in their turn. Go in peace! I have given you your life, but it is an existence worse than death."

vi Absolute monarchies had dishonored despotism; let us beware lest democratic republics should reinstate it and render it less odious and degrading in the eyes of the many by making it still more onerous to the few.

vii Works have been published in the proudest nations of the Old World expressly intended to censure the vices and the follies of the times: Labruyère inhabited the palace of Louis XIV when he composed his chapter upon the Great, and Molière criticized the courtiers in the plays that were acted before the court. But the ruling power in the United States is not to be made game of. The smallest reproach irritates its sensibility, and the slightest joke that has any foundation in truth renders it indignant; from the forms of its language up to the solid virtues of its character, everything must be made the subject of encomium. No writer, whatever be his eminence, can escape paying this tribute of adulation to his fellow citizens. The majority lives in the perpetual utterance of self-applause, and there are certain truths which the Americans can learn only from strangers or from experience.

viii If America has not as yet had any great writers, the reason is given in these facts; there can be no literary genius without freedom of opinion, and freedom of opinion does not exist in America. The Inquisition has never been able to prevent a vast number of anti-religious books from circulating in Spain. The empire of the majority succeeds much better in the United States, since it actually removes any wish to publish them. Unbelievers are to be met with in America, but there is no public organ of infidelity. Attempts have been made by some governments to protect morality by prohibiting licentious books. In the United States no one is punished for this sort of books, but no one is induced to write them; not because all the citizens are immaculate in conduct, but because the majority of the community is decent and orderly.

ix In this case the use of the power is unquestionably good; and I am discussing the nature of the power itself. This irresistible authority is a constant fact, and its judicious exercise is only an accident.

x The tendencies that I have just mentioned are as yet but slightly perceptible in political society, but they already exercise an unfavorable influence upon the national character of the Americans. I attribute the small number of distinguished men in political life to the ever increasing despotism of the majority in the United States.

xi When the American Revolution broke out, they arose in great numbers; for public opinion then served, not to tyrannize over, but to direct the exertions of individuals. Those celebrated men, sharing the agitation of mind common at that period, had a grandeur peculiar to themselves, which was reflected back upon the nation, but was by no means borrowed from it.

xii In absolute governments the great nobles who are nearest to the throne flatter the passions of the sovereign and voluntarily truckle to his caprices. But the mass of the nation does not degrade itself by servitude; it often submits from weakness, from habit, or from ignorance, and sometimes from loyalty. Some nations have been known to sacrifice their own desires to those of the sovereign with pleasure and pride, thus exhibiting a sort of independence of mind in the very act of submission. These nations are miserable, but they are not degraded. There is a great difference between doing what one does not approve, and feigning to approve what one does; the one is the weakness of a feeble person, the other befits the temper of a lackey.

XIII In free countries, where everyone is more or less called upon to give his opinion on affairs of state, in democratic republics, where public life is incessantly mingled with domestic affairs, where the sovereign authority is accessible on every side, and where its attention can always be attracted by vociferation, more persons are to be met with who speculate upon its weaknesses and live upon ministering to its passions than in absolute monarchies. Not because men are naturally worse in these states than elsewhere, but the temptation is stronger and at the same time of easier access. The result is a more extensive debasement of character.

XIV Democratic republics extend the practice of currying favor with the many and introduce it into all classes at once; this is the most serious reproach that can be addressed to them. This is especially true in democratic states organized like the American republics, where the power of the majority is so absolute and irresistible that one must give up one's rights as a citizen and almost abjure one's qualities as a man if one intends to stray from the track which it prescribes.

XV In that immense crowd which throngs the avenues to power in the United States, I found very few men who displayed that manly candor and masculine independence of opinion which frequently distinguished the Americans in former times, and which constitutes the leading feature in distinguished characters wherever they may be found. It seems at first sight as if all the minds of the Americans were formed upon one model, so accurately do they follow the same route. A stranger does, indeed, sometimes meet with Americans who dissent from the rigor of these formulas, with men who deplore the defects of the laws, the mutability and the ignorance of democracy, who even go so far as to observe the evil tendencies that impair the national character, and to point out such remedies as it might be possible to apply; but no one is there to hear them except yourself, and you, to whom these secret reflections are confided, are a stranger and a bird of passage. They are very ready to communicate truths which are useless to you, but they hold a different language in public.

XVI If these lines are ever read in America, I am well assured of two things: in the first place, that all who peruse them will raise their voices to condemn me; and, in the second place, that many of them will acquit me at the bottom of their conscience.

---

1) Our selection is typical of Tocqueville's method: the clear and vigorous statement of inductive generalizations, and pertinent comparison of American and European conditions. But he does not give us very much of

the observation itself, of the particulars on which the inductive generalization is based.

2) The validity of Tocqueville's contentions could be judged finally and fully only against a knowledge of conditions in the United States in 1831–2, the years in which he made his observations. But there is an approach more feasible for us. Since the majority exercises the same power that it did in 1831, we can see whether we think our own observations support what Tocqueville says.

3) That procedure is the more legitimate because Tocqueville's writing often has a prophetic quality. As an instance, take his remarks about the United States and Russia. He says that the two countries are the only countries still in the process of vital growth, and continues:

> The Anglo-American relies upon personal interest to accomplish his ends and give free scope to the unguided strength and common sense of the people; the Russian centers all the authority of society in a single arm. The principal instrument of the former is freedom; of the latter, servitude. Their starting-point is different and their courses are not the same; yet each of them seems marked out by the will of Heaven to sway the destinies of half the globe.[1]

Do you find any comparable prophetic quality in our selection?

4) Of course we should hardly expect such large generalization as Tocqueville's to stand up at every point. For instance, is VIII valid? Do you think of other reasons why the literature of the United States would not have been distinguished or extensive in 1831?

5) But we should come to the center of Tocqueville's thinking. Consider II. What exactly does he mean by saying that majority power "acts upon the will as much as upon the actions"? What is Tocqueville's assumption about the nature of power? An often quoted maxim by Lord Acton says: "Power tends to corrupt, and absolute power corrupts absolutely."

6) In this connection, consider also IX. What exactly does Tocqueville mean by the second sentence?

7) Tocqueville will be convincing to you in the degree that you can supply particulars that support his generalizations. Do you know examples of men in public life who have given up the integrity of their own thought in the face of the pressure of public opinion? Are academic standards or ideals ever compromised by a partial surrender, not to reasoned opposition, but just to the weight of majority attitudes? How about the fourth sentence in I—can it be substantiated? How about XIV? Political observers say that we have, more often than not, preferred mediocre Presidents—that great excellence and integrity may keep a man from being President. Would Tocqueville's contentions help to explain that observation?

8) Perhaps the contention that is most likely to surprise Americans is the contention that the tyranny of the majority tends to debase the character of individual Americans. Just how does Tocqueville argue it?

9) How is this selection connected in idea with our reading from John Stuart Mill?

[1] Reprinted from *Democracy in America* by Alexis de Tocqueville, edited by Phillips Bradley, by permission of Alfred A. Knopf, Inc. Copyright, 1945, by Alfred A. Knopf, Inc.

10) Tocqueville is not the only observer of American life who has seen in us a tendency toward self-congratulation. What do you think of the validity of the last sentence in VII?

11) If you raised your voice to condemn Tocqueville, you did what he says in XVI that he was sure you would do. Do you see why, if what Tocqueville says is true, it must follow that most American readers will resent what he says?

12) Assuming that Tocqueville's contentions are generally sound, could they have been presented more effectively? How?

13) You will have seen that this argument has a strictly limited intention. Tocqueville, in his role of observer, intends to convince his readers of the truth of certain contentions, but not, except perhaps by implication, to persuade them to any course of action. Do you think he is considering French readers primarily? Is he considering American readers at all?

14) You will be able to think of persons in the United States who have markedly independent minds, and of others (perhaps not so many) who are markedly independent in mind and in conduct. Suppose, for instance, that you think of a half dozen of the latter. Will that for you invalidate Tocqueville's contentions? Do exceptions to a generalization necessarily invalidate it? Does Tocqueville recognize exceptions to his own generalizations? Where?

The great problems of human life are never solved finally. They must be continually restated, and the principles that apply to them must be continually re-examined. Since Henry Steele Commager is a historian, he would not for a moment suppose or wish us to suppose that the central principles in his "Free Enterprise in Ideas" are new principles. Indeed, you will see that part of the argument is argument by authority, that Tocqueville is among the several writers cited, and that in two crucial passages the authority is John Stuart Mill. But every generation must understand what it accepts as truth in reference to its own conditions and special problems. If freedom is in danger in our time from persons who suppose themselves its friends, then we have the greater need to understand the problems of free thought and discussion.

In this essay, analysis of problems and argument come together in admirably clear exposition. It will be worth your while to study the technique as well as the ideas. The technique is adapted to the expected readers, for many persons feel deeply but think confusedly about the issue of intellectual freedom, which comes up continually in what seem to be new forms. Notice how Professor Commager, taking into account the state of mind of many of his readers, makes a careful initial analysis of his problems. And you would do well to make a list of the important premises in the order in which they appear, for, as you will soon discover, much of the reasoning is deductive.

We shall be reading part of Milton's *Areopagitica,* which is quoted at the close of this essay. Milton, too, pleads for free enterprise in ideas. This essay is good preparation for reading him, since Professor Commager states, simply and in reference to our time, the great principles that Milton states elaborately and in reference to his.

FROM *Freedom, Loyalty, Dissent* (1954)

HENRY STEELE COMMAGER

Free Enterprise in Ideas

I 'I sometimes think that when folks talk about things they've begun to lose them already,' says Stark Young's Hugh McGehee to his son after an evening of Southern rodomontade. It would be an exaggeration to say that we have begun to lose liberty in America, but it is sobering that there should be so much talk about it, just as it is sobering that there should be so much talk about Americanism and about loyalty. It was a happier time when these things could be taken for granted instead of being soiled and worn by every sunshine patriot eager for cheap applause. Nor is much of the talk itself reassuring. Liberty is enlisted in strange armies, pressed into service for curious causes, and as we listen to some of the arguments for censorship or exclusion or suppression, all in the name of liberty, we are reminded irresistibly of Madame Roland's cry on the scaffold, 'Liberty, what crimes are done in thy name.'

II Nor is the difficulty wholly with those who, in a sort of vindication of Orwell's *1984*, invoke liberty for oppression. Some of the difficulty comes from well-intentioned idealists who are content with familiar formulas, or who would interpret liberty as wholly a personal and individual affair—a matter of abstract principle rather than of conduct, of private rights rather than of general social responsibilities.

III When we consider civil and political liberties we must avoid the pleasant illusions of abstractions and get down to cases. We must look to the meaning of our freedoms in their present-day context, and in their operation. And when we do this we must remember what Harold Laski so insistently urged upon us (in *Reflections on the Revolution of Our Time*), that rights and liberties do not mean the same thing to all of us:

'The rule of law is a principle with a fairly long history behind it. And if the burden of that history has one outstanding lesson it is that, over the social process as a whole, the rule of law is only equally applied as between persons . . . whose claim on the state power is broadly recognized as equal. The rule of law is not an automatic principle of action which operates indifferently as to time and place and the persons to whom, as judges, its application is entrusted. It is very likely to be one thing for a Negro in Georgia and another thing for a white man in Georgia.'

The function of freedom—let us say of the guarantee of due process or of the right to vote—for the Negro and the white in the South is one very obvious example of why we have to look to the operation of the principle rather than to its mere formulation. Others come readily to mind: the difference in guarantees of freedom to white and to Oriental during World War II, for example, or the different treatment afforded the vagrant and the respectable citizen, or that difference in the attitude toward corporate crime and individual crime which Professor Sutherland has explored in his study of *White Collar Crime.*

IV We must recognize, too, at the outset that there are two very broad categories of violations of liberty: the political and the nonpolitical, or perhaps we should say the official and the unofficial. Only the first has received adequate attention—invasion of personal rights by the federal or state governments or by some administrative body. These are the impairments of liberty that are dramatized in the press and challenged in the courts—a flag-salute law, a segregation law, a white primary law, the censorship of a film, or the administrative seizure of an industry. Yet the second category of invasion and impairment, the unofficial, is more widespread and more effective than the first. It is invasion by social or community pressure, by the pressure of public opinion or of public customs and habits—the kind of invasion that Tocqueville described and warned against over a century ago. It is very difficult to get at this by law. Fair Employment Practice Acts may prevent a Negro or a Jew from getting fired for racial reasons, but they will not go far toward getting him a job in the first place. A teacher who has been guilty of dangerous thoughts can take a broken contract to court, but she cannot deal with community pressure that makes it advisable for her to move on, nor can she force other school boards to give her a job. We have only to read Norman Cousins' description [1] of the interplay of social and economic pressures in Peoria, Illinois, to realize how enormously effective these are and how difficult it is to do anything about them. As John Stuart Mill observed a century ago, 'The immense mass of mankind are, in regard to their usages, in a state of social slavery; each man being bound under heavy penalties to conform to the standard of life common to his own class.'

V Our basic freedoms, in short, are not as basic as we like to think, just as our passion for individualism is not as passionate as we suppose. If we content ourselves with abstractions we may go seriously astray; as Professor Denis Brogan has remarked in his recent book on revolutions, the American claim to—and hope for—a special place in the affections of Asian peoples is frustrated by the elementary fact that of all the powers of the world 'America is the most color conscious.' We may believe that our words—which we assume to express our principles—represent us more truly even than our actions, but to outsiders it is the actions that are more eloquent than the words.

VI Now it will be granted at once that our traditional liberties are not absolute—not in a mathematical sense, anyway. All of them are qualified by the rights of society, or of the state. There are limits on liberty, as there

[1] *Saturday Review,* 3 May 1952.

are limits on authority. The broad principle of those limits is generally recognized and accepted; no liberties may be exercised so as to injure others,
or injure the community.

VII Needless to say, this does not get us very far. That liberty is not absolute is one of those truisms that is almost always brought out and put to
work whenever somebody wants to censor a book or a film that he doesn't
like, or to throw a teacher or a librarian or a radio performer out of his job.
Actually it is worth stating only as an introduction to the real problems.
How do we determine the limits on liberty and the rights and interests of
the community? And who are the 'we' who determine? It is easy to fall
back on the generalization that the freedom of the individual must not be
used to injure the community, and easy enough to say that in the last analysis it is society which determines. But these vague answers are of no practical help. To draw the line between the exercise of freedom and the limitations on freedom is one of the most delicate tasks of statesmanship and
philosophy. And the power of drawing the line is one of the most complex
and sobering exercises of political authority.

VIII It is in the drawing of lines, the setting of boundaries, the fixing of
limits, the reconciliation of claims that the problems rise. Look where we
will, in our own society we will find that problems of freedom or of rights
revolve around this matter of fixing limits and drawing lines. Thus in the
conflicting claims of a free press and a responsible press, or of freedom and
license in the press. Thus in the conflicting claims of liberty and security
in diplomacy, or in science. Thus in the conflicting claims of artistic freedom and of the protection of the morals of the community, or of religious
freedom and protection against blasphemy or the stirring up of religious
hatreds. Thus in the conflicting claims of the right to public entertainment
and the right to privacy. Thus in the conflicting claims of the right to private organization and the interest of society in protecting itself against dangerous organizations. Thus in the conflicting claims of conscience—let us
say of conscientious objectors to military service or a flag salute—and of
national defense or of patriotism. Thus in the conflicting claims of academic freedom and of the right of a democracy to determine what should
be taught in its schools—and how.

IX Now we have been using the word 'conflicting' somewhat uncriti-
cally. But is not the conflict exaggerated, and have we searched intensively
enough for the reconciliation? We must keep in mind that the community
has a paramount interest in the rights of the individual, and the individual
a paramount interest in the welfare of the community of which he is a
part. The community cannot prosper without permitting, nay encouraging,
the far-reaching exercise of individual freedom; the individual cannot be
safe without permitting, nay supporting, the far-reaching exercise of authority by the state.

X There is, in short, too much emphasis on independence and not
enough on interdependence; too much emphasis on division and not
enough on unity. Actually it is only to the superficial view that there is any

genuine conflict between liberty and security, for example, or between academic freedom and social freedom.

xi For what is clear on closer examination is that we cannot have any one of these alleged goods without the other. There is no real choice between freedom and security. Only those societies that actively encourage freedom—that encourage, for example, scientific and scholarly research, the questioning of scientific and social orthodoxies and the discovery of new truths—only such societies can hope to solve the problems that assail them and preserve their security. The experience of Nazi Germany is all but conclusive on this (we are still required to wait until all the returns are in from Russia, but it is a reasonable prophecy that Russia will fall behind on scientific and social research just as Germany did). A nation that silences or intimidates original minds is left only with unoriginal minds and cannot hope to hold its own in the competition of peace or of war. As John Stuart Mill said in that essay on 'Liberty' to which we cannot too often repair, 'A state which dwarfs its men, in order that they may be more docile instruments in its hands . . . will find that with small men no great thing can really be accomplished.'

xii It is probable that other alleged alternatives so vehemently urged upon us are equally fictitious. Take, for example, the matter of the claims of 'academic freedom' and of a society concerned with the teaching of truth—as is every sound society. Clearly there is no genuine conflict here. All but the most thoughtless or the most ignorant know that unless education is free the minds of the next generation will be enslaved. Even in American Legion halls it is probably a bust of Socrates that stands in the niche—Socrates who was condemned because he was a corruptor of youth—rather than of those forgotten members of the tribunal who put him to death. We have always known that academic freedom, like other freedoms, was subject to abuse, but we have also known (up to now, in any event) that the abuse was part of the price paid for the use, and that it was not in fact a high price. The simple fact is that the kind of society that cherishes academic freedom is the kind that gets the best teachers and scholars and students, and the kind that tries to control what teachers may teach or students learn is the kind that ends up with mediocre teachers and mediocre students. A comparison of German science and scholarship in the generation before the First World War and the generation of Nazism should be conclusive on this.

xiii So, too, with the problem of freedom of the press as against the right of the community to protect itself against libel or obscenity or sedition or against similar dangers. Granted that there is no absolute freedom of the press—no right to proclaim blasphemy to church-goers or to distribute obscene literature to children—the alleged conflict is still largely fictitious. The hypothetical dangers linger in the realm of hypothesis; when they emerge from this to reality they can be dealt with by ordinary nuisance or libel or criminal laws, not by censorship laws. We are all familiar with Justice Holmes's graphic illustration of the man who cries 'fire' in a crowded theater, but the fact is that no sane man ever does this, and our ordinary laws should not be made for the hypothetical insane. The fact is that censorship always defeats its own purpose, for it creates, in the end, the kind of society that is incapable of exercising real discretion, incapable, that is, of doing an honest or intelligent job, and thus guarantees a steady intellectual decline.

xiv We must, then, keep in mind that we are dealing with realities, not abstractions. We must learn to think things, not words; we must fasten our attention on consequences, not on theories. We must keep ever in mind the warning of William James that meaningful discussion will 'hinge as soon as possible upon some practical or particular issue.'

xv The importance of this becomes clear when we realize that almost everyone agrees on the principles that should govern our conduct. At least almost all say and probably think that they agree. It is the application that is different. Southerners who deny Negroes a fair trial purport to be enthusiastic for the Bill of Rights but do not apply it in the same way to whites and Negroes. The Legislature of Texas which passed a resolution outlawing any party that 'entertained any thought or principle' contrary to the Constitution of the United States was doubtless sincere enough, but it did not intend to outlaw the Democratic party because that party 'entertains' a thought contrary to the Fifteenth Amendment. Senator McCarthy doubtless thinks of himself as a paladin of Constitutional liberties and so does Senator McCarran; Merwin K. Hart of the National Economic Council and Allen Zook of the notorious National Council for American Education invoke the Constitution, as do the editors of *Counterattack* and of *Red Channels*. All this is too obvious for rehearsal. We must get beyond the principles to their application in order to discover where the difficulty is, and to discover how to resolve it.

xvi When we approach the problem this way we can see that the most compelling argument for freedom is not the argument from theory or principle, but the argument of necessity. To put the issue as simply as possible: we maintain freedom not in order to indulge error but in order to discover truth, and we know no other way of discovering truth. It is difficult to think of any situation where this principle does not apply.

xvii This does not mean for a moment that the principles are unimportant. They are enormously important. They provide the framework of our thinking. They provide us with a common vocabulary. They crystallize for us the values we cherish. If we did not have a body of principles of freedom, we should not be discussing this matter at all. The principles are important, then, and essential. But it is in the application that we discover their meaning. It is the application that is the test. If we are to solve our problems, it must be by traveling the road of conduct and consequences. Theory may mislead us; experience must be our guide.

xviii Let us note three or four examples. Here, for instance, is perhaps the most important of all at the moment—the conflicting claims of scientific freedom and national security. To talk in abstract terms of the freedom of the scientist does not get us very far, for that is not an abstract freedom;

it is a freedom whose effective exercise requires a good deal of co-operation from the community. Nor does it get us very far to talk in abstract terms about national security. Everyone is in favor of national security, but Senators Morse and McCarthy have different notions about how it is to be achieved. The meaningful approach is that of consequences. What happens when you adopt a policy of freedom for research—freedom with commonsense regulations that any sensible man may be expected to observe? What happens when you permit the Government or the military to control the research? Fortunately, we need not speculate here; Walter Gelhorn's remarkable study of *Security, Loyalty, and Science* has covered the ground and furnished the moral.

'The costs of secrecy [he says] are high. When the freedom of scientific exchange is curtailed, an unfavorable reaction upon further scientific development is inevitable. We pay for secrecy by slowing the rate of our scientific progress, now and in the future. This loss of momentum may conceivably be disastrous, for even from the strictly military point of view "it is just as important for us to have some new secrets to keep as it is for us to hold on to the old ones." If it is unsound to suppress scientific knowledge during the long years of a cold war, the American people may one day discover that they have been crouching behind a protective wall of blueprints and formulas whose impregnability is an utter illusion.'

xix Or let us look to an equally familiar field—the effort to rid our school system of alleged 'subversives.' Ignore for the moment all questions about the definition of subversive (a term that has not yet been legally defined) or about the rights of teachers. Look solely to the social interest, the community interest, in the matter, and apply the test of consequences. What happens when a state tries to purge its state universities or a community tries to purge its public schools of alleged subversives?

xx We have a good deal of evidence on this matter by now, for the campaign against subversives has gone on for some time. We can therefore speak here with some assurance. What happens is not that the state or city gets rid of hordes of Communists. Not at all. It very rarely finds any,[1] and

---

[1] William B. Pendergast of the U.S. Naval Academy thus summarizes the situation as of 1950: 'In none of the states which enacted anti-subversive laws in 1949 was any need for the legislation demonstrated. Texas had one known Communist student in its state universities and colleges. Maryland . . . only one had held any public position in the recent past, and that as a kindergarten teacher in the Baltimore schools; this teacher was dismissed in 1948. . . . A survey made by *The New York Times* in September 1949 disclosed that no Communist problem existed in the school systems of twenty-nine of the nation's largest cities. . . . Governor Dever of Massachusetts declared that, to his knowledge there were no Communists in the ranks of his state's employees. . . . Proponents of the anti-subversive laws here discussed failed to name a single Communist employed by their states in 1949. They failed to cite a single dangerous act recently perpetrated by Communists within their states. Inquiry into the operation of the 1949 legislation . . . confirms the suspicion that there was no pressing need for the legislation. . . . Nothing resembling a Communist was turned up anywhere as a result of the operation of these laws. The only tangible effect of the legislation to date has been added work for file clerks who handle the loyalty declarations.' 'State Legislatures and Communism: The Current Scene,' XLIV, *American Political Science Review*, 571–2.

it rarely finds any subversives unless it wants to stretch that term to embrace anyone who rejoiced in Russian victories in 1943 or who reads *The Nation* or who favors socialized medicine. What happens is the demoralization and the eventual corruption of the school system. This is not a momentary or even a temporary affair; it is something the consequences of which may be felt for years. The search for subversives results in the intimidation of the independent, the original, the imaginative, and the experimental-minded. It discourages independence of thought in teachers and students alike. It discourages the joining of organizations that may turn out to be considered subversive. It discourages the reading of books that may excite the suspicion of some investigator or some Legionnaire. It discourages criticism of educational or of Governmental policies. It discourages the discussion of controversial matters in the classroom, for such discussion may be reported, or misreported, and cause trouble. It creates a situation where first-rate minds will not go into teaching or into administration and where students therefore get poor teaching. In the long run it will create a generation incapable of appreciating the difference between independence of thought and subservience. In the long run it will create a generation not only deprived of liberty but incapable of enjoying liberty.

xxi Turn where we will to apply the test of consequences, we discover that we must insist on freedom because we cannot do without it, because we cannot afford the price of its denial. Thus the most powerful argument against Congressional programs of investigation of Foundations ('To determine if they are using their resources for un-American and subversive activities or for purposes not in the interest or tradition of the United States') is that if it is put into effect it will endanger existing foundations and discourage philanthropists from setting up others and discourage that boldness and independence which foundations can provide more freely than almost any other institution. The most powerful argument against the censorship of textbooks and the elimination of 'un-American' ideas or of anything critical of the 'American spirit of private enterprise' is that such censorship will guarantee the elimination of textbooks with any ideas at all. The compelling argument against the purging of libraries is that if the kind of people who believe in purges have their way and work their will, our libraries will cease to be centers of light and learning and become instead instruments of party or church or class, or depositories of literature whose only merit is its innocuousness. The compelling argument against denying passports or visas on the grounds of unpopular political or economic ideas is that by silencing criticism in those who expect to travel from country to country we deprive ourselves of the value of what foreigners might have to tell us, discourage criticism in our own citizens, and deny to foreigners living evidence that the United States encourages intellectual independence. The decisive argument against the kind of censorship of radio and motion-picture performers that we are now witnessing is that it will leave us, in the end, with programs devoid of ideas and performers devoid of originality or of courage to apply originality.

XXII In every case it is society that is the loser. Our society can doubt-less afford to lose the benefits of ideas or character in any one instance, but the cumulative costs of the intimidation of thoughtful and critical men and women is something no society can afford.

XXIII A society that applies doctrinaire notions to social conduct will find itself in the end the prisoner of its own doctrines. A society that takes refuge in shibboleths like 'subversive' or 'un-American' will find itself unable to recognize reality when it appears—even the reality of danger. A society that discourages experiment will find that without experiment there can be no progress, and that without progress, there is regress. A society that attempts to put education and science and scholarship in strait jackets will find that in strait jackets there can be no movement, and that the re-sult will be intellectual atrophy. A society that repudiates free enterprise in the intellectual arena under the deluded notion that it can flourish in the economic alone will find that without intellectual enterprise, economic en-terprise dries up. A society that encourages state intervention in the realm of ideas will find itself an easy prey to state intervention in other realms as well.

XXIV That government which most scrupulously protects and encour-ages complete freedom of thought, expression, communication, investiga-tion, criticism is the one which has the best chance of achieving security and progress. 'They that can give up essential liberty to obtain a little tem-porary safety deserve neither liberty nor safety,' wrote Benjamin Franklin two centuries ago, and what he said is as valid now as it was then. Gov-ernment and society have a paramount interest in independence, original-ity, heterodoxy, criticism, nonconformity, because all experience teaches that it is out of these that come new ideas, and because every society needs a continuous re-examination of old ideas and a continuous flow of new ideas. And it is relevant to remember, too, that it is nonconformity that needs encouragement. As William Ellery Channing said over a century ago, 'We have conservatives enough.'

XXV Three centuries ago John Milton addressed himself to the problem that now confronts us, and what he said in *Areopagitica* is still valid:

'Believe it, Lords and Commons, they who counsel ye to such a sup-pressing do as good as bid ye suppress yourselves. . . . Ye cannot make us now less capable, less knowing, less eagerly pursuing of the truth, un-less ye first make yourselves, that made us so, less the lovers, less the found-ers of our true liberty.'

———————

Chronologically we should have read our selection from Milton before reading Tocqueville and Commager. But it offers some difficulty, which perhaps we can handle the better for our acquaintance, through the Com-mager essay, with its central concern. It is a brilliant piece of argument, and it will serve us also as a review of the problems of metaphor and allu-sion in reading.

When Milton wrote his great defence of the freedom of the press, he called it *Areopagitica,* in reference to the ancient court of Athens, the Areopagus. In 1643, during the time of the Commonwealth, the Parliament of England enacted a law requiring that all books be licensed by an official censor before publication. Milton's protest was published in 1644—and without the license the law required. Milton tells us in his *Second Defence of the English People:* "I wrote my 'Areopagitica' in order to deliver the press from the restraints with which it was encumbered; that the power of determining what was true and what was false, what ought to be published and what suppressed, might no longer be entrusted to a few illiterate and illiberal individuals, who refused their sanction to any work which contained views or sentiments at all above the level of the vulgar superstition." There may have been a time in America when it was possible to think of the *Areopagitica* as merely a great monument of English prose, with no particular pertinence to contemporary concerns. It is not so in our time.

But the *Areopagitica* is not easy to read. It belongs to an old tradition of English prose, a tradition to which we are unused. Moreover, Milton was directing it to the most fully adequate readers of his day. These readers knew the Latin classics and the Bible well. Milton's allusion would not have been of any special difficulty for them, as it is for us. We have here but a few passages, a small part of the whole, made into a pattern. Read over the selection to get a general control of it, and then read it with the questions. They will help you with the allusions and with some other matters.

FROM *Areopagitica* (1644)

JOHN MILTON

I . . . Be assured, Lords and Commons, there can no greater testimony appear than when your prudent spirit acknowledges and obeys the voice of reason, from what quarter soever it be heard speaking; and renders ye as willing to repeal any act of your own setting forth as any set forth by your predecessors.

II If ye be thus resolved, as it were injury to think ye were not, I know not what should withhold me from presenting ye with a fit instance wherein to show both that love of truth which ye eminently profess, and that uprightness of your judgement which is not wont to be partial to yourselves; by judging over again that order which ye have ordained *to regulate printing: that no book, pamphlet, or paper shall be henceforth printed, unless the same be first approved and licensed by such,* or at least one of such, as shall be thereto appointed.

III I deny not but that it is of greatest concernment in the church and commonwealth to have a vigilant eye how books demean themselves, as well as men, and thereafter to confine, imprison, and do sharpest justice on them as malefactors. For books are not absolutely dead things, but do contain a potency of life in them to be as active as that soul was whose progeny they are; nay, they do preserve as in a vial the purest efficacy and extraction of that living intellect that bred them. I know they are as lively, and as vigourously productive, as those fabulous dragon's teeth; and being sown up and down, may chance to spring up armed men. And yet, on the other hand, unless wariness be used, as good almost kill a man as kill a good book: who kills a man kills a reasonable creature, God's image; but he who destroys a good book, kills reason itself, kills the image of God, as it were, in the eye. Many a man lives a burden to the earth; but a good book is the precious life-blood of a master spirit, embalmed and treasured up on purpose to a life beyond life. 'Tis true, no age can restore a life, whereof, perhaps, there is no great loss; and revolutions of ages do not oft recover the loss of a rejected truth, for the want of which whole nations fare the worse. We should be wary, therefore, what persecution we raise against the living labours of public men, how we spill that seasoned life of man preserved and stored up in books; since we see a kind of homicide may be thus committed, sometimes a martyrdom; and if it extend to the whole impression, a kind of massacre, whereof the execution ends not in the slaying of an elemental life, but strikes at that ethereal and fifth essence, the breath of reason itself, slays an immortality rather than a life.

.   .   .   .

IV Good and evil we know in the field of this world grow up together almost inseparably; and the knowledge of good is so involved and interwoven with the knowledge of evil, and in so many cunning resemblances hardly to be discerned, that those confused seeds which were imposed on Psyche as an incessant labour to cull out and sort asunder, were not more intermixed. It was from out the rind of one apple tasted that the knowledge of good and evil, as two twins cleaving together, leaped forth into the world. And perhaps this is that doom which Adam fell into of knowing good and evil, that is to say, of knowing good by evil. As therefore the state of man now is, what wisdom can there be to choose, what continence to forbear, without the knowledge of evil? He that can apprehend and consider vice with all her baits and seeming pleasures, and yet abstain, and yet distinguish, and yet prefer that which is truly better, he is the true warfaring Christian. I cannot praise a fugitive and cloistered virtue, unexercised and unbreathed, that never sallies out and sees her adversary, but slinks out of the race where that immortal garland is to be run for, not without dust and heat. Assuredly we bring not innocence into the world, we bring impurity much rather; that which purifies us is trial, and trial is by what is contrary. That virtue therefore which is but a youngling in the contemplation of evil, and knows not the utmost that vice promises to her followers, and rejects it, is but a blank virtue, not a pure; her whiteness is but an excremental whiteness; which was the reason why our sage and serious poet Spenser, whom I dare be known to think a better teacher than Scotus or Aquinas, describing true temperance under the person of Guyon, brings him in with his palmer through the cave of Mammon and the bower of earthly bliss, that he might see and know, and yet abstain. Since therefore the knowledge and survey of vice is in this world so necessary to the constituting of human virtue, and the scanning of error to the confirmation of truth, how can we more safely, and with less danger, scout into the regions of sin and falsity than by reading all manner of tractates and hearing all manner of reason? And this is the benefit which may be had of books promiscuously read.

.   .   .   .   .

v And how can a man teach with authority, which is the life of teaching, how can he be a doctor in his book, as he ought to be, or else had better be silent, whenas all he teaches, all he delivers, is but under the tuition, under the correction, of his patriarchal licenser, to blot or alter what precisely accords not with the hidebound humour which he calls his judgement? When every acute reader, upon the first sight of a pedantic license, will be ready with these like words to ding the book a quoit's distance from him: "I hate a pupil teacher, I endure not an instructor that comes to me under the wardship of an overseeing fist. I know nothing of the licenser, but that I have his own hand here for his arrogance; who shall warrant me his judgement?" "The state, sir," replies the stationer, but has a quick return: "The state shall be my governors, but not my critics; they may be mistaken in the choice of a licenser, as easily as this licenser may be mistaken in an author. This is some common stuff." And he might add from Sir Francis Bacon, that "such authorized books are but the language of the times." For though a licenser should happen to be judicious more than ordinary (which will be a great jeopardy of the next succession), yet his very office and his commission enjoins him to let pass nothing but what is vulgarly received already.

vi Nay, which is more lamentable, if the work of any deceased author, though never so famous in his lifetime and even to this day, come to their hands for license to be printed or reprinted, if there be found in his book one sentence of a venturous edge, uttered in the height of zeal (and who knows whether it might not be the dictate of a divine spirit?), yet not suiting with every low decrepit humour of their own, though it were Knox himself, the reformer of a kingdom, that spake it, they will not pardon him their dash; the sense of that great man shall to all posterity be lost, for the fearfulness or the presumptuous rashness of a perfunctory licenser. And to what an author this violence hath been lately done, and in what book of greatest consequence to be faithfully published, I could now instance, but shall forbear till a more convenient season. Yet if these things be not resented seriously and timely by them who have the remedy in their power, but that such iron-moulds as these shall have authority to gnaw out the choicest periods of exquisitest books, and to commit such a treacherous fraud against the orphan remainders of worthiest men after death, the more sorrow will belong to that hapless race of men whose misfortune it is to have understanding. Henceforth let no man care to learn, or care to be more than worldly wise; for certainly in higher matters to be ignorant and slothful, to be a common steadfast dunce, will be the only pleasant life, and only in request.

.   .   .   .   .

VII And now the time in special is, by privilege to write and speak what may help to the further discussing of matters in agitation. The temple of Janus, with his two controversial faces, might now not unsignificantly be set open. And though all the winds of doctrine were let loose to play upon the earth, so truth be in the field, we do injuriously by licensing and prohibiting to misdoubt her strength. Let her and falsehood grapple; who ever knew truth put to the worse, in a free and open encounter? Her confuting is the best and surest suppressing. He who hears what praying there is for light and clearer knowledge to be sent down among us, would think of other matters to be constituted beyond the discipline of Geneva, framed and fabricked already to our hands.

VIII Yet when the new light which we beg for shines in upon us, there be who envy and oppose, if it come not first in at their casements. What a collusion is this, whenas we are exhorted by the wise man to use diligence, "to seek for wisdom as for hidden treasures" early and late, that another order shall enjoin us to know nothing but by statute? When a man hath been labouring the hardest labour in the deep mines of knowledge, hath furnished out his findings in all their equipage, drawn forth his reasons as it were a battle ranged, scattered and defeated all objections in his way, calls out his adversary into the plain, offers him the advantage of wind and sun, if he please, only that he may try the matter by dint of argument; for his opponents then to skulk, to lay ambushments, to keep a narrow bridge of licensing where the challenger should pass, though it be valour enough in soldiership, is but weakness and cowardice in the wars of truth. For who knows not that truth is strong, next to the Almighty? She needs no policies, nor stratagems, nor licensings to make her victorious; those are the shifts and the defences that error uses against her power. Give her but room, and do not bind her when she sleeps, for then she speaks not true, as the old Proteus did, who spake oracles only when he was caught and bound, but then rather she turns herself into all shapes except her own, and perhaps tunes her voice according to the time, as Micaiah did before Ahab, until she be adjured into her own likeness.

---

1) Notice in III—and throughout—how one metaphor is suggested by the foregoing metaphor and developed out of it.

2) You probably recognize "those fabulous dragon's teeth" as an allusion to the story of Jason and Medea. Any of the classical allusions in this selection can be identified in *The Oxford Companion to Classical Literature* or in Gayley's *Classic Myths*.

3) A great many persons who know nothing else about the *Areopagitica* know through quotation this passage: ". . . a good book is the precious life-blood of a master spirit, embalmed and treasured up on purpose to a life beyond life." Do you see any reason that this particular passage would be remembered?

4) Although a paradox is by definition a self-contradictory statement, it may resolve into meaning. We would surely call "slays an immortality

rather than a life" a paradox. Does it make sense in context? What, in literal terms, is Milton saying?

5) Perhaps you should make a little summary statement for iii—indeed, it might be well to make one for each of the subsequent paragraphs as you work through it.

6) In the first sentence in iv Milton alludes to the story of the various nearly impossible tasks that Venus, angry because her son Cupid loved Psyche, set Psyche to do. Notice the immediate shift to Biblical allusion.

7) What sort of image of virtue arises from the passage beginning "I cannot praise . . ."? A comparison of the moral life to a race seems to be a natural one; St. Paul speaks of running the race that is set before us (Hebrews 12:1). Toward the end of the paragraph Milton is saying that Edmund Spenser in his *The Faerie Queene* is a better moral teacher than Duns Scotus, a Scottish theologian, or St. Thomas Aquinas, the Italian author of a great discussion of Christian thought and conduct. Spenser is a better teacher, Milton believes, because as a poet he represents his teaching concretely. Guyon, the representation of the virtue of temperance, is subjected to the temptations of avarice and lust, so that his innocence is not ignorance.

8) What according to Milton in v will be the intellectual result of the licensing system? Perhaps this paragraph will explain to you why some academic persons are so much concerned today about academic freedom. In vi Milton is saying that the suppression of books will extend to old books as well as new. Have you ever heard of anything like that in our time?

9) In the second sentence in vii, the allusion is complex. The Roman temple of Janus had two doors, open in wartime, closed in peace. And Janus himself was represented with two faces. Milton seems to be saying that the time needs truth, and that since truth comes out of controversy, controversy ought to be allowed. In the last sentence of the paragraph he is saying that men really desire truth, truth beyond the Calvinistic theology ("the discipline of Geneva") which is already set down and known.

10) Did you ever know such a person as is described in the first sentence of viii—a person who resented any idea that came not first to his casement window? The point of the paragraph is a strong one: the person who is unwilling that what he believes in should encounter any opposition does not have much confidence in his belief.

11) Again—in the last sentence—we have both a classical allusion and a Biblical allusion. Proteus is the old man of the sea who can assume any shape he likes but who, if held down firmly, has to tell the truth. There is a fine story about him in the fourth book of the *Odyssey*. The prophet Micaiah, when he was first called before Ahab, bade him go forth to war; but when Ahab adjured him to tell the truth, he foretold Ahab's defeat (see 2 Chronicles 18, and especially verses 14–17).

12) This selection from the *Areopagitica* is rather like many poems in that one must do some work on it before he can begin to enjoy it. Now that you have the allusions clear and have followed through the ideas, go back and read the selection over, right straight along.

13) Most instructors will remember some student asking in reference to some piece of elaborate writing, "Why does he write like that?" Now of

course elaborate writing may be bad writing; but it may also be very good writing. Think about what has happened to you in reading this Milton selection. If you have really read it, you have been pretty active. And that is what Milton intended. There are two reasons. One is that pleasure is just the sign of a successful activity; no reading interests us greatly that does not require something of us. The other is that Milton wanted to touch our emotions as well as make a statement for our intellects; he put into his writing what would evoke images for us—if we keep alert enough to respond.

14) But—perhaps you will say—does he not limit his audience? He does in our time; indeed, he did in his own. Yet we know that language is a complex set of conventions, and part of our difficulty is merely that we have here conventions not much used in modern writing. And perhaps Milton would say that at no time is the number of persons vitally interested in the free play of ideas very great, that, on this question, it is important to speak impressively to the most adequate readers.

15) The matter of allusion needs one further remark. It was a great advantage to Milton to be able to allude to the Bible and to the Latin classics with confidence, knowing that his first readers would understand the allusions. Communication depends upon a common body of knowledge, of which literary knowledge may be an important part. But one of the special problems of the modern writer is that there is no body of literary knowledge that he can be sure any great number of his readers share.

16) You really should read a paragraph or two of this selection aloud; unless you are a very good reader you will not feel the sentence rhythm otherwise.

iii   SOME PROBLEMS IN READING ARGUMENT

If the matters at issue in a piece of argument are within the reader's experience or observation, he will of course judge its validity by what he knows. In "Let Mr. Chips Fall Where He May," for instance, we could often judge on the grounds of our own experience; so too in the selections on intellectual freedom. But you often find that you do not have grounds in your own knowledge on which to accept or reject a writer's contentions and supporting statements. Are you then helpless in judging an argument? You are not nearly so helpless as you may at first thought suppose.

You can ask, "Is this argument convincing on the face of it?" Now that is not to ask, "Do I feel convinced?" It is instead to ask some questions about the means the writer uses. If you find that the writer is presenting you with large generalizations that he does not tie to any instance and that, upon consideration, *you* cannot tie to any instance, you will of course decide that the generalization is not meaningful to you. It may be sound, but at least you ought not to be influenced by it. If you find that the writer is also more concerned to appeal to your emotions than he is to appeal to your judgment, you will question his generalizations very closely. And if you find that fact and judgment come in the context of the same sentence, you can insist on your privilege of making a separation.

Then, too, you can ask yourself, "Are there assumptions here that I should not accept?" We have remarked that some assumption is almost inevitable. In any discussion of one of the problems of democracy, for instance, we should expect the assumption that democracy is, in practice, the best form of government. But in such a discussion there might be also the assumption that democracy and unrestricted private enterprise are identical. A reader willing to make the first assumption might be unwilling to make the second—if he knew it was there. But if he is not quite conscious of its presence, he may be accepting conclusions from a premise he has not examined. Sometimes a writer is clever enough to let an idea remain an assumption in preference to giving it the explicit statement that a reader would examine. Then the reader must be clever enough to see what the writer is doing.

You have perhaps read articles by writers on propaganda analysis cautioning you against certain common techniques of persuasion. Such warnings are useful, and a sensible reader will not neglect them. But do not think of them as an all-sufficient formula that you can apply whenever, for some reason, you suppose you have need to approach an argument cautiously. Any formula for detecting illegitimate means of persuasion has the danger of over-simplification. A reader may be lulled into supposing that to recognize certain much-used devices and to detect obvious logical fallacies are all that he needs to do. What the reader needs above all is the habit of care, the habit of watching to see exactly what is being said, the habit we have been all along trying to establish.

That habit of care will protect you from a deceptive kind of statement, particularly common in argument, that we may call pseudo-statement— that is, writing that appears on its surface to make a meaningful statement, or to set forth valid evidence in favor of some point of view or course of action, when in fact it does nothing of the sort. You can find many examples of pseudo-statements in the advertisements; here is one: "Guard that throat, doctors say. And Thus-and-so Pipes give you one . . . two . . . *three* Throat-Guards, protecting your throat like no other smoke can! Making the smoke easier on your throat . . . keeping it cooler." You are probably already aware of the ad writer's trick of using an incomplete comparison to avoid making any real claim: easier on the throat than what? [1] But consider "protecting your throat like no other smoke can!" Never mind now about the use of "like" for "as"; think about the statement. Since no one supposes that any smoke *protects* the throat, no one should suppose that anything has been said.

Now you may feel—and rightly so—that you will not be taken in by such admen's tricks. But pseudo-statement is not always so obvious. Let us look at two excerpts from an article, written in the 1940's, opposing a law requiring the fingerprinting and registration of aliens. Just before our first

[1] Remember that the incomplete comparison is tricky all around; it can throw a writer. An instance, reported by *The New Yorker*, is a sign on a motor court: "A Better Place to Stay Costs No More."

example the writers had been saying—what was the fact—that in some states aliens were barred by law from certain professions and occupations. They continue:

What the States are doing now by law, private business has to a great extent been doing all along. As far back as 1928–29, with unemployment at a minimum, industry denied work to aliens in three out of every five cases and labor unions refused to accept aliens in four out of every five memberships. Since then this ratio has grown.

This statement looks much more specific than it is. What exactly does "industry denied work to aliens in three out of every five cases" mean? Are the writers saying that in 1928–29 three out of five aliens were unemployed? Or does the statement say that of every five applications for work by aliens, three were turned down? (If it means that, then all aliens who wanted to work might well have found jobs within a short time.) One cannot fix a meaning upon "cases." Is the rest of the sentence any better? It can hardly mean that one out of five union members was an alien—aliens made up only about 2 per cent of the total population. But what does it mean? And what ratio is it that we are told in the next sentence has grown?

Now do you see that we really could make some judgment about the passage above without any previous knowledge of its subject? We could say of some sentences, "These should not influence us; they seem to be making a point, but they really are not." Let us try another example. A paragraph in the same article begins with the question: "Does the alien lower the American standard of living?" Apparently not, the writers say, and offer this sentence in support: "The ten States with the highest proportion of foreign-born in their population have more than twice the per capita annual income of the ten States with the lowest proportion of foreign-born." Now did you see a shift of terms? You may have missed it by its very obviousness. The question is asked about the alien. It is answered with a statement about the foreign-born. Are "alien" and "foreign-born" equivalent terms? You know very well that they are not; you know that many persons who have been citizens for years are foreign-born. You can only conclude that you have really been told nothing about the alien and the American standard of living.

A kind of pseudo-statement that offers particular danger is the one containing statistical terms. This is true not so much because the ordinary reader does not understand statistical terms—after all, we have just seen that lack of information does not leave us defenceless against pseudo-statement—as because he has a sort of superstitious veneration for them, so that in their presence he tends to relax the defences he has. The notion that figures don't lie has had a long life. We shall end this chapter with a selection designed to create a healthy skepticism about that notion. It may even teach you how to identify particular pseudo-statements masquerading as statistical evidence.

FROM *How to Lie with Statistics* (1954)

DARRELL HUFF

The Well-Chosen Average

I You, I trust, are not a snob, and I certainly am not in the real-estate business. But let's say that you are and I am and that you are looking for property to buy along a road that is not far from the California valley in which I live.

II Having sized you up, I take pains to tell you that the average income in this neighborhood is some $15,000 a year. Maybe that clinches your interest in living here; anyway, you buy and that handsome figure sticks in your mind. More than likely, since we have agreed that for the purposes of the moment you are a bit of a snob, you toss it in casually when telling your friends about where you live.

III A year or so later we meet again. As a member of some taxpayers' committee I am circulating a petition to keep the tax rate down or assessments down or bus fare down. My plea is that we cannot afford the increase: After all, the average income in this neighborhood is only $3,500 a year. Perhaps you go along with me and my committee in this—you're not only a snob, you're stingy too—but you can't help being surprised to hear about that measly $3,500. Am I lying now, or was I lying last year?

IV You can't pin it on me either time. That is the essential beauty of doing your lying with statistics. Both those figures are legitimate averages, legally arrived at. Both represent the same data, the same people, the same incomes. All the same it is obvious that at least one of them must be so misleading as to rival an out-and-out lie.

V My trick was to use a different kind of average each time, the word "average" having a very loose meaning. It is a trick commonly used, sometimes in innocence but often in guilt, by fellows wishing to influence public opinion or sell advertising space. When you are told that something is an average you still don't know very much about it unless you can find out which of the common kinds of average it is—mean, median, or mode.

VI The $15,000 figure I used when I wanted a big one is a mean, the arithmetic average of the incomes of all the families in the neighborhood. You get it by adding up all the incomes and dividing by the number there are. The smaller figure is a median, and so it tells you that half the families in question have more than $3,500 a year and half have less. I might also have used the mode, which is the most frequently met-with figure in a series. If in this neighborhood there are more families with incomes of $5,000 a year than with any other amount, $5,000 a year is the modal income.

VII In this case, as usually is true with income figures, an unqualified "average" is virtually meaningless. One factor that adds to the confusion is that with some kinds of information all the averages fall so close together that, for casual purposes, it may not be vital to distinguish among them.

VIII If you read that the average height of the men of some primitive tribe is only five feet, you get a fairly good idea of the stature of these people. You don't have to ask whether that average is a mean, median, or mode; it would come out about the same. . . .

IX The different averages come out close together when you deal with data, such as those having to do with many human characteristics, that have the grace to fall close to what is called the normal distribution. If you draw a curve to represent it you get something shaped like a bell, and mean, median, and mode fall at the same point.

X Consequently one kind of average is as good as another for describing the heights of men, but for describing their pocketbooks it is not. If you should list the annual incomes of all the families in a given city you might find that they ranged from not much to perhaps $50,000 or so, and you might find a few very large ones. More than ninety-five per cent of the incomes would be under $10,000, putting them way over toward the left-hand side of the curve. Instead of being symmetrical, like a bell, it would be skewed. Its shape would be a little like that of a child's slide, the ladder rising sharply to a peak, the working part sloping gradually down. The mean would be quite a distance from the median. You can see what this would do to the validity of any comparison made between the "average" (mean) of one year and the "average" (median) of another.

XI In the neighborhood where I sold you some property the two averages are particularly far apart because the distribution is markedly skewed. It happens that most of your neighbors are small farmers or wage earners employed in a near-by village or elderly retired people on pensions. But three of the inhabitants are millionaire week-enders and these three boost the total income, and therefore the arithmetic average, enormously. They boost it to a figure that practically everybody in the neighborhood has a good deal less than. You have in reality the case that sounds like a joke or a figure of speech: Nearly everybody is below average.

XII That's why when you read an announcement by a corporation executive or a business proprietor that the average pay of the people who work in his establishment is so much, the figure may mean something and it may not. If the average is a median, you can learn something significant from it: Half the employees make more than that; half make less. But if it is a mean (and believe me it may be that if its nature is unspecified) you may be getting nothing more revealing than the average of one $45,000 income—the proprietor's—and the salaries of a crew of underpaid workers. "Average annual pay of $5,700" may conceal both the $2,000 salaries and the owner's profits taken in the form of a whopping salary.

XIII Let's take a longer look at that one. . . . The boss might like to express the situation as "average wage $5,700"—using that deceptive mean. The mode, however, is more revealing: most common rate of pay in this business is $2,000 a year. As usual, the median tells more about the situation than any other single figure does; half the people get more than $3,000 and half get less.

xiv How neatly this can be worked into a whipsaw device in which the worse the story, the better it looks is illustrated in some company statements. Let's try our hand at one in a small way.

xv You are one of the three partners who own a small manufacturing business. It is now the end of a very good year. You have paid out $198,-000 to the ninety employees who do the work of making and shipping the chairs or whatever it is that you manufacture. You and your partners have paid yourselves $11,000 each in salaries. You find there are profits for the year of $45,000 to be divided equally among you. How are you going to describe this? To make it easy to understand, you put it in the form of averages. Since all the employees are doing about the same kind of work for similar pay, it won't make much difference whether you use a mean or a median. This is what you come out with:

> Average wage of employees . . . . $ 2,200
> Average salary and profit of owners 26,000

That looks terrible, doesn't it? Let's try it another way. Take $30,000 of the profits and distribute it among the three partners as bonuses. And this time when you average up the wages, include yourself and your partners. And be sure to use a mean.

> Average wage or salary $2,806.45
> Average profit of owners 5,000.00

Ah. That looks better. Not as good as you could make it look, but good enough. Less than six per cent of the money available for wages and profits has gone into profits, and you can go further and show that too if you like. Anyway, you've got figures now that you can publish, post on a bulletin board, or use in bargaining.

xvi This is pretty crude because the example is simplified, but it is nothing to what has been done in the name of accounting. Given a complex corporation with hierarchies of employees ranging all the way from beginning typist to president with a several-hundred-thousand-dollar bonus, all sorts of things can be covered up in this manner.

xvii So when you see an average-pay figure, first ask: Average of what? Who's included? The United States Steel Corporation once said that its employees' average weekly earnings went up 107 per cent between 1940 and 1948. So they did—but some of the punch goes out of the magnificent increase when you note that the 1940 figure includes a much larger number of partially employed people. If you work half-time one year and full-time the next, your earnings will double, but that doesn't indicate anything at all about your wage rate.

xviii You may have read in the paper that the income of the average American family was $3,100 in 1949. You should not try to make too much out of that figure unless you also know what "family" has been used to mean, as well as what kind of average this is. (And who says so and how he knows and how accurate the figure is.)

xix This one happens to have come from the Bureau of the Census. If you have the Bureau's report you'll have no trouble finding the rest of the information you need right there: This is a median; "family" signifies "two or more persons related to each other and living together." (If persons living alone are included in the group the median slips to $2,700, which is quite different.) You will also learn if you read back into the tables that the figure is based on a sample of such size that there are nineteen chances out of twenty that the estimate—$3,107 before it was rounded—is correct within a margin of $59 plus or minus.

xx That probability and that margin add up to a pretty good estimate. The Census people have both skill enough and money enough to bring their sampling studies down to a fair degree of precision. Presumably they have no particular axes to grind. Not all the figures you see are born under such happy circumstances, nor are all of them accompanied by any information at all to show how precise or unprecise they may be. . . .

xxi Meanwhile you may want to try your skepticism on some items from "A Letter from the Publisher" in *Time* magazine. Of new subscribers it said, "Their median age is 34 years and their average family income is $7,270 a year." An earlier survey of "old TIMEers" had found that their "median age was 41 years. . . . Average income was $9,535. . . ." The natural question is why, when median is given for ages both times, the kind of average for incomes is carefully unspecified. Could it be that the mean was used instead because it is bigger, thus seeming to dangle a richer readership before advertisers? . . .

SUGGESTIONS FOR PAPERS

There are any number of subjects for papers in direct connection with the selections. One student may find he wishes to write a refutation of one of them; another student may find he wishes to write in support of another. Unless you purpose a fairly long paper, you will do best to limit yourself to one principle and deal with that in a concrete application. Remember Commager's insistence that principles are important but that "it is in the application that we discover their meaning." For instance, you may find a starting point in some passage in "Free Enterprise in Ideas" which you approve, or with which you disagree. You can make your discussion of it meaningful if you take it to a specific condition in your community, campus, or state.

Or if it is the Tocqueville piece that gives you a start, do not try to discuss the whole problem of the pressure of majority opinion and its effect on character. You will know enough instances that support or do not support Tocqueville in some particular regard so that you can write a concrete discussion. Limit yourself to what you can treat concretely, convincingly, and fairly fully. If a short paper is desired, you might write under the assumption that your reader has read the selection in question.

An exercise in connection with the selection from Milton might be this: Assume for your reader an intelligent person with little experience in reading anything but contemporary writing. Write an account of our selection for him. It will not be a summary quite, but rather a reduced and selected restatement. Use some quotation, but fit it carefully into your context so that it will make no difficulty for your reader. Or you might prepare an account of the selection for oral presentation. Then you might think of your account as your contribution to a panel discussion of the freedom of the press—a sort of argument by authority.

Most students can find many subjects for argument papers. Of course you need more than just an opinion to support; you need information, and probably the best subject is the one you know most about. But you will have to consider scope. If you try to write a short paper on some complex question, you will have room for only unsupported assertion—which may have no more effect than merely to irritate your reader. If you take a big subject, you will need a fairly long paper for it. Now it may occur to you that editorials are often very short treatments of very big subjects. But the editorial writer is in a special position. Commonly the news columns of the day on which he writes, or of the day or two before, furnish concrete background for his argument.

We have spoken of tact in argument; remember about it when you write. Student arguments very commonly fail in effect for want of tact. Successful argument requires that you envisage your reader as one who probably holds opinions different from yours. You want to convince him, not to offend him. Make every concession to his opinions that you can afford to make; try to foresee his objections and to deal with them before they arise in his mind. Above all, be clear. There is much unnecessary controversy, controversy that arises from misunderstanding and not from real difference of opinion. You need not add to it. Do not be afraid to keep restating your contention, and be sure you get it well stated at or near the end.

If the considerations in " Some Problems in Reading Argument" interested you, you may wish to do a little investigation. A simple but interesting exercise is to collect a number of pseudo-statements from advertisements and write a report on the ad writers' technique of pseudo-statement. A more difficult exercise is to take a piece of argument from a publication in which you do not have complete confidence. Examine it carefully, and decide what in it you can accept, what you feel you ought to suspend judgment about, and—perhaps—what you must reject. If you take a piece on some question you know little about, the exercise will be difficult, but the more valuable.

XIII

Writing in Answer to Questions

Probably the student's immediate use for the instruction in this chapter will be in answering examination questions. Nevertheless, the chapter is not called "How to Write Better Examinations," because the principles of restatement and approach discussed here have a wider application than their use in examinations, and because technique alone will not accomplish a good examination. Yet, although technique will not substitute for knowledge, it does make possible an effective use of one's information. Many college freshmen have had little opportunity in high school to write essay examinations, and sometimes they feel that they are suddenly expected to possess a technique they have not practiced. This chapter may help you to a technique.

Every college teacher of any experience knows that, in examinations, his students often make a poor use of information they really possess, and that they do not recognize, even when the papers have been returned, just where their writing has gone wrong. Some general advice is therefore appropriate, and we shall have to start with it. We are dealing with what most students have had to learn by experience; whatever you can learn by precept is so much clear gain.

Here is a list of five ways students commonly fail to use their information, or fail to use it effectively. It is a list of five examination troubles that you can avoid. Some of our previous discussions apply to them.

1. A student may misread or only partially read the question—a frequent trouble. It may be the result of examination tension; if you are a victim of such tension, school yourself to pause before starting an answer and to be sure you have read and considered every word of the question. Watch particularly for the technical terms of the subject matter. But just as often the trouble is that a word or expression in the question calls up in the student's mind a number of associations with material he has just reviewed, and these associations prevent him from finishing his reading of the question, or distract him from the intention of the question. The student who "learns his notes" without thinking much about their meaning is particularly subject to this trouble.

2. A student may answer the question but include in what he writes material not asked for and only generally related to the question. This trou-

ble, too, may come from uncontrolled associations, associations that come up as the student writes. An amiable instructor may search out the answer amid the extraneous material, but he can hardly give full credit for it if the student has pretty well concealed the point he should make. Another unhappy result of this sort of over-writing is that it usually takes more time than is allowed for the question and hence steals time from subsequent answers.

3. A student may write so slowly that he cannot get down a reasonable amount of material in the time allowed. Here the student must distinguish between a slowness consequent from inadequate preparation and a native slowness in expression and organization. But the slow writer usually knows his weakness. He should make writing about the topics he expects to be examined on a part of his examination preparation. The practice will help him toward a ready expression.

4. A student may write so vaguely that the instructor can only guess what information he possesses. In particular, he may neglect to define; or he may over-generalize, and write with such lack of concrete instance or example that the instructor remains in doubt whether the student's generalizations have meaning for the student himself.

5. A student who writes easily enough, and who has enough information for a good answer, may yet write in so disorganized a fashion that his presentation is ineffective. Indeed, his lack of organization may prevent the student himself from seeing that he has omitted important matters that he really knows should be part of his answer.

Now in most of these troubles the kind of remedy may be obvious. But one needs more than just the knowledge of what should be done. One needs certain habits of mind. We can make a start at developing them.

Of course we cannot in this book simulate exactly the conditions of an examination, but we can do something about practice in the analysis of questions and the writing of answers to them. We shall use a set of four related selections such as might be part of a student's reading in courses in history, political science, history of public education, sociology, or American literature. There are two by John Adams, and two by Thomas Jefferson. (A careful preparation will serve you twice, because the four selections are used again in the next chapter, there as a basis for instruction in the course paper.) Since ordinarily in writing an examination, a student depends upon both his reading and lecture material, we have in this chapter a few paragraphs that simulate a classroom lecture on the selections. They follow the selections, because a sensible student reads his assignment before his instructor talks about it. Finally there are a number of different sorts of examination questions, with some discussion of the problems they offer, and opportunities for practice in answering them.

The exercise will be most helpful if you will study the selections exactly as you would if they were assigned material for one of the courses listed above, getting such control of them that you feel yourself able to write on them without looking back at the text. Your instructor may wish to have you answer some of the questions in the classroom under examination conditions; and that exercise will be especially valuable if it gives you an opportunity to compare several papers and to decide which of them are the more effective, and why. Of course the principles involved in writing good examination answers are just the principles we have been using all along. Now we merely apply them to a particular academic task.

In the paragraph below, the selections are introduced by the sort of comment an instructor might make in assigning them. And the footnotes to the selections are such comments as he might make on the text.

i   THE READINGS

John Adams and Thomas Jefferson were contemporaries, political opponents, and, at least in the latter portion of their lives, good friends who discussed in an interesting series of letters their opinions on political and other matters. We are starting with two passages from Adams's *Defence of the Constitutions* because they make clear the central assumptions in his political thinking. Then we have a letter from Jefferson to Adams in which he develops his theory of natural aristocracy and describes an interesting plan of education. Jefferson's letter is followed by Adams's reply; the two make as significant a pair of letters as you are likely ever to find. Our last selection is from Jefferson's *Notes on Virginia*. It goes over some of the material in Jefferson's letter to Adams, but gives us a more detailed account of the way his plan was to work.

FROM

A Defence of the Constitutions of Government of the United States of America (1787)

JOHN ADAMS

[i]

1 We have all along contended, that the predominant passion of all men in power, whether kings, nobles, or plebeians, is the same; that tyranny will be the effect, whoever are the governors, whether the one, the few, or the many, if uncontrolled by equal laws, made by common consent, and supported, protected, and enforced by three different orders of men *in equilibrio*.[1] In Florence, where the administration was, by turns, in the nobles, the grandees, the commons, the plebeians, the mob, the ruling passion of each was the same; and the government of each immediately degenerated into a tyranny so insupportable as to produce a fresh revolution. We have all along contended, that a simple government, in a single assembly, whether aristocratical or democratical, must of necessity divide into two parties, each of which will be headed by some one illustrious

[1 This inclusive sentence is at the very center of Adams's thinking, and the argument from experience which follows is also most characteristic of him.]

family, and will proceed from debate and controversy to sedition and war. In Florence, the first dissension was among the nobility; the second between the nobles and commons; and the third between the commons and plebeians. In each of which contests, as soon as one party got uppermost, it split in two; and executions, confiscations, banishments, assassinations, and dispersions of families, were the fruit of every division, even with more atrocious aggravations than in those of Greece. Having no third order to appeal to for decision, no contest could be decided but by the sword.

[ii]

[Adams has cited Jonathan Swift and quoted Lord Bolingbroke's *Idea of a Patriot King* to the effect that there will always be, in any society, a small group of gifted and aggressive persons who, when they take part in public affairs, will inevitably dominate them, for good or for ill. Adams goes on:]

1 If there is, then, in society such a natural aristocracy as these great writers pretend, and as all history and experience demonstrate, formed partly by genius, partly by birth, and partly by riches, how shall the legislator avail himself of their influence for the equal benefit of the public? and how, on the other hand, shall he prevent them from disturbing the public happiness? I answer, by arranging them all, or at least the most conspicuous of them, together in one assembly, by the name of a senate; by separating them from all pretensions to the executive power, and by controlling in the legislative their ambition and avarice, by an assembly of representatives on one side, and by the executive authority on the other. Thus you will have the benefit of their wisdom, without fear of their passions. If among them there are some of Lord Bolingbroke's guardian angels, there will be some of his instruments of Divine vengeance too. The latter will be here restrained by a threefold tie,—by the executive power, by the representative assembly, and by their peers in the senate. But if these were all admitted into a single popular assembly, the worst of them might in time obtain the ascendancy of all the rest. In such a single assembly, as has been observed before, almost the whole of this aristocracy will make its appearance, being returned members of it by the election of the people. These will be one class. There will be another set of members, of middling rank and circumstances, who will justly value themselves upon their independence, their integrity, and unbiased affection to their country, and will pique themselves upon being under no obligation. But there will be a third class, every one of whom will have his leader among the members of the first class, whose character he will celebrate, and whose voice he will follow; and this party, after a course of time, will be the most numerous. The question then will be, whether this aristocracy in the house will unite or divide? and it is too obvious, that destruction to freedom must be the consequence equally of their union or of their division. If they unite generally in all things, as much as they certainly will in respecting each other's wealth, birth, and parts, and conduct themselves with prudence, they will strengthen themselves by insensible degrees, by playing into each other's hands more wealth and popularity, until they become able to govern elec-

tions as they please, and rule the people at discretion. An independent member will be their aversion; all their artifices will be employed to destroy his popularity among his constituents, and bring in a disciple of their own in his place.

11 But if they divide, each party will, in course of time, have the whole house, and consequently the whole state, divided into two factions, which will struggle in words, in writing, and at last in arms, until Caesar or Pompey must be emperor, and entail an endless line of tyrants on the nation. But long before this catastrophe, and indeed through every scene of the drama, the laws, instead of being permanent, and affording constant protection to the lives, liberties, and properties of the citizens, will be alternately the sport of contending factions, and the mere vibrations of a pendulum. From the beginning to the end it will be a government of men, now of one set, and then of another; but never a government of laws.

FROM *Letter to John Adams* (October 28, 1813)

THOMAS JEFFERSON

1 . . . I agree with you that there is a natural aristocracy among men. The grounds of this are virtue and talents. Formerly, bodily powers gave place among the aristoi. But since the invention of gunpowder has armed the weak as well as the strong with missile death, bodily strength, like beauty, good humor, politeness and other accomplishments, has become but an auxiliary ground for distinction. There is also an artificial aristocracy, founded on wealth and birth, without either virtue or talents; for with these it would belong to the first class. The natural aristocracy I consider as the most precious gift of nature, for the instruction, the trusts, and government of society. And indeed, it would have been inconsistent in creation to have formed man for the social state, and not to have provided virtue and wisdom enough to manage the concerns of the society. May we not even say, that that form of government is the best, which provides the most effectually for a pure selection of these natural aristoi into the offices of government? The artificial aristocracy is a mischievous ingredient in government, and provision should be made to prevent its ascendancy. On the question, what is the best provision, you and I differ; but we differ as rational friends, using the free exercise of our reason, and mutually indulging its errors. You think it best to put the pseudo-aristoi into a separate chamber of legislation, where they may be hindered from doing mischief by their co-ordinate branches, and where, also, they may be a protection to wealth against the agrarian and plundering enterprises of the majority of the people. I think that to give them power in order to prevent them from doing mischief is arming them for it, and increasing instead of remedying the evil. For if the co-ordinate branches can arrest their action, so may they that of the co-ordinates. Mischief may be done negatively as well as positively. Of this, a cabal in the Senate of the United States has furnished many proofs. Nor do I believe them necessary to protect the wealthy; be-

cause enough of these will find their way into every branch of the legislature to protect themselves. From fifteen to twenty legislatures of our own, in action for thirty years past, have proved that no fears of an equalization of property are to be apprehended from them. I think the best remedy is exactly that provided by all our constitutions, to leave to the citizens the free election and separation of the aristoi from the pseudo-aristoi, of the wheat from the chaff. In general they will elect the really good and wise. In some instances, wealth may corrupt, and birth blind them; but not in sufficient degree to endanger the society.

11 It is probable that our difference of opinion may, in some measure, be produced by a difference of character in those among whom we live. From what I have seen of Massachusetts and Connecticut myself, and still more from what I have heard, and the character given of the former by yourself, who know them so much better, there seems to be in those States a traditionary reverence for certain families, which has rendered the offices of the government nearly hereditary in those families. I presume that from an early period of your history, members of those families happening to possess virtue and talents have honestly exercised them for the good of the people, and by their services have endeared their names to them. In coupling Connecticut with you, I mean it politically only, not morally. For having made the Bible the common law of their land, they seem to have modeled their morality on the story of Jacob and Laban.[1] But although this hereditary succession to office with you may, in some degree, be founded in real family merit, yet in a much higher degree it has proceeded from your strict alliance of Church and State.[2] These families are canonised in the eyes of the people on common principles, 'you tickle me, and I will tickle you.' In Virginia we have nothing of this. Our clergy, before the revolution, having been secured against rivalship by fixed salaries, did not give themselves the trouble of acquiring influence over the people. Of wealth, there were great accumulations in particular families, handed down from generation to generation, under the English law of entails. But the only object of ambition for the wealthy was a seat in the King's Council. All their court was paid to the crown and its creatures; and they Philipised[3] in all collisions between the King and the people. Hence they were unpopular; and that unpopularity continues attached to their names. A Randolph, a Carter, or a Burwell must have great personal superiority over a common competitor to be elected by the people even at this day. At the first session of our legislature after the Declaration of Independence, we passed a law abolishing entails. And this was followed by one abolishing the privilege of

[1 Laban, Jacob's father-in-law, exploited Jacob, but Jacob at length outwitted him (Genesis 29–31). Jefferson is saying that the people of Connecticut have patterned their morality on an Old Testament story in which neither of the main characters seems very admirable.]
[2 Jefferson refers to a hold-over of the close relationship between church and state in Massachusetts and Connecticut established at their founding as colonies.]
[3 An allusion to Athenian history. Jefferson means that in all disputes between the British government and the Virginia colony, the wealthy supported the British government. Randolph, Carter, and Burwell are example names of old and wealthy Virginia families.]

primogeniture, and dividing the lands of intestates equally among all their children, or other representatives. These laws, drawn by myself, laid the axe to the root of pseudo-aristocracy. And had another which I prepared been adopted by the legislature, our work would have been complete. It was a bill for the more general diffusion of learning. This proposed to divide every county into wards of five or six miles square, like your townships; to establish in each ward a free school for reading, writing and common arithmetic; to provide for the annual selection of the best subjects from these schools, who might receive, at the public expense, a higher degree of education at a district school; and from these district schools to select a certain number of the most promising subjects, to be completed at an University, where all the most useful sciences should be taught. Worth and genius would thus have been sought out from every condition of life, and completely prepared by education for defeating the competition of wealth and birth for public trusts. My proposition had, for a further object, to impart to these wards those portions of self-government for which they are best qualified, by confiding to them the care of their poor, their roads, police, elections, the nomination of jurors, administration of justice in small cases, elementary exercises of militia; in short to have made them little republics, with a warden at the head of each, for all those concerns which, being under their eye, they would better manage than the larger republics of the county or State. A general call of ward meetings by their wardens on the same day through the State would at any time produce the genuine sense of the people on any required point, and would enable the State to act in mass, as your people have so often done, and with so much effect, by their town meetings. The law for religious freedom,[1] which made a part of this system, having put down the aristocracy of the clergy, and restored to the citizen the freedom of the mind, and those of entails and descents nurturing an equality of condition among them, this on education would have raised the mass of the people to the high ground of moral respectability necessary to their own safety, and to orderly government; and would have completed the great object of qualifying them to select the veritable aristoi, for the trusts of government, to the exclusion of the pseudalists; and the same Theognis who has furnished the epigraphs of your two letters, assures us that ["Good men, Cyrnus, have never ruined a state"]. Although this law has not yet been acted on but in a small and inefficient degree, it is still considered as before the legislature, with other bills of the revised code, not yet taken up, and I have great hope that some patriotic spirit will, at a favorable moment, call it up, and make it the key-stone of the arch of our government.

III With respect to aristocracy, we should further consider, that before the establishment of the American States, nothing was known to history but the man of the old world, crowded within limits either small or overcharged, and steeped in the vices which that situation generates. A govern-

[1 In colonial Virginia the Anglican Church was the established church, supported by all taxpayers. Jefferson refers to a law abolishing this relationship.]

ment adapted to such men would be one thing; but a very different one, that for the man of these States. Here every one may have land to labor for himself, if he chooses; or, preferring the exercise of any other industry, may exact for it such compensation as not only to afford a comfortable subsistence, but wherewith to provide for a cessation from labor in old age. Every one, by his property, or by his satisfactory situation, is interested in the support of law and order. And such men may safely and advantageously reserve to themselves a wholesome control over their public affairs, and a degree of freedom, which, in the hands of the *canaille* of the cities of Europe, would be instantly perverted to the demolition and destruction of everything public and private. The history of the last twenty-five years of France, and of the last forty years in America, nay of its last two hundred years, proves the truth of both parts of this observation.

IV But even in Europe a change has sensibly taken place in the mind of man. Science has liberated the ideas of those who read and reflect, and the American example has kindled feelings of right in the people. An insurrection has consequently begun, of science, talents, and courage, against rank and birth, which have fallen into contempt. It has failed in its first effort, because the mobs of the cities, the instrument used for its accomplishment, debased by ignorance, poverty, and vice, could not be restrained to rational action. But the world will recover from the panic of this first catastrophe. Science is progressive, and talents and enterprise on the alert. Resort may be had to the people of the country, a more governable power from their principles and subordination; and rank, and birth, and tinsel-aristocracy will finally shrink into insignificance, even there.[1] This, however, we have no right to meddle with. It suffices for us, if the moral and physical condition of our own citizens qualifies them to select the able and good for the direction of their government, with a recurrence of elections at such short periods as will enable them to displace an unfaithful servant, before the mischief he meditates may be irremediable.

V I have thus stated my opinion on a point on which we differ, not with a view to controversy, for we are both too old to change opinions which are the result of a long life of inquiry and reflection; but on the suggestions of a former letter of yours, that we ought not to die before we have explained ourselves to each other. We acted in perfect harmony, through a long and perilous contest for our liberty and independence. A Constitution has been acquired, which, though neither of us thinks perfect, yet both consider as competent to render our fellow citizens the happiest and the securest on whom the sun has ever shone. If we do not think exactly alike as to its imperfections, it matters little to our country, which, after devoting to it long lives of disinterested labor, we have delivered over to our successors in life, who will be able to take care of it and of themselves.

[1 Jefferson is of course referring to the French Revolution. He is saying that, although the Revolution seemed to end in futile violence and excess, the general change in thinking of which it was a part will inevitably move forward and ultimately succeed.]

FROM *Letter to Thomas Jefferson* (November 15, 1813)

JOHN ADAMS

1 We are now explicitly agreed upon one important point, viz., that there is a natural aristocracy among men, the grounds of which are virtue and talents. You very justly indulge a little merriment upon this solemn subject of aristocracy. I often laugh at it too, for there is nothing in this world more ridiculous than the management of it by all the nations of the earth; but while we smile, mankind have reason to say to us, as the frogs said to boys, what is sport to you are wounds and death to us. When I consider the weakness, the folly, the pride, the vanity, the selfishness, the artifice, the low craft and mean cunning, the want of principle, the avarice, the unbounded ambition, the unfeeling cruelty of a majority of those (in all nations) who are allowed an aristocratical influence, and, on the other hand, the stupidity with which the more numerous multitude not only become their dupes, but even love to be taken in by their tricks, I feel a stronger disposition to weep at their destiny, than to laugh at their folly. But though we have agreed in one point, in words, it is not yet certain that we are perfectly agreed in sense. Fashion has introduced an indeterminate use of the word talents. Education, wealth, strength, beauty, stature, birth, marriage, graceful attitudes and motions, gait, air, complexion, physiognomy, are talents, as well as genius, science, and learning. Any one of these talents that in fact commands or influences two votes in society gives to the man who possesses it the character of an aristocrat, in my sense of the word. Pick up the first hundred men you meet, and make a republic. Every man will have an equal vote; but when deliberations and discussions are opened, it will be found that twenty-five, by their talents, virtues being equal, will be able to carry fifty votes. Every one of these twenty-five is an aristocrat in my sense of the word, whether he obtains his one vote in addition to his own by his birth, fortune, figure, eloquence, science, learning, craft, cunning, or even his character for good fellowship, and a *bon vivant*. . . .

11 Your distinction between natural and artificial aristocracy does not appear to me founded. Birth and wealth are conferred upon some men as imperiously by nature as genius, strength, or beauty. The heir to honors, and riches, and power, has often no more merit in procuring these advantages than he has in obtaining a handsome face or an elegant figure. When aristocracies are established by human laws, and honor, wealth, and power are made hereditary by municipal laws and political institutions, then I acknowledge artificial aristocracy to commence; but this never commences till corruption in elections become dominant and uncontrollable. But this artificial aristocracy can never last. The everlasting envies, jealousies, rivalries, and quarrels among them; their cruel rapacity upon the poor ignorant people, their followers, compel them to set up Caesar, a demagogue, to be a

monarch, a master; *pour mettre chacun à sa place*.[1] Here you have the origin of all artificial aristocracy, which is the origin of all monarchies. And both artificial aristocracy and monarchy, and civil, military, political, and hierarchical despotism have all grown out of the natural aristocracy of virtues and talents. We, to be sure, are far remote from this. Many hundred years must roll away before we shall be corrupted. Our pure, virtuous, public-spirited, federative republic will last forever, govern the globe, and introduce the perfection of man; his perfectibility being already proved by Price, Priestley, Condorcet, Rousseau, Diderot, and Godwin.[2] Mischief has been done by the Senate of the United States. I have known and felt more of this mischief than Washington, Jefferson, and Madison, all together. But this has been all caused by the constitutional power of the Senate, in executive business, which ought to be immediately, totally, and essentially abolished. Your distinction between the [aristoi] and [pseudo-aristoi] will not help the matter. I would trust one as well as the other with unlimited power. The law wisely refuses an oath as a witness in his own case, to the saint as well as the sinner. . . .

III You suppose a difference of opinion between you and me on the subject of aristocracy. I can find none. I dislike and detest hereditary honors, offices, emoluments, established by law. So do you. I am for excluding legal, hereditary distinctions from the United States as long as possible. So are you. I only say that mankind have not yet discovered any remedy against irresistible corruption in elections to offices of great power and profit, but making them hereditary.

FROM *Notes on the State of Virginia* (1784)

THOMAS JEFFERSON

I Another object of the revisal[3] is to diffuse knowledge more generally through the mass of the people. This bill proposes to lay off every county into small districts of five or six miles square, called hundreds, and in each of them to establish a school for teaching reading, writing, and arithmetic; the tutor to be supported by the hundred, and every person in it entitled to

[1 The French expression means "to put everyone in his place."]
[2 In the three sentences beginning "We, to be sure . . ." and ending with the list of names, Adams is writing with a heavy sarcasm. The three English thinkers (Price, Priestley, and Godwin) and the three French thinkers (Condorcet, Rousseau, and Diderot) were part of the movement of mind that Jefferson refers to in IV of our selection from his letter to Adams. Adams probably believes Jefferson too close to their opinions. The belief in perfectibility typically arose from the conviction that man was not by nature bad, and that by the use of his reason he would ultimately make a good society. The six thinkers are not, however, so nearly identical in their views as the passage implies.]
[3 "The revisal" is a proposed revisal of Virginia law. Jefferson's *Notes on Virginia* is a collection of information about Virginia written in answer to questions from the secretary of the French legation in Philadelphia, and first published in France. Jefferson wrote the book in 1781–2, more than thirty years before his letter to Adams. You have seen that in 1813 he had by no means given up his plan.]

send their children three years gratis, and as much longer as they please, paying for it; these schools to be under a visitor who is annually to choose the boy of best genius in the school, of those whose parents are too poor to give them further education, and to send him forward to one of the grammar schools, of which twenty are proposed to be erected in different parts of the country, for teaching Greek, Latin, geography, and the higher branches of numerical arithmetic. Of the boys thus sent in any one year, trial is to be made at the grammar schools one or two years, and the best genius of the whole selected, and continued six years, and the residue dismissed. By this means twenty of the best geniuses will be raked from the rubbish annually, and be instructed, at the public expense, so far as the grammar schools go. At the end of six years' instruction, one half are to be discontinued (from among whom the grammar schools will probably be supplied with future masters); and the other half, who are to be chosen for the superiority of their parts and disposition, are to be sent and continued three years in the study of such sciences as they shall choose, at William and Mary College, the plan of which is proposed to be enlarged, as will be hereafter explained, and extended to all the useful sciences. The ultimate result of the whole scheme of education would be the teaching all the children of the state reading, writing, and common arithmetic; turning out ten annually, of superior genius, well taught in Greek, Latin, geography, and the higher branches of arithmetic; turning out ten others annually, of still superior parts, who to those branches of learning shall have added such of the sciences as their genius shall have led them to; the furnishing to the wealthier part of the people convenient schools at which their children may be educated at their own expense. The general objects of this law are to provide an education adapted to the years, to the capacity, and the condition of everyone, and directed to their freedom and happiness. . . . By that part of our plan which prescribes the selection of the youths of genius from among the classes of the poor, we hope to avail the state of those talents which nature has sown as liberally among the poor as the rich, but which perish without use, if not sought for and cultivated. But of all the views of this law none is more important, none more legitimate, than that of rendering the people the safe, as they are the ultimate, guardians of their own liberty. For this purpose the reading in the first stage, where *they* will receive their whole education, is proposed, as has been said, to be chiefly historical. History, by apprising them of the past, will enable them to judge of the future; it will avail them of the experience of other times and other nations; it will qualify them as judges of the actions and designs of men; it will enable them to know ambition under every disguise it may assume; and, knowing it, to defeat its views. In every government on earth is some trace of human weakness, some germ of corruption and degeneracy, which cunning will discover, and wickedness insensibly open, cultivate, and improve. Every government degenerates when trusted to the rulers of the people alone. The people themselves therefore are its only safe depositories. And, to render even them safe, their minds must be improved to a certain degree. This indeed is not all that is necessary, though it be essentially necessary. An amendment of our constitution must here come in aid of the public education. The influence over government must be shared among all the people. If every individual which composes their mass participates of the ultimate authority, the government will be safe; because the corrupting the whole mass will exceed any private resources of wealth; and public ones cannot be provided but by levies on the people. In this case every man would have to pay his own price. The government of Great Britain has been corrupted, because but one man in ten has a right to vote for members of Parliament. The sellers of the government, therefore, get nine tenths of their price clear. It has been thought that corruption is restrained by confining the right of suffrage to a few of the wealthier of the people; but it would be more effectually restrained by an extension of that right to such members as would bid defiance to the means of corruption.

11 Lastly, it is proposed, by a bill in this revisal, to begin a public library and gallery, by laying out a certain sum annually in books, paintings, and statues.

A CLASSROOM LECTURE   *ii*

Now we come to Adams and Jefferson on the idea of natural aristocracy. We shall remark on Adams's thought first. All Adams's political thinking was based upon his conviction that men are by nature not to be trusted with power, that their inherent selfishness will lead them usually to misuse whatever power they have. He would have vigorously applauded Lord Acton's maxim: "Power tends to corrupt, and absolute power corrupts absolutely." He was much concerned, therefore, with ways by which to guard against the concentration of power in persons or in groups. He desired a government in which there should be a balance of power, in which one interest might restrain another. For instance, Adams believed that, in the federal government, the directly elected House of Representatives should express with some immediacy the will of the great body of people. But he insisted that it ought to restrain, and to be restrained by, the Senate, which in his theory was the body by which the aristocracy were to be represented. (You will remember that, until the adoption of the seventeenth amendment to the Constitution in 1913, senators were elected by state legislatures.) Our first selection makes clear a central principle in Adams's thinking and then applies the principle to explaining the ills of a unicameral, that is, a one-house, legislature.

Jefferson's view of human nature was not completely opposed to Adams's. Certainly Jefferson believed that no group of men is good enough to be trusted with unrestrained power. His fear of centralized power in federal government is based on his recognition of the corrupting effect of power. If he was not much concerned with stability in government, he did wish to keep all the sovereignty possible in the hands of local governments, so that no group could acquire overwhelming power. Yet Jefferson had a far greater trust in the ordinary man's wisdom and ability to protect his own liberties than Adams had. (His suspicion of men in cities was his one great reservation.) Adams, indeed, believed that the people could never protect their own liberties, that their liberties would be preserved only under a government of law, and by constitutions not easily changed.

You can see, therefore, that when Jefferson wrote to Adams that in general the people "will elect the really good and wise," he was expressing a kind of confidence that Adams could not share. Adams believed that some aggressive aristocracy would always get power, and always need to be restrained. Jefferson's answer to this position comes in the first part of his letter to Adams; it takes the form of a distinction between an "artificial aristocracy, founded on wealth and birth," and a "natural aristocracy," the grounds of which are "virtue and talents."

Instead of the control of a vicious aristocracy by a balanced government, as Adams recommended, Jefferson had quite another program. With a part of this program he had already succeeded. He had got through the Virginia legislature bills abolishing certain laws which held together the estates of the great landed proprietors. These were laws concerning entail and primogeniture—surely you looked up these terms when you came to them in Jefferson's letter. He believed that he had, by this legislation, prevented a landed aristocracy from perpetuating itself for generation after generation. But that, after all, was only a negative measure. The more important part of his plan was not made into law. It was the establishment of a system of state-supported education designed to select and develop a natural aristocracy. This plan is not only the result of his theory of a natural aristocracy. It is the way in which he believed the natural aristocrats might be discovered and made a functioning group in the state.

But, as his reply shows, Adams remained unconvinced. He was no more in favor of hereditary aristocracy than Jefferson was. Yet his view of human nature, at once sober, realistic, and sceptical of theory, kept him from admitting the validity of Jefferson's distinction between two sorts of aristocracy. He saw that Jefferson's plan put into operation would result in two groups of aristocrats. He would, he said, as soon trust the one as the other with unchecked power. Adams's reply to Jefferson is so consistent with his general thought that a reader who had read our selections from Adams's *Defence of the Constitutions* and Jefferson's letter to Adams could easily predict the general argument of Adams's reply.

The selection from Jefferson's *Notes on Virginia* extends the thinking of his letter to Adams in two principal ways. In the first place, as we have said, it details the plan of rigorous selection which is vital to what Jefferson wanted to accomplish. From it we learn how really different Jefferson's proposal was from modern theories of public education. In the second place, it makes clear, as the letter to Adams does not, how important in his thinking was the elementary education that all the children of Virginia were to have. He believed that a democracy to succeed must have an informed electorate. Jefferson's thinking on education has greatly influenced educational thought in the United States. But you will realize, if you understand Jefferson's plan, that not all the persons who talk of "education for democracy" are Jeffersonians.

SAMPLE QUESTIONS AND DISCUSSION

Here we have a number of sample examination questions and discussion of the problems in answering them. Some of these questions are better than others; the intent is to sample the sort of questions with which a student may have to cope.

1. These two definition questions need no special discussion, since the ordinary principles of definition apply:

    A. Define "entail" and "primogeniture."

    B. Define "natural aristocracy" in the sense in which Adams uses the term, and then in the sense in which Jefferson uses the term.

2. These questions may be handled by summary restatement:

    A. How would Jefferson's Virginia Plan for education have accomplished a selection of capable students to be educated for the good of the state?

    B. What will inevitably happen, according to Adams, in a unicameral legislature?

In A the student will have to decide how detailed an account he is capable of giving. If he cannot remember the numbers of students to be selected, he can at least make the principle of selection clear—and that is the most important matter.

3. These questions are designed for brief answers, but they require the discrimination of essential points in Jefferson's thinking:

    A. What are the primary reasons, according to Jefferson, for his system of state-supported education?

    B. What are the two vital connections between Jefferson's plan for public education and good government? In other words, why does Jefferson believe public support for education necessary to the successful functioning of a democratic state?

The questions require about the same answer. A is probably the better test of a student's knowledge; B is a leading question, intended to give a student a start on his answer by indicating the number of connections he is expected to find. It states and restates the question in an effort to make it clear.

4. These questions are related in much the same way that the two questions in 3 are related:

    A. What did Adams consider the primary function of a senate?

    B. Jefferson wrote in a letter to Adams: "You think it best to put the pseudo-aristoi into a separate chamber of legislation, where they may be hindered from doing mischief. . . ." Explain the political theory to which Jefferson refers, making clear why Adams believes the aristocracy will be prevented from doing mischief by their representation in a separate chamber.

For immature students, B is better than A, since it indicates the extent of the treatment expected, and since it is a leading question. Question A might conceivably be answered: "Adams considered the primary function of a senate that of representing the aristocracy"; and if very little time were allowed for its answer, that might be the answer expected. But if, say, ten or fifteen minutes were allowed for it, one would take it for granted that he ought to discuss the relationships between the senate and the house. The intention of the question might well have been clearer—but you may encounter questions no better than this.

5. Here is a single question on Adams:

A. How was Adams's theory of mixed government connected with his conviction about the nature of man?

Although "mixed government" is a term Adams used, it has not appeared in this chapter, and you will have to infer its meaning. Since Adams's conviction about the nature of man is the premise, you would do well to establish that first.

We turn now to questions that offer certain problems in organization. An examination is not a place for an elaborate or a subtle organization; it is a place for a clear, definite organization. You will do best to think first just what points you wish to make in answer to a question—and then to consider the best order in which to make them. Perhaps it will be well to jot down the points on the margin of your bluebook. When you have made your decisions, construct a signpost sentence which makes clear what matters you will discuss *and* the order in which you will discuss them.

6. This is a comparative question of an ordinary sort:

A. Compare the methods by which Adams and Jefferson would restrain the ambitions of the rich and the well-born as they affect the welfare of the state.

Now in any short and simple comparison, one has a choice of two structures. He may give a part of his discussion to one element in the comparison, and a second part to the other: in this instance, a part to the method Adams proposes and a part to the method Jefferson proposes. Or he may in a continuous discussion make his comparison point by point.

7. Here is a question that asks for a rather complex comparison:

A. Compare Jefferson's plan for public education with public education in the United States today as you know it.

The student is asked to compare a plan with a system in general practice. He will have to make allowances for the differences in two periods. And he will have to decide what principles are implicit in present-day educational practice, for it is only in principles that the comparison asked for is possible. Then he will have to decide upon his structure. Although he might use successfully either of the two structures suggested above, let us suppose he designs one especially for this complex comparison. He decides to give one paragraph to the differences between Jefferson's educational thinking and the dominant principles of public education today, and to give one paragraph to the likenesses between them. His signpost sentence for the first paragraph (coming after an introductory sentence or two) might be this: "Jefferson's plan differs in principle in two ways: 1. in that it is highly selective, and 2. in that it is designed, not for the good of individuals, but for the good of the state." The student might begin his second paragraph with some such sentence as this: "Jefferson's plan and the theory of modern public education have in common. . . ."

8. An instructor may write a comparative question in which one half of the comparison is taken care of by a statement in the question. Here is an example:

> A. Jefferson says: "Every government degenerates when trusted to the rulers of the people alone. The people themselves therefore are its only safe depositories. And, to render even them safe, their minds must be improved to a certain degree." How far, judging from our selections from Adams, would Adams agree?

In answering this question, a student might think of the quotation as a first paragraph in a comparative discussion, and in what he writes give Adams's opinion on Jefferson's contentions, point by point. The question is difficult in that it requires some inference.

9. Sometimes examination questions require the application of one body of knowledge to another, or require the student to think out the probable effect of principles in practice. The student should remember that such questions are designed not merely to elicit his opinions, but to give him an opportunity to show that he has information, can use it, and can understand its purport. Here are examples:

> A. Sociologists recognize three classes, lower, middle, and upper, and divisions thereof. How would Jefferson's efforts to revise Virginia law, assuming them all successful, affect class structure?
>
> B. In practice, would Jefferson's "natural aristocracy" be less ambitious for power and thus less a danger to the state than any other sort of aristocracy? How far do you agree with Adams on this matter?
>
> C. How far does the thinking in Jefferson's Virginia Plan for education apply to the present-day discussion of federal aid for education?

The signpost sentence for an answer to any one of the above would probably be a contention; for instance, an answer to C might have the signpost sentence: "Although Jefferson was an opponent of the extension of federal power in general, much of what he says about the importance of education to the state might be used in recommending federal aid to education."

XIV

Restatement in College Papers

I n the writing for most of your college courses, you will be dealing with printed source material for carefully designated purposes. And in the writing one does after college, one often needs to use source material economically and effectively. The technique has to be learned. A part of it we have considered in the section on formal summary. And doubtless your practice writing has given you experience. But we are now ready to deal with the restatement of printed material in special sorts of contexts.

i INFORMAL SUMMARY

When we write a formal summary, we try to make the most complete cut-down statement we can, and to keep the summary in exact proportion to the original passage. Of course such a summary may have a place in a larger piece of writing. But whether it stands alone or functions as a part of a larger purpose, a formal summary is, by definition, a piece of writing that stands completely for an original passage and conveys to a reader the whole pattern of thought of that passage.

We shall use the term "informal summary" to designate a no less careful kind of writing, but one in which the technique of formal summary is modified to accomplish particular purposes. Informal summary is useful in academic writing, and in writing in general, when the writer's concern is with one or two aspects of the passage he is using. He will wish to give those aspects emphasis, but he will also need to give his readers some notion of the context of the whole. An informal summary, therefore, is likely to be descriptive of the whole passage, and to give special attention to a part or parts. It need not keep to the proportion of the original, and it may include interpretative comment. (Of course the writer will make clear that his comment *is* comment, not part of the original.)

We shall take as a first example an anecdote of Mark Twain's; you will see at once that a student might have any one of a number of kinds of interest in the passage and use for it in his writing.

FROM *Mark Twain's Autobiography* (1924)

MARK TWAIN

Notes on "Innocents Abroad"

I I will begin with a note upon the dedication. I wrote the book in the months of March and April, 1868, in San Francisco. It was published in August, 1869. Three years afterward Mr. Goodman of Virginia City, Nevada, on whose newspaper I had served ten years before and of whom I have had much to say in the book called *Roughing It*—I seem to be over-loading the sentence and I apologize—came East, and we were walking down Broadway one day when he said:

II "How did you come to steal Oliver Wendell Holmes's dedication and put it in your book?"

III I made a careless and inconsequential answer, for I supposed he was joking. But he assured me that he was in earnest. He said:

IV "I'm not discussing the question of whether you stole it or didn't—for that is a question that can be settled in the first bookstore we come to. I am only asking you *how* you came to steal it, for that is where my curiosity is focalized."

V I couldn't accommodate him with this information, as I hadn't it in stock. I could have made oath that I had not stolen anything, therefore my vanity was not hurt nor my spirit troubled. At bottom I supposed that he had mistaken another book for mine, and was now getting himself into an untenable place and preparing sorrow for himself and triumph for me. We entered a bookstore and he asked for *The Innocents Abroad* and for the dainty little blue-and-gold edition of Dr. Oliver Wendell Holmes's poems. He opened the books, exposed their dedications, and said:

VI "Read them. It is plain that the author of the second one stole the first one, isn't is?"

VII I was very much ashamed and unspeakably astonished. We continued our walk, but I was not able to throw any gleam of light upon that original question of his. I could not remember ever having seen Doctor Holmes's dedication. I knew the poems, but the dedication was new to me.

VIII I did not get hold of the key to that secret until months afterward; then it came in a curious way, and yet it was a natural way; for the natural way provided by nature and the construction of the human mind for the discovery of a forgotten event is to employ another forgotten event for its resurrection.

IX I received a letter from the Reverend Doctor Rising, who had been rector of the Episcopal church in Virginia City in my time, in which letter Doctor Rising made reference to certain things which had happened to us in the Sandwich Islands six years before; among other things he made casual mention of the Honolulu Hotel's poverty in the matter of literature. At first I did not see the bearing of the remark; it called nothing to my mind. But presently it did—with a flash! There was but one book in Mr. Kirchhof's hotel, and that was the first volume of Doctor Holmes's blue-and-gold series. I had had a fortnight's chance to get well acquainted with its contents, for I had ridden around the big island (Hawaii) on horseback and had brought back so many saddle boils that if there had been a duty on them it would have bankrupted me to pay it. They kept me in my room, unclothed and in persistent pain, for two weeks, with no company but cigars and the little volume of poems. Of course, I read them almost constantly; I read them from beginning to end, then began in the middle and read them both ways. In a word, I read the book to rags, and was infinitely grateful to the hand that wrote it.

x Here we have an exhibition of what repetition can do when persisted in daily and hourly over a considerable stretch of time, where one is merely reading for entertainment, without thought or intention of preserving in the memory that which is read. It is a process which in the course of years tries all the juice out of a familiar verse of Scripture, leaving nothing but a dry husk behind. In that case you at least know the origin of the husk, but in the case in point I apparently preserved the husk, but presently forgot whence it came. It lay lost in some dim corner of my memory a year or two, then came forward when I needed a dedication, and was promptly mistaken by me as a child of my own happy fancy.

xi I was new, I was ignorant, the mysteries of the human mind were a sealed book to me as yet, and I stupidly looked upon myself as a tough and unforgivable criminal. I wrote to Doctor Holmes and told him the whole disgraceful affair, implored him in impassioned language to believe that I never intended to commit this crime, and was unaware that I had committed it until I was confronted with the awful evidence. I have lost his answer. I could better have afforded to lose an uncle. Of these I had a surplus, many of them of no real value to me, but that letter was beyond price and unsparable. In it Doctor Holmes laughed the kindest and healingest laugh over the whole matter, and at considerable length and in happy phrase assured me that there was no crime in unconscious plagiarism; that I committed it every day, that he committed it every day, that every man alive on the earth who writes or speaks commits it every day, and not merely once or twice, but every time he opens his mouth; that all our phrasings are spiritualized shadows cast multitudinously from our readings: that no happy phrase of ours is ever quite original with us; there is nothing of our own in it except some slight change born of our temperament, character, environment, teachings, and associations; that this slight change differentiates it from another man's manner of saying it, stamps it with our special style, and makes it our own for the time being; all the rest of it being old, moldy, antique, and smelling of the breath of a thousand generations of them that have used it before!

XII In the thirty-odd years which have elapsed since then I have satisfied myself that what Doctor Holmes said was true.

————————

1) Twain's memory was always creative, and the detail here may not all be strictly accurate; the discussion of the working of the mind is convincing and instructive. Have you not yourself at some time discovered that an idea or expression was not so original as you had supposed it to be?

2) Now what are the possible uses of this passage? A student might be writing on Mark Twain himself: he might be interested in this anecdote as an illustration of Twain's personality, or of his skill in narration. Or he might be doing a study of Twain's experience in the Sandwich Islands (now called the Hawaiian Islands) and find that IX had some small usefulness. But the anecdote might also fit in a discussion of the whole question of literary indebtedness, of the relationship of literary works to their predecessors. Or it might fit quite as well into a paper on the psychology of memory. A student might write a paper on dedications in general — there are many interesting examples. He might be writing on Holmes, and find Twain's anecdote an interesting side light on Holmes's personality. In each of these papers, obviously, the passage should be treated in a fashion appropriate to the intention of the paper. And in none of them, probably, would there be space for a lengthy treatment.

3) We shall try examples of two informal summaries, assuming different kinds of interest in the anecdote. And the examples will also illustrate a technical matter: the way in which brief quotation may be combined with formal summary. You will find as a practical matter in writing that a little summary is often necessary in introducing a quotation, in order that it may have intelligible context.

4) Let us suppose a paper on literary indebtedness. Our anecdote might be handled in this fashion:

> An anecdote in Mark Twain's autobiography is a striking instance —perhaps an extreme instance—of literary indebtedness. Twain tells how a friend accused him of stealing the dedication of a volume of poems by Oliver Wendell Holmes and using it as the dedication for his own *Innocents Abroad*. Twain found that the accusation was true, but could not at first account for the theft. Then he was reminded by another friend of a fortnight he had spent, laid up with saddle boils, in a hotel in the Sandwich Islands, a fortnight in which he read and reread a volume of Holmes, the only reading matter the hotel offered. In chagrin Twain wrote to Holmes, but Holmes assured him that he had committed no crime. The letter from Holmes was lost, but Twain remembered him as saying most comforting things to the effect that "all our phrasings are spiritualized shadows cast multitudinously from our readings: that no happy phrase of ours is ever quite original with us."

5) Now we shall assume a quite different purpose for the informal summary. We are writing a paper called "The Genial Dr. Holmes." We

have been speaking of the qualities of his writing: the first sentence in the summary below is transitional.

> But Holmes's geniality and breadth of view may be illustrated by his relations with people quite as well as by his Breakfast Table series. Mark Twain tells us how, through a queer trick of memory, he reproduced the dedication of a volume of Holmes's poems as his own dedication for *Innocents Abroad*. When Twain discovered what he had done, he wrote to Holmes in abject apology, and Holmes consoled him in a letter the substance of which Twain remembered after some thirty years, a letter in which "Doctor Holmes laughed the kindest and healingest laugh over the whole matter." "I have lost his answer," Twain writes. "I could better have afforded to lose an uncle. Of these I had a surplus, many of them of no real value to me, but that letter was beyond price and unsparable."

The next selection is not an anecdote, but a miniature essay, a form in which E. B. White has a special skill. As you read it notice how Mr. White, starting personally and with a single concrete instance and never becoming impersonal nor abstract, yet manages to represent important social and political questions.

FROM *One Man's Meat* (1942)

E. B. WHITE

Lime

I Received my allotment of ground limestone from the government last month. They gave me three tons of it, and it cost me nothing save a nominal charge for trucking. I have already spread it on my upper field and harrowed it in. Thus the New Deal comes home to me in powdered form, and I gain a new alkalinity and acquire some fresh doubts and misgivings.

II I've been thinking a good bit about this lime, this handout; and it seems to me that it is the principal ingredient of the new form of government which Mr. Roosevelt is introducing, an ingredient which I must try hard to identify in order to clarify the stew on which I feed and on which the people of America (or Amarrica) are so sharply divided. By applying for and receiving this lime I have become a party to one of the so-called "social gains" which we heard so much about during the political campaign. I don't know whether I like it or not. The lime for my field was a gift to me from all the taxpayers of the United States, a grudging gift on the part of about half of them who disavow the principles of the AAA, a gift in the name of fertility, conservation, and humanity. In so far as it is to the advantage of the nation that the soil of America shall be maintained in all its chemical goodness, the dispensation from Mr. Roosevelt is justifiable. Most farmers need more fertilizer than they can afford to buy; when the government provides it free of charge the land improves. But this of course isn't the whole story.

III To be honest I must report that at the time I got the lime I experienced a slight feeling of resentment—a feeling not strong enough to prevent my applying for my share in the booty, but still a recognizable sensation. I seemed to have lost a little of my grip on life. I felt that something inside me, some intangible substance, was leaching away. I also detected a slight sense of being under obligation to somebody, and this, instead of arousing my gratitude, took the form of mild resentment—the characteristic attitude of a person who has had a favor done him whether he liked it or not. All I had to do was spread the lime on a five-acre piece, together with barn dressing; but the Federal government had a harder spreading job than that: the government had to spread the cost of it over the entire citizenry, over not only those who had reëlected Roosevelt but those who had despised him. So much Republican acidity for the lime to sweeten, it must have lost much of its strength before it reached my clay soil.

IV I don't know. It is something for every man to study over, with the help of his God and his conscience. I do begin to feel the friendly control over me and over my land which an Administration exerts in its eagerness to "adjust" me and to change the soil reaction of my upper field. I believe in this Administration, on the whole; in its vision and in its essential vigor. I even voted for it again. It has been called crackpot, but that doesn't disparage it for me. Genius is more often found in a cracked pot than in a whole one. In the main I prefer to be experimented on by an idealist than allowed to lie fallow through a long dry reactionary season. I believe in this Administration, but I am also trying to make out the implications in a load of limestone.

V I think it is an unusually important question, and I wish I could be as sure of it in my mind as the President is in his. (Query: does he ever get any free lime for his Hyde Park place?) The gift of fertilizer is an arbitrary benefit, bestowed by thinkers who agree that soil fertility is a national concern—a matter which touches *all* the people and, therefore, which may rightly be charged against all the people. That much is true, I think, even though there are millions of Americans who will never feel any direct gain from the increased alkalinity of my little bit of ground. But I believe it also is true that a government committed to the policy of improving the nation by improving the condition of *some* of the individuals will eventually run into trouble in attempting to distinguish between a national good and a chocolate sundae.

VI To take an extreme example: through indirect taxation my lime is paid for in part by thousands of young ladies many of whom are nursing a personal want comparable to my want of lime. We will say that they want a permanent wave, to bolster their spirits and improve the chemistry of their nature. Theirs is a real want, however frivolous. Hairdressing, like any other form of top dressing, is a vital need among many people, and the satisfaction of it, in a sense, may be termed a national good. It doesn't come first, as soil does, but it comes eventually at the end of a long line of reasoning or unreasoning. I think that one hazard of the "benefit" form of government is the likelihood that there will be an indefinite extension of benefits, each new one establishing an easy precedent for the next.

VII Another hazard is that by placing large numbers of people under obligation to their government there will develop a self-perpetuating party capable of supplying itself with a safe majority. I notice that a few days after my lime had come I received a letter from my county agent which started, "To Members of the H—— County Agricultural Conservation Association. Dear Member . . ." You see, already I was a paid-up Democrat, before ever the lime had begun to dissolve.

VIII Well, I'm not trying to take sides. I'm just a man who got a few bags of lime for nuthin', and whose cup runneth over, troubling his dreams.

------

1) Readers who confuse ponderousness with significance may not find this little essay important. But it does skillfully use a concrete instance to represent a problem, and it does clearly define that problem. Notice the way in which White's metaphors arise from the literal lime and the farm, and how they come to stand for the national "implications in a load of limestone."

2) The essay is doubtless quite clear in itself but, since you may be asked to make informal summaries of it for particular purposes, you may need a little more information than you have on the New Deal and agriculture. Look up, then, the Agricultural Adjustment Acts of 1933 and 1938, and the Soil Conservation and Domestic Allotment Act of 1936. A convenient place to do so is Richard B. Morris's *Encyclopedia of American History*.

3) Here are some titles that indicate subjects for papers in which informal summaries of this essay might be used:

A. E. B. White as Commentator on American Life
B. The Farmer in the Second Quarter of the Twentieth Century
C. American Life in the Forties
D. The New Deal and the American Farmer
E. The Role of the County Agent in Farm Affairs
F. The Force of Precedent in Politics
G. The Moral Results of Government Aid
H. The Proper Limits of Government

Now the ways in which the essay would be used in such papers would differ greatly, according to intention and subject matter. For instance, in A a rather full summary would be indicated; but in H a very brief informal summary would probably serve primarily as a context for a quotation the writer found to his purpose. Consider the other titles and decide how the essay might be used for the indicated purposes.

4) Let us assume a paper called "Contemporary Opinion of the AAA," and experiment with an informal summary of White's essay. For the intention this title indicates, the main purpose of the summary, obviously,

will be to provide context for quotation useful to that intention. Such a summary might be this:

> E. B. White's miniature essay, "Lime," is a shrewd comment on government benefits. Mr. White sees clearly enough that soil fertility is a national concern, "a matter which touches *all* the people and, therefore, which may rightly be charged against all the people." But he sees other "implications in a load of limestone." He sees that limits in the administration of government benefits are hard to fix; he believes that a government committed to a benefit policy will "eventually run into trouble in attempting to distinguish between a national good and a chocolate sundae." And he sees that as more and more persons are obligated to their government for benefits, the party in power may be able to develop itself as "a self-perpetuating party capable of supplying itself with a safe majority." White's feeling that he did not know whether or not he liked being a party to "social gains" which were a "grudging gift" on the part of about half the taxpayers must have been the feeling of many of the beneficiaries of the New Deal.

RESTATEMENT IN THE SOURCE PAPER   *ii*

The documented source paper in which the student investigates an assigned or chosen subject requires the restatement of material from a number of pieces of writing. The structure of the course paper as a whole is outside our scope, but the technique of restatement used in the course paper is very much within it. Since the course paper is a task that college students have in several courses throughout their college careers, students who learn as freshmen how to restate material from sources will find their skill useful when they become upperclassmen. For our illustration in the use of source material we shall assume a student writing a paper called "Adams and Jefferson on Natural Aristocracy"; we can therefore use material with which you are very familiar.

The instruction about informal summary above applies to our present concern. But there we were thinking of the use of source materials primarily as illustration or substantiation. In a formal documented paper long sections may be a reworking of source material—perhaps of many separate passages—into a new fabric designed to accomplish a defined and strictly limited purpose. The problem in such papers is to handle particular pieces of source material in a manner proportionate to their importance to the whole intention of the paper and to connect them clearly to that intention.

In writing a source paper, a student uses his source materials, mainly, in two ways. He will often quote directly, and indicate that he is doing so by quotation marks or, if the passage is long, by single-spacing it and setting it in from each margin. But even when he quotes, the student has the problem of making the quotation part of the pattern of his paper. More often he will be reducing his material by restating it, acknowledging his dependence upon his source by a footnote and, frequently, by using the writer's name in his own text.

Let us suppose that our student is writing the introductory part of his paper, and that he is, quite rightly, there concerned with some initial generalization about the development of Adams's political thought. He finds the following passage from V. L. Parrington's *The Colonial Mind* useful to his purpose:

During the revolutionary struggle he had been a member of the left wing; during the early struggles under the Constitution he was a member of the right wing. The young man had been a stalwart defender of human rights, the old man was a stalwart defender of property rights; and this shift of position was fatal to his reputation with the rising democratic party. The French Revolution marked the critical turning point in his intellectual development. As a politician he was well-nigh ruined by it; but as a political thinker he owed it much. Before that vast upheaval came to challenge his somewhat conventional mind, he was a hard-working lawyer-politician, with a liking for legalistic constitutional theory; but as the Revolution went forward, he was forced into uncompromising reaction.[1]

Our student does not have space enough to quote this passage in full, and he realizes that when he takes space for direct quotation it ordinarily should be quotation from his primary sources, the writings of Adams and Jefferson. He intends to use the passage, therefore, in summary restatement. He remembers and puts into practice a principle of summary: Make your own statement; do not patch together phrases from the original. He writes:

V. L. Parrington believes that the French Revolution was the turning point in the development of Adams's political views. He says that, although Adams had been considered a member of the left wing in his advocacy of the American Revolution, the French Revolution forced him to consider his political principles anew, and that he reached a position of "uncompromising reaction."

The student has rightly included Parrington's name in his restatement, since the passage makes a judgment (if the passage were merely recording undisputed fact, that would be unnecessary).

The purpose of our student's paper justifies this use of a secondary source; and sometimes direct quotation from a secondary source is justified. But the tendency of many students is to use so much secondary material that their papers seem to be written around instead of on subjects. A course paper has a defined and limited purpose that determines the material used and the extent of its treatment. The writer will probably quote more frequently from his primary sources than from his secondary sources, but even his primary sources he must deal with by restatement for the most part.

[1] Excerpted from *The Colonial Mind* by Vernon L. Parrington, copyright, 1927, by Harcourt, Brace and Company, Inc.; renewed, 1954, by Vernon L. Parrington, Jr., Louise P. Tucker, and Elizabeth P. Thomas. Reprinted by permission of the publishers.

We need to consider carefully, therefore, both economy and ethics in restatement. Now the sample restatement above seems in no way remarkable, does it? Yet a great many students never learn to reduce their source material properly, and wonder why their instructors think little of their course papers. The matter is so important that perhaps this time we need an illustration of what should *not* be done. Let us say we have another student working on the Parrington passage. He is rather too typical a student, and he produces a passage something like the following (which is not BURLESQUE, but which may be a little exaggerated):

During the revolution Adams had been a member of the left wing, but in the early struggles under the constitution he was a member of the right wing. The young man had been a stalwart defender of human rights; the old man was a stalwart defender of property rights. The French Revolution marked a turning point in his intellectual development, for although as a politician he was nearly ruined by it, he owed it much as a political thinker. Earlier he was a hardworking lawyer and politician who liked constitutional theory, but as the Revolution went forward, he was forced into uncompromising reaction.

Of course, the student writes a footnote acknowledging Parrington's book as his source.

What has this unfortunate fellow done? He has made an entirely improper use of his source, he has produced a queer hybrid sort of passage— neither quotation nor restatement, but a patchwork of both—and he has failed to attain any considerable reduction. When he came to his first work in the course paper, he forgot everything he had learned about summary. Had he used quotation marks around the parts of sentences lifted bodily from Parrington's text, he would have avoided the semi-plagiarism with which he is chargeable; his passage would have been honest, if ineffectual.

Now we return to our exemplary student. He learns as he goes along, and possibly he profits from instruction a little more rapidly than most students do. At any rate, by the time he has finished the introductory part of the paper he is proceeding in a workmanlike manner. We observe him next as he has come to the place in which he needs to define Jefferson's concept of "natural aristocracy." What he has learned about definition stands him in good stead now.

He decides, rightly, that at this crucial point he should quote Jefferson directly; but he realizes that he must weave the quotation skillfully into the fabric of the paper. And a little consideration shows him that his readers will need a distinction between "natural aristocracy" and "aristocracy" in the ordinary sense. He sees how he can make the distinction a starting point for the definition:

What is ordinarily called "aristocracy"—that group of persons powerful and distinguished by social position or inherited wealth—Jefferson in his letter to Adams calls "pseudo-aristocracy." But Jefferson does recognize another kind of superiority—one that might be politically and socially useful.

He insists that "there is a natural aristocracy among men. The grounds of this are virtue and talents. . . .[1] The natural aristocracy I consider as the most precious gift of nature, for the instruction, the trusts, and government of society." The status of a person as a natural aristocrat, then, has nothing to do with his means or social position, for it depends upon inherent excellence and ability. In his *Notes on Virginia* Jefferson speaks of "those talents which nature has sown as liberally among the poor as the rich."

Our student must of course also make clear what Adams means by "natural aristocracy." He sees that he must let his reader know that, for Adams, modifying "aristocracy" by "natural" does not really change the sense of the noun. After some reflection he writes:

When Adams uses the term "natural aristocracy" he intends us to understand that aristocracies are inevitable. As he sees it, all aristocracies are "natural" in their origin, for they begin when gifted persons take power and position, as they will always do. In his letter to Jefferson, he makes his idea clear in an account of a hypothetical republic:

> Pick up the first hundred men you meet, and make a republic. Every man will have an equal vote; but when deliberations and discussions are opened, it will be found that twenty-five, by their talents, virtues being equal, will be able to carry fifty votes. Every one of these twenty-five is an aristocrat in my sense of the word, whether he obtains his one vote in addition to his own by his birth, fortune, figure, eloquence, science, learning, craft, cunning, or even his character for good fellowship. . . .

Adams therefore says to Jefferson: "Your distinction between natural and artificial aristocracy does not appear to me to be founded." He is saying that men become aristocrats by their talents, to be sure, but that there are many talents besides those of the intellect.

Our student feels that he is learning how to put materials together and that he is getting along pretty well. Toward the end of his paper, however, he comes to a problem that gives him a good deal of trouble before he solves it. He has established Jefferson's concept of natural aristocracy; he has made clear the difference between the thought of Adams and Jefferson on the whole matter of aristocracy. It is now time to write an account of Jefferson's Virginia plan for education, to explain for his readers how Jefferson intended to discover natural aristocrats and to assure the state of their services.

Now at once our student sees that he has a choice. Jefferson's description of the plan in his letter to Adams (beginning "It was a bill . . .") is short enough to quote entire. His more extended account in *Notes on Virginia* would have to be handled in summary. Our student feels that it would surely be well to have the account in Jefferson's own words, and so he thinks at first that he will use the passage from Jefferson's letter. But he remembers that an important matter is not covered in the passage from

[1 Notice the periods indicating an omission in the quotation from the letter to Adams. Excisions within quotations are indicated by three periods; the fourth period here is the period required for end punctuation.]

the letter: that passage does not make at all clear the rigor of the selection Jefferson intends. Perhaps, he thinks, the better way would be to write a formal summary of the passage from *Notes on Virginia*. Yet he is reluctant to relinquish the quotation.

Then it occurs to him that perhaps he can use the quotation as a center for the discussion and extend it by reference to the *Notes on Virginia* passage. Such combination of sources is difficult, even for more experienced writers than our student; but after two or three false starts he finds the way he wants to do it. His final version is this:

An essential feature of Jefferson's plan was a system for rigorous selection of those students who should be educated at the state's expense and for its service. In his letter to Adams he describes the system in a general way. He proposes

> . . . to divide every county into wards of five or six miles square . . . ; to establish in each ward a free school for reading, writing and common arithmetic; to provide for the annual selection of the best subjects from these schools, who might receive, at the public expense, a higher degree of education at a district school; and from these district schools to select a certain number of the most promising subjects, to be completed at an University. . . .

In his *Notes on Virginia* Jefferson is much more specific. The free education provided by the wards is to be a three-year education (although a child may continue longer if his parents will pay). The "annual selection" from the ward schools is to be the selection in each of the best boy student among those from families of small means. These students are to be sent to one of the twenty district grammar schools that Jefferson hopes to have established. In the grammar schools these brilliant boys will have a trial year or two. Then, in each grammar school, the one best boy student among them will be selected to finish grammar school (six years in all). At the end of grammar school, these twenty will be divided in half: the ten "to be completed at an University" will go to William and Mary College at state expense; the other ten will end their formal education (and, Jefferson thinks, may well become grammar school teachers). At three times in the system, then, there will be a rather ruthless elimination; the survivors will be supposed to have demonstrated their status as "natural aristocrats."

What pleases the student about his final version is the close connection he has managed between the quoted passage and the development of it based on *Notes on Virginia*. He got that connection by picking up bits of the quoted passage in his development, and by keeping the development parallel to the quoted passage.

We shall not follow our student further in his labors—you will have been able to see how he is going at them. Not all his difficulties with restatement have been illustrated. Moreover, nothing at all has been said about the form of his footnotes; since practice in footnoting varies, advice on that matter had better come entirely from your instructor. But do notice that in these illustrative passages the reader is informed about sources by the text; even if he should skip the footnotes (as many readers do) he would be under no misapprehension about the student's debt to his sources. In general the footnotes will simply tell *where* the sources are to be found; and the reader need consult the notes only if he wishes to see in its original context one of the passages used by the student.

You would do well to find the passages our student uses in the selections themselves, and to consider the relationship of the student's paper to his sources. He has used his sources in a mature enough fashion. Really, however, it required no special gift on his part. He had paid attention to his previous instruction in definition and in organization, and he had got a thorough control of his source material before he began writing.

Of course we have been observing him at difficult and crucial points in his paper. Particularly we have watched him weave in quotation, always difficult for the unpracticed writer. Often in his paper he was able to write a running account of the thought of Adams or of Jefferson, or a running comparison; indeed, our examples contain much of his direct quotation.

SUGGESTIONS FOR PAPERS

Exercises in informal summary based on selections from this book will be easy for you or your instructor to devise. Of course in any such exercise, you will first envisage a purpose for the informal summary in a particular paper. Devise a title for that assumed paper that will clearly indicate its intention, and use it as a title for the exercise, so that your instructor can see what you are about.

Here are some suggestions for practice in restatement for the formal, documented source paper:

Selections in Chapter II: (1) The selection from Bryce's *The American Commonwealth.* (a) Assume that you are writing a paper on education in the United States in the late nineteenth century and that you wish to use Bryce's judgment briefly. Write a restatement of about 75 words (about half as many as there are in the example summary of the Bryce passage in Chapter V). (b) Assume a paper called "Foreign Opinion of American Education in the Nineteenth Century." For this paper Bryce's judgment is important. Write a summary of the passage that includes some quotation. (2) The selection from Rachel L. Carson's *The Sea Around Us.* Assume a paper on Bermuda for a geography course. The paper is on the modern geography of the island, but knowledge of the origin of the island is important to an understanding of its modern geography. Handle the Carson passage in about 150 words for the first section of the paper.

A selection in Chapter III: Thoreau's "Walking." (a) Assume a paper called "The Impetus of Westward Movement." Handle the Thoreau selection as it might be used in the introductory portion of the paper, using some quotation. (b) Assume a paper on the American West in literature. The first section considers work by men not themselves Westerners, such men as Irving, Thoreau, and Whitman. Handle the passage as it might be used in the first section of the paper.

Selections in Chapter V: (1) The fourth passage from Mill's *On Liberty*. Assume a paper for a political science course on ways of making minority opinion effective. Your first two paragraphs make up an argument by authority for the importance of minority opinion to the state, an argument in which you cite a number of writers. Begin with "According to Mill . . ." and reduce the passage to a very brief summary for use as part of your argument by authority. (2) Franklin's "Speech in the Constitutional Convention." (a) Assume a paper about the ratification of the Constitution by the states. In the introductory portion you wish to use the "Speech," since its principles apply to ratification as well as to adoption by the convention. Handle the selection for that purpose. (b) Assume that, as part of a study of Franklin, you are writing a section on his skill and tact as statesman and diplomat. Write such an account of the speech that a reader would realize its skill and the subtlety of its approach.

A selection in Chapter VI: Kittredge's *Witchcraft in Old and New England*. Assume a paper—perhaps for a sociology course—on superstitions, in which witchcraft is the topic of but a single section. In this section you have described English and continental beliefs about witchcraft before 1680, and you have space enough for about 300 words on the Salem outbreak. Write a discussion beginning in this fashion: "Everyone has heard of the witchcraft trials in Salem about 1692. According to George Lyman Kittredge. . . ."

You or your instructor can easily devise other such exercises, using material from this book or from the reading you are doing for other courses.

XV

Accounts of Books

One cannot read all the books he ought to know about; for a good many he must depend upon accounts in historical and critical works or, for new books, upon reviews. Recognizing that such knowledge is of a secondary sort, we will sometimes be content with it, sometimes be led by it to the books themselves.

Perhaps no sort of reading requires more discrimination. Accounts of books are seldom objective. The very necessity of selecting material from a book for treatment in a brief space precludes complete objectivity. The reader must ask whether the basis of the judgment about the book, even if it is only an implied judgment, is really clear to him. After he has read the account, his question ought always to be "Now just what do I know about this book?"

i   ## HISTORICAL ACCOUNTS OF BOOKS

We shall be concerned first of all with accounts of books that are part of a larger piece of writing, accounts that put the book into a historical context. Our first example is a masterly account of Sir Thomas (or St. Thomas) More's *Utopia,* 1516. It is a part of a section called "The New Learning 1509–1520" in a history of England. We can distinguish at least three purposes on the part of the historian: (1) He would review a notable example of the literature of the period. (2) He would give his readers some knowledge of the quality of More's mind and spirit. (3) He would have his readers compare the English society of the early sixteenth century with More's ideal society, and he would have them compare their own society with More's ideal society. Notice as you read how summary restatement and quotation are combined in the passage.

FROM   *A Short History of the English People*   (1874)

JOHN RICHARD GREEN

[More's *Utopia*]

1 It was on one of his diplomatic missions that More describes himself as hearing news of the Kingdom of "Nowhere." "On a certain day when I

had heard mass in Our Lady's Church, which is the fairest, the most gorgeous and curious church of building in all the city of Antwerp, and also the most frequented of people, and service being over I was ready to go home to my lodgings, I chanced to espy my friend Peter Gilles talking with a certain stranger, a man well stricken in age, with a black sun-burnt face, a large beard, and a cloke cast trimly about his shoulders, whom by his favour and apparell forthwith I judged to be a mariner." The sailor turned out to have been a companion of Amerigo Vespucci in those voyages to the New World "that be now in print and abroad in every man's hand," and on More's invitation he accompanied him to his house, and "there in my garden upon a bench covered with green turves [turfs] we sate down, talking together" of the man's marvellous adventures, his desertion in America by Vespucci, his wandering over the country under the equinoctial line [south of the equator], and at last of his stay in the Kingdom of "Nowhere." It was the story of "Nowhere," or Utopia, which More embodied in the wonderful book which reveals to us the heart of the New Learning. As yet the movement had been one of scholars and divines. Its plans of reform had been almost exclusively intellectual and religious. But in More the same free play of thought which had shaken off the old forms of education and faith turned to question the old forms of society and politics. From a world where fifteen hundred years of Christian teaching had produced social injustice, religious intolerance, and political tyranny, the humourist philosopher turned to a "Nowhere" in which the mere efforts of natural human virtue realized those ends of security, equality, brotherhood, and freedom for which the very institution of society seemed to have been framed. It is as he wanders through this dreamland of the new reason that More touches the great problems which were fast opening before the modern world, problems of labour, of crime, of conscience, of government. Merely to have seen and to have examined questions such as these would prove the keenness of his intellect, but its far-reaching originality is shown in the solutions which he proposes. Amidst much that is pure play of an exuberant fancy, much that is mere recollection of the dreams of bygone dreamers, we find again and again the most important social and political discoveries of later times anticipated by the genius of Thomas More. In some points, such as his treatment of the question of Labour, he still remains far in advance of current opinion. The whole system of society around him seemed to him "nothing but a conspiracy of the rich against the poor." Its economic legislation was simply the carrying out of such a conspiracy by process of law. "The rich are ever striving to pare away something further from the daily wages of the poor by private fraud and even by public law, so that the wrong already existing (for it is a wrong that those from whom the State derives most benefit should receive least reward) is made yet greater by means of the law of the State." "The rich devise every means by which they may in the first place secure to themselves what they have amassed by wrong, and then take to their own use and profit at the lowest possible price the work and labour of the poor. And so soon as the rich decide on adopting these devices in the name of the public, then they become law." The result was the wretched existence to which the labour-class was doomed, "a life so wretched that even a beast's life seems enviable." No such cry of pity for the poor, of protest against the system of agrarian and manufacturing tyranny which found its expression in the Statute-book, had been heard since the days of Piers Ploughman. But from Christendom More turns with a smile to "Nowhere." In "Nowhere" the aim of legislation is to secure the welfare, social, industrial, intellectual, religious, of the community at large, and of the labour-class as the true basis of a well-ordered commonwealth. The end of its labour-laws was simply the welfare of the labourer. Goods were possessed indeed in common, but work was compulsory with all. The period of toil was shortened to the nine hours demanded by modern artizans, with a view to the intellectual improvement of the worker. "In the institution of the weal public this end is only and chiefly pretended and minded that what time may possibly be spared from the necessary occupations and affairs of the commonwealth, all that the citizens should withdraw from bodily service to the free liberty of the mind and garnishing of the same. For herein they conceive the felicity of this life to consist." A public system of education enabled the Utopians to avail themselves of their leisure. While in England half of the population could read no English, every child was well taught in "Nowhere." The physical aspects of society were cared for as attentively as its moral. The houses of Utopia "in the beginning were very low and like homely cottages or poor shepherd huts made at all adventures of every rude piece of timber that came first to hand, with mud walls and rigid roofs thatched over with straw." The picture was really that of the common English town of More's day, the home of squalor and pestilence. In Utopia however they had at last come to realize the connexion between public morality and the health which springs from light, air, comfort, and cleanliness. "The streets were twenty feet broad; the houses backed by spacious gardens, and curiously builded after a gorgeous and gallant sort, with their stories one after another. The outsides of the walls be made either of hard flint, or of plaster, or else of brick; and the inner sides be well strengthened by timber work. The roofs be plain and flat, covered over with plaster so tempered that no fire can hurt or perish it, and withstanding the violence of the weather better than any lead. They keep the wind out of their windows with glass, for it is there much used, and sometimes also with fine linen cloth dipped in oil or amber, and that for two commodities, for by this means more light cometh in and the wind is better kept out."

11 The same foresight which appears in More's treatment of the questions of Labour and the Public Health is yet more apparent in his treatment of the question of Crime. He was the first to suggest that punishment was less effective in suppressing it than prevention. "If you allow your people to be badly taught, their morals to be corrupted from childhood, and then when they are men punish them for the very crimes to which they have been trained in childhood—what is this but to make thieves,

and then to punish them?" He was the first to plead for proportion between the punishment and the crime, and to point out the folly of the cruel penalties of his day. "Simple theft is not so great an offense as to be punished with death." If a thief and a murderer are sure of the same penalty, More shows that the law is simply tempting the thief to secure his theft by murder. "While we go about to make thieves afraid, we are really provoking them to kill good men." The end of all punishment he declares to be reformation, "nothing else but the destruction of vice and the saving of men." He advises "so using and ordering criminals that they cannot choose but be good; and what harm soever they did before, the residue of their lives to make amends for the same." Above all, he urges that to be remedial punishment must be wrought out by labour and hope, so that "none is hopeless or in despair to recover again his former state of freedom by giving good tokens and likelihood of himself that he will ever after that live a true and honest man." It is not too much to say that in the great principles More lays down he anticipated every one of the improvements in our criminal system which have distinguished the last hundred years. His treatment of the religious question was even more in advance of his age. If the houses of Utopia were strangely in contrast with the halls of England, where the bones from every dinner lay rotting in the dirty straw which strewed the floor, where the smoke curled about the rafters, and the wind whistled through the unglazed windows; if its penal legislation had little likeness to the gallows which stood out so frequently against our English sky; the religion of "Nowhere" was in yet stronger conflict with the faith of Christendom. It rested simply on nature and reason. It held that God's design was the happiness of man, and that the ascetic rejection of human delights, save for the common good, was thanklessness to the Giver. Christianity, indeed, had already reached Utopia, but it had few priests; religion found its centre rather in the family than in the congregation: and each household confessed its faults to its own natural head. A yet stranger characteristic was seen in the peaceable way in which it lived side by side with the older religions. More than a century before William of Orange, More discerned and proclaimed the great principle of religious toleration. In "Nowhere" it was lawful to every man to be of what religion he would. Even the disbelievers in a Divine Being or in the immortality of man, who by a single exception to its perfect religious indifference were excluded from public office, were excluded, not on the ground of their religious belief, but because their opinions were deemed to be degrading to mankind, and therefore to incapacitate those who held them from governing in a noble temper. But even these were subject to no punishment, because the people of Utopia were "persuaded that it is not in a man's power to believe what he list." The religion which a man held he might propagate by argument, though not by violence or insult to the religion of others. But while each sect performed its rites in private, all assembled for public worship in a spacious temple, where the vast throng, clad in white, and grouped round a priest clothed in fair raiment wrought marvellously out of

birds' plumage, joined in hymns and prayers so framed as to be acceptable
to all. The importance of this public devotion lay in the evidence it afforded that liberty of conscience could be combined with religious unity.

1) More's book has given us a noun, "utopia," and an adjective, "utopian." Define the words as you think they would be used, not in direct reference to More's book, but in reference to social thinking. Then look them
up in your dictionary and see how close you came to its definitions.

2) The paragraph that introduced our selection distinguished three
purposes on Green's part. The first of them must be understood, of course,
in relation to his general purpose as a historian. He would not pay a great
deal of attention to More's effort to attain verisimilitude for his utopia, as
a literary historian might; and his main interest would naturally be in the
ideas of the book. But does not the account give some notion of the literary
quality of *Utopia,* and even of its degree of verisimilitude? How?

3) Point out passages which are specific evidence of the second and
third purposes on Green's part.

4) More held positions of honor under Henry VIII and was lord chancellor for a few years. But when he refused to take any oath that would
call into question the Pope's authority over the Church in England and refused to affirm that Henry's divorce from Queen Catherine was justified,
he was tried, found guilty of high treason, and beheaded (1535). Does
Green's account of *Utopia* suggest to you a man of great moral earnestness
as its writer—one who would die for his convictions?

5) *The Oxford Companion to English Literature* speaks of the "simple
style and generous outlook" of *A Short History of the English People,* of
its inclusive scope "social, political, economic, and intellectual," and of
Green's interest in "the life of the humbler classes of the population." How
much of this judgment is illustrated by our selection?

6) A final judgment of the adequacy and relative excellence of Green's
account of *Utopia* would take a knowledge of More's book in its original
Latin. Yet practically we are often faced with the problem of judging the
dependability of accounts of books we have not read. Can you find evidence
within the account itself that would lead you to judge it dependable (or
not dependable)?

7) Can you discern any general principle (or principles) that Green is
using in his combination of quotations from the *Utopia* with sentences of
his own? (You might for a start consider the first half of II.) Do you think
the principles you discern would be useful to you in writing an account of
a book?

8) What have you noted about the structure of the selection? (It is in
very long paragraphs, but their length is apparently determined by the organization of the history itself.) Soon after the introductory description of
the meeting with the mariner who had visited Nowhere and of the general
plan of the book, there is a passage which functions as a signpost for the
subsequent discussion. Do you find it?

We turn to V. L. Parrington's account of *Modern Chivalry* by Hugh
Henry Brackenridge. The first two parts of *Modern Chivalry* were pub-

lished in 1792, and additions to it appeared later, the last in 1815. The 1805 edition which Parrington mentions was a revision.

FROM *The Colonial Mind* (1927)

V. L. PARRINGTON

[Brackenridge's *Modern Chivalry*]

I *Modern Chivalry* is our first backcountry book. It is redolent of stump-lands and their rude leveling ways, and for years it was immensely popular along the western frontier. It is a satire aimed primarily at back-woods shortcomings, but with an eye that kept turning towards the older settlements to scrutinize their equal shortcomings. Its main theme is concerned with certain weaknesses of popular sovereignty already unpleasantly evident as a result of the extension of suffrage; and in particular with the unseemly office-hunting zeal of coonskin candidates. The preposterous spectacle of a pushing fellow with no qualifications setting himself up for high office was to become more frequent with the later rise of Jacksonian democracy; but already there was abundant justification for the satire of Brackenridge. The records of the time are loud in criticism of the demagoguery that resulted from the sudden shift of leadership in consequence of the social upheaval following the Revolutionary War. The old leaders of the aristocratic tradition had fled or had fallen into disfavor, and new men, too often of small capacity and less breeding, had pushed into the seats of authority. With the triumph of Jefferson this transfer of power went forward briskly to the scandal of all aristocrats. The lust of office spread like the plague, and demagogues caught the popular ear, none too nice to distinguish between sense and fustian. Irving brushed against the democratic weakness in his brief venture into politics, and vented his spleen in *Rip Van Winkle.* It is this which Brackenridge deals with primarily in *Modern Chivalry,* the first part of which was published in 1792 and the second in 1805. The general leveling of offices, he pointed out, was not democracy, but the abuse and ruin of democracy. America was engaged in a great and noble experiment; the success of that experiment depended upon an honest and intelligent electorate; it must not be brought to failure by demagogues through the incapacity of the voter.

II Brackenridge had come in later years to be a pacifist. He had had his fill of revolutions and armed revolts. As a principal arbitrator during the tumult of the Whisky Insurrection, he had come to fear popular lawlessness; and as a friend of the French Revolution he was concerned at the methods of the Jacobin leaders. Commenting on the Whisky Insurrection he said in later years:

I saw before me anarchy, a shock to the government, a revolution im-
pregnated with the Jacobin principles of France. . . . Let no man suppose I coveted a revolution; I had seen the evils of one already in the American; and I had read the evils of another, the French. My imagination
presented the evils of the last strongly to my view, and brought them so
close to a possible experience at home, that during the whole period of the
insurrection, I could scarcely bear to cast my eye on a paragraph of French
news.

A reasonable and intelligent democracy, holding steadily to the purpose
of the common good, was his cherished ideal. He was not a political philosopher interested in general principles. His purpose was to satirize manners, not to speculate on causes; and in the days of triumphant republicanism the most conspicuous target was offered by the tousled head of the
demagogue, "the courtier of democracy." In the preface to the 1846 edition, the editor thus summarizes the political views of Brackenridge:

An enlightened democracy was looked upon by him as the true nobility.
He considered the true democrat as the true gentleman, who *ought* to feel
a stain on his fair reputation, "as a wound." He maintained "that democracy is not in its nature coarse, and vulgar, or destitute of high integrity
and honor." The aim and end of his writings was to raise the standard of
democracy, and to elevate "the noble of nature" to the same level with any
other noble, in those qualities which constitute true nobility. The noble of
nature, in his opinion, ought not to yield to the noble of aristocracy or monarchy, in strict integrity, in liberal and benevolent feelings, in propriety of
manners and general intelligence.

III The work is a string of adventures, interspersed with miscellaneous
discussion, of Captain John Farrago—who is evidently Brackenridge himself—and his bog-trotting servant Teague O'Regan. The Captain is an intelligent person, well read in the literature of the times, and "a good deal
disposed to subscribe to the elementary principles" of Paine's *Rights of
Man*. He can summarize neatly the arguments on both sides of the political
questions of the day, but he retains the open mind and cautious judgment
of the independent. He is a free-lance critic, democratic in sympathies but
unsparing in exposure of absurdity. His hits fall right and left, on the country yokel, the city speculator, members of Congress, the institution of slavery. He is greatly concerned to preserve his servant from the temptations
of ambition which assail him in the backwoods as well as in Philadelphia.
The career of Teague O'Regan is a broad satire on the mounting ambition
of old-world peasants to push their way up. That the underling should rise
in a democratic country was well; but that he should be in unseemly haste
to scramble into positions beyond his capacities, that in pushing his private
fortunes he should bring ridicule upon the democratic experiment, was
not well. Teague O'Regan's desire to scramble discovered quite too fertile a
field for his own or the country's good. He is nearly sent to Congress by a
backwoods constituency, listens to other seductive appeals, and in the end

is sent by President Washington to the West as a revenue officer, where he falls into the untender hands of the whisky rioters, and finds his Irish beauty marred by a coat of tar and feathers.

IV It is in his burlesque of electorate methods that Brackenridge hits most sharply at the current tendencies of republicanism. The ways of the backwoods he caricatures by describing a contest between an honest deacon and an ignorant Scotch-Irishman, which he came upon in his peregrinations.

When they looked upon the one, they felt an inclination to promote him. But when, again, on the other hand, they saw two kegs which they knew to be replenished with a very cheering liquor, they seemed to be inclined in favor of the other. The candidates were called upon to address the people, and the grave person mounted the stump of a tree, many of them standing round, as the place was a new clearing. His harangue was listened to by some of the older and more sedate, and one man, hard of hearing, seemed to make great effort to catch the sounds. As soon as the man of the two kegs took a stump, he was surrounded by an eager crowd.—"Frinds," said he, in the native Scotch-Irish, "I'm a good dimicrat, and hates the Brattish— I'm an elder of the meetin', forby, and has been overseer of the roads for three years:—An' ye all know, that my mammy was kilt o' the Ingens— now all ye that's in my favor, come forit an' drenk." Appetite, or rather thirst, prevailed, and the voters gave their votes to the man with the two kegs.

If whisky decided elections in the backcountry, business controlled them in the city. The following is almost modern in its caricature:

The candidates were all remarkably pot-bellied; and waddled in their gait. The captain inquiring what were the pretensions of these men to be elected; he was told, that they had all stock in the funds, and lived in brick buildings; and some of them entertained fifty people at a time, and ate and drank abundantly; and living an easy life, and pampering their appetites, they had swollen to this size.

"It is a strange thing," said the captain, "that in the country, in my route, they would elect no one but a weaver or a whisky-distiller; and here none but fat squabs, that guzzle wine, and smoke segars.". . . "No, faith" (said his friend), "there is na danger of Teague here, unless he had his scores o' shares in the bank, and was in league with the brokers, and had a brick house at his hurdies, or a ship or twa on the stocks . . . all is now lost in substantial interest, and the funds command everything."

V That there might be no mistake as to the meaning of his satire Brackenridge set down at the end an explicit statement of his purpose.

As already hinted by some things put into the mouth of the captain, I could make it a principal matter to form the heart of *a republican government*. And in order to this, keep out all that nourishes *ambition, the poison of public virtue*. . . . In the American republics, we retain yet a great deal of the spirit of monarchy. The people are not aware of the phraseology

itself, in some instances. . . . The first lesson I would give to a son of
mine would be to have nothing to do with public business, but as a duty to
his country. To consider service in civil life, no more to be desired than
service in the military. . . . Those who say to them, *vox populi vox dei,*
offer up an incense to flattery, as impious as the worshippers of the Cæsars.
They should be warned to beware of flatterers, whose object is not to serve
them, but themselves. The demagogue in a democracy, and the courtier in
a monarchy, are identical. They are the same, plying the same arts in different situations. . . . I shall have accomplished something by this book,
if it shall keep some honest man from lessening his respectability by pushing himself into public trusts for which he is not qualified; or when pushed
into public station, if it shall contribute to keep him honest by teaching him
the folly of ambition, and farther advancement. . . . This is in great
part, the moral of this book; if it should be at all necessary to give a hint
of it.

vɪ One may do a worse service to democracy than to point out its faults.
Brackenridge was no truckler either to King George or to his neighbors.
Living in the midst of a coonskin democracy, he refused to believe that
there was any particular virtue in coonskin. It is not the cap but what is
under it that signifies. He was a vigorous individualist, a confirmed democrat, a friend of all honest liberalisms, a man who honored his own coun-
sels and went his own way. We could better spare more pretentious books
from the library of our early literature than these clever satires that preserve for us some of the homely ways of a time when American institutions
were still in the making.

---

1) What does "backcountry" mean? Does the term "stump-lands" help
to define it? What would "coonskin candidates" be? If Captain Farrago
subscribed to "the elementary principles" of Paine's *Rights of Man,* what
would he believe? (If you have no acquaintance with Paine's thought, *The
Oxford Companion to American Literature* will help you.) How does your
dictionary define "satire"? How far does *Modern Chivalry* seem to illustrate
the definition?

2) If you have read *Don Quixote,* you are probably aware that there is
a parallel between Cervantes' characters, the Don and his squire Sancho,
and Brackenridge's characters, the Captain and his Irish servant Teague.
And you will have seen that the structure of *Modern Chivalry* must be like
that of *Don Quixote.* There is also a resemblance to the first part of Samuel
Butler's verse satire, *Hudibras* (1663)—a satire of some elements in the
Cromwellian party. But Parrington, although he would have been aware of
these parallels and of Brackenridge's debt to Cervantes and Butler, mentions neither author. What do you conclude about Parrington's interests as
a literary historian? What seem to be Parrington's social and political convictions?

3) We found that the structure of Green's account of *Utopia* was governed by a signpost passage. Although in the Parrington selection 1 is de-

veloped by the subsequent paragraphs, it does not govern the structure as a signpost. How shall we describe the organization here? What is the relationship between III and IV?

4) How, do you suppose, were the two quotations in IV chosen? What is their purpose? Does Parrington offer them as examples of the best, or the most interesting, parts of *Modern Chivalry*?

5) In literary history and in critical writing, quotation is almost an art, for the success of an account of a book may depend on a writer's ability to pick out passages that illustrate for his reader the ideas or the quality of the book. And notice how carefully the quotations are introduced here. That is part of the art, and a part, as we have seen, that most students have to learn. Notice, too, that Parrington excises parts of the passages he quotes, presumably parts that do not directly bear upon his purpose. How is excision indicated?

6) Perhaps the judgment of Brackenridge in VI is based on more knowledge of him than is given to us in Parrington's account of *Modern Chivalry*. But how much of the judgment is supported by what has been said in the account?

7) Answer the question that was suggested in the headnote for this chapter: "Now just what do I know about this book?"

THE JOURNALISTIC BOOK REVIEW   *ii*

Although the good journalistic book review may have some of the same virtues as the accounts of books by Green and Parrington we have just examined, its intent is different. Nor is it the same thing as the critical essay, although the two forms may come close together in the leading reviews in book supplements to newspapers and in the principal reviews in *The New Yorker*. The journalistic book review is first of all a news story about a new book. It should describe the book in such fashion that the reader can tell whether or not he would be interested in reading the book. If it fails to do that, it fails in its main purpose, no matter what erudition or sensitivity on the part of the reviewer it may display.

In general, examples of journalistic book reviews are best found by the student himself, since the best examples for him will be reviews of books he has read, or at least reviews of books in the fields of his interests.[1] (And he would be interested—and sometimes perhaps surprised—to read two or three reviews of the same book.) But here is a review that will be useful to us, for we know something about the book reviewed. It is a good example of reviews in professional journals.

[1] The student will find reviews in the New York *Times Book Review*, the New York *Herald Tribune Books*, the London *Times Literary Supplement*, the *Saturday Review*, the *New Yorker* magazine, *Harper's Magazine*, the *Atlantic Monthly*, the *Scientific American*, in a number of specialized publications, technical and scholarly journals, and perhaps in his local newspaper. In *Harper's* and the *Atlantic* important new books are reviewed in a running account of the month's crop of new books—an interesting form, but not a form available for student exercises.

History and Nature of the Ocean (1951)

R. TUCKER ABBOTT

I Rarely has the soul of the sea been so adequately fathomed or its thousand faces so delightfully pictured as Rachel Carson has done in her latest book, *The Sea Around Us*. The many technical divisions of ocean-ography have been blended in a manner that gives the reader a full appreciation of the history, nature, and cyclic functions of the ocean.

II The book is divided into three main sections, the first dealing in eight chapters with various modern phases of oceanic biology and marine geography, the second part picturing the dynamics of waves, currents, and tides, and the last three chapters discussing man and the sea about him.

III Although the chapter on The Birth of an Island won for its author the 1950 George Westinghouse Science Writing Award, several other chapters are of equal, if not superior, caliber, as, for example, her treatment of marine sediments in The Long Snowfall. The normally staid story of sedimentary rocks has been presented in living fashion. The reader feels the spirit of the timeless and inexorable rain of myriads of dying planktonic lives descending from the surface ceiling of the sea to the ever-thickening sediments on the ocean floor. "It is interesting to think that even now, in our own lifetime, the flakes of a new 'snowstorm' are falling, falling, one by one, out there on the ocean floor. The billions of Globigerina are drifting down, writing their unequivocal record. . . ." As in so many of her other chapters, the author has interlaced the most recent advances in oceanography. In her descriptions of unseen life in the sea, she presents an up-to-date account of the work being done in underwater sounds. Hydrophone techniques are revealing a new world under the sea, from the froggy croaks of the fish and the whistles and squeals of porpoise to the fat-frying sizzle heard from beds of snapping shrimp.

IV The importance of the sea to man is forcefully demonstrated in the chapters on The Global Thermostat and Wealth from the Salt Seas. An account is given of the long-range cyclic effects of tides and currents on European climate and the history of modern man. In the final chapter, The Encircling Sea, man's knowledge and legends of the mysterious sea are entertainingly presented in a historical review extending from the time of the ancient Greeks' ocean, which was an endless stream flowing around the border of the earth, to the first works of Matthew Maury and present-day sailing directions and coast pilots.

V It is singularly refreshing to find a popular book on a scientific subject which can carry the reader so gently and pleasantly through the mazes of science and yet maintain such a high degree of accuracy. This is because the author is a poet and scientist.

The next selection is a review of a different sort. It is a review of a new edition of the letters of the Reverend Sydney Smith, a well-known figure in English literary and social history. The reviewer does not assume that he is introducing Smith to his readers, and he deals with the editor's work on the edition in just one approving phrase. He is sampling the book for his readers, and he intends a piece that will have an interest and a completeness in itself.

The Reverend Sydney Smith is remembered in the history of American literature. He much offended Americans by his famous question: "In all the four quarters of the globe, who reads an American book?" Fortunately, just as the question was asked, Washington Irving and James Fenimore Cooper were making possible a satisfactory answer.

Sydney (1954)

BERTON ROUECHÉ

I Clergyman, libertarian, and a founder of the *Edinburgh Review,* Sydney Smith was born in 1771 at Woodford, in Essex, and died in London in 1845. "The Smith of Smiths," Macaulay called him. To Byron, he was "the loudest wit I e'er was deafened with." "He is a very clever fellow," George III once cheerfully conceded, "but he will never be a bishop." They all were more or less right. He was invariably passed over when the richer ecclesiastical preferments were handed out, he was often loud and he could be deafening, and he was certainly the most notable Smith of his day. But he was also something more. He was a man of good will and a man of good works, and, above all, a man of good humor. The evidence, if any is needed, may be found in "The Letters of Sydney Smith," just published, under the scrupulous editorship of Nowell C. Smith, by the Oxford University Press. It runs to two thick volumes, it consists of over a thousand substantial letters (half of which have only recently come to light), and it constitutes a thousand proofs that he was probably the most consistently amusing Englishman that ever lived.

II Smith's capacity as a dinner-table and drawing-room entertainer has never been much of a secret. The memoirs of all his more memorable contemporaries are salted with specimens of his wit. Some of his conceits ("Bishop —— deserves to be preached to death by wild curates," for example, and "Brighton Pavilion looks as if St. Paul's Cathedral had come down and littered") have gone through dozens of editions. His letters, however, tell us something that we could hardly have been sure of until now. Smith was not, like Rogers and Luttrell and Wilde and so many other diners-out of reputation, a horticulturist of humor. He didn't plant and prune and nurse his comedy into bloom. It sprang from his lips or fell from his pen spontaneously, naturally, and incessantly. We find it as early as 1794, when he was a mere twenty-three, in the first but one of his extant letters ("Your offer of a horse to carry my portmanteau I cannot accept, and for two reasons. . . . The first is you have no horse here, the next, I have no portmanteau"), and it lasted him all his long life.

III The chronic exuberance that characterized Smith could only have been natural. There was little in his life to induce it. It is true he made a happy marriage, but one of his four children died young and another turned out worthless. Moreover, he was for many years poor almost to privation. What was worse, to a man with a taste for high jinks and high society, was that he was doomed until nearly the end of his days to the gray routine of a country parson—first in Wiltshire, then in Yorkshire, and finally in Somerset, but always a hundred miles or so from London. Yet Smith's bad luck was our good fortune. Had he been as able as he was welcome to spend more than a few short weeks a year at Holland House and Lady Blessington's and the King of Clubs and all the rest, we could hardly have had this gleaming cascade of correspondence to enliven our own gray days. We would not have this (to Lady Holland): "I have no doubt from what you say that the Archbp. acted conscientiously. I will do human nature the justice to say that we are all prone to make other people do their duty." Or this (to Lord Grey): "We are told that Man is not to live by bread alone; this is comfortable for there will be very little of it this year." Or this (to Lady Holland): "Philosopher Malthus came here last week. I got an agreeable party for him of unmarried people. There was only one Lady who had had a Child, and for her I apologised . . . but he is a very good-natured man, and if there are no appearances of approaching fertility is civil to every lady." And we would certainly not have this (to J. A. Murray): "Your grouse are not come by this day's mail, but I suppose they will come tomorrow. Even the rumor of grouse is agreeable."

IV Picking our way through this bonanza of ebullience, we soon cease to wonder why Smith failed to rise in his profession. The marvel is that he was allowed to remain even in the countryside. He is as candid as a secret diarist. Writing to a friend at the peak of the Napoleonic threat, he has this to say of Pitt: "For 15 years I have found my income dwindling away under his eloquence, and regularly in every Session of Parliament he has charmed every classical feeling and stript me of every guinea I possest. At the close of every brilliant display an expedition failed or a Kingdom fell, and by the time that his Style had gained the summit of perfection Europe was degraded to the lowest abyss of Misery. God send us a stammerer." But it was for churchmen and religion that he reserved his tartest treats. "The Upper Parsons live vindictively," he observes to Murray, "and evince their aversion . . . by an improved health. The Bishop of Ely has the rancor to recover after three paralytic strokes, and the Dean of Lichfield to be vigorous at 82—and yet these are the men who are called Christians." To

Lady Holland: "Nothing can be more disgusting than an Oratorio. How absurd, to see 500 people fidling like madmen about the Israelites in the Red Sea." To Murray: "Every fresh accident on the railroads is an advantage, and leads to an improvement. What we want is an overturn which would kill a bishop, or at least a dean. This mode of conveyance would then become perfect." To Lady Mary Bennet: "I am going to preach a charity sermon next Sunday. I desire to make three or four hundred weavers cry, which it is impossible to do since the late rise in cottons." To John Allen: "We are going to educate the poor in York as elsewhere. The Church attempting to be useful, is much as if Sheridan were to take to keeping accounts." And he adds, evolving what is surely one of the most Surrealist of images, to Lady Holland: "I believe it is only a plan to prevent the little Boys from learning . . . and that a sort of Sham Multiplication Table will be introduced."

v There is no end; everything interests him ("Miss —— abuses the privilege of literary women to be plain"), everything inspires him ("Luttrell came over for the day; he was very agreeable, but spoke too lightly, I thought, of veal soup"), and everything, even the necessity of a remark to an artist engaged in painting his portrait, is transformed by his pen. "Whatever you do," he wrote, "preserve the orthodox look." Until the end. And even then his powers refused to fail him. "If you hear of sixteen or eighteen pounds of human flesh," he wrote from his sickbed to Lady Carlisle, "they belong to me. I look as if a curate had been taken out of me." A few weeks later, he was dead.

Here is a short article on the book review as a literary form. It is by a distinguished writer of both reviews and critical essays. You might see whether you think the foregoing reviews and the others you are reading are written in accord with the principles here set down. And if you are to write reviews of your own, you will find practical help in what Mr. Krutch has to say on the function and procedure of the reviewer.

What Is a Good Review? (1937)

JOSEPH WOOD KRUTCH

1 Of all literary forms the book review is the one most widely cultivated and least often esteemed. To many the very phrase "literary form" may smack of pretense when applied to a kind of writing which is usually so casual; and formlessness may, indeed, be the only form of many commentaries on books. Book reviewing can, nevertheless, become an art in itself and would be such more often if the ambitious reviewer would only devote himself to the cultivation of its particular excellences instead of attempting, as he so often does, to demonstrate his capacities by producing something "more than a mere review." The best review is not the one which is trying

Reprinted from *The Nation*, April 17, 1937, by permission of *The Nation*.

to be something else. It is not an independent essay on the subject of the book in hand and not an esthetic discourse upon one of the literary genres. The best book review is the best review of the book in question, and the better it is the closer it sticks to its ostensible subject.

II To say this is not to say that a good review is easy to write; in certain technical respects it is, indeed, the most difficult of all forms of literary criticism for the simple reason that in no other is the writer called upon to do so many things in so short a space. The critical essay, no matter how extended it may be, is not compelled to aim at any particular degree of completeness. It may—in fact it usually does—assume that the reader is sufficiently familiar with the work under discussion to make description unnecessary, and it may also confine itself to whatever aspects of the subject the critic may choose.

III But the book review as a literary form implies completeness; it has not really performed its function unless, to begin with, it puts the reader in possession of the facts upon which the criticism is based, and unless—no matter upon how small a scale—its consideration is complete. However penetrating a piece of writing may be, it is not a good review if it leaves the reader wondering what the book itself is like as a whole or if it is concerned with only some aspects of the book's quality.

IV I shall not pretend to say how large a proportion of the so-called reviews published . . . actually achieve the distinguishing characteristics of the book-review form, but a certain number of them do, and the sense of satisfactoriness which they give can always be traced to the fact that, whatever other qualities they may have, they accomplish the three minimum tasks of the book reviewer. They describe the book, they communicate something of its quality, and they pass a judgment upon it.

V Each of these things is quite different from the others, but only the last is usually considered as carefully as it ought to be by either reader or writer. Adequate description implies a simple account of the scope and contents of the book; its presence guarantees that the reader will not be left wondering what, in the simplest terms, the book is about. "Communication of quality" implies, on the other hand, a miniature specimen of what is commonly called "impressionistic criticism"; it means that the reviewer must somehow manage to recreate in the mind of the reader some approximation of the reaction produced in his own mind by the book itself. And in however low esteem this form of criticism may be held as a be-all and end-all (Mr. Eliot calls it the result of a weak creative instinct rather than of a critical impulse), it is indispensable in a book review if that review is to perform the function it is supposed to perform, and if it is to become what it is supposed to be—namely, not merely an account of a book on the one hand or an independent piece of criticism on the other, but a brief critical essay which includes within itself all that is necessary to make the criticism comprehensible and significant.

VI Your "reviewer" often envies the more lofty "critic" because the critic is supposed to be read for his own sake while the reviewer must assume that the reader is attracted more by his interest in the book discussed than

by the reviewer himself. For that very reason he is likely either to treat reviewing as a casual affair or to seek for an opportunity to write something
else under the guise of a review. He might be happier himself and make
his readers happier also if he would, instead, take the trouble to ask what
a review ought to be and if he would examine his own work in the light of
his conclusions. It is not easy to do within the space of a thousand words
or less the three things enumerated. It is less easy still to combine the description, the impression, and the judgment into a whole which seems to
be, not three things at least, but one.

vii How many reviewers of novels, for instance, seem to know how
much of a particular story has to be told in order to provide a solid basis
for the impression they intend to convey? And if it is decided that some
part of the story must be told, how many know, as a story-teller must,
whether the incidents are striking enough to come first or must be introduced with some comment which creates the interest? Yet a first-rate review, despite its miniature scale, raises precisely the same problems as long
narratives or expositions raise, and each must be solved as artfully if the review is to have such beauty of form as it is capable of. Doubtless the finest
reviewer can hardly hope to have his art fully appreciated by the public.
But there is every reason why he should respect it himself.

THE CRITICAL ESSAY   *iii*

The book review and the critical essay may come close together—they
do in Mr. Roueché's "Sydney." But the term "critical essay" often designates a discussion of a book, or of the work of a writer, with which, it is
assumed, the reader of the essay is familiar. The intent is not so much description then, but instead interpretation, definition of quality, and judgment. And since for judgment some context of values is necessary, good
criticism is, to some extent at least, comparative criticism.

Our example of the critical essay is by W. H. Auden, a distinguished
contemporary poet. Mr. Auden's assumption is that his readers have read
Herman Melville's great novel, *Moby-Dick* (1851). If you have not, you
will still be able to follow, but an indication of the action may help. The
novel is an account, accompanied by much reflection, and much detail
about whaling (which Mr. Auden's essay does not consider), of Captain
Ahab's quest for a great white whale, Moby-Dick. The account comes to
us through a narrator, Ishmael. Captain Ahab has lost a leg by Moby-Dick,
and he is determined to kill the whale on this voyage. He communicates
his mania to the crew of his ship, the *Pequod*. The *Pequod* searches long
for the whale, and finally finds him. There is an exciting three-day chase,
but Moby-Dick wins in the end: the *Pequod* is destroyed with all the crew
but Ishmael, who remains to tell the story. (We have a chapter from *Moby-
Dick* in Chapter XVIII. Perhaps you will wish to read it before you read
Mr. Auden's essay. It is important to his interpretation.)

Now here we have a general problem in reading. The problem, as it
may be stated in reference to Mr. Auden's essay, is this: Have you enough

background to read and understand a comparison of *Moby-Dick* and Greek tragedy? You may say, I have not read *Moby-Dick,* I know nothing about Greek tragedy and, for that matter, little about any tragedy—I cannot follow such a comparison. Of course it is not sensible to try to read too far ahead of oneself. Yet if one waited to have an entirely adequate background before he read, perhaps he would not get anything of much importance read. Such an essay as we have here may very well be an approach to further reading, and it is informative and stimulating just in itself. An adequate desk dictionary will help a good deal; and *The Oxford Companion to Classical Literature* will supply identifications of names and definitions of terms in Greek tragedy. And Mr. Auden does not assume much knowledge of Greek tragedy; he even writes an account of so well-known a story as that of Oedipus.

The Christian Tragic Hero (1945)

W. H. AUDEN

I "Moby Dick" is at once an heroic epic like the "Iliad," an heroic tragedy like the "Oresteia," an heroic quest like the legend of the "Golden Fleece," and an allegorical religious quest like "Pilgrim's Progress"; it is also a nineteenth-century American novel. Even if it were not the great book it is, it would therefore be of unusual interest to the critic who would compare the values believed in and the attitudes held at different stages in Western civilization. I propose in this article to consider only one of them, the concept of the Tragic Hero in Greece and in Christendom. Most of the characteristics one observes in Melville's hero can also be seen in, say, the heroes of Shakespeare's tragedies, but Melville's choral asides make them more explicit in his own case.

II To sum them up in advance, the conclusions I shall try to demonstrate are these: first, Greek tragedy is the tragedy of necessity; i.e., the feeling aroused in the spectator is "What a pity it had to be this way"; Christian tragedy is the tragedy of possibility, "What a pity it was this way when it might have been otherwise"; secondly, the hubris which is the flaw in the Greek hero's character is the illusion of a man who knows himself strong and believes that nothing can shake that strength, while the corresponding Christian sin of Pride is the illusion of a man who knows himself weak but believes he can by his own efforts transcend that weakness and become strong.

III In using the term Christian I am not trying to suggest that Melville or Shakespeare or any other author necessarily believed the Christian dogmas, but that their conception of man's nature is, historically, derived from them.

IV As an example of Greek tragedy let us take "Oedipus Rex." As a young man, Oedipus learns from a prophecy that he is fated to murder his

Reprinted from *The New York Times Book Review,* December 16, 1945. By permission of *The New York Times Book Review,* and of Mr. W. H. Auden.

father and marry his mother. Believing that his foster parents are his real parents he leaves Corinth. He meets an old man on the road; they quarrel about who shall give way to the other, and Oedipus kills him. He comes to Thebes, saves it from a monster, and is rewarded by the hand of its Queen, Jocasta. Thebes is stricken with plague, and the Oracle declares the cause to be the undetected presence of a criminal. Oedipus undertakes an investigation and discovers that the criminal is himself. In expiation of his crime he puts out his eyes, and Jocasta hangs herself.

v A modern reader, accustomed to the tragedy of possibility, instinctively asks, "Where and when did he make the wrong choice?" and as instinctively answers, "He should not have listened to the prophecy in the first place, or, having done so, then he should never have struck the old man or anyone else, and should never have married Jocasta or anyone else." But such thoughts would never have occurred to Sophocles or his audience. Macbeth and Captain Ahab are wrong to listen to the prophecies about them, because they are equivocal, and each reads into his a possibility he is wrong to desire; the prophecy Oedipus hears is not only unequivocal but something he is right to wish to avoid. When he kills the old man he feels no guilt, neither is he expected to feel any, and when he marries Jocasta there is nothing the matter with the relation as such. It is only when it turns out that, as a matter of fact, the former was his father and the latter is his mother that guilt begins.

vi The tragedy is that what had to happen happened, and if one asks what was wrong with Oedipus, that such a terrible fate should be assigned to him, one can only say that it is a punishment for a hubris which was necessarily his before he learnt of the prophecy at all; i.e., had he not had such a character, the prophecy would never have been made.

vii Other Greek heroes are faced with the tragic choice between two evils: Agamemnon must either sacrifice his daughter or fail in his duty to the Greek Army; Antigone must be false either to her loyalty to her brother or to her loyalty to her city.

viii The tragic situation, of learning that one is a criminal or of being forced to become one, is not created by the flaw in the hero's character, but is sent him by the gods as a punishment for having such a flaw.

ix The pessimistic conclusion that underlies Greek tragedy seems to be this: that if one is a hero, i.e., an exceptional individual, one must be guilty of hubris and be punished by a tragic fate; the only alternative and not one a person can choose for himself is to be a member of the chorus, i.e., one of the average mass; to be both exceptional and good is impossible.

x How does "Moby Dick" compare with this?

xi The hero, Captain Ahab, far from being exceptionally fortunate, is at the beginning, what in a Greek tragedy he could only be at the end, exceptionally unfortunate. He is already the victim of what the modern newspaper, which is Greek in this respect, would call a tragedy; a whale has bitten off his leg. What to the Greeks could only have been a punishment for sin is here a temptation to sin, an opportunity to choose; by making the wrong choice and continuing to make it, Ahab punishes himself. To say that a character is tempted means that it is confronted by possibility, that it is not a fixed state but a process of becoming: the possibilities are not infinite; i.e., Ahab cannot become Starbuck or Pip or Ishmael or anyone else except Ahab, but the possibilities are eternal; the past is irrevocable but always redeemable now.

XII Thus we can at every moment answer the question, "What should Ahab do now?" Before the story opens he has suffered and made his first wrong choice. He was not wrong to make Moby Dick into a symbol of all the inexplicable suffering in the world; on the contrary, the capacity to see the universal in the particular is the mark of human greatness, and it is only Flask, the Philistine trimmer, who says, "A whale is only a whale"; he was wrong, however, to insist on his own explanation, that the motive behind the whale's act and behind all suffering is personal malevolence. Once he has done so, he can still be saved, but he has made his salvation a much harder task, for he is now required to forgive the whale personally, in contrast, for instance, to Captain Boomer, who, like Ahab, has been deprived of a limb by Moby Dick, but in his pragmatic English way explains the whale's ferocity as mere clumsiness which is easier to forgive than malice.

XIII In Greek tragedy are two kinds of characters, the exceptional hero and the average chorus, and neither can become the other; in Christian tragedy there is not only an infinite variety of possible characters, varying all the way from Ahab, the captain, who defiantly insists on being absolutely unique, down to Pip, the cabin boy, who is too afraid to claim even his own name, but overshadowing them all is the possibility of each becoming both exceptional and good; this ultimate possibility for hero and chorus alike is stated in Father Mapple's sermon, and it is to become a saint—i.e., the individual who of his own free will surrenders his will to the will of God. In this surrender he does not become a ventriloquist's doll, for the God who acts through him can only do so by his consent; there always remain two wills, and the saint, therefore (unlike the late Greek conception of the undramatic Sage who is good by necessity because he knows), never ceases to be tempted to obey his own desires.

XIV Of this possibility Ahab's career is at every point a negative parody.

XV The saint does not ask to be one, he is called to become one, and assents to the call. The outward sign that Ahab is so called, is the suffering which is suddenly intruded into his life. What he is called to become, we do not, of course, know for certain—all we know for certain is that he rejected it—but we can guess that he was called to give up hunting whales—i.e., the normal cannibalistic life of this world, a life which is permitted, for instance, to Queequeg (who, though sinless, is not a saint, but the innocent man before the fall) but no longer to Ahab once he has been made uniquely conscious of the suffering it inflicts. Of the others, less is required: of Starbuck that he face evil instead of superstitiously avoiding it, of Stubb that he face his fears instead of whistling in the dark; but of Ahab alone is it required, because he alone has the necessary heroic passion, to become a real and not a merely respectable Quaker.

xvi Ahab is not deaf; he hears the call and refuses it with all the passion with which he might have accepted it; like the saint he wills one thing, to kill Moby Dick. For this he leaves his wife and child; for this his first act in the book is to throw away his pipe, his last physical addiction, his last relation with the element of earth; for this he destroys the ship's quadrant, its relation to the element of air so that the Pequod can only know the universe through compass and line in terms of the dualistic antagonism of fire and water.

xvii The saint, knowing his will to be weak, may express his external resolve by a temporal or bodily ritual act, but his vow and his act concern his own will alone. Ahab attempts to use ritual as a magical means of compelling the wills of others, as when he forces the crew to swear on their harpoons, and finally even to compel lifeless things, as when he baptizes a harpoon itself.

xviii Just as the saint never ceases to be tempted to forsake his calling, so, vice versa, Ahab is never free from the possibility of renouncing his refusal. Divine grace offers itself, now in the nostalgic beauty of fine weather, now as Gabriel, the mad idolater of the whale, an unlovely reflection of himself, and finally, in its strongest and least disguised form, as the cry for help of a friend in distress when the Pequod meets the Rachel, and it is only after he has refused this last offer that his doom becomes necessary. Melville portrays this decisive change with great subtlety. For it is at this point that Ahab places the idiot Pip in his cabin and, in a grotesque parody of the saint as the servant of servants, takes for himself the humble position of lookout on the mast which is the negative image of the martyr's cross. Instead of gaining a martyr's crown, however, his hat, the badge of his authority, is snatched from his head by the Jovian eagle, and from this moment Fedallah, the slave, the projection of Ahab's will, seems suddenly to have taken charge of his creator, or rather his summoner. Fedallah is clearly intended by Melville, I think, to represent the demonic, i.e., that which (unlike Ahab, who is tempted by suffering) tempts itself and denies for the sake of denying, and about which, therefore, nothing historic can be said; we are only told his religion.

xix So Ahab, refusing life, goes unrepentant, like all of Shakespeare's tragic heroes, to the unnecessary death he has chosen, dragging with him all his companions, and the only survivor is, as in Greek tragedy, the Chorus, the spectator, Ishmael. But Ishmael is not, like the Greek Chorus, the eternal average man, for he isn't a character at all. To be a character one must will and act, and Ishmael has no will, only consciousness; he does not act, he only knows, and what he knows is good *and* evil, i.e., possibility. He cannot die because he has not yet begun to live, and he ends the book as a baby reborn from the sea in Queequeg's coffin, thrust back into life as an orphan with his first choice still to make.

----

1) First of all, are you sure of the literary and theological terms in the first three paragraphs? Perhaps three of them need comment. "Hubris" and "the sin of Pride" really designate the same propensity in man; they differ

as that propensity is understood in two theologies. "Hubris," defined in II, is used almost exclusively in reference to Greek literature, and indicates a "blindness of heart," a confidence inappropriate to the human condition. "The sin of Pride" is not mere vanity; it is rather the erection of the human spirit in its own will, a denial of man's dependence on God.

2) When in II Mr. Auden speaks of "the flaw in the Greek hero's character," he is using a technical term. Aristotle tells us in his *Poetics* that there is in the nature of the tragic hero a trait by which he contributes to his catastrophe (the tragic hero is "a person neither eminently virtuous or just, nor yet involved in misfortune by deliberate vice or villainy, but by some error or human frailty; and this person should be some one of high fame and flourishing prosperity").

3) Paragraph IV reviews not Sophocles' play but the story of Oedipus. Sophocles' *Oedipus Rex* begins as Thebes is stricken with a plague, and the play is concerned with the revelation to Oedipus of his real identity and his guilt.

4) Too often people get a notion that all one needs to understand of Greek tragedy is that it is "fatalistic." Now Greek tragedy is not just an account of man in the grip of a mysterious and malignant power called fate. As Auden makes clear, the Greek tragic poets faced the problem of the interplay between character and circumstance in individual lives, but they saw character as an inevitable propensity. Nevertheless, Oedipus is highly representative of our human predicament. Prosser Hall Frye says:

> We are all of us without exception in Oedipus' case—rounded like him with ignorance and mystery, and yet obliged to act incessantly and at our own hazard, so that our every step seems a presumption deserving of disaster and our every judgment an arrogance inviting rebuke and humiliation. Of all Greek tragedy the *Oedipus Tyrannus* seems to me not only the most characteristic of the genius which produced it, but also most applicable to our hapless human lot.

Do you see what Frye means? We are all ignorant of the potentialities of our nature, which have come down to us from unknown forebears. We are all ignorant of the next moment of our future. On the razor edge between two mysteries we must all make our decisions. Of this human predicament Christian thought is, of course, entirely aware. But do you see what, according to Auden, Christian thought offers further? What exactly is meant by the last sentence in XI?

5) What is meant in XII when Flask, the third mate, is called a "Philistine trimmer"? Do you see that throughout it is plain that Ahab is a great person, greater than the rest of the ship's company, and that therefore more is required of him? Is it also true, do you think, that the great person is particularly liable to the sin of Pride, even while he may easily be free of the lesser sins? Do you see the symbolism of the incident of Ahab's throwing away his pipe, mentioned in XVI? And do you see what is meant when Auden says in XI that "Ahab punishes himself"? Certainly part of that punishment is his separating himself, not only from all the ordinary human weaknesses, but from humanity itself: the erection of his will results in an awful aloneness. You will have noticed in XVIII that in the last of his career Ahab increasingly turns to those with whom by birth and training he

has least in common. (Fedallah is a Parsee, a Zoroastrian from India— when Ahab separates himself from the will of God, he turns to what is for one of his tradition superstition.)

6) Now suppose a student felt that he really was not prepared to read this piece, but that he has done as much as he could with it. How much has it profited him? At the least he has read an interesting comparison of two great interpretations of human experience, Greek and Christian. And even if he has not read the works considered, that comparison probably arises more intelligibly for him than it would in abstract discussion. Moreover he can use this essay as an introduction to *Moby-Dick* and to Greek tragedy: he will know what sort of ideas the works present, and what their interest might be for him. But he should realize that reading literary criticism is no adequate substitute for reading literature, any more than reading about philosophy is a substitute for reading the philosophers. Literary criticism, like all sorts of studies of literature, is an important but secondary kind of knowledge. To know *Moby-Dick* one must read it. Yet the educated person must know about more things than he knows intimately; and a good piece of literary criticism does indicate the place of a work in its culture.

7) Now that we have been over the piece, let us consider in more detail just what its assumptions are. If Auden assumes that his readers have read *Moby-Dick* (and a great many of the readers of the *Times Book Review* have), does he assume a recent reading? Is he at all concerned for the reader who has never read it? Do any of the references to Greek tragedy remain unclear to you? If Auden had been assuming readers with no acquaintance with *Moby-Dick,* do you think the structure of the piece would have been different, and that he might have included additional material? How and of what sort? Define the differences in intention between such an account of a book as Green's account of *Utopia* and this piece. Define the differences in intention between this piece and a journalistic book review.

8) *Moby-Dick* was first published in 1851 and pretty much neglected in the nineteenth century; it is indeed only within the last twenty-five years that it has come to be considered generally one of the three or four greatest American novels. The reasons for its delayed recognition are various and complex. One of them is that it is a book that rather extends the reader. But can you see, on the basis of what Auden says, any reason or reasons why the book has spoken to our time with particular insistence?

SUGGESTIONS FOR PAPERS

Here are suggestions for short exercises in connection with Green's account of *Utopia:* (a) Write a one-sentence logical definition of the term "utopian novel" and extend it by a short discussion of More's book. (b) Write a paragraph drawn from this selection appropriate to a paper on the history of criminology. (c) Assume that you are writing a paper on some nineteenth-century utopian novel and that you wish in your introductory paragraphs to discuss the history of the utopian novel as literary kind. Draw a paragraph from the selection for this purpose.

Papers connected with the Green selection may be these: (a) If you have read William Morris's *News from Nowhere* (1891) or Edward Bellamy's *Looking Backward: 2000–1887* (1888), write an account of it. Determine the purpose of your account—is your interest primarily literary or social? (b) If you have read Aldous Huxley's *Brave New World* (1932) or George Orwell's *Nineteen Eighty-Four* (1949), you will realize that contemporary novels cast in the future predict a future hostile to freedom and decency. And you know about the appalling future imagined by science fiction writers. Write a paper comparing the life that More imagines with modern fictional projections into a future. (E. M. Forster's short story entitled "The Machine Stops," 1928, is a highly intelligent and literate piece of science fiction. It is short enough so that you could read it in preparation for a comparative paper.)

And here are some short exercises in connection with Parrington's account of *Modern Chivalry:* (a) Take the political term "stump speaker" or "on the stump" and write a definition of it, illustrating its origin by material drawn from the selection. (b) Assume that Parrington's book is one of your textbooks and that you have this question on an examination: "Identify Captain Farrago and Teague, making clear their representative quality." Answer it. (c) Assume that you are writing a paper called "The Demagogue" for a course in political science and that, in the introductory portion, you begin a paragraph: "Apparently the demagogue has been a part of our political life since the very beginning of the national period." Develop the sentence with material drawn from the selection, making due acknowledgment.

As a subject for a paper, you might consider this: Although Parrington gives us a good notion of *Modern Chivalry,* his primary interest is in its ideas, not in its literary quality. Read a few episodes from the book itself and, drawing both from your experience with the book and Parrington's account, write a discussion of the literary quality of *Modern Chivalry.* Of course you will not then exclude discussion of its ideas—the book is designed as a vehicle for ideas.

For the student's work in his own accounts of books, or in journalistic book reviews, there are so many possibilities that suggestion must be very general. If the instructor knows that his students will face special requirements and forms in book reports for courses they will take, he may wish to make assignments with regard to them. If reading a book and writing about it takes more time than the assignment schedule will allow, students may write about a book they already know. And the journalistic book review may be practiced quite as well with an old book as a new one—it is only necessary to assume for the purposes of the review that the book is new.

Accounts of books and journalistic book reviews may, of course, be extended papers, but they are not necessarily so. Short accounts, or short reviews, are excellent exercises in economy. For reviews, the short reviews in *The New Yorker* and in the *Scientific American* are often excellent models. And excellent practice may be gained from accounts of magazine articles, or reviews of them, instead of accounts or reviews of books—there is no difference in principle, merely a difference in scale.

For many students the most valuable practice might be a book review designed for oral presentation to a club or a discussion group—or, for that matter, to his own composition class.

In the "Suggestions for Papers" in Chapter VIII there are suggestions for some pieces of fairly obvious comparative criticism in connection with two selections. If one of them was attractive to you but not used then, it might appropriately be used now. Critical essays on other works are quite possible for students, but need careful consideration. One would not write a critical essay without a good deal of preparation, and some time for reflection.

XVI

Analogy

When we say that two things or processes or conditions are analogous, we mean that they are alike in some important respects but not in all. When we designate a passage as "an analogy," we are recognizing the writer's use of such likeness for a particular purpose. Of course an analogy frequently may be expressed in a simile or in a metaphor. But in this section we shall let "an analogy" designate an analogy that controls the structure of a piece of writing. Such an analogy is one efficient way of using the reader's experience toward new knowledge. We have seen that all successful writing must in some way use the reader's experience. That is why it is profitable for us to examine some analogies formally and explicitly worked out.

i SOME SHORT ANALOGIES

Often the primary purpose of an analogy is explanatory. If we are discussing for a reader or hearer a thing or process quite unfamiliar to him, we naturally approach it through what is familiar. Much classroom teaching proceeds by analogy; you may probably remember your high school science teacher, as he was beginning a discussion of the way in which sound waves behave, talking about dropping a pebble in a pool. He was using the familiar thing to make clear the unfamiliar. Sound waves and the little waves from a dropped pebble are not even in the same medium, but the very word "waves" in "sound waves" recognizes the parallel relationships, the analogy. Here is an analogy of the same sort:

FROM *The Stars in Their Courses* (1931)

SIR JAMES JEANS

[The Blue of the Sky]

1 Imagine that we stand on any ordinary seaside pier, and watch the waves rolling in and striking against the iron columns of the pier. Large waves pay very little attention to the columns—they divide right and left

Reprinted from *The Stars in Their Courses* by Sir James Jeans, by permission of the Cambridge University Press.

and re-unite after passing each column, much as a regiment of soldiers would if a tree stood in their road; it is almost as though the columns had not been there. But the short waves and ripples find the columns of the pier a much more formidable obstacle. When the short waves impinge on the columns, they are reflected back and spread as new ripples in all directions. To use the technical term, they are "scattered." The obstacle provided by the iron columns hardly affects the long waves at all, but scatters the short ripples.

II We have been watching a sort of working model of the way in which sunlight struggles through the earth's atmosphere. Between us on earth and outer space the atmosphere interposes innumerable obstacles in the form of molecules of air, tiny droplets of water, and small particles of dust. These are represented by the columns of the pier.

III The waves of the sea represent the sunlight. We know that sunlight is a blend of lights of many colours—as we can prove for ourselves by passing it through a prism, or even through a jug of water, or as Nature demonstrates to us when she passes it through the raindrops of a summer shower and produces a rainbow. We also know that light consists of waves, and that the different colours of light are produced by waves of different lengths, red light by long waves and blue light by short waves. The mixture of waves which constitutes sunlight has to struggle through the obstacles it meets in the atmosphere, just as the mixture of waves at the seaside has to struggle past the columns of the pier. And these obstacles treat the light-waves much as the columns of the pier treat the sea-waves. The long waves which constitute red light are hardly affected, but the short waves which constitute blue light are scattered in all directions.

IV Thus, the different constituents of sunlight are treated in different ways as they struggle through the earth's atmosphere. A wave of blue light may be scattered by a dust particle, and turned out of its course. After a time a second dust particle again turns it out of its course, and so on, until finally it enters our eyes by a path as zigzag as that of a flash of lightning. Consequently the blue waves of the sunlight enter our eyes from all directions. And that is why the sky looks blue.

---

1) Sir James is using in his analogy two processes that are dissimilar in many ways, indeed in most ways. What he requires is that there be a set of relationships in one process that is parallel to a set of relationships in the other. We can say that the first element of the analogy is handled in I, and that the two elements are handled together in II–III.

2) Here is an explanation of the same phenomenon, written by Frits W. Went in an article called "Air Pollution":

> . . . the famous discovery concerning the blueness of the sky . . . was made in the 1860s by the well-known English physicist and lecturer John Tyndall. He demonstrated experimentally that when a strong beam of light was passed through air containing small amounts of organic vapors, a "blue cloud" formed. The air was completely transparent, but it had a bluish tinge, which Tyndall surmised was

due to the formation of submicroscopic particles from the organic molecules. He concluded that most of the sky's blue color had to be attributed to the reflection of sunlight by minute particles in the sky.[1]

Try to decide exactly what Sir James's analogy does for a reader that the above account does not. But what do we learn from this account that we do not learn from the analogy?

3) *The Stars in Their Courses,* dealing as it does with material difficult for its intended readers, proceeds continually by analogy. If you will read this little book, you will learn much about analogy as a resource in writing, and much about astronomy. But you must understand that, in any science, analogy, convenient and even necessary for the beginner, must after a time be abandoned. When one has control of a science, he must think of its phenomena in and for themselves.

Our next analogy is designed to represent the kind of difficulty the physicist faces in atomic study. The analogy has far-reaching implications. The nineteenth-century scientist lived in a nice tight universe of law and solid matter. Relatively few persons have any notion of the universe contemporary science is beginning to envisage.

FROM *What Holds the Nucleus Together?* (1953)

HANS A. BETHE

[Strange Ball Game] [2]

I We are confronted with a problem which is just the opposite of the one physicists had when they began to study the atom as a whole. They were completely familiar with the forces (electric) at play, but had to discover the laws (quantum mechanics) that governed the operation of these forces. In the case of the nucleus, we are fairly confident about the governing laws (again quantum mechanics), but must discover the force.

II One might picture the situation in this way. You are walking in the park and come upon a group of men playing baseball. After watching for a few minutes you decide that it is a match between lunatics. The batters seem to run to any base that pleases them; the fielders throw the ball at random; the object of the game is utterly obscure, and the score, impossible to compute. But by long, intense observation you finally figure out the strange rules of the game. That is where atomic physics had arrived 20 years ago. We have now moved along to another place in the park and discovered a second game more insane than the first. The rules seem to be the same, but the players are playing without a ball! Something—we do not know just what—is passing back and forth among the players, and to un-

[1] Reprinted with permission of *Scientific American,* May, 1955, Volume #192, No. 5.

[2] Reprinted with permission of *Scientific American,* September, 1953, Volume #189, No. 3.

derstand the game we must find out what that something is. The invisible ball shuttling among the players corresponds to the force between particles in the nucleus.

III Our problem is twofold: (1) to measure the force and determine its other properties, and (2) to probe into the "cause" of the nuclear force, as it were, by studying its connections with other physical phenomena.

You will remember Mark Twain's remarks on the river pilot's memory in our selection from *Life on the Mississippi* in Chapter VIII. Now since the trained memory of the pilot is his distinguishing quality, Twain is not content with describing the way in which that memory functions on the river. Twain wants to make the reader realize the quality of the pilot's memory as fully as is possible. To accomplish that he finds—or, it is more accurate to say, he constructs—some analogies. How many are there in the following selection? Is this selection analogy for explanation in quite the same sense that the analogy by Sir James Jeans is?

FROM *Life on the Mississippi* (1875, 1883)

MARK TWAIN

A Pilot's Needs

I . . . First of all, there is one faculty which a pilot must incessantly cultivate until he has brought it to absolute perfection. Nothing short of perfection will do. That faculty is memory. He cannot stop with merely thinking a thing is so and so; he must *know* it; for this is eminently one of the "exact" sciences. With what scorn a pilot was looked upon, in the old times, if he ever ventured to deal in that feeble phrase "I think," instead of the vigorous one "I know!" One cannot easily realize what a tremendous thing it is to know every trivial detail of twelve hundred miles of river and know it with absolute exactness. If you will take the longest street in New York, and travel up and down it, conning its features patiently until you know every house and window and lamp-post and big and little sign by heart, and know them so accurately that you can instantly name the one you are abreast of when you are set down at random in that street in the middle of an inky black night, you will then have a tolerable notion of the amount and the exactness of a pilot's knowledge who carries the Mississippi River in his head. And then, if you will go on until you know every street crossing, the character, size, and position of the crossing-stones, and the varying depth of mud in each of those numberless places, you will have some idea of what the pilot must know in order to keep a Mississippi steamer out of trouble. Next, if you will take half of the signs in that long street, and *change their places* once a month, and still manage to know their new positions accurately on dark nights, and keep up with these re-peated changes without making any mistakes, you will understand what is required of a pilot's peerless memory by the fickle Mississippi.

II I think a pilot's memory is about the most wonderful thing in the world. To know the Old and New Testaments by heart, and be able to recite them glibly, forward or backward, or begin at random anywhere in the book and recite both ways and never trip or make a mistake, is no extravagant mass of knowledge, and no marvelous facility, compared to a pilot's massed knowledge of the Mississippi and his marvelous facility in the handling of it. I make this comparison deliberately, and believe I am not expanding the truth when I do it. Many will think my figure too strong, but pilots will not.

III And how easily and comfortably the pilot's memory does its work; how placidly effortless is its way; how *unconsciously* it lays up its vast stores, hour by hour, day by day, and never loses or mislays a single valuable package of them all! Take an instance. Let a leadsman cry, "Half twain! half twain! half twain! half twain! half twain!" until it becomes as monotonous as the ticking of a clock; let conversation be going on all the time, and the pilot be doing his share of the talking, and no longer consciously listening to the leadsman; and in the midst of this endless string of half twains let a single "quarter twain!" be interjected, without emphasis, and then the half twain cry go on again, just as before: two or three weeks later that pilot can describe with precision the boat's position in the river when that quarter twain was uttered, and give you such a lot of head-marks, stern-marks, and side-marks to guide you, that you ought to be able to take the boat there and put her in that same spot again yourself! The cry of "quarter twain" did not really take his mind from his talk, but his trained faculties instantly photographed the bearings, noted the change of depth, and laid up the important details for future reference without requiring any assistance from *him* in the matter. If you were walking and talking with a friend, and another friend at your side kept up a monotonous repetition of the vowel sound A, for a couple of blocks, and then in the midst interjected an R, thus, A, A, A, A, A, R, A, A, A, etc., and gave the R no emphasis, you would not be able to state, two or three weeks afterward, that the R had been put in, nor be able to tell what objects you were passing at the moment it was done. But you could if your memory had been patiently and laboriously trained to do that sort of thing mechanically.

IV Give a man a tolerably fair memory to start with, and piloting will develop it into a very colossus of capability. But *only in the matters it is daily drilled in.* A time would come when the man's faculties could not help noticing landmarks and soundings, and his memory could not help holding on to them with the grip of a vice; but if you asked that same man at noon what he had had for breakfast, it would be ten chances to one that he could not tell you. Astonishing things can be done with the human memory if you will devote it faithfully to one particular line of business.

This next example is from *Moby-Dick*. The "I" of the passage is Ishmael, the narrator of the story, an educated young American on his first voyage on a whaler. Queequeg is a native of the South Seas.

FROM *Moby-Dick* (1851)

HERMAN MELVILLE

The Mat-Maker

I It was a cloudy, sultry afternoon; the seamen were lazily lounging about the decks, or vacantly gazing over into the lead-colored waters. Queequeg and I were mildly employed weaving what is called a sword-mat, for an additional lashing to our boat. So still and subdued and yet somehow preluding was all the scene, and such an incantation of revery lurked in the air, that each silent sailor seemed resolved into his own invisible self.

II I was the attendant or page of Queequeg, while busy at the mat. As I kept passing and repassing the filling or woof of marline between the long yarns of the warp, using my own hand for the shuttle, and as Queequeg, standing sideways, ever and anon slid his heavy oaken sword between the threads, and idly looking off upon the water, carelessly and unthinkingly drove home every yarn: I say so strange a dreaminess did there then reign all over the ship and all over the sea, only broken by the intermitting dull sound of the sword, that it seemed as if this were the Loom of Time, and I myself were a shuttle mechanically weaving and weaving away at the Fates. There lay the fixed threads of the warp subject to but one single, ever returning, unchanging vibration, and that vibration merely enough to admit of the crosswise interblending of other threads with its own. This warp seemed necessity; and here, thought I, with my own hand I ply my own shuttle and weave my own destiny into these unalterable threads. Meantime, Queequeg's impulsive, indifferent sword, sometimes hitting the woof slantingly, or crookedly, or strongly, or weakly, as the case might be; and by this difference in the concluding blow producing a corresponding contrast in the final aspect of the completed fabric; this savage's sword, thought I, which thus finally shapes and fashions both warp and woof; this easy, indifferent sword must be chance—aye, chance, free will, and necessity—no wise incompatible—all interweavingly working together. The straight warp of necessity, not to be swerved from its ultimate course—its every alternating vibration, indeed, only tending to that; free will still free to ply her shuttle between given threads; and chance, though restrained in its play within the right lines of necessity, and sideways in its motions directed by free will, though thus prescribed to by both, chance by turns rules either, and has the last featuring blow at events.

---

1) In I a mood is established, a mood in which an occupation that does not require much attention becomes fused with Ishmael's thoughts. How far did you read into the passage before you became aware of the general intention of the analogy?

2) The analogy is, of course, between the weaving of the mat and the interplay of necessity, will, and chance in human experience. But you will,

first of all, need to visualize the mat-making clearly. It may be well for you to write a brief account of the physical process itself.

3) How far does this analogy serve an explanatory purpose?

4) The speculation with which we are here concerned has—in one form or another—fascinated and baffled generations of men; and men have come to very different conclusions. How does the analogy help Melville to make precisely clear his conclusion about the relationship of necessity, will, and chance in human affairs? Would it be true to say that it has something of the function of a diagram? Why or why not?

5) Perhaps we need to pursue question 4 a bit further. This is by no means the first time the loom has been used as a symbol of human destiny. Usually, however, the operator of the loom is a supernatural being, weaving the fate of humans. Consider such questions as these: What is the effect of "using my own hand for the shuttle" in the second sentence in 11? In view of Melville's ideas, why does the analogy, as well as the literal mat-making, require that two persons be concerned in the weaving? Would it make any difference how the two functions were assigned? For the purposes of the analogy could Ishmael—the "I"—just as well use the wooden sword? Would some sailor who hailed from Nantucket do just as well as Queequeg for the sword-wielder? What is Melville enforcing in the sentence which begins "Meantime, Queequeg's impulsive, indifferent sword . . . "?

6) Can you apply this analogy to your own experience? What in it corresponds to the warp? For instance, if you chose the college you now attend, was that your own hand at the shuttle? What then is the warp? And what the action of the wooden sword?

7) Does Melville say in the last sentence that chance is the most important of the three elements in human destiny?

8) Just to be sure of your control of this passage, make a short statement of Melville's ideas about human destiny without using the analogy.

The following analogy, a famous one, is a striking presentation of the faith of the rationalist. This belief in the triumph of human reason, with its accompanying faith in the future, is older than Holmes; the attitude in this analogy seems really an eighteenth-century one. See whether you think this analogy has any comparable function to the analogy by Melville. And consider why the first element in the analogy might have been chosen (notice the description of the insects). Decide whether the analogy has any purpose as explanation.

FROM *The Autocrat of the Breakfast-Table* (1857–8)

OLIVER WENDELL HOLMES

[The Flat Stone Overturned]

1 Did you never, in walking in the fields, come across a large flat stone, which had lain, nobody knows how long, just where you found it, with the

grass forming a little hedge, as it were, all round it, close to its edges,— and have you not, in obedience to a kind of feeling that told you it had been lying there long enough, insinuated your stick or your foot or your fingers under its edge and turned it over as a housewife turns a cake, when she says to herself, "It's done brown enough by this time"? What an odd revelation, and what an unforeseen and unpleasant surprise to a small community, the very existence of which you had not suspected, until the sudden dismay and scattering among its members produced by your turning the old stone over! Blades of grass flattened down, colorless, matted together, as if they had been bleached and ironed; hideous crawling creatures, some of them coleopterous or horny-shelled,—turtle-bugs one wants to call them; some of them softer, but cunningly spread out and compressed like Lepine watches; (Nature never loses a crack or a crevice, mind you, or a joint in a tavern bedstead, but she always has one of her flat-pattern live timekeepers to slide into it;) black, glossy crickets, with their long filaments sticking out like the whips of four-horse stage-coaches; motionless, slug-like creatures, young larvæ, perhaps more horrible in their pulpy stillness than even in the infernal wriggle of maturity! But no sooner is the stone turned and the wholesome light of day let upon this compressed and blinded community of creeping things, than all of them which enjoy the luxury of legs—and some of them have a good many—rush round wildly, butting each other and everything in their way, and end in a general stampede for underground retreats from the region poisoned by sunshine. *Next year* you will find the grass growing tall and green where the stone lay; the ground-bird builds her nest where the beetle had his hole; the dandelion and the buttercup are growing there, and the broad fans of insect-angels open and shut their golden disks, as the rhythmic waves of blissful consciousness pulsate through their glorified being. . . .

II . . . there is meaning in each of those images,—the butterfly as well as the others. The stone is ancient error. The grass is human nature borne down and bleached of all its color by it. The shapes which are found beneath are the crafty beings that thrive in darkness, and the weaker organisms kept helpless by it. He who turns the stone over is whosoever puts the staff of truth to the old lying incubus, no matter whether he do it with a serious face or a laughing one. The next year stands for the coming time. Then shall the nature which had lain blanched and broken rise in its full stature and native hues in the sunshine. Then shall God's minstrels build their nests in the hearts of a newborn humanity. Then shall beauty—Divinity taking outlines and color—light upon the souls of men as the butterfly, image of the beatified spirit rising from the dust, soars from the shell that held a poor grub, which would never have found wings had not the stone been lifted.

III You never need think you can turn over any old falsehood without a terrible squirming and scattering of the horrid little population that dwells under it.

ii   ARGUMENT BY ANALOGY

You are familiar with analogies used for argument—you have probably argued some question by analogy within the last day or two. Suppose a student says: City A is happy under the city manager plan of government, but city B is badly governed under a mayor and a city council of the traditional sort; therefore city B ought to adopt the city manager plan. You can see that if A and B stand for actual cities that are analogous in important respects—size, special problems, traditions, and so on—the argument will have some validity. And you can see the assumption in such argument. A logician might state it: if two things agree with one another in one respect, or in some respects, they will probably agree in others. Since analogical reasoning makes an immediate, easy use of experience, we use it often in our everyday thinking.

Now of course an argument by analogy may be deceptive (as may, indeed, any other sort of argument). A careless reader may neglect to examine the kind and degree of likeness between the elements in the analogy. A clever writer may succeed in making the two elements in his analogy seem more completely or more really similar than they are—or a writer may be himself deceived. But if an analogy is worked out at any length, the reader has opportunity to examine it—and he should. Our examples of argument by analogy have a good deal of technical interest.

In his "Preface" to *Mere Christianity*, C. S. Lewis uses an analogy between the word "gentleman" and the word "Christian" as a means of enforcing his definition of the latter. The two words mean quite different things; but they are analogous in their histories. Now we might call what Mr. Lewis has written "an extended definition by analogy." But the first paragraph of our selection makes its purpose as argument as well as definition manifest. Lewis needs to make clear a matter of terminology that, besides being generally confused, has a great deal of emotional implication.

FROM *Mere Christianity* (1952)

C. S. LEWIS

[The Word "Christian"]

1 . . . Objections may be felt—and have been expressed—against my use of the word *Christian* to mean one who accepts the common doctrines of Christianity. People ask: "Who are you, to lay down who is, and who is not a Christian?" or "May not many a man who cannot believe these doctrines be far more truly a Christian, far closer to the spirit of Christ, than some who do?" Now this objection is in one sense very right, very chari-

table, very spiritual, very sensitive. It has every amiable quality excepts that of being useful. We simply cannot, without disaster, use language as these objectors want us to use it. I will try to make this clear by the history of another, and very much less important, word.

11 The word *gentleman* originally meant something recognisable; one who had a coat of arms and some landed property. When you called someone "a gentleman" you were not paying him a compliment, but merely stating a fact. If you said he was not "a gentleman" you were not insulting him, but giving information. There was no contradiction in saying that John was a liar and a gentleman; any more than there now is in saying that James is a fool and an M.A. But then there came people who said—so rightly, charitably, spiritually, sensitively, so anything but usefully—"Ah, but surely the important thing about a gentleman is not the coat of arms and the land, but the behaviour? Surely he is the true gentleman who behaves as a gentleman should? Surely in that sense Edward is far more truly a gentleman than John?" They meant well. To be honourable and courteous and brave is of course a far better thing than to have a coat of arms. But it is not the same thing. Worse still, it is not a thing everyone will agree about. To call a man "a gentleman" in this new, refined sense, becomes, in fact, not a way of giving information about him, but a way of praising him: to deny that he is "a gentleman" becomes simply a way of insulting him. When a word ceases to be a term of description and becomes merely a term of praise, it no longer tells you facts about the object: it only tells you about the speaker's attitude to that object. (A "nice" meal only means a meal the speaker likes.) A *gentleman,* once it has been spiritualised and refined out of its old coarse, objective sense, means hardly more than a man whom the speaker likes. As a result, *gentleman* is now a useless word. We had lots of terms of approval already, so it was not needed for that use; on the other hand if anyone (say, in a historical work) wants to use it in its old sense, he cannot do so without explanations. It has been spoiled for that purpose.

111 Now if once we allow people to start spiritualising and refining, or as they might say "deepening," the sense of the word *Christian,* it too will speedily become a useless word. In the first place, Christians themselves will never be able to apply it to anyone. It is not for us to say who, in the deepest sense, is or is not close to the spirit of Christ. We do not see into men's hearts. We cannot judge, and are indeed forbidden to judge. It would be wicked arrogance for us to say that any man is, or is not, a Christian in this refined sense. And obviously a word which we can never apply is not going to be a very useful word. As for the unbelievers, they will no doubt cheerfully use the word in the refined sense. It will become in their mouths simply a term of praise. In calling anyone a Christian they will mean that they think him a good man. But that way of using the word will be no enrichment of the language, for we already have the word *good.* Meanwhile, the word *Christian* will have been spoiled for any really useful purpose it might have served.

IV We must therefore stick to the original, obvious meaning. The name *Christians* was first given at Antioch (Acts xi. 26) to "the disciples," to those who accepted the teaching of the apostles. There is no question of its being restricted to those who profited by that teaching as much as they should have. There is no question of its being extended to those who in some refined, spiritual, inward fashion were "far closer to the spirit of Christ" than the less satisfactory of the disciples. The point is not a theological, or moral one. It is only a question of using words so that we can all understand what is being said. When a man who accepts the Christian doctrine lives unworthily of it, it is much clearer to say he is a bad Christian than to say he is not a Christian.

---

1) The problem of definition here is surely clear to you. The important question for our present purpose is, why does Mr. Lewis find the use of his analogy necessary or desirable?

2) However you answer that question, you can hardly say that he uses the word "gentleman" because it is more familiar than "Christian." And to show the analogous development of the two words, he has had to write a long paragraph on the history of "gentleman." (See what your dictionary has to say about the derivation of "gentle.")

3) Perhaps the last sentence in 1 suggests our answer. "Gentleman" is a less important word than "Christian" in several ways. And one way is that the modern reader is not likely to feel very deeply about it. Do you see, then, that its use as an analogy allows Lewis to discuss the principle with which he is concerned without the likelihood that his reader's emotional commitments will get in the way? If the reader sees the principle for "gentleman," he can hardly help seeing it for "Christian," no matter how vaguely he has been using the term.

4) In your own writing, you will do well to remember that if your reader has a misapprehension, his emotions will urge him to defend it. If you can for a while take the discussion out of any emotional context, that will be an advantage to him and to you.

As a convenient way of enforcing an important point, our second selection is divided into two parts, and we have some questions about the first part before we consider the second. The selection is from an address by John Ruskin. He has just been saying, "All economy, whether of states, households, or individuals, may be defined to be the art of managing labour." And he has been describing an ideal mistress of a household who, because she keeps all the servants well occupied, overburdens no one of them. It is to her household that the first sentence of our selection refers, and it is from the idea in the sentence quoted above that the argument by analogy proceeds. Watch it carefully.

FROM *The Discovery and Application of Art* (1857)

JOHN RUSKIN

[The Great Farm]

[i]

1 Now, the precise counterpart of such a household would be seen in a nation in which political economy was rightly understood. You complain of the difficulty of finding work for your men. Depend upon it the real difficulty rather is to find men for your work. The serious question for you is not how many you have to feed, but how much you have to do; it is our inactivity, not our hunger, that ruins us: let us never fear that our servants should have a good appetite—our wealth is in their strength, not in their starvation. Look around this island of yours, and see what you have to do in it. The sea roars against your harbourless cliffs—you have to build the breakwater, and dig the port of refuge; the unclean pestilence ravins in your streets—you have to bring the full stream from the hills, and to send the free winds through the thoroughfare; the famine blanches your lips and eats away your flesh—you have to dig the moor and dry the marsh, to bid the morass give forth instead of engulfing, and to wring the honey and oil out of the rock. These things, and thousands such, we have to do, and shall have to do constantly, on this great farm of ours; for do not suppose that it is anything else than that. Precisely the same laws of economy which apply to the cultivation of a farm or an estate apply to the cultivation of a province or of an island. Whatever rebuke you would address to the improvident master of an ill-managed patrimony, precisely that rebuke we should address to ourselves, so far as we leave our population in idleness and our country in disorder. What would you say to the lord of an estate who complained to you of his poverty and disabilities, and, when you pointed out to him that his land was half of it overrun with weeds, and that his fences were all in ruin, and that his cattle-sheds were roofless, and his labourers lying under the hedges faint for want of food, he answered to you that it would ruin him to weed his land or to roof his sheds—that those were too costly operations for him to undertake, and that he knew not how to feed his labourers nor pay them? Would you not instantly answer, that instead of ruining him to weed his fields, it would save him; that his inactivity was his destruction, and that to set his labourers to work was to feed them? Now you may add acre to acre, and estate to estate, as far as you like, but you will never reach a compass of ground which shall escape from the authority of these simple laws. The principles which are right in the administration of a few fields, are right also in the administration of a great country from horizon to horizon: idleness does not cease to be ruinous because it is extensive, nor labour to be productive because it is universal.

1) A student, asked to state the essence of this passage, wrote: "A well-run nation will not have idleness and strife. A nation of idlers cannot be a well-organized nation. Each cog must work to make a smooth running whole." Did the student understand what Ruskin was driving at? Did he see what the analogy was?

2) Certainly the analogy is intended to do more than just to enforce the idea that working hard is good. Can we put this argument in the form of a proportion? Suppose we say: "The inactivity of citizens is to a nation as the inactivity of servants is to an estate." But that is only a negative idea, and Ruskin seems to be arguing *for* something. Can you put what he is arguing *for* in the form of a proportion? Perhaps you need to consider the analogy further: What is analogous to the servants on the farm? And to the farmer?

3) What sentences are the central statements of the argument by analogy? What is their relationship to the organization of the whole passage?

4) Abandoning the terms of the analogy, make a brief statement of the contention about government that Ruskin is here making.

5) Is this, in your opinion, an acceptable argument by analogy? Is there anything deceptive about it? The two elements in the analogy do have some real likeness. Is that likeness great enough?

6) A farm is a small and familiar social organization; we may suppose we can understand what goes on there. It is reassuring to be told that a national economy works the same way. And in this regard you should notice particularly the effect of the direct address; consider, for instance, the questions beginning "What would you say to the lord of an estate who . . ." and "Would you not instantly answer. . . ." Do you see that, if the reader assents to the answer the writer supplies him, his assent is likely to carry over to the writer's next statement, too?

In Ruskin's address, passage ii follows passage i without break.

[ii]

I Nay, but you reply, there is one vast difference between the nation's economy and the private man's: the farmer has full authority over his labourers; he can direct them to do what is needed to be done, whether they like it or not; and he can turn them away if they refuse to work, or impede others in their working, or are disobedient, or quarrelsome. There *is* this great difference; it is precisely this difference on which I wish to fix your attention, for it is precisely this difference which you have to do away with. We know the necessity of authority in farm, or in fleet, or in army; but we commonly refuse to admit it in the body of the nation. Let us consider this point a little.

II In the various awkward and unfortunate efforts which the French have made at the development of a social system, they have at least stated one true principle, that of fraternity or brotherhood. Do not be alarmed; they got all wrong in their experiments, because they quite forgot that this fact of fraternity implied another fact quite as important—that of paternity, or fatherhood. That is to say, if they were to regard the nation as one

family, the condition of unity in that family consisted no less in their having a head, or a father, than in their being faithful and affectionate members, or brothers. But we must not forget this, for we have long confessed
it with our lips, though we refuse to confess it in our lives. For half an
hour every Sunday we expect a man in a black gown, supposed to be telling us truth, to address us as brethren, though we should be shocked at the
notion of any brotherhood existing among us out of church. And we can
hardly read a few sentences on any political subject without running a
chance of crossing the phrase "paternal government," though we should be
utterly horror-struck at the idea of governments claiming anything like a
father's authority over us. Now, I believe those two formal phrases are in
both instances perfectly binding and accurate, and that the image of the
farm and its servants which I have hitherto used, as expressing a wholesome national organization, fails only of doing so, not because it is too domestic, but because it is not domestic enough; because the real type of a
well-organized nation must be presented, not by a farm cultivated by servants who wrought for hire, and might be turned away if they refused to
labour, but by a farm in which the master was a father, and in which all
the servants were sons; which implied, therefore, in all its regulations, not
merely the order of expediency, but the bonds of affection and responsibilities of relationship; and in which all acts and services were not only to
be sweetened by brotherly concord, but to be enforced by fatherly authority.

III   Observe, I do not mean in the least that we ought to place such an
authority in the hands of any one person, or of any class, or body of persons. But I do mean to say that as an individual who conducts himself
wisely must make laws for himself which at some time or other may appear
irksome or injurious, but which, precisely at the time they appear most
irksome, it is most necessary he should obey, so a nation which means to
conduct itself wisely, must establish authority over itself, vested either in
kings, councils, or laws, which it must resolve to obey, even at times when
the law or authority appears irksome to the body of the people, or injurious
to certain masses of it.

------

1) Did you reply, as Ruskin tells us in I that he expected his hearers
and readers to reply, that the argument by analogy was unsound? Did you
say that a nation and a farm are not analogous enough to support the contention, and that the kind of authority a nation has over its citizens is not
the kind of authority a farmer has over his employees?

2) What Ruskin has done is of great technical interest. In our passage i
he has made a faulty argument by analogy as persuasive as he could—indeed for some readers it might be wholly persuasive. Then in passage ii
Ruskin changes his ground.

3) Ruskin says in passage ii that in a good society—in the society he
would have us labor to achieve—his analogy would be a sound analogy.
But notice that it is pointed out in the last half of paragraph II that in this
good society both elements of the analogy would change somewhat—the
farm would not be run for the profit motive.

4) But an opponent could change his ground, too. He might contend that any political development that made the relationship of a citizen to the state analogous to the relationship of a dependent son to his father would be a bad development. In other words, the analogy would still be in question if the opponent denied that what is desirable in a family is also desirable in a state.

5) Is the state that Ruskin urges a totalitarian state? If it is not, how does it differ? Exactly what is said in III? Is not this paragraph in itself a brief argument by analogy? What is the analogy?

Argument by analogy is often not so fully and so fairly worked out as it is in the Ruskin passage. And an argument by analogy that is merely implied in a metaphor is likely to be deceptive, because it depends upon an association that the reader makes unconsciously. For instance, a group of industrialists may talk about their "pioneering on the frontiers of progress," and intend thus to exalt their researches or their new products. Since we have been taught to revere the pioneers in our history, our favorable responses to "pioneering" and "frontiers" may carry over to our feeling about industrial endeavors, although the likeness between them and the individualistic efforts of frontiersmen is slight or non-existent.

In somewhat the same fashion advertisers and public relations writers use a favorable response to "geared to." We are mechanically minded enough to think of a gear ratio as something inherently right. When an advertiser says his product is geared to modern living, he does not expect us to consider whether the expression has much meaning; he merely hopes for a favorable association. A more striking example [1] is the term "pump-priming." During the depression years of the 1930's people used to talk of "pump-priming" when they meant the spending of federal money on public works in an effort to get the nation's economy properly functioning. The implied argument by analogy was an effective one. Most people knew about pouring a little water in a pump to prime it—that priming usually works and that thereupon one gets a lot of water from the pump. As long as one did not consider how far analogous a pump and the economic system were, the metaphor implied simplicity and success.

The importance of implied analogy in metaphor is illustrated in an interesting fashion in a passage from Thomas Paine's *Common Sense*. You will remember that Paine wrote his *Common Sense* at the crucial period of tension between the colonies and Great Britain, and that his intention was to persuade his readers that an immediate break with Great Britain was logical, advantageous to the colonies, and inevitable—and you will remember what a very effective piece of writing *Common Sense* was. Notice how anxious Paine is to counteract the effect of an implied analogy in an established metaphor, and to substitute other metaphors. Consider the logic of the argument throughout.

[1] Borrowed from Winthrop Tilley's *Basic English for College Freshmen* (Rinehart and Company).

FROM *Common Sense* (1776)

THOMAS PAINE

[Mother Country]

I It hath lately been asserted in Parliament, that the colonies have no relation to each other but through the parent country, i.e. that Pennsylvania and the Jerseys, and so on for the rest, are sister colonies by the way of England; this is certainly a very roundabout way of proving relationship, but it is the nearest and only true way of proving enmity (or enemyship, if I may so call it). France and Spain never were, nor perhaps ever will be, our enemies as *Americans,* but as our being the *subjects of Great Britain.*

II But Britain is the parent country, say some. Then the more shame upon her conduct. Even brutes do not devour their young, nor savages make war upon their families; wherefore, the assertion, if true, turns to her reproach; but it happens not to be true, or only partly so, and the phrase *parent* or *mother country* hath been jesuitically adopted by the King and his parasites, with a low papistical design of gaining an unfair bias on the credulous weakness of our minds. Europe, and not England, is the parent country of America. This new world hath been the asylum for the persecuted lovers of civil and religious liberty from *every part* of Europe. Hither have they fled, not from the tender embraces of the mother, but from the cruelty of the monster; and it is so far true of England, that the same tyranny which drove the first emigrants from home, pursues their descendants still.

III In this extensive quarter of the globe, we forget the narrow limits of three hundred and sixty miles (the extent of England) and carry our friendship on a larger scale; we claim brotherhood with every European Christian, and triumph in the generosity of the sentiment.

ANALOGY BECOMING ALLEGORY   *iii*

We turn to a famous analogy from Edward Bellamy's *Looking Backward: 2000–1887,* a nineteenth-century use of the literary kind we discussed in connection with John Richard Green's account of More's *Utopia.* Bellamy's "utopian romance" was once a very influential book, and it is still read. In our selection the "I" is Julian West, a citizen of Boston of the late nineteenth century, who, through a series of remarkable events, finds himself living in the year 2000. In 2000 private capitalism has been replaced by a democratic form of state capitalism. Every citizen is at once an employee and a member of the state, and many of the ills of civilization have been done away with. In our selection West is writing for the people of 2000 and explaining to them the social structure of 1887. The selection purports to be an analogical explanation of a difficult subject through a simple and familiar object. But as you read, watch what happens—you will find it more complex than that.

FROM *Looking Backward: 2000–1887* (1888)

EDWARD BELLAMY

[The Stagecoach of Capitalism]

I By way of attempting to give the reader some general impression of the way people lived together in those days, and especially of the relations of the rich and poor to one another, perhaps I cannot do better than to compare society as it then was to a prodigious coach which the masses of humanity were harnessed to and dragged toilsomely along a very hilly and sandy road. The driver was hunger, and permitted no lagging, though the pace was necessarily very slow. Despite the difficulty of drawing the coach at all along so hard a road, the top was covered with passengers who never got down, even at the steepest ascents. These seats on top were very breezy and comfortable. Well up out of the dust, their occupants could enjoy the scenery at their leisure, or critically discuss the merits of the straining team. Naturally such places were in great demand and the competition for them was keen, every one seeking as the first end in life to secure a seat on the coach for himself and to leave it to his child after him. By the rule of the coach a man could leave his seat to whom he wished, but on the other hand there were many accidents by which it might at any time be wholly lost. For all that they were so easy, the seats were very insecure, and at every sudden jolt of the coach persons were slipping out of them and falling to the ground, where they were instantly compelled to take hold of the rope and help to drag the coach on which they had before ridden so pleasantly. It was naturally regarded as a terrible misfortune to lose one's seat, and the apprehension that this might happen to them or their friends was a constant cloud upon the happiness of those who rode.

II But did they think only of themselves? you ask. Was not their very luxury rendered intolerable to them by comparison with the lot of their brothers and sisters in the harness, and the knowledge that their own weight added to their toil? Had they no compassion for fellow beings from whom fortune only distinguished them? Oh, yes; commiseration was frequently expressed by those who rode for those who had to pull the coach, especially when the vehicle came to a bad place in the road, as it was constantly doing, or to a particularly steep hill. At such times, the desperate straining of the team, their agonized leaping and plunging under the pitiless lashing of hunger, the many who fainted at the rope and were trampled in the mire, made a very distressing spectacle, which often called forth highly creditable displays of feeling on the top of the coach. At such times the passengers would call down encouragingly to the toilers of the rope, exhorting them to patience, and holding out hopes of possible compensation in another world for the hardness of their lot, while others contributed to buy salves and liniments for the crippled and injured. It was agreed that it was a great pity that the coach should be so hard to pull, and there was a sense of general relief when the specially bad piece of road was gotten over.

This relief was not, indeed, wholly on account of the team, for there was always some danger at these bad places of a general overturn in which all would lose their seats.

III It must in truth be admitted that the main effect of the spectacle of the misery of the toilers at the rope was to enhance the passengers' sense of the value of their seats upon the coach, and to cause them to hold on to them more desperately than before. If the passengers could only have felt assured that neither they nor their friends would ever fall from the top, it is probable that, beyond contributing to the funds for liniments and bandages, they would have troubled themselves extremely little about those who dragged the coach.

IV I am well aware that this will appear to the men and women of the twentieth century an incredible inhumanity, but there are two facts, both very curious, which partly explain it. In the first place, it was firmly and sincerely believed that there was no other way in which Society could get along, except the many pulled at the rope and the few rode, and not only this, but that no very radical improvement even was possible, either in the harness, the coach, the roadway, or the distribution of the toil. It had always been as it was, and it always would be so. It was a pity, but it could not be helped, and philosophy forbade wasting compassion on what was beyond remedy.

V The other fact is yet more curious, consisting in a singular hallucination which those on the top of the coach generally shared, that they were not exactly like their brothers and sisters who pulled at the rope, but of finer clay, in some way belonging to a higher order of beings who might justly expect to be drawn. This seems unaccountable, but, as I once rode on this very coach and shared that very hallucination, I ought to be believed. The strangest thing about the hallucination was that those who had but just climbed up from the ground, before they had outgrown the marks of the rope upon their hands, began to fall under its influence. As for those whose parents and grand-parents before them had been so fortunate as to keep their seats on the top, the conviction they cherished of the essential difference between their sort of humanity and the common article was absolute. The effect of such a delusion in moderating fellow feeling for the sufferings of the mass of men into a distant and philosophical compassion is obvious. To it I refer as the only extenuation I can offer for the indifference which, at the period I write of, marked my own attitude toward the misery of my brothers.

---

1) In the first sentence Bellamy's hero and narrator, Julian West, seems to say that he is writing an ordinary analogy for explanation: the social structure of the last quarter of the nineteenth century may be compared to a great coach. But, although his purported readers in 2000 perhaps would have seen a stagecoach in a museum, it would not have been a familiar object. And Bellamy's real readers, for the most part at least, did not see stagecoaches on the roads. Why do you suppose Bellamy chose it?

2) Do you think it may be that, since Bellamy considers the capitalistic

system outworn and antiquated, he feels that the proper analogy for it is something else antiquated? Or is he primarily interested in the vivid image of injustice the analogy makes possible?

3) But of course we have been overlooking something. The analogy is not really between a stagecoach and the social structure of the late nineteenth century. One element of the analogy is an account of some persons pulling a stagecoach and some other few riding on top. It is in that account that we see an obvious injustice. Now if the capitalistic system works in a fashion analogous to that account, must it not be unjust, too? What purported at the outset to be an analogy for explanation has turned into an implied argument by analogy. How would you state the argument by analogy explicitly?

4) This analogy is so completely worked out, prolonged into such detailed narrative, that it passes into ALLEGORY, in which a set of persons, actions, and details are symbols for another set of persons, actions, and details. Bunyan's *Pilgrim's Progress,* once known to almost all who read English, represents man's effort to attain salvation by an account of a man called Christian who journeys long through difficult country and must face the greatest impediments on his way to the Celestial City. In our selection what (to take but a few symbols) is represented by "every sudden jolt," "highly creditable displays of feeling," and "salves and liniments"? And what, exactly, is the comment on our social system (and human nature) made in the third sentence of v?

5) But a writer is not limited to one device at a time, and Bellamy can do through West, his narrator, things he could not do if he were writing in his own person. Do you see the advantage? Bellamy is discussing injustices familiar to him, and quite as familiar to his readers, *as if* he were explaining them to persons to whom the injustices were new and surprising. We shall watch Jonathan Swift use a similar device when he has his narrator, Gulliver, describe warfare in Europe to the king of Brobdingnag, who knows nothing about it and is therefore shocked at what Gulliver takes as commonplace. It is a device to make the reader see freshly and from a new point of view an injustice custom has dulled for him.

6) If you cannot yet parallel what Bellamy is doing from your literary experience, you probably can from your everyday experience. Have you never explained a familiar injustice to a child and realized that, even as you were speaking, you were seeing it anew? In what passages particularly does Bellamy make effective use of this device of point of view? Where are we made aware of probable shock and surprise on the part of the purported readers?

7) But may the matter be a little more complex than the considerations of questions 5 and 6 indicate? West would presumably have some emotional attachment to the generation in which he was born, even though he is intellectually convinced of the excellence of the system of 2000. Do you think Bellamy may be using that conflict for his own purposes? For instance, we realize such an expression as "a very distressing spectacle" as an ironic UNDERSTATEMENT. And we suspect some ironic reservation in "highly creditable displays of feeling on the top of the coach." Are they ironic in effect because we understand West to have a satirical intent? Or are they ironic in effect because we understand that West would naturally

prefer somewhat neutral language? In either case, the reader himself is left to supply a more adequate judgment.

8) Bellamy expected that a system of state capitalism would have replaced private capitalism by our time. Although it has not, the social structure has undergone some changes, and some of Bellamy's own predictions have been fulfilled in part. For instance, in one part of his book he predicts the system we call social security. Could Bellamy's analogy be adapted to represent the social structure of our own time? Could one trying to use it so find a way to represent the place of labor unions? Of unemployment insurance? What would one do with the working man who is also, since he has some investments, in a small way a capitalist?

9) Bellamy and Ruskin have something in common; at least both look forward to a collectivist society, and both use analogy as a means of persuasion. Is our selection from one more likely to be persuasive than our selection from the other? Can you defend your opinion?

SUGGESTIONS FOR PAPERS

Writing a formal summary of an analogy is a fairly difficult and a rewarding exercise. The trick is to make the structure of the original come clear in the summary, and perhaps we need an example. Here is a summary of the analogy from *The Autocrat of the Breakfast-Table:*

When you turn over a flat stone, you find under it the grass matted and dead, and the space it had occupied full of repulsive insect creatures— hard-shelled, many-legged, or slug-like—who hate and fear the sun. There will be wild commotion as they retreat from the light. But when you return the next year, you find that all is changed: the grass is green, and flowers and birds and butterflies live there.

In the same way, when an old, established error is done away with, you see that it had sheltered the wicked who profited by it, and the weak who were inhibited by it, and that both resent the truth. But when the error has been long-enough destroyed, you find that all is changed: the error is of no effect, and human nature freed from it develops toward full stature and beauty.

You may wish to try writing analogies of your own. Assume a particular purpose for any analogy you write: an explanation, or a vivid image of an idea, for a reader you can envisage. If you try a piece of argument by analogy, then make sure you have a sound analogy.

For an extended paper, you might do this: Look up "analogy" in your desk dictionary and quote the first definition you find, which will be a definition in a general sense, not a definition of "analogy" as a literary device. Working from that definition, write a discussion of the way in which a writer may use analogy. You may use as examples analogies from this text, from your general reading, or of your own devising. Assume readers with less literary experience than your own. Or you may wish to adapt this suggestion to a paper called, say, "Analogy as a Teaching Device."

A paper requiring further reading might be a study of Sir James Jeans's use of analogy in *The Stars in Their Courses,* in which there are, besides briefly extended analogies like the one in our selection, scores of analogies stated in a sentence or a very few sentences. It would be a particularly rewarding study because Sir James's subject is difficult for readers both intellectually *and* imaginatively. For such a paper, assume that your readers are the members of the class.

The suggestions for papers concerning utopian stories in Chapter XV might appropriately be adapted for use now in special connection with *Looking Backward.* Or you might read all or part of William Dean Howells's interesting adaptation of the technique of the utopian novel, *A Traveler from Altruria* (1894), and write a report for the class.

XVII

Ironic Satire

Ironic satire" describes a literary kind, and the term needs definition at the start. Satire is rather a broad term. We mean by "a satire" a piece of writing directed toward human vice, folly, or confusion, intellectual or moral. The intention of a satire is so to ridicule its object that the reader will despise it, scorn it, or—if these words are too strong in reference to the object—see it as it really is. A completely successful satire makes the reader feel about its object just as the writer does. Now a satire may use one or more of several means, even quite direct ones. In our title the term "satire" designates the end, and "ironic" the means. From time to time the term "irony" has come up for us. It must have done so, for a touch of irony is a frequent element in good writing. When the term did appear, its particular meaning and application were clear, let us hope, from the context. But for the purposes of this chapter we shall have to consider the question "What makes a statement ironic?"

The difficulty is that the ironic reaction depends, in a special way, upon the activity of both reader and writer. We shall get on well, however, if we keep in mind that irony in literature, whatever its mode, inheres in a contrast for which *the writer provides the materials,* but which *the reader makes.* In irony used with satirical intent, the contrast is usually between two meanings in the same statement. When that contrast is very obvious, you call the statement, rightly, sarcasm. When the contrast is not obvious, when, indeed, it may be missed, the statement is ironic. But when the second meaning *is* missed, there is, for the reader who misses it, no irony. Thoreau says, "It takes two to speak truth—one to speak and another to hear." Irony requires the same two.

Sometimes this sort of irony is described as a statement that on the surface, or literally, says one thing, but actually means another. But that is not quite precise. The literal meaning is "actual" enough and may be for some readers the only meaning. It seems better to say that in an ironic statement two meanings arise, a literal meaning and another. Of course for the perception of the second meaning, there must be some community of knowledge and attitude between the writer and his reader. We shall see how this perception arises in the reading of our selections.

i   TWO EIGHTEENTH–CENTURY SATIRISTS

The first of our selections is from Jonathan Swift's *Gulliver's Travels*. In it Gulliver is the guest of the king of Brobdingnag, a land of giants. Swift gives Gulliver the characteristic limitations of mind of eighteenth-century Englishmen, or indeed, Europeans. But Gulliver is loyal to his own place and time, and he would like to convince the enlightened king that Europe is in some points superior to Brobdingnag.

FROM *Gulliver's Travels* (1726)

JONATHAN SWIFT

I . . . Great allowances should be given to a King who lives wholly secluded from the rest of the world, and must therefore be altogether unacquainted with the manners and customs that most prevail in other nations; the want of which knowledge will ever produce many prejudices, and a certain narrowness of thinking, from which we and the politer countries of Europe are wholly exempted. And it would be hard indeed, if so remote a prince's notions of virtue and vice were to be offered as a standard for all mankind.

II To confirm what I have now said, and further, to show the miserable effects of a confined education, I shall here insert a passage which will hardly obtain belief. In hopes to ingratiate myself farther into his Majesty's favour, I told him of an invention discovered between three and four hundred years ago, to make a certain powder, into an heap of which the smallest spark of fire falling, would kindle the whole in a moment, although it were as big as a mountain, and make it all fly up in the air together, with a noise and agitation greater than thunder. That a proper quantity of this powder rammed into an hollow tube of brass or iron, according to its bigness, would drive a ball of iron or lead with such violence and speed, as nothing was able to sustain its force. That the largest balls thus discharged, would not only destroy whole ranks of an army at once, but batter the strongest walls to the ground, sink down ships, with a thousand men in each, to the bottom of the sea; and, when linked together by a chain, would cut through masts and rigging, divide hundreds of bodies in the middle, and lay all waste before them. That we often put this powder into large hollow balls of iron, and discharged them by an engine into some city we were besieging, which would rip up the pavements, tear the houses to pieces, burst and throw splinters on every side, dashing out the brains of all who came near. That I knew the ingredients very well, which were cheap, and common; I understood the manner of compounding them, and could direct his workmen how to make those tubes of a size proportionable to all other things in his Majesty's kingdom, and the largest need not be above an hundred foot long; twenty or thirty of which tubes, charged with the proper quantity of powder and balls, would batter down the walls of the strongest town in his dominions in a few hours, or destroy the whole metropolis, if ever it should pretend to dispute his absolute commands. This I humbly offered to his Majesty, as a small tribute of acknowledgment in return of so many marks that I had received of his royal favour and protection.

III The King was struck with horror at the description I had given of those terrible engines, and the proposal I had made. He was amazed how so impotent and grovelling an insect as I (these were his expressions) could entertain such inhuman ideas, and in so familiar a manner as to appear wholly unmoved at all the scenes of blood and desolation, which I had painted as the common effects of those destructive machines, whereof he said some evil genius, enemy to mankind, must have been the first contriver. As for himself, he protested that although few things delighted him so much as new discoveries in art or in nature, yet he would rather lose half his kingdom than be privy to such a secret, which he commanded me, as I valued my life, never to mention any more.

IV A strange effect of narrow principles and short views! that a prince possessed of every quality which procures veneration, love, and esteem; of strong parts, great wisdom, and profound learning, endued with admirable talents for government, and almost adored by his subjects, should from a nice unnecessary scruple, whereof in Europe we can have no conception, let slip an opportunity put into his hands, that would have made him absolute master of the lives, the liberties, and the fortunes of his people.

---

1) Parts of *Gulliver's Travels* are satire of particular matters in English life; other parts are directed toward humanity in general. How would you say this piece is directed?

2) We had some little characterization of Gulliver as the piece was introduced. What in the selection itself implies his character?

3) The irony here is easy to perceive, because we see at once that what Gulliver says is not necessarily what Swift thinks, and because Swift is careful to make us realize Gulliver's limitations of mind. As we shall see, irony is a little harder to perceive when the writer appears to be speaking in his own person.

4) What does the king stand for? Think of it this way: Suppose we did not have III; suppose Swift had merely written at the end of II: "But the King refused my offer." What would be the difference in the effect of the whole? Would the irony be easier or harder to perceive?

5) What has happened to the ironic effect of this piece since 1726? Is it possible that it has increased, not lessened? We expect a certain exaggeration in satire; the satirist may write things large in order to enforce his design upon us. But is Gulliver's quality of mind much exaggerated? Have you never seen in our own time, say in magazines that deal with science in a very popular fashion, new atomic weapons described with such gusto that one would think the writer supposed the chief end of science to be quick and easy destruction?

6) Gulliver says the king called him an impotent, grovelling insect.

Now of course the king is a giant; Gulliver is minute in comparison. Is remarking Gulliver's size all of the king's intention? All of Swift's?

7) Suppose we try to say in explicit language just what human failings and limitations Gulliver represents. How would you state them?

8) What attitude toward these failings and limitations has Swift? How does he want us to feel?

9) One failure of Gulliver's is clearly his assumptions about human greatness, his stupidity about what it consists of. Let us look at another piece of writing which also considers what greatness is. The passage is from Rabelais's *Gargantua;* the speaker is a king addressing a captured enemy, whom he intends to release:

> The time is not now as formerly, to conquer the kingdoms of our neighbor princes, and to build up our own greatness upon the loss of our nearest Christian brother. This imitation of the ancient Herculeses, Alexanders, Hannibals, Scipios, Caesars, and other such heroes, is quite contrary to the profession of the gospel of Christ, by which we are commanded to preserve, keep, rule, and govern every man his own country and lands, and not in a hostile manner to invade others; and that which heretofore the Barbarians and Saracens called prowess and valor, we now call robbing, thievery, and wickedness. It would have been more commendable in him [the invading king] to have contained himself within the bounds of his own territories, royally governing them, than to insult and domineer in mine, pillaging and plundering every where like a most unmerciful enemy; for, by ruling his own with discretion, he might have increased his greatness. . . .

Perhaps a comparison of this passage with the Swift piece will throw some of the qualities of the latter into relief. What ideas do the two writers have in common? What is Rabelais's assumption about the nature of man and how does it differ from Swift's? Rabelais apparently thinks of war as an outworn custom, surviving as a sort of anachronism. Would such an attitude or hope be ever likely in Swift, do you think? Is the speaker here anything like the king of Brobdingnag? But can the king of Brobdingnag be thought of as typical of humanity? Of any part of it? What attitude is Rabelais trying to evoke in the reader?

Here is another selection by Swift, a famous example of sustained irony. In 1729 when this piece was published, Swift was Dean of St. Patrick's Cathedral in Dublin. He wrote in a period of great distress in Ireland, a distress caused by three years of famine, by the callousness of Englishmen, and by the selfishness and folly of Irishmen, too. Conditions in Ireland had long been appalling. To see what Swift intends, you must remember that when an injustice persists long enough, men may get used to it and accept it as part of the nature of things. We shall use the whole of Swift's elaborate title, for the irony starts there.

A Modest Proposal

for preventing the children of poor people in Ireland
from being a burden to their parents or country, and
for making them beneficial to the public (1729)

JONATHAN SWIFT

I It is a melancholy object to those who walk through this great town, or travel in the country, when they see the streets, the roads, and cabin-doors, crowded with beggars of the female sex, followed by three, four, or six children, all in rags, and importuning every passenger for an alms. These mothers, instead of being able to work for their honest livelihood, are forced to employ all their time in strolling to beg sustenance for their helpless infants; who, as they grow up, either turn thieves for want of work, or leave their dear native country to fight for the Pretender in Spain, or sell themselves to the Barbadoes.

II I think it is agreed by all parties, that this prodigious number of children in the arms, or on the backs, or at the heels of their mothers, and frequently of their fathers, is, in the present deplorable state of the kingdom, a very great additional grievance; and, therefore, whoever could find out a fair, cheap, and easy method of making these children sound, useful members of the commonwealth, would deserve so well of the public, as to have his statue set up for a preserver of the nation.

III But my intention is very far from being confined to provide only for the children of professed beggars; it is of a much greater extent, and shall take in the whole number of infants at a certain age, who are born of parents in effect as little able to support them, as those who demand our charity in the streets.

IV As to my own part, having turned my thoughts for many years upon this important subject, and maturely weighed the several schemes of our projectors, I have always found them grossly mistaken in their computation. It is true, a child, just dropped from its dam, may be supported by her milk for a solar year, with little other nourishment; at most, not above the value of two shillings, which the mother may certainly get, or the value in scraps, by her lawful occupation of begging; and it is exactly at one year old that I propose to provide for them in such a manner, as, instead of being a charge upon their parents, or the parish, or wanting food and raiment for the rest of their lives, they shall, on the contrary, contribute to the feeding, and partly to the clothing, of many thousands.

V There is likewise another great advantage in my scheme, that it will prevent those voluntary abortions, and that horrid practice of women murdering their bastard children, alas, too frequent among us! sacrificing the poor innocent babes, I doubt, more to avoid the expense than the shame, which would move tears and pity in the most savage and inhuman breast.

VI The number of souls in this kingdom being usually reckoned one million and a half, of these I calculate there may be about two hundred thousand couple whose wives are breeders; from which number I subtract thirty thousand couple, who are able to maintain their own children, (although I apprehend there cannot be so many, under the present distresses of the kingdom); but this being granted, there will remain a hundred and seventy thousand breeders. I again subtract fifty thousand, for those women who miscarry, or whose children die by accident or disease within the year. There only remain a hundred and twenty thousand children of poor parents annually born. The question therefore is, How this number shall be reared and provided for? which, as I have already said, under the present situation of affairs, is utterly impossible by all the methods hitherto proposed. For we can neither employ them in handicraft or agriculture; we neither build houses (I mean in the country), nor cultivate land: they can very seldom pick up a livelihood by stealing, till they arrive at six years old, except where they are of towardly parts; although I confess they learn the rudiments much earlier; during which time they can, however, be properly looked upon only as probationers; as I have been informed by a principal gentleman in the county of Cavan, who protested to me, that he never knew above one or two instances under the age of six, even in a part of the kingdom so renowned for the quickest proficiency in that art.

VII I am assured by our merchants, that a boy or a girl before twelve years old is no saleable commodity; and even when they come to this age they will not yield above three pounds, or three pounds and half-a-crown at most, on the exchange; which cannot turn to account either to the parents or kingdom, the charge of nutriment and rags having been at least four times that value.

VIII I shall now, therefore, humbly propose my own thoughts, which I hope will not be liable to the least objection.

IX I have been assured by a very knowing American of my acquaintance in London, that a young healthy child, well nursed, is, at a year old, a most delicious, nourishing, and wholesome food, whether stewed, roasted, baked, or boiled; and I make no doubt that it will equally serve in a fricassee or a ragout.

X I do therefore humbly offer it to public consideration, that of the hundred and twenty thousand children already computed, twenty thousand may be reserved for breed, whereof only one-fourth part to be males; which is more than we allow to sheep, black-cattle, or swine; and my reason is, that these children are seldom the fruits of marriage, a circumstance not much regarded by our savages; therefore one male will be sufficient to serve four females. That the remaining hundred thousand may, at a year old, be offered in sale to the persons of quality and fortune through the kingdom: always advising the mother to let them suck plentifully in the last month, so as to render them plump and fat for a good table. A child will make two dishes at an entertainment for friends; and when the family dines alone, the fore or hind quarter will make a reasonable dish, and, seasoned with a little pepper or salt, will be very good boiled on the fourth day, especially in winter.

XI I have reckoned, upon a medium, that a child just born will weigh twelve pounds, and in a solar year, if tolerably nursed, increaseth to twenty-eight pounds.

XII I grant this food will be somewhat dear, and therefore very proper for landlords, who, as they have already devoured most of the parents, seem to have the best title to the children.

XIII Infants' flesh will be in season throughout the year, but more plentiful in March, and a little before and after: for we are told by a grave author, an eminent French physician, that fish being a prolific diet, there are more children born in Roman Catholic countries about nine months after Lent, than at any other season; therefore, reckoning a year after Lent, the markets will be more glutted than usual, because the number of Popish infants is at least three to one in this kingdom; and therefore it will have one other collateral advantage, by lessening the number of Papists among us.

XIV I have already computed the charge of nursing a beggar's child (in which list I reckon all cottagers, labourers, and four-fifths of the farmers) to be about two shillings per annum, rags included; and I believe no gentleman would repine to give ten shillings for the carcass of a good fat child, which, as I have said, will make four dishes of excellent nutritive meat, when he hath only some particular friend, or his own family, to dine with him. Thus the squire will learn to be a good landlord, and grow popular among his tenants; the mother will have eight shillings net profit, and be fit for work till she produces another child.

XV Those who are more thrifty (as I must confess the times require) may flay the carcass; the skin of which, artificially dressed, will make admirable gloves for ladies, and summer boots for fine gentlemen.

XVI As to our city of Dublin, shambles may be appointed for this purpose in the most convenient parts of it, and butchers, we may be assured, will not be wanting; although I rather recommend buying the children alive, and dressing them hot from the knife, as we do roasting pigs.

XVII A very worthy person, a true lover of his country, and whose virtues I highly esteem, was lately pleased, in discoursing on this matter, to offer a refinement upon my scheme. He said, that many gentlemen of this kingdom, having of late destroyed their deer, he conceived that the want of venison might be well supplied by the bodies of young lads and maidens, not exceeding fourteen years of age, nor under twelve; so great a number of both sexes in every country being now ready to starve for want of work and service; and these to be disposed of by their parents, if alive, or otherwise by their nearest relations. But, with due deference to so excellent a friend, and so deserving a patriot, I cannot be altogether in his sentiments; for as to the males, my American acquaintance assured me, from frequent experience, that their flesh was generally tough and lean, like that of our schoolboys, by continual exercise, and their taste disagreeable; and to fatten them would not answer the charge. Then as to the females, it would, I think, with humble submission, be a loss to the public, because they soon would become breeders themselves: and besides, it is not improbable that some scrupulous people might be apt to censure such a practice, (although indeed very unjustly), as a little bordering upon cruelty; which, I confess, has always been with me the strongest objection against any project, however so well intended.

xviii But in order to justify my friend, he confessed that this expedient was put into his head by the famous Psalmanazar, a native of the island Formosa, who came from thence to London above twenty years ago; and in conversation told my friend, that in his country, when any young person happened to be put to death, the executioner sold the carcass to persons of quality as a prime dainty; and that in his time the body of a plump girl of fifteen, who was crucified for an attempt to poison the emperor, was sold to his imperial majesty's prime minister of state, and other great mandarins of the court, in joints from the gibbet, at four hundred crowns. Neither indeed can I deny, that, if the same use were made of several plump young girls in this town, who, without one single groat to their fortunes, cannot stir abroad without a chair, and appear at playhouse and assemblies in foreign fineries which they never will pay for, the kingdom would not be the worse.

xix Some persons of a desponding spirit are in great concern about that vast number of poor people, who are aged, diseased, or maimed; and I have been desired to employ my thoughts, what course may be taken to ease the nation of so grievous an encumbrance. But I am not in the least pain upon that matter, because it is very well known, that they are every day dying, and rotting, by cold and famine, and filth and vermin, as fast as can be reasonably expected. And as to the young labourers, they are now in almost as hopeful a condition: they cannot get work, and consequently pine away for want of nourishment, to a degree, that if at any time they are accidentally hired to common labour, they have not strength to perform it; and thus the country and themselves are happily delivered from the evils to come.

xx I have too long digressed, and therefore shall return to my subject. I think the advantages by the proposal which I have made are obvious and many, as well as of the highest importance.

xxi For first, as I have already observed, it would greatly lessen the number of Papists, with whom we are yearly over-run, being the principal breeders of the nation, as well as our most dangerous enemies; and who stay at home on purpose to deliver the kingdom to the Pretender, hoping to take their advantage by the absence of so many good Protestants, who have chosen rather to leave their country than stay at home and pay tithes against their conscience to an Episcopal curate.

xxii Secondly, The poorer tenants will have something valuable of their own, which by law may be made liable to distress, and help to pay their landlord's rent; their corn and cattle being already seized, and money a thing unknown.

xxiii Thirdly, Whereas the maintenance of a hundred thousand children, from two years old and upward, cannot be computed at less than ten shillings a piece per annum, the nation's stock will be thereby increased fifty thousand pounds per annum, besides the profit of a new dish introduced to the tables of all gentlemen of fortune in the kingdom, who have any refinement in taste. And the money will circulate among ourselves, the goods being entirely of our own growth and manufacture.

xxiv Fourthly, The constant breeders, besides the gain of eight shillings sterling per annum by the sale of their children, will be rid of the charge of maintaining them after the first year.

xxv Fifthly, This food would likewise bring great custom to taverns; where the vintners will certainly be so prudent as to procure the best receipts for dressing it to perfection, and, consequently, have their houses frequented by all the fine gentlemen, who justly value themselves upon their knowledge in good eating: and a skilful cook, who understands how to oblige his guests, will contrive to make it as expensive as they please.

xxvi Sixthly, This would be a great inducement to marriage, which all wise nations have either encouraged by rewards, or enforced by laws and penalties. It would increase the care and tenderness of mothers toward their children, when they were sure of a settlement for life to the poor babes, provided in some sort by the public, to their annual profit instead of expense. We should see an honest emulation among the married women, which of them could bring the fattest child to the market. Men would become as fond of their wives during the time of their pregnancy as they are now of their mares in foal, their cows in calf, or sows when they are ready to farrow; nor offer to beat or kick them (as is too frequent a practice) for fear of a miscarriage.

xxvii Many other advantages might be enumerated. For instance, the addition of some thousand carcasses in our exportation of barrelled beef; the propagation of swine's flesh, and improvement in the art of making good bacon, so much wanted among us by the great destruction of pigs, too frequent at our tables, which are no way comparable in taste or magnificence to a well-grown, fat, yearling child, which, roasted whole, will make a considerable figure at a lord mayor's feast, or any other public entertainment. But this, and many others, I omit, being studious of brevity.

xxviii Supposing that one thousand families in this city would be constant customers for infants' flesh, besides others who might have it at merry-meetings, particularly at weddings and christenings, I compute that Dublin would take off annually about twenty thousand carcasses; and the rest of the kingdom (where probably they will be sold somewhat cheaper) the remaining eighty thousand.

xxix I can think of no one objection, that will possibly be raised against this proposal, unless it should be urged, that the number of people will be thereby much lessened in the kingdom. This I freely own, and it was indeed one principal design in offering it to the world. I desire the reader will observe, that I calculate my remedy for this one individual kingdom of Ireland, and for no other that ever was, is, or, I think, ever can be, upon earth. Therefore let no man talk to me of other expedients: of taxing our absentees at five shillings a pound: of using neither clothes, nor household furniture, except what is our own growth and manufacture: of utterly rejecting the materials and instruments that promote foreign luxury: of curing the expensiveness of pride, vanity, idleness, and gaming in our women: of introducing a vein of parsimony, prudence, and temperance: of learning to love our country, in the want of which we differ even from LAPLANDERS, and the inhabitants of TOPINAMBOO: of quitting our animosities and factions, nor acting any longer like the Jews, who were murdering one another at the very moment their city was taken: of being a little cautious not to sell our country and consciences for nothing: of teaching landlords to have at least one degree of mercy toward their tenants. Lastly, of putting a spirit of honesty, industry, and skill into our shopkeepers; who, if a resolution could now be taken to buy only our native goods, would immediately unite to cheat and exact upon us in the price, the measure, and the goodness, nor could ever yet be brought to make one fair proposal of just dealing, though often and earnestly invited to it.

xxx Therefore I repeat, let no man talk to me of these and the like expedients, till he hath at least some glimpse of hope, that there will be ever some hearty and sincere attempt to put them in practice.

xxxi But, as to myself, having been wearied out for many years with offering vain, idle, visionary thoughts, and at length utterly despairing of success, I fortunately fell upon this proposal; which, as it is wholly new, so it has something solid and real, of no expense and little trouble, full in our own power, and whereby we can incur no danger in disobliging ENGLAND. For this kind of commodity will not bear exportation, the flesh being of too tender a consistence to admit a long continuance in salt, although perhaps I could name a country, which would be glad to eat up our whole nation without it.

xxxii After all, I am not so violently bent upon my own opinion as to reject any offer proposed by wise men, which shall be found equally innocent, cheap, easy and effectual. But before something of that kind shall be advanced in contradiction to my scheme, and offering a better, I desire the author, or authors, will be pleased maturely to consider two points. First, as things now stand, how they will be able to find food and raiment for a hundred thousand useless mouths and backs. And, secondly, there being a round million of creatures in human figure, throughout this kingdom, whose whole subsistence put into a common stock would leave them in debt two millions of pounds sterling, adding those who are beggars by profession, to the bulk of farmers, cottagers, and labourers, with the wives and children, who are beggars in effect; I desire those politicians who dislike my overture, and may perhaps be so bold as to attempt an answer, that they will first ask the parents of these mortals, whether they would not at this day think it a great happiness to have been sold for food at a year old, in the manner I prescribe, and thereby have avoided such a perpetual scene of misfortunes, as they have since gone through, by the oppression of landlords, the impossibility of paying rent without money or trade, the want of common sustenance, with neither house nor clothes to cover them from the inclemencies of the weather, and the most inevitable prospect of entailing the like, or greater miseries, upon their breed for ever.

xxxiii I profess, in the sincerity of my heart, that I have not the least personal interest in endeavouring to promote this necessary work, having no other motive than the public good of my country, by advancing our trade, providing for infants, relieving the poor, and giving some pleasure to the rich. I have no children by which I can propose to get a single penny; the youngest being nine years old, and my wife past child-bearing.

———————

1) Paragraph 1 describes quite objectively the conditions in Ireland at the time Swift wrote. Irishmen who went to fight for the Pretender joined the supporters of James Stuart, son of James II, who was plotting to regain the throne from which his father had been deposed; those who sold themselves to the Barbadoes sold themselves as laborers in the West Indies.

2) One sometimes finds this sort of statement about irony: irony is marked by the detachment of the writer, the coolness of his expression at a time when he really feels deeply. Now do you see that this statement, applied to "A Modest Proposal," completely misses the point? Swift has created a character and writes from that character's point of view. Although the character is not named, we must recognize him, or our discussion will be confused. For convenience, we shall call that character "the proposer."

3) The proposer begins with an air of dispassionate reasonableness: "this prodigious number of children . . . is, in the present deplorable state of the kingdom, a very great additional grievance"; he has a suggestion. Suppose an intelligent reader with no knowledge of Swift and no warning that this piece was ironic. How far would he read, do you think, before he became aware of the ironic intent? Is there anything in IV, for instance, that might disturb him? If he gets over IV without being disturbed, how about VI?

4) Let us suppose our intelligent reader has been disturbed to find terms ordinarily reserved to the reproduction of domestic animals. He does not speak of human birth in that fashion; still the proposer's attitude is so impersonally scientific that perhaps *he* does. And the proposer speaks of the training of children to be thieves as if—were it only feasible—that might be a solution. Yet the reader recognizes the proposer's question— how this number shall be reared and provided for—as a very real problem. He comes to the "modest proposal" in x in some distress of mind, particularly after the preparatory shock of IX.

5) And is not the great shock here that the condition of Ireland is so bad—as even the modern reader realizes from the essay—that the "modest proposal" makes a kind of horrid sense? It is consistent with the callousness with which the problem has been treated, and seems to be merely an extension of it. "I grant," says the proposer, "this food will be somewhat dear, and therefore very proper for landlords, who, as they have already devoured most of the parents, seem to have the best title to the children." Is not the proposer only suggesting that if "devoured" is an entirely appropriate metaphor for what has happened to parents, it might as well be literal for their children?

6) After the statement of the proposal in x, Swift makes his proposer develop it in detail and dispassionately consider possible objections to it. Why? Are XI–XXVIII intended only to distress the reader? What gets said in this long passage about the condition of Ireland?

7) Now the condition of Ireland had been described before this essay. The jar that is characteristic in our response to irony is here strong enough

to shake the reader out of his ordinary inability to imagine the distress of others, and out of his ability to ignore suffering when it is so long continued as to become commonplace. And that is why irony may be an effective means to awaken the social conscience.

8) Of course Swift had some ideas about what really might be done to improve the state of Ireland. Do they come into this essay at all? How?

9) But why state them in that fashion? Would not Swift's real proposals have been clearer to most of his readers had he simply written a serious essay to urge his remedies? What is the effect of the proposer's "Therefore let no man talk to me of other expedients . . ."?

10) What is the relation of xxxii to the rest of the essay?

11) "A Modest Proposal" is often cited as the most remarkable example of sustained irony in English, and indeed there seems no point at which Swift slips out of the DRAMATIC PROPRIETY of his role as proposer, save perhaps in xxxii. The last sentence of the essay, the proposer's final affirmation of his entire disinterestedness, is an especially effective stroke.

12) This essay is a particularly good example of the way in which irony depends upon a community of attitude between writer and reader. In it, the community of ordinary humane feeling is between Swift and his reader; the proposer seems to stand outside it. (That is why it is bad criticism to equate Swift and the proposer.) It is when the reader sees that the proposer speaks outside the usual moral and emotional context of civilization that he sees the ironic intention. The remarkable thing about the essay is Swift's success in consistently keeping him outside, and yet in making him logical, cogent, incisive.

13) What have our selection from *Gulliver's Travels* and "A Modest Proposal" in common? How do they differ in method? Which is the more effective? For all readers? There are a number of things to be considered in a careful comparison of the two.

In a special sense, our reading of Swift is a preparation for reading Benjamin Franklin's ironic satire. Franklin had a remarkable gift for understanding a literary technique and adapting it to his own purposes. Although his pieces of ironic satire are in debt to Swift and might not have existed but for his reading of Swift, they have the same kind of excellence. Perhaps they have as much. Our first example uses a satiric means we have not before examined, the device of PARODY.

On the Slave-Trade (1790)

BENJAMIN FRANKLIN

To the Editor of the Federal Gazette

March 23rd, 1790.

SIR,

1 Reading last night in your excellent Paper the speech of Mr. Jackson in Congress against their meddling with the Affair of Slavery, or attempting

to mend the Condition of the Slaves, it put me in mind of a similar One made about 100 Years since by Sidi Mehemet Ibrahim, a member of the Divan of Algiers, which may be seen in Martin's Account of his Consulship, anno 1687. It was against granting the Petition of the Sect called *Erika,* or Purists, who pray'd for the Abolition of Piracy and Slavery as being unjust. Mr. Jackson does not quote it; perhaps he has not seen it. If, therefore, some of its Reasonings are to be found in his eloquent Speech, it may only show that men's Interests and Intellects operate and are operated on with surprising similarity in all Countries and Climates, when under similar Circumstances. The African's Speech, as translated, is as follows.

"Allah Bismillah, &c. God is great, and Mahomet is his Prophet.

II "Have these *Erika* considered the Consequences of granting their Petition? If we cease our Cruises against the Christians, how shall we be furnished with the Commodities their Countries produce, and which are so necessary for us? If we forbear to make Slaves of their People, who in this hot Climate are to cultivate our Lands? Who are to perform the common Labours of our City, and in our Families? Must we not then be our own Slaves? And is there not more Compassion and more Favour due to us as Mussulmen, than to these Christian Dogs? We have now above 50,000 Slaves in and near Algiers. This Number, if not kept up by fresh Supplies, will soon diminish, and be gradually annihilated. If we then cease taking and plundering the Infidel Ships, and making Slaves of the Seamen and Passengers, our Lands will become of no Value for want of Cultivation; the Rents of Houses in the City will sink one half; and the Revenues of Government arising from its Share of Prizes be totally destroy'd! And for what? To gratify the whims of a whimsical Sect, who would have us, not only forbear making more Slaves, but even to manumit those we have.

III "But who is to indemnify their Masters for the Loss? Will the State do it? Is our Treasury sufficient? Will the *Erika* do it? Can they do it? Or would they, to do what they think Justice to the Slaves, do a greater Injustice to the Owners? And if we set our Slaves free, what is to be done with them? Few of them will return to their Countries; they know too well the greater Hardships they must there be subject to; they will not embrace our holy Religion; they will not adopt our Manners; our People will not pollute themselves by intermarrying with them. Must we maintain them as Beggars in our Streets, or suffer our Properties to be the Prey of their Pillage? For Men long accustom'd to Slavery will not work for a Livelihood when not compell'd. And what is there so pitiable in their present Condition? Were they not Slaves in their own Countries?

IV "Are not Spain, Portugal, France, and the Italian states govern'd by Despots, who hold all their Subjects in Slavery, without Exception? Even England treats its Sailors as Slaves; for they are, whenever the Government pleases, seiz'd, and confin'd in Ships of War, condemn'd not only to work, but to fight, for small Wages, or a mere Subsistence, not better than our Slaves are allow'd by us. Is their Condition then made worse by their falling into our Hands? No; they have only exchanged one Slavery for another, and I may say a better; for here they are brought into a Land where the Sun of Islamism gives forth its Light, and shines in full Splendour, and they have an Opportunity of making themselves acquainted with the true Doctrine, and thereby saving their immortal Souls. Those who remain at home have not that Happiness. Sending the Slaves home then would be sending them out of Light into Darkness.

v "I repeat the Question, What is to be done with them? I have heard it suggested, that they may be planted in the Wilderness, where there is plenty of Land for them to subsist on, and where they may flourish as a free State; but they are, I doubt, too little dispos'd to labour without Compulsion, as well as too ignorant to establish a good government, and the wild Arabs would soon molest and destroy or again enslave them. While serving us, we take care to provide them with every thing, and they are treated with Humanity. The Labourers in their own Country are, as I am well informed, worse fed, lodged, and cloathed. The Condition of most of them is therefore already mended, and requires no further Improvement. Here their Lives are in Safety. They are not liable to be impress'd for Soldiers, and forc'd to cut one another's Christian Throats, as in the Wars of their own Countries. If some of the religious mad Bigots, who now teaze us with their silly Petitions, have in a Fit of blind Zeal freed their Slaves, it was not Generosity, it was not Humanity, that mov'd them to the Action; it was from the conscious Burthen of a Load of Sins, and Hope, from the supposed Merits of so good a Work, to be excus'd Damnation.

vi "How grossly are they mistaken in imagining Slavery to be disallow'd by the Alcoran! Are not the two Precepts, to quote no more, '*Masters, treat your Slaves with kindness; Slaves, serve your Masters with Cheerfulness and Fidelity,*' clear Proofs to the contrary? Nor can the Plundering of Infidels be in that sacred Book forbidden, since it is well known from it, that God has given the World, and all that it contains, to his faithful Mussulmen, who are to enjoy it of Right as fast as they conquer it. Let us then hear no more of this detestable Proposition, the Manumission of Christian Slaves, the Adoption of which would, by depreciating our Lands and Houses, and thereby depriving so many good Citizens of their Properties, create universal Discontent, and provoke Insurrections, to the endangering of Government and producing general Confusion. I have therefore no doubt, but this wise Council will prefer the Comfort and Happiness of a whole Nation of true Believers to the Whim of a few *Erika,* and dismiss their Petition."

vii The Result was, as Martin tells us, that the Divan came to this Resolution; "The Doctrine, that Plundering and Enslaving the Christians is unjust, is at best *problematical;* but that it is the Interest of this State to continue the Practice, is clear; therefore let the Petition be rejected."

viii And it was rejected accordingly.

ix And since like Motives are apt to produce in the Minds of Men like Opinions and Resolutions, may we not, Mr. Brown, venture to predict, from this Account, that the Petitions to the Parliament of England for abolishing the Slave-Trade, to say nothing of other Legislatures, and the Debates upon them, will have a similar Conclusion? I am, Sir, your constant Reader and humble Servant,

HISTORICUS.

---

1) Franklin's last public act was to sign, as president of the Abolition Society ("the Sect called *Erika*"), a memorial to the House of Representatives. The speech of Mr. Jackson, of Georgia, was in opposition to this memorial. We have here an ironic parody of Jackson's speech, but the sort of argument parodied was typical of pro-slavery argument down to the War between the States, and was too often heard from pulpits. What does the FRAME (as Historicus's covering letter to the editor may be called) contribute to the effect of the whole? Just what sort of person is Historicus?

2) Two arguments parodied in the speech of Sidi Mehemet Ibrahim were, unhappily, common. One was that Negro slaves were benefited, even blessed, by being slaves of Christians. The other was that the Bible justified slavery. The two precepts in VI really refer to passages from the Bible frequently cited out of context and without regard to their time and place, such passages as Ephesians 6:5–9, 1 Timothy 6:1–2, and Titus 2:9–10.

3) If this ironic parody worked as intended, it should have been an aid to those contemporaries of Franklin with sluggish imaginations. Certainly the failure of Christians who favored slavery must have been their inability to think how it would feel to be enslaved themselves. But cannot this piece be read in reference to more than the slave trade? Can you think of contemporary manifestations of the human propensities that Franklin here satirizes?

4) Like some other of Franklin's ironic satires, this one was, apparently, taken at face value by some persons; we are told by a contemporary that it "caused many persons to search the bookstores and libraries for the work from which it was said to be extracted." But what, say in the first paragraph of the frame, should have made the ironic intent clear to anyone reading with care?

Our next selection is in one way a little more subtle than any of the ironic satires we have so far considered. In "A Modest Proposal" we have the proposer, in the selection from *Gulliver's Travels* we have Gulliver, in "On the Slave-Trade" we have Sidi Mehemet Ibrahim—no person of any perception is likely to attribute to the author the ideas of the figure he creates as a vehicle for the satire. But here the reader may at first suppose that all the ideas are Franklin's own.

As you read, look for the first indications of ironic intent. When you have read the piece, you should be able to see that the title itself is ironical —if you do not, then that is a sure sign you need to reread. And do not neglect Franklin's note, for it is part of the satire. (For St. Paul's voyage and shipwreck there mentioned, see Acts 28:1–10.)

Remarks Concerning the Savages of North America (1784)

BENJAMIN FRANKLIN

I Savages we call them, because their Manners differ from ours, which we think the Perfection of Civility; they think the same of theirs.

II Perhaps, if we could examine the Manners of different Nations with Impartiality, we should find no People so rude, as to be without any Rules of Politeness; nor any so polite, as not to have some Remains of Rudeness.

III The Indian Men, when young, are Hunters and Warriors; when old, Counsellors; for all their Government is by Counsel of the Sages; there is no Force, there are no Prisons, no Officers to compel Obedience, or inflict Punishment. Hence they generally study Oratory, the best Speaker having the most Influence. The Indian Women till the Ground, dress the Food, nurse and bring up the Children, and preserve and hand down to Posterity the Memory of public Transactions. These Employments of Men and Women are accounted natural and honourable. Having few artificial Wants, they have abundance of Leisure for Improvement by Conversation. Our laborious Manner of Life, compared with theirs, they esteem slavish and base; and the Learning, on which we value ourselves, they regard as frivolous and useless. An Instance of this occurred at the Treaty of Lancaster, in Pennsylvania, *anno* 1744, between the Government of Virginia and the Six Nations. After the principal Business was settled, the Commissioners from Virginia acquainted the Indians by a Speech, that there was at Williamsburg a College, with a Fund for Educating Indian youth; and that, if the Six Nations would send down half a dozen of their young Lads to that College, the Government would take care that they should be well provided for, and instructed in all the Learning of the White People. It is one of the Indian Rules of Politeness not to answer a public Proposition the same day that it is made; they think it would be treating it as a light matter, and that they show it Respect by taking time to consider it, as of a Matter important. They therefore deferr'd their Answer till the Day following; when their Speaker began, by expressing their deep Sense of the kindness of the Virginia Government, in making them that Offer; 'for we know,' says he, 'that you highly esteem the kind of Learning taught in those Colleges, and that the Maintenance of our young Men, while with you, would be very expensive to you. We are convinc'd, therefore, that you mean to do us Good by your Proposal; and we thank you heartily. But you, who are wise, must know that different Nations have different Conceptions of things; and you will therefore not take it amiss, if our Ideas of this kind of Education happen not to be the same with yours. We have had some Experience of it; Several of our young People were formerly brought up at the Colleges of the Northern Provinces; they were instructed in all your Sciences; but, when they came back to us, they were bad Runners, ignorant of every means of living in the Woods, unable to bear either Cold or Hunger, knew neither how to build a Cabin, take a Deer, or kill an Enemy, spoke our Language imperfectly, were therefore neither fit for Hunters, Warriors, nor Counsellors; they were totally good for nothing. We are however not the less oblig'd by your kind Offer, tho' we decline accepting it; and, to show our grateful Sense of it, if the Gentlemen of Virginia will send us a Dozen of their Sons, we will take great Care of their Education, instruct them in all we know, and make *Men* of them.'

IV Having frequent Occasions to hold public Councils, they have acquired great Order and Decency in conducting them. The old Men sit in the foremost Ranks, the Warriors in the next, and the Women and Children in the hindmost. The Business of the Women is to take exact Notice of what passes, imprint it in their Memories (for they have no Writing), and communicate it to their Children. They are the Records of the Council, and they preserve Traditions of the Stipulations in Treaties 100 Years back; which, when we compare with our Writings, we always find exact. He that would speak, rises. The rest observe a profound Silence. When he has finish'd and sits down, they leave him 5 or 6 Minutes to recollect, that, if he has omitted any thing he intended to say, or has any thing to add, he may rise again and deliver it. To interrupt another, even in common Conversation, is reckon'd highly indecent. How different this is from the conduct of a polite British House of Commons, where scarce a day passes without some Confusion, that makes the Speaker hoarse in calling *to Order;* and how different from the Mode of Conversation in many polite Companies of Europe, where, if you do not deliver your Sentence with great Rapidity, you are cut off in the middle of it by the Impatient Loquacity of those you converse with, and never suffer'd to finish it!

V The Politeness of these Savages in Conversation is indeed carried to Excess, since it does not permit them to contradict or deny the Truth of what is asserted in their Presence. By this means they indeed avoid Disputes; but then it becomes difficult to know their Minds, or what Impression you make upon them. The Missionaries who have attempted to convert them to Christianity, all complain of this as one of the great Difficulties of their Mission. The Indians hear with Patience the Truths of the Gospel explain'd to them, and give their usual Tokens of Assent and Approbation; you would think they were convinc'd. No such matter. It is mere Civility.

VI A Swedish Minister, having assembled the chiefs of the Susquehanah Indians, made a Sermon to them, acquainting them with the principal historical Facts on which our Religion is founded; such as the Fall of our first Parents by eating an Apple, the coming of Christ to repair the Mischief, his Miracles and Suffering, &c. When he had finished, an Indian Orator stood up to thank him. 'What you have told us,' says he, 'is all very good. It is indeed bad to eat Apples. It is better to make them all into Cyder. We are much oblig'd by your kindness in coming so far, to tell us these Things which you have heard from your Mothers. In return, I will tell you some of those we have heard from ours. In the Beginning, our Fathers had only the Flesh of Animals to subsist on; and if their Hunting was unsuccessful, they were starving. Two of our young Hunters, having kill'd a Deer, made a Fire in the Woods to broil some Part of it. When they were about to satisfy their Hunger, they beheld a beautiful young Woman descend from the Clouds, and seat herself on that Hill, which you see yonder among the blue Mountains. They said to each other, it is a Spirit that has smelt our broiling Venison, and wishes to eat of it; let us offer some to her. They presented her with the Tongue; she was pleas'd with the Taste of it, and said, "Your kindness shall be rewarded; come to this Place after thirteen Moons, and you shall find something that will be of great Benefit in nourishing you and your Children to the latest Generation." They did so, and, to their Surprise, found Plants they had never seen before; but which, from that ancient time, have been constantly cultivated among us, to our great Advantage. Where her right Hand had touched the Ground, they found Maize; where her left hand had touch'd it, they found Kidney-Beans; and where her Backside had sat on it, they found Tobacco.' The good Missionary, disgusted with this idle Tale, said, 'What I delivered to you were sacred Truths; but what you tell me is mere Fable, Fiction, and Falsehood.' The Indian, offended, reply'd, 'My brother, it seems your Friends have not done you Justice in your Education; they have not well instructed you in the Rules of Common Civility. You saw that we, who understand and practise those Rules, believ'd all your stories; why do you refuse to believe ours?'

VII When any of them come into our Towns, our People are apt to crowd round them, gaze upon them, and incommode them, where they desire to be private; this they esteem great Rudeness, and the Effect of the Want of Instruction in the Rules of Civility and good Manners. 'We have,' say they, 'as much Curiosity as you, and when you come into our Towns, we wish for Opportunities of looking at you; but for this purpose we hide ourselves behind Bushes, where you are to pass, and never intrude ourselves into your Company.'

VIII Their Manner of entring one another's village has likewise its Rules. It is reckon'd uncivil in travelling Strangers to enter a Village abruptly, without giving Notice of their Approach. Therefore, as soon as they arrive within hearing, they stop and hollow, remaining there till invited to enter. Two old Men usually come out to them, and lead them in. There is in every Village a vacant Dwelling, called *the Strangers' House*. Here they are plac'd, while the old Men go round from Hut to Hut, acquainting the Inhabitants, that Strangers are arriv'd, who are probably hungry and weary; and every one sends them what he can spare of Victuals, and Skins to repose on. When the Strangers are refresh'd, Pipes and Tobacco are brought; and then, but not before, Conversation begins, with Enquiries who they are, whither bound, what News, &c.; and it usually ends with offers of Service, if the Strangers have occasion of Guides, or any Necessaries for continuing their Journey; and nothing is exacted for the Entertainment.

IX The same Hospitality, esteem'd among them as a principal Virtue, is practis'd by Private Persons; of which Conrad Weiser, our Interpreter, gave me the following Instance. He had been naturaliz'd among the Six

Nations, and spoke well the Mohock Language. In going thro' the Indian Country, to carry a Message from our Governor to the Council at Onondaga, he call'd at the Habitation of Canassatego, an old Acquaintance, who embrac'd him, spread Furs for him to sit on, plac'd before him some boil'd Beans and Venison, and mix'd some Rum and Water for his Drink. When he was well refresh'd, and had lit his Pipe, Canassatego began to converse with him; ask'd how he had far'd the many Years since they had seen each other; whence he then came; what occasion'd the Journey, &c. Conrad answered all his Questions; and when the Discourse began to flag, the Indian, to continue it, said, 'Conrad, you have lived long among the white People, and know something of their Customs; I have been sometimes at Albany, and have observed, that once in Seven Days they shut up their Shops, and assemble all in the great House; tell me what it is for? What do they do there?' 'They meet there,' says Conrad, 'to hear and learn *good Things*.' 'I do not doubt,' says the Indian, 'that they tell you so; they have told me the same; but I doubt the Truth of what they say, and I will tell you my Reasons. I went lately to Albany to sell my Skins and buy Blankets, Knives, Powder, Rum, &c. You know I us'd generally to deal with Hans Hanson; but I was a little inclin'd this time to try some other Merchant. However, I call'd first upon Hans, and asked him what he would give for Beaver. He said he could not give any more than four Shillings a Pound; "but," says he, "I cannot talk on Business now; this is the Day when we meet together to learn *Good Things*, and I am going to the Meeting." So I thought to myself, "Since we cannot do any Business to-day, I may as well go to the meeting too," and I went with him. There stood up a Man in Black, and began to talk to the People very angrily. I did not understand what he said; but, perceiving that he look'd much at me and at Hanson, I imagin'd he was angry at seeing me there; so I went out, sat down near the House, struck Fire, and lit my Pipe, waiting till the Meeting should break up. I thought too, that the Man had mention'd something of Beaver, and I suspected it might be the Subject of their Meeting. So, when they came out, I accosted my Merchant. "Well, Hans," says I, "I hope you have agreed to give more than four Shillings a Pound." "No," says he, "I cannot give so much; I cannot give more than three shillings and sixpence." I then spoke to several other Dealers, but they all sung the same song,—Three and sixpence,—Three and sixpence. This made it clear to me, that my Suspicion was right; and, that whatever they pretended of meeting to learn *good Things,* the real purpose was to consult how to cheat Indians in the Price of Beaver. Consider but a little, Conrad, and you must be of my Opinion. If they met so often to learn *good Things,* they would certainly have learnt some before this time. But they are still ignorant. You know our Practice. If a white Man, in travelling thro' our Country, enters one of our Cabins, we all treat him as I treat you; we dry him if he is wet, we warm him if he is cold, we give him Meat and Drink, that he may allay his Thirst and Hunger; and we spread soft Furs for him to rest and sleep on; we demand nothing in return. But, if I go into a white Man's House at Albany, and ask for Victuals and Drink, they say, "Where is your Money?" and if I have none, they say, "Get out, you Indian Dog." You see they have not yet learned those little *Good Things,* that we need no Meetings to be instructed in, because our Mothers taught them to us when we were Children; and therefore it is impossible their Meetings should be, as they say, for any such purpose, or have any such Effect; they are only to contrive *the Cheating of Indians in the Price of Beaver.'*

NOTE.—It is remarkable that in all Ages and Countries Hospitality has been allow'd as the Virtue of those whom the civiliz'd were pleas'd to call Barbarians. The Greeks celebrated the Scythians for it. The Saracens possess'd it eminently, and it is to this day the reigning Virtue of the wild Arabs. St. Paul, too, in the Relation of his Voyage and Shipwreck on the Island of Melita says the Barbarous People shewed us no little kindness; for they kindled a fire, and received us every one, because of the present Rain, and because of the Cold.—F.

ii THREE TWENTIETH–CENTURY SATIRISTS

Twentieth-century satire should be, one might think, easier to apprehend than eighteenth-century satire. You may not always find it so. You look at eighteenth-century satire historically, but you may find twentieth-century satire directed toward what you believe or take for granted. We shall start with an amusing piece by a brilliant writer, Morris Bishop, one that has an importance beyond the entertainment it furnishes. It is one of several pieces in which Mr. Bishop has his Professor Entwhistle comment on the academic life.

A question likely to arise for you is this: "Just what, or who, is being satirized?" Now a satire may cut several ways at once. Is Mr. Bishop directing this piece at football, students, faculty, or just some members of the faculty? Where does Mr. Bishop, himself a college professor, stand—with the Professor of Social Sciences, or perhaps with the Professor of Moral Philosophy? Or not with either?

Perhaps the term SATIRIC TYPE will be useful in your discussion. Some, at least, of these professors are types; they are generalized from observation of a number of persons. For instance, the Professor of Social Sciences is no one professor, and not your professor of social sciences. But he is made of the traits that the group of social science professors exhibit. Since your instructor knows the genus professor better than you do, he may see things here that you do not. Almost surely his experience will make him appreciate the last touch in the piece more than you can.

Football in the Faculty Club (1953)

MORRIS BISHOP

A sour November rain washed the windows of the Faculty Club. In the lounge, a half-dozen pipes made their burnt offerings, in ritual gratitude for dinner. A zealot for pipes would have recognized the imported straight grain of the Professor of Social Sciences, the bubbling fifty-center of the

Professor of Chemistry, the nicotine-secreting health pipe of the Professor of Moral Philosophy, the gnarled antique, bound with adhesive tape, of Professor Entwhistle.

"See the game Saturday?" said the Professor of Social Sciences, catching the eye of the Professor of Chemistry.

"Yuh. Pretty sad spectacle," said the Professor of Chemistry.

The Professor of Social Sciences had his opening, and he took the conversational ball for an end run. "It all depends on how you look at it. From the point of view of a faithful follower of the Team, a sad spectacle indeed. But as a cultural phenomenon, very absorbing. In fact, when we are behind by two touchdowns, I take comfort in regarding the game as a form of the initiation ceremonies, or *rites de passage,* which are, of course, almost universal among primitive peoples."

"What do you mean, primitive peoples?" said the Professor of Chemistry. "I should say that a football crowd—"

"I agree with you entirely," said the Professor of Social Sciences, raising his voice a trifle. " 'Primitive' is merely a convenient term, not a scientific classification. The same drives are at work in all societies, whatever their degrees of evolution. There seems to be some profound impulse that bids the tribe withdraw its young men at their coming of age and put them through the severest tests of manhood. They are segregated and fed on special foods, as at our training tables. Certain other foods are taboo; among the Mycoolon tribe of Australia, for example, the initiates are forbidden snakes, turtles, anteaters, and emu eggs. And in our own tribe, alcohol, tobacco, and pastry. The initiates are given instruction by selected elders, who have distinguished themselves in the performance of tribal rites. Coaches. They are trained in maintaining group consciousness; they are taught that success resides in conformity. Team play. Often they receive new names."

"Numbers," contributed the Professor of Chemistry.

"Precisely. Numbers. And when their training is completed—"

"Funny thing," interrupted Professor Entwhistle, who had been vainly adjusting the adhesive tape that bound his pipe bit to the briar. "Numbers for players were first introduced by the University of Pittsburgh in 1908, in order to stimulate the sale of programs. We may take this date as the moment when football ceased to be a game and became a spectacle."

"And when their training is completed," pursued the Professor of Social Sciences firmly, "they are given a public test of virility. This test is always painful and often bloody. It frequently includes ritual mutilation. Compare the honorable sabre slashes of the German students and the honorable wounds our squad members display so proudly in our classrooms. The initiates gladly endure their pains, because the entire clan is watching at the initiation rites, shouting its encouragement in rhythmic form."

"All together, fellows, give 'em the old locomotive!" intoned the Professor of Chemistry, in genial burlesque of a cheerleader.

Unheeding, the Professor of Social Sciences continued: "The totem of the clan is paraded, with much beating of tomtoms, rattling of gourds, and ritual acrobatics by the drum majors—or I should say the shamans. The totem is commonly a fierce hunting animal, whose qualities the tribesmen desire for themselves. Thus our colleges choose for their totems the lion, the tiger, the bear, the wolverine; so far as I know, no educational institution has adopted as its totem the virtuous horse, the playful panda."

"What you going to do about the football?" said the Professor of Chemistry.

"Thank you," said the Professor of Social Sciences. "I see you recognize that the game is a war game, a substitute for the test of actual war. Now, among most primitive peoples the young warrior is expected to bring back a trophy as the proof of his manhood. Among the American Indians, the trophy was a scalp. And in New Guinea and in many other places it was an enemy's head. I suggest, therefore, that the football is a substitute, a surrogate, for a human head."

Professor Entwhistle had renounced the effort to repair his pipe with adhesive tape and was wiring it precariously with paper clips. "The ancestor of our game of football," he said, "was a game called Kicking the Dane's Head. It was played in England in the eleventh century, and consisted of kicking a human skull between two towns, which were the goals. If you happened to see Reisman's article in the *American Quarterly*—"

His pipe fell apart, and the Professor of Social Sciences regained control. "The game of football, as I was saying, is the old drama of the headhunters. At the stadium Saturday, I shut my eyes and imagined I was in New Guinea, hearing the animal cries of the tribesmen, watching the young heroes carrying their dripping burden, passing it from hand to hand, dodging the savage enemy, and endeavoring by strength or craft to bring the precious trophy safely to their home territory."

"Touchdown!" cried the Professor of Chemistry.

"Your analogy is very ingenious," broke in the Professor of Moral Philosophy. "But if I were looking for the symbolism of football, I should be inclined to go deeper."

"Watch out for the things of the spirit," muttered the Professor of Chemistry to the Professor of Social Sciences.

"I should be inclined to find the ultimate significance of the football game in the things of the spirit," pursued the Professor of Moral Philosophy. "Football is a struggle, as life is a struggle. We see afar the Goal, and between us and it stands the Enemy, ever ready to drag us down into the mire and thrust us backward, throwing us for a loss. But we fight our way forward, hardly hoping to attain the distant Goal, striving only to gain a yard or two, to make a first down, to obtain a breathing space in the long struggle—a reprieve, a new opportunity to win some more yardage. Why, football is the modern 'Pilgrim's Progress,' the new Dante! I must remember to tell my class, I like to brighten things up with modern parallels."

"What do you make of the football?" inquired the Professor of Chemistry.

"The football? The football I take to be the spirit. For *pneuma* in Greek is 'spirit,' and is not the football primarily pneumatic?"

"What happens if you can't make a first down with your pneumatic spirit?" said the Professor of Chemistry.

"You have to kick," said the Professor of Moral Philosophy firmly.

Professor Entwhistle had wound a handkerchief about his pipe. He held the device with both hands as he smoked. He was obviously in an ugly humor. "All very pretty," he exploded. "But you can go crazy with symbolism, as people usually have. Look here—" He laid his pipe tenderly down and scribbled hastily in the lavish white space of a magazine advertisement, which he thrust under the eye of the Professor of Chemistry. "What does this represent?"

The Professor of Chemistry looked at this diagram:

O—O—O—O—O—O—O
            |
            O
            |
      O—O—O

Suspecting, with good reason, a trap, the Professor of Chemistry slowly replied, "Why, it looks like a diagram of a football team."

"My dear fellow, I'm amazed!" cried Professor Entwhistle in triumph. "That's the molecular structure of 4-isobutylheptane! Don't you recognize 4-isobutylheptane?"

The Professor of Chemistry turned crimson. "Here, give it here a minute! You took me by surprise."

"What is the deeper symbolism of a football team?" continued Professor Entwhistle. "It's merely a molecular arrangement. And I could show you how, by a simple displacement of the molecular structure, you obtain an A formation, or a single wing to the right. Don't look for any other significance. Just a lot of molecules, in opposition to another lot of molecules. And on Saturday our molecules were simply not active enough."

"Of course I recognize 4-isobutylheptane," said the Professor of Chemistry sulkily. "That was a trick play of yours, Entwhistle. A deception. Like when, in the third period, everybody thought we were going to kick and then Quackenbush flipped a pass to Harper."

"If Harper hadn't muffed that pass, the whole game might have gone differently," said the Professor of Moral Philosophy.

"The pass was too high," said the Professor of Chemistry. "Harper couldn't have caught it."

"Harper couldn't catch it because he was too slow getting down under it," said the Professor of Moral Philosophy warmly. "He's always too slow getting under them."

"Harper was all right," rejoined the Professor of Chemistry. "The trouble was, Quackenbush misjudged and threw it too high. Quackenbush nearly always throws them too high."

"On the contrary—" began the Professor of Moral Philosophy.

Professor Entwhistle sighed, and rose from his wicker chair, which also sighed. "Well, I've got to be off to the Committee on the Revision of the Curriculum."

"I thought we'd just got the curriculum revised," said the Professor of Chemistry.

"We did," said Professor Entwhistle. "Now we're revising it back."

"Good night, Entwhistle," said the occupants of the reading room sympathetically.

"Good night, molecules," said Professor Entwhistle.

Mr. C. S. Lewis's *The Screwtape Letters* is one of the few pieces of sustained irony that have had a wide popularity in our time. Reprinted here are three of the letters, any one of which may be read by itself if one understands the frame of the irony.

In his preface Mr. Lewis says he will not tell us how the manuscript of these letters came into his hands. In them Screwtape, a personage among the devils, advises his nephew, Wormwood, a young and inexperienced tempter, how to handle the commonplace young man trying to be a Christian who is always referred to as the "patient."

The central device is a simple one: the Christian's experience and problems are written about from the devils' point of view, an inversion of the point of view from which these matters are ordinarily discussed. Screwtape and Wormwood own their allegiance to Satan himself, called "Our Father below." God is always referred to by Screwtape as "the Enemy." But a simple device may be subtly worked out, and Mr. Lewis warns us in his preface that "there is wishful thinking in Hell as well as on Earth"—perhaps not everything that Screwtape hopes is true about the patient and his associates is true.

FROM *The Screwtape Letters* (1944)

C. S. LEWIS

II

MY DEAR WORMWOOD,

I I note with grave displeasure that your patient has become a Christian. Do not indulge the hope that you will escape the usual penalties; indeed, in your better moments, I trust you would hardly even wish to do so. In the meantime we must make the best of the situation. There is no need to despair; hundreds of these adult converts have been reclaimed after a brief sojourn in the Enemy's camp and are now with us. All the *habits* of the patient, both mental and bodily, are still in our favour.

II One of our great allies at present is the Church itself. Do not misunderstand me. I do not mean the Church as we see her spread out through all time and space and rooted in eternity, terrible as an army with banners.

That, I confess, is a spectacle which makes our boldest tempters uneasy. But fortunately it is quite invisible to these humans. All your patient sees is the half-finished, sham Gothic erection on the new building estate. When he goes inside, he sees the local grocer with rather an oily expression on his face bustling up to offer him one shiny little book containing a liturgy which neither of them understands, and one shabby little book containing corrupt texts of a number of religious lyrics, mostly bad, and in very small print. When he gets to his pew and looks round him he sees just that selection of his neighbours whom he has hitherto avoided. You want to lean pretty heavily on those neighbours. Make his mind flit to and fro between an expression like "the body of Christ" and the actual faces in the next pew. It matters very little, of course, what kind of people that next pew really contains. You may know one of them to be a great warrior on the Enemy's side. No matter. Your patient, thanks to Our Father below, is a fool. Provided that any of those neighbours sing out of tune, or have boots that squeak, or double chins, or odd clothes, the patient will quite easily believe that their religion must therefore be somehow ridiculous. At his present stage, you see, he has an idea of "Christians" in his mind which he supposes to be spiritual but which, in fact, is largely pictorial. His mind is full of togas and sandals and armour and bare legs and the mere fact that the other people in church wear modern clothes is a real—though of course an unconscious—difficulty to him. Never let it come to the surface; never let him ask what he expected them to look like. Keep everything hazy in his mind now, and you will have all eternity wherein to amuse yourself by producing in him the peculiar kind of clarity which Hell affords.

III Work hard, then, on the disappointment or anticlimax which is certainly coming to the patient during his first few weeks as a churchman. The Enemy allows this disappointment to occur on the threshold of every human endeavour. It occurs when the boy who has been enchanted in the nursery by *Stories from the Odyssey* buckles down to really learning Greek. It occurs when lovers have got married and begin the real task of learning to live together. In every department of life it marks the transition from dreaming aspiration to laborious doing. The Enemy takes this risk because He has a curious fantasy of making all these disgusting little human vermin into what He calls His "free" lovers and servants—"sons" is the word He uses, with His inveterate love of degrading the whole spiritual world by unnatural liaisons with the two-legged animals. Desiring their freedom, He therefore refuses to carry them, by their mere affections and habits, to any of the goals which He sets before them: He leaves them to "do it on their own." And there lies our opportunity. But also, remember, there lies our danger. If once they get through this initial dryness successfully, they become much less dependent on emotion and therefore much harder to tempt.

IV I have been writing hitherto on the assumption that the people in the next pew afford no *rational* ground for disappointment. Of course if they do—if the patient knows that the woman with the absurd hat is a fanatical bridge-player or the man with squeaky boots a miser and an extortioner—then your task is so much the easier. All you then have to do is to keep out of his mind the question "If I, being what I am, can consider that I am in some sense a Christian, why should the different vices of those people in the next pew prove that their religion is mere hypocrisy and convention?" You may ask whether it is possible to keep such an obvious thought from occurring even to a human mind. It is, Wormwood, it is! Handle him properly and it simply won't come into his head. He has not been anything like long enough with the Enemy to have any real humility yet. What he says, even on his knees, about his own sinfulness is all parrot talk. At bottom, he still believes he has run up a very favourable credit-balance in the Enemy's ledger by allowing himself to be converted, and thinks that he is showing great humility and condescension in going to church with these "smug," commonplace neighbours at all. Keep him in that state of mind as long as you can,

Your affectionate uncle
SCREWTAPE

XI

MY DEAR WORMWOOD,

I Everything is clearly going very well. I am specially glad to hear that the two new friends have now made him acquainted with their whole set. All these, as I find from the record office, are thoroughly reliable people; steady, consistent scoffers and worldlings who without any spectacular crimes are progressing quietly and comfortably towards our Father's house. You speak of their being great laughers. I trust this does not mean that you are under the impression that laughter as such is always in our favour. The point is worth some attention.

II I divide the causes of human laughter into Joy, Fun, the Joke Proper, and Flippancy. You will see the first among friends and lovers reunited on the eve of a holiday. Among adults some pretext in the way of Jokes is usually provided, but the facility with which the smallest witticisms produce laughter at such a time shows that they are not the real cause. What that real cause is we do not know. Something like it is expressed in much of that detestable art which the humans call Music, and something like it occurs in Heaven—a meaningless acceleration in the rhythm of celestial experience, quite opaque to us. Laughter of this kind does us no good and should always be discouraged. Besides, the phenomenon is of itself disgusting and a direct insult to the realism, dignity, and austerity of Hell.

III Fun is closely related to Joy—a sort of emotional froth arising from the play instinct. It is very little use to us. It can sometimes be used, of course, to divert humans from something else which the Enemy would like them to be feeling or doing: but in itself it has wholly undesirable tendencies; it promotes charity, courage, contentment, and many other evils.

IV The Joke Proper, which turns on sudden perception of incongruity, is a much more promising field. I am not thinking primarily of indecent or bawdy humour, which, though much relied on by second-rate tempters, is often disappointing in its results. The truth is that humans are pretty clearly divided on this matter into two classes. There are some to whom "no passion is as serious as lust" and for whom an indecent story ceases to produce lasciviousness precisely in so far as it becomes funny; there are others in whom laughter and lust are excited at the same moment and by the same things. The first sort joke about sex because it gives rise to many incongruities: the second cultivate incongruities because they afford a pretext for talking about sex. If your man is of the first type, bawdy humour will not help you—I shall never forget the hours which I wasted (hours to me of unbearable tedium) with one of my early patients in bars and smoking-rooms before I learned this rule. Find out which group the patient belongs to—and see that he does *not* find out.

v The real use of Jokes or Humour is in quite a different direction, and it is specially promising among the English who take their "sense of humour" so seriously that a deficiency in this sense is almost the only deficiency at which they feel shame. Humour is for them the all-consoling and (mark this) the all-excusing, grace of life. Hence it is invaluable as a means of destroying shame. If a man simply lets others pay for him, he is "mean"; if he boasts of it in a jocular manner and twits his fellows with having been scored off, he is no longer "mean" but a comical fellow. Mere cowardice is shameful; cowardice boasted of with humorous exaggerations and grotesque gestures can be passed off as funny. Cruelty is shameful— unless the cruel man can represent it as a practical joke. A thousand bawdy, or even blasphemous, jokes do not help towards a man's damnation so much as his discovery that almost anything he wants to do can be done, not only without the disapproval but with the admiration of his fellows, if only it can get itself treated as a Joke. And this temptation can be almost entirely hidden from your patient by that English seriousness about Humour. Any suggestion that there might be too much of it can be represented to him as "Puritanical" or as betraying a "lack of humour."

vi But Flippancy is the best of all. In the first place it is very economical. Only a clever human can make a real Joke about virtue, or indeed about anything else; any of them can be trained to talk *as if* virtue were funny. Among flippant people the Joke is always assumed to have been made. No one actually makes it; but every serious subject is discussed in a manner which implies that they have already found a ridiculous side to it. If prolonged, the habit of Flippancy builds up around a man the finest armour-plating against the Enemy that I know, and it is quite free from the dangers inherent in the other sources of laughter. It is a thousand miles away from joy: it deadens, instead of sharpening, the intellect; and it excites no affection between those who practice it,

Your affectionate uncle
SCREWTAPE

XXIII

MY DEAR WORMWOOD,

I Through this girl and her disgusting family the patient is now getting to know more Christians every day, and very intelligent Christians too. For a long time it will be quite impossible to *remove* spirituality from his life. Very well then; we must *corrupt* it. No doubt you have often practiced transforming yourself into an angel of light as a parade-ground exercise. Now is the time to do it in the face of the Enemy. The World and the Flesh have failed us; a third Power remains. And success of this third kind is the most glorious of all. A spoiled saint, a Pharisee, an inquisitor, or a magician, makes better sport in Hell than a mere common tyrant or debauchee.

II Looking round your patient's new friends I find that the best point of attack would be the border-line between theology and politics. Several of his new friends are very much alive to the social implications of their religion. That, in itself, is a bad thing; but good can be made out of it.

III You will find that a good many Christian-political writers think that Christianity began going wrong, and departing from the doctrine of its Founder, at a very early stage. Now this idea must be used by us to encourage once again the conception of a "historical Jesus" to be found by clearing away later "accretions and perversions" and then to be contrasted with the whole Christian tradition. In the last generation we promoted the construction of such a "historical Jesus" on liberal and humanitarian lines; we are now putting forward a new "historical Jesus" on Marxian, catastrophic, and revolutionary lines. The advantages of these constructions, which we intend to change every thirty years or so, are manifold. In the first place they all tend to direct men's devotion to something which does not exist, for each "historical Jesus" is unhistorical. The documents say what they say and cannot be added to; each new "historical Jesus" therefore has to be got out of them by suppression at one point and exaggeration at another, and by that sort of guessing (*brilliant* is the adjective we teach humans to apply to it) on which no one would risk ten shillings in ordinary life, but which is enough to produce a crop of new Napoleons, new Shakespeares, and new Swifts, in every publisher's autumn list. In the second place, all such constructions place the importance of their Historical Jesus in some peculiar theory He is supposed to have promulgated. He has to be a "great man" in the modern sense of the word—one standing at the terminus of some centrifugal and unbalanced line of thought—a crank vending a panacea. We thus distract men's minds from Who He is, and what He did. We first make Him solely a teacher, and then conceal the very substantial agreement between His teachings and those of all other great moral teachers. For humans must not be allowed to notice that all great moralists are sent by the Enemy not to inform men but to remind them, to restate the primeval moral platitudes against our continual concealment of them. We make the Sophists: He raises up a Socrates to answer them. Our third aim is, by these constructions, to destroy the devotional life. For the real presence of the Enemy, otherwise experienced by men in prayer and sacrament, we substitute a merely probable, remote, shadowy, and uncouth figure, one who spoke a strange language and died a long time ago. Such an object cannot in fact be worshipped. Instead of the Creator adored by its creature, you soon have merely a leader acclaimed by a partisan, and finally a distinguished character approved by a judicious historian. And fourthly, besides being unhistorical in the Jesus it depicts, religion of this kind is false to history in another sense. No nation, and few individuals, are really brought into the Enemy's camp by the historical study of the biography of Jesus, simply as biography. Indeed materials for a full biography have been withheld from men. The earliest converts were converted by a single historical fact (the Resurrection) and a single theological doctrine (the Redemption) operating on a sense of sin which they already had—and sin, not against some new fancy-dress law produced as a novelty by a "great man," but against the old, platitudinous, universal moral law which they had been taught by their nurses and mothers. The "Gospels" come later and were written not to make Christians but to edify Christians already made.

iv The "Historical Jesus" then, however dangerous he may seem to be to us at some particular point, is always to be encouraged. About the general connection between Christianity and politics, our position is more delicate. Certainly we do not want men to allow their Christianity to flow over into their political life, for the establishment of anything like a really just society would be a major disaster. On the other hand we do want, and want very much, to make men treat Christianity as a means; preferably, of course, as a means to their own advancement, but, failing that, as a means to anything—even to social justice. The thing to do is to get a man at first to value social justice as a thing which the Enemy demands, and then work him on to the stage at which he values Christianity because it may produce social justice. For the Enemy will not be used as a convenience. Men or nations who think they can revive the Faith in order to make a good society might just as well think they can use the stairs of Heaven as a short cut to the nearest chemist's shop. Fortunately it is quite easy to coax humans round this little corner. Only today I have found a passage in a Christian writer where he recommends his own version of Christianity on the ground that "only such a faith can outlast the death of old cultures and the birth of new civilisations." You see the little rift? "Believe this, not because it is true, but for some other reason." That's the game,

Your affectionate uncle
SCREWTAPE

We have said that such a sustained ironic structure as Mr. Lewis's is rare in modern writing. You will more often encounter irony as one of several elements in a piece of satiric writing; and so it figures in the two groups of selections which close this chapter.

James Thurber examines twentieth-century experience in his own way.

In his *Let Your Mind Alone!* he considers a number of books in popular psychology. You need not worry about any possible unfairness to the writers of them; they get along very well indeed. Thoreau says, "The mass of men lead lives of quiet desperation," and the immense popularity of inspirational psychology seems to show that at least hundreds of thousands do. These inspirational books exploit a human need, and they are therefore a fair mark for the satirist. Some of the more recent and dismaying examples of the kind still await him.

It would be a brave critic who tried to define Mr. Thurber's special skill. As it is exhibited here, it seems in part a kind of concreteness of mind. Mr. Thurber takes the popular psychologist's abstract pronouncements and his contrived anecdotes literally, and then extends them. The extension does not become exaggeration quite; nor does it need to be exaggeration, for both pronouncement and anecdote are often on the brink of absurdity.

FROM *Let Your Mind Alone!* (1937)

JAMES THURBER

[i]
The Conscious vs. The Unconscious

I It is high time that we were getting around to a consideration of the magnum opus of Louis E. Bisch, M.D., Ph.D., formerly Professor of Neuropsychiatry at the New York Polyclinic Medical School and Hospital, and Associate in Educational Psychology at Columbia University, and the author of "Be Glad You're Neurotic." Some of the reassuring chapter titles of his popular treatise are "I'm a Neurotic Myself and Delighted," "You Hate Yourself. No Wonder!," "No, You're Not Going Insane Nor Will Any of Your Fears Come True," "Are Your Glands on Friendly Terms?," and "Of Course Your Sex Life Is Far from Satisfactory." Some of you will be satisfied with just these titles and will not go on to the book itself, on the ground that you have a pretty good idea of it already. I should like, however, to have you turn with me to Chapter VII, one of my favorite chapters in all psychomentology, "Your Errors and Compulsions Are Calls for Help."

II The point of this chapter, briefly, is that the unconscious mind often opposes what the conscious mind wants to do or say, and frequently trips it up with all kinds of evasions, deceits, gags, and kicks in the pants. Our popular psychiatrists try to make these mysteries clear to the layman by the use of simple, homely language, and I am trying to do the same. Dr. Bisch relates a lot of conflicts and struggles that take place between the Hercules of the Conscious and the Augean Stables of the Unconscious (that is my own colorful, if somewhat labored, metaphor and I don't want to see any of the other boys swiping it). "I myself," writes Dr. Bisch, "forgot the number of a hospital where I was to deliver a lecture when I was about to apologize for my delay. I had talked to that particular hospital perhaps a hundred times before. This was the first time, however, that I was consciously trying to do what unconsciously I did not want to do." If you want unconsciously as well as consciously to call a hospital one hundred times out of one hundred and one, I say your conscious and unconscious are on pretty friendly terms. I say you are doing fine. This little experience of Dr. Bisch's is merely to give you a general idea of the nature of the chapter and to ease you into the discussion gently. There are many more interesting examples of conflict and error, of compulsion and obsession, to come. "A colleague," goes on Dr. Bisch, "told me that when he decided to telephone his wife to say he could not be home for dinner he dialled three wrong numbers before he got his own. 'It's because she always flares up when I'm detained at the office,' he explained." This shows that psychiatrists are just as scared of their wives as anybody else. Of course, I believe that this particular psychiatrist dialled the three wrong numbers on purpose. In the case of all husbands, both neurotic and normal, this is known as sparring for time and has no real psychological significance.

III I almost never, I find in going slowly and carefully through Dr. Bisch's chapter, taking case histories in their order, agree with him. He writes, "The appearance of persons whom one dislikes or is jealous of, who have offended in some way or whom one fears, tend to be blotted from the mind." Well, some twelve years ago I knew, disliked, was jealous of, feared, and had been offended by a man whom I shall call Philip Vause. His appearance has not only not been blotted from my mind, it hasn't even tended to be. I can call it up as perfectly as if I were holding a photograph of the man in my hand. In nightmares I still dream of Philip Vause. When, in these dreams, I get on subways, he is the guard; when I fly through the air, the eagle that races with me has his face; when I climb the Eiffel Tower, there he is at the top, his black hair roached back, the mole on the left cheek, the thin-lipped smile, and all. Dr. Bisch goes on to say that "the more disagreeable an incident, the deeper is it finally repressed." To which he adds, "The recollection of the pain attending child-birth never lingers long." He has me there.

IV Dr. Bisch proceeds from that into this: "A man who mislays his hat either dislikes it, wants a new one, experienced unpleasantness when last he wore it, or he does not want to go out. And what you lose you may be sure you do not value, even if it be your wedding ring. Psychologists claim that we lose things because we want to be rid of them or the association they carry, but that we are unwilling to admit the fact to ourselves and actually throw the thing away." This shows you pretty clearly, I think, the point psychologists have reached. I call it mysticism, but I am a polite fellow; you can call it anything you want to. Under any name, it isn't getting us anywhere. Every husband whose tearful wife has lost her wedding ring will now begin to brood, believing (if he strings along with the psychologists instead of with me) that the little darling threw it away, because she is really in love with Philip Vause, and that her tears over her loss are as phony as the plight of a panhandler's family. Let us leave all the sad young couples on the point of separating and go on to Dr. Bisch's analysis of a certain man.

v "A certain man," writes Dr. Bisch, "forgot to wind the alarm on several occasions, in consequence of which he was late for work. He also forgot his keys on two occasions and had to wake up his wife in the early hours of the morning. Twice he forgot the furnace at night with the result that there was no heat the next day. In this case the unconscious was trying to tell him that he did not like living in the country although consciously he maintained that he did, for the good of the children." There are, from the standpoint of my own school of psychology, so many fallacies in this piece of analysis that I hardly know where to begin. But let us begin at the beginning, with the failure to wind the alarm clock. Now, a man who does not want to stay home winds the clock so that it will wake him and he can get the hell out and go to the office. There is surely nothing sounder than this. Hence the failure to wind the alarm clock shows that his unconscious was trying to tell him that he did not want to go to the office any more but wanted to stay at his house in the country all the time. The key-forgetting business I simply do not believe. A man who has had to rout out his wife once in the early hours of the morning is not going to forget his key a second time. This is known as Thurber's Empirical Law No. 1. If Dr. Bisch had lived in the country as long and as happily as I have, he would know this simple and unmystical fact: any man can forget to fix the clock and the furnace; especially the furnace, because the clock is usually right where it can be seen, whereas the furnace isn't. Some husbands "forget" to bank the furnace because they have kept hearing funny noises in the cellar all evening and are simply scared to go down there. Hundreds of simple little conscious motives enter into life, Dr. Bisch, hundreds of them.

vi "A woman," goes on Dr. Bisch, "who wished to consult an attorney about a divorce wrote to him: 'I have been married 22 years.' But the second 2 had evidently been added afterward, indicating that probably she was embarrassed to admit not being able to make a go of it after living with the man so long." How's that again, Doctor? I may be dumb, but I don't exactly catch all that. Couldn't the woman have really been married only 2 years, and couldn't she have added the second 2 indicating that probably she was embarrassed to admit that she was giving up trying to make a go of it after living with the man so *short* a time? Maybe we better just drop this one.

vii "A woman," continues Dr. Bisch (this is another woman), "who was talking to me about an intended trip to the lakes of northern Italy said: 'I don't wish to visit Lavonia Bay.' She, herself, was surprised, as no such place exists. Inasmuch as the trip was to be a honeymoon, it was 'love, honor, and obey' that really was bothering her." I take off my hat to the Doctor's astonishing powers of divination here, because I never would have figured it out. Now that he has given me the key, I get it, of course. "Love, honor, and obey," love-honor-obey, Lavonia Bay. I wonder if he knows the one about the woman who asked the librarian for a copy of "In a Garden." What she really wanted was "Enoch Arden." I like Lavonia Bay better,

though, because it is psycho-neurotic, whereas there was nothing the matter with the other poor woman; she just thought that the name of the book
was "In a Garden." Dr. Bisch might very likely see something more in this,
but the way I've always heard it was that she just thought the name was
"In a Garden."

VIII "When a usually efficient secretary," writes Dr. Bisch, "makes errors in typing or shorthand, the excuse of fatigue or indisposition should
be taken with a grain of salt. Resentment may have developed toward the
employer or the work, or something may unconsciously be bothering her.
Some years ago my own secretary often hit the *t* key by mistake. I discovered a young man by the name of Thomas was courting her." That doesn't
explain the mistakes of a secretary I had five or six years ago. I had never
had a secretary before, and had, indeed, never dictated a letter up to that
time. We got some strange results. One of these, in a letter to a man I
hoped I would never hear from again, was this sentence: "I feel that the
cuneo has, at any rate, garbled the deig." This was not owing to fatigue or
indisposition, or to resentment, although there *was* a certain resentment—
or even to a young man named Cuneo or Deig. It was simply owing to the
fact that my secretary, an Eastern girl, could only understand part of what
I, a Middle-Westerner, was saying. In those days, I talked even more than
I do now as if I had steel wool in my mouth, and the young lady just did
not "get" me. Being afraid to keep asking me what I was trying to say, she
simply put down what it sounded like. I signed this particular letter, by
the way, just as she wrote it, and I never heard again from the man I sent
it to, which is what I had **hoped** would happen. Psychiatrists would contend that I talked unintelligibly because of that very hope, but this is because they don't know that in Ohio, to give just one example, the word "officials" is pronounced "fishuls," no matter what anybody hopes.

IX We now go on to the case of a gentleman who deviated from the normal, or uninteresting. "In dressing for a formal dinner," says Dr. Bisch, "a
man put on a bright red bow tie. His enthusiasm was self-evident." That is
all our psychiatrist says about this one, and I think he is letting it go much
too easily; I sense a definite drop here. If I were to say to you that in dressing for a formal dinner last night I put on a bright red bow tie and you
were to say merely, "Your enthusiasm was self-evident," I would give you
a nasty look and go on to somebody else who would get a laugh out of it,
or at least ask what the hell was the idea. For the purpose of analysis in this
particular case, I think you would have to know who the man was, anyway. If it was Ernest Boyd, that's one thing; if it was Jack Dempsey, that's
another thing; if it was Harpo Marx or Dave Chasen, that's still another
thing, or two other things. I think you really have to know who the man
was. If the idea was to get a laugh, I don't think it was so very good. As for
Dr. Bisch's notion that the man was enthusiastic, I don't see that at all. I
just don't see it. Enthusiastic about what?

X Our psychiatrist, in this meaty chapter, takes up a great many more
cases, many more than I can disagree with in the space at my disposal, but
I can't very well leave out the one about the man and the potatoes, be-

cause it is one of my favorites. It seems that there kept running through this unfortunate gentleman's mind the words "mashed potatoes, boiled potatoes, mashed potatoes, boiled potatoes"—*that* old line. This went on for days, and the poor fellow, who had a lot of other things he wanted to keep repeating, could only keep repeating that. "Here," says Dr. Bisch, "the difficulty lay in the fact that the man had previously received a reprimand from his employer regarding his easy-going ways with the men who were under him in his department. 'Don't be too soft!' the employer had shouted. 'Be hard!' That very evening his wife served French fried potatoes that were burnt. 'I should be hard with her, too,' he mused. The next day the 'mashed potatoes, boiled potatoes' had been born." Now my own analysis is that the fellow really wanted to kill (mash) his wife and then go out and get fried or boiled. My theory brings in the fried potatoes and Dr. Bisch's doesn't, or not so well, anyway. I might say, in conclusion, that I don't like fellows who muse about getting hard with their wives and then take it out in repeating some silly line over and over. If I were a psychiatrist, I would not bother with them. There are so many really important ailments to attend to.

[ii]

Sample Intelligence Test

I The fuzziness that creeps into the thought processes of those inspirationalists who seek to clarify the human scene reaches an interesting point in Chapter XIV of "How to Develop Your Personality," by Sadie Myers Shellow, Ph.D. Dr. Shellow was formerly psychologist with the Milwaukee Electric Railway & Light Company. These things happen in a world of endless permutations. I myself was once connected with the Central Ohio Optical Company. I was hired because I had a bicycle, although why an optical company would want a bicycle might appear on the face of it as inexplicable as why a railway-and-light company would want a psychologist. My experience of motormen leads me to believe that they are inarticulate to the point of never saying anything at all, and I doubt if there is a motorman in all Wisconsin who would reveal the story of his early childhood to a psychologist. Dr. Shellow, of course, may have proceeded along some other line, but most psychologists start with your childhood. Or with your sex life. I somehow have never thought of motormen as having sex lives, but this doesn't mean that they don't have them. I feel that this speculation is not getting us anywhere.

II Let us return to Dr. Shellow's book. It was first published five years ago, but her publishers have just brought out a dollar edition, which puts the confusion in Chapter XIV within reach of everyone. In 1932, the book went into six printings. The present edition was printed from the original plates, which means that the mistakes which appear in it have gone on and on through the years. The book begins with a prefatory note by Albert Edward Wiggam, a foreword by Morris S. Viteles, and an introduction by Dr. Shellow herself. In Chapter I, first paragraph, Dr. Shellow gives the dictionary definition of "personality" as follows: "The sum total of traits necessary to describe what is to be a person." Unless I have gone crazy reading all these books, and I think I have, that sentence defines personality as the sum total of traits necessary to describe an unborn child. If Dr. Shellow's error here is typographical, it looms especially large in a book containing a chapter that tells how to acquire reading skill and gives tests for efficiency in reading. Dr. Shellow tells of a young woman who "was able to take in a whole page at a glance, and through concentrated attention relate in detail what she had read as the words flashed by." If Dr. Shellow used this system in reading the proofs of her book, the system is apparently no good. It certainly *sounds* as if it were no good. I have started out with an admittedly minor confusion—the definition of personality—but let us go on to something so mixed up that it becomes almost magnificent.

III Chapter XIV is called "Intelligence Tests," and under the heading "Sample Intelligence Test" twelve problems are posed. There are some pretty fuzzy goings-on in the explanation of No. 11, but it is No. 12 that interests me most; what the Milwaukee motormen made of it I can't imagine. No. 12 is stated as follows: "Cross out the *one* word which makes this sentence absurd and substitute one that is correct: A pound of feathers is lighter than a pound of lead." Let us now proceed to Dr. Shellow's explanation of how to arrive at the solution of this toughy. She writes, "In 12 we get at the critical ability of the mind. Our first impulse is to agree that a pound of feathers is lighter than a pound of lead, since feathers are lighter than lead, but if we look back, we will see that a *pound* of feathers could be no lighter than a *pound* of lead since a pound is always the same. What one word, then, makes the whole sentence absurd? We might cross out the second pound and substitute ounce, in which case we would have: A pound of feathers is heavier than an ounce of lead, and that would be correct. Or we might cross out the word heavier and substitute bulkier, in which case we would have eliminated the absurdity."

IV We have here what I can only call a paradise of errors. I find, in Dr. Shellow's presentation of the problem and her solution of it, Transference, Wishful Thinking, Unconscious Substitution, Psychological Dissociation, Gordian Knot Cutting, Cursory Enumeration, Distortion of Focus, Abandonment of Specific Gravity, Falsification of Premise, Divergence from Consistency, Overemphasis on Italics, Rhetorical Escapism, and Disregard of the Indefinite Article. Her major error—the conjuring up of the word "heavier" out of nowhere—is enough to gum up any problem beyond repair, but there are other interesting pieces of woolly reasoning in No. 12. Dr. Shellow gets off on the wrong foot in her very presentation of the problem. She begins, "Cross out the *one* word which makes this sentence absurd." That means there is *only* one word which can be changed and restricts the person taking the test to that one word, but Dr. Shellow goes on, in her explanation, to change first one and then another. As a matter of fact, there are five words in the sentence any one of which can be changed to give the sentence meaning. Thus we are all balled up at the start. If Dr. Shellow had written, "Cross out one word which makes this sentence absurd," that would have been all right. I think I know how she got into trouble. I imagine that she originally began, "Cross out one of the words," and found herself face to face with that ancient stumbling block in English composition, whether to say "which *makes* this sentence absurd" or "which *make* this sentence absurd." (I don't like to go into italics, but to straighten Dr. Shellow out you got to go into italics.) I have a notion that Dr. Shellow decided that "make" was right, which of course it is, but that she was dissatisfied with "Cross out one of the words which make this sentence absurd" because here "words" dominates "one." Since she wanted to emphasize "one," she italicized it and then, for good measure, put the definite article "the" in front of it. That would have given her "Cross out the *one* of the words which make this sentence absurd." From there she finally arrived at what she arrived at, and the problem began slowly to close in on her.

v I wouldn't dwell on this at such length if Dr. Shellow's publishers had not set her up as a paragon of lucidity, precision, and logical thought. (Come to think that over, I believe I would dwell on it at the same length even if they hadn't.) Some poor fellows may have got inferiority complexes out of being unable to see through Dr. Shellow's authoritative explanation of No. 12, and I would like to restore their confidence in their own minds. You can't just go batting off any old sort of answer to an intelligence test in this day when every third person who reads these books has a pretty firm idea that his mind is cracking up.

vi Let us go on to another interesting fuzziness in the Doctor's explanation. Take her immortal sentence: "We might cross out the second pound and substitute ounce," etc. What anybody who followed those instructions would arrive at is: "A pound of feathers is lighter than *a* ounce of lead." Even leaving the matter of weight out of it (which I am reluctant to do, since weight is the main point), you can't substitute "ounce" for "pound" without substituting "an" for "a," thus changing two words. If "an" and "a" are the same word, then things have come to a pretty pass, indeed. If such slipshoddery were allowed, you could solve the problem with "A pound of feathers is lighter than two pound of lead." My own way out was to change "is" to "ain't," if anybody is interested.

vii Let us close this excursion into the wonderland of psychology with a paragraph of Dr. Shellow's which immediately follows her explanation of No. 12: "If the reader went through this test quickly before reading the explanation, he may have discovered some things about himself. A more detailed test would be even more revealing. Everyone should at some time or other take a good comprehensive intelligence test and analyze his own defects so that he may know into what errors his reasoning takes him and of what faulty habits of thought he must be aware." I want everybody to file out quietly, now, without any wisecracks.

This next group of short pieces is from the *Ladies' and Gentlemen's Guide to Modern English Usage.* Mr. Thurber says in a note to the title that the work is "Inspired by Mr. H. W. Fowler's excellent 'Dictionary of

Modern English Usage.'" Mr. Fowler is not the target of the satire, and his book has no absurdity except the intrinsic absurdity of the English language. Since Mr. Thurber writes very well, we can be sure he has trouble with grammar and syntax—only a poor sort of writer does not. The harder you have tried to write well, the more you will enjoy these pieces.

But you will find some touches of satire. There is implied satire of the user of what *The New Yorker* calls "the ubiquitous whom"—the person whose grammar breaks down in an especially pretentious fashion. There is satire of the primer sentences of Ernest Hemingway and the too many persons influenced by them. And there is satire on us all in our stumbling pursuit of grammatical precision.

It is not recommended that you learn your grammar from Mr. Thurber's *Guide*. But the grammatical dilemmas represented there are very real. The sentence in "Which" about the pew in the gallery, for instance, is but a slight exaggeration of a sentence in G. K. Chesterton's story "The Hammer of God." Moreover, the implied grammatical moral is a good one: if you get into serious trouble in a sentence, throw it all away and start over. And if these pieces lead you to Fowler's *Dictionary of Modern English Usage*, they will have done you a service.

FROM *Ladies' and Gentlemen's Guide to Modern English Usage* (1929)

JAMES THURBER

[i]
Who and Whom

1 The number of people who use "whom" and "who" wrongly is appalling. The problem is a difficult one and it is complicated by the importance of tone, or taste. Take the common expression, "Whom are you, anyways?" That is of course, strictly speaking, correct—and yet how formal, how stilted! The usage to be preferred in ordinary speech and writing is "Who are you, anyways?" "Whom" should be used in the nominative case only when a note of dignity or austerity is desired. For example, if a writer is dealing with a meeting of, say, the British Cabinet, it would be better to have the Premier greet a new arrival, such as an under-secretary, with a "Whom are you, anyways?" rather than a "Who are you, anyways?"—always granted that the Premier is sincerely unaware of the man's identity. To address a person one knows by a "Whom are you?" is a mark either of incredible lapse of memory or inexcusable arrogance. "How are you?" is a much kindlier salutation.

11 The Buried Whom, as it is called, forms a special problem. This is where the word occurs deep in a sentence. For a ready example, take the common expression: "He did not know whether he knew her or not be-

cause he had not heard whom the other had said she was until too late to see her." The simplest way out of this is to abandon the "whom" altogether and substitute "where" (a reading of the sentence that way will show how much better it is). Unfortunately, it is only in rare cases that "where" can be used in place of "whom." Nothing could be more flagrantly bad, for instance, than to say "Where are you?" in demanding a person's identity. The only conceivable answer is, "Here I am," which would give no hint at all as to whom the person was. Thus the conversation, or piece of writing, would, from being built upon a false foundation, fall of its own weight.

III A common rule for determining whether "who" or "whom" is right is to substitute "she" for "who," and "her" for "whom," and see which sounds the better. Take the sentence, "He met a woman who they said was an actress." Now if "who" is correct then "she" can be used in its place. Let us try it. "He met a woman she they said was an actress." That instantly rings false. It can't be right. Hence the proper usage is "whom."

IV In certain cases grammatical correctness must often be subordinated to a consideration of taste. For instance, suppose that the same person had met a man whom they said was a street-cleaner. The word "whom" is too austere to use in connection with a lowly worker, like a street-cleaner, and its use in this form is known as False Admiration or Pathetic Fallacy.

V You might say: "There is, then, no hard and fast rule?" ("was then" would be better, since "then" refers to what is past). You might better say, then (or have said): "There was then (or is now) no hard and fast rule?" Only this, that it is better to use "whom" when in doubt, and even better to re-word the statement, and leave out all the relative pronouns, except ad, ante, con, in, inter, ob, post, prae, pro, sub, and super.

[ii]

Which

I The relative pronoun "which" can cause more trouble than any other word, if recklessly used. Foolhardy persons sometimes get lost in which-clauses and are never heard of again. My distinguished contemporary, Fowler, cites several tragic cases, of which the following is one: "It was rumoured that Beaconsfield intended opening the Conference with a speech in French, his pronunciation of which language leaving everything to be desired . . ." That's as much as Mr. Fowler quotes because, at his age, he was afraid to go any farther. The young man who originally got into that sentence was never found. His fate, however, was not as terrible as that of another adventurer who became involved in a remarkable which-mire. Fowler has followed his devious course as far as he safely could on foot: "Surely what applies to games should also apply to racing, the leaders of which being the very people from whom an example might well be looked for . . ." Not even Henry James could have successfully emerged from a sentence with "which," "whom," and "being" in it. The safest way to avoid such things is to follow in the path of the American author, Ernest Hemingway. In his youth he was trapped in a which-clause one time and barely escaped with his mind. He was going along on solid ground until he got into this: "It was the one thing of which, being very much afraid—for whom has not been warned to fear such things—he . . ." Being a young and powerfully built man, Hemingway was able to fight his way back to where he had started, and begin again. This time he skirted the treacherous morass in this way: "He was afraid of one thing. This was the one thing. He had been warned to fear such things. Everybody has been warned to fear such things." Today Hemingway is alive and well, and many happy writers are following along the trail he blazed.

II What most people don't realize is that one "which" leads to another. Trying to cross a paragraph by leaping from "which" to "which" is like Eliza crossing the ice. The danger is in missing a "which" and falling in. A case in point is this: "He went up to a pew which was in the gallery, which brought him under a colored window which he loved and always quieted his spirit." The writer, worn out, missed the last "which"—the one that should come just before "always" in that sentence. But supposing he had got it in! We would have: "He went up to a pew which was in the gallery, which brought him under a colored window which he loved and which always quieted his spirit." Your inveterate whicher in this way gives the effect of tweeting like a bird or walking with a crutch, and is not welcome in the best company.

III It is well to remember that one "which" leads to two and that two "whiches" multiply like rabbits. You should never start out with the idea that you can get by with one "which." Suddenly they are all around you. Take a sentence like this: "It imposes a problem which we either solve, or perish." On a hot night, or after a hard day's work, a man often lets himself get by with a monstrosity like that, but suppose he dictates that sentence bright and early in the morning. It comes to him typed out by his stenographer and he instantly senses that something is the matter with it. He tries to reconstruct the sentence, still clinging to the "which," and gets something like this: "It imposes a problem which we either solve, or which, failing to solve, we must perish on account of." He goes to the water-cooler, gets a drink, sharpens his pencil, and grimly tries again. "It imposes a problem which we either solve or which we don't solve and . . ." He begins once more: "It imposes a problem which we either solve, or which we do not solve, and from which . . ." The more times he does it the more "whiches" he gets. The way out is simple: "We must either solve this problem, or perish." Never monkey with "which." Nothing except getting tangled up in a typewriter ribbon is worse.

[iii]

Whether

I A certain type of person is wont to let "whether" get him down. For one thing, he will wear himself out doubling the alternative. That is, he will write some such clause as "Whether or not the birds will or will not come north this year." Either "or not" or "or will not" should be dropped. If one or the other isn't dropped, an ornithologist can get into all sorts of trouble, such as "Whether or not the nuthatch will or will not hatch, is not known." If the thing goes as far as that, a person should drop ornithology too. A good ornithologist doesn't need "whethers." He should know whether or not the bird will hatch, and say so.

II The use of "whether" after "doubt" is another troublesome matter. Yet the rule is simple. When the sentence is affirmative, use "whether"— "I doubt whether he will go." When the sentence is negative, use "that"—"I do not doubt that he will go." Practically nobody remembers this rule, however, and the best thing to do is carry it on a little slip of paper in your pocket and refer to it when needed. In great crises, it is well not to bother with either one. For example, if a gentleman wishes to address a lady as follows, "I no longer doubt whether (that) I love you," the best modern usage is simply to place his arms around her waist. In this case her arms should go around his shoulders. Occasionally a gentleman will put his arms around a lady's shoulders and expect her to put hers around his waist. Since this is contrary to accepted custom, the result often is that both parties reach for the same place, i.e., waist or shoulders, at the same time, and thus appear to be boxing. Nothing can end a courtship any faster than to appear to be boxing. If a gentleman is going to depart from the common practice he should give warning.

III The question of when to use "whether or no" instead of "whether or not" will likely never be decided now. Grammarians have avoided the subject since the deplorable experience of Dr. Amos Crawley, M.A., LL.D., who, in his invaluable but, alas, uncompleted monograph, "Clarified Expression," unaccountably got involved, while his wife and servants were away and he was alone in the house, in a construction beginning: "Whether or not 'whether or no' is ever preferable to 'whether or not' depends on whether or not . . ." at which point he was stricken. The best advice is make up your mind and avoid doubt-clauses.

SUGGESTIONS FOR PAPERS

If your instructor is willing that you try a piece of ironic satire, you will have to find your own subject, for you know best what you can write ironically about. An experiment you might try, if you and your instructor think well of it, is to modernize our selection from *Gulliver's Travels*— have Gulliver recommend to the king's admiration flame-throwers, submarines, atomic weapons, and the like. And students sometimes do pretty well with what is called "a transparency." A transparency usually presents someone speaking from a common and typical point of view not at all that of the writer, but so managed that the reader "sees through" to the writer's real attitude. Sinclair Lewis's "The Man Who Knew Coolidge" may be considered a transparency. The device works well for short pieces. For example, a transparency using a college subject might take as the speaker a recent alumnus, and make him say:

I always say the really important thing you get out of going to college is it's so broadening—even the professors when you get to know them. My dad always used to talk about what he called the queer ducks he had for profs. But it isn't that way any more—you take some of my profs, why they'd do all right in business. Good many of them belong to service clubs. But of course college isn't all studies. My fraternity now—why there were fellows from all over. Of course we didn't pledge just anybody, and most of the fellows were from close around Smugburg, but you certainly learned how to get along with people. Of course sometimes we got a fellow with queer ideas—couldn't really understand fraternity spirit, or took religion seriously, or kept talking about racial discrimination, or something. But mostly . . . etc.

Or you might find it interesting to adapt C. S. Lewis's technique to a college subject. For example, you have heard a lot of official good advice about getting the most out of college—and you know how ineffectual it seems usually to be. Suppose you write a letter purporting to be from a recent graduate to a nephew or niece, a letter written under the assumption that the whole endeavor of a boy or girl in college ought to be to avoid any enlightenment therefrom. See if you can make the right attitudes and ideas implicit in a letter in which you urge all the wrong ones. (Of course this technique may be used for other than college subjects.)

Here are suggestions for other sorts of exercises:

An exercise in extended definition: Find in your desk dictionary the definition that seems best to cover irony of statement. Taking it for a starting point, write a consideration of irony of statement, illustrating by reference to our selections and other examples that you find or devise.

An exercise in interpretation: There are persons who are nearly impervious to irony—they may be fine persons, too. Assume one of them as your reader, and write a critical discussion of any one of our selections. Try to make clear to your reader—without talking down to him—what the writer is getting at. Or, if you take "Football in the Faculty Club," you will not need to assume a reader impervious to irony, but merely one quite unacquainted with academic things and people.

Exercises requiring further reading: (a) Read Franklin's "Edict of the King of Prussia" or his "Rules by Which a Great Empire May Be Reduced to a Small One" or his "The Sale of the Hessians." Write an account of it for the members of the class. You can get sufficient background from any textbook in American history. The first two were written when Franklin was London agent for four of the American colonies in the years just before the Revolution. (b) Read all of *The Screwtape Letters*—a small book —and write a critical account, with such quotation as may indicate its quality. (c) One of the most effective of eighteenth-century ironic satires is Daniel Defoe's "The Shortest Way with the Dissenters" (1702). Reading it and writing an account of it would be an interesting exercise, and one which would extend you. You would need background on the troubles of nonconformists around the time of the essay, background which you could easily get from any textbook history of England. (d) Examine one of the currently popular inspirational books and write an account of it for the class. Try to explain its popularity and to decide what it actually offers its readers.

An exercise in comparative criticism: Compare the work of Swift and Franklin in the ironic satire, and make an estimate of the kind and degree of Franklin's debt to Swift. Remember that such criticism is hardly intelligible without illustrative quotation.

XVIII

Interpretation

I n this chapter we shall not be doing anything that is really new to us. But it may be that you will find the level of difficulty, and of interest, a bit higher than it has been in most of the material we have been over. Or, perhaps it is better to say, you will find that level higher if you read actively enough to get to it. Certainly the selections here may be read on more than one level. In them ideas are represented as well as stated. In them there are implications beyond the surface meaning—beyond the meaning one apprehends with ordinary attention the first time through.

TWO EXCERPTS FROM WALDEN

i

These selections from *Walden* by Henry David Thoreau (1817–62) are chosen for their intrinsic interest and because they offer certain problems that you ought to have some practice in solving. You are likely to find that upon a first reading you gather what may seem a sufficient meaning, but that with closer attention you realize implications you were unaware of at first. These implications depend upon metaphor, upon allusion, and upon Thoreau's way of representing ideas concretely and leaving generalization about them up to the reader.

Our selections stand well by themselves, since they are units of writing, complete treatments of the matters Thoreau has in hand. Yet you will get a better control of them for knowing something about *Walden* and about its author's intention.

Thoreau lived nearly all his forty-five years in Concord, Massachusetts; "I have travelled a good deal," he says, "in Concord." He was for a long time "reporter to a journal of no very wide circulation"—his own—and never in his time did he make much impression upon the thought of his countrymen. But what he made out of a consideration of his own life has come to seem increasingly pertinent to our time, and *Walden* grows in importance to us year by year.

"To be a philosopher," Thoreau says, "is not merely to have subtle thoughts, nor even to found a school, but so to love wisdom as to live according to its dictates, a life of simplicity, independence, magnanimity, and trust. It is to solve some of the problems of life, not only theoretically, but practically." *Walden* is the record of an effort to live such a life; Thoreau, convinced that an abundance of things made for a poverty of spirit, tested his belief by living for two years in a cabin he built on the shore of Walden Pond.

Since *Walden* is a disturbing book, readers have often erected a defence of misunderstanding. Thoreau was not a primitivist—he does not preach a return to some past era of simplicity; he urges instead "the unquestionable ability of man to elevate his life by a conscious endeavor." He did not even suggest that his life at Walden Pond was a pattern of life for all men; "I would not have any one," he says, "adopt *my* mode of living on any account; for, beside that before he has fairly learned it I may have found out another for myself, I desire that there may be as many different persons in the world as possible." Thoreau is not primarily important as a naturalist; his reflection on man is more important to him and to his readers than his observation of plants and animals. He is an egoist only in the fashion he would have all men be egoists, for he believed that human potentiality could be realized only in the individual. If he believed that he had a better sense of values than his neighbors, he felt no spiritual separation from them; "I never knew," he says, "and never shall know, a worse man than myself." But he offers no system to change society; he believes men cannot be reformed—though men can reform themselves.

Yet the reader of *Walden* who understands all these things is likely to find himself resentful, for what Thoreau asks of us is difficult: he asks us really to consider what we have always taken for granted. We live, he insists, "this mean life that we do because our vision does not penetrate the surface of things." And the things that stop our vision are for the most part those material things of which we suppose civilization consists. He offers us a theory of value, a principle each man can apply only for himself: "the cost of a thing is the amount of what I will call life which is required to be exchanged for it, immediately or in the long run." This principle will not much resemble the theory of value in your economics textbook; but you can find principles like it in the New Testament, for instance Luke 12:15.

Our first selection is an ironic consideration of man in a heroic role; the second selection represents the industrial and commercial developments of the mid-nineteenth century which have culminated in the civilization in which we live.

FROM *Walden* (1854)

HENRY DAVID THOREAU

[i]

[The Battle of the Ants]

1 . . . One day when I went out to my wood-pile, or rather my pile of stumps, I observed two large ants, the one red, the other much larger, nearly half an inch long, and black, fiercely contending with one another.

Having once got hold they never let go, but struggled and wrestled and rolled on the chips incessantly. Looking farther, I was surprised to find that the chips were covered with such combatants, that it was not a *duellum,* but a *bellum,* a war between two races of ants, the red always pitted against the black, and frequently two red ones to one black. The legions of these Myrmidons covered all the hills and vales in my wood-yard, and the ground was already strewn with the dead and dying, both red and black. It was the only battle which I have ever witnessed, the only battle-field I ever trod while the battle was raging; internecine war; the red republicans on the one hand, and the black imperialists on the other. On every side they were engaged in deadly combat, yet without any noise that I could hear, and human soldiers never fought so resolutely. I watched a couple that were fast locked in each other's embraces, in a little sunny valley amid the chips, now at noon-day prepared to fight till the sun went down, or life went out. The smaller red champion had fastened himself like a vice to his adversary's front, and through all the tumblings on that field never for an instant ceased to gnaw at one of his feelers near the root, having already caused the other to go by the board; while the stronger black one dashed him from side to side, and, as I saw on looking nearer, had already divested him of several of his members. They fought with more pertinacity than bulldogs. Neither manifested the least disposition to retreat. It was evident that their battle-cry was Conquer or die. In the mean while there came along a single red ant on the hill-side of this valley, evidently full of excitement, who either had despatched his foe, or had not yet taken part in the battle; probably the latter, for he had lost none of his limbs; whose mother had charged him to return with his shield or upon it. Or perchance he was some Achilles, who had nourished his wrath apart, and had now come to avenge or rescue his Patroclus. He saw this unequal combat from afar,— for the blacks were nearly twice the size of the red,—he drew near with rapid pace till he stood on his guard within half an inch of the combatants; then, watching his opportunity, he sprang upon the black warrior, and commenced his operations near the root of his right fore-leg, leaving the foe to select among his own members; and so there were three united for life, as if a new kind of attraction had been invented which put all other locks and cements to shame. I should not have wondered by this time to find that they had their respective musical bands stationed on some eminent chip, and playing their national airs the while, to excite the slow and cheer the dying combatants. I was myself excited somewhat even as if they had been men. The more you think of it, the less the difference. And certainly there is not the fight recorded in Concord history, at least, if in the history of America, that will bear a moment's comparison with this, whether for the numbers engaged in it, or for the patriotism and heroism displayed. For numbers and for carnage it was an Austerlitz or Dresden. Concord Fight! Two killed on the patriots' side, and Luther Blanchard wounded! Why here every ant was a Buttrick,—"Fire! for God's sake fire!"—and thousands shared the fate of Davis and Hosmer. There was not one hireling there. I have no doubt that it was a principle they fought for, as much as our ancestors, and not to avoid a three-penny tax on their tea; and the results of this battle will be as important and memorable to those whom it concerns as those of the battle of Bunker Hill, at least.

II I took up the chip on which the three I have particularly described were struggling, carried it into my house, and placed it under a tumbler on my window-sill, in order to see the issue. Holding a microscope to the first-mentioned red ant, I saw that, though he was assiduously gnawing at the near fore-leg of his enemy, having severed his remaining feeler, his own breast was all torn away, exposing what vitals he had there to the jaws of the black warrior, whose breast-plate was apparently too thick for him to pierce; and the dark carbuncles of the sufferer's eyes shone with ferocity such as war only could excite. They struggled half an hour longer under the tumbler, and when I looked again the black soldier had severed the heads of his foes from their bodies, and the still living heads were hanging on either side of him like ghastly trophies at his saddle-bow, still apparently as firmly fastened as ever, and he was endeavoring with feeble struggles, being without feelers and with only the remnant of a leg, and I know not how many other wounds, to divest himself of them; which at length, after half an hour more, he accomplished. I raised the glass, and he went off over the window-sill in that crippled state. Whether he finally survived that combat, and spent the remainder of his days in some Hotel des Invalides, I do not know; but I thought that his industry would not be worth much thereafter. I never learned which party was victorious, nor the cause of the war; but I felt for the rest of that day as if I had had my feelings excited and harrowed by witnessing the struggle, the ferocity and carnage, of a human battle before my door.

III Kirby and Spence tell us that the battles of ants have long been celebrated and the date of them recorded, though they say that Huber is the only modern author who appears to have witnessed them. "Æneas Sylvius," say they, "after giving a very circumstantial account of one contested with great obstinacy by a great and small species on the trunk of a pear tree," adds that " 'This action was fought in the pontificate of Eugenius the Fourth, in the presence of Nicholas Pistoriensis, an eminent lawyer, who related the whole history of the battle with the greatest fidelity.' A similar engagement between great and small ants is recorded by Olaus Magnus, in which the small ones, being victorious, are said to have buried the bodies of their own soldiers, but left those of their giant enemies a prey to the birds. This event happened previous to the expulsion of the tyrant Christiern the Second from Sweden." The battle which I witnessed took place in the Presidency of Polk, five years before the passage of Webster's Fugitive-Slave Bill.

---

1) The allusion to the first battle of the Revolutionary War at Lexington and Concord (April 19, 1775) is probably clear to you. The first stanza of Emerson's "Concord Hymn," once a favorite quotation for orators, is

By the rude bridge that arched the flood,
Their flag to April's breeze unfurled,
Here once the embattled farmers stood
And fired the shot heard round the world.

Perhaps the allusions to Homer's *Iliad* (Myrmidons, Achilles, Patroclus) are also clear to you. If they are not, do what you can to repair the lack by using *The Oxford Companion to Classical Literature.* Consider the importance of allusion to the selection. Are not the allusions of particular and unusual importance here? Why?

2) What is the intention (or, what are the intentions) of this selection? Is it important only as a piece of careful observation? Has it an importance as natural history? Do you discern more than one level of meaning?

3) Consider the sentence: "The more you think of it, the less the difference." How is the idea in the sentence suggested before the sentence appears? How is the idea enforced after the sentence appears?

4) When unimportant matters are described with apparent seriousness and in an exalted manner we may have, as in Washington Irving's *Knickerbocker's History of New York* or Pope's *The Rape of the Lock,* a MOCK-HEROIC style. A somewhat similar technique is used here—at least you will have observed an ironic effect in the juxtaposition of references to Achilles or Davis and Hosmer and descriptions of struggling insects. Yet what does the irony point up? The insignificance of ants?

5) Notice the focus of attention. We observe first the struggle of two ants, then observe the legions of ants on both sides, and concentrate on three, which are finally observed under a microscope. Is the microscope important to any purpose besides a scientific one?

6) James K. Polk, mentioned in the last sentence of the selection, was President 1845–49. He was a militant nationalist, and the Mexican War, of which Thoreau and many other conscientious New Englanders entirely disapproved, was fought during his administration. Thoreau calls the Fugitive-Slave Bill "Webster's" not because Daniel Webster proposed the measure, but in reference to Webster's acquiescence in it in his Seventh of March Speech in support of the Compromise of 1850. The more you know about these matters, the more pointed the last sentence in the selection becomes.

7) The last paragraph would be interesting without the last sentence. But how far is the reference to Kirby and Spence (authors of *Introduction to Entomology,* 1815–26) designed to introduce and make occasion for the last sentence in the selection?

8) Consider the selection entire. What is the comment on human affairs and human qualities implicit in it? Make that comment explicit in a sentence or a few sentences.

9) Can this selection be discussed as an analogy? Here is an overt analogy between rats and men for comparison. It is from Hans Zinsser's *Rats, Lice and History* (1935).

I . . . It will be profitable to consider the striking analogy between rats and men. More than any other species of animal, the rat and mouse have become dependent on man, and in so doing they have developed characteristics which are amazingly human.

II In the first place, like man, the rat has become practically omnivorous. It eats anything that lets it and—like man—devours its own kind, under stress. It breeds at all seasons and—again like man —it is most amorous in the springtime. It hybridizes easily and, judging by the strained relationship between the black and the brown rat, develops social or racial prejudices against this practice. The sex proportions are like those among us. Inbreeding takes place readily. The males are larger, the females fatter. It adapts itself to all kinds of climates. It makes ferocious war upon its own kind, but has not, as yet, become nationalized. So far, it has still stuck to tribal wars—like man before nations were invented. If it continues to ape man as heretofore, we may, in a few centuries, have French rats eating German ones, or Nazi rats attacking Communist or Jewish rats; however, such a degree of civilization is probably not within the capacities of any mere animal. Also—like man—the rat is individualistic until it needs help. That is, it fights bravely alone against weaker rivals, for food or for love; but it knows how to organize armies and fight in hordes when necessary.

III Donaldson [in his *Memoir on the Rat*], basing his calculations mainly on stages in the development of the nervous system, reckons three years of a rat life as ninety years for man. By this scale, the rat reaches puberty at about sixteen, and arrives at the menopause at the equivalent of forty-five. In following man about all over the earth, the rat has—more than any other living creature except man—been able to adapt itself to any conditions of seasonal changes or climate.[1]

How much do the two passages have in common? What is required of the reader in the Thoreau passage that is not required of him in the Zinsser passage? Which seems at first reading to have the more intense effect? Which writer makes the greater demand on his reader's intelligence and perception?

[ii]

[The Fitchburg Railroad]

I The Fitchburg Railroad touches the pond about a hundred rods south of where I dwell. I usually go to the village along its causeway, and am, as it were, related to society by this link. The men on the freight trains, who go over the whole length of the road, bow to me as to an old acquaintance, they pass me so often, and apparently they take me for an employee; and so I am. I too would fain be a track-repairer somewhere in the orbit of the earth.

II The whistle of the locomotive penetrates my woods summer and winter, sounding like the scream of a hawk sailing over some farmer's yard, informing me that many restless city merchants are arriving within the circle of the town, or adventurous country traders from the other side. As they come under one horizon, they shout their warning to get off the track

[1] Reprinted from *Rats, Lice and History* by Hans Zinsser, by permission of Little, Brown and Company. Copyright, 1934, 1935, by Hans Zinsser.

to the other, heard sometimes through the circles of two towns. Here come your groceries, country; your rations, countrymen! Nor is there any man so independent on his farm that he can say them nay. And here's your pay for them! screams the countryman's whistle; timber like long battering rams going twenty miles an hour against the city's walls, and chairs enough to seat all the weary and heavy laden that dwell within them. With such huge and lumbering civility the country hands a chair to the city. All the Indian huckleberry hills are stripped, all the cranberry meadows are raked into the city. Up comes the cotton, down goes the woven cloth; up comes the silk, down goes the woolen; up come the books, but down goes the wit that writes them.

III When I meet the engine with its train of cars moving off with planetary motion,—or, rather, like a comet, for the beholder knows not if with that velocity and with that direction it will ever revisit this system, since its orbit does not look like a returning curve,—with its steam cloud like a banner streaming behind in golden and silver wreaths, like many a downy cloud which I have seen, high in the heavens, unfolding its masses to the light,—as if this travelling demigod, this cloud-compeller, would ere-long take the sunset sky for the livery of his train; when I hear the iron horse make the hills echo with his snort like thunder, shaking the earth with his feet, and breathing fire and smoke from his nostrils (what kind of winged horse or fiery dragon they will put into the new Mythology I don't know), it seems as if the earth had got a race now worthy to inhabit it. If all were as it seems, and men made the elements their servants for noble ends! If the cloud that hangs over the engine were the perspiration of heroic deeds, or as beneficent as that which floats over the farmer's fields, then the elements and Nature herself would cheerfully accompany men on their errands and be their escort.

IV I watch the passage of the morning cars with the same feeling that I do the rising of the sun, which is hardly more regular. Their train of clouds stretching far behind and rising higher and higher, going to heaven while the cars are going to Boston, conceals the sun for a minute and casts my distant field into the shade, a celestial train beside which the petty train of cars which hugs the earth is but the barb of the spear. The stabler of the iron horse was up early this winter morning by the light of the stars amid the mountains, to fodder and harness his steed. Fire, too, was awakened thus early to put the vital heat in him and get him off. If the enterprise were as innocent as it is early! If the snow lies deep, they strap on his snow-shoes, and with the giant plough plough a furrow from the mountains to the seaboard, in which the cars, like a following drill-barrow, sprinkle all the restless men and floating merchandise in the country for seed. All day the fire-steed flies over the country, stopping only that his master may rest, and I am awakened by his tramp and defiant snort at midnight, when in some remote glen in the woods he fronts the elements incased in ice and snow; and he will reach his stall only with the morning star, to start once more on his travels without rest or slumber. Or perchance, at evening, I hear him in his stable blowing off the superfluous energy of the day, that he may calm his nerves and cool his liver and brain for a few hours of iron slumber. If the enterprise were as heroic and commanding as it is protracted and unwearied!

v Far through unfrequented woods on the confines of towns, where once only the hunter penetrated by day, in the darkest night dart these bright saloons without the knowledge of their inhabitants; this moment stopping at some brilliant station-house in town or city, where a social crowd is gathered, the next in the Dismal Swamp, scaring the owl and fox. The startings and arrivals of the cars are now the epochs in the village day. They go and come with such regularity and precision, and their whistle can be heard so far, that the farmers set their clocks by them, and thus one well-conducted institution regulates a whole country. Have not men improved somewhat in punctuality since the railroad was invented? Do they not talk and think faster in the depot than they did in the stage-office? There is something electrifying in the atmosphere of the former place. I have been astonished at the miracles it has wrought; that some of my neighbors, who, I should have prophesied, once for all, would never get to Boston by so prompt a conveyance, are on hand when the bell rings. To do things "railroad fashion" is now the by-word; and it is worth the while to be warned so often and so sincerely by any power to get off its track. There is no stopping to read the riot act, no firing over the heads of the mob, in this case. We have constructed a fate, an *Atropos,* that never turns aside. (Let that be the name of your engine.) Men are advertised that at a certain hour and minute these bolts will be shot toward particular points of the compass; yet it interferes with no man's business, and the children go to school on the other track. We live the steadier for it. We are all educated thus to be sons of Tell. The air is full of invisible bolts. Every path but your own is the path of fate. Keep on your own track, then.

vi What recommends commerce to me is its enterprise and bravery. It does not clasp its hands and pray to Jupiter. I see these men every day go about their business with more or less courage and content, doing more even than they suspect, and perchance better employed than they could have consciously devised. I am less affected by their heroism who stood up for half an hour in the front line at Buena Vista, than by the steady and cheerful valor of the men who inhabit the snow-plough for their winter quarters; who have not merely the three o'clock in the morning courage, which Bonaparte thought was the rarest, but whose courage does not go to rest so early, who go to sleep only when the storm sleeps or the sinews of their iron steed are frozen. On this morning of the Great Snow, perchance, which is still raging and chilling men's blood, I hear the muffled tone of their engine bell from out the fog bank of their chilled breath, which announces that the cars *are coming,* without long delay, notwithstanding the veto of a New England northeast snow storm, and I behold the ploughmen covered with snow and rime, their heads peering above the mould-board which is turning down other than daisies and the nests of field-mice, like boulders of the Sierra Nevada, that occupy an outside place in the universe.

vii Commerce is unexpectedly confident and serene, alert, adventurous, and unwearied. It is very natural in its methods withal, far more so than many fantastic enterprises and sentimental experiments, and hence its singular success. I am refreshed and expanded when the freight train rattles past me, and I smell the stores which go dispensing their odors all the way from Long Wharf to Lake Champlain, reminding me of foreign parts, of coral reefs, and Indian oceans, and tropical climes, and the extent of the globe. I feel more like a citizen of the world at the sight of the palm-leaf which will cover so many flaxen New England heads the next summer, the Manilla hemp and cocoa-nut husks, the old junk, gunny bags, scrap iron, and rusty nails. This carload of torn sails is more legible and interesting now than if they should be wrought into paper and printed books. Who can write so graphically the history of the storms they have weathered as these rents have done? They are proof-sheets which need no correction. Here goes lumber from the Maine woods, which did not go out to sea in the last freshet, risen four dollars on the thousand because of what did go out or was split up: pine, spruce, cedar,—first, second, third, and fourth qualities, so lately all of one quality, to wave over the bear, and moose, and caribou. Next rolls Thomaston lime, a prime lot, which will get far among the hills before it gets slacked. These rags in bales, of all hues and qualities, the lowest condition to which cotton and linen descend, the final result of dress,—of patterns which are now no longer cried up, unless it be in Milwaukee, as those splendid articles, English, French, or American prints, ginghams, muslins, &c., gathered from all quarters both of fashion and poverty, going to become paper of one color or a few shades only, on which forsooth will be written tales of real life, high and low, and founded on fact! This closed car smells of salt fish, the strong New England and commercial scent, reminding me of the Grand Banks and the fisheries. Who has not seen a salt fish, thoroughly cured for this world, so that nothing can spoil it, and putting the perseverance of the saints to the blush? with which you may sweep or pave the streets, and split your kindlings, and the teamster shelter himself and his lading against sun, wind, and rain behind it,—and the trader, as a Concord trader once did, hang it up by his door for a sign when he commences business, until at last his oldest customer cannot tell surely whether it be animal, vegetable, or mineral, and yet it shall be as pure as a snowflake, and if it be put into a pot and boiled, will come out an excellent dun fish for a Saturday's dinner. Next Spanish hides, with the tails still preserving their twist and the angle of elevation they had when the oxen that wore them were careering over the pampas of the Spanish main,—a type of all obstinacy, and evincing how almost hopeless and incurable are all constitutional vices. I confess that, practically speaking, when I have learned a man's real disposition, I have no hopes of changing it for the better or worse in this state of existence. . . . Here is a hogshead of molasses or of brandy directed to John Smith, Cuttingsville, Vermont, some trader among the Green Mountains, who imports for the farmers near his clearing, and now perchance stands over his bulk-head and thinks of the last arrivals on the coast, how they may affect the price for him, telling his customers this moment, as he has told them twenty times before this morning, that he expects some by the next train of prime quality. It is advertised in the Cuttingsville Times.

VIII While these things go up other things come down. Warned by the whizzing sound, I look up from my book and see some tall pine, hewn on far northern hills, which has winged its way over the Green Mountains and the Connecticut, shot like an arrow through the township within ten minutes, and scarce another eye beholds it; going

> "to be the mast
> Of some great ammiral."

And hark! here comes the cattle-train bearing the cattle of a thousand hills, sheepcots, stables, and cow-yards in the air, drovers with their sticks, and shepherd boys in the midst of their flocks, all but the mountain pastures, whirled along like leaves blown from the mountains by the September gales. The air is filled with the bleating of calves and sheep, and the hustling of oxen, as if a pastoral valley were going by. When the old bell-wether at the head rattles his bell, the mountains do indeed skip like rams and the little hills like lambs. A car-load of drovers, too, in the midst, on a level with their droves now, their vocation gone, but still clinging to their useless sticks as their badge of office. But their dogs, where are they? It is a stampede to them; they are quite thrown out; they have lost the scent. Methinks I hear them barking behind the Peterboro' Hills, or panting up the western slope of the Green Mountains. They will not be in at the death. Their vocation, too, is gone. Their fidelity and sagacity are below par now. They will slink back to their kennels in disgrace, or perchance run wild and strike a league with the wolf and the fox. So is your pastoral life whirled past and away. But the bell rings, and I must get off the track and let the cars go by:

> What's the railroad to me?
> I never go to see
> Where it ends.
> It fills a few hollows,
> And makes banks for the swallows,
> It sets the sand a-blowing,
> And the blackberries a-growing,

but I cross it like a cart-path in the woods. I will not have my eyes put out and my ears spoiled by its smoke and steam and hissing.

IX Now that the cars are gone by and all the restless world with them, and the fishes in the pond no longer feel their rumbling, I am more alone than ever. For the rest of the long afternoon, perhaps, my meditations are interrupted only by the faint rattle of a carriage or team along the distant highway.

---

1) Walt Whitman, who intended to include in his poetry all those vital and typical things in American life that he felt poets in his time had neglected, writes in his "To a Locomotive in Winter":

Type of the modern—emblem of motion and power—pulse of the con-
tinent,
For once come serve the Muse and merge in verse, even as here I see
thee, . . .
Fierce-throated beauty!
Roll through my chant with all thy lawless music, thy swinging lamps
at night,
Thy madly-whistled laughter, echoing, rumbling like an earthquake,
rousing all,
Law of thyself complete, thine own track firmly holding. . . .

In reading the selection from Thoreau, we must remember that for mid-
nineteenth-century America the railroad was the most impressive symbol
of the new age of power, and of industrial and commercial development.
How, throughout the selection, is the representative quality of the Fitchburg Railroad made clear?

2) Thoreau's writing needs most careful attention. Did you, for instance, get the full significance of the comparison of the durability of a
salt fish and "the perseverance of the saints" in vii? To do so you need to
know the theological definition of "perseverance." Or did you realize the
image of the plowman turning down daisies and nests of field mice against
the image of the snowplow and its crew in vi?

3) What is the full meaning of the last sentence in i? (Consider it in
the context of the whole selection.)

4) Paragraphs ii, iii, and iv have as one of their intentions the giving
of a firm impression of the power and the glory and the wonder of the
railroad. Consider the means by which this intention is accomplished.
Note how we are led to think of the locomotive as a living being. The metaphor "iron horse" was conventional, but it is here developed in an impressive fashion. Has the new mythology Thoreau foresees developed?
What is it?

5) What is the effect of the allusions? Do the place names have the
effect of allusions? What sort of reader is Thoreau assuming? ("Cloud-
compeller" in iii is a Homeric EPITHET for Zeus. For "to be the mast/Of
some great ammiral" in viii see Milton's *Paradise Lost,* Book I, lines 283–
313. Notice that such brief, unidentified quotations have the effect of allusion.)

6) What is the effect of the antithesis in the last sentence of ii? Where
is this antithesis used again? What other sentences suggest reservations
which modify what may seem to be the dominant attitude of admiration?

7) "Law of thyself complete," Whitman writes, "thine own track firmly
holding"; and in v Thoreau, too, pays tribute to the precision and efficiency of the railroad: "We live," he says, "the steadier for it." But he also
says: "We have constructed a fate, an *Atropos,* that never turns aside. (Let
that be the name of your engine.)" What is an Atropos? In what way are
we sons of Tell (William Tell)? What is one's own track? How do we
construct a fate? Do you see that this paragraph has far-reaching implications, central to the full understanding of the selection? Notice the return
to the idea of one's own track at the end of the selection.

8) In vi and vii we have a remarkably vivid account of the romance

of commerce as it is represented by the variety of freight the Fitchburg Railroad carries. What are some of the ways in which Thoreau gives us a realization of the far-flung activities of trade and their relation to the lives of men?

9) "While these things go up other things come down." Literally this first sentence in VIII says that such things as molasses are sent to Vermont and such things as pine trees to Massachusetts shipyards. What else does it say? How is the idea concretely represented in the paragraph?

10) Perhaps you have already noted a special quality of structure. In V, for instance, did you not conclude that "we have constructed a fate" *before* you came to that statement? Thoreau is likely to withhold his general statement until the perceptive reader has had time to formulate the idea for himself. When the statement appears, therefore, it comes as confirmation of what is in the reader's mind. The effect is almost as if one were thinking *with* Thoreau. Can you find this effect elsewhere in the selection? Have you ever observed it in another writer?

11) There is a pretty sure test of literary excellence—a test at least of what is excellent for oneself. But it takes some time. If one can return again and again to the same writing and find it, each time, fresh and new, he must conclude that it is good writing. In some work, one discovers at each return something he had not seen before. Make an appointment with yourself to return to these Thoreau selections three months hence and see how they stand up.

ii   AN ESSAY BY STEVENSON

Robert Louis Stevenson had a great following in the latter years of his short life and for some years after his death. Then, perhaps because he had been overpraised, there was a reaction, and his work was undervalued. But there are signs of a juster appraisal. Stevenson once remarked, "Though we are mighty fine fellows nowadays, we cannot write like Hazlitt"—and some persons add, "nor like Stevenson, either." In "The Lantern-Bearers" he is writing about a matter near his heart, and important to the rest of us, too. But he intends to gain for the presentation of his ideas all of the interest that style and form have for readers. We shall work through the essay carefully. You will find that we are continuing the study of a number of matters with which we have been before concerned, and that in particular we are examining a subtle use of analogy.

In one of its intentions, "The Lantern-Bearers" is a piece of argument. Stevenson is opposing the position of writers of realistic fiction, and that of the critics who praise them. But however deeply Stevenson felt about realism, and however resentful he may have been toward certain critics, his essay is not an attempt to berate realists, or not primarily. It is an attempt to bring readers to his belief about the use of fiction.

William Dean Howells, a great realist, tells us in his *Criticism and Fiction* that the fiction writer as realist ought to work in the commonplace and with average experience, that he should "front the every-day world and catch the charm of its work-worn, care-worn, brave, kindly face":

In life he finds nothing insignificant; all tells for destiny and character; nothing that God has made is contemptible. He cannot look upon human life and declare this thing or that thing unworthy of notice, any more than the scientist can declare a fact of the material world beneath the dignity of his inquiry. He feels in every nerve the equality of things and the unity of men; his soul is exalted, not by vain shows and shadows and ideals, but by realities, in which alone the truth lives. In criticism it is his business to break the images of false gods and misshapen heroes, to take away the poor silly toys that many grown people would still like to play with.

Now Howells's statement is admirable, and Stevenson does not say that the ideal is all wrong. He does say that in practice the realist's method of observation and report is most inadequate, and that it often fails to see the truth about men. As you read the essay you should watch particularly to see how Stevenson endeavors to cut the ground from under the realist's theory. He does so by leading the reader to feel that, whatever its pretensions, whatever its name, realism is, more often than not, essentially untrue to life.

The Lantern-Bearers (1887)

ROBERT LOUIS STEVENSON

i

1 These boys congregated every autumn about a certain easterly fisher-village, where they tasted in a high degree the glory of existence. The place was created seemingly on purpose for the diversion of young gentlemen. A street or two of houses, mostly red and many of them tiled; a number of fine trees clustered about the manse and the kirkyard, and turning the chief street into a shady alley; many little gardens more than usually bright with flowers; nets a-drying, and fisher-wives scolding in the backward parts; a smell of fish, a genial smell of seaweed; whiffs of blowing sand at the street-corners; shops with golf-balls and bottled lollipops; another shop with penny pickwicks (that remarkable cigar) and the *London Journal,* dear to me for its startling pictures, and a few novels, dear for their suggestive names: such, as well as memory serves me, were the ingredients of the town. These, you are to conceive posted on a spit between two sandy bays, and sparsely flanked with villas—enough for the boys to lodge in with their subsidiary parents, not enough (not yet enough) to cocknify the scene: a haven in the rocks in front: in front of that, a file of grey islets: to the left, endless links and sand-wreaths, a wilderness of hiding-holes, alive with popping rabbits and soaring gulls: to the right, a range of seaward crags, one rugged brow beyond another; the ruins of a mighty and ancient fortress on the brink of one; coves between—now charmed into sunshine quiet, now whistling with wind and clamorous with bursting surges; the dens and sheltered hollows redolent of thyme and southernwood, the air at the cliff's edge brisk and clean and pungent of the

sea—in front of all, the Bass Rock, tilted seaward like a doubtful bather, the surf ringing it with white, the solan-geese hanging round its summit like a great and glittering smoke. This choice piece of seaboard was sacred, besides, to the wrecker; and the Bass, in the eye of fancy, still flew the colours of King James; and in the ear of fancy the arches of Tantallon still rang with horseshoe iron, and echoed to the commands of Bell-the-Cat.

II There was nothing to mar your days, if you were a boy summering in that part, but the embarrassment of pleasure. You might golf if you wanted; but I seem to have been better employed. You might secrete yourself in the Lady's Walk, a certain sunless dingle of elders, all mossed over by the damp as green as grass, and dotted here and there by the stream-side with roofless walls, the cold homes of anchorites. To fit themselves for life, and with a special eye to acquire the art of smoking, it was even common for the boys to harbour there; and you might have seen a single penny pickwick, honestly shared in lengths with a blunt knife, bestrew the glen with these apprentices. Again, you might join our fishing-parties, where we sat perched as thick as solan-geese, a covey of little anglers, boy and girl, angling over each other's heads, to the much entanglement of lines and loss of podleys and consequent shrill recrimination—shrill as the geese themselves. Indeed, had that been all, you might have done this often; but though fishing be a fine pastime, the podley is scarce to be regarded as a dainty for the table; and it was a point of honour that a boy should eat all that he had taken. Or again, you might climb the Law, where the whale's jaw-bone stood landmark in the buzzing wind, and behold the face of many counties, and the smoke and spires of many towns, and the sails of distant ships. You might bathe, now in the flaws of fine weather, that we pathetically call our summer, now in a gale of wind, with the sand scourging your bare hide, your clothes thrashing abroad from underneath their guardian stone, the froth of the great breakers casting you headlong ere it had drowned your knees. Or you might explore the tidal rocks, above all in the ebb of springs, when the very roots of the hills were for the nonce discovered; following my leader from one group to another, groping in slippery tangle for the wreck of ships, wading in pools after the abominable creatures of the sea, and ever with an eye cast backward on the march of the tide and the menaced line of your retreat. And then you might go Crusoeing, a word that covers all extempore eating in the open air: digging perhaps a house under the margin of the links, kindling a fire of the sea-ware, and cooking apples there—if they were truly apples, for I sometimes suppose the merchant must have played us off with some inferior and quite local fruit, capable of resolving, in the neighbourhood of fire, into mere sand and smoke and iodine; or perhaps pushing to Tantallon, you might lunch on sandwiches and visions in the grassy court, while the wind hummed in the crumbling turrets; or clambering along the coast, eat geans (the worst, I must suppose, in Christendom) from an adventurous gean-tree that had taken root under a cliff, where it was shaken with an ague of east wind, and silvered after gales with salt, and grew so foreign among its bleak surroundings that to eat of its produce was an adventure in itself.

III There are mingled some dismal memories with so many that were joyous. Of the fisher-wife, for instance, who had cut her throat at Canty Bay; and of how I ran with the other children to the top of the Quadrant, and beheld a posse of silent people escorting a cart, and on the cart, bound in a chair, her throat bandaged, and the bandage all bloody—horror!—the fisher-wife herself, who continued thenceforth to hag-ride my thoughts, and even to-day (as I recall the scene) darkens daylight. She was lodged in the little old jail in the chief street; but whether or no she died there, with a wise terror of the worst, I never inquired. She had been tippling; it was but a dingy tragedy; and it seems strange and hard that, after all these years, the poor crazy sinner should be still pilloried on her cart in the scrap-book of my memory. Nor shall I readily forget a certain house in the Quadrant where a visitor died, and a dark old woman continued to dwell alone with the dead body; nor how this old woman conceived a hatred to myself and one of my cousins, and in the dread hour of the dusk, as we were clambering on the garden-walls, opened a window in that house of mortality and cursed us in a shrill voice and with a marrowy choice of language. It was a pair of very colourless urchins that fled down the lane from this remarkable experience! But I recall with a more doubtful sentiment, compounded out of fear and exultation, the coil of equinoctial tempests; trumpeting squalls, scouring flaws of rain; the boats with their reefed lugsails scudding for the harbour mouth, where danger lay, for it was hard to make when the wind had any east in it; the wives clustered with blowing shawls at the pier-head, where (if fate was against them) they might see boat and husband and sons—their whole wealth and their whole family—engulfed under their eyes; and (what I saw but once) a troop of neighbours forcing such an unfortunate homeward, and she squalling and battling in their midst, a figure scarcely human, a tragic Mænad.

IV These are things that I recall with interest; but what my memory dwells upon the most, I have been all this while withholding. It was a sport peculiar to the place, and indeed to a week or so of our two months' holiday there. Maybe it still flourishes in its native spot; for boys and their pastimes are swayed by periodic forces inscrutable to man; so that tops and marbles reappear in their due season, regular like the sun and moon; and the harmless art of knucklebones has seen the fall of the Roman empire and the rise of the United States. It may still flourish in its native spot, but nowhere else, I am persuaded; for I tried myself to introduce it on Tweedside, and was defeated lamentably; its charm being quite local, like a country wine that cannot be exported.

V The idle manner of it was this:—

VI Toward the end of September, when school-time was drawing near and the nights were already black, we would begin to sally from our respective villas, each equipped with a tin bull's-eye lantern. The thing was so well known that it had worn a rut in the commerce of Great Britain; and the grocers, about the due time, began to garnish their windows with our particular brand of luminary. We wore them buckled to the waist upon a cricket belt, and over them, such was the rigour of the game, a buttoned top-coat. They smelled noisomely of blistered tin; they never burned aright, though they would always burn our fingers; their use was naught; the pleasure of them merely fanciful; and yet a boy with a bull's-eye under his top-coat asked for nothing more. The fishermen used lanterns about their boats, and it was from them, I suppose, that we had got the hint; but theirs were not bull's-eyes, nor did we ever play at being fishermen. The police carried them at their belts, and we had plainly copied them in that; yet we did not pretend to be policemen. Burglars, indeed, we may have had some haunting thoughts of; and we had certainly an eye to past ages when lanterns were more common, and to certain story-books in which we had found them to figure very largely. But take it for all in all, the pleasure of the thing was substantive; and to be a boy with a bull's-eye under his top-coat was good enough for us.

VII When two of these asses met, there would be an anxious "Have you got your lantern?" and a gratified "Yes!" That was the shibboleth, and very needful too; for, as it was the rule to keep our glory contained, none could recognize a lantern-bearer, unless (like the pole-cat) by the smell. Four or five would sometimes climb into the belly of a ten-man lugger, with nothing but the thwarts above them—for the cabin was usually locked, or choose out some hollow of the links where the wind might whistle overhead. There the coats would be unbuttoned and the bull's-eyes discovered; and in the chequering glimmer, under the huge windy hall of the night, and cheered by a rich steam of toasting tinware, these fortunate young gentlemen would crouch together in the cold sand of the links or on the scaly bilges of the fishing-boat, and delight themselves with inappropriate talk. Woe is me that I may not give some specimens—some of their foresights of life, or deep inquiries into the rudiments of man and nature, these were so fiery and so innocent, they were so richly silly, so romantically young. But the talk, at any rate, was but a condiment; and these gatherings themselves only accidents in the career of the lantern-bearer. The essence of this bliss was to walk by yourself in the black night; the slide shut, the top-coat buttoned; not a ray escaping, whether to conduct your footsteps or to make your glory public: a mere pillar of darkness in the dark; and all the while, deep down in the privacy of your fool's heart, to know you had a bull's-eye at your belt, and to exult and sing over the knowledge.

ii

1 It is said that a poet has died young in the breast of the most stolid. It may be contended, rather, that this (somewhat minor) bard in almost every case survives, and is the spice of life to his possessor. Justice is not done to the versatility and the unplumbed childishness of man's imagination. His life from without may seem but a rude mound of mud; there will be some golden chamber at the heart of it, in which he dwells delighted; and for as dark as his pathway seems to the observer, he will have some kind of a bull's-eye at his belt.

11 It would be hard to pick out a career more cheerless than that of Dancer, the miser, as he figures in the "Old Bailey Reports," a prey to the

most sordid persecutions, the butt of his neighbourhood, betrayed by his hired man, his house beleaguered by the impish school-boy, and he himself grinding and fuming and impotently fleeing to the law against these pin-pricks. You marvel at first that any one should willingly prolong a life so destitute of charm and dignity; and then you call to memory that had he chosen, had he ceased to be a miser, he could have been freed at once from these trials, and might have built himself a castle and gone escorted by a squadron. For the love of more recondite joys, which we cannot estimate, which, it may be, we should envy, the man had willingly foregone both comfort and consideration. "His mind to him a kingdom was"; and sure enough, digging into that mind, which seems at first a dust-heap, we un-earth some priceless jewels. For Dancer must have had the love of power and the disdain of using it, a noble character in itself; disdain of many pleasures, a chief part of what is commonly called wisdom; disdain of the inevitable end, that finest trait of mankind; scorn of men's opinions, an-other element of virtue; and at the back of all, a conscience just like yours and mine, whining like a cur, swindling like a thimble-rigger, but still pointing (there or thereabout) to some conventional standard. Here were a cabinet portrait to which Hawthorne perhaps had done justice; and yet not Hawthorne either, for he was mildly minded, and it lay not in him to create for us that throb of the miser's pulse, his fretful energy of gusto, his vast arms of ambition clutching in he knows not what: insatiable, insane, a god with a muck-rake. Thus, at least, looking in the bosom of the miser, consideration detects the poet in the full tide of life, with more, indeed, of the poetic fire than usually goes to epics; and tracing that mean man about his cold hearth, and to and fro in his discomfortable house, spies within him a blazing bonfire of delight. And so with others, who do not live by bread alone, but by some cherished and perhaps fantastic pleasure; who are meat salesmen to the external eye, and possibly to themselves are Shakespeares, Napoleons, or Beethovens; who have not one virtue to rub against another in the field of active life, and yet perhaps, in the life of contemplation, sit with the saints. We see them on the street, and we can count their buttons; but heaven knows in what they pride themselves! heaven knows where they have set their treasure!

III There is one fable that touches very near the quick of life: the fable of the monk who passed into the woods, heard a bird break into song, hark-ened for a trill or two, and found himself on his return a stranger at his convent gates; for he had been absent fifty years, and of all his comrades there survived but one to recognize him. It is not only in the woods that this enchanter carols, though perhaps he is native there. He sings in the most doleful places. The miser hears him and chuckles, and the days are moments. With no more apparatus than an ill-smelling lantern I have evoked him on the naked links. All life that is not merely mechanical is spun out of two strands: seeking for that bird and hearing him. And it is just this that makes life so hard to value, and the delight of each so incom-municable. And just a knowledge of this, and a remembrance of those for-tunate hours in which the bird has sung to us, that fills us with such wonder when we turn the pages of the realist. There, to be sure, we find a picture of life in so far as it consists of mud and of old iron, cheap desires and cheap fears, that which we are ashamed to remember and that which we are careless whether we forget; but of the note of that time-devouring nightingale we hear no news.

IV The case of these writers of romance is most obscure. They have been boys and youths; they have lingered outside the window of the beloved, who was then most probably writing to some one else; they have sat before a sheet of paper, and felt themselves mere continents of congested poetry, not one line of which would flow; they have walked alone in the woods, they have walked in cities under the countless lamps; they have been to sea, they have hated, they have feared, they have longed to knife a man, and maybe done it; the wild taste of life has stung their palate. Or, if you deny them all the rest, one pleasure at least they have tasted to the full—their books are there to prove it—the keen pleasure of successful literary composition. And yet they fill the globe with volumes, whose cleverness inspires me with despairing admiration, and whose consistent falsity to all I care to call existence, with despairing wrath. If I had no better hope than to continue to revolve among the dreary and petty businesses, and to be moved by the paltry hopes and fears with which they surround and animate their heroes, I declare I would die now. But there has never an hour of mine gone quite so dully yet; if it were spent waiting at a railway junction, I would have some scattering thoughts, I could count some grains of memory, compared to which the whole of one of these romances seems but dross.

V These writers would retort (if I take them properly) that this was very true; that it was the same with themselves and other persons of (what they call) the artistic temperament; that in this we were exceptional, and should apparently be ashamed of ourselves; but that our works must deal exclusively with (what they call) the average man, who was a prodigious dull fellow, and quite dead to all but the paltriest considerations. I accept the issue. We can only know others by ourselves. The artistic temperament (a plague on the expression!) does not make us different from our fellow-men, or it would make us incapable of writing novels; and the average man (a murrain on the word!) is just like you and me, or he would not be average. It was Whitman who stamped a kind of Birmingham sacredness upon the latter phrase; but Whitman knew very well, and showed very nobly, that the average man was full of joys and full of a poetry of his own. And this harping on life's dulness and man's meanness is a loud profession of incompetence; it is one of two things: the cry of the blind eye, *I cannot see,* or the complaint of the dumb tongue, *I cannot utter.* To draw a life without delights is to prove I have not realized it. To picture a man without some sort of poetry—well, it goes near to prove my case, for it shows an author may have little enough. To see Dancer only as a dirty, old, small-minded, impotently fuming man, in a dirty house, besieged by Harrow boys, and probably beset by small attorneys, is to show myself as keen an observer as . . . the Harrow boys. But these young gentlemen (with a more becoming modesty) were content to pluck Dancer by the coat-tails; they did not suppose they had surprised his secret or could put him living in a book: and it is there my error would have lain. Or say that in the same romance—I continue to call these books romances, in the hope of giving pain—say that in the same romance, which now begins really to take shape, I should leave to speak of Dancer, and follow instead the Harrow boys; and say that I came on some such business as that of my lantern-bearers on the links; and described the boys as very cold, spat upon by flurries of rain, and drearily surrounded, all of which they were; and their talk as silly and indecent, which it certainly was. I might upon these lines, and had I Zola's genius, turn out, in a page or so, a gem of literary art, render the lantern-light with the touches of a master, and lay on the indecency with the ungrudging hand of love; and when all was done, what a triumph would my picture be of shallowness and dulness! how it would have missed the point! how it would have belied the boys! To the ear of the stenographer, the talk is merely silly and indecent; but ask the boys themselves, and they are discussing (as it is highly proper they should) the possibilities of existence. To the eye of the observer they are wet and cold and drearily surrounded; but ask themselves, and they are in the heaven of a recondite pleasure, the ground of which is an ill-smelling lantern.

iii

ɪ For, to repeat, the ground of a man's joy is often hard to hit. It may hinge at times upon a mere accessory, like the lantern, it may reside, like Dancer's, in the mysterious inwards of psychology. It may consist with perpetual failure, and find exercise in the continued chase. It has so little bond with externals (such as the observer scribbles in his note-book) that it may even touch them not; and the man's true life, for which he consents to live, lie altogether in the field of fancy. The clergyman, in his spare hours, may be winning battles, the farmer sailing ships, the banker reaping triumph in the arts: all leading another life, plying another trade from that they chose; like the poet's housebuilder, who, after all is cased in stone,

> By his fireside, as impotent fancy prompts,
> Rebuilds it to his liking.

In such a case the poetry runs underground. The observer (poor soul, with his documents!) is all abroad. For to look at the man is but to court deception. We shall see the trunk from which he draws his nourishment; but he himself is above and abroad in the green dome of foliage, hummed through by winds and nested in by nightingales. And the true realism were that of the poets, to climb up after him like a squirrel, and catch some glimpse of the heaven for which he lives. And the true realism, always and everywhere, is that of the poets: to find out where joy resides, and give it a voice far beyond singing.

ɪɪ For to miss the joy is to miss all. In the joy of the actors lies the sense of any action. That is the explanation, that the excuse. To one who has not the secret of the lanterns, the scene upon the links is meaningless. And hence the haunting and truly spectral unreality of realistic books. Hence, when we read the English realists, the incredulous wonder with which we observe the hero's constancy under the submerging tide of dulness, and how he bears up with his jibbing sweetheart, and endures the chatter of idiot girls, and stands by his whole unfeatured wilderness of an existence, instead of seeking relief in drink or foreign travel. Hence in the French, in that meat-market of middle-aged sensuality, the disgusted surprise with which we see the hero drift sidelong, and practically quite untempted, into every description of misconduct and dishonour. In each, we miss the personal poetry, the enchanted atmosphere, that rainbow work of fancy that clothes what is naked and seems to ennoble what is base; in each, life falls dead like dough, instead of soaring away like a balloon into the colours of the sunset; each is true, each inconceivable; for no man lives in the external truth, among salts and acids, but in the warm, phantasmagoric chamber of his brain, with the painted windows and the storied walls.

III Of this falsity we have a recent example from a man who knows far better—Tolstoi's *Powers of Darkness*. Here is a piece full of force and truth, yet quite untrue. For before Mikita was led into so dire a situation he was tempted, and temptations are beautiful at least in part; and a work which dwells on the ugliness of crime and gives no hint of any loveliness in the temptation, sins against the modesty of life, and even when a Tolstoi writes it, sinks to melodrama. The peasants are not understood; they saw their life in fairer colours; even the deaf girl was clothed in poetry for Mikita, or he had never fallen. And so, once again, even an Old Bailey melodrama, without some brightness of poetry and lustre of existence, falls into the inconceivable and ranks with fairy tales.

iv

I In nobler books we are moved with something like the emotions of life; and this emotion is very variously provoked. We are so moved when Levine labours in the field, when André sinks beyond emotion, when Richard Feverel and Lucy Desborough meet beside the river, when Antony, "not cowardly, puts off his helmet," when Kent has infinite pity on the dying Lear, when, in Dostoieffsky's *Despised and Rejected*, the uncomplaining hero drains his cup of suffering and virtue. These are notes that please the great heart of man. Not only love, and the fields, and the bright face of danger, but sacrifice and death and unmerited suffering humbly supported, touch in us the vein of the poetic. We love to think of them, we long to try them, we are humbly hopeful that we may prove heroes also.

II We have heard, perhaps, too much of lesser matters. Here is the door, here is the open air. *Itur in antiquam silvam.*[1]

---

1) What is accomplished toward the purpose of the essay in the first three paragraphs? You will have noticed that the matter of the boys' lanterns is not introduced until the fourth paragraph.

[1 It leads into the ancient wood.]

2) In all of section i of the essay there is no mention of fiction or of writers, and indeed the analogy is not immediately established in section ii. Just where in section ii is it established?

3) What is gained by not revealing at once that the matter of the boys and their lanterns has an analogical purpose? Is it perhaps that Stevenson hopes that the reader's acceptance of what is said about the two views of the boys with lanterns will carry over to what is said about two views in writing fiction? Or think of the matter this way: suppose Stevenson had chosen to call his essay "Romance and Realism." Do you see that for Stevenson's purpose that would be a poor title? (Stevenson must assume, if he thinks his opinions important enough to write about, that some of his readers have preconceptions different from his own.) Explain how *both* title and structure are designed to be disarming.

4) But we may have assumed too much. Just to be sure that we see the full meaning of the analogy, let us restate it, giving a paragraph to each element of the analogy. We might begin our first paragraph: *There are two ways to look at boys carrying lanterns hidden under their coats.* . . . You continue the restatement.

5) We have seen that analogy may have a purpose as explanation, as argument, as a way of supplying an image. How about this analogy? In how many of these ways does it function? And in this regard, notice how, even before the analogy is established, the boys and their lanterns become a source of metaphor: for instance, "he will have some kind of a bull's-eye at his belt." Cite other examples of metaphors that depend upon the account of those lanterns.

6) But Stevenson chooses to enforce his thesis by means beyond the central analogy. There is his use of the fable of the monk, and, perhaps more impressive, his treatment of Dancer (Daniel Dancer, a famous eighteenth-century miser in England). If you have read Frank Norris's *Mc-Teague,* you will know an instance of a miser in fiction (a woman) whose essential motive never does become clear, whose miserliness seems incredible. Or perhaps you know George Eliot's *Silas Marner.* How about Silas's motivation? Was that imaginatively clear to you? At any rate, is what Stevenson means clear to you when he says: "The observer (poor soul, with his documents!) is all abroad"?

7) What is the full implication of Stevenson's remark toward the end of section ii: "I continue to call these books romances, in the hope of giving pain"?

8) The Zola mentioned a few lines later is Émile Zola (1840–1902), a French novelist whose realism is often called NATURALISM, a term which designates a development in realism. Naturalism aims at a scientific sort of observation, it assumes that man's conduct is determined by forces outside his will—his heredity and his environment—and it typically deals with unpleasant sorts of experience. Now with the questions of free will and determinism Stevenson does not directly deal. What do you infer are his assumptions about the nature of man? We can put that question in concrete terms: Stevenson suggests the sort of novel he might write about Dancer were he a realist. Can you envisage the sort of novel he, or a novelist with his view of experience, would write?

9) What exactly is Stevenson's objection to Tolstoi's *Powers of Darkness?* Do you know enough about Tolstoi to understand what Stevenson means when he says Tolstoi knows far better? Even a brief account of Tolstoi's work in a reference book would be of some help.

10) Considering what is said in the whole essay, what would you say Stevenson believes the function of the fiction writer to be?

11) Now we should have in mind pretty well the ideas Stevenson wishes to enforce. We may return to some questions about method, questions best answered in regard to the essay entire. First of all, consider the four-section structure. We have recognized that paragraphs are for the convenience of the reader, to mark out how the thought progresses. Are these larger divisions also for his convenience? What part of the whole purpose is accomplished in each of the four sections?

12) What sort of relationship is Stevenson attempting to establish with his reader? Does he, for instance, think of him as an opponent to be overwhelmed or to be convinced? Or does he succeed in establishing some common ground with him? Do you find the personal nature of some passages intrusive? Some persons feel that in some of his essays Stevenson exploits his personality too much. Would that, in your opinion, be a legitimate censure of this essay?

13) We have often noted that in good exposition of an ordinary sort generalization is immediately followed by instance, and definition by example. Have you been aware that that is not quite the pattern here? Here, very often, the general idea arises from the concrete and comes to us immediately in an image. In few sentences can you find an idea stated abstractly, and in those you will usually find that Stevenson has worked toward and not from the generalization. In what writers we have read can you find parallels for Stevenson's practice in this regard?

14) Since Stevenson is a stylist of note, we need to consider a quality of his style. Some persons find the writing in some of his essays PRECIOUS, that is, over-patterned and self-conscious. And indeed there are passages like the following from "Aes Triplex" which may be a little precious:

> We have all heard of cities in South America built upon the side of fiery mountains, and how, even in this tremendous neighbourhood, the inhabitants are not a jot more impressed by the solemnity of mortal conditions than if they were delving gardens in the greenest corner of England. There are serenades and suppers and much gallantry among the myrtles overhead; and meanwhile the foundation shudders underfoot, the bowels of the mountain growl, and at any moment living ruin may leap sky-high into the moonlight, and tumble man and his merry-making in the dust.

Perhaps the ALLITERATION and other play with sounds in the second sentence is a little intrusive; perhaps the reader is made a little too conscious of its pattern.

15) Yet Stevenson would probably have defended the sentence. A writer, he says in his "On Some Technical Elements of Style in Literature," is like a man who juggles two oranges, for a writer must maintain meaning and pattern at once, never sacrificing one for the other. And pattern for him is largely a matter of the structure of sentences:

so that each sentence, by successive phrases, shall first come into a kind of knot, and then, after a moment of suspended meaning, solve and clear itself. In every properly constructed sentence there should be observed this knot or hitch; so that (however delicately) we are led to foresee, to expect, and then to welcome the successive phrases. The pleasure may be heightened by an element of surprise, as, very grossly, in the common figure of the antithesis, or, with much greater subtlety, where an antithesis is first suggested and then deftly evaded.

Is there antithesis in the second sentence quoted from "Aes Triplex"? Where, would you say, is the knot?

16) Try and find a number of sentences in "The Lantern-Bearers" which clearly conform to the principle quoted above. Do you find them effective? But notice too that Stevenson occasionally uses a short and simply constructed sentence as a sort of change of pace. Do you find instances in which these sentences are also used for emphasis?

17) William James, one of the greatest of American philosophers, has an essay called "On a Certain Blindness in Human Beings," an essay concerned with "the blindness with which we are all afflicted in regard to the feelings of creatures and people different from ourselves." Now this essay furnishes us an excellent example of the use by one writer of the work of another. James sees that "The spectator's judgment is sure to miss the root of the matter, and to possess no truth." And his perception is so coincident with Stevenson's that James uses a very long quotation from "The Lantern-Bearers," excising most of the references to fiction writing, with which James is not in his essay concerned. In introducing that quotation, James says that he really thinks "The Lantern-Bearers" "deserves to become immortal, both for the truth of its matter and the excellence of its form."

18) Now consider first what James's attitude toward Stevenson's essay is. He finds it important quite apart from any consideration of fiction writing. Can you identify it with your own experience? Do you know that you have failed really to see what the lives of others mean to them? You surely know that others have failed to see what some part of your life means to you.

19) Is James's estimate of the essay too high? Not a great many pieces of writing, certainly, do really deserve "to become immortal" and only a very small proportion of the work any generation of writers does.

20) James says that "The Lantern-Bearers" deserves immortality "both for the truth of its matter and the excellence of its form." As we can see from the passage cited in question 15, Stevenson would have been gratified by the double praise. But consider whether truth of matter and excellence of form are—from the point of view of the reader—finally separable. Would we, would James, know the truth of the matter without the excellence of form? If Stevenson is writing about what we ordinarily do not see because we are afflicted with a certain blindness, is it then the excellence of form that has enabled us this time to see?

A LITERARY USE OF THE BOOK OF JONAH   *iii*

In the general present-day ignorance of the Old Testament, the Book of Jonah is hardly known except as the basis of poor jokes about Jonah and the whale. But traditionally for both Jews and Christians it is an important book. It is read by the Jews as a lesson in the afternoon service on the Day of Atonement. Two of the Gospels report a citation by Christ himself (Matthew 12:38–41; Luke 11:29–32).

The Book of Jonah comes among the prophetic books in the Old Testament, but that is because its author took the name of a prophet, Jonah the son of Amittai, a historical personage (see 2 Kings 14:25) as the name of his central character. The book itself is not prophecy; it is a story told to enforce a great concept of the nature of God. Scholars think the book was written toward the end of the fifth or in the fourth century B.C.

As the book opens, the Lord instructs Jonah to go to Nineveh and warn that great city of its wickedness; but Jonah does not think of the people of Nineveh as his people, and he does not want the worship of the Lord extended to them.

The Book of Jonah

Chapter 1

1 Now the word of the Lord came unto Jonah the son of Amittai, saying,

2 Arise, go to Nineveh, that great city, and cry against it; for their wickedness is come up before me.

3 But Jonah rose up to flee unto Tarshish from the presence of the Lord, and went down to Joppa; and he found a ship going to Tarshish: so he paid the fare thereof, and went down into it, to go with them unto Tarshish from the presence of the Lord.

4 But the Lord sent out a great wind into the sea, and there was a mighty tempest in the sea, so that the ship was like to be broken.

5 Then the mariners were afraid, and cried every man unto his god, and cast forth the wares that were in the ship into the sea, to lighten it of them. But Jonah was gone down into the sides of the ship; and he lay, and was fast asleep.

6 So the shipmaster came to him, and said unto him, What meanest thou, O sleeper? arise, call upon thy God, if so be that God will think upon us, that we perish not.

7 And they said every one to his fellow, Come, and let us cast lots, that we may know for whose cause this evil is upon us. So they cast lots, and the lot fell upon Jonah.

8 Then said they unto him, Tell us, we pray thee, for whose cause this evil is upon us; What is thine occupation? and whence comest thou? what is thy country? and of what people art thou?

9 And he said unto them, I am an Hebrew; and I fear the Lord, the God of heaven, which hath made the sea and the dry land.

10 Then were the men exceedingly afraid, and said unto him, Why hast thou done this? For the men knew that he fled from the presence of the Lord, because he had told them.

11 Then said they unto him, What shall we do unto thee, that the sea may be calm unto us? for the sea wrought, and was tempestuous.

12 And he said unto them, Take me up, and cast me forth into the sea; so shall the sea be calm unto you: for I know that for my sake this great tempest is upon you.

13 Nevertheless the men rowed hard to bring it to the land; but they could not: for the sea wrought, and was tempestuous against them.

14 Wherefore they cried unto the Lord, and said, We beseech thee, O Lord, we beseech thee, let us not perish for this man's life, and lay not upon us innocent blood: for thou, O Lord, hast done as it pleased thee.

15 So they took up Jonah, and cast him forth into the sea: and the sea ceased from her raging.

16 Then the men feared the Lord exceedingly, and offered a sacrifice unto the Lord, and made vows.

17 Now the Lord had prepared a great fish to swallow up Jonah. And Jonah was in the belly of the fish three days and three nights.

Chapter 2

1 Then Jonah prayed unto the Lord his God out of the fish's belly,

2 And said, I cried by reason of mine affliction unto the Lord, and he heard me; out of the belly of hell cried I, and thou heardest my voice.

3 For thou hadst cast me into the deep, in the midst of the seas; and the floods compassed me about: all thy billows and thy waves passed over me.

4 Then I said, I am cast out of thy sight; yet I will look again toward thy holy temple.

5 The waters compassed me about, even to the soul: the depth closed me round about, the weeds were wrapped about my head.

6 I went down to the bottoms of the mountains; the earth with her bars was about me for ever: yet hast thou brought up my life from corruption, O Lord my God.

7 When my soul fainted within me I remembered the Lord: and my prayer came in unto thee, into thine holy temple.

8 They that observe lying vanities forsake their own mercy.

9 But I will sacrifice unto thee with the voice of thanksgiving; I will pay that that I have vowed. Salvation is of the Lord.

10 And the Lord spake unto the fish, and it vomited out Jonah upon the dry land.

Chapter 3

1 And the word of the Lord came unto Jonah the second time, saying,

2 Arise, go unto Nineveh, that great city, and preach unto it the preaching that I bid thee.

3 So Jonah arose, and went unto Nineveh, according to the word of the Lord. Now Nineveh was an exceeding great city of three days' journey.

4 And Jonah began to enter into the city a day's journey, and he cried, and said, Yet forty days, and Nineveh shall be overthrown.

5 So the people of Nineveh believed God, and proclaimed a fast, and put on sackcloth, from the greatest of them even to the least of them.

6 For word came unto the king of Nineveh, and he arose from his throne, and he laid his robe from him, and covered him with sackcloth, and sat in ashes.

7 And he caused it to be proclaimed and published through Nineveh by the decree of the king and his nobles, saying, Let neither man nor beast, herd nor flock, taste any thing: let them not feed, nor drink water:

8 But let man and beast be covered with sackcloth, and cry mightily unto God: yea, let them turn every one from his evil way, and from the violence that is in their hands.

9 Who can tell if God will turn and repent, and turn away from his fierce anger, that we perish not?

10 And God saw their works, that they turned from their evil way; and God repented of the evil, that he had said that he would do unto them; and he did it not.

Chapter 4

1 But it displeased Jonah exceedingly, and he was very angry.

2 And he prayed unto the Lord, and said, I pray thee, O Lord, was not this my saying, when I was yet in my country? Therefore I fled before unto Tarshish: for I knew that thou art a gracious God, and merciful, slow to anger, and of great kindness, and repentest thee of the evil.

3 Therefore now, O Lord, take, I beseech thee, my life from me; for it is better for me to die than to live.

4 Then said the Lord, Doest thou well to be angry?

5 So Jonah went out of the city, and sat on the east side of the city, and there made him a booth, and sat under it in the shadow, till he might see what would become of the city.

6 And the Lord God prepared a gourd, and made it to come up over Jonah, that it might be a shadow over his head, to deliver him from his grief. So Jonah was exceeding glad of the gourd.

7 But God prepared a worm when the morning rose the next day, and it smote the gourd that it withered.

8 And it came to pass, when the sun did arise, that God prepared a vehement east wind; and the sun beat upon the head of Jonah, that he fainted, and wished in himself to die, and said, It is better for me to die than to live.

9 And God said to Jonah, Doest thou well to be angry for the gourd? And he said, I do well to be angry, even unto death.

10 Then said the Lord, Thou hast had pity on the gourd, for the which thou hast not laboured, neither madest it grow; which came up in a night, and perished in a night:

11 And should not I spare Nineveh, that great city, wherein are more

than six score thousand persons that cannot discern between their right hand and their left hand; and also much cattle?

---

1) By fleeing to Tarshish in Spain, the farthest port that Jonah knows about, he supposes that he is beyond the reach of the Lord, who Jonah thinks—or wishes to think—is the God of Israel and of no other people.

2) Jonah's conduct in being willing to sacrifice himself for the good of the crew (1:11–12) is heroic enough; his sin is a sin of pride, the besetting sin of great spirits.

3) Has the argument that used to go on about the possibility of a whale swallowing Jonah any real basis? Scholars tell us that there is no word in the Hebrew that may be translated "whale." What is the implication of 1:17?

4) Scholars think that 2:2–9 is perhaps not a part of the original, but a later addition to it. The passage has the form of a psalm, and is indeed made up of material gathered from the Book of Psalms. Do you see that the imagery does not fit Jonah's situation? In what verses particularly?

5) Nevertheless the psalm is in spiritual harmony with the original: when Jonah is fleeing the Lord, he is spiritually separate from Him; at his repentance he is taken back into communion with Him. And the fish's belly is the place of his repentance.

6) When in Chapter 3 the people of Nineveh turn from their evil ways, the Lord "repents" his purpose to punish them. We can understand 3:10 by comparing Jeremiah 18:7–8: "At what instant I shall speak concerning a nation, and concerning a kingdom, to pluck up, and to pull down, and to destroy it; If that nation, against whom I have pronounced, turn from their evil, I will repent of the evil that I thought to do unto them."

7) "But it displeased Jonah exceedingly, and he was very angry." What is the matter with Jonah?

8) Do you know anybody like Jonah? Part of his trouble is his professional pride as a prophet; he had proclaimed the destruction of Nineveh, but the city had been forgiven. Do you feel the comic implication in Chapter 4? Jonah feared the Lord would not do as he, Jonah, would have Him; when the Lord asks "Doest thou well to be angry?" Jonah evidently replies something like this: yes, indeed I do. But the Lord understands Jonah, and does not try to reason with pride. We have in 4:5–11 a sort of dramatized PARABLE or analogy.

9) Jonah's "pity" for the gourd (4:10) is not quite pity in the ordinary sense, for Jonah benefits by the gourd. The Lord's pity for Nineveh is pity; yet it is parallel to Jonah's feeling for the gourd, too, since the Lord's creation delights Him and is—in a mysterious way—necessary to Him. The idea that is represented here is made eloquently explicit in a book in the Old Testament Apocrypha, The Wisdom of Solomon, 11:23–26:

> But thou hast mercy upon all; for thou canst do all things, and winkest at the sins of men, because they should amend. For thou lovest all the things that are, and abhorrest nothing which thou hast made: for never wouldst thou have made any thing, if thou hadst hated it. And how could any thing have endured, if it had not been thy will? or

been preserved, if not called by thee? But thou sparest all: for they are thine, O Lord, thou lover of souls.

10) But do you see that this great idea is embodied in a story that intends a gentle satire on men who do not comprehend the idea? Jonah is a type of Israelite who thinks of the Lord as the exclusive possession of himself and his group; and his kind is by no means limited to Israel or to the fourth or fifth century B.C.

Herman Melville in his *Moby-Dick* has reworked the story of Jonah in a remarkable way. His ninth chapter is the sermon of Father Mapple, minister to seafarers, who takes for his text: "And God had prepared a great fish to swallow up Jonah." The chapter will stand quite well by itself as a unit of writing, but it is also important in the interpretation of the novel. You may remember that W. H. Auden says that the ideal of life expressed in the sermon is the ideal of which Captain Ahab is potentially capable, but which he refuses. Before you read the chapter, perhaps you should review Mr. Auden's essay (in Chapter XV), particularly paragraphs XIII–XVII.

The person of Father Mapple seems to be based upon that of Father [Edward Thompson] Taylor, preacher at the Seamen's Bethel in Boston. Father Taylor was a Protestant; "Father" was a title given him in affection by his congregations. Richard Henry Dana in his *Two Years before the Mast* tells us that the first inquiry of sailors on the California coast was for Father Taylor; indeed, he was a famous person. But Professor Willard Thorp believes that Melville was also thinking of the Reverend Enoch Mudge, chaplain of a bethel in New Bedford, Massachusetts, where the action of the first chapters of *Moby-Dick* goes on.

FROM *Moby-Dick* (1851)

HERMAN MELVILLE

The Sermon

I Father Mapple rose, and in a mild voice of unassuming authority ordered the scattered people to condense. "Starboard gangway, there! side away to larboard—larboard gangway to starboard! Midships! midships!"

II There was a low rumbling of heavy sea-boots among the benches, and a still slighter shuffling of women's shoes, and all was quiet again, and every eye on the preacher.

III He paused a little; then kneeling in the pulpit's bows, folded his large brown hands across his chest, uplifted his closed eyes, and offered a prayer so deeply devout that he seemed kneeling and praying at the bottom of the sea.

IV This ended, in prolonged solemn tones, like the continual tolling of a bell in a ship that is foundering at sea in a fog—in such tones he commenced reading the following hymn; but changing his manner towards the concluding stanzas, burst forth with a pealing exultation and joy—

> "The ribs and terrors in the whale,
>   Arched over me a dismal gloom,
> While all God's sun-lit waves rolled by,
>   And lift me deepening down to doom.

> "I saw the opening maw of hell,
>   With endless pains and sorrows there;
> Which none but they that feel can tell—
>   Oh, I was plunging to despair.

> "In black distress, I called my God,
>   When I could scarce believe him mine,
> He bowed his ear to my complaints—
>   No more the whale did me confine.

> "With speed he flew to my relief,
>   As on a radiant dolphin borne;
> Awful, yet bright, as lightning shone
>   The face of my Deliverer God.

> "My song for ever shall record
>   That terrible, that joyful hour;
> I give the glory to my God,
>   His all the mercy and the power."

v Nearly all joined in singing this hymn, which swelled high above the howling of the storm. A brief pause ensued; the preacher slowly turned over the leaves of the Bible, and at last, folding his hand down upon the proper page, said: "Beloved shipmates, clinch the last verse of the first chapter of Jonah—'And God had prepared a great fish to swallow up Jonah.'

vi "Shipmates, this book, containing only four chapters—four yarns is one of the smallest strands in the mighty cable of the Scriptures. Yet what depths of the soul does Jonah's deep sea-line sound! what a pregnant lesson to us is this prophet! What a noble thing is that canticle in the fish's belly! How billow-like and boisterously grand! We feel the floods surging over us, we sound with him to the kelpy bottom of the waters; sea-weed and all the slime of the sea is about us! But *what* is this lesson that the book of Jonah teaches? Shipmates, it is a two-stranded lesson; a lesson to us all as sinful men, and a lesson to me as a pilot of the living God. As sinful men, it is a lesson to us all, because it is a story of the sin, hard-heartedness, suddenly awakened fears, the swift punishment, repentance, prayers, and finally the deliverance and joy of Jonah. As with all sinners among men, the sin of this son of Amittai was in his wilful disobedience of the command of God—never mind now what that command was, or how conveyed —which he found a hard command. But all the things that God would have us do are hard for us to do—remember that—and hence, he oftener commands us than endeavors to persuade. And if we obey God, we must disobey ourselves; and it is in this disobeying ourselves, wherein the hardness of obeying God consists.

VII "With this sin of disobedience in him, Jonah still further flouts at God, by seeking to flee from Him. He thinks that a ship made by men, will carry him into countries where God does not reign, but only the Captains of this earth. He skulks about the wharves of Joppa, and seeks a ship that's bound for Tarshish. There lurks, perhaps, a hitherto unheeded meaning here. By all accounts Tarshish could have been no other city than the modern Cadiz. That's the opinion of learned men. And where is Cadiz, shipmates? Cadiz is in Spain; as far by water, from Joppa, as Jonah could possibly have sailed in those ancient days, when the Atlantic was an almost unknown sea. Because Joppa, the modern Jaffa, shipmates, is on the most easterly coast of the Mediterranean, the Syrian; and Tarshish or Cadiz more than two thousand miles to the westward from that, just outside the Straits of Gibraltar. See ye not then, shipmates, that Jonah sought to flee world-wide from God? Miserable man! Oh! most contemptible and worthy of all scorn; with slouched hat and guilty eye, skulking from his God; prowling among the shipping like a vile burglar hastening to cross the seas. So disordered, self-condemning in his look, that had there been policemen in those days, Jonah, on the mere suspicion of something wrong, had been arrested ere he touched a deck. How plainly he's a fugitive! no baggage, not a hat-box, valise, or carpet-bag,—no friends accompany him to the wharf with their adieux. At last, after much dodging search, he finds the Tarshish ship receiving the last items of her cargo; and as he steps on board to see its Captain in the cabin, all the sailors for the moment desist from hoisting in the goods, to mark the stranger's evil eye. Jonah sees this; but in vain he tries to look all ease and confidence; in vain essays his wretched smile. Strong intuitions of the man assure the mariners he can be no innocent. In their gamesome but still serious way, one whispers to the other—'Jack, he's robbed a widow;' or, 'Joe, do you mark him; he's a bigamist;' or, 'Harry lad, I guess he's the adulterer that broke jail in old Gomorrah, or belike, one of the missing murderers from Sodom.' Another runs to read the bill that's stuck against the spile upon the wharf to which the ship is moored, offering five hundred gold coins for the apprehension of a parricide, and containing a description of his person. He reads, and looks from Jonah to the bill; while all his sympathetic shipmates now crowd round Jonah, prepared to lay their hands upon him. Frighted Jonah trembles, and summoning all his boldness to his face, only looks so much the more a coward. He will not confess himself suspected; but that itself is strong suspicion. So he makes the best of it; and when the sailors find him not to be the man that is advertised, they let him pass, and he descends into the cabin.

VIII " 'Who's there?' cries the Captain at his busy desk, hurriedly making out his papers for the Customs—'Who's there?' Oh! how that harmless question mangles Jonah! For the instant he almost turns to flee again. But he rallies. 'I seek a passage in this ship to Tarshish; how soon sail ye, sir?' Thus far the busy Captain had not looked up to Jonah, though the man now stands before him; but no sooner does he hear that hollow voice, than he darts a scrutinizing glance. 'We sail with the next coming tide,' at last he slowly answered, still intently eyeing him. 'No sooner, sir?'—'Soon enough for any honest man that goes a passenger.' Ha! Jonah, that's another stab. But he swiftly calls away the Captain from that scent. 'I'll sail with ye,'—he says,—'the passage money, how much is that?—I'll pay now.' For it is particularly written, shipmates, as if it were a thing not to be overlooked in this history, 'that he paid the fare thereof' ere the craft did sail. And taken with the context, this is full of meaning.

ix "Now Jonah's Captain, shipmates, was one whose discernment detects crime in any, but whose cupidity exposes it only in the penniless. In this world, shipmates, sin that pays its way can travel freely, and without a passport; whereas Virtue, if a pauper, is stopped at all frontiers. So Jonah's Captain prepares to test the length of Jonah's purse, ere he judge him openly. He charges him thrice the usual sum; and it's assented to. Then the Captain knows that Jonah is a fugitive; but at the same time resolves to help a flight that paves its rear with gold. Yet when Jonah fairly takes out his purse, prudent suspicions still molest the Captain. He rings every coin to find a counterfeit. Not a forger, any way, he mutters; and Jonah is put down for his passage. 'Point out my state-room, sir,' says Jonah now, 'I'm travel-weary; I need sleep.' 'Thou look'st like it,' says the Captain, 'there's thy room.' Jonah enters, and would lock the door, but the lock contains no key. Hearing him foolishly fumbling there, the Captain laughs lowly to himself, and mutters something about the doors of convicts' cells being never allowed to be locked within. All dressed and dusty as he is, Jonah throws himself into his berth, and finds the little state-room ceiling almost resting on his forehead. The air is close, and Jonah gasps. Then, in that contracted hole, sunk, too, beneath the ship's water-line, Jonah feels the heralding presentiment of that stifling hour, when the whale shall hold him in the smallest of his bowel's wards.

x "Screwed at its axis against the side, a swinging lamp slightly oscillates in Jonah's room; and the ship, heeling over towards the wharf with the weight of the last bales received, the lamp, flame and all, though in slight motion, still maintains a permanent obliquity with reference to the room; though, in truth, infallibly straight itself, it but made obvious the false, lying levels among which it hung. The lamp alarms and frightens Jonah; as lying in his berth his tormented eyes roll round the place, and this thus far successful fugitive finds no refuge for his restless glance. But that contradiction in the lamp more and more appals him. The floor, the ceiling, and the side, are all awry. 'Oh! so my conscience hangs in me!' he groans, 'straight upward, so it burns; but the chambers of my soul are all in crookedness!'

xi "Like one who after a night of drunken revelry hies to his bed, still reeling, but with conscience yet pricking him, as the plungings of the Roman race-horse but so much the more strike his steel tags into him; as one who in that miserable plight still turns and turns in giddy anguish, praying God for annihilation until the fit be passed; and at last amid the whirl of woe he feels, a deep stupor steals over him, as over the man who bleeds to death, for conscience is the wound, and there's naught to staunch it; so, after sore wrestlings in his berth, Jonah's prodigy of ponderous misery drags him drowning down to sleep.

XII "And now the time of tide has come; the ship casts off her cables; and from the deserted wharf the uncheered ship for Tarshish, all careening, glides to sea. That ship, my friends, was the first of recorded smugglers! the contraband was Jonah. But the sea rebels; he will not bear the wicked burden. A dreadful storm comes on, the ship is like to break. But now when the boatswain calls all hands to lighten her; when boxes, bales, and jars are clattering overboard; when the wind is shrieking, and the men are yelling, and every plank thunders with trampling feet right over Jonah's head; in all this raging tumult, Jonah sleeps his hideous sleep. He sees no black sky and raging sea, feels not the reeling timbers, and little hears he or heeds he the far rush of the mighty whale, which even now with open mouth is cleaving the seas after him. Aye, shipmates, Jonah was gone down into the sides of the ship—a berth in the cabin as I have taken it, and was fast asleep. But the frightened master comes to him, and shrieks in his dead ear, 'What meanest thou, O sleeper! arise!' Startled from his lethargy by that direful cry, Jonah staggers to his feet, and stumbling to the deck, grasps a shroud, to look out upon the sea. But at that moment he is sprung upon by a panther billow leaping over the bulwarks. Wave after wave thus leaps into the ship, and finding no speedy vent runs roaring fore and aft, till the mariners come nigh to drowning while yet afloat. And ever, as the white moon shows her affrighted face from the steep gullies in the blackness overhead, aghast Jonah sees the rearing bowsprit pointing high upward, but soon beat downward again towards the tormented deep.

XIII "Terrors upon terrors run shouting through his soul. In all his cringing attitudes, the God-fugitive is now too plainly known. The sailors mark him; more and more certain grow their suspicions of him, and at last, fully to test the truth, by referring the whole matter to high Heaven, they fall to casting lots, to see for whose cause this great tempest was upon them. The lot is Jonah's; that discovered, then how furiously they mob him with their questions. 'What is thine occupation? Whence comest thou? Thy country? What people?' But mark now, my shipmates, the behavior of poor Jonah. The eager mariners but ask him who he is, and where from; whereas, they not only receive an answer to those questions, but likewise another answer to a question not put by them, but the unsolicited answer is forced from Jonah by the hard hand of God that is upon him.

XIV " 'I am a Hebrew,' he cries—and then—'I fear the Lord the God of Heaven who hath made the sea and the dry land!' Fear him, O Jonah? Aye, well mightest thou fear the Lord God *then!* Straightway, he now goes on to make a full confession; whereupon the mariners became more and more appalled, but still are pitiful. For when Jonah, not yet supplicating God for mercy, since he but too well knew the darkness of his deserts,—when wretched Jonah cries out to them to take him and cast him forth into the sea, for he knew that for *his* sake this great tempest was upon them; they mercifully turn from him, and seek by other means to save the ship. But all in vain; the indignant gale howls louder; then, with one hand raised invokingly to God, with the other they not unreluctantly lay hold of Jonah.

xv "And now behold Jonah taken up as an anchor and dropped into the sea; when instantly an oily calmness floats out from the east, and the sea is still, as Jonah carries down the gale with him, leaving smooth water behind. He goes down in the whirling heart of such a masterless commotion that he scarce heeds the moment when he drops seething into the yawning jaws awaiting him; and the whale shoots-to all his ivory teeth, like so many white bolts, upon his prison. Then Jonah prayed unto the Lord out of the fish's belly. But observe his prayer, and learn a weighty lesson. For sinful as he is, Jonah does not weep and wail for direct deliverance. He feels that his dreadful punishment is just. He leaves all his deliverance to God, contenting himself with this, that spite of all his pains and pangs, he will still look towards His holy temple. And here, shipmates, is true and faithful repentance; not clamorous for pardon, but grateful for punishment. And how pleasing to God was this conduct in Jonah, is shown in the eventual deliverance of him from the sea and the whale. Shipmates, I do not place Jonah before you to be copied for his sin but I do place him before you as a model for repentance. Sin not; but if you do, take heed to repent of it like Jonah."

xvi While he was speaking these words, the howling of the shrieking, slanting storm without seemed to add new power to the preacher, who, when describing Jonah's sea-storm, seemed tossed by a storm himself. His deep chest heaved as with a ground-swell; his tossed arms seemed the warring elements at work; and the thunders that rolled away from off his swarthy brow, and the light leaping from his eye, made all his simple hearers look on him with a quick fear that was strange to them.

xvii There now came a lull in his look, as he silently turned over the leaves of the Book once more; and, at last, standing motionless, with closed eyes, for the moment, seemed communing with God and himself.

xviii But again he leaned over towards the people, and bowing his head lowly, with an aspect of the deepest yet manliest humility, he spake these words:

xix "Shipmates, God has laid but one hand upon you; both his hands press upon me. I have read ye by what murky light may be mine the lesson that Jonah teaches to all sinners; and therefore to ye, and still more to me, for I am a greater sinner than ye. And now how gladly would I come down from this mast-head and sit on the hatches there where you sit, and listen as you listen, while some one of you reads *me* that other and more awful lesson which Jonah teaches to *me*, as a pilot of the living God. How being an anointed pilot-prophet, or speaker of true things, and bidden by the Lord to sound those unwelcome truths in the ears of a wicked Nineveh, Jonah, appalled at the hostility he should raise, fled from his mission, and sought to escape his duty and his God by taking ship at Joppa. But God is everywhere; Tarshish he never reached. As we have seen, God came upon him in the whale, and swallowed him down to living gulfs of doom, and with swift slantings tore him along 'into the midst of the seas,' where the eddying depths sucked him ten thousand fathoms down, and 'the weeds were wrapped about his head,' and all the watery world of woe bowled over him. Yet even then beyond the reach of any plummet—'out of the belly of hell'— when the whale grounded upon the ocean's utmost bones, even then, God heard the engulphed, repenting prophet when he cried. Then God spake unto the fish; and from the shuddering cold and blackness of the sea, the whale came breeching up towards the warm and pleasant sun, and all the delights of air and earth; and 'vomited out Jonah upon the dry land;' when the word of the Lord came a second time; and Jonah, bruised and beaten— his ears, like two sea-shells, still multitudinously murmuring of the ocean— Jonah did the Almighty's bidding. And what was that, shipmates? To preach the Truth to the face of Falsehood! That was it!

xx "This, shipmates, this is that other lesson; and woe to that pilot of the living God who slights it. Woe to him whom this world charms from Gospel duty! Woe to him who seeks to pour oil upon the waters when God has brewed them into a gale! Woe to him who seeks to please rather than to appal! Woe to him whose good name is more to him than goodness! Woe to him who, in this world, courts not dishonor! Woe to him who would not be true, even though to be false were salvation! Yea, woe to him who, as the great Pilot Paul has it, while preaching to others is himself a cast-away!"

xxi He drooped and fell away from himself for a moment; then lifting his face to them again, showed a deep joy in his eyes, as he cried out with a heavenly enthusiasm,—"But oh! shipmates! on the starboard hand of every woe, there is a sure delight; and higher the top of that delight, than the bottom of the woe is deep. Is not the main-truck higher than the kelson is low? Delight is to him—a far, far upward, and inward delight—who against the proud gods and commodores of this earth, ever stands forth his own inexorable self. Delight is to him whose strong arms yet support him, when the ship of this base treacherous world has gone down beneath him. Delight is to him, who gives no quarter in the truth, and kills, burns, and destroys all sin though he pluck it out from under the robes of Senators and Judges. Delight,—top-gallant delight is to him, who acknowledges no law or lord, but the Lord his God, and is only a patriot to heaven. Delight is to him, whom all the waves of the billows of the seas of the boisterous mob can never shake from this sure Keel of the Ages. And eternal delight and deliciousness will be his, who coming to lay him down, can say with his final breath—O Father!—chiefly known to me by Thy rod—mortal or immortal, here I die. I have striven to be Thine, more than to be this world's, or mine own. Yet this is nothing: I leave eternity to Thee; for what is man that he should live out the lifetime of his God?"

xxii He said no more, but slowly waving a benediction, covered his face with his hands, and so remained kneeling, till all the people had departed, and he was left alone in the place.

---

1) Consider for a moment the hymn that Father Mapple reads. How does the hymn writer understand Jonah's psalm? Does he rightly interpret the meaning of Jonah in the fish's belly?

2) Father Mapple says (vi) that there is a "two-stranded lesson" in the Book of Jonah. He begins to develop the first strand at once. Where does the development of the second strand begin?

3) How much of the Book of Jonah is Father Mapple using in his sermon? If he does not use all of the story, does he use all of the meaning?

4) Why does Father Mapple say in vi "never mind now what that command was"? Does he ever say what it was?

5) We may, in comparing the first two chapters of the Book of Jonah and Father Mapple's account of them, compare two narrative methods. The story of Jonah is told us by the original writer in the objective narration characteristic of Old Testament writers. We are not told what Jonah thinks or feels, or what his motives are. We are told merely what he says and does. What narrative assumptions are made in Father Mapple's account?

6) Compare the treatment of a number of incidents in the two versions. How firmly based on the Old Testament account is Father Mapple's? If it is interpretative, is it justly so? For instance, is Jonah's appearance of guilt a legitimate inference from what is said in the Book of Jonah?

7) Or how about the detail in Father Mapple's sermon (ix) that Jonah paid thrice the usual sum? Does the Book of Jonah say merely that Jonah paid *his* fare? There are no other passengers. Do you take it, as some commentators do, that we are to understand that Jonah chartered the ship?

8) Father Mapple in ix tells us a good deal about the captain's character. Is there any basis in the original for what he tells?

9) Or again, how about xiv? Is the interpretation of the sailors' attitude toward Jonah right according to your reading of the Book of Jonah? (Notice that these sailors are not Jonah's countrymen, and that in the original they speak of the Lord as *"thy* God.")

10) When the added detail is not an inference from the text of the Book of Jonah alone, it is the what-must-have-been according to Father Mapple's knowledge of the sea, ships, sailors, and human nature. For instance, the swinging light of x has no basis in the original. Is the symbolic meaning Father Mapple makes Jonah see in it consonant with character and situation? Or take another sort of instance. Father Mapple's notion of the captain and his attitude toward Jonah seems not to be based upon the original. Is it humanly convincing? Does it conform to your observation of men?

11) How does Father Mapple interpret Jonah's unwillingness to go to Nineveh? Is the motive he gives Jonah the motive you see in the original? Is it the motive our questions and discussion suggested? But notice that even if there is a difference in the way a particular motive is understood, Father Mapple certainly sees the general human and spiritual meaning: "And if we obey God, we must disobey ourselves; and it is in this disobeying ourselves, wherein the hardness of obeying God consists."

12) Now each of the methods we have been comparing has its own kind of interest. In which of them does the reader have most to do? Do you see that the narrative writer who offers so full an interpretation as Father Mapple's gives up something in doing so? And do you see that the reader's activity when he reads the Book of Jonah is an important part of his experi-

ence? Still, it may well be that the reader of Father Mapple's sermon will go back to the Book of Jonah with the text enriched for him.

13) Yet there remains a problem. Do you think that the Jonah of Father Mapple's sermon is more concrete, more real to us than the Jonah of the original? If he is, does he—even while he gains reality—lose something of his representative significance? Of course Father Mapple does treat him as a representative character, particularly in vi and xix. And of course a character is often both individual and representative; indeed the greatest characters in literature are both, for in a really great character we recognize ourselves and our concerns. Nevertheless, what happens as a consequence of the wealth of circumstance with which Father Mapple tells the story? Does the personality of Father Mapple ever get between us and the story?

14) Melville was all his life preoccupied with the problem of evil. Do you think, in view of that preoccupation, that he may mean xx to have a reference to organized religion in his time? Certainly the religion of most New England intellectuals then was bland and amazingly confident of the essential goodness of man; this bland confidence was "the most curious social phenomenon," wrote Henry Adams looking back on it, "that he had to account for in a long life."

15) If Father Mapple had used the rest of the Book of Jonah, would his interpretation of Jonah's experience and character have been so well supported? (That is not to suggest that there is anything illegitimate about an interpretative account of the first episode by itself.) But do you see that in the Book of Jonah, Jonah's experience has two quite separate stages, the last of them not completely worked out? And do you see that only in the last two chapters is the satirical intent at all plain?

16) Would the dramatized parable of the gourd have lent itself well to the sort of expanded treatment that Father Mapple gives to the first two chapters? Why or why not?

17) Probably Father Mapple's style, in its use of nautical language and its occasional COLLOQUIALISM, has something of that of his PROTOTYPES; but it has Melville's characteristic rhetoric, too. Do you find passages that seem self-consciously "literary"—not what a sincere, unlettered sailor's preacher would naturally say? Consider this clause: "Jonah's prodigy of ponderous misery drags him drowning down to sleep." Do you find other examples of such calculated alliteration? Or consider Father Mapple's metaphors. Of course he draws on two great sources: his seaman's experience and the Bible. Anyone very familiar with the King James version of the Bible is likely to use a vivid English; perhaps we can quite well suppose an unlettered preacher saying, "Terrors upon terrors run shouting through his soul." But how about such sentences as the last in xii? And how about Father Mapple's diction in general? The diction of the King James version is a relatively simple diction and not highly latinized. What would you say about Father Mapple's vocabulary? But even if we agree that the prototypes of Father Mapple probably would have spoken more simply than he does, is that a reason that Melville should not have used his own resources in this chapter?

18) Melville introduces Chapter IX by two short chapters describing the chapel and the pulpit in it. Yet there are a number of paragraphs here

that are not part of the sermon itself. What is their function? Suppose they had been omitted. What, if anything, would have been lost to you as a reader? Why does the most considerable interruption of the sermon come just after xv?

SUGGESTIONS FOR PAPERS

The Thoreau selections will yield a good many exercises. Here are suggestions for exercises in connection with "The Battle of the Ants": (a) Assume an intelligent but unpracticed reader (your brother in high school, say) who has read the selection and has it before him. Write *for him* an interpretative restatement. Recall to him what he has read and indicate its significance. (b) Assume a reader who has not read the selection, and write for him an account of it in which Thoreau's intention comes clear. (c) Assume an examination in a literature course with these questions: 1. Discuss Thoreau's account of "The Battle of the Ants." (You might answer this question assuming there were ten minutes allowed for the answer, and then work your answer over assuming a question for which twenty minutes were allowed.) 2. Mock-heroic writing may be defined as writing, intended to amuse, in which a trivial subject is treated in an exalted manner and by the use of epic conventions. Consider Thoreau's account of "The Battle of the Ants" in regard to this definition. 3. Emerson says: "Man is an analogist, and studies relations in all objects. . . . All the facts in natural history taken by themselves, have no value, but are barren, like a single sex. But marry it to human history, and it is full of life." Discuss "The Battle of the Ants" as an example of the marriage of natural history and human history.

Exercises a and b above may be carried out quite as well with "The Fitchburg Railroad." And written answers to questions 3, 6, 7, and 9 on "The Fitchburg Railroad" will be interpretative restatement of parts of the selection. Examination questions for practice might be these: 1. Thoreau says "But lo! men have become tools of their tools." How is this idea that men may be controlled by forces they suppose they control developed in "The Fitchburg Railroad"? 2. Discuss "The Fitchburg Railroad" as it illustrates Thoreau's way of concretely representing ideas in his social criticism.

A paper of some little length might be one of these: (a) Discuss together some nineteenth-century imaginative treatments of the railroad, for instance "The Fitchburg Railroad," Whitman's "To a Locomotive in Winter," and Emily Dickinson's "I like to see it lap the miles" (a recent poem by an English writer, Stephen Spender's "The Express," is interesting for comparison). (b) Write a discussion of Thoreau's use of metaphor and allusion in our selection from "Walking" (in Chapter III), "The Battle of the Ants," and "The Fitchburg Railroad."

If your instructor is willing to have papers only generally connected with the "The Lantern-Bearers," he might allow you to write an account of some boys' or girls' activity which parallels the lantern-bearing of Stevenson's youth. Or perhaps he might allow you to write a chapter for a novel about Dancer, using what Stevenson says about him as a sort of context for it. If you find yourself in disagreement with Stevenson's thesis, you might write a piece which is, explicitly or implicitly, an answer to it. But you should hardly try that unless you have read some realistic novels.

Suggestions for papers more specifically connected with "The Lantern-Bearers" are these: (a) Assume that you are writing a paper for a literature course in which you are considering the arguments against the realistic novelist's position. Write a brief account of the essay for such a purpose. (b) Take this quotation from William James: "Wherever a process of life communicates an eagerness to him who lives it . . . there *is* 'importance' in the only real and positive sense in which importance ever anywhere can be." Develop and enforce the sentence by a selected account of Stevenson's essay. (c) Take question 4 and your work in connection with it. Expand your brief statement of the analogy into a paper of 200–300 words, keeping the two elements of the analogy in pretty close balance. (d) Go back to question 15. Take the material quoted in reference to the "knot" in an effective sentence, and go on to develop it in a piece in which you quote and analyze illustrative sentences from the essay.

And here are two suggestions for papers that will require further reading: (a) Read Stevenson's "A Gossip on Romance," from his *Memories and Portraits*. This essay, too, has to do with the romance writer's procedure, but Stevenson's concern is other than his concern in our essay. Write a brief account of it, assuming as your readers the members of the class. (b) Or, instead of a summary account, discuss "A Gossip on Romance" as it may explain the appeal of Stevenson's *Treasure Island* or *Kidnapped* or both. Assume as your readers the members of the class.

Suggestions for papers leading from the story of Jonah are these: (a) Write an account of the Book of Jonah, interpreted as is appropriate, for readers nine to twelve years old. (b) Write a sermon for Father Mapple to preach on the episode of Jonah and the gourd. (c) Quote W. H. Auden's reference to Father Mapple's sermon in paragraph XIII of "The Christian Tragic Hero" (p. 368) and then discuss the sermon for a reader who has not read it. Make clear to him what there is in the sermon that substantiates Auden's judgment. (d) Read the story of Joseph (Genesis 37, 39–46:7) and write a short account of it, making clear the ideals of character and conduct it represents. (e) Read the Book of Ruth (it is short) and then reread it with the aid of a good Old Testament commentary. Write an interpretative account of the book.

Index of Authors